TRAUMA AND UPROOTING

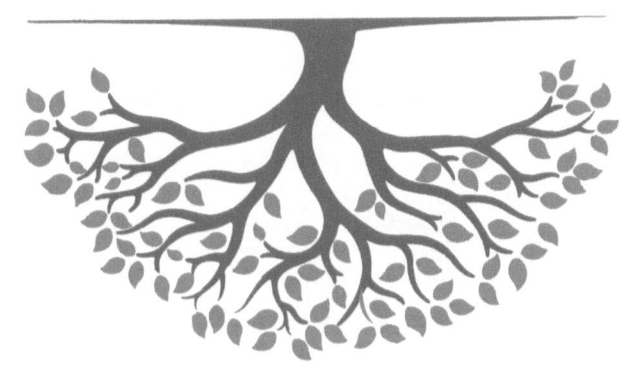

DIANA MISEREZ

Inquiries and Book Orders should be addressed to:

Great Writers Media
Email: info@greatwritersmedia.com
Phone: 877-600-5469

ISBN: 978-1-960939-90-6 (sc)
ISBN: 978-1-960939-91-3 (ebk)

ACKNOWLEDGEMENTS

There are many people to whom I am indebted in relation to the writing of this book. Above all, there have been researchers and practitioners who have generously agreed to my quoting quite substantial portions of their texts. I wish to mention, first and foremost, Dr Bessel van der Kolk, whose ground breaking book *The Body Keeps the Score* tells the whole story of how in the 1970s alarming phenomena of post-traumatic stress became apparent but were very far from being understood – and then how, in the course of a few years, he and other psychiatrists plumbed the depths of these phenomena, making some extraordinary discoveries. I wish to thank very warmly a number of doctors for allowing me to bring many of their findings into this book, especially Dr van der Kolk, of course, and Drs Richard F. Mollica, Judith L. Herman, Inger Agger, Peter Handford, Heide Rieder and Thomas Ebert. Then there is a host of other authors, whose texts bring to life a variety of situations, not least Nadia Murad, who depicts the horror of the IS genocide of the Yazidis of northern Iraq in August 2014, and Colette Braeckman and others, who depict the remarkable work of Dr Mukwege in the teeth of the danger and horror of mass rapes of women in Kivu. I wish I could thank them all in person!

Finally, I thank my daughter and two lifelong friends for encouraging me to keep on writing this account, and thank Matador for taking on the production of this rather long book.

CONTENTS

AUTHOR'S NOTE

When Trauma and Uprooting was first published in October 2020, no one could have imagined that within just a few months, Afghanistan, for twenty years enjoying a life of meaningful freedom and progress, would fall to the Taliban militants, or that the massive Russian army would soon be directed by a powerful dictator to attack Ukraine, a sovereign country.

Because of the graphic media reporting on each of these calamitous events, broadcast daily across the western world, in August/September 2021 on the plight of Afghanistan, then from 24 February 2022 on the brutal Russian invasion of Ukraine, it is safe to assume that readers will already have become familiar with events so shocking that not only may the survivors lose their peace of mind, but so may many observers across our troubled world. Nevertheless it has seemed reasonable to add a brief summary to the book.

August 2021 And The Taliban Takeover Of Afghanistan

Amnesty International (AI), the United Nations, MSF and Human Rights Watch amongst others have provided the world with an overview of the situation in Afghanistan at the time of the Taliban takeover, when the government collapsed, President Ghani fled, international troops were withdrawn and thousands stampeded to get out of the country. A subsequenet wave of reprisal killings, the forcible eviction of thousands of people and the imposition of strict limits on human rights illustrated the radical changes in the country, at a time that the suspension of international aid meant that people's access to food and to health care became severely limited. Though some 123,000 people were airlifted from Kabul airport in chaotic conditions - on one day a bomb blast in the vicinity of the airport killed over a hundred would-be travellers – others have attempted to leave on foot, hoping that the borders would not be sealed off.

In an atmosphere of fear, and even of terror, people associated with the previous government, particularly women, have since the takeover been trying to hide, conscious of what can happen if the Taliban find them. As AI has reported, women lawyers, judges and prosecutors, immediately forced from their jobs, have gone into hiding. These women were particularly vulnerable, facing reprisals from individuals whom they had once convicted and imprisoned, but subsequently freed from prison by the Taliban. Violence against women and girls has been widespread, if sorely under reported, though in the majority of cases no action is taken against perpetrators. In any case, women's legal and other support mechanisms have been shut down, and girls of secondary school age are denied schooling. Many of the men who served in the Afghan police and armed forces have been singled out for 'punishment' after failing in their attempts to remain hidden from the Taliban.

Barely have I finished writing the above than the shocking news flashes across the world of a devastating earthquake in Afghanistan that has killed a thousand people and injured at least 1500 others. It makes one wonder how much more agony the poor country can possibly endure.

24 February 2022 And The Brutal Russian Attack On Ukraine

No one the world over, apart from the former soviet spy Vladimir Putin, whose status as president – and dictator - of Russia relied on managed elections, ever imagined that war would again break out in Europe. It was generally assumed that the 1990s Balkan violence could not be replicated.

But once all the untiring diplomatic efforts of the West had failed and Putin launched his war, with Ukraine's armed forces and their president doing their best against vastly superior forces, who could have foreseen the level of unmitigated violence of the Russian occupiers? – such as the use of cluster weapons, banned under international law, sent to explode in the centre of residential areas? or the missile attack on the Kramatorsk railway station – that like so many of the recent Russian attacks, stands out for heartless brutality. Evidence from places in the region of the capital Kiev such as Bucha, Irpin, Hostomel and Borodianka, where Russian forces were present for weeks before being turned back by the Ukrainian army, bear evidence of senseless executions, rape and the looting of all the possessions people had had before the Russian forces pushed into unprecedented and unwarranted occupation.

Over the last four long months, traumatic scenes of the horrific destruction of property, uprooting and flight, along with testimonies of genocidal acts and rape as a weapon of war, have been allied with the spectacle of the unbearable distress of men, women and children. Within a few weeks, the United Nations Refugee Agency (UNHCR) put at over four million the number of people who had left Ukraine for safety and – one hopes – for some solace, while countless millions of others have been displaced within their country.

We have seen European countries, both those neighbouring Ukraine and others, taking in large numbers of those making up the unprecedented refugee exodus. Poland has taken in over two million, with Romania, Hungary and Moldavia also opening their doors wide to the Ukrainians fleeing massive violence. The United Kingdom, France, Spain, Italy, and Scandinavian countries are all playing a part, while Switzerland, the country in which I live, has so far admitted over 30,000 Ukrainian refugees – such a small number in relation to the four million needing asylum, but probably the most a small country can do. Three of the thirty thousand came to live here with me, along with the first 'refugee dog' I have ever encountered, a beautiful Golden Retriever. It seems symptomatic of the people of Ukraine that on fleeing, they have given preference over all their possessions to their cats, dogs and pet rabbits.

As Putin's war dragged on, people the world over held their breath for the port of Mariupol, where the well-trained Ukrainian soldiery was holding out against ceaseless bombardment by the Russian encircling forces, with missiles arriving from Russian ships out at sea to destroy most of the city. Hundreds of thousands of Mariupol residents were prevented from escaping conditions of fear, famine and homelessness and many are still imprisoned in the remnants of that once-fine city that is now in the hands of the Russians. In similar circumstances, countless residents of shattered buildings – people of all ages, down to babies - have somehow managed to eke out a precarious existence in the basements, often short of electricity, food and water. Some have succumbed to injuries, shock and the awful state of deprivation that they have been forced into. As I write this, the Guardian reports that the military situation for Ukraine's defenders in the eastern Donbas is "extremely difficult", as Russian attacks have intensified in an effort to capture the cities of Sievierodonetsk and Lysychansk.

Decent Russians who manage to obtain any knowledge of what is being done in the name of their country suffer from a deep sense of shame and many have gone abroad, but with tens of thousands of Russian protestors in prison the Kremlin has muzzled all those who would want the truth to emerge about the reality of war and the suffering it is causing. Most other Russians are apparently still taken in by Putin's outrageous propaganda.

In time, international judicial authorities will determine the extent of war crimes and crimes against humanity, and it is hoped that those responsible will face justice. Meanwhile, we are living in unnerving times.

May Heaven help the people of Afghanistan, and Ukraine and its diaspora.

D.M., late June 2022

ABOUT TRAUMA AND UPROOTING

Many of us are far from sanguine about the way things are going nowadays on this planet – quite apart from the recent appearance of the horrifying Coronavirus – "COVID-19" – which has radically changed the way people of practically every nation are thinking and behaving, and which is causing unprecedented stress, distress and trauma – in the medical services as well as in the general public.

By the time this book appears in print, we dare hope that the fight against this obscene virus is being won on all fronts, and not only in China and Singapore. But at the time of writing, the news is terrifying sombre, and this makes it difficult to concentrate as fully as before on the theme of trauma and uprooting. We must, however, proceed!

The Belated Recognition Of Trauma

We believe that the world could be a far better place, but all too much of the news is disquieting, and, alas, too many people – we ourselves, perhaps, or people we know – suffer from one form or another of trauma. And trauma and post-traumatic stress are very difficult to live with.

This book came to be written to show how universal trauma has now become, with a principal focus on man-made events that have forced millions of people to be uprooted from their homes, and often from their countries. Euripides said in 431 BC, "There is no greater sorrow on earth than the loss of one's native land." We know that this sorrow was felt by people wrenched away over centuries by Arabs and Europeans from their surroundings in Africa and forced into slavery, and by natives of the American continent whose lands were confiscated by Europeans who intruded and forcibly dominated people of many tribes who over thousands of years had created their own civilisations.

One need not necessarily read all the long and disturbing accounts of how, at various times between 1914 and the present, considerable devastation came about in all parts of Europe, Chile, Argentina, the former Indochina, Rwanda, Congo and northern Iraq (apart from the other recent and even contemporary scenes of horror, such as Syria, Yemen, Afghanistan…) as a result of fascism, political extremism and religious intolerance. But we have to recognize that the extreme forms of violence described in this book affected (or in some cases may still affect) whole populations with unavoidable psychological and physiological consequences that have been truly recognized only over the last thirty to forty years. So, whether or not we bring ourselves to plunge into the painful history of our world's last hundred or so years, we should read about the research undertaken and the experience gained since 1978. That will bring us to reflect not only on the suffering but also on the resilience of the human spirit, described by researcher-practitioners, abler authors than I, in fascinating books that I very warmly recommend.

Why especially 1978? Well, in July of that year a former combat soldier of the American armed forces came to a young Dutch psychiatrist working at the Boston Veterans Administration Clinic asking for help over the alarming behaviour that he had inexplicably and suddenly developed years after leaving Vietnam – namely manifestations of what later came to be called post-traumatic stress disorders, PTSD. Dr Bessel van der Kolk was totally perplexed, but he was determined to get to grips with the phenomenon and find ways of helping the perturbed young man, who it very soon turned out was one of many "vets" in similarly deep trouble. In parallel, other psychiatrists and practitioners such as the highly experienced American psychiatrists Dr Judith Lewis Herman and Dr Richard F. Mollica were turning their attention to this whole new area of investigation: trauma – massive, severe or acute trauma – what its causes and manifestations are and how its effects can be alleviated. In fact, they have virtually given their lives to this hitherto ignored area of work. Their invaluable findings, recorded in exceptionally valuable books that will loom large in the final chapters of this one,[1] have been written as a result of decades of research, observation and therapy among men, women and children of very different ages and cultural backgrounds.

It was also in 1978, in March, that I was catapulted by the United Nations Refugee Agency (UNHCR) to Mendoza, Argentina, to compile

---

[1] Dr van der Kolk's remarkable account, entitled *The Body Keeps the Score: Brain, Mind, and Body in the Healing of Trauma* (Penguin Books, 2014), about the effects of trauma that results from abuse, neglect and a range of other disasters, was the first that I found. It takes us stage by stage through the discoveries made in neuroscience, developmental psychopathology and interpersonal neurobiology.

resettlement documentation for Chilean refugees trapped in Argentina who were required by the military junta to leave the country as rapidly as possible. Encountering in this refugee population various manifestations of psychiatric illness, I was glad to have these explained to me in simple terms, on a case-by-case basis, by a young Argentine psychologist. But it was subsequently shocking to find on getting back to Geneva that what is *now* known as PTSD seemed as yet to be unheard of in Europe. In fact, two years went by before in 1980 the American Psychiatric Association gave post-traumatic stress disorder(s) (PTSD) a name, by which time research had got underway in the USA.

At about the same time, Dr Peter Handford, a professor of law at the University of Western Australia who happens to be a cousin of mine, was beginning to recognize a need to write about this new phenomenon of post-traumatic stress that he and his students found cropping up in relation to some of the legal procedures with which they were concerned.

Recognition Of Trauma At Last

Today, trauma has almost become commonplace – regrettably, for it is not something one would wish even on one's worst enemy! – but of course it was high time that it should come to be recognized and talked about, since it drastically affects so many lives. We get references to some of its causes in the media, coming across facts such as these, grouped under a Red Cross "Humanitarian index" in the *Red Cross Red Crescent Magazine*,[2] the cover page of which has the titles "Seeking Peace of Mind – Coping with the Psychological and Mental Health Impacts of Crisis":

> Percentage of states in conflict that have more than ten parties fighting on their territory: 25. Percentage of conflicts that have between three and nine opposing forces: 44. Number of separate armed groups registered in the city of Misrata, Libya: 236.

Next come serious articles such these:

SEEKING PEACE OF MIND: Psychological first aid needs to be at the forefront of humanitarian response. But how do we address the challenge of bringing it to the front lines of today's conflicts and crises? Meanwhile, people affected by

---

[2]   *RCRC*, Issue 1 (2018), www.rcrcmagazine.org.

conflict, the disappearance of loved ones, detention and social isolation caused by conflict and natural disasters tell their stories.

A CITY OF MISERY – Bangladesh photographer Munem Wasif shows how life in camps outside Cox's Bazar – where some 680,000 people are struggling to survive – compounds the psychological stresses faced by families who fled violence in Myanmar.

We have only to glance at the long list in Chapter 1 of traumatizing events of the twentieth century and early years of the twenty-first to realize that trauma has come to stay. The sufferings of Syrians are appalling as the war in their country drags on, hopes of the creation of a representative government having been dashed. The plight of people in Yemen, where attempts to bring in humanitarian aid to starving populations have frequently been thwarted by one or the other belligerent, conjures up other unbearable images. Terrorist acts seem to be in the news every second day (not least in Afghanistan, valiantly attempting as I write this to elect a representative government), along with shootings in various places, especially the USA.

On the positive side, we applaud Prince Harry for his contribution to making trauma known through his strong focus on mental illness. He still recently had the courage to let it be known how acutely he suffered for twenty years from the death of his mother, how he tried unsuccessfully to ignore his anguish, and how, strongly encouraged by his brother, Prince William, he decided at long last to address it – and get to be free of it. Prince William himself spoke publicly on 18 May 2019 about the enormous pain he too suffered over the death of Diana, a wonderful mother to her two boys. His pain, he said, on losing his mother was greater than any other form of pain one could conceivably suffer. And the prince is currently engaged across Britain on a campaign, waged through the world of football, to help men harbouring anxiety to find the means of expressing strong sentiments that, if left "bottled up", could lead to mental breakdown (and, sad to say, sometimes to suicide).

There are nowadays courses on which one can enrol and study over the internet, such as these glimpsed recently: "Positive psychology", University of Carolina; "Positive psychology, applications and interventions", University of Pennsylvania; and "Positive psychiatry and mental health", University of Sydney. The many books about trauma that are now available offer introductions to the subject from different angles, many of them offering helpful ways and means of dealing with one's PTSD if one is unfortunate enough to have it.

* * * * * *

On Identity And Effects

"Trauma" is a noun that in the 1990s suddenly became familiar in our Western world, and one could say too familiar, along with the corresponding adjective, "traumatic". I remember hearing from a friend back then that relationships within her church had been "traumatic", while for some people just the day in the office or the routine drive home through traffic congestion may have been described as "traumatic". More appropriately, however, one started to hear these terms in relation to women who had been victims of rape attacks or attempts, children who had been neglected or abused, people whose homes had been repossessed and veterans of various wars. House moves, marriage breakdowns and job losses have all, at one time or another, been qualified as "traumatic", which quite possibly they have been.

Trauma, in its psychological sense (as opposed to that of a physical shock), is defined by the Oxford English Reference Dictionary as "**a** – an emotional shock following a stressful event, sometimes leading to long-term neurosis and **b** (in general use) a distressing or emotionally disturbing experience" (Gk. *Trauma traumatos*, wound). In either case, it can mean a highly stressful event that overwhelms a person's ability to cope, and that furthermore has physiological as well as psychological effects.

The American Psychiatric Association, after bringing out a first definition of PTSD in 1980, has over the years brought out a *Diagnostic and Statistical Manual of Mental Disorders* (DSM), updating it from time to time. It states that PTSD is a psychiatric disorder that can occur in people who have experienced or witnessed a traumatic event such as a natural disaster, a serious accident, a terrorist act, war/combat, rape or other violent personal assault. Circumstances typically involve the loss of control, betrayal, abuse of power, helplessness, pain, confusion and/or loss.

The DSM text adds that people with PTSD have intense, disturbing thoughts and feelings related to their experience that last long after the traumatic event has ended. They may relive the event through flashbacks, nightmares or insomnia; they may feel sadness, fear, shame or anger; and they may feel detached or estranged from other people, suffer from emotional outbursts and suffer from anxiety or depression. People with

15

PTSD may avoid situations or people that remind them of the traumatic event, and they may have strong negative reactions to something as ordinary as a loud noise or being touched accidentally.

PTSD can also occur among members of the "helping professions" as a result of repeated exposure to shocking scenes. Not only that: post-traumatic stress can occur among animals, particularly among wild animals that are being abused by man, such as herds of elephants decimated by attacks from helicopter gunships in the interests of obtaining more ivory, and the bears kept in Vietnam in cages so small that they cannot even stand or stretch out, being periodically cut open to extract the bile believed by certain communities to be beneficial to human health. The traumatic fate of countless other species cruelly and even sadistically treated by mankind unfortunately goes beyond the scope of this book.

* * * * * *

A Personal Note

On embarking on the writing of a book on trauma that readers might expect to be written by someone with medical qualifications, I should point out that I have never been other than a generalist. However, from the age of seventeen onwards I happened to live alongside refugees – people from Russia and other countries of Eastern Europe, Africans, Asians and Latin Americans, on occasion almost sharing in their flight! This helps explain why I have been strongly urged to write, sketching the elements that have led to the perception that, while very large numbers of people have been traumatized at some stage – people in almost every part of the world – there is still in this twenty-first century too little understanding of the multiple stages of suffering that people frequently go through, and of the phenomenon of post-traumatic stress (PTSD).

When the United Nations Organization launched the first of a long series of UN "years", it was World Refugee Year, 1959–60, and the symbol chosen was that of an uprooted tree – representing the refugee. The symbolism is important, for people forced to flee their countries have of course had to uproot themselves, leaving behind all that symbolized their lives up to that fatal day. So this expression in its various forms – uprooted, uprooting, uprootedness – will reappear in relation to the millions of people about whom this book is being written, who in very many cases suffered, or are suffering, from post-traumatic stress, PTSD.

My encounters with uprooting and flight began when, on leaving school, I was warmly welcomed for a month by a family that had fled their aristocratic home in East Prussia (now a part of Poland). They had had to start life all over again in West Germany – from nothing except their health and determination. Then in my first year at Bristol University I found I was side by side with many other East European refugees, and came to hear what they had been through before they got to Bristol. It wasn't long before it seemed that to reconcile myself with the much more favourable circumstances of my own life I would do well to get into work to do with refugees. Setting my heart on joining the Office of the United Nations High Commissioner for Refugees (UNHCR), I took a UN secretarial examination in Birmingham and got what seemed to be a promise of employment once I had graduated, albeit at a very junior level – but to get into UNHCR through any door was all that seemed to matter. Meanwhile, the first UN year, World Refugee Year, demonstrated to the world that large numbers of people uprooted by the Second World War were still trapped in abject conditions in refugee camps in Austria, Germany, Greece and Italy. I could hardly wait to get to Geneva.

Good fortune was certainly on my side, for within a couple of weeks of entering the majestic Palais des Nations (the European Office of the United Nations, built originally for the ill-fated League of Nations), I was given challenging work and never looked back.[3] While in a job of resettlement assistant, dealing with sheaves of case notes of elderly and so-called "handicapped" refugees (people with a physical, social or mental handicap), I got to know outside work hours a marvellous Russian woman of sixty-three who had become a refugee twice in her lifetime. Fleeing her country in the early 1920s as a young widow, obliged, along with hundreds of thousands of other Russians, to travel further and further east, she had lived for forty years in Harbin, China (studying dentistry, then working as a dentist), before again needing to escape terrifying intimidation. She had and her second husband had recently been brought across the world to Switzerland, and fourteen years later she told me that she was still having nightmares. What? Still having nightmares after having lived in peaceful Switzerland for so long? I couldn't get my head round this. Thanks to

---

[3]   Except that my British nationality militated against my recruitment being adjusted to that of professional officer, despite the very warm recommendations of my supervisors, so I took other work to await the retirement of the many "Brits" who, having been taken in from the post-war International Refugee Organization (IRO), occupied posts now needed inter alia for "Third World" people.

Alexandra Vavilova, I began to hear more about what we can call "the refugee experience".

This courageous and loveable woman wrote me charming letters while I was on extended missions to the Great Lakes area of Africa (Burundi, 1964/65, and Congo, 1976/77) and the former Indochina (Laos and Vietnam, 1975/76). More and more, both the work and my spare time involved quite close relationships with people who had become refugees – or, in the case of Laos, who were about to become refugees, their country, along with Vietnam and Cambodia, having become communist while I was there.

Then in March 1978, UNHCR sent me at short notice to Argentina, where several thousand Chileans, after escaping the fascist regime of General Augusto Pinochet in power after the *coup d'état* of 11 September 1973, were now in jeopardy after Isabel Perón's government had been overturned by the equally fascist military junta. Most of them were not so very far from their home country, living in Mendoza, a city at the foot of the Andes, and given help to subsist by UNHCR funding administered by an agency, CEAS (Centro de Estudios y Acción Social). Now they would somehow have to get to another country, their choices being limited to Europe, Scandinavia and Canada. Not one of them wished to go to the USA (correctly believed to have been guilty of involvement in Pinochet's *coup d'état*). And they needed UNHCR's help for this.

It soon emerged as I prepared resettlement files with CEAS that many of the refugees, an all-too-high proportion of them in fact, were suffering from a series of symptoms that corresponded to what the future term PTSD, post-traumatic stress disorder, would signify. Many of the children were wetting their beds, even a girl of sixteen who, with her siblings, had seen their father dragged away in the night by armed men. People were suffering from frequent headaches, nightmares, insomnia, flashbacks (reliving the traumatic event), back and stomach pain, irritability, epileptiform fits, a loss of self-esteem and a series of other ills, including survivor guilt (the suffering people may have when they have survived when so many others, perhaps close family members or friends, did not). Some of the children had been misguidedly told by their mothers that their absent father was on a journey and would be back, but after months, or sometimes years (this was more than four years after the initial terror), many of the children, no longer able to believe what they had been told, were becoming seriously perturbed. A single woman, Silvia M-H., had developed epileptiform fits after learning that the man she had been working with – and loved – a social worker, had been shot in the first week of the military coup. She became aware of other disappearances among neighbours, and her association with them had been enough for her to be watched. Her own family, feeling that they too could be suspect by association, had begged her to leave Chile.

This was perhaps the most radical of all my "learning experiences". Returning to Europe that summer and faced, to my consternation, with a realization that trauma was apparently unknown to the European medical field, I determined to try to do something about it. Not unexpectedly, this took all too long. I switched to the international Red Cross (the part known as the IFRC)[4] – far from imagining that, in those UNHCR corridors, two inspirational people were soon to meet who, despite considerable scepticism from all around, would eventually become instrumental in making refugee trauma known across a very broad front: they were (and still are!) a Cypriot clinical psychologist, Mary Petevi, and an American psychiatrist, Dr Richard A. Mollica. Chapter 20 describes some of their incomparable work and its results.

Something Of A Breakthrough

I met with some scepticism too: the Red Cross head of relief who had recruited me three years earlier called me in to reprove me for "going off at a tangent" (his words) by wanting to give time and effort to psychological needs. The Red Cross mandate, he reminded me, was to provide distressed populations with food and clothing, shelter and medical services, *full stop*. Nevertheless, with the encouragement of the Norwegian Secretary General, Hans Høegh, and the ICRC, and thanks to expert organizational help received from the Swedish Red Cross, the International Catholic Child Bureau and the World Health Organization, I set up a five-day international workshop on what we termed "the psychological problems of refugees and asylum seekers". The focus was on the mental health status of people living in Western countries or who were hoping, while in far-distant camps, to get there. In October 1987, bringing together at the Hotel Terrasse, Vitznau, on the banks of Lake Lucerne, sixty professionals from sixteen countries from a broad range of backgrounds, we found that the participants, meeting daily for breakfast (even though lodged in two different hotels!) and spending the rest of each day together until about 11 p.m., needed every bit of those five days to communicate the extensive experience that they were only too

---

[4] The International Red Cross Movement, created in 1863, consists of the ICRC (International Committee of the Red Cross), the IFRC (International Federation of Red Cross and Red Crescent Societies) and National Red Cross or Red Crescent Societies

eager to share. On the half-day we had allotted to leisure, half went up the Rigi on the oldest mountain railway in the world, the other half onto the lake, when as the in-depth conversations continued: no time was lost at all! Those were five very momentous days.

Participants reflected on the traumatic events, past and present, affecting people – in their countries of origin, during flight, in first asylum camps and upon arrival in what they expected would be a safe haven. They suggested appropriate methods of assisting these people so that their trauma would not become something with which they would have to contend for the rest of their lives. As Vitznau church bells tolled the angelus, cowbells were heard from nearby pastures and lake steamers drew silently into the jetty below our meeting room, participants heard about some of the worst forms of evil man can perpetrate against man: physical and psychological torture, incarceration in inhuman conditions, forced separation of families, sudden deportation, violence on the high seas... recalling that it was only a proportion of those subjected to such treatment who actually reached host countries. Some who wanted to flee had no opportunity of doing so, dying in prison (or being murdered), getting left behind in the panic of flight, or being intercepted during flight attempts and turned back, if not killed. Many of the victims of gross human rights abuses are children, some of whom have been forced to witness unspeakable horrors and may even have been induced to flee without the reassuring company of a parent or other close relative. The day we assembled at Vitznau that autumn day of 1987, a Vietnamese woman took her life only a few miles away from where we were meeting. She was one of the innumerable refugees for whom life had finally become intolerable.

The book that resulted from the workshop, published in 1988 in French and English,[5] recorded some of the important papers presented in plenary sessions. The authors based their addresses on their deep professional involvement, which in most cases included a research approach combined with unique personal experience. The chapters, a few excerpts of which will appear in this book, share a common theme – the need of those who have been through traumatic experiences to rebuild their personalities and their lives in a secure environment. This theme had implications for the refugees' families, the personnel of organizations assisting them, medico-social personnel in the public services, representatives of local, regional or national authorities, and the general public. A selection of the workshop conclusions and recommendations – still valid today – is given as Annex 1A to this book.

---

[5] *Refugees, the Trauma of Exile* (ed.) (Martinus Nijhoff) and *Réfugiés, les traumatismes de l'exil* (réd) (Emil Bruylant, 1988). The IFRC has authorized me to quote from it.

Although it had taken all too long after my own introduction to trauma in Mendoza in 1978 to reach this very satisfactory result, it became evident that it was only the very same year of our workshop (1987) that the prestigious London Tavistock Psychiatric Clinic was setting up a "Unit for the Study of Trauma and Its Aftermath", receiving two years later a research grant for work "to clarify developing ideas on the nature of trauma, and the way in which it affects subsequent mental and emotional functioning", to quote its head, Mrs Caroline Garland. Mrs Garland shared with me her draft chapter for a book to be published by Churchill Livingstone in 1991 entitled *Handbook of Psychotherapy for Psychiatrists*, Ms. Garland's part being "External Disasters and the Internal World: An Approach to Understanding Survivors". From this time on, a number of aid organizations, among them the Red Cross, began to focus on trauma. In 1990 the British Red Cross brought out *Coping with a Personal Crisis*, just as the Danish Red Cross produced *Psychological First Aid – and Other Humane Support*. The British Save the Children, having given support to the Mozambican Ministry of Education by financing an adviser in child mental health, translated resultant material under the title *Helping Children in Difficult Circumstances* (1991). In 1992 the ICCB published *The Psychological Well-Being of Refugee Children*.

In October 1993, the Council of Delegates of the International Red Cross and Red Crescent Movement, in a meeting in Birmingham, adopted an important new resolution, of which the following are two extracts:

> Reaffirming that armed conflicts and violations of international humanitarian law are among the main causes of forced population movements:
>
> Strongly encourages the National Societies: …
>
> (e) to focus attention on the psychological problems encountered by most refugees, asylum seekers, displaced persons and returnees.[6]

A resolution adopted several months earlier at the East African Red Cross and Red Crescent Societies Regional Meeting, Addis Ababa, March 1993, had stated, inter alia:

---

[6] Set down in *Guide for Planning Operations for Refugees, Displaced Persons and Returnees, International Federation of Red Cross and Red Crescent Societies* (Geneva, December 1993).

> That the Red Cross or Red Crescent should develop culturally sensitive programmes of psychological support to the refugees, displaced and returnees.

Then, in 1995, a draft of mine entitled "Organised Violence and Trauma", co-written with a distinguished Afghan psychiatrist before I left,[7] got to be expertly dealt with by my successor, Dr Ulrike von Buchwald, who received valuable comments and suggestions from people in the National Societies of Germany, Denmark, USA, Sri Lanka, Macedonia, Serbia, Croatia and Sweden. The finished product was circulated to National Societies worldwide in the four Red Cross languages, with the title *Working with Victims of Organised Violence from Different Cultures: A Red Cross and Red Crescent Guide*. A section of this guide features as Annex B, along with its reading list, but as the Movement continued to focus on the psychological needs of damaged populations over the intervening years, it was superseded to some extent by two excellent Red Cross and Red Crescent publications: *Community Based Psychological Support, A Training Manual* (IFRC, 1st edition, January 2003); and *IFRC Framework for Community Resilience* (2018). Both readily accessible on the internet, they will be referred to again later.

Concurrently, other NGOs have made the provision of psychological support one of their priorities in both their publications and their activities.

* * * * * *

It Seems Tragic That It Took So Long

One may well wonder how it is only over the four recent decades that the Western world, racked throughout the twentieth century and into the twenty-first by situations of massive violence, has become conscious of trauma. After all, it is far from being a recent phenomenon. It appears that the Greeks and Romans were familiar with it at least to a degree, for there are passages in the *Aeneid* and the *Odyssey*, I am told, that point to experience of such suffering in the Trojan War. There are clear references to it in Shakespeare, such as Kate Percy's speech in *Henry IV Part I* (Act 2 Scene 3); and Charles Dickens clearly suffered PTSD as a result of being

---

[7] Dr Mohammad Azam Dadfar, psychiatrist and once minister of higher education and minister of refugees and repatriation in his country, with five languages at his command, was for a period a prisoner of the communist-backed regime. He later worked at the Treatment and Research Center of Mental Disorders for Afghans in Peshawar.

involved in a railway accident at Staplehurst in 1865, as we can learn from Wikipedia or from biographies of Dickens.

My cousin Professor Peter Handford, who made his life in Australia after joining the University of Western Australia's School of Law, published in 1993 the first edition of the book that he and his co-author had entitled *Tort Liability for Mental Harm*. A section from this publication's third edition is featured in Chapter 5 of this book.

Back in the late 1970s, Dr Bessel van der Kolk and his contemporaries at first felt totally ill-equipped to help men who had developed alarming behavioural conditions, for there was no previously recorded knowledge about post-traumatic stress. The Veterans Association was not even ready to give support to research that Dr van der Kolk proposed to undertake on the phenomenon. We learn from books like *The Body Keeps the Score* that nineteenth-century attempts to bring to light the reality of post-traumatic stress (for example by French scientists working with the famous Dr Charcot, the French neurologist and professor of anatomical pathology at the Salpétrière Hospital, best known today for his work on hypnosis and hysteria) had been stifled by scepticism and a general lack of interest on the part of those who could have given researchers support. Discoveries about the retention of experiences made by the Russian scientist Ivan Pavlov, working with dogs in the early twentieth century, also went unrecognized. And, right into the 1980s, scepticism continued to keep hidden the real discoveries by other medical practitioners, as Dr van der Kolk writes when referring to misguiding statements made in high places that retarded the acknowledgement of trauma.[8]

Certainly prior to 1978 there had been great concern about the destructive and all-too-common practice of torture and the needs of torture survivors to receive specialized care. In Chapter 7, we shall see moves that

---

[8] "I vividly recall a phone call from a well-known newsweekly in London, telling me that they planned to publish an article about traumatic memory in their next issue and asking me whether I had any comments on the subject. I was quite enthusiastic about their question and told them that memory loss for traumatic events had first been studied in England well over a century earlier. I mentioned John Eric Erichsen and Frederic Myers' work on railway accidents in the 1860s and 1870s and Charles Samuel Myers' and W.H.R. Rivers' extensive studies of memory problems in combat soldiers of World War I. I also suggested they look at an article published in *The Lancet* in 1944, which described the aftermath of the rescue of the entire British army from the beaches of Dunkirk in 1940. More than 10 per cent of the soldiers who were studied had suffered from major memory loss after the evacuation. The following week, the magazine told its readers that there was no evidence whatsoever that people sometimes lose some or all memory for traumatic events." *The Body Keeps the Score*, p.191.

led to the creation of the Rehabilitation and Research Centre for Torture Victims, Copenhagen.

Obviously, we live in a period that sees more and more uprooting than ever before. The reality of mass flight and migration, of which we see continuous proof in the media, is as stark as was foreseen many years ago when factors such as the worldwide demographic upsurge and the ever-widening gap between the richer and the poorer nations, along with far from sufficient development aid, were recognized and used increasingly to warn the world of what was bound to happen. Those people who risk their lives trying to cross the Mediterranean to Europe are, for the most part, uprooted because of economic conditions in their countries. They have gone to endless trouble to reach the north coast of Africa, in the hope of getting to countries that can give them work and a decent life away from the hunger, unemployment and lack of prospects at home; then they have faced merciless exploitation and the daunting perils of the dangerous sea crossing.

But huge numbers of people correspond to the internationally recognized definition of refugee, namely a person who:

> As a result of events occurring before 1 January 1951 and owing to well-founded fear of being persecuted for reasons of race, religion, nationality, membership of a particular social group or political opinion, is outside the country of his nationality and is unable or, owing to such fear, is unwilling to avail himself of the protection of that country; or who, not having a nationality and being outside the country of his former habitual residence as a result of such events, is unable or, owing to such fear, is unwilling to return to it.

> United Nations Convention Relating to the Status of Refugees, Geneva, 28 July 1951, and Protocol relating to the Status of Refugees, New York, 31 January 1967.

The critical situation of people who fled the endless conflict in Syria, or who are trying to reach Europe after leaving Afghanistan, Vietnam or Niger, are more likely to be declared in due course to be refugees (though it may take years of waiting, of frustration and of unmet needs). The current situation of those currently incited to leave Turkey and to cross over into Greece is abhorrent as attempts are made strenuously by Greek patrols to push women, children and men away from the shores. As if they have not suffered enough already, as if they are not human beings like the rest of us.

The above definition was first adopted in 1951, the year that the Office of the United Nations High Commissioner (UNHCR) was created. It is incorrect to call people who are on the move largely because of poor economic conditions back home "refugees", however much they may nevertheless need tremendous levels of help.

UNHCR, changing its name some years ago to "The Refugee Agency", has become concerned both with refugees who fall within its mandate, and – over recent years – with survivors of calamities occurring within their country's own borders such as drought, floods, volcanic eruptions or earthquakes – people known in UN language as "internally displaced persons" or IDPs.

* * * * * *

So much for this account of how the reality of trauma and post-traumatic stress came to surface at last! But there is much more in Chapters 19 and 20, and some readers may actually wish to read those two chapters first, particularly as the final chapter outlines healing possibilities and practices. In any case, it is certainly not imperative to read the chapters in sequence! Readers can pick and choose what might be of most interest.

The underlying idea in creating this book has been to sketch a number of the most significant situations that people have lived through over the last hundred or so years, pointing to some of the psychological consequences that could hardly fail to ensue. At the time of writing, there are still populations with untold suffering in Syria, Yemen, Bangladesh and all the other places where people are deprived of human dignity. "People smuggling" has become a lucrative business that all too often has tragic consequences. But at the same time, and this is of course supremely important, along with the organization of massive aid, methods of healing have been gaining momentum, as descriptions in the last chapter of this book are meant to show. There is now international recognition of the need to address mental health issues right at the start of humanitarian activities mounted to bring relief to distressed populations.

However hard people may find it to turn these pages – that were far from easy to write! – I hope that *Trauma and Uprooting* will prove to be revealing, and useful to those who aim to get into international humanitarian work.

Riaz, Switzerland, spring 2020

CHAPTER 1

Who Is Affected By Trauma?
A Litany Of Suffering Over The Last 100 Years

I t is increasingly understood nowadays that people who have lived through traumatic experiences are marked by them, and deserve understanding, respect and the chance to resume a normal life. To suffer post-traumatic stress (PTSD) is likely to have been, or to be, the lot of many of the millions of people who have been victims of organized violence – in the two world wars, in the countless civil wars that have never ceased to erupt in various parts of the world, in situations of massive political repression that have involved the practice of torture and in activities of terrorists. This is without listing events closer to home, such as dreadful accidents, criminal activities, marriage breakdowns, job losses and other disasters in our societies that may affect us deeply.

(1) SITUATIONS OF ORGANIZED VIOLENCE[1]

The First World War (1914–19) and its aftermath

If we try to grasp the appalling cost to the human race of the First World War,[2] we have to take on board the fact that the total number of both civilian and military casualties is estimated at around 37 million people.

The Battle of the Somme, spanning 141 days (1 July 1916–18 November 1916) cost the British army some 420,000 casualties.[3] The French suffered another estimated 200,000 casualties and the Germans an estimated 500,000. Gunfire wasn't the only factor taking lives; the diseases that emerged in the trenches were a major killer on both sides. The living conditions in the trenches made men vulnerable to countless health hazards such as trench foot, shell shock, blindness and burns from mustard (poison) gas, lice, trench fever and influenza. Prisoners of war were treated inhumanely both then and, to a large extent, during the Second World War.

Of the millions who survived those war years, countless men returned having been wounded, some being crippled for life. For many of them, their experiences lived with them for the rest of their lives in nightmares and other forms of post-traumatic stress (PTSD) – but this was not understood. Dr Judith Herman, in her book *Trauma and Recovery*,[4] writes of the fact that "under conditions of unremitting exposure to the horrors of trench warfare men began to break down in shocking numbers. … Many soldiers began to act like hysterical women. They screamed and wept uncontrollably. They froze and could not move. They became mute and unresponsive. They lost their memory and their capacity to feel…" She reports that, according to one estimate, mental breakdowns represented 40% of British battle casualties,

---

[1]   We see the World Health Organization's definition of organized violence in the context of many extreme situations. Inger Agger refers to it in *The Blue Room* (1992), p.55, as follows: "In 1986, a World Health Organization (WHO) working group introduced the concept 'organized violence' to describe societal violence, defined as the conscious and deliberate infliction of pain and suffering by an organized group according to a declared or implied strategy and/or system of ideas and attitudes (van Geuns 1987). The WHO group emphasized that violence also can be psychological. The heartbeat can be stopped by other means than a bullet."

[2]   Not to mention the tremendous suffering of hundreds of thousands of horses and a number of dogs.

[3]   1 July 1916 was reported to be the bloodiest day in the history of the British army, with 57,470 casualties, including 19,240 dead – one of whom was my father's only brother.

[4]   Judith Lewis Herman, *Trauma and Recovery, from Domestic Abuse to Political Terror* (Pandora, 1992).

but "Military authorities attempted to suppress reports of psychiatric casualties because of their demoralizing effect on the public."[5] The British psychologist Charles Myers examined some of the initial cases, attributing their symptoms to the concussive effects of exploding shells, hence the term "shell shock", but as time went on military psychiatrists realized that the symptoms came from psychological trauma, especially the emotional stress of prolonged exposure to violent death. Unfortunately, the seriously affected soldiers, expected to glory in war and show no sign of emotion, were initially looked down upon. Some were put through agonizing electric shock treatment, with the aim of preparing them for a return to the trenches. If medical attitudes were gradually to become more enlightened, the general attitude was still "Let them put it all behind them, and make a new start."

Many of the families left without a breadwinner lived on the edge of poverty.

The Armenian Genocide: Many sources, including Wikipedia, report how over several years from April 1915, 1.5 million Armenians, mostly citizens of the Ottoman Empire were killed, the Ottoman authorities rounding up, arresting, and deporting from Constantinople (present-day Istanbul) to the region of Ankara over two hundred Armenian intellectuals and community leaders. The majority of them were eventually murdered. Then after the wholesale killing of the able-bodied male population, women, children, the elderly and the infirm were deported on death marches in the direction of the Syrian Desert. Most Armenian diaspora communities around the world came into being as a direct result of the genocide. Turkey still does not accept the word *genocide*, despite being faced with repeated calls to recognize the mass murders as genocide.

The Russian Revolution And Civil War (1917–22), The Gulags (1917–56)

The Russian Revolution of 1917 came about in a way that no one, not even Lenin, had altogether predicted. Its immediate impetus was the First World War, which was taking a heavy toll on Russian soldiers at the front and on peasants at home. As we read in the *Encyclopaedia Brittanica*, corruption and inefficiency were widespread in the imperial government, and ethnic minorities were eager to escape Russian domination. Peasants, workers and soldiers rose up after the enormous and largely pointless slaughter of the initial First World War years had destroyed Russia's economy as well as

---

5   Elaine Showalter, *The Female Malady* (1988), pp.168–170.

its prestige as a European power. After the imperial government had been overthrown, Vladimir Lenin's Bolsheviks seized power at the expense of the social democrats (Mensheviks) and conservative "Whites".

It was the world's costliest civil war in terms of the number of lives lost during combat and in events relating to the war. It is estimated that the country lost some 1.5 million combatants, and around eight million civilians died following armed attacks, famine and disease. Large numbers of White Russians fled the newly established Soviet Union (USSR), seeking refuge far from their homes, even as far away as China, where a large Russian enclave came about in the city of Harbin.

The prison camps instigated by Lenin and mainly situated in remote Siberian regions to which tens of millions would be sent throughout the next four decades account (according to Western scholarly estimates), for between 1.2 and 1.7 million deaths from executions, starvation and the harsh slave labour conditions. Men and women filled the sixty or so camps that the writer Alexandr Solzhenitsyn called "The Gulag Archipelago" in three major waves: in 1929–32, the years of the collectivization of Soviet agriculture; in 1936–38, at the height of Stalin's purges; and in the years following the Second World War, when those arrested and interned in camps included Soviet soldiers and other citizens who had been taken prisoner or used as slave labourers by the Germans during the war, people suspected of anti-Soviet attitudes, including Greeks, Bulgarians, Armenians, Turks, Kurds, Ukrainians and inhabitants of Soviet republics.

People sent to the Gulags in the early days had included the better-off strata of society and opponents of the Bolsheviks, while soon there would also be purged Communist Party members and military officers, members of ethnic groups suspected of disloyalty, suspected saboteurs, dissidents, ordinary criminals and many innocent people who were victims of Stalin's purges.[6]

Hitler, National Socialism And The Second World War, 1933–45

From the time Adolf Hitler became chancellor of Germany in January 1933, Nazi violence was directed against Jews, initially by means of countless restrictions and propaganda. Then, on the night of 9/10 November 1938 the violence became overt: in what became known as "Kristallnacht" (the "Night of Broken Glass"), Nazis torched synagogues, vandalized Jewish homes, schools and businesses, and killed close to a hundred Jews. In the aftermath of Kristallnacht, some 30,000 Jewish men were arrested and

---

[6] Encyclopaedia Britannica, internet.

sent to Nazi concentration camps. Chapter 3 takes this tragic story on, for throughout the hallucinating years that followed came the unimaginable suffering and murder of six million Jews of all ages, known as the Holocaust. The Nazis murdered people with disabilities, gypsies and most of those who had expressed opposition to their policies.

Hitler, after making a case against the heavy penalties imposed on Germany by the Allies' Versailles Treaty that Germany had been forced to sign, on 2 September 1939 carried the German population forward and into the Second World War with the unprovoked invasion of Poland. As late as 8 August 1939, Winston Churchill, denied a voice both on the BBC and in *The Times* newspaper, had broadcast a speech to the United States, using an American network: "In Germany, on a mountain peak, there sits one man, who in a single day can release the world from the fear which now oppresses it; or in a single day can plunge all that we have and are into a volcano of smoke and flame. If Herr Hitler does not make war, there will be no war. No one else is going to make war."[7] It was what Churchill later called "the unnecessary war", saying, "There never was a war more easy to stop than that which has just wrecked what was left of the world from the previous struggle. The human tragedy reaches its climax in the fact that after all the exertions and sacrifices of hundreds of millions of people... we have still not found Peace and Security."[8]

The Red Army was "the main engine of Nazism's destruction," writes British historian and journalist Max Hastings in his book *Inferno: The World at War, 1939-1945*. "The Soviet Union paid the hardest price: though the numbers can never be precise, an estimated 26 million Soviet citizens died during World War II, including as many as 11 million soldiers. ... The Russians paid almost the entire 'butcher's bill' for defeating Nazi Germany, accepting 95 per cent of the military casualties of the three major powers of the Grand Alliance." The Russian prisoners of war were treated inhumanly by the German state, while the estimated four million prisoners of war captured by the Soviets from all over Europe may not have fared much better.

One finds war memorials in countless places in today's Russia to commemorate the millions of dead. Particularly moving is the one featuring the courageous opposition to the Nazis during the siege of Leningrad

---

[7] Quoted in *Churchill, the Power of Words* by Sir Martin Gilbert.

[8] *The Gathering Storm*, Winston Churchill (1948). Throughout the period 1933–38, the successive governments under Ramsay MacDonald, Stanley Baldwin and Neville Chamberlain were blind to realities, choosing not to heed the increasingly urgent warnings of Winston Churchill, the clear-sighted, well-informed backbencher who, earlier, had held several ministerial posts in government.

(today's Saint Petersburg): after the German forces invaded the Soviet Union in the summer of 1941, an army surrounded the city of Leningrad in an extended siege that began in September and lasted nearly 900 days. It resulted in the death from starvation of more than a million of the brave citizens who had refused to give in. The Germans before retreating ruined the royal palaces situated twenty or more kilometres from the centre of the former capital, stealing the gold that had embellished them. It took over fifty years to restore those magnificent buildings.

Britain was of course under siege for a long time, as soon as what we had called the "phony war" had been succeeded by the heavy bombing of all our cities. The Nazi bombers gave Britain a tremendous pounding for months on end. The German bombings caused 43,000 civilian deaths, 137,000 wounded and the loss of a million homes in London alone. But even worse for many people of Europe was to have the Nazis occupy their countries, watching their every move and arresting anyone suspected of having Jewish blood or sympathies with Jews or with the opposition. Hitler's indiscriminate bombing of fine cities like Rotterdam had been the forerunner to occupation and the terrifying presence of the Wehrmacht, the SS and the Gestapo. It was tragic that, after five years of war, to get rid of the Nazi presence all over occupied Europe the Allies in 1944–45 had to bomb some civilian areas, especially the Channel ports in Normandy. The seventy-fifth anniversary of the Normandy landings, celebrated on and around 6 June 2019, was a moving experience for many. People were impressed by the modest testimonies of the remaining veterans, most of them in their 90s, and appreciated once again the heroism of the men who had faced tremendous odds in tackling the Nazi hordes to free Europe after the five years of occupation.

The forty to fifty million deaths incurred in the Second World War made it the bloodiest conflict and the largest war in history. Every family in practically every part of the world was involved in one way or another. Millions of people, including the survivors of the Holocaust, must have suffered from post-traumatic stress, receiving little real understanding of their state and certainly no therapy. As would happen in the late 1970s with former Vietnam veterans of the US armed forces, some Allied military personnel suffered the onset of PTSD many years after the end of hostilities. In 1964, an Anglican curate in Swindon, UK, was suddenly taken seriously ill. A New Zealander, he had flown innumerable Lancaster trips but survived. His surgeons commented to him that many who had served in those crews were now presenting life-threatening illness – two decades after the end of the war.

Two Atomic Bombs Dropped On Hiroshima And Nagasaki

On 6 and 9 August 1945, after Japan had failed to react positively to a demand to declare defeat, atomic bombs developed from 1942 onwards in the USA were dropped, first on Hiroshima, then on Nagasaki. They caused massive destruction in terms of human lives – many tens of thousands of deaths occurring instantly, at least an equivalent number subsequently as a result of radiation – and there was unimaginable environmental damage.

Repressive Regimes And Wars Of Independence: 1954–62 Algerian War Of Independence

The war saw atrocities committed on both sides, with Algerian historians putting the death toll at 1.5 million Algerian victims, while French historians say that around 400,000 people from both sides were killed. There was a mass exodus of French citizens and of Algerians who had supported the French, most of them as soldiers in France's army contingents. Henceforward, largely Muslim communities sprang up in most parts of France, which thus became the first European country with a strong Muslim population.

1959: China And Tibet

In March 1959, the Dalai Lama and thousands of his followers left Tibet, after Tibet had been overrun by communist China and its government abolished. China calls Tibet an "autonomous region" of China, and exercises strong repression on the country. Thousands of Tibetans have been imprisoned and tortured, many killed. The Dalai Lama, greatly respected by most world leaders, had to base his life in India, glad that many of his thousands of followers eventually received the necessary assistance to cultivate land and eke out a living.

Vietnam, Cambodia And Laos

From 1954 to 1975, the three countries of Indochina lived through war years in which they suffered intensely from heavy US bombings and ground conflict. Then all three countries were taken over by communist forces.

All the Cambodians who survived the subsequent four years under the Pol Pot regime, which was responsible for the deaths of a third of the entire population of Cambodia, had continually been in life-threatening situations, and rightly considered themselves victims of violence. The huge numbers of Vietnamese "boat people" who, from 1978 onwards, left their homes in small boats in the hope of achieving a better life in the West, were in danger of drowning in the South China Sea, their women preyed on by Thai pirates. Both lowland Lao and large numbers of the hill tribes fled into Thailand, claiming repression in Laos. For years, there were camps all over South East Asia giving only temporary asylum to many hundreds of thousands of fugitives.

Coups D'état: Chile (1973) And Argentina (1976)

General Pinochet's violent *coup d'état* of 11 September 1973 caused the imprisonment, torture, death and exile of tens of thousands of Chileans. Three years later, the 24 March 1976 military *coup d'état* in Argentina that overthrew the government of Isabel Perón also led to unquantifiable suffering. Countless inhabitants of both countries as well as those who managed to flee were seriously traumatized.

Rwanda, From 1959 To The 1990s

Ethnic violence between the majority Hutu tribe and the minority Tutsi population first broke out in 1959, and found expression again in 1963, 1974 and 1993, before reaching its horrific climax in the form of genocide in the three months of April, May and June 1994. In a later chapter we shall see how all this came about, but, obviously, a high proportion of the eight million Rwandans who survived the years of war, random assassinations, rape and finally genocide suffered – and may well still be suffering – the sequelae of those years, whether they lived on in a shattered Rwanda or fled to the four countries surrounding Rwanda before returning two years later.

Acts Of Terrorism: The "Nine Eleven" Twin Towers Attack, 11 September 2001

After two hijacked airliners crashed into the twin towers of the World Trade Center, New York, the Pentagon was struck by a third hijacked plane. A fourth hijacked aircraft, suspected to be bound for a high-profile target in Washington, DC, crashed into a field in southern Pennsylvania. The attacks killed 3,025 US citizens and other nationals. President Bush and Cabinet officials now considered the United States to be in a state of war with international terrorism, and indicated that Usama bin Laden, founder of the terrorist organization al Qaeda, was their prime suspect. In the aftermath of the "nine eleven" attacks, the United States formed the Global Coalition Against Terrorism.

Terrorist acts had been perpetrated with increasing frequency in a number of countries of the world, with waves of coordinated gun attacks and suicide bombings occurring. Subsequent to 2001, Spain, Great Britain and France have been among the countries viciously attacked by terrorists with links to Islamic cells, but they are by no means alone: there have been indiscriminate attacks on Christian women, children and men in countries south of the Sahara – and in other countries of the world. In Nigeria alone, between November 2017 and October 2018 Boko Haram terrorists killed over 3,700 Christians (90% of all the Christians killed across the world in that period)[9]

Wars In Iraq, Afghanistan, Syria, Yemen; Ethnic Repression In Myanmar

There cannot be any doubt that the distressing turmoil in Iraq and in Afghanistan, following years of conflict in both countries, laid the way to extreme acts of terrorism and resulted in new refugee flows. The genocide perpetrated by ISIS terrorists on the peaceful Yazidi people in northern Iraq and the trauma of survivors will be referred to later in this book.

Who can doubt that many of the millions of Syrians whose country after almost ten years of war is not at peace are traumatized, whether they are still in their ravaged country or are among the several million who got out and survive in virtually destitute conditions in refugee camps, with no chance of either return or resettlement? In Yemen, the worst humanitarian situation the world has known for decades has left 80% of the population in great distress, while the warring sides have blocked the delivery of desperately needed assistance. As for the 800,000 Rohingya people who fled Myanmar as a result of violent persecution, both what they have suffered before getting to Cox's Bazaar, Bangladesh, and the conditions in which they are forced to live are traumatic factors more than likely leading eventually to post-traumatic stress.

South–North Migration

Naturally, the same could be said of migrants fleeing conditions in a variety of countries, who, for several years, have been ending up in Libya, where

---

[9]   *Open Doors*, speaking of the United Nations General Assembly commemoration on 23 August of people killed for their religion.

they have found themselves violently exploited and robbed and their women raped before getting out in frail boats to cross the Mediterranean Sea – or to drown.

(2) THEN THERE ARE THE HORRIFYING ACCIDENTS

The Sinking Of Ships And Ferries

Although the greatest shipwreck on record, that of the *Titanic*, happened over a hundred years ago, almost everyone in Europe must have become familiar through the several films that have been produced with what happened to *RMS Titanic* in the night of 14/15 April 1912 on the great ship's maiden voyage between Southampton and New York with 2,224 people on board. The death toll was put at between 1,490 and 1,635.

The still comparatively recent wrecking of the *Costa Concordia* on the rocks of an island, Isola del Giglio, that had not been on the ship's true path stands in many people's memories. All the drama of the event, with people scrambling to get off the great ship as others drowned in their cabins, could certainly be felt through the massive television coverage of that totally unnecessary shipwreck. The death toll was thirty-three. The captain was sentenced to sixteen years in prison.

Human error also accounts for numerous tragic ferry disasters, such as those in Indonesian waters, on Lake Victoria and in the Channel between England and the continent of Europe.

Nuclear Disasters

The Chernobyl disaster of April 1986 at a Ukraine power plant was the first terrifying nuclear "accident" (after the devastating bombings in 1945). At first denied by the Soviet Union authorities, it was subsequently found to have caused unquantifiable damage to populations and to territory across a wide swathe of Eastern Europe. In March 2011, a tsunami sweeping over the coastline of Japan caused the disaster at the Fukushima nuclear power station, the very serious effects of which took years to assess.

Airline Crashes

Over the last twenty years, world opinion has been horrified and thousands of people traumatized by what has happened to airliners that crashed – or even disappeared. For examples of major crashes since 1998 see the box below:

In July 1998, Swissair Flight 111 crashed in the Atlantic soon after taking off at New York's J.F. Kennedy Airport on its way to Geneva. All 229 passengers and crew on board the McDonnell Douglas aircraft were killed.

In March 2014, Malaysia Airlines Flight 370 on a scheduled international passenger flight from Kuala Lumpur Airport, Malaysia, to Beijing with 227 passengers and twelve crew on board, simply disappeared from radar screens and the mystery of its disappearance has never been solved.

Then, only a few months later, on 17 July 2014 while flying over eastern Ukraine, Malaysia Airlines Flight 17, a scheduled passenger flight by Boeing 777 from Amsterdam Airport to Kuala Lumpur with 283 passengers and fifteen crew, was shot down by a missile. There were no survivors. Russia has been accused of being involved.

On 24 March 2015, an Airbus A320 211 operated as Flight 9525 by Germanwings, a low-cost carrier owned by Lufthansa, crashed 100 kilometres north-west of Nice in the French Alps. All 144 young passengers and six crew members were killed. It was established that the young German co-pilot had deliberately crashed the aircraft.

On 29 October 2018, a Lion Air flight with a brand-new Boeing 737 MAX 8 crashed thirteen minutes after take-off from Jakarta, the capital of Indonesia, into the Java Sea. It should have gone on to land at Pagkal Pinang at the end of a one-hour drive. There were 189 people on board.

On 10 March 2019, a Boeing 737 MAX 8 of Ethiopian Airlines crashed shortly after take-off in the direction of Nairobi, with 157 people on board. All Boeing 737 MAX 8 aircraft were subsequently grounded while the cause of the two Boeing 737 MAX crashes was being investigated.

Both the crashes of the Malaysian Airlines flights and that of the Germanwings flight were undoubtedly the result of deliberate acts of destruction.

The Aeroflot flight of 5 May 2019, cut short on take-off from Moscow by fire, caused the death of forty-one passengers when the emergency landing saved only a third of the passengers evacuated in extreme haste while the rear half of the aircraft was engulfed in flames.

The Football Stadium Disasters

The Heysel Stadium disaster occurred on 29 May 1985 in the Heysel Stadium in Brussels, resulting in thirty-nine deaths and thirty-four arrests. Huge numbers of fans had arrived from Milan and Liverpool. The deadly crush came about when mostly Juventus fans escaping from a breach by Liverpool fans were pressed against a collapsing wall.

Then, less than four years later, the Hillsborough disaster was a fatal human crush during an FA Cup semi-final match between Liverpool and Nottingham Forest at Hillsborough Stadium in Sheffield, England, on 15 April 1989. With ninety-six fatalities and 766 injuries, it was the worst disaster in British sporting history. The police match commander, David Duckenfield, was put on trial over his role at the match, accused of gross negligence and manslaughter. Jurors heard vivid descriptions of the "vice-like" crushing of Liverpool football fans in a "scene of horror" at the stadium.

The Piper Alpha Disaster, 1988

An explosion on Piper Alpha, an oil production platform in the North Sea on 6 July 1988, resulted in oil and gas fires that destroyed the platform, killing 167 people, including two crewmen of a rescue vessel; sixty-one workers escaped and survived. Thirty bodies were never recovered. Piper Alpha had once been Britain's biggest single oil- and gas-producing platform, bringing more than 300,000 barrels of crude a day – 10% of the country's total – from below the seabed 125 miles north-east of Aberdeen. The accident is the deadliest offshore oil rig accident ever.[10]

Fires In High-Rise Apartment Buildings

No one in Britain is likely ever to forget that, on 14 June 2017, a fire broke out in the twenty-four-storey Grenfell Tower block of flats in North Kensington, West London, just before 1:00 a.m. BST. It caused seventy-two deaths, including those of two victims who later died in hospital. More than seventy others were injured and 223 people escaped. It is recognized as having been the deadliest structural fire in the United Kingdom since the 1988 Piper Alpha disaster and the worst UK residential fire since the Second World War. The fire is the subject of a public inquiry, police investigations and coroners' inquests. Elsewhere in Europe there have been other significant fires, though fortunately not as destructive as this one.

The anguish of relatives and friends of all these disaster victims, not to mention other air and sea disasters and the all-too-frequent road deaths, is easily imagined. Many of them – as well as the members of emergency services who are often confronted by unimaginable sights – may suffer from post-traumatic stress. Add to all the above examples of human disasters the grotesque actions of terrorists, and acts of criminality in our midst, and we see that more people than could ever have been imagined may, after

---

[10]   *The Guardian.*

being subjected to traumatic stress in various forms, suffer the multiple consequences of PTSD.

(3) BUT EVEN THAT IS – UNFORTUNATELY – NOT ALL

Of course, large populations are subjected to the effects of terrifying natural disasters such as the Kobe earthquake of 1995 and the tsunamis of 2004 and 2018 in Asia (the latter combined with an earthquake and landslides), causing death and destruction on a hitherto unimagined scale. There continue to be the uncontrollable bush and forest fires that at various times have taken over huge areas of Australia, Brazil, Greece, Portugal and the USA. Such disasters, forcing survivors to face total loss and an uncertain future, can in a sense be equated with the effects of organized violence.

Turning to other areas of our lives, we have this year had to face the reality of the coronavirus (Covid-9). We have become aware that bereavement, like the often sudden onset of cancer and that of other debilitating, life-threatening diseases can be traumatizing both for the unfortunate sufferer and for his or her relatives and close friends. We need also to take on the fact that the loss of a home and domestic violence – marriage breakdown, the neglect and abuse of children – are serious ills in our Western societies that are responsible for post-traumatic stress in a high number of our fellow human beings.

Shocks to a human being's psyche can take many forms. And it is perhaps relatively rare that one realizes that a shock, or a series of shocks, can so damage what had been our excellent mental health that we end up – sometimes years after the event – with previously unimagined symptoms, not just headaches or back pain but other insidious forms of PTSD.

And furthermore it is not only human beings who suffer from traumatic experiences. Though studies undertaken over the last few years have been limited to the effects on human beings of violence, tragic accidents, serious illness, bereavement or other forms of loss, there is evidence that countless animals can also suffer from PTSD. The suffering in captivity of wild animals such as bears, lions, tigers, elephants and sea mammals, and that of domestic and farm animals, where cynically and cruelly treated by man, can certainly result in post-traumatic stress.

(4) REFUGEES AND ASYLUM SEEKERS

Uprooting and flight consequent to some of the situations of organized violence briefly described above can lead to problems relating to people's arrival in other countries, such as the rigours of camp life or, in the case of people arriving in Western countries, detention, interrogation, the withholding of refugee status and a degree, sometimes a marked degree, of incomprehension on the part of many of the representatives of host communities. The disasters people have had to live through have already had a tremendous and lasting impact on them, breaking down established defences and leaving them extremely vulnerable. Coupled with paralysing uncertainty both about their families left behind and about their future, people's trauma can all too easily be exacerbated.

It is only the last three or four decades that there has been any detailed scientific investigation of the mental health of refugees and asylum seekers, a complicated task as many of the subjects studied lived through situations of extreme stress before leaving their countries. There have been discernible patterns in the thousands of personal testimonies, affidavits and statements that have reached human rights organizations, including the United Nations Commission on Human Rights and the International Committee of the Red Cross. Many of those sequestered have been men and women with a high level of education, professional skills and social goals. But, just as often, they have been ordinary country people, such as farmers and village shopkeepers, living, however, in an area controlled by opposition groups, or belonging to the same ethnic group as opponents of the regime. Totalitarian regimes look upon these people as real or potential rivals or opponents.

As happened routinely in Chile and Argentina after 1973, armed squads snatched individuals from their place of work or from the street or, more commonly, broke into their homes at dead of night, and terrorized the spouse and the children by beating up their victim before their eyes. The slightest opposition on the part of unfortunate onlookers would be rewarded with blows. The intruders would blindfold and handcuff their prisoner, later perhaps ransacking the house to look for anything they could use as incriminating evidence in the event of a trial.

Exile may be the only alternative to facing ongoing danger. But no one wants to be a refugee or asylum seeker. People do not willingly uproot themselves, leaving behind everything that is familiar, unless there is no alternative. It would make no sense to leave your country, your culture and your social status to become dependent on people in an alien environment. It may be that you are not received very sympathetically in the country you hoped would prove to be a safe haven. Your story of what you have been through, of why you are here, is treated with obvious suspicion. You cannot bring yourself to talk about some of the treatment you received. In any case, you haven't much of the language; you know you are expressing yourself clumsily and are not getting through to them. You sense some sarcasm, and in any case these immigration officers seem to be in a hurry to get the interview over.

You begin to feel an object of contempt. You are ushered through the airport by people who could not remotely guess at your state of mind. You are put in a reception centre in a seedy part of town with people from other countries who seem as dispirited as you feel. The staff seems quite nice, but in one way or another you gradually become aware of the climate of rejection of refugees. You sleep badly, suffer from nightmares and headaches. You don't know what has happened to your family. You have problems digesting the food. You are not allowed to work and you cannot find anything to occupy your time. You receive no news as to what's happening on your case, and maybe there's no news from home. Months go by. The agonizing uncertainty has some of the same effects as the imprisonment and torture you had perhaps been through.

When your case comes up at last, you are required to provide evidence to substantiate your story. It is only because a human rights group comes to your aid that you can prove you had really been through a very bad time. You are told you will not be deported, news that comes as an immense relief. But the added stress has told on you. You have seen some aspects of the new society's worst side first. You have felt alienated, and have lost your self-esteem. Worrying about everything, day and night, you haven't had a chance to make much progress with the new language. Things are so different from anything you ever experienced that you are really suffering from culture shock.

However, you now know that you can stay and you do your best to pull yourself together. No one can ever give you back what you have lost, but you are going to find a place to live, establish a new sense of identity and community, redefine your social relationships and find at least some continuity between the past, the present and the future. You will try to find meaning in your life.

Uprooting from one's traditional milieu with all its personal and social ramifications, and adaptation to a new way of life, are among the complex issues featured in this book.

CHAPTER 2

My Family And Trauma Related To The War Years

The American Psychiatric Association in 1980 determined the following to be post-traumatic stress disorders, by now recognized across a broad front as PTSD:

1. Intrusive thoughts such as repeated, involuntary memories; distressing dreams; or flashbacks of the traumatic event. Flashbacks may be so vivid that people feel they are reliving the traumatic experience or seeing it before their eyes.
2. Avoidance: avoiding people, places, activities, objects and situations that bring on distressing memories; avoiding remembering or thinking about the traumatic event; or resisting talking about what happened or how they feel about it.
3. Negative thoughts and feelings may include ongoing and distorted beliefs about oneself or others; ongoing fear, horror, anger, guilt or shame; taking much less interest in activities previously enjoyed; or feeling detached or estranged from others.
4. Arousal and reactive symptoms may include being irritable and having angry outbursts; behaving recklessly or in a self-destructive way; being easily startled; or having problems concentrating or sleeping.

Reflecting a great deal on the whole subject of trauma after being urged to write this book brought to mind several elements of the life of my own family that had mostly been left undisturbed for years. In particular, my grandmother's experiences as a night-time ambulance driver throughout the Nazi blitzes of British cities deserve more than a passing mention, especially given the parallels with search and rescue efforts elsewhere in this damaged world, Syria in particular.

My Father

Eric Willday, born in 1903 in Stechford, Birmingham, was only ten years old when his father of only forty-seven died of pneumonia, and had just had his thirteenth birthday when his twenty-five-year-old brother was killed in the Battle of the Somme. With no breadwinner left, young Eric opted to leave school to help his mother take in lodgers. In his teenage years my father did his best to study unaided, while taking an active part in local sports activities. Eventually he got work representing in London a firm called "London Aluminium". My parents got married in 1931, by which time Eric had become the proud owner of a new house seven miles north of Marble Arch. From the house and the colourful garden that he created from an area at first littered with building rubbish, my parents looked over the fields to Harrow.

My brother David was born the following year, and started school in 1937. The three of them had a happy, fulfilled life, making friends with people in the area and receiving visits from family and friends from the Midlands. All seemed to be well, and a brother or sister for five-year-old David was on the way.

No one but those who actually listened to Winston Churchill's increasingly urgent warnings about Hitler's preparations for war seemed to be unduly worried about the future. But, just before I arrived in June 1938, Hitler's aggressive plans seemed far more real as he took over Austria (the "Anschluss"). My father's firm cancelled his London job because of the growing international uncertainty, offering him one in Birmingham, but in a fit of annoyance, refusing the idea of pulling up the roots he had put down in London for almost ten years, Eric unwisely turned the offer down, assuming that he would be able to find other work.

The climate was such that not only did he not find another job but no one was buying houses in the London area. Suddenly, my father found that he had lost everything he had had managed to build up in London. He was devastated and never truly recovered from this shock, nor would he talk about it. Obliged to return to Birmingham with his wife, a five-year-old son and a newborn baby, he borrowed or rented a house from his father-in-law and looked for work. Work came to him a few months later: before the outbreak of war his old firm had turned over to manufacturing Lancaster bombers, Hurricanes and Spitfires in Castle Bromwich factories, and took him on. When war on Germany was declared on 2 September 1939, the day after Hitler's unprovoked attack on Poland, Eric evacuated his little family to the safety of the Cotswolds, a hilly area some thirty miles south of Birmingham. The three of us moved into a room of a family called Keeley, and benefited from the extreme calm and beauty of Chipping Campden. But, for months, what Britons called the "Phony War" meant that there was as yet no real danger to civilians in cities. So, to avoid needless expense, we resumed life in Birmingham. An Anderson shelter had been erected in a ground-floor room of the house and a "blast wall" built in front of the windows, to take the shock if and when bombs fell in the garden.

The months of the heavy bombing of Britain, starting in September 1940 and going on relentlessly to May 1941, caused massive destruction and loss of life in our capital city and our industrial heartland and seaports. Nor were Wales and Scotland overlooked by the Nazis. The massive night squadrons of Heinkels, Dorniers or Junckers stationed in Normandy were to fly over us nightly throughout those eight months to flatten as many of our cities as possible,[1] the Birmingham area being on most of the Nazis' flight paths. Air raid warnings sounded practically every night, whereupon Mother first woke David, then took me in her arms down to the air-raid shelter. We passed the hours until the "all clear" sounded telling stories, playing with little Christmas bells and other small toys and practising putting on our gas masks. Our father was either on night work at the aircraft factory or out as a street warden, so we saw him very little. But he managed in some of the daylight hours to dig up what had been a lawn tennis court in the back garden to plant a wide variety of vegetables and herbs. There were already raspberry canes in that garden, as well as loganberry plants and redcurrant and blackcurrant bushes. Having also two big Cox's orange apple trees, we were really blessed with fruit when all other kinds of foodstuffs meant standing in interminable queues – something that, to this day, I hate doing!

Our father, always inclined to be tense and rather silent, was declared redundant when the war ended, and had an uncertain and therefore stressful work life until he took retirement at sixty-three. Throughout his life, he was prone to angry outbursts that were not easy to live with. He never really came to terms with what he lost that fateful year of my birth: a good father, generous to the extent that his limited means allowed, thoughtful and

---

[1]   They applied a new verb to this kind of activity: *coventrieren*, having reduced Coventry and its lovely cathedral to rubble.

sometimes humorous, he remained affected by the involuntary uprooting of that year. My mother confided towards the end of her life that, from 1938 onwards, she and my father were "just good friends". But how terrible for any man to lose his virility at only thirty-five! My parents had originally hoped to have four children.

As for the rest of the family, it seemed that Mother, who lived through both world wars, had coped well with all the hard work and stress. We took in lodgers, both because so many people lost their homes during the Blitz and because of the ruinous financial loss in London. Twelve-year-old David, proud on 8 May 1945 to announce the news of the end of the war to his (almost) seven-year-old sister, went through life without ever referring to any real stress connected with the war. And, as for me, for well over sixty years it so happened (curiously) that hearing any aero engine noise at night produced an immediate and vivid vision of our times in that cramped little Anderson air-raid shelter. Having always assumed that this had nothing to do with trauma, I should probably realize now that what I was getting so often were flashbacks, a feature of PTSD that in my case was perfectly harmless but nevertheless real.

The Uncles

My uncle Ted Nichols was in the British Expeditionary Forces that came to be trapped in Dunkirk in spring 1940, but rescued from the beaches against all the odds – 340,000 British and French soldiers, less those, alas, who died from machine-gun fire or bombings by German aircraft.[2] Ted was not among the 10% of evacuees who reportedly suffered from PTSD. He subsequently undertook certain very perilous missions that could have been traumatic, but came through the war years with his characteristic cheerfulness and without overt harm.

My mother's younger brother Norman Renton, after training men in Aldershot from 1939 to 1942, was sent to Singapore and arrived just as the colony was overrun by the Japanese. He became one of the relatively few survivors of the years of captivity by the Japanese, first being incarcerated in the notorious Changi prison camp, then sent among hundreds of Allied prisoners to work sixteen- to eighteen-hour days on the Death Railway

---

[2]   When over 300,000 Allied soldiers were trapped by the German army on Dunkirk beaches, Winston Churchill ordered all available ships and boats to head for Dunkirk to evacuate as many men as possible. Between 26 May and 4 June 1940, over 900 fishing and pleasure boats and some larger ships formed a flotilla and evacuated under fire 200,000 British and 140,000 French soldiers.

at Sonkurai/River Kwai. A very high proportion of the prisoners of war died of disease, chronic malnutrition, overwork, beatings and executions. Norman managed to avoid the most chronic stress that was the lot of the captured officers, on the one hand by starting to compose, in his head, what came to be a definitive book on telecommunications,[3] and, on the other, by listening on a radio that he built inside a broom head to concerts from the Albert Hall. This was despite damage to his ears from beatings, as we learned only decades later.[4] How well I remember his imminent return, and his sister Evelyn cautioning us not to ask him any questions "Let him put it all behind him…" Her words expressed the universal approach in those days to potential psychiatric harm. Visiting this brave uncle with my mother very many years later, I commented that he had never talked about his war experiences, and to this he replied "I would have been glad to talk about them, but no one asked me."

Two other uncles, Alec and Eddie, were in war service throughout the Second World War, Alec posted to India, Eddie serving in minesweepers in the North Sea. Both seem to have survived without developing post-traumatic stress.

Our aunt Dagny Klaveness Ambjornsen married our Uncle Alec in Norway in June 1947, and became someone I admired immensely. She was nineteen when war broke out. In 1940, when she had been about to go to Oslo University to study humanities, the Germans invaded Norway. She joined the Norwegian resistance, becoming a member of a cell based deep in the forest near her home, and her work involved running as a courier and passing messages. Throughout the winters, she and her fellow resistance colleagues dressed in all-white clothes to ski long distances without being seen, and would often have to sleep in snow-holes to avoid detection. Some of her missions took her across enemy lines. We know that she was arrested once, but managed to escape.

Dagny was then asked to work in London for the Norwegian government-in-exile, on the surface working with import–export files, but

---

[3]   Norman Renton: *Telecommunications Principles, etc.* (1958). The book went into three editions. Years later, Norman was head of the British delegation at the annual meetings of the International Telecommunications Union, Geneva (ITU – the oldest of the fifteen specialized agencies of the United Nations).

[4]   Norman told our cousin John how a Japanese weather balloon fell into the camp and, thanks to his telecommunications expertise, he was able to turn the transmitter into a receiver. Had he been caught listening to a concert being broadcast by the BBC, Norman could have been shot or beaten to death. As John said, he risked his life for a little beauty and sanity.

in fact still involved in resistance missions. After the war, she returned to the UK and she and our Uncle Alec met while she was studying sociology at a Quaker college near Birmingham. He had been in Norway on post-war work, and it was there that they were married, from a beautiful family home that not long before had been recuperated from the Nazis. Every one of the wedding guests, according to my mother, who represented our family, expressed the immense gratitude Norwegians felt towards the British for having delivered Norway from the Nazis.

No more rational, brave, dignified and humorous person could ever have joined our family! With regard to those war years, Dagny told me that she and her companions in the Norwegian resistance had vowed never to talk about their war work. In her old age, our dear Dagny, widowed in February 1999 and suffering from dementia, was once or twice found by her daughter to be trying to start out on clandestine missions in the middle of the night.

Relics from the past...

Our Grandmother, Claudia Frances Renton, 1883–1968

The following account covers several pages of this book, but I think this is justified to illustrate the kind of traumatic experiences people have in wartime. Writing about my grandmother to give readers insights into her war experiences brings us, in a sense, close to survivors of the horrific conflicts in Syria and elsewhere that – prior to the Coronavirus pandemic – were in the news perpetually for years.

"Nan" became for her eight children and nineteen grandchildren a fascinating person with whom, in ones and twos, we used to love staying in her tiny Chipping Campden cottage. Having in 1931 driven into the Cotswold area south of Birmingham with two or three of her younger children, and finding that the two Chipping Campden gatehouses of the former manor house were to be let, she unhesitatingly signed a forty-year lease on them. Campden House, the once-impressive home of a prominent wool merchant ennobled by James I, had burned down during the Civil War, and the gatehouse cottages, like the principal outbuildings, had been closed up for 300 years. Though they had nothing more than "one up, one down", with a winding stone staircase to link the two rooms, they had immense charm, and, once extended, North Gate House provided a quiet country haven for Nan, during the war years in particular.

When Hitler was on the warpath and war looked imminent, Nan had intended the family to make Chipping Campden their home. But, with our grandfather refusing to leave their Stechford home and other family members also electing to stay in Birmingham, she wrote to the army offering her services and started work as an ambulance driver at Bordesley Green Birmingham ambulance station, a few months later being drafted into the Mechanised Transport Corps, with which she worked until the MTC closed on 30 June 1945.

Her diary describes her experiences driving ambulances during Hitler's blitz on Britain with bombing raids on Birmingham almost every night for months. On 14 November 1940, following the intense Nazi raid that destroyed Coventry's medieval cathedral and city centre, on what should have been a much-needed day off she drove straight there, the first ambulance driver from outside the stricken city. People of my generation still speak of the orange flames on the skyline that night that were visible from many miles away. By 1941 my grandmother really felt she had had enough and handed in her notice, but it was not accepted. Instead, her job changed, and for the rest of the war she remained in army uniform and drove key people on undisclosed missions, particularly to Allied meetings in remote parts of Scotland.

The only entry in the diary after 1941 was a few paragraphs written in October 1945 summarizing the last four years of the war. As she said, she did not have the heart to write anything after her son Norman, sent to Singapore, was reported missing. The years of trauma told on her, depriving her of years of normal sleep, but she never referred to that fact, and would simply show visitors a new curtain she had made or a new hat she had crocheted during the night hours.

Enrolled from the start of the war in the "Fannys" (short for First Aid Nursing Yeomanry) and wearing army uniform for the next six years, Claudia Renton really needed her village home some fifty kilometres away for periods, however short (even sometimes just a few hours) to recover from the nightly scenarios.

Nan's War Diary

Oct.20th 1940

> I have been on ambulance work at Bordesley Green 1 year from 16th Oct. [1939] and I have decided to write here some of my experiences of the results of war – in order that Alec (in India) and Freda in Australia may one day read them, for naturally I am not telling them in letters much about it all. In

fact I couldn't because letters are censored and news of raids etc. not sent on.

Going on to indicate where several other members of the family were now living, she continued:

> When the fear of invasion arose, our depot was the Headquarters for the Home Guard on night duty. Oh what a lot they were – the weeks I spent on night duty will always be a nightmare to me. After the raids started we all had to take cover in the cellars amongst the huge water pipes, all huddled together on the floors. It was horrible. If a bomb had hit us we would have been drowned or scalded to death. The greater the noise of the bombs falling, the louder these people used to sing and shout. One night in particular bombs were falling thick and fast; I thought each one was for us.
>
> Having been there a year I was entitled to 6 days' leave. Oh how I longed to get to Campden to stay put – but instead I took a 5 days' intensive officer training course.

She spent the sixth day cleaning both Clover Bank, the home of which she was not very fond, and her cottage, barely getting any sleep.

> About the middle of Oct I arrived on early morning shift at 7 a.m. and Mr. Cansell rushed me off at once to an incident and to relieve those who had been there all night. It was in Bishop St./Gooch St. Several had been buried in cellars there and gas and water pipes had burst, so the poor people had no chance. I saw them bring about 15 out, one at a time – and helped to tie them up in their shrouds. Oh the terrible sights! As we were fastening one up and examining her, thinking her dead, she turned her head and opened her poor swollen black eyes and asked for a cup of tea. She was rushed off to hospital (after a sip or two of tea). But it was so sad to see the people standing about waiting for their children and mothers to be dug out. One poor man was only allowed to see his daughter's shoe – they wouldn't let him see her face to identify her. She was too terrible to look at. I followed him into his house, the rescue men had to nearly carry him and his old wife was weeping in her apron. I patted them and took their hands and said "Let

it comfort you to know she was killed outright, she would not have suffered." "Oh do you think so, Ma'am?" the old lady said looking up from her apron. I said "Yes, most certainly" and she said "Those are the most comforting words I have heard." As I passed through the barriers where hundreds of people were standing, they called to me "God bless you for what you are doing". I couldn't keep the tears back. One woman came clambering up from the back of the ruins with her face all cut and coat torn. She had found her own way out somehow. It was just like someone rising from a grave. Five of the rescue men went over the pile of ruins to get her and helped her over into the street where such a cheer went up from the crowd at the sight of her, and a man ran forward and kissed her, and another boy too. One white-faced lad about 17 had been standing around looking at each corpse as they were brought up, then seeing one cried "My Mam" and went away. I wanted to go after him but I was too busy, I couldn't leave. A lot of the dead could not be identified, even the neighbours could not identify them, they were so knocked about. We searched their pockets for any sign of identification but in some cases it was quite hopeless. I was there from 7 a.m. until 1.30 p.m. and still they had not dug them all out. Being the only one in khaki such a lot of people evidently thought I was in charge; ever so many parsons among the crowd came to me and I sent them into the homes of the bereaved… That was a ghastly grim business and made one realise what war is.

About the next night after that there was a heavy raid around Stechford and Yardley. Two or three houses opposite Dorothy's old house in Vera Rd. were down. Dorothy had only left about a week before. A bomb fell in Mary Rd. I was in the hall at the time and it felt as though the lounge and dining room were falling together, the hall seemed to sink, I gripped the door of the dining room. Several of our windows were broken with it. Just round the corner from Richmond Rd 3 or 4 houses were down. Seven children and a father were all killed in one house. Our night shift had to turn out and the 7 children were all laid out under our shed. The garage where we get our A.R.P. petrol was completely on the ground, and lots of houses in Bordesley. …

During the last week or two there have been awful raids in B'ham. Shops and factories down everywhere. Fires going all night. On Sat night I stood in the veranda watching the bombs dropping over B'ham. You would see flashes like sheet lightning lighting up everywhere, then "bang" the bomb had dropped, and a *tr r r r r* – the building falling, collapsing like a pack of cards – or toy bricks.

I am not on night duty, but those who were went out. A bomb dropped close behind the escort car (which would have been mine had I been on) and it raised it high in the air, and down it came with a bump – the driver thought it was "all up". Our ambulances picked up a lot of dead from the Picture House, Stratford Rd. and had to take them to mortuary where floors were full of dead people, hundreds of them I was told, they just took them in and dumped them down – no one here to receive them, and a girl of 20 had to help carry them in!

Dec. 18 So much has been happening to poor old Birmingham the past month and more, and I have not had the least inclination to write it down, but I will recall just a few of the experiences – giving description of one week only.

About 5 weeks ago I went to Coventry – the Coventry that was – to give my off-duty day – to help in any way I could. No traffic at all was allowed past Stonebridge, but being in uniform and having our sectional flag on the car I was allowed to pass without even showing my identification cards. In fact the policemen made way for me. When I got to Coventry I could not tell where I was, every street and building was down to the ground, all gutted, smoking and smouldering. It was a pitiful sight to see the Cathedral down, where Alec took us one Sunday afternoon about 3 years ago to a recital. I reported to Police Headquarters and there were hundreds of people waiting in queues to get a hearing – homeless people. A way was made for me by police and I walked straight through and offered my services. I was sent to Hospital Infirmary, and from there was given a list of people to look after and find homes for. The address of refuge homes were given to me but as all phones were down it meant actually going to these places to see how many they could take, and oh it was so difficult to find the places and all roads blocked.

I got hold of the First Aid man from Courtaulds who was also on the same job and he was a great help in showing me the way. We found the slum district we were looking for, and the people there were just sheltering under bits of corrugated iron – their walls, ceilings, doors & windows were all out & if the beds were left they were drenched with water & bricks & rubbish. One old man in particular, he was nearly dead, he was sitting in a chair by a fire for his fire grate was left but no walls around it, & there he had sat since the place was bombed... He was too weak to stand. The doctor had seen him & said he must be got away somewhere – but where – all hospitals were full. ... I had to climb over piles of bombed buildings to get to him, so I knew it would be a stretcher case. I want to the RP for an ambulance, but the whole place and ambulances had been bombed, all of them. ... There was no water, gas or food in the town. ... The miles of people waiting for buses to get them away carrying their pet cats & canaries & pots & pans & all kinds of things, where they were going goodness knows, they didn't know themselves. They were all black from the bombing & no water to wash, yet you could see & hear rushing water at the bottom of all bombed premises. The Ministry of Information had a van there driven by one of our M.T.C. ladies, & he was speaking through a loudspeaker telling the people all their children were to be at such and such a place to be taken away at once, they feared an epidemic, and he said no one must use their lavatories, they must do as their grandfathers did, dig a hole in the garden. There were craters everywhere & I saw a van had run down into one & a car in another. I had to leave Coventry before dark, leaving all the desolation behind me.

The next day... this Tuesday night raid started early, bombs dropped all around this school (our post). Every house in the street at the side of school (Drummond Rd) was struck & several on fire. The screams & shrieks of the people were only drowned by bombs falling all the time. ... We were all sent down into the cellars & the men called up to go out. They returned on the verge of collapse & looking so black & sooty that you would hardly recognise them as the full-of-life fellows they were when they went out. There were fires, fires everywhere. ... Then the call came down the trap door for Mrs. Renton. So I had to climb up thro' this trap door & drive my own car & follow the ambulance to Cherry Wood Rd. Dordrough Lane P.O. Stores had been bombed & was burning – in fact everywhere was burning. We had to drive on the footpath all the way up the road, & when we got to Cherry Wood Rd. where people were trapped under a house the men took the stretchers & clambered over the fallen house & I had to stand by ambulance & pass anything they called for. They had gone out of sight & hearing over the wreckage to back of house & as I sat on back of ambulance gripping on, screaming bombs fell all around me, lights blazed from every window as the glass & blackout fell out & houses crashed all around me. I was spellbound & not afraid as I watched walls bulge, then collapse. I had a man with a cut eye to take to 1st aid for treatment, & the way I had come was all blocked. I had to go another way then found a house right down across the road. Two men helped me to move some of the bricks to get over.[1] I thought every minute the car would overbalance – then I got thro' & another bomb in front of me blew down one of the big green standards & cables for trams, & a fire started. I had to drive between fire & craters & over these overheated cables. Whether they were dangerous or not I knew not, but thought the rubber tyres were non-conductors & I also had rubber boots on – & so I got back to depot with my patient. Then I had to return to scene of incident. Still they had not got people out, they could hear cries & a baby crying.

Our men were returning all from different places, and were all on the verge of collapse. Many did – & one driver told me only yesterday that he had been sent out again he would be in a lunatic asylum by now. That terrible night has played havoc with our personnel. Such a lot have turned the job in since then, one of our men drivers had been 4 years in last war, yet said that all those years put together he never saw half as much as he saw in Bordesley Green that night. He has been off ever since & we hear he can never face it again. Every time he heard a bomb drop he shrinks into as corner

---

[1] Three months later, Nan saw her patient again. He told her that only a minute or two after she had gone, a bomb had fallen and killed the two men.

on the floor & cries, & they dare not leave him. Yet he was a hardened old soldier. I got home about 3.30 a.m. Dorothy & Peg were sleeping under dining room table. Pat in pantry. Father & Claude in bed. I felt like patting myself on back for coming thro' it so well – yet I could not sleep. I worried about those trapped people and wondered if they had been got out alive, & regretted I was unable to lift the tons & tons of bricks under gunfire & bombs. As the bombs fell I gripped on to back of ambulance & it was lifted – it just bounced. I had only been back a few minutes when the school, our depot, was actually struck.

The diary goes on, with graphic descriptions of more frightful scenes, and relating how on one occasion she did collapse. She had to take periods of rest, but did not give up her service until the end of the war, six years from the start of it all. The diary includes details of our rationing (which continued until 4 July 1954).

Nan never made any direct allusions to the chronic insomnia that resulted from her involvement in the war. For many years, she took on driving duties to ferry people in her own car from their Cotswold homes to hospital, or vice versa. I remember her keeping a spade in the boot during winter months, in case of need if the car were to get stuck in snowdrifts along those remote unlit country lanes. We grandchildren whenever we were with her in her little cottage had such wonderful times, imbibing some of her spirit, enjoying the whole of the big, colourful garden that she had laid out herself from a section of field, playing around the ruins of Campden House, watching the sheep-shearers, wandering across fields, exploring the village scene or taking part in haymaking. And to this day, our annual family reunions have all taken place in magical Chipping Campden.

If I have talked too much about my family, I apologize. I have left until later any reference to my son-in-law, who with the members of his family lived through the Serb repression of Albanian speakers in beleaguered Kosovo.

CHAPTER 3

The Holocaust

At the time of writing this chapter, there has just been the commemoration of the discovery by Allied forces, 75 years ago, of Auschwitz extermination camp. The memory of six million Jews, and of the other people Hitler had decided should be murdered, was honoured in various ceremonies attended by people of note, including a number of heads of state, notably that of Germany, Chancellor Angela Merkel.

The enormity of what Germany under Adolf Hitler did to the Jews of Europe is difficult to grasp, even if one equates the numbers of the victims with those for example of the whole population of Norway (4.5 million today) or Panama (four million), adding 1.5 million people and two million people, respectively, to reach that appalling total of six million Jews. Six million men, women, children and babies annihilated, wiped off the face of the earth in conditions of unimaginable violence and treachery.

The immeasurable suffering of thousands of millions of people in the course of the Second World War resulted from the creation by the Austrian First World War corporal Adolf Hitler of the German Nationalist Socialist Party. Proclaiming anti-Semite policies, Hitler, initially not much more than a shiftless rabble-rouser, obtained a sufficient following over the years to rise to become chancellor of Germany in a period in which, as a result of the 1929 Wall Street Crash, the world had entered a ten-year period of serious economic depression. The longest, deepest and most widespread depression of the twentieth century, with its drastically damaging effect on industry, finance and agriculture across the whole Western world, lasted right up to the outbreak of the Second World War.

From the early 1930s, Hitler's policies of violence and repression saw the murders of his early opponents, the brutalization of Jews, and the organization of the concentration camps (*Konzentrationslager*) that before long would spring up all over occupied Europe. Many of them were soon to be used for the mass murder of Jews, gypsies, opponents, and people with handicaps.

State-enforced racism resulted in anti-Jewish legislation, boycotts, the nationwide propagation of Hitler's theory of the superiority of "Aryans", and the "Night of Broken Glass" pogrom, all aimed to remove the Jews from German society. Both in Germany and subsequently in all the occupied lands, the Nazi government implemented a series of laws to exclude Jews from political, economic and social life. Jewish books were burned, anti-Semitism took hold and synagogues were desecrated or burned to the ground. Gentiles (the Nazi government's "Aryans"), were encouraged to inform on Jews, and everywhere the earlier relaxed atmosphere of the various communities vanished. Jews were stripped of their citizenship and, along with communists, political activists, alcoholics, prostitutes, beggars and the homeless, they could be arrested without warning and taken off to one of the concentration camps, where the cruel treatment given them included measures to humiliate them to the greatest imaginable degree (for example being forced to stand by helplessly to witness atrocities committed against people they loved). Jewish homes were looted by people who burst in and helped themselves to anything they wanted. Aryans were prohibited from employing Jews, who were barred from their own professions as lawyers, doctors or journalists, were banned from state hospitals and were not allowed to travel. Countless other degrading restrictions on Jews were brought in. The Nazis confiscated Jewish bank accounts and valuables and so had funds for all their projects.

Hitler could have been stopped. But unfortunately, throughout the 1930s both Britain and France were weak, while Germany was rearming secretly in flagrant violation of the Versailles Treaty of 1919. As the facts gradually came to light (in London consistently communicated by civil servants to Winston Churchill – who unfortunately no longer enjoyed his earlier prestige), the governments of Britain and France, both pledged to pacifism, avoided recognition of the fact that Hitler represented a distinct danger to peace. In Paris there had been for years a rapid succession of governments, some of which lasted only a few weeks – or even only a few days – while in London, throughout the 1930s, none of the successive British prime ministers heeded the increasingly urgent warnings of Winston Churchill about Germany's mounting military strength. Churchill the visionary was frustrated year after year over getting his warnings received in the House of Commons.[1]

The Nazi armies took over Austria, and then Czechoslovakia after the British and French agreed in 1938 to Hitler's demand for what he called the Sudetenland. Jews in the new Nazi "client states" became outcasts overnight. Hitler wanted both to eliminate all the Jews and to take over huge tracts of other countries' lands, for *Lebensraum*, living space. His obsession with the idea of eliminating all the Jews and expanding the populations of so-called "Aryans" led to the destructive Nazi policies that caused incalculable suffering and death. His armies invaded Poland in a *Blitzkrieg* at dawn on 1 September 1939, showing off their massive military superiority. Infantry invaded across the northern and southern borders and there were multiple bombardments, with the loss of very many civilian lives.

Entire Polish communities fled on bicycles, on foot or on carts, praying that the Polish army might halt the German advance. Many crossed the borders to Romania, Lithuania and Hungary. After massive bombing of the capital city, Warsaw was under siege for three weeks until Polish forces finally capitulated and 100,000 prisoners of war were taken. The following day, 1 October 1939, German Panzer tanks rolled through the streets. Within days of the invasion, forced labour was imposed on all Jews under the age of sixty, homes were looted and thousands lost their livelihoods and most of their belongings.

In line with their treaty obligations, France and Britain declared war on Germany on 2 September. In 1940 Winston Churchill, so long ostracized by the governments of the day for his very pertinent warnings about Hitler, was appointed prime minister to handle the war with Germany. It was fortunate that he was, for many members of the Conservative government and of the British aristocracy still envisaged caving in to the tyrannical German dictator (who with hindsight has been seen as possessed of madness).

On 10 May 1940, the Nazi army and air force threw themselves against Holland and in no time encircled the French and British forces and forced

---

[1] Churchill couched one of his very first warnings in March 1933, *barely six weeks* after Adolf Hitler had become chancellor of Germany. In speech after speech, he sought to warn of the dangers of allowing Germany to steal a march on Britain in military and air preparations, but no one listened. Britain's Conservative government remained blind to realities until it was far too late to put obstacles across Hitler's path, and saw appeasement as the only way forward. The fascist dictator who, along with Mussolini, helped General Franco take over Spain at the cost of well over 500,000 lives and another 500,000 refugees, would soon dominate – and terrorise – virtually the whole of Europe and cause chaos even further afield.

them to retreat to the coast at Dunkirk. On 15 May, the French premier Paul Reynaud called Churchill, who had become British prime minister only five days earlier, to say "we have been defeated. We are beaten!" So France – a co-signatory of the guarantee of the borders of the Polish state – collapsed. The Nazis, aided and abetted by Italy's dictator Mussolini, and aligned by treaty with the Soviet Union, were free to do just what they wanted. Following their unprovoked attacks on Germany's neighbours, they sent in occupying forces, initiating barbaric methods against the populations of occupied Europe, including Norway

Then in 1941 Hitler, failing to invade Great Britain, took the fatal step of ordering a powerful onslaught on the Soviet Union. This for Josef Stalin was naturally a totally unexpected move on Hitler's part in view of the Treaty of Non-Aggression signed in 1939 between Germany and the USSR. Hitler's ambitions of world dominance led to the loss of an as yet undetermined number of Russian lives.[2]

The times were certainly threatening, to say the least. But no one, even after reading Hitler's *Mein Kampf*, could really grasp the reality of what lay ahead.

The "Final Solution"

The genocide of the Jews was the culmination of a decade of Nazi policy under the rule of Adolf Hitler. After the Second World War began, the Nazis gradually inaugurated plans to annihilate the whole of European Jewry.

They established ghettos in occupied countries, starting with Poland in 1940. During the German invasion of the Soviet Union in 1941, mobile killing squads (*Einsatzgruppen* in German) began killing entire Jewish communities. The methods used, shooting victims or killing them with exhaust fumes in sealed vans, were soon regarded as inefficient – and as a psychological burden on the killers. By the spring of 1943, these squads were responsible for the deaths of over a million Jews and tens of thousands of partisans, Roma (Gypsies) and Soviet political officials.[3]

---

[2] The Russian Ministry of Defence puts the figure of military personnel who died or were killed at 8.7 million (General G.F. Krivosheev, 1997, in *Soviet Casualties and Combat Losses in the Twentieth Century*, London. Greenhill Books). However, concordant reports found on internet quote another figure given by the Central Defence Ministry of fourteen million dead and missing, mentioning that 800,000 women served in the Soviet Armed Forces.

[3] *The Holocaust Encyclopedia.*

In January 1942, after what became known as the Wannsee Conference attended by the senior Nazis, the systematic deportation of Jews from all over Europe to six extermination camps established in what had been Polish territory began: Chelmno, Belzee, Sobibor, Treblinka, Auschwitz-Birkenau and Majdanek. The Chelmno killing centre had already begun operations on 8 December 1941, using gas vans. The other death camps used carbon monoxide gas, Zyklon B or a combination of the two. Mauthausen (Austria) too had killing facilities.

When rumours began to emerge asserting that Germany had started to use industrial means to kill the Jews, no one could believe them. The Nazi genocide was the first mass slaughter designed to exterminate a group of millions of people – the European Jews – through careful and detailed planning, organization and industrial implementation. It was all mounted on a mercilessly vast scale, and if the very idea seemed to defy credibility, the combination of Nazi deceit, ruthlessness and German efficiency with the cooperation of the authorities in occupied countries ensured its success. Before Nazism could finally be crushed, more than six million Jews from every part of Europe had been killed, the majority gassed to death, their bodies initially being tossed into mass graves. Subsequently, they were reduced to ashes by being taken by Jewish slave labour ("capos") from the specially constructed gas chambers to be burned in the huge industrial ovens nearby. Others were killed by starvation and beatings while forced to work as slave labourers on various industrial sites. German industry, aware that the captives had absolutely no rights, was glad to make full use – and abuse – of free labour.

Some of Europe's most brilliant men and women were among the thousands herded daily into cattle trucks at various strategic points and taken on the long journey to a death camp. On arrival at the subsequently notorious Auschwitz-Birkenau after several suffocating days and nights without food, water or sanitation, people were met by SS men with fierce Alsatians and would soon learn what their real fate was going to be. Far from it being to work, as previously announced by Nazi propaganda,[4] unless they were found to be fit and were chosen for the role of slave labourers, they were to be killed forthwith. Children, women and men of all ages were murdered en masse by the Nazis within hours of arriving in those sealed goods wagons.

Earlier, many of these same victims after Hitler's rise to power had sought to emigrate. But world powers were extremely reluctant to admit them in

---

4   The revolting motto over the entrance gate to the death camp, *Arbeit macht frei* ("Work makes you free"), left in place subsequently, must have been just about the most cynical of all the treacherous Nazi lies.

reasonable numbers: at a conference in Evian (France) in July 1938, each government representative produced reasons as to why his or her country could not help to save Jews from further persecution. Those who did get out of Germany in time went either to other countries of Europe, or crossed the Atlantic. The latter would be safe, but it was a different fate for all those who had assumed that, in a country like Holland or France,[5] they need no longer have fears of being victims of the Nazi tyranny. Sooner or later, the Nazi machine was to catch up with them. Only in Sweden and the United Kingdom, where hundreds of children had been taken in towards the end of the 1930s, were Jewish people safe. Switzerland also admitted a limited number of desperate border-crossers, repelling others, however, at the borders.

Many of the Jews in Europe, before they found themselves in the notorious cattle trucks being taken east, had first been herded into ghettos, the best-known having been the Warsaw ghetto, created in 1940 and where there was a dramatic uprising in 1943.[6] Jews who had not so far been killed or taken to unknown destinations were forced to leave their homes and most of their belongings, and live in close proximity with other Jews in a limited area guarded by the Nazi SS. They were used for work, and initially could come and go day by day within certain hours, returning to the same corner of the ghetto, where, for the time being, they were with members of their families but lacked any normal services or any basic forms of comfort. This was the pattern created in the occupied territories. A visit by representatives of the International Red Cross to a ghetto meant that it would be made superficially to look totally different, and the Nazi officers would assure the visitors that there would be no more transports to the east. But thousands more Jews would be sent east as soon as the delegates' backs were turned. Nazi deceit had worked as well on the Red Cross delegates as it had elsewhere.

There were few survivors of the ghettos, for in time, as the tide of war turned in favour of the Allies, the occupants of the ghettos were loaded onto cattle trucks and taken to the death camps.

The man Churchill once described as "a bloodthirsty guttersnipe" had instituted a diabolical regime all over Europe, most of his adepts learning

---

[5] France had already taken in between 20,000 and 30,000 Jews from Germany–Austria or Eastern Europe.

[6] The Warsaw Ghetto uprising broke out on Passover eve, 19 April 1943. It was the first urban uprising in occupied Europe, and the largest act of resistance carried out by Jews during the Holocaust. In time, the Warsaw Ghetto uprising came to be one of the best-known events in the history of the Holocaust. For both Jews and non-Jews this event has become the symbol of the desperate heroism and resolute struggle of the Jewish spirit. From the *Holocaust Encyclopaedia*.

to be cynically and ruthlessly heartless towards everyone in their power. The diverse Nazi atrocities perpetrated for instance in Holland, where after a time, the population came to be subjected to the most extreme war conditions and by spring 1945 was reduced to starvation levels, are described through the recently published biographical account of Audrey Hepburn's wartime experiences.[7] It is not surprising that many of the Nazis' victims, utterly deprived of their dignity and of their bodies' most basic needs, lost the will to live. In the Nazi death camps, and even in occupied territories, many died or killed themselves, all their strength of body and spirit now gone.

After liberation by the Allies, the Bergen-Belsen and Mauthausen camps served for a time as two of the 2,500 displaced person camps set up right across Europe to house the estimated eleven million displaced war survivors who had nowhere to go.

* * * * * *

After the Holocaust, Jewish survivors could not fully realize for some time that they were among the very few Jews who had not been murdered by the Nazis. Perhaps while in prolonged confinement, when thinking about the past or about a possible future brought about by unbearably intense longings, they had developed the capacity to restrict and suspend their thoughts. The now-famous American psychiatrist and author Dr Judith Herman suggests that in some cases the chronic trauma of captivity cannot be integrated into a person's ongoing life if the former prisoner refuses to speak of the past, in which case memories of the past can prove to be intrusive and override current preoccupations. "Prolonged captivity produces profound alterations in the victim's identity. All the psychological structures of the self... have been invaded and systematically broken down. In many totalitarian systems this dehumanizing process is carried to the extent of taking away the victim's name."[8] We know that in Auschwitz everyone had a number tattooed on an arm, and that all personal possessions, including clothes and shoes, watches and jewellery were confiscated, while those not sent to the gas chambers had all their body hair shaved off.

---

[7] *Dutch Girl Audrey Hepburn and World War II*, by Robert Matzen, Goodnight Books, 2019. Audrey Hepburn, born in Belgium of a Dutch mother and English father, was taken to Holland in 1939 when she was 10.

[8] Judith Herman MD, *Trauma and Recovery from Domestic Abuse to Political Terror* (1992), p.93.

In the depths of their souls, survivors of the concentration camps desperately wanted to be reunited with members of their families. Those who returned to their home areas hoped for a semblance of normality in those environments, only to find that there had been substantial changes: most of them no longer had any living relatives, and some of the townspeople were far from showing welcoming behaviour when they got back from their terrible ordeals. Of course, it was difficult for anyone really to imagine what these returning Jewish remnants had had to endure throughout the six nightmare years.

They undoubtedly suffered tremendous psychological harm. The Nazis had succeeded in breaking people, driving them to the point of degradation in which they had lost all will to live. According to two Auschwitz survivors, they were regarded as the living dead.[9] Before them now lay a long period of grieving, and of overcoming an array of obstacles to achieving any kind of normal life. In the new realities they had to face were the absence of family members and friends, of real health and of any belongings (substantial or otherwise). Businesses they had owned before the war had been taken over by the Nazis, and subsequently by the Communists, and their houses were occupied by strangers. In most cases, they had no financial means either. Only some Jewish survivors attained – after several decades of effort – any satisfactory outcome to claims they made as their parents' heirs. The banks, particularly in Switzerland, managed to put every possible obstacle in their path, of which the most cynical was a demand for the death certificates of their parents.[10] All this without any doubt tended to compound their trauma.

For – need it be said? – many or most of the Jewish survivors must have been suffering from chronic trauma after being the captives of merciless jailors for so long, seeing those around them taken away, or either then or later from beatings, starvation and exhaustion. Most people did not, either then or later, have access to any real form of help with their psychological scars. If sometimes the worst effects of trauma remain latent for some time and surface at a later stage in people's lives, many must meanwhile

---

[9] Levi Primo, *Survival in Auschwitz: The Nazi Assault on Humanity* (1958, trans. Stuart Woolf, Collier, 1961) and Wiesel, *Night*, Krystal, quoted by Judith Herman MD in *Trauma and Recovery* (Pandora, 1992).

[10] This in the end became a scandal that added to the ignominy of Swiss banks in relation to their having bought Hitler's stolen gold, which enabled Switzerland, professing to be neutral, to send to Germany both valuable raw materials and manufactured parts for arms. C.f. Tom Bower's *Blood Money – the Swiss, the Nazis and the looted billions.*

have suffered from some of these manifestations of PTSD, probably accompanying psychosomatic reactions (the body's distress symptoms):

- Deep emotional and affective disturbances.
- Depressive reactions accompanying multiple somatic complaints.
- Paranoid and startle thoughts with chronic dysphoric mood (that is to say, the inability to laugh).
- Low self-esteem, altered perception and withdrawal; people who have been through extreme forms of stress are likely to feel unsure of their own identity, feeling threatened by others and unsure as to how to react to them.
- Behavioural disturbances (intolerance of noise and stress, for example[11]), intellectual disturbances (like memory and concentration difficulties) and obsessional thoughts about what happened, often causing people to withdraw within themselves, losing any real interest in life.
- Survivor guilt: refugees and people displaced by war often suffer from this.

Among the survivors of the Nazi concentration camps, many continued to experience depression and PTSD throughout the four or more decades that followed their liberation. But they were not understood. As Dr Richard Mollica has observed, "For traumatized persons who leave a world like Auschwitz, the ultimate fear is being unable to ever reconnect with the normal world. They dread that those closest to them will turn away in neglect or indifference when they try to share their most intimate experiences," reinforcing the survivors' feelings of humiliation instilled by their captors.[12]

In this context, Dr Judith Herman refers to something Leo Eitinger, a psychiatrist who has studied survivors of the Nazi concentration camps, said in describing the cruel conflict of interest between victim and bystander, namely that, as war is something the community wants to forget, a "veil of oblivion" is drawn over everything painful and unpleasant. The survivor wants to forget but would be glad to talk; the community wants to forget and hopes he will not talk. Yet it has been pointed out that "the features of post-traumatic stress disorder that become most exaggerated in chronically traumatized people

---

[11] Even unborn babies suffered from noise and stress in the Nazi slave labour camp of Freiburg, manifesting symptoms of post-traumatic stress in childhood. Wendy Holden, *Born Survivors* (Sphere, 2015).

[12] Richard Mollica MD, *Healing Invisible Wounds – Paths to Home and Recovery in a Violent World* (2006).

are avoidance or construction. When the victim has been reduced to a goal of simple survival, psychological constriction becomes an essential form of adaptation," and this applies to every aspect of life, including the ability to plan ahead. Indeed, it can lead to the over-development of a solitary inner life, prolonged captivity having so disrupted human relationships that it is now difficult to establish any in the new surroundings.[13]

The international organizations did what they could in seeking opportunities for displaced people to start a new life, but, until the late 1950s and even into the 1960s, some of them were still eking out a miserable existence in the displaced persons camps in Greece, Italy, Austria and Germany. In the post-war years, most of these unfortunate people had few opportunities to recreate social bonds and to build a new family as they must have longed to do. They did their best, despite finding themselves after their liberation in adverse situations that were liable to militate against success.

The Second Generation

Before the Nazi oppression began, the survivors had historical and socio-economic backgrounds in their homelands that could not be replicated after Europe had been torn apart by the Second World War. After the liberation, the map of Europe having been redrawn, although some of the survivors returned to what had been their homelands and large numbers were taken in by Western countries, many had nowhere to go and everything that had epitomized the old way of life – jobs and social status, intimacy with family and friends – had gone. A life in involuntary exile seemed the final failure. They had lost the world they had known, one of mostly large close-knit families with a cultural and perhaps religious background that that had come to be totally devastated by Nazi repression. They were left disoriented and often isolated since they had found that most, if not all, of their family members had been murdered, and because, for the most part, the people around them, however much they had been affected by the six years of war, had not suffered persecution and could not be expected to understand what it was to have survived the extreme forms of Nazism to which these survivors of the camps had been exposed.

As for receiving any help with their psychological needs, it seems that right up to the 1980s/1990s the medical profession, unversed in giving any appropriate help to severely traumatized people, believed anyway that Holocaust survivors had limited capacity to resolve trauma-related problems

---

[13]   Judith Herman MD, *op. cit.*, p.8.

except in somatic complaints and illnesses. In 1981, Leo Eitinger observed that psychiatry had become aware that for any traumatized person there was a great difference between being bound to live without close personal ties and living in contact with others who can be a personal support in daily life or in difficult situations.[14] So some thought started to be given to the psychological needs of uprooted people, although it had not yet got very far. It is very fortunate that in subsequent years psychiatrists like Doctors Richard Mollica, Bessel van der Kolk and Judith Herman, along with Leo Eitinger himself, have carried out in-depth studies about these needs, and means have been devised of providing invaluable support to uprooted victims of man-made disasters.

Dr Richard Mollica has also testified to the deep belief in medicine and psychiatry in the early 1980s that people who had experienced horrific atrocities could not be rehabilitated, that Holocaust survivors expressed their distress through physical and bodily complaints and illnesses, and that their capacity to resolve their trauma-related problems was severely limited. But as he writes, "These beliefs were found to be wrong, as our clinic successfully treated more than ten thousand survivors of mass violence and torture over the next two decades."[15] Nevertheless, appropriate support to Holocaust survivors had been lacking for over forty years.

Over the post-war years, there were cases of survivors who had difficulty in relating to the second generations of their families, and even to members of the third generations. There were sad cases such as that of the grandmother in Britain, an Auschwitz survivor, who though she had brought up her own children she did not feel able to establish a relationship with her grandchildren. The explanation was that when she saw them, delayed PTSD caused her to suffer from intense flashbacks of children being pushed into the gas chambers. Then there was the poor man who, in his retirement years, applied for psychotherapy: he was alone, his wife having died, and he had failed to establish a good relationship with their children. It was only after two years in therapy that he was able to talk about having been shut in a cupboard throughout his childhood, rather than be discovered by the Gestapo. It had made him an insecure adult who found it very difficult to get on with anyone. His wife had been the exception, and she had been the only person to love and interact with him.

---

[14] Chapter 1. L. Eitinger: "Foreigners of Our Time: Historical Survey on Psychiatry's Approach to Migration and Refugees", p.20 in *Strangers of the world*, Leo Eitinger and David Schwarz (eds) (Hans Huber, 1981).

[15] Richard F. Mollica, MD, *Healing Invisible Wounds – Paths to Hope and Recovery in a Violent World* (2006).

People naturally wanted to rebuild their lives. Lacking many of the original components, they tried to put together what they could recover and start their lives again somehow: found a new family perhaps, hoping that psychological difficulties in relation to their new partners could be overcome. Often, in the quest for a person with a similar cultural, socio-economic and educational background, they would find the new partner among fellow survivors.

Many new couples were anxious to bring children into the world quite soon after liberation, as soon, in fact, as their emaciated bodies had acquired sufficient strength and they felt prepared psychologically to become parents. However, in some cases this turned out to be too soon. One or perhaps both parents, lacking any supportive network, were not really ready psychologically to attend to the needs of new little human beings. If the children seemed to fill the vacuum left in the parents' lives by the Holocaust, they tended to become, more than individuals in their own right, symbolic replacements for those who had gone. And, tragically, it seems that some of the trauma got to be passed on to these children, on both conscious and unconscious levels. Researchers have found that parents might choose a child, often the eldest, or the one who somehow resembled a relative (such as an earlier child who had been murdered) as the one chosen to be a kind of "memorial candle" (Wardi 1992[16]). These children might even be named after someone whose life had been taken in the Holocaust, and provide the only real meaning in the parents' life.

The children of the second generation could not always be conscious that their mission was to replace the ones who vanished in the Holocaust, and shoulder the task of maintaining not only family history but even the history of Judaism. Some second-generation children got so bonded with their parents that they remained dependent on them even after attaining adulthood. The parents' inability to bring up their children without expressing their repressed "pathological grief" for the lost family members seems to have made it very difficult for the second generation to choose their own partners, to be able to love as adults, to mark out an independent path.

These are generalizations with which however not all researchers and practitioners concur. An extensive review of the research literature from the period 1973–99 made by Natan Kellerman[17] observes that although

---

[16] Quoted by Judit Horvath-Lindberg in her doctoral thesis, *Swedish Identities in Sweden after the Holocaust* (1995): unpublished/part of PhD studies, Department of Psychology Stockholm University, Sweden.

[17] Natan P.R. Kellerman, Psychopathology in Children of Holocaust Survivors: A Review of the Research Literature, *Isr. J. Psychiatry Relat. Sci.*, Vol. 38 No. 1 (2001) 36–46.

there has been an impressive body of work done on the transgenerational transmission of Holocaust trauma that has resulted in almost four hundred publications, it remains a subject of considerable controversy. The main question, he writes, involves the presence or absence of specific psychopathology in this population, and while psychotherapists keep reporting various characteristic signs of distress, research has failed to find significant differences between the offspring of Holocaust survivors and comparative groups. In the summary of his review that covers the findings of thirty-five comparative studies published between 1973 and 1999 on the mental state of offspring of Holocaust survivors, he remarks that all that extensive research indicates rather conclusively that the non-clinical population of children of Holocaust survivors does not show signs of more psychopathology than others do, and that in fact children of Holocaust survivors tend to function rather well!

We see in other contexts, for example those of second-generation Vietnamese or Cambodians, that there is at least a degree of psychopathology (that we shall revert to in later chapters).

CHAPTER 4

The Life And Work Of Dr Helen Bamber, OBE (1925-2014)

One of the people who particularly impressed us all at the five-day workshop on refugee trauma mentioned in the Introduction was Helen Bamber, a pioneer in the area of trauma, who shortly before we met had set up the Medical Foundation for the Care of Victims of Torture in London. Helen spoke off the cuff at Vitznau, but she contributed two meaningful papers to the subsequent book, *Refugees – the Trauma of Exile*. And over subsequent years, my family had the privilege of receiving several visits from her.

This chapter tries to encapsulate the life and work of one of the most outstanding women of our time. It outlines Helen Bamber's experiences from the war years in London to the palpable mental agony of Holocaust survivors that she met with in the camp of Bergen-Belsen, Germany, in 1945–47, then it follows her through the years in which she gradually prepared the ground to set up measures that could meet the needs of traumatized survivors of man's inhumanity, namely the creation of the Medical Foundation for the Care of Victims of Torture, London.

In Chapter 6, we present Helen's papers on the subject of torture, and on the work of the Medical Foundation and of the Swedish Red Cross to meet the needs of torture survivors.

Helen's Heroic Action Of 1945–47

As soon as the war was over, the young Jewish woman of twenty, brought up in London with the knowledge of what was going on in Germany, travelled through shattered Europe to participate in the delivery of assistance to survivors of the death camps. Over the final weeks of the war countless thousands had been brutally forced by the Nazis to drag themselves on foot from the various concentration camps to those of Bergen-Belsen and Mauthausen.[1] Helen had immediately to face the suffering of the haggard, starving survivors, and would henceforward devote her life, stage by stage, to finding means of helping victims of organized violence.

Helen's background was that of the only child of parents of Polish origin who grew up in London. Throughout her teenage years, her father made her aware of the dangers of Nazism. He would read her pages of Hitler's *Mein Kampf* and share with her Josef Goebbels's incendiary speeches. As she would say to me one day, "We knew exactly what was going on in Germany. One had only to listen to German radio." Her biographer, Neil Belton,[2] tells us a great deal about Helen's childhood and adolescent years, how her experiences in wartime Britain formed her character, and how throughout those critical years Helen prepared herself psychologically to go to Germany as soon as war ended.

She set off in mid-1945 as the youngest member of a rehabilitation team sent from Britain to help survivors of the Holocaust. She went in British army uniform – with a Star of David sewn on the sleeve, to let the Germans know that she too was Jewish. Her supervisor, Henry Lunzer, in the Jewish Relief Unit, who many years later still thought of her as a "lovely, vivacious little girl", would describe her as a natural organizer. "Helen just took charge of headquarters, administered the whole thing. It was amazing at that age. God only knows what made her so efficient."[3]

Helen spent all the time she possibly could in the camp, to which in the last weeks of the war the Germans, hoping to efface all traces of their depravity and extreme inhumanity, had forced the survivors of many of the other camps to go, on foot. Many emaciated prisoners died – or were shot – on the way; some died after they had managed to get there. It was a place of horror, totally unnerving to the men of the British and Canadian armed

---

[1] On the last day before the Nazi surrender, Mauthausen death camp received over a thousand sick and starving women taken by goods train from their existence as slave labourers in Freiberg, near Dresden where many women had died of starvation coupled with fourteen-hour shifts in freezing temperatures – or had been taken back to Auschwitz to be killed. The account of three "walking skeletons" who managed to survive that nightmare two-week rail journey and protect the babies, born in the very last days of the war, each weighing under three pounds (one of them born in that open coal wagon!), is poignantly told in *Born Survivors*, by Wendy Holden (Sphere, 2015).

[2] Neil Belton, *The Good Listener, Helen Bamber, A Life against Cruelty* (1998).

[3] *The Guardian* (11 March 2000).

forces who liberated it on 15 April 1945.[4] There were bodies everywhere, where people had collapsed from starvation and disease. There were huge pits containing the remains of dozens or perhaps hundreds of bodies, of Jews of many different nationalities who had been in that infernal place. It has been estimated that 50,000 or more people were killed in that concentration camp alone – which, unlike the numerous extermination camps such as Auschwitz-Birkenau or Mauthausen, had not been set up with gas chambers.

Helen was soon aware of how essential it was for many of the survivors to tell someone about their unimaginable sufferings. She told a *Guardian* interviewer about how inexperienced she had been, how she had had to learn quickly. "I realised after a time that I couldn't take away their suffering, or their images of their losses, or their terrible sense of unresolved grief. People would tell you their story and it would spill out like a kind of vomit. They would go on talking, talking, talking…" A haggard woman Helen spoke to me about would seize her by the arm, and let her go only after she had told her story, not once but at least three times. The prints this poor woman must have left on Helen's arm no doubt testified to the extreme desperation she felt to talk to someone, anyone, about the horrors she had experienced. "And what they were telling you was sometimes quite dreadful", she told me, so that after a while she began to realize that the most important role for her was to bear witness.

Bearing witness to the vulnerability of humanity became a motto for Helen, who had experienced acute loss and grief herself during the war: her vivacious young aunt Mina, who had been her role model, died when a bomb made a direct hit on a four-floor London building, exploding in the basement where Mina and her companion had gone to attend a concert at the popular Café de Paris. One night Helen herself, out as a firefighter, had a shock when a wooden staircase she was on lurched from under her feet and she fell to the bottom. For the rest of her life, as I saw when Helen stayed with us, she was very wary of stairs.

In a laureation address for the degree of doctor of laws to be bestowed on Helen, Professor Peter Hower, deputy principal of the University of

---

[4]   In an interview in 2008, LeRoy Petersen, a young member of the medical corps of the US 11th Armored Division that liberated Mauthausen, spoke sixty years later of the breakdown he had suffered after putting in long hours there and desperately needing some rest. He said that he had bled from the nose, bled from the inner ears, and just couldn't sleep. His commanding officer told him to rest. Nevertheless, he remained traumatized, and said that over the years his post-traumatic stress had grown worse, in particular the nightmares that always featured the appalling scenes of that death camp. Wendy Holden, *Born Survivors*.

Dundee, said, in referring to her time at Belsen, that she learned one crucial lesson, namely that the physical scars inflicted by torture and cruelty heal more quickly than the damage to the mind and the soul, and that the victims of cruelty and torture must be listened to before any start can be made to rehabilitation.

Nevertheless, on leaving Belsen in the extreme cold of early 1947, Helen told her biographer that she had felt utterly drained – incapable either of seeing beyond her reunion with Rudi Bamberger, her future husband, a German Jewish refugee who when in his teens had seen his father murdered by Hitler's Brown Shirts and his mother and sister taken away; or of relating what she had been through to the rest of her life. She said that she hadn't done it for Rudi, And she didn't think that she had gone to Germany because of any feeling that she was doing the bidding of her father: "I did it for myself", she said, and she did it because the truth was that the only way she felt she could survive was to find a way to avoid being overwhelmed, to do something while she could, maybe work with some of the afflicted people instead of despairing about them all. She concluded, with astounding modesty, "And that's all really that I've ever been able to do."[5]

Helen continued on her return from Belsen first to espouse the needs of the abused, by working with orphaned Jewish adolescents brought to the UK after the war, helping to meet their physical and emotional needs. Then, working in hospital administration, she became involved in different health care issues, campaigning against the policy which separated mothers from their distressed children in hospital, becoming one of the founding members of the National Association for the Welfare of Children in Hospital that helped create the more sympathetic practices of today. From 1958, Helen worked as an almoner at St. George's Hospital in the East End, and then at the Middlesex Hospital. Both working with and spending a good deal of valuable "learning time" with Dr Maurice Pappworth, a Jewish doctor who had passed the Royal College of Surgeons examination but was refused a consultancy because of his origins, she shared his concern about the number of clinical research projects by doctors that abused human rights. The two of them, not surprisingly facing strong criticism, drew public attention to these abuses, and as a result medical research ethics committees came to be created that would give vital protection to the public. Somehow, Helen found time to get married and bring up two sons, David and Jonathan. She was a very devoted mother, working part-time, and Rudi was a devoted father.

---

[5] Neil Belton, *op. cit.*, pp.3–7 and 114.

Throughout the 1950s and 1960s, while working alongside doctors and gaining more and more experience of medical challenges, Helen became aware that many countries used torture, imprisonment without trial and similar measures to suppress dissident opinion. Meeting through her work countless victims of extreme cruelty who were seeking help to rebuild their broken lives, she resolved to totally oppose human cruelty in all its forms. She met some remarkable, like-minded people, among them John Schlapobersky, who had experienced imprisonment and torture in South Africa, and Perico Rodríguez, imprisoned and tortured for three years by the Argentine junta. With them and under the auspices of the newly formed Amnesty International,[6] becoming a leading figure as secretary of the Medical Campaign of Amnesty's British Medical Group, she tried to bring support to a number of damaged individuals, realizing eventually that it was vital to find a place to which such people could come for help. "On her own she could not change the world but she could be a bearer of evidence; far more ambitious and dangerous, she could also try to undo the work of the torturer. This was her aim in setting up the Foundation for the Care of Victims of Torture," her biographer wrote.[7]

Helen founded the Medical Foundation for Care of Victims of Torture in 1985. It was established as a registered charity, providing medical treatment, counselling and therapy to torture survivors, and the preparation of documentation providing evidence of torture became an essential service. Sponsorship came from the heads of the Royal College of Physicians, Royal College of Psychiatrists and Royal College of Surgeons of England. Foundation staff and volunteers worked at first in two rooms in the former National Temperance Hospital, off Hampstead Road in north-west London. By 1990, it was treating 750 clients before moving to a building in Grafton Road, Kentish Town.

A Remarkable And Very Necessary Place
For Damaged Survivors To Go

I visited the Medical Foundation in 1988, to take a small suitcase full of *Refugees – the Trauma of Exile*. "This book," she exclaimed with her usual humour, "ought to be on the bedside table of every government minister!"

---

[6]   Amnesty International, the London-based non-governmental organization created in July 1961 and now recognized worldwide, focuses on human rights, with more than seven million members and supporters around the world. Its motto is "It is better to light a candle than to curse the darkness".

[7]   From the back cover of Neil Belton's book *The Good Listener*.

She told me about the innumerable specialists working there, some full-time and some part-time, some on salaries, but many as volunteers. They were psychotherapists, physiotherapists, surgeons, gynaecologists and other specialists. Helen introduced me to someone who practised the Alexander technique, namely a therapy that enables the survivor of torture, whose body had once been subjected to atrocious pain at the hands of torturers, to begin to accept other people's touch in the gentle ministrations of the hands of the therapist, and thereby gradually gets release from intense stress and bodily rigidity. Naturally that day, as every day, there were clients present, people from many different countries of the world.

In general, Helen, when not campaigning, which is what she mostly did from Monday to Friday (raising awareness of needs, raising funds and leading appeals against negative decisions on asylum claims), spent Saturdays and Sundays with clients. It was to be said of her in the obituary published by her second foundation, "Helen's attentiveness and focus on the individual gave her the ability to navigate the complexity of trauma and the human responses to it. She remained unyielding in her instinct to understand, and pioneered methods to help those she worked with to achieve what she termed 'creative survival'. ... The gift that Helen gave to so many was to enable them to find their own way of surviving. Helen always led by example, selfless with her time and energy until she retired due to ill-health aged 88." The integrated model of care that Helen developed went on being used after her death.[8]

Perico Rodríguez, a man who had been in an Argentine prison in the late 1970s but got to Britain partly thanks to Amnesty International, then worked alongside Helen for forty years. His background equipped him uniquely to give support, understanding and even love to the people in great need who came for help. He paid a moving tribute to Helen when she died: "Last night, when I learnt that Helen had died, I began thinking about her life and the real meaning of life. I always admired her incredible sense of commitment to the causes she felt were important. I remember her determination to help everybody – I mean everybody, not just those 'deserving of help' people but everybody who needed help. We also learnt from her that there is no such thing as large or little suffering. For Helen, suffering in whatever form was enough to trigger the compassion that we are now sharing with her. This is the gift I got from Helen. Not that I was

---

[8] *Helen Bamber OBE Has Passed Away*, Helen Bamber Foundation, May 2014.

alien to commitment, but she enforced and consolidated the ethos that life is not worth living if you are indifferent to people."[9]

Helen may have lacked formal training as a psychotherapist, but as her head of child and adolescent psychotherapy at the foundation, Sheila Melzak, said, "I don't know how she does it, but people just open up to her. All sorts of people feel safe with her. … They'll talk to her about the most private experiences," and she added that no level of training could equip someone with this skill. Helen, she said, somehow managed to hear tales that most of us would be unable to listen to, believing that it was anger that fuelled her gruelling schedule. But she could say that even in the midst of such evil and suffering, or perhaps especially in such places, "there's something very good to be retrieved from people".

Nevertheless, a close observer told *The Guardian* that Helen was more vulnerable than she let on. "I think there are times when she is very upset by the intolerable experiences people go through." Her son Jonathan described her as "driven, focused, dedicated, slightly obsessive…" and said that she had an unimaginable amount of energy, going off to all the most horrible, devastated places in the world. Helen was travelling widely, especially to Chile, Uganda, Kosovo, Northern Ireland and the Middle East, to investigate gross violations of human rights, and was a member of human rights committees from Belfast to Gaza.

Helen felt great affinity with men living in the border areas around Berwick who had returned to Britain in 1945–46 from the war in Asia to a welcome that was barely lukewarm. These elderly men still had searing memories of their treatment by the Japanese. In the 1980s she travelled at least twice to Berwick to be with them and listen to their stories – in most cases, stories that their relatives had not wished (or not dared) to hear when they had got home after six years away. Neil Belton, who travelled with Helen, wrote about the brotherhood of these men, fifty years after the end of the war with Japan, noting that for the most part they had shared the past only with one another, perhaps feeling closer to their former comrades-in-arms than they could to their wives. He saw that they touched Helen Bamber for more personal reasons too: she could understand the necessary discipline of their women who could not share in this brotherhood and, as she had known to her own cost, could not heal their minds as well as mother them and their children. She told him that she had lived with a

9   *Perico Rodriguez Pays Tribute to Helen Bamber OBE*, Helen Bamber Foundation, May 2014. In a testimony that he gave to the world in a thirteen-minute video on his retirement in 2016, Perico spoke of the need for love in human relationships, and in particular with regard to people who have been to hell and back.

man who could not speak for many years about what had happened to him in Nazi Germany, and she had realized the capacity people have to survive and apparently survive well – but it's at the price of numbing and depression. Those former prisoners of war had come back, as the Holocaust survivors had, with memories of brutality, of grotesque death, and nobody really wanted to hear about it all any more than they wanted to hear from the Holocaust survivors. Helen knew how very difficult it was to deal with this in a marriage, and she could guess the price the women paid.[10]

By 2000, the Medical Foundation had eighty-five paid staff and 110 volunteers, receiving some 2,000 clients per year and, by means of a most impressive variety of measures, bringing understanding and hope to people who had been feeling nothing but despair and isolation. One of these methods that took people out of the modest foundation accommodation was the creation of allotments, each attributed to someone seriously damaged by his or her experiences, who was now given the opportunity to vent some of the accumulated anger on the weeds, to have the pleasure of once again having his or her hands in the soil, and of sowing seeds and having them grow.[11]

By the time Helen handed the Foundation over to a new director, shortly to create another Foundation to care for people who did (or do) not fall directly into the category of torture survivors, the Medical Foundation had received tens of thousands people from countless countries of the world who had come to Britain to seek help. It came to be renamed "Freedom from Torture". At the time of writing, its internet site states that since the inception of the foundation in 1985, over 57,000 survivors of torture have been referred to it for help. It adds that is one of the world's largest torture treatment centres – I would think that it is probably the largest, receiving people from ninety-six countries.

Freedom from Torture began a regional programme in late 2003 with the opening of a centre in Manchester, treating clients living in the north-west. This followed the government's dispersal scheme, which saw asylum seekers relocated outside London. In 2004, the London headquarters moved into a £5.8m treatment centre in Isledon Road, Finsbury Park. The building was purpose-built by architect Paul Hyett. Freedom from Torture's Scotland centre opened in Glasgow in 2004, followed by a Newcastle centre in 2006 and a Birmingham centre in 2009.

---

[10] Neil Belton, *op. cit.*, pp.3–7.

[11] Sonja Linden and Jenny Grut, *The Healing Fields, Working with Psychotherapy and Nature to Rebuild Shattered Lives.*

A Very Broad Mandate

Today's Freedom from Torture website states that "the organization provides services that include medical consultation, examination and forensic documentation of injuries through medico-legal reports, psychological and physical treatment and support, and practical help. It employs over 156 staff and 140 volunteers across its five centres in London, Birmingham, Manchester, Newcastle and Glasgow. These include medical doctors, caseworkers, counsellors, legal advisers, physiotherapists, psychotherapists, psychologists, interpreters, child and family therapists and group workers." The list of materials one may wish to consult is truly impressive.

Reference to just one of these, a five-page document entitled "Submission of Freedom from Torture to the Joint Committee for Human Rights Inquiry into Immigration Detention" (August 2018) is indicative of some of the in-depth professional work that is carried out. As I have been authorized to include it in this chapter, let us look at it, for it is important and it reflects the type of activity that Helen involved herself in over so many years!

Freedom from torture cites its credentials[12] before explaining that the submission will focus on torture survivors and primarily address the two issues of:

> I. Whether current legal and policy frameworks are sufficient in preventing people from being detained wrongfully and whether current practices in the detention system protect human rights;

> II. Whether the initial decision to detain an individual should be made independently, such as by requiring prior judicial approval.

---

[12] Namely "Freedom from Torture is a UK-based human rights organisation and one of the largest torture rehabilitation centres in the world. Each year we provide clinical services to more than 1,000 survivors of torture in the UK, the majority of whom are asylum seekers or refugees."

Key Issue	Recommendation
Current legal and policy framework of immigration detention is flawed, leading to poor decisions to detain and continue detention	1. Torture survivors should not be detained under any circumstances & should be prioritised in alternatives to detention. 2. Decisions to detain should be made independently. Representations should be permitted by the individual and their lawyer. 3. In detention reviews, vulnerability should outweigh immigration factors, unless there are exceptional circumstances.
Adults at Risk Policy fails to protect vulnerable people and raises the evidentiary burden to a degree that it restricts access to those in need	1. Remove the evidence levels from the Adults at Risk policy 2. Replace the broad range of immigration factors with the previous threshold of "exceptional circumstances" to justify continued detention
Rule 35 safeguard measure does not work, leaving torture survivors suffering harm to their health in detention	1. Remove the requirement to comment on the likely impact of ongoing detention 2. Properly resource the process 3. Independent monitoring
"Torture" definition undermines aim of primary legislation to protect vulnerable people	1. Statutory Instruments 2018/410 and 2018/411 should be annulled immediately with administrative guidance subsequently amended. 2. The UNHCR detention guidelines definition should be used.

The remaining four pages set out the logical and legal bases of the above recommendations. There seems to be no doubt that such approaches carry substantial weight – though naturally, they involve a considerable amount of prior study, reflection and consultation.

Helen set in motion back in the 1980s and 1990s a formidable array of responsibilities that the staff working under her direction assumed, and that have been assumed by those now carrying the work further and further forward.

Chapter 6 reproduces the papers that Helen Bamber contributed to the book *Refugees – The Trauma of Exile*. I have felt it legitimate to include them in this book on trauma and uprooting, believing that the material presented all those years ago has still a great deal of validity, however notable the subsequent evolution of the foundation that came to be renamed "Freedom from Torture".

Indefatigable Helen

In April 2005, Helen created her second foundation, the Helen Bamber Foundation, which she explained was to provide support to the very many people seeking help who needed the same kinds of understanding and help to rebuild their lives as the clients of the first, and who were not survivors of torture in the accepted sense. At the top of the Foundation's current list of publications is "The Trauma-Informed Code of Conduct – For All the Professionals Working with Survivors of Human Trafficking & Slavery", the clearest of indications of the breadth of Helen's concerns.

Soon after the opening, Helen and Dr Michael Korzinski, who had already worked together for fifteen years, wrote as co-directors of the Helen Bamber Foundation on 15 July 2005:

> Since opening our doors in April 2005, it has been our aim to respond rapidly and creatively to the constant changes in government legislation that have a direct impact on the health and welfare of the population we are committed to serve. The problems people face have become increasingly complex and too numerous for any one organisation to work in isolation. We reach out to other professionals and groups to provide a comprehensive service through a network of support.
>
> Our traditional network with human rights lawyers and country experts is becoming increasingly important as current circumstances in a particular country are often in dispute. We are also forming new and sometimes unexpected connections. For example, the Sports Performance Rehabilitation Centre in Roehampton, which usually works with elite athletes like Kelly Holmes, is now involved in providing movement analysis to some of our Chechen clients who have suffered massive physical injuries.
>
> We are breaking new ground...
>
> Our raison d'être is to treat all cases with respect to their specific needs. ... Cases range from those whose experience of atrocity was as long ago as WWII to present-day survivors of gross human rights violations from countries as diverse as North Vietnam, Chechnya, Nepal, Iran, Zimbabwe, Ethiopia,

and Eritrea, to name just a few. We have also been working with those affected by the recent bombings in London.

The Helen Bamber Foundation's measures of working with and for clients are many and varied, as appears from the following schema and of course from the website:

The aspirations set out in that schema were those that Helen hoped would come into being little by little, and do not correspond exactly to what the foundation is doing nowadays.

Getting To Know Helen

The five-day Red Cross workshop at Vitznau was set up with the help of Red Cross funds entrusted to me by the Swedish Red Cross, which sent two expert members of staff to Geneva to help with the planning. I asked national societies of the seventeen or so countries expected to attend to nominate only one person from Red Cross, the other two invited to attend should represent other NGOs (non-governmental organizations) or even individuals. I had for example heard of the wonderful therapeutic work being carried out in Belgium by Dr Jorge Barudy, himself a torture survivor from Chile, and knew that it would be essential to have people like him at the workshop. Someone working temporarily at the British Red Cross conveyed an invitation to Helen, who only eighteen months earlier had set up the Medical Foundation for the Care of Victims of Torture. This initiative was extraordinarily fortunate.

Helen through her secretary asked me to book her into a hotel a week ahead, as she needed rest. She came and rather fell in love with Vitznau! She apologized for not having been able to prepare a paper from which to speak in the plenary sessions – but she hardly needed a paper! Helen and I subsequently kept in touch and in 1994, she managed a short break and came to stay with us in Devon, where I lived with my daughter and mother for a limited period. She was good enough to read through parts of the manuscript of the book I was writing. We enjoyed walks together in the countryside, took cream teas in a beautiful hotel garden that was full of magnificent rhododendrons, and shared a great deal. Years later, Helen started coming to stay with us in the Gruyère region of Switzerland, intending to come frequently, as she had been advised so often to take regular breaks, though she very rarely did. She told us that several decades earlier, she had so loved the trips with her young husband, racing across France on a post-war American motorbike to Switzerland, where Rudi was very happy to use his mother tongue, German.

But though Helen managed two visits that year, each of only one week in February and May, combining them with a day at the United Nations, she never managed to get away again. Some of her belongings remained with us "for the next visit". She had very much enjoyed walking along the little river here and in the Bernese Oberland, where on her February visit, Helen was amazed to be able to sit outside in warm sunshine. We went to Vitznau, by train and boat, being given lunch in the oldest house in the village by my friend Monika, erstwhile owner and manager of the Hotel Terrasse, where the 1987 workshop had been held.

Unique Helen. When on her arrival at Geneva Airport I had wanted to ask her about herself and the work, within five minutes she knew everything about my health and well-being, that of my husband, that of our daughter and that of our two dogs! Helen was reticent about Neil Belton's book *The Good Listener* on my bookshelves: "THAT BOOK!" she exclaimed when she caught sight of it. She perhaps had no real quarrel with the book (that the biographer had taken three years to write, researching it carefully and minutely), but she felt that he had not fully grasped her marital situation. She spoke to me of Rudi, of how the two of them met, of how little they communicated – and how difficult it had in fact been for each of them to convey to the other the immense burden of the previous years. I remember how very sad Helen was when Rudi died.

Helen's young life and her marriage seem to have been bereft of fun and laughter – though Helen loved both! Knowing that she listened over so many years to accounts of suffering, it may be hard for us to imagine that this unique woman had a great sense of fun and laughed easily. She was a delight to be with. Going back to years in her earlier life, she had told a *Guardian* reporter that after the breakdown of her marriage, she was short of money and rented rooms to foreign students, and "I suppose I began to laugh a lot when they were around. We had fun, we danced, we cooked, I used to book the entire launderette on a Sunday afternoon. ... There hadn't been much laughter in my parents' home or in my married life." The report went on, "Bamber has a lovely girlish giggle, and can extract humour from the grimmest situations. She says the ability to laugh is terribly important, especially in someone so prone to crying. Does she cry at work? 'No, I can listen to the most appalling stories that people tell me, I can bear it.' She says the one thing she can't cope with is hearing people sing. ... 'There's something about the human voice; seeing what capacity people have for creativity and what's denied them. Perhaps it's about what people might be if left alone.'"

I remain deeply grateful for having met Helen and for having had the privilege of her friendship. It was a pleasure to hear just the other day from Dr Richard A. Mollica, an outstanding psychiatrist about whose work I have written what I can in Chapters 19 and 20 of this book, that he and Helen were great friends and associates.

This remarkable woman, who throughout her life seems to have worked seven days a week, died in 2014 after a period of illness. She is owed a tremendous debt of gratitude for the outstanding work she did, for the inspiration and guidance she gave to countless people in the medical and allied fields, and for representing in many different fora the need for understanding and support of people damaged by the circumstances of their lives. Helen, appointed European Woman of Achievement in 1993, was awarded an OBE, an Award for a Lifetime's Achievement in Human Rights in 1998 and no fewer than nine honorary degrees for her work, inter alia from Oxford University, Dundee University, Glasgow University, the University of Ulster, Kingston University, the Open University and Oxford Brookes University.

Over the past several years, there have been several very special events in London commemorating Helen's life and work. Trustees of the two foundations are active in these celebrations, among them the distinguished actress Emma Thompson and the British journalist, writer and broadcaster John McCarthy, often remembered as the longest-held British hostage in the Lebanon hostage crisis of the 1980s, when over a period of several years Islamic Jihad terrorists seized a number of hostages.

The extraordinary work that Helen created through the two foundations is of course continued by dedicated people who continue to use the techniques that had evolved over all the earlier years. These are the websites:

www.helenbamber.org

www.freedomfromtorture.org

Both foundations are naturally deserving of the fullest support.

CHAPTER 5

Trauma, Psychiatric Harm And Litigation

The Nature Of Trauma And Post-Traumatic Stress (PTSD)

When from 1978 onwards I was becoming increasingly aware of the aspect of trauma in refugees' lives and the apparent ignorance of it by the medical profession, I found no indications that any research was being carried out on it anywhere! Much of the thinking about psychological illness in the form that interested and concerned people like me in working with refugees still lay in the future. What could be the cause of the mental distress that seemed to take on different forms, sometimes actually changing people's personalities? Something obviously very serious had happened that had apparently led to psychiatric illness and suffering.

It seemed natural that some of the refugees were loath to talk about their mental health, but if they took refuge in silence, how could they hope to be helped (assuming that help could be at hand)? Little by little, a list of some of the problems was emerging: elements such as headaches, stomach and back pain, anxiety, irritability, forgetfulness, insomnia, nightmares, epileptiform fits or seizures, enuresis (bed-wetting), aggressiveness, violence, suicidal tendencies, depression – and those frightening flashbacks that it seems often surge into the lives of people who have experienced massive trauma. All this seemed to be evidence of very troubling experiences.

This was the critical period in which Dr Bessel van der Kolk had come face to face with former combat soldiers who, though initially successful in leading normal lives after their return from Vietnam, had suddenly become victims of flashbacks so disturbing that they feared they were a danger to their own families. The experienced young psychiatrist, searching in places in which he could have expected to find some relevant literature on different forms of psychiatric illness, was frustrated and there remained for some time real perplexity as to how these men, virtually tortured by their own uncontrollable behaviour, could be helped. If in 1980 the term PTSD came to be coined by the American Psychiatric Association, a list of symptoms was published only seven years later, but by then serious minds had been brought to focus on the phenomenon, particularly in the USA.

It began to appear that where traumatized individuals are both resilient and receive the understanding and support of family and friends, the stress can be eased even though, inevitably, memories of the traumatic event or period remain; but, when traumatic events such as prolonged ill-treatment or exposure to war conditions are experienced in conditions that are far from conducive to a return to normality, there may frequently be dramatic long-term effects categorized as PTSD.

The Mayo Clinic in the USA gives us helpful insights on its website, stating that post-traumatic stress disorder (PTSD) is a mental health condition triggered by a terrifying event – or series of events such as war or persecution – that people have either experienced or witnessed. Symptoms may include flashbacks, nightmares and severe anxiety, as well as uncontrollable thoughts about the event. The symptoms, lasting for months or even years, may get worse and interfere with day-to-day functioning.

As we have seen, symptoms may appear only years after the event, at which point they can cause significant problems in social or work situations and in relationships, interfering with people's ability to go about their normal daily tasks. If grouped into the four types categorized by experts, they can produce intrusive memories, avoidance, negative changes in thinking and mood, and changes in physical and emotional reactions. They can vary over time or vary from person to person.

Symptoms of **intrusive memories** may include:

- Recurrent, unwanted distressing memories of the traumatic event
- Reliving the traumatic event as if it were happening again (flashbacks)
- Upsetting dreams or nightmares about the traumatic event
- Severe emotional distress or physical reactions to something that reminds you of the traumatic event

Symptoms of **avoidance** may include:

- Trying to avoid thinking or talking about the traumatic event
- Avoiding places, activities or people that remind you of the traumatic event

Symptoms of **negative changes in thinking and mood** may include:

- Negative thoughts about yourself, other people or the world
- Hopelessness about the future
- Memory problems, including not remembering important aspects of the traumatic event
- Difficulty maintaining close relationships
- Feeling detached from family and friends
- Lack of interest in activities you once enjoyed
- Difficulty experiencing positive emotions
- Feeling emotionally numb

Symptoms of **changes in physical and emotional reactions (also called arousal symptoms)** may include:

- Being easily startled or frightened
- Always being on guard for danger
- Self-destructive behaviour, such as drinking too much or driving too fast
- Trouble sleeping
- Trouble concentrating
- Irritability, angry outbursts or aggressive behaviour
- Overwhelming guilt or shame

The Mayo Clinic website continues by stating that PTSD symptoms can vary in intensity over time. People may have them when already stressed, or when there are reminders of what they had been through. For example for an ex-combatant, the sound of a car backfiring could revive combat experience; or, for a woman, seeing a report on the news about a sexual assault could make her overcome by memories of what had happened to her.

Timely help and support may prevent normal stress reactions from deteriorating and developing into PTSD. Turning to family and friends who will listen and offer comfort may be enough, but it may mean that finding a mental health professional for a course of therapy will be critical to recovery.

The kinds of traumatic events to which people have been exposed are listed in Chapter 1. But what about PTSD and the law?

Trauma In The Context Of Litigation

Who has not known someone, be it only through literature, who has experienced the long-drawn out process of seeking satisfaction for redress through the courts? In this changing world of ours, more and more cases reach the courts in relation to domestic violence, marriage breakdown, children taken into care, property, accidents, and of course crimes of all sorts. In parallel, recent years have seen changes being made in Britain to facilitate access to legal aid. The Legal Aid, Sentencing and Punishment of Offenders Act 2012 ("Laspo") is a statute of the Parliament of the United Kingdom, creating reforms to the justice system. Elspeth Thomson, chair of the British legal aid committee at the family law organization Resolution, has said, "We've been calling for changes to the evidence gateway since Laspo was implemented in 2013." She said that, as Parliament has committed to protecting victims of domestic abuse, ministers have a duty to ensure that those who need legal aid are able to access it, and she went on to say, "These changes, made in consultation with Resolution[1] and others, are a step in the right direction, allowing the justice system to better support at-risk and vulnerable people at perhaps the most difficult time of their lives – when the family unit is breaking down." Joe Egan, president of the Law Society of England and Wales, also supported wider access to legal aid: "Legal aid is a lifeline for those who have suffered abuse. It is often the only way someone can bring their case before the courts."

But to be able to have comparatively easier access to the courts is one thing. To imagine getting redress for psychiatric harm is another. We can consider, shortly, what it may be like in countries like the United Kingdom or Australia to seek compensation for damage inflicted on one's mind.

A few months ago, I renewed contact with my distant cousin Dr Peter Handford, emeritus professor of law at the University of Western Australia, Perth. Each of us had known since the 1980s of the other's interest in trauma. Peter had been going on with his teaching, research and writing throughout the intervening years, and I naturally wondered whether he might give me some expert advice on this chapter – then realizing that I had virtually hit the jackpot! Peter told me that he had recently written the third edition of a book entitled *Tort Liability for Mental Harm* (published by Thomson Reuters (Professional) Australia Ltd. in 2017). The first edition, entitled *Tort Liability for Psychiatric Damage*, had been written with a former student

---

[1]   PTSD Resolution is a charity that makes health help available for members of UK forces who are in need of it.

of his twenty-four years earlier, then he had brought out the two subsequent editions on his own. The book, he explained, deals with liability for what had traditionally been called "nervous shock" – in relation to Australian law but also reflecting terminology and practice in the United States and Britain. The book since its initial publication in 1993 has certainly met a need, being cited by courts in England, Australia and elsewhere.

My cousin's authoritative writing turns out to be critical to give real meaning and substance to this chapter, not least the descriptions of efforts to have recognized in the courts what has variously been termed "nervous shock", "psychiatric harm", "emotional distress", "psychiatric injury" and so on. It is fascinating to hear about the gradual changes in the laws (particularly those of Australia and Britain), some advocated by none other than my cousin, to take psychiatric harm into account to a greater extent.

Peter introduced me to Chapter 5 of his book, entitled "A Medical Perspective", explaining, "It seeks to set out some information about medical and psychiatric research into psychiatric injury, *in case it is any use to you*" (my italics). He went on to write, "The original version of the first part of the chapter was written by my co-author Nicholas Mullany. For the second and third editions, this material was revised and rewritten by Professor Philip Mitchell AM, FASSA, FRANZCP, FRCPych, Scientia Professor and Head of the School of Psychiatry at the University of New South Wales, which I think gives some assurance of soundness and usefulness. I contributed a few passages and a few footnotes scattered within this section, and I wrote the second main section of the chapter."

"Any use?! Dear Cousin Peter, naturally this chapter written for lawyers on the nature of trauma and post-traumatic stress is of real interest to us here. So, with your permission, I'd like to choose your material for this chapter, leaving aside at present the many other sources available to me, on aspects of PTSD – on our bodies' nervous system, and on the fact that trauma and PTSD have been shown to make changes in our brains."

The same Chapter 5 goes on to include accounts of brave individuals tackling airlines for compensation after suffering serious stress while passengers on one of their flights, and we can perhaps look at one of those shortly. But, well before we get to that point, let us first look at PTSD and then see from *Tort Liability for Mental Harm* how the law has been taken on board the reality of psychiatric harm. At Peter's suggestion, in the interests of space I have deleted the majority of the prolific footnotes.

[5.10] The purpose of this chapter is to examine the medical and psychiatric research into psychiatric injury, in order that lawyers may better understand what is involved in categorising particular conditions as recognisable psychiatric disorders and distinguishing them from lesser states which are said to amount only to mental or emotional distress. An understanding of these issues assists us to deal with the question whether, for purposes of legal liability, it is rational to identify psychiatric injury as a category separate from physical harm.

Under the sub-heading "Psychiatric injury and medical research", the question of terminology is dealt with at some length, some of which reads:

[5.40] While definitions of psychiatric (or mental) disorder differ, that used by the *American Diagnostic and Statistical Manual of Mental Disorders – Fifth Edition* (DSM-5)[2] is indicative:

A syndrome characterized by clinically significant disturbance in an individual's cognition, emotion regulation, or behaviour that reflects a dysfunction in the psychological, biological, or developmental processes underlying mental functioning. Mental disorders are usually associated with significant distress or disability in social, occupational, or other important activities.[3]

DSM-5 further emphasises that this syndrome or pattern must not be either merely an expectable or culturally approved response to a common stressor or loss, such as the death of a loved one, or socially deviant behaviour (for example, political, religious, or sexual) and conflicts that are primarily between the individual and society.

[5.50] It should also be noted from the outset that, as is the case with "recognisable (or recognised) psychiatric illness", expressions such as "mental distress" and "emotional suffering" are not terms of either art or medical science: there is no universally accepted language to characterise these states of the human mind. One often finds "mental suffering", "mental anguish", "emotional distress" and the like both in the case law and the literature and there does not appear to be any discernible difference between them. Objections

---

[2] American Psychiatric Association, Diagnostic and Statistical Manual of Mental Disorders, Fifth Edition: DSM-5 (American Psychiatric Association, Washington DC, 2013).

[3] See DSM-5, Section I: DSM-5 Basics – Use of the Manual.

can be raised to the use of both "mental" and "emotional" in this context. The term "mental" to some may convey a psychological or psychiatric condition (and, as we have noted, "mental disorders" and "psychiatric disorders" are synonymous terms), thereby making distinction between the two identified categories more difficult than need be. It may also be said that the use of the word "emotional" to describe a person's mood or spirits is better avoided because it is often used to indicate a state of agitation or excitement, perhaps with pejorative overtones. However, no better terms appear to be available, and they are sanctioned by long usage. As there is no clear reason for preferring one term to the other, terms such as "mental distress" or "emotional distress" have therefore generally been used interchangeably to characterise states of the human mind which lack objective and recognisable syndromal characteristics, other than the primary instinctive reactions outlined below.

Terminology is obviously crucial, but unfortunately the same terms do not always mean the same things in different jurisdictions, even though efforts have no doubt been made internationally towards conformity.

Under the sub-heading "Emotions", we read,

[5.70] The best way to appreciate the ambit of what is recoverable under the current law is to examine from a medical perspective the "mental distress" or "emotional suffering" that most common law systems have viewed as unworthy of compensation. Mental distress has been described as any **"disagreeable disturbance of emotional or mental tranquillity"** or "traumatically induced reaction which is medically detrimental to the individual". It is thus best understood as a comprehensive label covering a variety of unpleasant emotional reactions.

[5.80] There does not appear to be any universally accepted classification of human emotions. The respected United States neuroscientist Antonio Damasio distinguishes between *primary or universal emotions* (happiness, sadness, fear, anger, surprise or disgust), *secondary or social emotions* (such as embarrassment, jealousy, guilt or pride) and *background emotions* (well-being or malaise; calm or tension). The mental distress that is the origin of the harm suffered in the cases we will be considering usually consists of a combination of the following unpleasant emotions: 1. Fear or apprehension. 2. Horror. 3. Grief, sorrow and loneliness. 4. Shame, humiliation and embarrassment. 5. Anger, annoyance and vexation. 6. Disappointment and frustration. 7. Worry and anxiety.

Moving on to what my cousin's book has to tell us about the human nervous system, obviously vital information in the context of trauma, giving us new understanding, we read:

[5.90] For a proper understanding of what follows it is important first to have some knowledge of the human nervous system. This consists of the central nervous system and the peripheral nervous system. It may be further subdivided functionally into the somatic and autonomic nervous systems. These various systems are anatomically and physiologically distinct. The central nervous system comprises the cerebral hemispheres (comprised of the cerebral cortex, white matter and subcortical regions), the rest of the forebrain (thalamus, hypothalamus and pituitary gland), the midbrain, the brain stem and the spinal cord, which are the main centres where correlation and integration of nervous information occurs. Injury to this system, particularly trauma to the brain, is mainly a matter for the neurologist, though damage to areas such as the frontal lobes may lead to personality and behavioural change. The peripheral system consists of the nerves emerging from the brain (cranial nerves) and from the spinal cord (spinal nerves) which convey neural messages from the sense organs and sensory receptors inward to the central nervous system and from the central nervous system outward to the muscles and glands of the body. The somatic nervous system comprises those peripheral systems responsible for conveying and processing conscious and unconscious sensory information (such as vision, touch, pain and unconscious muscle sense) from the head, body wall and extremities to the central nervous system, and the motor control of the voluntary muscles. In other words, it innervates the body (for example, the skin and skeletal muscles) but not the viscera or blood vessels. We are here chiefly concerned with the remaining category – the autonomic nervous system, which involves innervation of involuntary structures within the body. It operates independently of the volition on these structures and is responsible for conveying and processing sensory input from the visceral organs (for example, the digestive and cardiovascular systems), and the motor control of the involuntary (smooth) and cardiac muscles and of glands of the viscera (for example, the large internal organs found in the abdominal cavity or "guts").

Tort Liability for Mental Harm goes on to tell us about effects of emotions on the body:

[5.100] In 1902 Gillett J in *Kline v Kline*, attempting to describe mental or emotional distress, said that there was "a touching of the mind, if not of the body". However, from the scientific point of view, it is incorrect to think of any sort of emotional response as purely *mental* suffering. A considerable amount of medical evidence has been assembled since the beginning of the last century to demonstrate that all emotions have physical effects. The basis of our knowledge of this subject remains the pioneering work of Dr Walter B Cannon of the Harvard Medical School who, during the early years of the 20th century, conducted extensive investigations into the physical effects of various emotions and produced very convincing evidence that emotions bring about important bodily changes. Although more is now known about physiology, modern research has done nothing to invalidate his thesis. But even before his study there was significant scientific opinion that supported such a contention. William Harvey in the 17th century recognised that affections of the mind were accompanied by bodily responses, and in the 19th century what was probably the first serious study of the physical effects of fright was carried out by Charles Darwin. Damasio describes this graphically: "All emotions use the body as their theatre (internal milieu, visceral, vestibular and musculoskeletal systems)."

In certain other publications, we learn about the extent to which, given our far-distant roots as hunter-gatherers, our human make-up, because of our ancient double role as both predator and prey, is very much like that of other animals. Our nervous reactions to acute stress can be similar, but unlike other animals, we human beings are – unfortunately, of course – liable to remain traumatized, sometimes suffering the consequences of shock for years after the event, in some form or other of PTSD. Peter A. Levine's *Waking the Tiger* is one of these publications that teach us a good deal about our own make-up – and how to deal with post-traumatic stress. As for the cost to the body (as distinct from the mind, the emotions, but not separate from them) we have much to learn from the book *The Body Keeps the Score*, by Dr Bessel van der Kolk, the Dutch-American doctor mentioned earlier, who has shown in his initial chapters how very reluctant the medical profession was for several decades to accept the idea that the body and mind are inseparable.

The brilliantly researched *Tort Liability for Mental Harm* goes on to say, in paragraph **[5.110]**:

> Much of the scientific evidence on the effects of emotions on the body deals with fear. Fear may be of many types but it inevitably involves the *threat* of loss or damage to something that the individual greatly values and to which he or she is strongly attached. It may be for one's own personal safety or that of another, for loss of a prized possession or even an abstract ideal such as honour, reputation or a political or religious canon. Fear causes various bodily changes…

There follows a detailed description of the changes our bodies can undergo as a result of a traumatic event. Perhaps we can return to paragraph 5.110 later in this book. But meanwhile, very significantly, we see from paragraph 5.130 that, whereas *in the short term* these changes are not harmful, in the long term these bodily changes may cause serious and permanent damage. Several authors have pointed out that, when nature developed the physical reactions following fear, fear usually meant fight or flight – as in the animal world – but in the case of human beings it seldom means either. So the infliction of emotional distress, if serious or intense enough, or repeated often enough, may cause debilitating and permanent harm.

We have a valuable explanation here of how PTSD can come about:

> **[5.140]** There is thus a primary, automatic and instinctive reaction to traumatic stimuli, involving conscious and unconscious components, which may be seen as the body's

attempt to combat and protect the individual from the stress associated with the situation in question. This may be followed by a longer-term reaction, which occurs when the body can no longer overcome the problem of ongoing emotional stress or adequately cope with the traumatic event.

This fascinating Chapter 5 of my cousin's book goes into further interesting material under the heading "Anxiety disorders, somatic disorders and psychoses", speaking of psychoses of which the most serious are schizophrenia and bipolar disorder, that however do not concern us here. And then, under the heading "Post-traumatic stress disorder", we read:

[5.210] Of all the "recognisable psychiatric illnesses", of particular significance for our purposes is the very considerable interest focused in the last two or three decades on post-traumatic stress disorder ("PTSD") and it is on this anxiety disorder that we will concentrate our discussion. Although the clinical features of PTSD have been observed for hundreds of years, the psychiatric nomenclature is of recent vintage. It was only in 1980 that American psychiatrists introduced this new diagnostic category into the third edition of the *Diagnostic and Statistical Manual of Mental Disorders* (DSM-III) – the diagnostic system of the American Psychiatric Association.[4] Previously what is really a relatively common human post-trauma problem had been known under a variety of different names such as "post-traumatic neurosis", "post-accident syndrome", "fright neurosis" or "shell shock". One catalyst for its inclusion was the result of growing research being carried out on combat veterans and in particular into the catastrophic effects of the Vietnam War.

[5.220] Some continue to debate the validity of this syndrome but the vast majority of the scientific community accept it as a psychiatric entity, pointing to repeated observation and description of identical sets of symptoms following traumatic events. It is included in DSM-5, and was added to the 10th edition of the World Health Organisation's *International*

---

[4] The most recent version, known as DSM-5, was published in 2013: American Psychiatric Association, Diagnostic and Statistical Manual of Mental Disorders, Fifth Edition: DSM-5 (American Psychiatric Association, Washington DC, 2013).

Classification of Diseases (ICD-10) – the standard psychiatric classification used in the Australian public health system. Although courts have been somewhat hesitant to utilise the benefits of the latest developments in this field, there are signs that this is changing. Starting in the late 1980s, judges began to identify the sufferings of plaintiffs as PTSD. The DSM-III-R criteria were expressly adopted for the first time in an Irish decision, and since then judges have regularly referred to the diagnostic criteria in DSM-III-R, DSM-IV, DSM-IV-TR and now DSM-5, and also to ICD-10 and other medical literature, to assist in the determination of whether a recognisable psychiatric illness has been established. The authors of DSM-5 suggest caution in the way in which this material should be used:

> Clinical training and experience are needed to use DSM for determining a diagnosis. The diagnostic criteria identify symptoms, behaviours, cognitive functions, personality traits, physical signs, syndrome combinations, and durations that require clinical expertise to differentiate from normal life variation and transient responses to stress.

Judges have also recognised the limitations of such sources. In the words of Thorpe LJ in *Vernon v Bosley (No 1)*:

> DSM-III-R may provide the medical profession with a useful diagnostic tool but PTSD and its DSM-III-R classification should not, in my judgment, be adopted in personal injury litigation as the yardstick by which the plaintiffs' success or failure is to be measured.

[5.230] DSM-5 defines PTSD as requiring: (i) exposure to actual or threatened death, serious injury, or sexual violence; (ii) the presence of intrusion symptoms associated with the traumatic event(s); (iii) persistent avoidance of stimuli associated with the traumatic event(s); (iv) negative alterations in cognitions and mood associated with the traumatic event(s); (v) marked alterations in arousal and reactivity associated with the traumatic event(s); (vi) a duration of disturbance of more than one month; and (vii) clinically significant distress or impairment in social, occupational or other important areas of functioning. ICD-10 requires an event or situation of an exceptionally threatening or catastrophic nature that is likely to cause pervasive illness in almost anyone. These definitions recognise that not all trauma victims are necessarily normal individuals, although the stressor must be of sufficient severity to invoke the symptoms in normal persons. Consequently, PTSD may be diagnosed in those who have had previous psychiatric problems. Importantly, it is also recognised that the trauma may be experienced through direct physical perception or on learning of it through third parties, alone or in the company of others.

Stressors capable of producing the condition include military combat, natural disasters, intentionally caused disasters (such as confinement in concentration camps, subjection to torture or presence at bombing sites), and the situation with which we are chiefly concerned, accidental disasters. Exposure to such phenomena must lead to a characteristic collection of symptoms involving mental re-experience of the traumatic event, numbing of responsiveness to the external world, the avoidance of stimuli associated with the trauma and increased arousal. These states do not always occur in a prescribed pattern, there being variations in the oscillations between them.

Tort Liability for Mental Harm deals more authoritatively with PTSD than any publication I got hold of when first setting out to write this book. In the next section, we read about symptoms and how individuals experience them:

> **[5.240]** PTSD thus focuses on specific psychological responses to an extreme environmental condition that would evoke distress symptoms in almost everyone. It consists of a combination of "tonic" features (those that the victim manifests all or most of the time) and "phasic" features (those that are manifested intermittently). Although comprised of the trilogy of intrusion (phasic), avoidance (tonic) and arousal (a mixture of phasic and tonic) symptoms, it is the first of these that is the characteristic feature of the disorder. Unwelcomed memories of the traumatic event may manifest themselves in recurrent and distressing recollections (in young children, in the form of

repeated engagement in play in which themes or aspects of the trauma are expressed), nightmares, sudden acting or feeling as if the event were recurring in the form of a sense of reliving the experience, visual and auditory flashbacks not unlike those experienced by LSD users, dissociative states lasting from a few seconds to several hours or even days, and intense distress at exposure to events that symbolise or resemble an aspect of the trauma (such as anniversaries of the trauma).

[5.250] The unconscious defence mechanisms of general non responsiveness and avoidance strategy may manifest themselves in deliberate efforts to avoid thoughts or feelings about the event in question and activities or situations that arouse recollections of it. PTSD victims may even experience memory fragmentation, developing psychogenic amnesia for an important aspect of the trauma. Commonly there is a markedly diminished interest in significant activities which in the case of children may result in the loss of recently acquired developmental skills such as toilet training or improvement in language. Feelings of detachment or estrangement from others, "emotional blunting", inability to express loving feelings and a sense of a life without future (for example, empty of marriage, children or career) are also signs of the existence of these components of the disorder.

I know from observations of a number of these symptoms that the description is "spot-on":

[5.260] Persistent symptoms of increased arousal that were not present prior to the trauma include irritability, difficulty in falling or staying asleep, problems with concentration, hypervigilance and exaggerated startle response. Sufferers may also experience negative alterations in cognitions and mood associated with the traumatic event, such as inability to remember some important aspects of the event, decreased interest in significant activities, and feelings of detachment from others.

The chapter goes on to indicate what intervals may occur between the traumatic event and the experience of a post-traumatic stress disorder:

[5.270] The original definition of PTSD drew a distinction between three subtypes: an acute disorder that began within six months of the trauma and lasted less than six months; a chronic disorder lasting six months or longer; and delayed PTSD that had its onset at least six months after the event in question. The literature reveals that most researchers conceptualise PTSD as a syndromal progression of clinical features from the acute to the chronic stage, although it is certainly true that this progression may be affected by secondary "symptoms" such as involvement in continuing or prospective litigation. DSM-5 stipulates that the symptoms outlined above must be present for at least one month before the diagnosis of PTSD will be made, although it is silent on the question of the time of the disturbance's onset. The capacity of PTSD to occur with a delayed start – it can be as little as a week or as long as 30 years – remains one of the puzzling aspects of the condition.

Let us now turn to what we learn from Chapters 1 of this learned book on how the lawmakers have come to recognize the need to bring laws in line with current realities.

Exercising The Law:
The Search For (New?) Limits: "The Boundary Stone"

We learn in *Tort Liability for Mental Harm* that since liability for "nervous shock" was initially recognized by courts at the end of the nineteenth century, the law of psychiatric injury has been dominated by the perceived need to impose limits on the scope of that liability. At the very beginning of the book, the author quotes a significant statement made in the 1988 court case *Attia v British Gas plc* by Lord Justice Bingham, later, as Lord Bingham, senior presiding judge of the House of Lords, the highest court in the UK:

> It is submitted, I think rightly, that this claim breaks new ground. No analogous claim has ever, to my knowledge, been upheld or even advanced. If, therefore, it were proper to erect a doctrinal boundary stone at the point which the onward march of recorded decisions has so far reached, we should answer the question of principle in the negative and dismiss the plaintiff's action. ... But I should for my part erect the boundary stone with a strong presentiment that it would not be long before a case would arise so compelling on its facts as to cause the stone to be moved to a new and more distant resting place.

My cousin Professor Peter Handford has devoted at least twenty-five years to the cause of broadening the law in relation to psychiatric injury. In the first edition of his book (1993) the concluding sentence reads, "At the first opportunity, the boundary stone must be moved again", and referred to shortly afterwards are the "reluctance of the courts to recognise the individual's interest in mental tranquillity, and the influence of underlying concerns that continued to cultivate undue judicial caution and foster the imposition of inappropriate doctrinal restrictions on recovery". While recognizing that considerable advances had been made in psychiatric damage law since such claims first emerged, it seems that they have been "piecemeal and slow in coming".

Of course, as we have seen, it was only in some of the later years of the twentieth century that PTSD came to be realized by the medical profession. Nevertheless, with regard to the law, "the more telling reason was *society's failure to appreciate, or refusal to admit, that serious disruption to peace of mind is no less worthy of community and legal support than physical injury to the body*, even given that priorities in accident compensation require careful thought in the face of limited resources". And the book boldly went on to say that "a more desirable position… would be for the law to treat psychiatric damage in the same way as cases of physical injury. The two kinds of personal harm should not be treated differently in terms of the rules governing responsibility at law."

Another significant statement had been made in 1992 by Lord Oliver of Aylmerton in *Alcock v Chief Constable of South Yorkshire Police* (the action brought by the relatives of those killed in the Hillsborough football disaster):

> There is… nothing unusual or peculiar in the recognition by the law that compensatable injury may be caused just as much by a direct assault upon the mind or the nervous system as by direct physical contact with the body. This is no more than the natural and inevitable result of the growing appreciation by modern medical science of recognisable causal connections between shock to the nervous system and physical or psychiatric illness. Cases in which damages are claimed for directly inflicted injuries of this nature may present greater difficulties of proof but they are not, in their essential elements, any different from cases where the damages claimed arise from direct physical injury.

The 1980s/1990s research into post-traumatic stress began to bear fruit in the shape of numerous publications and a broad start-up of psychosocial aid measures to stricken victims of disasters. Then it began to be realized that rescuers too – police, doctors and nurses, family members and others who had been involved in disaster scenes – also needed support. The Red Cross and Red Crescent Movement was in the vanguard in all these respects, largely no doubt as a result of all the work done at Vitznau in 1987, which resulted in important recommendations on policy and practice that were circulated to all national societies worldwide, also brought up in international meetings.

Similarly, the law had begun to concede that "secondary victims", i.e. persons who suffered some form of mental harm as a result of another person being killed, injured or put in peril, ought also to be taken into account. This led to a series of other suggested limitations, and over and over again "it became necessary to move the boundary stone to a new and more distant resting place". My cousin's book had, as he wrote, the object of examining the issues raised in this area of liability and of exploring "the appropriateness of the then-current boundary marks, suggesting a more liberal direction that the law should take in the future".

Over thirty years earlier, a distinguished comparative law scholar, having made a detailed comparative study of the contrasting approaches of civil and common law systems to liability for negligence, said:

> One wonders… if the time has not come to say that if the plaintiff, as a result of the defendant's conduct, has suffered some kind of serious and "recognisable psychiatric illness" he should be allowed to recover damages irrespective of his relationship with the victims, his physical position at the time of the accidents, or even his personal propensities towards such type of injury. Indeed, the law may be slowly moving in that direction.

Our two authors of the first edition endorsed this general approach, suggesting "the abandonment of most of the control mechanisms that in the words of Lord Hoffmann 'disfigure the law of liability for psychiatric injury'". Evidently, these proposals rapidly received a good deal of attention, but a different proposal, by a certain Professor Jane Stapleton quoted in *The Frontiers of Liability* (Oxford University Press, 1994) suggested that the only possible solution was "to abolish recovery for psychiatric injury altogether". In the context of a second Hillsborough case that was dealing with the claims of police officers (*White v Chief Constable of South Yorkshire Police*), Lord Steyn addressed the two proposals, referring to the one made by "our" two authors as "a bold innovation" but saying that, in his view, the only sensible general strategy for the courts would be to say "thus far and no further". However, by the time the second edition of the book appeared seven years later there had been considerable progress in some jurisdictions, notably in Australia, towards the objective stated in the first edition, though the response was more cautious in England. The High Court of Australia in *Tame v New South Wales; Annetts v. Australian Stations Pty Ltd (2002)* expanded and restated liability on a rational basis, while in England the House of Lords in a series of important cases imposed new restrictions on the ambit of liability. In Canada, the Supreme Court in *Saadati v Moorhead (2017)* has now opened up the law by stating that compensation may be available for any form of serious mental harm, and not just a "recognizable psychiatric illness".

In a sub-section in the book entitled "Traditional arguments against recovery" on the problem of setting limits to liability for psychiatric injury and on what limits, if any, are appropriate, courts (in considering where to set down the boundary stone) have had to contend with the arguments against allowing recovery for mental harm, or against allowing recovery for such harm on the same basis as for physical injury. They are simply the traditional reasons referred to by certain judges unprepared to extend the law, whereas in Australia modern judges are seen to take a much more enlightened approach.

To bring this part of the chapter to its conclusion, I would like to quote one more passage from *Tort Liability for Mental Harm*:

> **[1.190]** Damage to the psyche has throughout history provoked apprehension, induced a sense of uncertainty and been shrouded in ignorance. People have always feared what they do not understand and been sceptical of that which they cannot "verify" by sight. Such attitudes are by no means extinct today. However, the fact that an injury cannot always be seen by the naked eye does not mean that it is any less of a "real" injury than those that involve the breaking of bones, the spilling of blood, the scarring of tissue or physical pain. Indeed, it can be argued that the mental repercussions of trauma are more serious, more deserving of the law's attention than those of a physical nature. Mental conditions frequently persist long after organic injuries have disappeared. Broken bones knit, wounds heal often without scarring or permanent disability and those that do scar, although unsightly, leave less of a

mark than scars on the mind. Physical pain usually subsides, often long before the psychological impact of distressing events disappears. The after-effects of trauma may never fully dissipate.[5] Certainly, not every form of psychiatric abnormality will be permanent or even long-lasting, and tragically there are physical conditions such as paraplegia and quadriplegia that remain with victims until death. But as a general observation, an injured mind is far more difficult to nurse back to health than an injured body and is arguably more debilitating and disruptive of a greater number of aspects of human existence.

Given the increasing volume of stressful factors in today's world affecting more and more people, one may imagine that there might be frequent recourse to the courts for injury to the mind. We are however reassured by what we read in this book that this is a relatively rare phenomenon, not least because pragmatic and personal considerations often lead people to refrain from instituting proceedings. Moreover, very many of those in our societies who have suffered considerable psychiatric harm are people who have been tortured in countries from which they probably had no alternative but to flee. Some such countries' courts are far more likely to have had the role of condemning innocents to torture, prison and/or death than to be courts in which there may be the hope and comfort of any form of redress – even after a change of regime.

It is worth mentioning here that many asylum seekers, threatened with expulsion in countries such as Britain and Switzerland (to take the two examples with which I have been most familiar), have over the years been saved, sometimes *in extremis*, from a forcible return to their countries of origin by expert testimonies provided by agencies such as the Medical Foundation for the Care of Victims of Torture in London (recently renamed "Freedom from Torture"), which proved that they had been tortured and suffered from PTSD. A Swiss lawyer told me many years ago that material published in the report on the Vitznau workshop had been used with effect to pre-empt rejection of some asylum seekers. The ability of some refugees who reach our countries (initially called "asylum seekers", of course) to show[6] that PTSD is part of their unwelcome "baggage" seems to augur well

---

[5]   For example, some of the sailors who suffered post-traumatic stress disorder as a result of their involvement in the Voyager disaster, a collision between two warships during a training exercise, were still being treated twenty years after the disaster.

[6]   As we shall see later in this book, there are many elements that militate against refugees/asylum seekers getting the kind of help that they (often desperately)

for the future at a time that it has become increasingly difficult to get a sympathetic hearing.

A Certain Ambivalence In Some Countries' Law Courts
In Relation To The Importance Of Psychiatric Harm

[5.510] The question that then arises is whether it is still possible to suggest, at least for the law's purposes, that there is such a thing as purely mental harm. In terms of legal conceptualisation and classification it still seems convenient to focus on mental harm (or psychiatric injury) as a discrete negligence category. There is much to be said for Lord Goff of Chieveley's view as expressed in *White v Chief Constable of South Yorkshire Police*:

[A] particular type of personal injury, viz, psychiatric injury, may... properly be differentiated from other types of personal injury. It appears to be in no way inconsistent with the making of that common sense judgment, as a matter of practical justice, that scientific advances are revealing that psychiatric illnesses may have a physical base, or that psychiatric injury should be regarded as another form of personal injury.

What is unacceptable is not this separate treatment, but rather the argument that liability for psychiatric injury, because it is psychiatric, should be much more limited than liability for physical harm. Courts in Australia and elsewhere have managed to rebut this argument. The English courts have not been as successful.

We can (if we wish) speculate on what success any of us might hope to achieve if we were to take to court a person or company that had done us wrong and caused us to suffer symptoms of PTSD. There must be many instances, now that the courts have become familiar with the reality of psychiatric harm, in which people could give thought to taking their persecutors to court – which presumably would never have been possible before about 1990. However, taking the discussion on further, we read:

[5.300] Despite the recognition of PTSD in both DSM-5 and ICD-10, and the growing sophistication of psychology

---

require. If they can get through to the authorities at all, it is usually thanks to the presence and help of translators and of course medical personnel.

and psychiatry over the years, a number of PTSD cases go unrecognised by experts in both disciplines. The disorder's symptoms are similar to other complaints and it is sometimes confused with other anxiety disorders, anti-social personality disorders, schizophrenia, alcoholism and other substance abuse, and depression. The identification difficulties are compounded by the fact that PTSD may coexist with any of these and with other psychiatric disorders (the phenomenon of comorbidity). One reason for diagnostic inaccuracy stems from the nature of psychopathology.[7] Where an x-ray clearly reveals evidence of fracture, or laboratory testing denotes abnormal growth hormone levels in atypically short or tall patients, there can be no doubt as to the nature of the particular complaint. Such unequivocal and reliable evidence is not always ascertainable when assessing mental disturbance.

A Specific Case

Chapter 5 features trials and appeals relating to several cases brought against airlines by their erstwhile passengers. *King v Bristow Helicopters Ltd* was a case before the Scottish courts brought by a Mr King after a helicopter on which he was a passenger landed heavily on a helideck on a North Sea oil rig platform in poor weather. PTSD developed subsequently, and the stress led to Mr King suffering peptic ulcer disease. Initially, it was held that his claim under Article 17 of the Warsaw Convention[8] was confined to the peptic ulcer disease, a ruling that excluded Mr King's claim for psychological injury. He could not accept it and his defence argued that the ulcer was triggered by psychiatric and not bodily injury. The First Division of the Court of Session reversed the first-instance decision that his claim was confined to the peptic ulcer condition and held that he was also entitled to claim damages for psychiatric injury.[9] The appeal went to the House of Lords, requiring, along with another appeal on behalf of an appeal on behalf of a Ms. Morris (*Morris v KLM Royal Dutch Airlines Ltd*), a ruling on the meaning of "bodily injury". The story goes on:

---

[7] Psychopathology is the study of abnormal states of mind.
[8] The Warsaw Convention is an international convention which regulates liability for air carriers who cross international boundaries.
[9] *King v Bristow Helicopters Ltd* 2001 SC 54.

[5.420] During the hearing in the House of Lords, a point emerged that had not been previously considered. It was based on *Weaver v Delta Airlines Inc*, where a federal court in Montana was dealing with a claim by a passenger for PTSD resulting from an emergency landing. The issue was whether the plaintiff suffered "bodily injury" – a requirement that United States courts, following the leading United States Supreme Court decision in *Eastern Airlines Inc v Floyd*, had held to rule out claims for purely mental injury unaccompanied by physical injury or some physical manifestation thereof. Lord Hobhouse of Woodborough described the special nature of the evidence in this case:

The plaintiff filed affidavits providing uncontradicted expert evidence that "extreme stress causes actual physical brain damage, ie, physical destruction or atrophy of portions of the hippocampus of the brain". "The impact upon [the plaintiff] of the events which occurred on that flight was extreme and included biochemical reactions which had physical impacts upon her brain and neurological system." She had thus presented evidence of "physical injury" and was entitled to say that "her diagnosed post-traumatic stress disorder arose from the physical changes in her brain brought on during the extreme stress of the emergency landing". ... The judge therefore distinguished her case from "*Floyd* and its progeny": she was relying upon "an injury to her brain, and the only reasonable conclusion is that it is, in fact, a bodily injury". ... It is hard to see any basis for disagreeing with the conclusion that, if the passenger can prove that his or her brain was damaged as a result of the accident, the passenger has suffered a *bodily injury*.

This was the argument that had been accepted by Shanstrom CJ in *Weaver*:

Weaver's action is here distinguishable from previous cases, because her claim is presented as a physical injury and she relies on recent scientific research explaining that post-traumatic stress disorder evidences actual trauma to brain cell structures. Weaver's post-traumatic stress disorder evidences an injury to her brain, and the only reasonable conclusion is that it is, in fact, a bodily injury.

More particularly, the injury to her brain should be considered a "bodily injury" as defined under the *Warsaw Convention*. Granted, Weaver's injury manifests itself in ways that are similar to the "injuries" previously found not compensatable in similar cases under the *Warsaw Convention*. However, the central factor here is not legal, but medical. The legal question in this case is simply whether the *Warsaw Convention* allows recovery for this particular kind of bodily injury, ie a brain injury (even with slight physical effects). The answer must be yes.

... Fright alone is not compensatable, but brain injury from fright is. Unlike the plaintiffs in *Floyd* and its progeny, Weaver's injury is a "bodily injury" as defined by the *Warsaw Convention*.

[5.430] Evidence such as that presented in *Weaver v Delta Airlines Inc.* has the potential not only to expand the interpretation of "bodily injury" in art 17 of the *Warsaw Convention* but also perhaps to expand the conception of what is understood by a "recognisable psychiatric illness" at common law, to strengthen the case for recognition of liability for pure mental distress and other mental injuries not amounting to recognisable psychiatric illness, and possibly even to render the distinction between physical and psychiatric injuries almost meaningless.

Ultimately, the House of Lords found against both Mr King and Miss Morris, holding that, where mental injury or illness lacked a physical cause or origin, it could not constitute "bodily injury" in the terms required by the Warsaw Convention. The judges expressed different views on the point raised in the *Weaver* case, but agreed that on the facts of the cases before them it was not necessary to reach a concluded view.

The fact that many court cases drag on for years means that contenders are under additional strain and may eventually develop PTSD. Whether specifically identified or not, PTSD must be a feature in many such court cases, and what was not known about it towards the end of the twentieth century has since become known across quite a broad spectrum of medical and social work specialities. In the field of law, we can admit that there has been quite some progress, in the face however of a degree of reluctance on the part of some experienced lawmakers to take into account a hitherto unrecognized form of damage. In criminal law, defences based on PTSD have become increasingly common, being used as the standard defence in selected situations; while in the USA, although a psychiatric diagnosis is not required to bring action, PTSD has become the favoured diagnosis in cases of emotional distress.

There is so much that can be said and written about PTSD in the context of litigation that I warmly recommend the book *Tort Liability for Mental Harm* to everyone with an interest in the subject.

Brief Summary Of A Contemporary Case

As a barrister friend has confirmed to me, considerations of confidentiality mean that it is usually not possible to quote "chapter and verse" when writing about traumatized individuals who are in the hands of the law. Perhaps, however, this summary reflecting the difficulty of providing timely help to a young immigrant is of some interest.

A young girl, born and brought up by her parents initially in their war-torn country, then spends several of her growing years in England before being taken back for a period to their home country. The family, realizing that it is too dangerous to remain there, returns to Europe and applies for refugee status, but their application coincides with the onset of serious mental agitation on the part of the girl, who in fact becomes very violent. As a result of her manifesting unmanageable behaviour, including making several suicide attempts, the parents apply for placement for her, but this proves more difficult than had been imagined despite the involvement of several parties, all manifesting evident goodwill. It comes to be realized that trauma arising from acute memories of war atrocities has been at the root of the young person's problematic behaviour. Over a period of months, different entities are involved in trying to find a solution, and time required to help the girl with her PTSD is lost. A statement in one of the law records that even the most rudimentary understanding of the girl's psychological needs remains far from clear demonstrates how difficult it proves to analyse and treat PTSD. At the time of writing, no satisfactory solution for the girl has been found.

The case has some parallels with those of former war combatants in the USA in the 1980s and 1990s, with the reported sudden outbursts of very dangerous behaviour on the part of certain individuals that baffled the men themselves, their families and those who were confronted with the need to try to help them. As has already been mentioned, these former combat soldiers suddenly started suffering from flashbacks so devastating that they were now, in a sense, reliving that period of their past that had been both meaningful and excruciatingly distressing.

CHAPTER 6

Organized Violence: Torture And Its Consequences

This chapter, based partly on addresses at the 1987 Vitznau workshop on refugee trauma, describes one of the most atrocious aspects of man's inhumanity to man. Then it goes on to describe some of the measures that are available to torture survivors – as touched upon in Chapter 4.

Although to date 157 countries[1] have ratified the United Nations Convention against Torture, Amnesty International has found that, within the last five years, torture has been practised in 141 countries. The Freedom from Torture Foundation in London (the current name of the Medical Foundation, spoken of earlier) has reported that in 2017, it received people from ninety-six countries who asked for "help to overcome torture" – a really shocking fact.

Torture As A Mechanism For Political Control, By Helen Bamber

The separation of body from mind is nowhere less appropriate than in the treatment of torture victims, where the body has been abused to gain access to the mind.

> Torture does not occur simply because individual torturers are sadistic, even if testimonies verify that they often are. Torture is usually part of state-controlled machinery to suppress dissent. Concentrated in the torturer's electrode or syringe is the power and responsibility of the state.
>
> However perverse the actions of individual torturers, torture itself has a rationale: isolation, humiliation, psychological

---

1 Of the 195 countries in the world, of which 193 are Member States of the United Nations.

pressure, and physical pain are means to obtain information, to break down the prisoner, and to intimidate those close to him or her. The torturer may be after something specific, like a signature on a confession, a renunciation of beliefs, or the denunciation of relatives, colleagues, and friends who in turn may be seized, tortured, and if possible, broken. Torture may also be a method of subduing a population through terror. Torture is usually an integral part of a government's security strategy. The problem is global.

Methods Of Torture

No experience of torture is typical, but there are discernible patterns in the thousands of personal testimonies, affidavits, and statements that reach human rights organizations like the Medical Foundation for the Care of Victims of Torture in London.

Torture usually means isolation, abduction, and *incommunicado* detention beyond the reach of family, friends, and legal assistance. Blindfolding during days of interrogation and torture serves to increase the prisoner's sense of being alone and defenceless. Essential to torture is the sense that the interrogator controls everything, even life itself.

The Medical Foundation for the Care of Victims of Torture in London has treated patients who have been subjected to the torture methods listed below.

Beatings: the prolonged beating of the soles of the feet with truncheons or other heavy implements, beating the body with wire cables, repeated blows with rifle butts and heavy army boots, repeated and violent banging of a victim's head against a wall, public floggings.
Burning: with acid, molten rubber, red-hot metal, cigarettes, paraffin-soaked rags.
Electrical torture: electrodes are placed on the sensitive areas of the body, including the lips, ears, mouth, and genitalia.
Hanging: the victim is suspended from the wall or ceiling for prolonged periods, often in awkward positions by the hands or feet.
Sexual torture: rape of both men and women is common. Sexual torture may also involve bestiality using dogs and the

insertion of broken bottles, rifles, truncheons, or other objects into the vagina and/or anus of the victim. Bicycle spokes may be forced into the urethra; heavy weights may be suspended from the victim's testicles, causing injury.

Mutilation: amputations and other injuries inflicted with sharp instruments including knives; the removal of finger nails and toe nails.

Suffocation: repeated immersion in water, often contaminated by sewage; the use of plastic bags or tight wet hoods.

Psychological torture: mock execution, torture of family members, threats to family members and friends, gross humiliation.

The use of torture and other forms of ill-treatment brutalizes and dehumanizes all those who inflict it. It affects their families and communities. It corrupts those responsible for decisions that lead to torture and ill-treatment and those who condone it. Work being done to help survivors of torture, within a state where torture has been or is being practised, of necessity includes working towards a general recognition of these facts.

It has been said that torture is "the most terrible event remaining in man's memory". It dominates and overshadows a survivor's life. The individual therapist or therapeutic team has to enable victims of torture to become creative survivors.

Torture Intends To Destroy, By Dr Paul Movschenson[2]

Naturally most of the countries that practise torture deny that they resort to it. The fact that torture is practised in secret has implications for the victims' credibility: they are faced with having to *prove* that they have been tortured.[3]

We must look at the intention of the torturers. During torture, the intention is not only to cause a person pain, but to *destroy*

---

[2] Dr Paul Movschenson was in the 1980s a psychiatrist at the Swedish Red Cross Centre for Tortured Refugees, which he helped establish. His background in the field of refugees and survivors of torture was with Amnesty International.

[3] Perico Rodríguez, mentioned elsewhere in this book and himself a torture survivor, spoke recently of having once received at the Foundation where he was a counsellor a young Iranian, who now told him, "You were the first person to believe me. Nobody had believed me. I want you to meet my wife and children." For in the intervening years, having been free of his post-traumatic stress, the young man had been able to live a normal life at last.

a person. From ill-treatment a victim could perhaps have the same pains or complaints, but the results are not the same because the intention was not to break the person.

It is important to remember that most torture victims are not refugees; they are people who remain in their country of origin, and they should not be forgotten. It has however proved very difficult to establish rehabilitation centres in those countries. ...

Not all those who have suffered torture necessarily have psychological problems. There are those who have come through severe torture without any lingering pains or problems. Having said that, however, it has been demonstrated by victims of the Second World War that health problems may occur many years after the torture was inflicted. People who have been in a good state of health for forty years suddenly develop problems after reaching retirement and perhaps after losing touch with their few remaining relatives.

Yet it would be dangerous to give the impression that all victims of torture inevitably get health problems, or to brand all torture victims as sick people. This could lead to a stigmatisation of the victims, and we want to avoid that.

If one has read about the reality of torture, it is most important to know what can be done to relieve survivors of their heavy burden of what Helen called "sequelae", their physical damage if it persists, their fears, and in many cases their post-traumatic stress. The content of this paper is as apposite now in the context of this book as it ever was.

Rehabilitation work with survivors of torture, by John Schlapobersky[4] and Helen Bamber

The reclamation of time and space

The majority of those tortured do not survive. The testimony of those who do, seen in the Medical Foundation, London

---

4   John Schlapobersky, who when a student was imprisoned in South Africa for his political work, was for many years from 1985 onwards a consultant psychotherapist and sometime member of the Board of Trustees of the Medical Foundation (renamed Freedom from Torture). He set up a wide range of teaching programmes in group and family therapy at for example London University and City University, and helped establish the European Network of Training Institutions for Group Psychotherapy and the British Network of Training Institutions in Marital Therapy.

and other agencies like ours, casts a shadow upon us all. In his conclusion to *Spanish Testimony* Arthur Koestler, writing of his detention whilst awaiting execution during the Spanish Civil War, described himself and his fellow inmates as "men without shadows". They were restricted in both time and space. Waiting for death they felt themselves deprived of the substance even to cast shadows in the space they occupied in prison. Their lives were also insubstantial in time, for they had no sense of the future and their past was of meaning only to their interrogators.

In the Medical Foundation we bear witness to the testimony of those who have had Koestler's experience, but who are without his voice. We see our responsibility, partly, in reclaiming time and space for those who have suffered the loss of both. We attempt to help those who have lived "without shadows" to discover a voice with which to speak of themselves:

> A young man, consumed by intensely-injured emotions that followed torture and exile, said, "I've lost my life. I've lost my plan. When you have a plan for life and the base is broken, nothing is left. I wanted to build my future and have an education but now everything is lost."
>
> Another person talked about becoming "zero". First he had been a student. He would have been an economist, he said, or perhaps even a lawyer. But now, he said, "I have become a zero." Sometimes, he said, he did not want to live. "If you aren't happy, if you aren't glad in the world, then you might as well die." Then he laughed and said he had his youth and his freedom and wanted to make a new beginning.

We find that as people begin to speak for themselves they reclaim time and space. Like the men described above, they retrieve from the consequences of torture their entitlement to a lifespan which the process was intended to destroy.

When people who have endured a nightmare begin to talk about survival, it behoves us all to take account of what they have to say. The poet Akhmatova writes that if you listen to

---

He is inter alia chairman of the German Society of Group Analysis and Group Psychotherapy (D3G), founded in 2011.

her, "You will hear thunder." And so it is with the perversion of human relationships. The damage done in hours, days, or months remains in the bodies and minds of those who survive. Torment is internalized and profound injuries are either disavowed at great personal expense, or are lived out through biological and psychological processes, until such time as an audience is found that can bear to pay attention. To listen, however, one must be ready "to hear thunder".

Torture – a perverted form of intimacy, a secular inquisition

Torture frequently involves an intimate and intense relationship between an individual and one or several others. The body and mind of the victim are a focus for concentrated attention, either in the form of an onslaught or assault, or in a process which is sustained over time and repeatedly applied. Injury thus arises in a direct and personal relationship whose purpose is the deliberate destruction of bodily and psychic integrity. Where the body is the primary site of attack, it is the torturer's point of access to the victim's identity and mind – and every physical scar has an emotional scar.

Torture has always been an instrument of war. It is today also the means for maintaining a particular kind of "peace" and achieving social control through coercion or terror; the state has established itself as the contemporary secular inquisition in many countries. The suffering of the individual is thus the torturer's access to the community. The victims of torture are always individuals, but never individuals alone. For every person detailed, there are mothers and fathers and spouses and children who wait. Torturers deprive the community of its individuals. Just as significantly, they deprive the individual of community by attacking the trust and coherence which make the fabric of any society.

As a personal and intimate violation, the torture process "steals" from the prototype of a healing relationship between a person and their doctor, confessor, or counsellor. And in doing so it perverts the benign intentions of the healing relationship to induce the very state from which the healer is committed to free his patient. This can leave the victim maimed, incapacitated, disabled, cowed, dispossessed of information, or the victim can be forced to witness or participate in such action against others.

If torture is survived at all, what features of the post-traumatic situation are specific to it? Amongst the most insidious consequences is the injury that torture victims suffer in their capacity for relationships. This poses a particular challenge to rehabilitative staff whose medical and psychological services are offered through relationships intended to be healing. When such relationships have been perverted or abused, those who come after, genuine as our reconstructive intention may be, must take account of serious and specific obstacles to progress.

The Medical Foundation And Its Commitments To Human Rights And Rehabilitation

This part of the chapter is a description of therapeutic and rehabilitative work undertaken by the Medical Foundation, London.

We shall review our policies, programmes, personnel, clients, and an illustrative range of typical treatments. Taken as a whole, the organization's development represents a modest attempt to answer the question: what can medicine, psychiatry and psychotherapy provide, as scientific disciplines based on humanistic principles, to protect the human body and the individual mind from the secular inquisition that faces us?

The Foundation was established in December 1985 to continue work first carried out by volunteer practitioners under the auspices of the Medical Group of Amnesty International. The organization works to relieve the physical, social and psychological suffering of individuals and their families who have been subjected to torture and other forms of organized violence. As well as its direct clinical responsibilities, the Medical Foundation has come to play an important national and international role in documentation and verification of torture, education and publicity about the problem worldwide, and consultation and advice to other agencies and personnel. Through a combination of medicine, casework, and a range of psychological and social therapies, we aim to encompass the needs of the whole person. By integrating self-help principles with the specialist services of a multi-professional team, we have found that almost all our clients can be helped in some way to overcome problems that are frequently severe and sometimes apparently intractable.

Policy

We see torture as a social, political, and moral problem that arises on coordinates in terms of time and geography which are frequently planned as a political strategy at local and global levels. Whenever it is applied on a systematic basis, torture has historical precedents and well-designed social consequences. In these cases it is usually associated with other major features of political instability, and the individual sequelae of torture are therefore often difficult to disentangle from trauma associated with other man-made calamities like warfare, political conquest and dispossession, concentrations camps, solitary confinement and other forms of imprisonment, exile, deportation, and refugee status in a foreign land. Our experience confirms that meaningful progress in rehabilitative work with torture victims requires an understanding by all concerned that such work is part of a broader human rights commitment to address these issues.

Many of those we see have suffered extensive physical trauma. In these and in all other cases of torture, there is massive psychic trauma which, if unattended, will almost certainly be compounded rather than alleviated in time. We work to the principle of positive intervention through medical attention and through sustained and structured emotional support in all those cases where people express a need that allows us to engage with them in constructive terms.

The concept of cure is in many cases inappropriate. Such post-traumatic sequelae are not the conditions of an illness so much as a form of bondage through which the torturer ensures that his interventions will last over time. The rehabilitative aim is centred on the purpose of freeing victims rather than "curing" them. Damage is in many cases profound and extensive, but in almost all those who come to our attention there is something constructive to be done.

In all those cases in which physical trauma is implicated, the principle of positive intervention begins from a medical consultation. We find this plays a part in legitimising help-seeking behaviour across a wide range of cultures. Furthermore, as a specialist in physical disorder the physician has a direct and practical role to play – as well as an indirect symbolic one – in helping restore to individuals the privacy and integrity of their own bodily processes. The separation of body from mind is nowhere less appropriate than in the treatment of torture where the body has been abused to gain access to the mind. From this basic principle of positive intervention, an integrated physical and psycho-social approach is developed involving the combined endeavours of a multi-professional team.

Separate individual treatments and discrete, unrelated resources are less useful than the resources of a team. Survivors' feelings of grief, rage, and helplessness need a containing environment where staff can accept and work with them.

> A young man spoke of the process of "decompensation", the abreaction of profound trauma, not long after arriving in London from his home in Central America where he had been tortured and had seen others suffer. Until he was seen at the Medical Foundation some months later, there was no one who could encompass the terms of his anguish. And so he told us, "the forest was my doctor". He would visit a patch of beech-wood nearby where he would run about, cry and shout in great distress, relieving pent-up emotions. "The Medical Foundation", he was later to say, "took over from the forest".

> Another man spoke in the metaphors that typified his Middle Eastern diction when he described the Foundation as a place in which, different as people's cultures were, they might find the same kind of sanctuary that they did in the holy places in their countries of origin, but here secular and open to all.

We are increasingly committed to the view that survivors need a relationship with a community rather than with a specific treatment, and that only in a therapeutic community can staff feel sufficiently supported by one another to endure repeated exposure to extreme experience.

Survival As A Creative Act

People's responses to stress are influenced by their own appraisal of the situation and their capacities to process the experience, to attach meaning to it and to incorporate it in their belief systems. Resilience in adversity is not only a strategy for coping but a creative challenge. People's development histories, cognitive set, affectional base, relationship network, and prior experience of mastery and self-confidence through challenge and adaptation are determining factors in their reactions to massive trauma. In the range of therapies offered, we have found it essential to make contact with people's prior forms of adjustment and to re-activate internal and adaptive strategies for further recovery.

We have been profoundly impressed by the dignity of those who survive torture and by the importance they attach to transcending the victim identity and to re-acquiring a sense of action and creative endeavour in their lives. We have come to regard the services we offer as aids for the sometimes remarkable powers of self-renewal that our clients bring to us. Ordinary social relationships contain those agencies for change which, when tapped, can release profound self-healing, regenerative resources. We see our professional skills as a means towards this end.

> One of our clients, incarcerated in the Middle East after serious injuries under torture, comforted a friend whom he had watched being hurt. "Old man", he said, "we cannot strike them back now. But whilst we are here in prison I shall teach you to read and write, and that will be our victory over them."

He had been a teacher and so by teaching others he found himself able to survive. Group therapy played an important role in his subsequent rehabilitation, for it helped him to re-discover strengths and resources in himself that the needs of others drew from him. He had lost most of what he loved and valued, and a sense of inconsolable loss pervaded the other features of post-traumatic stress from which he suffered. But he was startled by the growing recognition in the group that he had not lost the capacity to be of use to others, and on this discovery he began to rebuild his life.

Disaster imposes a sense of isolation on each survivor. The reduction of this isolation must be a central part of the process of recovery if people are to make genuine adjustments. The sustained and structured emotional support available at the Foundation is intended to meet this need, with the recognition that survivors have each witnessed disaster of incomprehensible magnitude. Many come to see that the testimony they provide in the process of bearing witness carries a responsibility towards the past which is one of the keys towards adjustment in the future. This can become one of the most powerful antidotes to the guilt of survival; the telling of stories, the recounting of narrative has become an integral and engaging aspect of the Foundation's life.

The Medical Foundation's Programmes[5]

The Medical Foundation has four basic programmes in its structure of work with torture victims:

- A rapid medico-legal assessment service in support of measures to protect refugees and asylum seekers;
- A professional crisis intervention programme offering medical, psychological, and social services on an immediate basis;
- Physical and psycho-social rehabilitation, including long-term medical treatment and a range of psychological therapies;
- Consultative and advisory facilities for other agencies and personnel.

The medico-legal assessment service

An assessment procedure to ascertain the details of torture allegations, to vindicate or disconfirm the claim, and to

---

[5] I just wish to remind readers that this chapter quotes material presented at the Red Cross Workshop of 1987, since when the Medical Foundation/Freedom from Torture has naturally continued to develop policies and practices (as reflected in Chapter 4 on Dr Helen Bamber).

maintain reliable documents which verify torture and injuries are an integral part of the Foundation's function. This work is carried out at the request of other agencies, including Amnesty International, and serves a variety of purposes.

Firstly, verification confirms the experience of victims and, in providing permanent and objective testimony, assists in the individual's process of recovery. Secondly, it assists the legal process. Scrupulous forensic assessments and records are compiled at the request of protection agencies during a period in Europe when safeguards to protect refugees and indicate their requests for asylum have been greatly reduced. By demonstrating the grounds for people's fear of further persecution, we have been able to strengthen their case for asylum. Thirdly, assessments of this kind maintain corroborative records about torture for historical purposes and stand as permanent documents. Torturers and those to whom they are responsible should know that evidence of their conduct is on permanent record.

The professional crisis intervention programme

A family may arrive at Heathrow airport, having perhaps transited in some other country *en route*, with documentation at once considered insufficient to grant normal entry, but with a claim for asylum deemed insufficient at least to avert immediate deportation. Nevertheless, they might be held in a detention centre pending investigation by the Home Office, and the terms of their custody might evoke the torture experience in the father, who had earlier been imprisoned for some time. He may suffer flashbacks, stop eating, or develop other symptomatology; if presented by officials with the prospect of inevitable return to a home country where there was genuine danger to himself and his family, a suicide attempt could follow. Such attempts whilst in this kind of detention have become much more frequent.

In situations such as this, the Foundation's staff services the requirements of the major refugee organisations: Amnesty International, the British Refugee Council, the Joint Council for Welfare of Immigrants, the United Kingdom Immigrants Advisory Service, the United Nations High Commission for Refugees and other refugee community organisations. Eighty per cent of our referrals are from these organisations. The remaining twenty per cent are from other sources which include: general practitioners, hospital departments of psychiatry, other medical specialists, the legal profession, social services, and self-referrals. The Foundation's reports are included in representations made to the Home Office by these organisations on behalf of individual asylum seekers. The reports contain requests for individuals and families to receive special consideration in their immediate care and future disposition. Careful and systematic reporting to government agencies by qualified professionals of clients' past experience of either torture or other forms of organised violence can ameliorate the terms under which they are held. They can also contribute towards a government decision to grant temporary admission whilst the case is being considered. Practitioners in the Foundation from the relevant professions are ready to travel long distances to detention centres in different parts of the country – often at short notice – to undertaken investigation and assessments.

Personnel and clients

All new referrals have an initial "reception" interview with the social worker, or director, or, under their guidance, with one of the administrative staff. Those who might be in need of medical attention are moved directly into the medical programme which might run concurrently with measures being undertaken on their behalf falling within the term "protection work", e.g. documentation and verification of their asylum applications, and liaison and consultation with lawyers, social services, and other agencies caring for refugees and asylum seekers.

Clients might reach the mental health programme via this route, or go directly to a consultation with one of the mental health professionals. In any event, an individual or family could, depending on the complexity of the case, be seen simultaneously by a social caseworker engaged in protection work or practical liaison on their behalf, by a general practitioner, by a psychiatrist, and by a psychotherapist. Team meetings and case discussions are essential and the progress of each case is regularly reviewed.

Where language problems arise which cannot be dealt with from amongst the staff, additional interpreters are brought in for specific needs. London has become an important location for refugees and asylum seekers from a uniquely varied range of countries and cultures, and in the main, this is the population from which the Medical Foundation's clients are drawn. The oldest people we see are generally those with late sequelae from the European Holocaust or Japanese concentration camps. The youngest are the children of current torture victims, or children amongst the current population of asylum seekers who have themselves been direct victims of torture or assault.

Treatment

Individual psychotherapy in the crisis intervention and long-term rehabilitation programme:

A young man arrived in London after a complicated series of moves between various countries and was living with family friends. He had been held in prison for some three years after his initial detention and torture, and owed his escape and freedom to an accident.

Until his imprisonment at about twenty years of age, he was physically robust and problem-free in psychological terms. He was a sports enthusiast, played football, and was interested in women. On referral we found him anorexic, significantly below his optimal weight, incapacitated by a poorly healed fracture to one wrist and by soft-tissue damage to the soles of his feet, which had split after they had been beaten whilst he was in prison. Walking any distance presented a problem, he suffered from recurrent headaches, a disordered sleeping pattern, and morbid ruminations. Exploration of traumatic associations aggravated a tremor which produced a dramatic convulsion for which he had been taken to several casualty department who found him neurologically well. This was his story:

On being arrested he was blindfolded, taken to a building where the blindfold was removed, and locked in a cell where he found a friend who had had four toes cut off. He was later taken down some stairs to a small room covered with blood. There was broken glass on the floor and three people not in uniform whom he would recognise if he saw them again.

He was stripped naked, his hands and feet were bound, and he was hung upside down from a bar on the ceiling with a rope around his feet. The torturers beat him with wire cable and cut the soles of his feet with glass pieces. With lighted cigarettes they burnt him between his fingers and on the backs of his hands. A bloodstained blanket was stuffed in his mouth to prevent his cries.

At a later point urine was passed in his mouth, he was punched in the mouth, six teeth were broken and were pulled out of his mouth with a pair of pliers. Twenty-four hours later he was subjected to a mock execution. Together with five other prisoners, he was tied to a pole, blindfolded, and when the shots rang out he alone was alive. He was then locked up in the back of a van with the corpses.

There are events in the course of human conduct to which, as witnesses, the only appropriate responses can be the silence of respect or the indignation of tears. In our work at the Medical Foundation, testimony of this kind is in no way unrepresentative. We are still very often speechless or distressed.

Work with this man began with a detailed history by one of our examining doctors and a caseworker. A great deal of time was spent establishing a relationship of familiarity. When we were confident he would not experience medical investigation as further bodily intrusion, further neurological tests were performed in the presence of the caseworker he had come to trust. In the setting he had come to trust, he was seen by a physiotherapist and osteopath for treatment to his feet and to his wrist. Staff secured for him a special set of shoes with built-up soles which reduced the discomfort of walking, and a bicycle which reduced the amount of walking necessary.

We began a course of individual psychotherapy with the assistance of a translator who was one of his family friends. The translator became part of the treatment process and continued the dialogue when they left us. Priority in our sessions was given to establishing a convivial and trusting relationship through a dialogue in which the future was more important than the past. Close attention was given to his family history, early, life, and the period prior to detention. Only six months into his therapy were the details of his torture explored, at which point there was a reoccurrence – as we had anticipated – of the convulsive seizure described above.

Together with the translator, a routine was established by which, when the seizure occurred, our client was firmly held and massaged on those muscle sites which had gone into spasm. Whilst doing so, the subject matter which had provoked the seizure was kept under discussion. The assistance of friends and family were engaged to sustain this sort of response at home. During our sessions we turned increasingly towards an exploration of the symbolic content of his vivid and tormented dreams. Much later in our sessions, when he had learnt enough English to attend without the translator, we would pass a large dictionary backwards and forwards between us. It became a transitional object, a bridge by which to cross from his experience in the past to our experience now in the present.

He made slow, consistent progress evidenced by changes in his mood, sleeping and eating patterns. His aversion to hot food, the consequence of (amongst other things) years of a cold diet in prison, steadily diminished and he was able to begin eating solids after some dental reconstruction. We knew he was getting better when his weight went up, when narrative about imprisonment no longer produced seizures, and when he was able to join a long-term therapy group, joke about an interest in women, and use our staff to begin planning a career and study programme.

Marital And Family Therapy In The Course Of
Protection Work And Long-Term Rehabilitation

A protection agency referred to us for documentation a man whose initial application for asylum had been turned down. On investigating his case to produce verification of his torture experience for protection purposes, major psychological and relationship problems came to light. In addition, we found a diffuse range of somatic complaints were associated with the bodily sites that had been injured but which were now, in physical terms, entirely well.

Medical investigation, as an essential routine, was a way of clearing the path towards a psychological exploration of the problem. The man's face, injured when he had been forced through a window by his torturers, and an area around the kidney where he had been stabbed, radiated pain for which investigations could not find a physical basis. His level of unresolved grief came to the surface early in explorations in which his wife joined us. Only through her disclosure about his heavy drinking and his description of her over-eating did their maladaptive collusion to protect each other come to light.

He had never been able to share with her the pain of what he had seen and suffered whilst in prison. He wished to protect her from this but was, at the same time, desperately in need of her understanding and presence in the internal world of his memories and losses. He drank to diminish the pain of this conflict. She wished to protect him from the loneliness and fear she had lived through when he had disappeared and there had been no evidence whether he was dead or alive. She had become depressed and could not eat. Now, to keep those associations "at bay", she over-ate.

Their daughter's anxiety state reflected the level of unacknowledged conflict and unhappiness at home. But she was most reluctant, at eleven years of age, to join us in the sessions. Our interpreter, a crucial member in these sessions, helped us frame a formulation by which an examination of the family's history was compared to an investigation of a "haunted house" in which, by opening all the cupboards and looking under beds, one could prove to oneself that there were no more ghosts. The daughter entered these discussions in this spirit with relish and humour. Their drinking and eating problems were translated into their own psychological language, and as they learnt to be open with one another, the situation changed dramatically. When the couple, seen on their own, were able to experience and share the pain they had been protecting each other from, the husband's somatic symptoms were fully resolved and the question of eating and drinking became one for humour and teasing, rather than shame and privacy.

Group Analytic Psychotherapy

We maintain an active programme of group work in which people from different cultures and nationalities work on a self-help basis, together with a therapist, to share and extend their coping resources and to unburden themselves of their histories.

During a discussion about language difficulties in one group, one of the members said that there was no problem about language. "People who have been injured have their own language," he said. "We communicate with each other like deaf people do, without hearing; our experiences speak to each other in our own signs. This is our language", he said. "It is like this." And he reached out and took the hands of the two people sitting on either side of him in a gesture of affirmation. They in turn reached out and took the hands of those who sat beside them. In a moment all the members of the group were holding hands in a silent gesture of affirmation.

At the conclusion of the first meeting of this group, the sense of confirmation that went round as people shook hands with each other was profound. We were, in a sense, saying to one another, "This is who we are. This is our group. We are not strangers to one another, and in one another's eyes we are not mutilated or scarred."

The next week one of the members referred to the dignity and care with which he had been helped by the Foundation when he arrived in London.

Through a bleak winter he had been seen for regular psychotherapy, had had many visits to doctors, and had received regular support on the telephone when it was needed. He was dispossessed and lonely, members of his family were dead or dying. He had little wish to live himself. But when his mood shifted in the spring, and he began to emerge as a person, he said to us, "Yours is the hand of humanity that reaches out to save me from drowning in my sorrow."

In the group, this man reached just such a hand out to a woman whose husband had suffered permanent brain damage as a result of torture and assault. She was wretched and disconsolate, and the hand he reached out to her was of real assistance. He referred back to the hand he had been offered earlier as a link. He described his own as another.

"This is a chain," he said, "one link and then another. It will be a great chain. When we eventually shake this chain it will be like thunder. You will hear thunder. The world will stop to listen. Humanity will come to its senses and there will be no more torture..."

Victims Of Torture – The Swedish Experience, By Judit Horvath-Lindberg[6]

After giving a short summary of the refugee situation in Sweden in a historical perspective, the speaker referred to the fact that many of the refugees had suffered massive trauma. The initial attitude, for years, was "Yes, you went through terrible times, but now you are safe, so you need no longer think about it. You ought to forget what you have been through: Sweden is a peaceful country and you can build up a new life. Don't even mention that your family was killed." All of us know now that this view is no longer acceptable.

Health provisions

It eventually came to be realized that the Swedish social and medical care system was not fitted to the needs of immigrants, refugees, and asylum seekers.

> For many years, doctors and nurses did not dare to ask "How are you?" because they were afraid they would not know what to do with the answer – particularly as asylum seekers were not entitled to receive medical attention other than for

---

[6] Judit Horvath-Lindberg is an experienced psychologist and anthropologist whose initiative was the basis of the creation of the Swedish Red Cross Centre for Tortured Refugees. After the Second World War, Sweden accepted between 150,000 and 200,000 refugees, including quite large groups from concentration camps. These were the first of the groups of refugees admitted to have gone through massive psychic trauma before coming to Sweden. Then came the Hungarians, Czechs and Poles. During the 1970s, the pattern changed: we began to see Christians from Turkey, Christians and others from Lebanon, South American refugees, then Kurds, Africans, and Vietnamese boat people (mostly of Chinese ethnic origin). In the 1980s, numbers of Iranians have been coming, along with the nationalities received earlier and a few others besides.

emergency needs. A group of professional volunteers was set up to work with them and liaise with the government health team. They began to voice the question "How are you?" – a very big step forward! If the asylum seekers say that they have been tortured, the group personnel can offer to put them in touch with the Swedish Red Cross volunteer group, and it is then up to each asylum seeker to decide whether he or she wants this. The doctors interviewing asylum seekers came to the same conclusion as the Danish Red Cross doctors: that twenty percent have been in prison and twenty-three per cent tortured. These were shocking statistics: we had expected the proportion to be not more than about ten per cent.

Somatic and psychosomatic symptoms

Judit stressed that not everyone who has been tortured has problems; not everyone needs a psychologist. But what we can expect in Sweden is that these people may sometimes be in need of some special help.

> What are their problems? You see the same pattern for asylum seekers as for refugees accepted under government programmes: they have pain, sometimes undefined pain in the head or stomach. Some people have a different view of pain, according to their culture. For example, South Americans know that they need a psychologist, but Kurds or Africans seldom come and say that they have psychological problems: instead they come with pain in various forms. They often have memory and concentration problems, which are sometimes assumed by asylum seekers to be a result of their current uncertainty. However, the same problems may persist for years after they have obtained refugee status and have begun to lead a settled life in Sweden. Then they realise that they have to look elsewhere for the cause.
>
> In the Swedish Red Cross Centre where we work with recognised refugees, we do not usually find outward signs of torture requiring medical care, for by then the refugees have generally been in Sweden for several years, maybe even twelve or fifteen. However, among the asylum seekers referred to our professional support group about fifty percent have some outward, physical signs of torture.

What happens to these people? They very often have problems in the family context. There are some who shirk the company of others and, in an attempt not to be noticed, creep along the walls. ... Others show a high incidence of aggression towards members of the family, or towards society, or towards themselves. People who before their imprisonment and torture had a normal family and professional life may find, after coming out of prison, that they have difficulties in suppressing aggressive impulses towards their family and towards society.

One question which this raises relates to people who have committed violent crimes; in Sweden they are sentenced to a prison term or to psychiatric treatment. Then sometimes it suddenly emerges that the offender had undergone torture, and the question arises whether there is a connection between the criminal act and his torture; we have had three or four such cases in the last two years. The change in personality caused by the torture experience can be a major problem.

Another aspect of the problem which may arise within the family occurs with men and women who were sexually tortured. They have difficulties in living a normal sexual life after that, either with the old partner or with a new one. (We have seen this especially with women from South America.) Then comes isolation – both physical and psychological, marital breakdown, and inevitably, repercussions for the children.

The content of this chapter, consisting largely of addresses made at Vitznau, finds echoes elsewhere in this book. We will now look briefly in Chapter 7 at the overall human rights picture as represented by United Nations bodies and non-governmental organizations, particularly the Red Cross/Red Crescent Movement and Amnesty International. Some "human interest" accounts will then lead into what had happened in Chile and Argentina – Chapter 8 – in events so violent that they overwhelmed their respective populations, causing large numbers of mostly traumatized people to flee.

CHAPTER 7

Human Rights

When we are aware of the destructive, dehumanizing activities of torturers and of all those who have wrought other forms of organized violence on hapless populations, we need to know what bodies exist to defend the citizens of our troubled world. There are United Nations bodies, there are non-governmental organizations (NGOs) and there are centres set up to help and as far as possible rehabilitate survivors of massive violence.

I. United Nations bodies and international Conventions

A most important basis for the work of the United Nations, and indeed for the innumerable other bodies throughout the world that care for the individual, is **the Universal Declaration of Human Rights**.

The Universal Declaration of Human Rights (UDHR) is a milestone document in the history of human rights. Drafted by representatives with different legal and cultural backgrounds from all regions of the world, the Declaration was proclaimed by the United Nations General Assembly in Paris on 10 December 1948 (General Assembly Resolution 217 A) as a common standard of achievements for all peoples and all nations. It sets out, for the first time, the fundamental human rights to be universally protected. It has been translated into over 500 languages.

The Declaration with its thirty articles is found easily on the internet.

The United Nations Commission on Human Rights, replaced in 2006 by the United Nations Human Rights Council, was established in 1946 to weave the international legal fabric that protects our fundamental rights and freedoms. Composed of fifty-three States members, its brief has been expanded over time to allow it to respond to the whole range of human rights problems. It sets standards to govern the conduct of States. It has acted as a forum where countries large and small, non-governmental groups and human rights defenders from around the world, voice their concerns.

The Office of the United Nations High Commissioner for Refugees (UNHCR), now known as **the Refugee Agency**, was founded in December 1950, in principle for a period of only three years. Decades later, after being renewed time after time for five-year periods by the UN General Assembly, it was seen to be needed permanently. It has a mandate to protect refugees, forcibly displaced communities, and stateless people, and assist in their voluntary repatriation, local integration or resettlement to a third country. Its Headquarters is in Geneva. **The current UN High Commissioner is Mr Filippo Grandi**, who had worked for many years as a staff member. Over the past sixty years, UNHCR has found it necessary to establish regional and/or branch offices in most parts of the world.

As long ago as the 1960s, and some time before trauma and PTSD were recognized in the Western world, the then United Nations High Commissioner for Refugees, Prince Sadruddin Aga Khan, was concerned about the mental health of refugees.[1] All these years later trauma has come to be among the major concerns of the United Nations bodies.

The Office of the United Nations High Commissioner for Human Rights (UNHCHR), created in 1993 and based in Geneva, is a department of the Secretariat of the United Nations that works to promote and protect the human rights that are guaranteed under international law and stipulated in the UDHR of 1948. In August 2018, the UN Secretary-General, António Guterres, following approval by the General Assembly, appointed **Michelle Bachelet of Chile as the next UN High Commissioner for Human**

---

[1]   In the mid-1960s the high commissioner, Prince Sadruddin Aga Khan, in a meeting with his representative stationed at Bukavu, in the Kivu Province of the Congo, asked about the extent to which Rwandans who had fled their country after outbreaks of severe inter-ethnic strife were suffering the effects of trauma. Years later, the prince wrote to the Secretary General of the (then) League of Red Cross Societies to express warm congratulations on the book *Refugees – The Trauma of Exile*. He was of course ahead of his time on practically every subject. His successor reportedly declined to meet a psychiatrist concerned about refugee trauma on the basis that "he firmly believed that refugees did not have emotional problems or psychological distress associated with their displacement and homeless state". The psychiatrist, Dr Richard F. Mollica, goes on to observe that "at that time, it was impossible for international and American policymakers and humanitarian relief agencies to accept the invisible psychological wounds affecting traumatized persons throughout the world. Today there is instead a demand for scientific methods and practices to help heal those wounds." *Healing Invisible Wounds – Paths to Hope and Recovery in a Violent World* (2006).

Rights. Dr Bachelet was twice president of Chile (2006–10 and 2014–18), the first woman to be elected to Chile's highest office. A long-term champion of human rights, Dr Bachelet is a paediatrician who began her government career as an adviser in the Health Ministry. She was involved from the early 1970s in human rights activism. She and both parents were political prisoners under the dictatorship of General Pinochet. I believe that her father died in prison.

The UNHCHR has published a 116-page book, entitled *Human Rights: A Basic Handbook for UN Staff*. In its Annex I (of six annexes) is a list of international human rights instruments. The UNHCHR also publishes Human Rights Fact Sheets, which "deal with selected questions of human rights under active consideration or are of particular interest". There are twenty-five of these so far, listed on the website.

International conventions are described briefly below, in chronical order of their creation:

The Convention on the Prevention and Punishment of the Crime of Genocide is an international human rights treaty approved unanimously by the UN General Assembly on 9 December 1948. It came into force on 12 January 1951, and now has 149 States parties. It seeks to prevent "the commission of certain acts with the intent to destroy a national, ethnic, racial or religious group" and commits States to bring alleged perpetrators to justice.

Since the Nuremberg Tribunal of 1945 and 1946, when judges from the Allied powers – Great Britain, France, the Soviet Union and the United States – presided over the hearings of twenty-two major Nazi criminals, and sentenced twelve prominent Nazis to death, other tribunals have been set up: the International Tribunal for the Former Yugoslavia, The Hague, to try Slobodan Milosević, president of former Yugoslavia and other Serb political and military leaders, notably Radovan Karadjić and Ratko Mladić, responsible for the genocide in Bosnia and Herzegovina; the Arusha Criminal Tribunal for Rwanda, and the Khmer Rouge Tribunal, Cambodia.

Four Geneva Conventions were created in 1949 to cover war situations, and are the fundamental instruments of the work of the International Committee of the Red Cross (ICRC). The First Geneva Convention related to the wounded on the battlefield, the Second to the wounded on wrecked ships, the Third to prisoners of war and the Fourth to civilian populations.

The 1951 Convention on the Status of Refugees and its 1967 Protocol provide protection to refugees. 147 States are parties to one or other of these. The importance of this convention and its protocol cannot be overstated. It has been in relation to them that since 1964, certain staff of UNHCR have been attacked or have even lost their lives.

The OAU Convention: In September 1969, the Organisation of African Unity (OAU) passed a Convention Governing the Specific Aspects of Refugee Problems in Africa.

The International Convention on the Elimination of All Forms of Racial Discrimination (ICERD) is a human rights instrument that commits its members to the elimination of *racial discrimination* and the promotion of understanding among all races. The Convention also requires its parties to outlaw *hate speech* and criminalize membership in racist organizations.

The convention was adopted and opened for signature by the *United Nations General Assembly* on 21 December 1965, and entered into force on 4 January 1969. As of April 2019, it has eighty-eight signatories and 180 States parties. It is monitored by the *Committee on the Elimination of Racial Discrimination* (CERD).

Two important covenants came into being in December 1966: **the International Covenant on Economic, Social and Cultural Rights (CESCR) and the International Covenant on Civil and Political Rights**. These, with the UDHR of 1948, are considered to make up the International Bill of Human Rights. In accordance with the Universal Declaration, the covenants recognize that the ideal of free human beings enjoying civil and political freedom and freedom from fear and want can be achieved only if conditions are created whereby everyone may enjoy civil and political rights, as well as economic, social and cultural rights.

The CESCR, first drafted in 1954, entered into force on 3 January 1976. It has 169 States Parties. It is one of the most important human rights treaties because it has been widely accepted, delineates a large number of rights, and translates them into binding commitments that are monitored by the CESCR's Committee on Economic, Social and Cultural Rights, founded in 1985.

The International Covenant on Civil and Political Rights, also first drafted in 1954, entered into force on 23 March 1976. It has 172 States Parties. Among its many provisions, it sets the rights of freedom of movement, equality before the law, the right to a fair trial and presumption of innocence, freedom of thought, conscience and religion, freedom of opinion and expression, and freedom of association.

The Convention against Torture and Other Cruel, Inhuman or Degrading Treatment or Punishment (commonly known as the United Nations Convention against Torture (UNCAT) is an *international human* *rights treaty.* It aims to prevent *torture* and other acts of *cruel, inhuman, or degrading treatment or punishment*, requiring States to take effective measures to prevent torture in any *territory* under their *jurisdiction*, and forbidding them to transport people to any country where there is reason to believe they will be tortured.

The text of the Convention was adopted by the *United Nations General Assembly* on 10 December 1984 and came into force on 26 June 1987. It defines torture as follows:

> The term "torture" means any act by which severe pain or suffering, whether physical or mental, is intentionally inflicted on a person for such purposes as obtaining from him or a third person information or a confession, punishing him for an act he or a third person has committed or is suspected of having committed, or intimidating or coercing him or a third person, or for any reason based on discrimination of any kind, when such pain or suffering is inflicted by or at the instigation of or with the consent or acquiescence of a public official or other person acting in an official capacity.

As of June 2019, the Convention has 166 States parties. Despite the provisions of the Convention, many governments do not respect their obligations and unfortunately, torture is probably more widespread today than it has ever been.

The 1989 Convention on the Rights of the Child (CRC) was approved by the UN General Assembly on 20 November 1989 and entered into force on 2 September 1990. States Parties now number 196 – all except the United States! The convention emphasizes the importance and vulnerability of children and delineates in one code laws that protect children across all classes of human rights. Specifically, "parties are to provide guarantees for children's survival, development, protection and participation" and are required to ensure "the best interests of the child must guide all actions", with particular attention being paid to refugee, minority and disabled children. Its two Optional Protocols (2000) "prohibit the recruitment of children under 18 into armed forces" and "strengthen prohibitions and penalties concerning the sale of children, child prostitution and child pornography".

United Nations Voluntary Fund For Victims Of Torture

The UN Voluntary Fund for Victims of Torture is a unique and universal humanitarian tool available to the United Nations and the Office of the High Commissioner for Human Rights (OHCHR), providing direct assistance to victims of torture and their family members wherever torture occurs – as outlined in its mission statement. The Fund aims at healing the physical and psychological consequences of torture on victims and their families, and thus restoring their dignity and role in society.

Since its establishment by the General Assembly in 1981 by *Resolution 36/151*, the Fund has made awards to more than 620 organizations and rehabilitation centres around the world, reaching out to over 50,000 victims every year. It is managed by the Office of the UNHCHR, with the advice of a *Board of Trustees* composed of independent experts from the five world regions.

The principal objective of the work given support by the UN Torture Fund is to assist torture survivors and their family members to rebuild their lives, providing immediate and accessible remedies. Grants are awarded to a variety of channels of assistance, including civil society organizations, associations of victims and their family members, private and public hospitals, law clinics, public interest law firms and individual lawyers.

Further information about the UN Voluntary Fund for Victims of Torture is given in Annex 2.

Other vitally important intergovernmental agencies working for and with refugees and displaced persons are:

- UNICEF – the United Nations Fund for Children, with headquarters in New York
- WHO – the World Health Organization (WHO), with headquarters in Geneva
- The World Food Programme (WFP), with headquarters in Rome
- The International Organization for Migration (IOM), based in Geneva[2]

---

[2] Apart from the above, there are numerous UN organizations, each with its mandate, for example 1) the International Labour Organization, the only tripartite UN agency. Since 1919 the ILO brings together governments, employers and workers of **187 member states**, to set labour standards, develop policies and devise programmes promoting decent work for all women and men; 2) the UN Development Programme (UNDP), which works to eradicate poverty and

The International Court of Justice, The Hague (Netherlands)

The International Court of Justice, established at San Francisco in 1945 by Article 92 of the United Nations Charter with its seat in The Hague, Netherlands, is the principal judicial court of the United Nations.

The International Criminal Court (ICC), The Hague (Netherlands)

The ICC was founded in Rome in 2002 and has 123 States Parties. It investigates and, where indicated, tries individuals who are charged with the gravest crimes of concern to the international community.

In accordance with Article 112 of the Rome Statutes, the Assembly of States Parties meets at the seat of the Court in The Hague or at the United Nations Headquarters in New York one a year. When circumstances so require, it may hold special sessions. The Assembly is tasked with providing management oversight to the Presidency, the Prosecutor and the Registrar regarding administration of the Court. It adopts the Rules of Procedure and Evidence and the elements of crime.

Human rights abuses and armed conflicts are of concern to the ICC. On 7 November 2019, the ICC condemned to thirty years' imprisonment one of the notorious warlords in Congo who had exercised his power to murder, rape, recruit boy soldiers and exploit mineral deposits in Eastern Congo (reported more fully in Chapter 17). The ICC is concerned at the time of writing with the four people deemed responsible for shooting down using a ground-to-air missile Malaysian Airlines Flight 17 (MH 17) over eastern Ukraine in 2014. None of the four has presented himself at the trial.

II. NGOs

1. The Red Cross and Red Crescent Movement:

The **International Red Cross and Red Crescent Movement** is an international humanitarian movement founded in 1863 after a Swiss citizen, Henry Dunant, appalled at the suffering on the battlefield at Solferino, campaigned for a national volunteer organization to be set up in every country. The two world bodies are **the International Committee of**

---

reduce inequalities through the sustainable development of nations; 3) the UN Development Fund for Women (UNIFEM), an associated fund of UNDP that has a human rights perspective, working to promote gender equality and women's empowerment, including within UN operational activities.

the Red Cross (ICRC) and **the International Federation of Red Cross and Red Crescent Societies (IFRC)**. The Movement's National Societies number 190. Its fundamental principles on which its action is based are humanity, impartiality, neutrality, independence, voluntary service, unity and universality. A high proportion of its work is carried out by its millions of volunteers across the globe.

Both the ICRC and the IFRC, along with the relevant National Societies, are involved in disaster relief worldwide, including work with displaced people and refugees. ICRC carries out a most important function in visiting detainees in prisons, in principle having the right to send delegates right into these places accessible to no one other than prison personnel – some of whom may be torturers.

While the international protection of refugees is pre-eminently the responsibility of UNHCR, the ICRC has a special role to play for refugees in situations involving armed conflict. International humanitarian law does not define refugees as such, but the Fourth Geneva Convention of 1949 sets as a criterion the need for protection of civilian persons who are not protected by any government. As a matter of practice, and under international humanitarian law, ICRC protection of civilians is extended to those civilians who are in the power of the enemy and to those civilians affected by hostilities. Concerning displaced persons, specifically those persons internally displaced by armed conflict, the ICRC, as a specifically humanitarian neutral and independent institution under the provisions of the Geneva Conventions of 1949, provides protection to these people. Military attacks on refugee camps in border areas have in recent years been of increasing concern to the ICRC (as of course to UNHCR).

The Red Cross And Red Crescent Movement And Trauma

As mentioned in the introduction, in 1987 the League of Red Cross and Red Crescent Societies (IFRC as of 1991) ran a five-day workshop that brought together people of sixteen countries concerned about the trauma suffered by many refugees and asylum seekers. The following reproduces the Preamble to the Conclusions and Recommendations of this International Red Cross Workshop on Psychological Problems of Refugees and Asylum Seekers held in 1987:

Bearing in mind that the Fundamental Principles of the Red Cross and Red Crescent Movement are the basis for the Movement's work;

that Resolution XVII of the Twenty-fifth International Red Cross Conference on the International Red Cross and Refugees *inter alia* encouraged the Movement "both to set up its own information and training activities and to take a greater part in providing information aimed at better understanding and mutual acceptance between refugees and their host communities";

that Resolutions XIV on torture of the Twenty-fourth International Conference of the Red Cross and X, XI, and XII of the Twenty-fifth International Conference are concerned with the intense suffering of not only the immediate victims of this practice but also of their families;

that the numbers of refugees and asylum seekers (particularly the latter) in industrialized countries have increased radically in the last three years and that a high proportion have been found to suffer from psychological problems;

the League of Red Cross and Red Crescent Societies convened at Vitznau, Switzerland, from 6 to 11 October 1987, a workshop on the psychological problems of refugees and asylum seekers, with a view to bringing about the broadest possible sharing of knowledge and of proven work methods, in the best interests of all those refugees and asylum seekers requiring understanding and help both now and in the future. At the League's suggestion, National Red Cross Societies extended the invitation to non-Red Cross professionals interested to contribute to the workshop.

Representatives of twelve National Red Cross Societies of western Europe, meeting with resource persons and staff of the United Nations High Commissioner for Refugees (UNHCR), the Intergovernmental Committee for Migration (ICM), several non-governmental agencies, and counterparts from government services or academic institutions in fifteen countries (including the United States and Canada) as well of the ICRC and the League – made the following forty observations, conclusions, and recommendations.

The first twenty of these are listed in Annex 1A.

In subsequent years, as mentioned in the Introduction, many National Societies and the ICRC gave support to the IFRC in publishing further significant guidelines that were the fruit of months of consultations with staff and volunteers of the movement, notably:

Working with Victims of Organized Violence from Different Cultures – a Red Cross and Red Crescent Guide (IFRC, 1995). A selected portion of this document is in Annex 1B.

Community Based Psychological Support, A Training Manual (IFRC, 1st edition, January 2003), written in conjunction with an expert from academia, Professor Gilbert Reyes, and *IFRC Framework for Community Resilience* (2018) (see Annex 1C).

These, like the earlier publications, were given the widest distribution throughout the movement.[3]

2. Amnesty International (AI), Human Rights Watch

Amnesty International (AI) is a worldwide non-governmental organization based in London. Its website speaks of how it all began, when in 1961 British lawyer Peter Benenson was outraged when two Portuguese students were jailed just for raising a toast to freedom. He wrote an article in *The Observer* newspaper and launched a campaign that provoked an incredible response. Reprinted in newspapers across the world, his call to action sparked the idea that people everywhere can unite in solidarity for justice and freedom. This inspiring moment didn't just give birth to an extraordinary movement; it was the start of extraordinary social change. Peter Benenson has said: Only when the last prisoner of conscience has been freed, when the last torture chamber has been closed, when the United Nations UDHR is a reality for the world's people, will our work be done.

AI is a global movement of more than seven million people who take injustice personally. It asserts "We are campaigning for a world where human rights are enjoyed by all. We are funded by members and people like you. We are independent of any political ideology, economic interest or religion." AI affirms that no government is beyond scrutiny and no situation is beyond hope. Torturers have become international outlaws.[4] Most countries have abolished the *death penalty.*

Candles in the dark: Amnesty's logo, a candle wrapped in barbed wire, was inspired by the ancient Chinese proverb "It is better to light a candle

---

[3] The last two of these valuable documents, accessible on the internet, are freely available, there being no need for users to request release from copyright, provided the source is clearly stated.

[4] In 2014, Amnesty International published a fifty-page report on torture entitled *Torture In 2014: 30 Years of Broken Promises.*

than to curse the darkness". In 1962, just a year after its foundation, AI had seventy groups in seven countries, and began to issue periodic reports on human rights abuses in various parts of the world. It adopted 210 prisoners and documented 1,200 cases in the Prisoners of Conscience Library. In 1977, Amnesty was awarded the Nobel Peace Prize for having "contributed to securing the ground for freedom, for justice, and thereby also for peace in the world".

"I was taken to a secret camp and tortured. No one can describe the pain. I'd hear a child crying and they'd say, 'This is your son.' They allowed me one call. I phoned Amnesty…" *Ursula K.*

Human Rights Watch is an international human rights activist NGO with headquarters in New York City that conducts research and advocacy on human rights. It was founded in 1978 by Robert L. Bernstein, Aryeh Neier and Jeri Laber.

There are hundreds of other valuable NGOs working to relieve needs. Most of them, initially created as national NGOs, soon became international, such as the now well-known Médecins sans Frontières (MSF – Doctors Without Borders). They are simply too numerous to mention by name.

3. A unique network: The International Rehabilitation Council for Torture Victims (IRCT), Copenhagen: An independent, international health organization that supports the rehabilitation of torture victims and works for the prevention of torture worldwide.

The creation of the IRCT goes back to 1974, when there was great concern about the destructive and all-too-common practice of torture and the needs of torture survivors to receive specialized care. A Danish doctor, Inge Genefke, and three of her fellows responded to a call by AI to help diagnose torture victims and produce forensic evidence that could help hold torturers to account in a court of law. In 1980, Dr Genefke and her colleagues were given permission to admit torture survivors to the University Hospital in Copenhagen. The creation of a rehabilitation centre in Copenhagen for torture survivors was "a first". Subsequently – and fairly soon – others were created, such as the Swedish Red Cross Centre for Torture Victims in Stockholm, and the Medical Foundation for the Care of Victims of Torture in London. By now, as the IRCT says of itself, "As a network of more than 160 torture rehabilitation centres in over 70 countries, it is the world's largest membership-based civil society organisation specialised in the field of torture rehabilitation" – a fact that impresses on us, as nothing else could, how widespread the practice is that the head of AI in a 2014 report termed "a worldwide crisis of barbarity, of political failure and of fear".

III. Individual Testimonies Of Torture Survivors

The two testimonies that follow in shortened form were the first of five published in *The Guardian* on 27 May 2001.

Perico Rodríguez was imprisoned and repeatedly tortured for three years following the 1976 military coup in Argentina led by General Jorge Videla. When he was fifty-nine and lived and worked in London, he described to *The Guardian* what had happened to him.5

> I was town clerk at the time, in a place called Cinco Saltos in Patagonia. I was arrested six days after the coup. I was an active socialist, working hard towards change, but repression was widespread; you were either a friend of the military or their enemy.
>
> The local police came to my home and took me away in front of my children. They took me to the local police station and as they questioned me they started beating me. When I look back, I realize it was then that I was most terrified. Until I felt the first blow I had thought, in a very stupid way, that they would conduct a civilized interrogation, that they would say they were sorry and that I would go home.

Perico stated that, after that, he was moved around a lot and tortured repeatedly. The torturers wanted names and information, which he never gave them, and he said that it was not just because he didn't want to jeopardize the lives of other people but because he knew that, once he did, he would die.

> They would tie my hands behind my back and force my head into a bucket of water. It was a terrifying experience of near death, which causes terrible pain in your lungs. In one prison I slipped and broke my arm. Five hours later, they took me to the local hospital to be put in plaster. When I got back, the interrogation started again, and they gave me electric shocks inside my plaster. Even during a journey to another prison

---

5   Today Perico, in his 70s, lives in retirement.

they chained us to the floor of the plane and beat us. These people were professional. They would torture us, and then have tea and a chat about fishing or their families and then they would start again.

Perico went on to explain that, when he was released from prison, it was thanks to AI. He and his wife some time earlier had picked up some hitchhikers, who, when they heard from his wife about his imprisonment, contacted Amnesty, who launched an urgent-action appeal and succeeded in getting him released.

"Amnesty is so important because it has brought the notion of human rights to a wider audience," he said, grateful to have been brought to Britain and to work at the Medical Foundation with Helen Bamber.

María N. was arrested at fifteen and tortured when the Uruguayan army seized power from figurehead president Juan María Bordaberry in 1973. Now forty-three, she lives near Liverpool.

> 'I was a teenager when I got married to a trade unionist in Montevideo in 1972, but I had no interest or involvement in politics whatsoever. The military took over a year later, and my husband and I found out that he was wanted by the authorities. It was very scary. I was 15 and pregnant with my first daughter." The couple decided that the best thing would be for the young wife to go and stay with her parents and for her husband to leave the country. The police came asking for him a few days later. She told them he had left the country and they said that if he didn't come back, they would arrest her instead.
>
> My daughter was born in January 1974 and the police came when she was 21 days old. Initially, I was taken to a police station and then to court, where I was charged and then sent to prison. I was very much in shock but I still believed in justice; I thought that at any minute they would realize they had made a mistake and release me. …

She was in prison for almost eighteen months, interrogated regularly. Mostly they wanted to know where her husband was and the names of various people, but she simply didn't know. She related how she lost most of her teeth while she was there, for every time they asked her a question that she couldn't answer they pulled one of her teeth out. They would also put a hood over her head and say: "We're going to shoot you now because you're not co-operating," and she would hear them get the gun ready. Then they would say: "It's lunchtime, we'll do it tomorrow." It was terrifying. The poor girl – just a teenager – suffered from malnutrition and hygiene was non-existent.

"Then, one day, one of the wardens gave me a postcard saying: 'Dear Maria, Thinking of you, Margaret.'" So many people wrote who had learnt of Maria's situation that the prison authorities released her, and, thanks to AI, she obtained asylum in England.

Three other testimonies from torture survivors (Chile, Zimbabwe, Sudan) were published by *The Guardian* the same day.

IV. Just a few of the individual researchers, practitioners, trainers and writers on trauma **Judith Lewis Herman, MD**, is an American professor of psychiatry with the Cambridge Health Alliance, Cambridge Hospital, Cambridge, MA, and an award-winning author. Her book *Trauma and Recovery – From Domestic Abuse to Political Terror* (Pandora, 1992) has been termed by the *New York Times Book Review* "One of the most important psychiatric works since Freud". We read on the cover of her book that Dr Herman "repeatedly challenges established orthodoxies, identifies a new diagnostic category for those suffering from 'hidden' traumas and proposes a ground-breaking recovery programme that favours a process of reintegration to one of catharsis. A deeply compassionate and readable work, required reading for all those who seek a deeper understanding of the psychology of men and women."

Bessel van der Kolk, MD, has been mentioned in the Introduction, and some of his very valuable work is described in Chapter 19. He is an American psychiatrist, researcher, author and worldwide speaker, based in Boston. His book *The Body Keeps the Score* (Penguin, 2014) is a masterpiece that shows how trauma literally reshapes both body and brain, and explores innovative treatments – from neurofeedback and meditation to sports, drama and yoga. He and Dr Judith Herman cooperated over several years in their early exploration of trauma. His book has been termed "An authoritative guide to the effects of trauma, and pathways to recovery. A must read for mental health and other health care professionals, trauma survivors, their loved ones, and those who seek… solutions to the cycle of trauma and violence in our society" (Dr Rachel Yehuda).

Richard F. Mollica, MD, is professor of psychiatry at Harvard Medical School, and directs the Harvard Program in Refugee Trauma. He is the recipient of the Human Rights Award from the American Psychiatric

Association. He has undertaken over thirty years of clinical work with victims of genocide, torture and abuse in the United States, Cambodia, Bosnia, and other parts of the world, and describes the surprising capacity of traumatized people to heal themselves. Dr Mollica studied not only medicine and psychiatry but also theology and psychology. Archbishop Desmond M. Tutu, speaking of Dr Mollica's extraordinary book *Healing Invisible Wounds – Paths to Hope and Recovery in a Violent World*, asserts that the stories recounted bear eloquent and often moving testimony to the resilience of human beings in the face of awful traumatic experiences, and their remarkable capacity to heal themselves.

Dr Mollica over the last few decades worked extensively and very effectively with the World Health Organization, in particular with the WHO Global Coordinator for Mental Health in Conflict and Disasters, Mary Petevi (see Chapter 20).

Other author-practitioners feature in Chapters 19 and 20.

CHAPTER 8

Coups D'etat In Chile And Argentina

Chile: Background To The September 1973 *Coup D'état*

The history of the Americas goes back, of course, to well before the fifteenth century of our era. Proofs have been unearthed that during the Ice Age, some intrepid human beings actually travelled along the western coastline of the Americas and established small settlements where the ice had begun to retreat inland. Then a few decades ago, it was discovered that there had been a Norse colonization of North America in the late tenth century AD,[1] when Norsemen explored and settled areas of the North Atlantic including the north-eastern fringes of North America.

When European explorers such as Christopher Columbus and Ferdinand Magellan landed in South America, the southern cone was inhabited by the Araucanian Indians, who continued to control the region until the nineteenth century. To the north, there had been the Atacama Indians, but they were subjugated by the Incas, who in turn (as most people know) were very roughly treated by the Spaniards, whose conquest of huge areas of South America meant exploitation and massacre. The Aztecs and Maya hardly fared better. There is still an ethnic minority of approximately a million people in existence, the Mapuche. While Chile has long portrayed itself as a nation founded upon European immigration and the assimilation of indigenous culture, since the return to democracy in 1990 the Mapuche have affirmed and sustained their difference within the dominant ideologies of national unity, writes a North American author.[2]

---

[1] Herman Palsson, *The Vinland Sagas: the Norse Discovery of America* (Penguin Classics, 1965), p.28.
[2] Joanne Crow, *The Mapuche in Modern Chile* (2013).

In 1541 Spain founded a colony at Santiago, which became the capital city. Struggles for independence took form early in the nineteenth century throughout South America, and Chile won its victory over the Spaniards in 1817. For many decades the country, dominated by the Andes and with its 2,500-mile (4,000-km) seaboard, was governed by a small oligarchy of landowners. It generally enjoyed political stability and prosperity, even though the peasantry, working under feudal conditions on the large estates, had few rights, and many of those who drifted to the towns did not prosper.[3] Chile, being the world's leading nitrate and copper producer, became increasingly industrialized, bringing about the creation of a new working class and the expansion of the towns, while there was a flight of capital to other countries.

Nevertheless, Chile came to be thought of as one of the most democratic and cultured countries of Latin America. Pablo Neruda (1904–73), Chilean poet, writer, diplomat, campaigner and politician, became the foremost writer of a large number of erudite men and women, many of whom came in their writings to point to the imbalance between rich and poor.

In 1964, the Christian Democrats led by Eduardo Frei Montalva[4] won the election and remained in office for six years, a period in which reforms in agriculture, housing and education were brought in, but then Frei's earlier opponent, Dr Salvador Allende, won the 1970 election – the first democratically elected Marxist head of state.

Allende governed a coalition of five left-wing parties (which included the Partido Comunista de Chile), and put into effect a number of radical nationalization policies, with a view to counteracting the flight of capital to the United States and other capitalist countries. Extensive land reforms to promote the enormous agricultural potential of the country were brought in, but not surprisingly were very unpopular with those who had held onto large areas of the country through several generations. Capitalism and socialism were on a crash course that would erupt overnight into a brutal *coup d'état* proving fatal for thousands of people, and causing millions to live in dread.

The Chilean refugees I was sent to Mendoza to document for resettlement told me that Allende's reforms, introduced by constitutional means, were in line with what the president's predecessor, Eduardo Frei, had envisaged but had not had sufficient time to bring in. However, there was a great deal of carefully orchestrated opposition to Allende, starting with a strike by transporters that totally paralysed the economy. The Chilean peso

---

[3] Close to five million Chileans were said in the 1990s to live below the UN poverty line – including a high proportion of the Mapuche: Inger Agger and Søren Buus Jensen, *Trauma and Healing under State Terrorism* (1996).

[4] Eduardo Frei was assassinated in January 1982.

plummeted, and as we could see from abroad the scene was being set for a takeover by right-wing forces, underwritten to a degree, but of course in secret, by the governments of the United States and Switzerland.

The Coup And Its Immediate Effects

On 11 September 1973,[5] General Augusto Pinochet, head of the army, a man who had failed at school and in civilian life, launched a vicious military coup in which President Allende was murdered in the presidential palace, dozens of people were shot and thousands were taken prisoner, being kept for weeks in the national football stadium. From there they were subjected to interrogation sessions, often carried out under torture. Women were systematically raped, as were some of the men. The horror of the post-11 September period is hard to imagine for anyone who has not been exposed to repression. Some of it came through the eyewitness accounts that it was part of my job to listen to, and through the Costa-Gavras film about the young North American intellectual who, living in Chile at the time with his young wife, had had the misfortune of hearing about the US clandestine involvement in the military coup and the temerity to ask questions.

Inger Agger and Søren Buus Jensen, in their 1996 book *Trauma and Healing under State Terrorism*, explain how an important inspiration for the Chilean armed forces was the Prussian military culture, even if it was mixed up with Chilean nationalism. These authors frequently refer to views of Pamela Constable and Arturo Valenzuela,[6] in saying that until the coup, the Chilean democratic tradition was quite strong and differed from the widespread military dictatorships in neighbouring countries. They quote an elderly human rights activist as saying to them, "I remember Augusto from school. He was not very bright, I always wondered how he was able to climb up through the military system," and they add, "Vertical obedience, disrespect of civilians – especially of politicians – suspiciousness against the academic world, and a massive, paranoia-like disgust of communists and

---

[5]   This was twenty-eight years to the day before the four coordinated terrorist attacks by members of al-Qaeda at the command of airliners on the Twin Towers in New York and the Pentagon. These tragic events have since been referred to by Americans as "Nine eleven".

[6]   *A Nation of Enemies: Chile under Pinochet* by Pamela Constable and Arturo Valenzuela (1991). Constable and Valenzuela chronicle the hate-driven campaign of oppression that sharpened divisions between left and right, rich and poor, civilian and military, and "turned the state into a monster" capable of torture and mass killings.

the 'reds' were basic elements in the military spirit, and – we may surmise – in the minds of Pinochet and his aides." Then they go on to say:

> One could also analyse the military spirit according to a psychological frame of reference. Maybe this perspective could add to our understanding of the psychological warfare of state terrorism. Concepts of borderline pathology seem applicable to the meanings and rationality of the military culture... for example:
>
> - The mechanism of *splitting*, by which the world is perceived in its extremes: as either black or white, good or evil.
> - The *paranoid tendency*, which makes all opponents resemble communists, terrorists or just "reds".
> - *Projective defence mechanisms*, which place the blame on everybody else but oneself. ...
> - The narcissistic aspect...
> - The *sado-masochistic position*, in which humiliating others and being humiliated yourself is an interdependent source of satisfaction. In the military, where it is necessary to lick upwards and spit downwards, this position is obvious.

They go on to say that, "in this culture, people could be pushed into roles in which they acted as psychopaths (seen from a 'usual' perspective) but in which they – from their own military perspective – acted as heroes."

An inescapable fact is that quite large numbers of Nazis are known to have escaped to Latin America at the end of the Second World War.

In any case, for over sixteen years, from 11 September 1973 to 11 March 1990, Chilean armed forces, the police and all those aligned with the military were involved in institutionalizing fear and terror across the unfortunate country. The systematic human rights violations that were committed included gruesome acts of physical and sexual abuse, as well as considerable psychological damage. The persecution of opponents (imagined or real, including assassinations carried out in Buenos Aires, Rome and Washington), political repression and state terrorism by the Chilean armed forces, members of Carabineros de Chile and the secret police came to be qualified as **crimes against humanity** by two commissions established several years later.

One of the places to which for seventeen years, from 1973 to 1990, General Pinochet's people would take victims to be tortured was (to all intents and purposes) a farming complex first set up a dozen years earlier in deep forest some 300 km south of the capital, Santiago. It was initiated and then run for the next thirty-six years by a former SS corporal, Paul Schäfer, who had fled Germany to avoid serving a prison sentence for child molestation. This Paul Schäfer called his sect and his followers "la Colonia Dignidad". They had started with nothing, but they carried out amazing work wresting land from the forest, building dormitories and storerooms, sowing wheat, potatoes and other crops and in principle helping the local population. All 300 German followers of the man who (like other gurus) had a unique gift for communication, turned over to him such wealth as they had had in Germany, and obeyed him blindly. They worked all hours without any pay, were deprived of the right to own any property whatsoever, and lived as single individuals in dormitories where conversations, and in fact any contact between the sexes, were strictly forbidden. Young children brought to the colony by German colonists and babies born on site were taken from their parents. Witnesses declared that no one trusted any other member of the sect, and in any case, ruled with a rod of iron, they were obliged to "confess" regularly to Schäfer. With the exception of the 200 boys he damaged, including Chilean children, it appears that most of the members of the singular community were made to believe that Paul Schäfer's methods were in their best interests – strange though that seems.

Never could any but Schäfer's closest aides have believed – at any rate at first – that people would be brought to Colonia Dignidad to be tortured, although Schäfer had set up a sophisticated system of electric torture that some of the colonists, reduced to slavery, had found their guru using on them. In a four-hour film, produced and shown on 10 March 2020 on the French-German TV channel Arte, we learn that Schäfer benefited from the full protection of Augusto Pinochet, who we see visiting the Colonia with senior officers and the head of the secret police. So there was no limit as to what he could do with impunity, and the Colonia was run as one of the regime's torture centres for seventeen years. A witness explains how deep trenches were dug, used to dispose of the bodies of men and women who would never again see the light of day. Later, when at long last democracy returned to Chile, Schäfer rapidly had these disintegrating bodies dug up and burned, the ashes being flung into the river.

It proved very difficult for most of the years that Colonia Dignidad existed to pin down what was going on there, despite the new minister of justice's best efforts. Schäfer's naïve disciples stood by him (or were forced to stand by him) throughout the years that the Chilean Justice department was trying to find out the truth through various investigations. The German State for its part did not really give credence to complaints that reached Bonn, and never did anything to disturb Schäfer's peace, the former Nazi having the German ambassador in his pocket. By the time the Chilean police did make arrests, the guru had escaped to Argentina, and was found and arrested only in 2005. But, subsequently revealing more of the horror of the place, one of his henchmen stated, in writing, that Colonia Dignidad had been used on a huge scale to import arms of every description for Pinochet, and had even got to manufacturing sophisticated weaponry on site. Furthermore, the colony had been manufacturing bacteriological gas intended to be available to General Pinochet if he decided to declare war on Argentina.[7]

These alarming facts came to light only fairly recently, and were therefore not known when the two commissions referred to just now were established. First, the National Commission for Truth and Reconciliation, the Rettig Commission, set up by President Patricio Aylwin (1990–94), involved eight commissioners from both sides of the political spectrum. It aimed to create as complete a picture as possible of the most serious human rights violations, gathering detailed evidence to list each victim's name, fate, and whereabouts, to recommend reparations for the families of victims and to recommend legal and administrative measures to prevent future violations.[8] It concluded in a report dated 2001 that 2,279 persons had been killed for political reasons, 957 had disappeared and 164 had been victims of political violence. Hundreds of military personnel and civilians were involved in subsequent trials.

The second, the National Commission on Political Imprisonment and Torture, called the Valech Commission, reporting on 29 November 2004 on the abuses committed in Chile between 1973 and 1990 by agents of Augusto Pinochet's military regime, found that 38,254 people had been imprisoned for political reasons, of whom most (27,255) had been tortured, while there was evidence of 2,279 executions. It also found that thirty people "disappeared" or had been executed in addition to those recorded by the earlier *Rettig Report*. The Valech Commission's report ran to 1,128 pages.

---

[7] *Colonia Dignidad, une secte allemande au Chili*, a four-part documentary by Annette Baumeister and Wilfried Huismann (2019, co-production Looksfilm, Surreal Films, WDR, SWR, in association with Arte, Canal 13).

[8] Ensalaco, Mark, Truth Commissions for Chile and El Salvador: A Report and Assessment, *Human Rights Quarterly*, Vol. 16 No. 4 (1994) 656–675.

Long before these two reports were envisaged, the Chilean human rights group CODEPU (the Committee in Defense of the People's Rights, 1989) "sought to make the dictatorship's violence visible by analyzing its components", asserting that "violence can be classified in two main groups: direct and indirect repression. *Direct repression* includes such phenomena as: assassination; kidnapping; disappearance; detention; torture; exile; internal exile (relegation); house searches without a warrant; intimidation (surveillance and continuous harassment). ... One of direct repression's most horrible weapons is to make a person *disappear* completely."[9] CODEPU (1989) listed some of the indirect techniques of repression: dismissal from work; deprivation of housing, health services, food; severance from social, political and labour associations; and total or partial loss of individual and collective freedom of expression, sometimes imposed under the pretence of legal principles, sometimes through self-censorship provoked by fear.[10]

CODEPU estimated subsequently that 500,000 of thirteen million Chileans had been affected by torture – either having been tortured themselves or having had people close to them tortured. With regard to the Rettig Commission's report, it esteemed that it showed only the tip of the iceberg; it did not deal with the use of torture as a strategy to create fear and terror on a societal scale. This strategy was linked to the particular image that the Chilean armed forces held of themselves and of their fellow citizens: they viewed themselves as fighting a battle to cure the twin social ills of political activity and Marxist ideology.

The psychological pressure created by torture of fear and terror was intended to dismantle civil society and its institutions, and recast them in a hierarchical, controllable form. In disregarding the widespread use of torture not resulting in death, the report ignored the primary human rights violation of the military regime.[11]

The Refugees' Accounts

So from 11 September 1973, torture, disappearances and assassinations were the background to these Chilean refugees' lives. I was told that some of the victims had been taken out over the sea in helicopters and pushed overboard. Many years later, when democracy nervously returned while Pinochet remained head of the army, mass graves were discovered containing the remains of political opponents of the military regime. No

[9] Inger Agger, *The Blue Room*, pp.56–57.
[10] Ibid., p.59.
[11] Found on https://solidarity-us.org/atc/59/p.2555.

one dared protest, and it was not only those who had openly supported the elected government who went in fear of their lives; it was also their families and friends, or anyone with whom they associated. Death squads prowled the streets. Masked men battered down people's doors at dead of night and beat up suspects in front of their terrified children. As the months went by, many more men and women simply "disappeared".[12] For their families, the agony of uncertainty was added to the horror of recent events. After husbands were taken, their wives were placed in the dilemma of what to tell the children. There seemed to be no escape from trauma, unless it was in flight. And an estimated 200,000 Chileans did flee. Initially, a number sought asylum in foreign embassies; the others crossed to Peru to the north, and to Argentina, on the other side of the Andes.

Furthermore, as prior to 1973 democratic Chile had become a safe haven for people fleeing the repressive regimes of other countries of Latin America, Paraguayans, Uruguayans and others also found that their lives were suddenly on the line, and they turned to church bodies for protection and assistance. Through the emergency action of the Roman Catholic Church and the Lutherans, in cooperation with UN representatives, a "Comité nacional de Ayuda a los Refugiados" (CONAR) was set up to create safe havens, fortunately recognized by the military government following representations by the United Nations High Commissioner for Refugees, Prince Sadruddin Aga Khan. From these safe havens, the refugees were gradually evacuated to other countries under UNHCR auspices.

Change In Argentina

The Chileans who had fled to Argentina initially found the atmosphere under President Isabel Perón relatively sympathetic to their plight. Then on 24 March 1976 a three-man military junta – the three heads of the army, navy and air force, led by Lt Gen Jorge Rafael Videla – carried out a *coup d'état* and took over the reins of power. Vowing to stamp out political violence and industrial unrest in Argentina, they put in train similar measures to those of their neighbour Pinochet to counteract the forces of the left and centre. People began to disappear without trace. Children were left fatherless and often motherless too. Their grandmothers began to share their common and agonizing concerns in weekly meetings on May Square in Buenos Aires, the Plaza de Mayo. Every Friday they brought to the same

---

[12] In Latin America, "disappearance" was a widely used power technique, through kidnapping people who were never found or by murdering them and refusing to acknowledge their deaths.

spot blown-up photographs of their missing sons and daughters, vocalizing their demands for an explanation of these disappearances. Soon the regime, cynically impervious to the distress behind the presence of these dignified women on the Plaza, would dub them *la Locas de la Plaza de Mayo* – the mad women of May Square.

It was to emerge very much later that not only had the junta killed those young people, many of them parents of babies – babies born to young women within the bars of secret prisons – but they had sold the newborns to high-ranking officers, who had brought them up as their own. Thanks to ceaseless exploratory work carried on at the international level and to the wonders of DNA identification, some of those grandchildren have come to be identified as having been born to victims of the regime and, in a few cases, they have been reunited with their biological families.

The fine Argentinian I met in the late 1980s, Perico Rodríguez, mentioned earlier as a member of Helen Bamber's team at the Medical Foundation for the Care of Victims of Torture, was a torture survivor, released from prison and brought to the UK with the help of Amnesty International. His story has been summarized in Chapter 7 and I have realized that he must have been a prisoner when I was in Mendoza.[13]

Now the refugees from Chile began to be called *guerilleros, subversivos, Marxistas, Communistas*. It became obvious that they were not going to be tolerated for very long. Indeed, soon after its *coup d'état* the regime, ruling by decree, required everyone residing in Argentina without permanent residence permits who could not return home because of fear of persecution to register with the authorities within three months. It began to screen each one, examining his or her past and issuing a blacklist of those who would be expelled from the country. UNHCR was obliged to ensure that everyone given the unpleasant status of "*Decreto negativo*" obtained an offer of a visa to go elsewhere.

My Mission

Kevin Lyonette, UNHCR's regional representative, suggested I go to Mendoza, Argentina's third city, at the foot of the Cordillera, for ten days to document the Chileans living up there. I would be working with the agency CEAS (Comité Ecumenico de Acción Social), UNHCR's operational partner, which was responsible for administering care and maintenance

---

13 Years later, we met several times in Geneva, London and Oxford, and one day he told me that he had been the only survivor of six men arrested and jailed together after the 1976 *coup d'état*.

funds allocated to mandate refugees, and for providing counselling. After the flight from Buenos Aires, I was made very welcome by CEAS and delivered to a hotel practically next door to the agency. A French speaker was appointed as interpreter until my inadequate university Spanish of many years earlier got going. All the staff were tremendously likeable, from the effective and somewhat charismatic young head of the agency, known as "Coca", a practising lawyer by the name of Juliana Juri, to the many social workers, all eager to learn what they could about "processing" refugees for resettlement. Their offices, waiting room, corridors and stairs were all full of Chileans of various ages down to young children, and all eyes focused on the newcomer. I hoped they wouldn't try to speak to me yet!

Though it seemed that no one had sufficiently informed CEAS previously (or informed them at all), the countries willing to issue entry visas to Chilean refugees were Sweden, Switzerland, France, Belgium, Britain, Australia, Canada and the United States. Each had their individual procedures and needs. Romania had made a grand gesture earlier in offering 1,500 visas, and many Chileans had gone there.[14]

I found no one willing to go to the USA.

Many of the refugees were keen to go to Sweden. They knew that Sweden was politically neutral and had a particularly welcoming programme for Chileans (who referred to this exemplary country as "colour TV Sweden"!) Later on, when in Stockholm, I was to meet the Swedish minister for immigration, Anita Gradin, and learned that she had many friends in the Latin American community. Switzerland stoically continued to offer fifty places per year for any refugees with a "handicap", be it physical, mental or social. I believed we could count on the Swiss to accept practically any "case" we might present to them.

France was sympathetic to the Latin American refugees and had already taken a large number. Its many voluntary agencies could cater for people of any political persuasion, and France was popular because the language was easier to learn than a non-Latin language. In Belgium, there was a wonderful group of people engaged in helping refugees recover from trauma, formed, I had heard, by a Chilean doctor by the name of Jorge Barudy. What he had set up as a pilot project had not ceased to gather momentum, and some of the more severe cases CEAS and UNHCR were concerned to help get out of Argentina could be submitted for consideration by the government in Brussels.

---

[14] But the Ceausescu dictatorship did little to comfort the Chileans for their loss of a socialist ideal, and we subsequently heard that before long many of them did their best to get out of Romania.

Australia, though a country that had already provided a permanent haven for many Latin Americans, had the disadvantage of making many of them feel, once there, achingly far from their home country, and rather cut off from the rest of the world.

Canada was a real hope for many of the Chileans I was to help document in Mendoza, and several weeks after the start of my mission a Canadian selection mission was announced. This was excellent news, and provided me with a good reason to stay on in Mendoza, for the Canadians supplied us with their own blank immigration forms, to be filled out in advance of the selection team's arrival.

From the first, my allotted ten days in Mendoza looked far from adequate, for there were as many refugees to document here as in the capital, Buenos Aires. Coca was one of those remarkable people who by their demeanour and intelligent leadership exert a quiet authority which is never questioned. We launched into a systematic registration of all the "*Decreto negativo*" cases and planned a heavy schedule of interviews.

Any individual or family constituting a straightforward case could be described on a single A4 sheet: family "biodata", a short social history, a clean health record. However, we found that many people needed special care, and in some cases it took the equivalent of a couple of days to write up a single dossier, because of the amount of interview time required, both with the refugees themselves and with medical advisers, such as the young psychologist who put his services at the disposal of CEAS one day a week.

A pleasant father of five had two daughters, aged sixteen and seven, manifesting symptoms of what has since been termed post-traumatic stress disorder (PTSD): bed-wetting, nightmares and seizures. They had seen their father, a film director, ill-treated in the middle of the night by hooded men. It seemed a miracle that he was now with them. A man, Antonio, who had been working illegally in Mendoza as an electrician in an effort to support his wife and two little girls, had been tending a 13,200 kW cable when someone turned on the power. The shock had nearly torn off his right arm, and he had fallen several feet from the top of the ladder to the floor, landing on his head. He had had two operations on his arm, but suffered from chronic headaches, anxiety and irritability. No wonder! An older man – he was fifty-eight – suffered from chronic asthma and poor eyesight, and in addition was illiterate (the only unlettered Chilean I met). He might have been a candidate for a retired people's home, had he not had a wife of twenty-nine and three very young children. A young blond fellow named Stanley had been a polio sufferer, and walked with difficulty. He said that his grandfather had come from Yorkshire and there need have been no real difficulty over his case vis-à-vis resettlement in Britain had his marital situation not been so complicated: he was accompanied by a girlfriend who wished to spend the rest of her life with him, but his loving and forgiving wife, a schoolteacher back in Chile by whom he had two young children, came to Mendoza to see if their situation could not somehow be resolved.

There was a courteous little couple of around sixty, very shy and retiring, but, like so many others, apparently viewed as a threat to Argentina's security. There was a woman, Viviane, with a handsome but physically handicapped adult son. She had been the politically active member of the family, and her husband, son and beautiful teenage daughter had had to follow her into exile. It transpired that she was suffering from seizures, though she did not care to admit it.

This mission was really an induction course for me into the subject of refugee trauma and post-traumatic stress. The person from whom perhaps I learned most was a youngish woman on her own, Silvia, whose case was a particularly complicated one but who accompanied me on some of my explorations when I needed to visit refugees in their temporary homes. She seemed to derive a certain satisfaction from being my guide, and was highly diverted that a UN official should sufficiently lack dignity as to hitchhike back to Mendoza from some outlandish spot we had needed to visit and from which there was no return bus. She was equally amused one Thursday, a day normally reserved for interviews, when, after the word had gone around that the staff was too busy, the doors opened after all – as soon as I had discovered that these conscientious young social workers were doggedly engaged on… compiling monthly statistics for UNHCR! It was Silvia who showed me around Mendoza, including the shanty town area. She pointed out some strict parallels between the situation in Chile and that in Argentina: for example, if you were looking for a flat or house you would not attempt to rent one if the previous tenant had been arrested. If the authorities found no link between you and the prisoner, they were quite capable of inventing one. Nor would you dare to possess, let alone use, gramophone records by a certain folk singer or books by a series of authors.

And it was Silvia who a few months later, in Switzerland, brought home to me more than anyone the fact that trauma was an element of the refugee experience insufficiently appreciated – or as yet not appreciated at all! – by people in the helping professions in Europe.

Introduction To Post-Traumatic Stress

Mendoza was a city of strange contrasts. Judging from the all-too-perfect tiled pavements, it was a rich city. But there were plenty of other signs pointing to the poverty of a majority. Magnificent old Fords of 1929 and 1930 vintage ran to and fro as though imbued with eternal life, their coachwork certainly benefiting from the very dry climate – but how they and other road users avoided frequent accidents, when at crossroads there were no rules and everyone seemed to shoot across virtually without looking or even slowing down, I could not guess. Eating in Argentina was an experience never to be forgotten, with the over-abundance of meat – in a country in which traditionally, any traveller could, at will, kill any animal in one of the immense herds in order to satisfy his hunger with a single steak.

All this made for a very rich experience. But what was most significant, of course, was the anguish – and in some cases apparent hopelessness – of many of the Chileans, spurs to ever-greater efforts to get them documented and away from the repression. Like my Pathet Lao sentinels of two years earlier, the plain clothes men in the Hotel Argentina reception area probably noted the time that I let myself out to start work on the files.[15]

Why was there such hopelessness on some faces? And what were these seizures so many of the Chileans seemed to be suffering from? I had some long talks with the psychologist. He explained his professional standpoint, one shared, he said, by neurologists and fellow psychologists: while they were epileptiform fits, the sufferers were *not epileptic*. He called the phenomenon "disritmia", explaining that there was a momentary arrest in the supply of blood to the brain. It caused instant unconsciousness, but the sufferer did not have convulsions as an epileptic does, and – most importantly – was likely to be perfectly curable, but curable only if there was an absence of traumatic circumstances and an environment conducive to the building up of trusting and loving relationships, to the re-establishment of self-confidence and to the recreation of an acceptable life mode.

As for the apparent apathy, it had to be attributed to the fact that some of these Chileans had now been in Argentina for several years, with no real prospect of a settled life. One woman, Monica, whose twin brother had been evacuated from a Chilean prison direct to the Netherlands, despaired of ever seeing him again, because Holland, having participated in the

---

[15] I was unaware then that UNHCR staff had been considered by the Junta to be at the very least suspect, if not actually subversive. Then I was shown some newspaper articles about UNHCR staff in which the word "guerrilleros" was used.

prisoner-release programme soon after the *coup d'état*, was not expected to accept any more refugee families from Latin America.

How unnerving it must be here in Argentina, I realized, both for people suffering from massive trauma and for their families! Their current circumstances were such that their mental health could hardly be expected to improve. For each and every one, the best solution would of course have been to be free to return home to a peaceful Chile. But the repressive dictator showed every sign of staying: he had found his niche, consolidated his power and, indeed, he remained in supreme control for a total of sixteen years.

In the circumstances, it was terribly important to do justice to each refugee on that newly compiled dossier, and to try to see that the person's wishes were taken into account to the fullest extent possible. As there were virtually no openings within Latin America, the Chilean refugee would have to face an uncertain future in a country of which he or she would have to learn the language, become acquainted with the culture and yet try to remain in touch with fellow countrymen and women, and with news from home. It was going to be no easy ride for any of these brave Chileans.

On one of the public holidays – it may have been May Day or Independence Day – Coca urged me to take a coach trip into the Andes, and thanks to this suggestion I saw some of the most majestic scenery in the world. The highest point of the Andes is the summit of the Aconcagua (6,960 m, 22,835 feet, above sea level). Glorious autumn tints merged with the many different colours of the rock faces, and contrasted with the shimmering white of fresh snow on the summits. The high point of the day's tour was to be set down just below the glaciers at 13,000 feet above sea level, on the border with Chile.

Standing between an immense monument to "Christo Redentor" (Christ the Redeemer) and a huge green-and-yellow panel wishing one "Bienvenido a Chile" (Welcome to Chile), I mused on the fact that, just as the Spanish Inquisitors had done terrible things in the name of Catholicism, as had some of the colonizers, the junta dared to proclaim that it was protecting the Church's interests by persecuting and murdering thousands of people. I pondered also on how the people of these rugged countries must feel when their world fell apart and they were forced out. What would they long for most – their mountains? The sea? Natives of the country with the longest Pacific seaboard, several of the Chileans had told me what the sight and smell of the sea meant to them, not to mention their enjoyment of seafoods and the fact that their children were brought up to enjoy life on the coast. Their culture? Coca took me to a concert of music from the Altiplano, the high plateaux of Bolivia and the borders of Chile, Peru and Argentina, and transported by the beauty of those pipes I knew that nothing in any other part of the world could replace the haunting associations of music like that.

No experiences abroad were likely to be able to duplicate those that the refugees had had before they were ejected from their homeland by a cruel dictatorship. Many a refugee, whatever his or her nationality, must have felt, while grasping the courage to break with the present for an uncertain future, that the only reality would be found after an eventual return home. Yes, grasping the courage… for of course it does take great courage to turn your back on everything you have known, leaving behind people you love, possessions you prized and scenes you know you will always long for.

Many Chilean exiles were to return in years to come from the forty or so countries to which they had gone. But for the children born in countries of resettlement, and even for those children who had been very young when they were torn from their homes, this return was tantamount to exile.

The Netherlands accepted Monica and her family, so they were reunited with the twin brother. Sweden included Antonio and his little family among the several hundred Chileans they were admitting, and I know that they were soon happy there. Two single girls with major mental health problems went to Belgium, and were helped by Dr Barudy and his group. Many of those I had met went to Canada. And Silvia and several others were taken in by Switzerland. It would be of interest to relate how people like this young Chilean woman coped with life from that time on. The account would have to show that successful integration is far from being a foregone conclusion for damaged refugees.[16] So although this chapter is already long enough, I have elected to add on a summary of Silvia's experiences.

In Chapter 20, we can see what courageous work was undertaken by health practitioners to assuage the suffering of many Chileans, both during

---

[16] For the nearly three years that I worked in UNHCR's Resettlement Section, the head of section was a woman who since leaving Greece thirty years earlier had never worked in the field, but had nevertheless achieved seniority. Though it had seemed obvious that, with regard to integration questions, for the Indochinese (in particular), there would be multiple hurdles that some of them would find it very difficult to surmount, she failed to realize it and delayed for a year the international meeting on integration that the British delegation had called for as a matter of urgency – and that she had promised to convene. The suggested blueprint for such a meeting I provided her with lay unheeded while hundreds of thousands of Indochinese were being transferred from various camps in South East Asia to thirty countries of resettlement – which really needed to know what to do with them. I had meanwhile left and gone to work with the International Red Cross.

the sixteen years of the repression and subsequently. My principal source is the book mentioned earlier, *Trauma and Healing under State Terrorism* (Inger Agger and Søren Buus Jensen, Zed Books, 1996).

Now, in late 2019, Chile after practically thirty years of peace is once again in ferment. The population has become increasingly indignant about the inequalities between the "haves" and the "have nots" and the unrest has come to be fiercely countered by violence. The reforms that President Sebastián Piñera has been anxious to promise may not be enough to ensure the return of calm.

Silvia's Experiences

Circumstances of my life combined to bring about a close association with Silvia. Our association, which started in March 1978 in Argentina, actually lasted for over thirty years. I know that she would have no objection to my writing about her, for long ago she had asserted that I should feel free to share her experiences in the interests of doing anything that might help others.

In the cramped little CEAS office where I conducted interviews, Silvia, a short, compact, intelligent woman of thirty-two, related her life story for the purposes of the comprehensive dossier we needed to compile. CEAS had asked me to consider this case a priority, both because Silvia was quite alone and because she was suffering from frequent blackouts, similar to epileptic fits.

She related how, the third child of a bricklayer, she had grown up in a coastal town of central Chile, San Antonio. There was a vestige of Indian blood in the family, and I could discern it in the jet-black hair and the dark eyes. She was still quite young when her younger brother, a merry little boy of eight who had been his elder sister's shadow, died as a result of a fall from a horse. Silvia was still a teenager. She said that her mother never recovered from the shock of this loss, and contracted terminal cancer. Silvia gave up her job to nurse her mother throughout her last months of life. Later, she nursed her father, who had contracted pneumonia one winter as a result of returning to work too soon after an attack of influenza, and he also died.

From the first, life had been hard. Poor families could not afford to put their children through secondary school. Silvia, leaving school at the age of twelve and finding work in many different places, tried to complete the secondary school syllabus outside work hours, and succeeded in this by the time she was twenty – then entertaining hopes of paying her way through university eventually. She took up employment in a port office in a small coastal town, driving a taxi after hours to earn extra money.

Organized Violence, Flight

Nothing could sufficiently have prepared Chileans for the 11 September 1973 *coup d'état*. Silvia had been a supporter of the first democratically elected Marxist head of state, Dr Salvador Allende, and she spoke of him often. When she heard on returning to her coastal town from a visit to Santiago that the man she loved and with whom she had worked had been shot, she had the first of the seizures that now dogged her life. She was then aware of other "disappearances", and even tried to find some of these former neighbours by going to the principal prisons to ask about them. No doubt she was carefully watched by the police.

She had not at all wished to leave Chile, but her married sister Rachel, feeling panic-stricken on seeing so many people arrested lest the same thing happen to herself and her family, insisted she leave. It seemed that they had relatives living in Mendoza, who however did nothing whatsoever to help Silvia throughout her four years of solitude and sickness. But she was of special concern to CEAS because she was quite alone and prone to frequent fits. The psychologist who received me regularly to go over the facts of various cases assured me that Silvia was not epileptic, and that given the kind of support and sense of security that she certainly lacked in Mendoza she could, in time, recover: what she needed was tranquillity and a good personal life, a return to as normal a life as possible, along with the support of specialists who, for a time, would have to prescribe appropriate medication. I was cheered by this analysis and included it in the dossier being prepared for use vis-à-vis the immigration authorities of any country liable to consider accepting Silvia for resettlement.

On my return from Argentina, the parish council of the village in which I lived, Céligny, seemed keen, on hearing from me about my unusual experiences on the other side of the Atlantic, to help one of these refugees. On getting back to my office, I had had reason to be annoyed on finding that the several dossiers I had forwarded to the UNHCR Resettlement Section to be sent on to Berne were gathering dust on the desk of a Filipino professional.[17] At all events, Silvia's file now got forwarded to the Swiss

---

[17] Challenging her to explain why nothing had been done with them, she actually resorted to a lie, pretending that she had had to work on them because they were too detailed. She could not know that many years before, I had had experience with what had come to be called "Jensen dossiers", files so carefully and professionally compiled by a Dr Jensen that every necessary element in a person's case was made available for use by a government department requested by UNHCR to examine the case seriously. In Mendoza I had made up the equivalent of those Jensen dossiers for

Department of Justice and Police, which duly examined her case, within three weeks issuing a visa in her name to the Swiss embassy in Buenos Aires. In Céligny, it was agreed that accommodation, help with finding medical specialists, help with the French language and other ways of providing the young woman refugee support would be shared around. I had a spacious flat and Silvia could live with me for a time.

The Chance Of A New Life

It had rained solidly for four days and nights before Silvia's plane touched down in sunshine in Geneva, and we were then delighted that the first month that Silvia was with us, we had marvellous summer weather. All seemed to go well at the start. We all assumed that, in Switzerland, Silvia would receive competent medical support. However, further shocks were to come. The neurologist to whom our pastor arranged to have Silvia referred, and to whom we gave a full copy of the medical file from Argentina with my report of the prognosis, pronounced her after an EEG examination to be epileptic. I was with her as interpreter: we were both taken aback, and in a rather delicate discussion with the neurologist, who seemed not to appreciate having his diagnosis queried, I got him to agree to a further examination. He suggested that this be immediately after the next loss of consciousness, whenever it should occur – be it over a weekend, he said rather grimly.

We duly reported to him the following Sunday morning, after Silvia blacked out on the top stair of my two-tier flat, and slid down the wooden staircase to the grandfather clock at the bottom. After looking at the new EEG graph, the neurologist startled us even more than he had the first time, saying curtly, "You are not epileptic, there's nothing wrong with you. Just get rid of your medication and stop behaving childishly!"

I got to be both shocked and incredulous when on accompanying her to a consultation with a second neurologist, it became obvious that these specialists were unaware of trauma. Silvia's hopes of an early cure were fast being dashed. If these people could not identify the illness, who would? Had no one here heard of trauma? Latin Americans knew about it – why not the Swiss? But the term "post-traumatic stress disorder" (PTSD) had not yet been coined, and much of the thinking about psychological illness lay years

---

at least a dozen "difficult cases" (as the terminology went). It is tempting to add that UNHCR's Resettlement Section had for years failed to use the fifty places that the Swiss government had made available year by year for what were then called "hardcore cases" (what a term!) Fifty precious places left unused – through ignorance, perhaps. The section was at that time rather poorly managed.

ahead. How was it possible in a century that had had two world wars that mental health experts did not recognize the crippling reality of trauma?

I was of course in no position to hold a discussion with professionals, but certainly shared Silvia's frustration. Naturally she could not wait to be rid of these sudden fits. How could she even think of living a normal life while they dogged her? But alas, for years, poor Silvia would not get to be helped with her psychological problems in any meaningful way – even after she began receiving psychotherapy in Geneva from an *Argentine* psychologist! – for there were unfortunately too many negative factors in her life for her to begin to shake off the PTSD.

This young woman, initially lodging under my roof, was being helped by various very pleasant Céligny residents, including our pastor, who had explored ways that he assumed would give her suitable medical support (the two neurologists), our postmaster, ready to help her with various formalities, and a dear lady of over sixty, Valentine, who helped Silvia for a very long time with her French language study – cycling down to the village from her outlying vintage home on an ancient bicycle and actually managing to return with Silvia on the back of it! The chairman of our parish council, Monsieur Widmer, gave her a job in his vineyards for several weeks. This was the only kind of safe job Silvia could handle for the time being, but the poor young woman, when travelling on a bus, was unaware that someone actually removed the money she had earned from her bag. For even in Switzerland there are thieves!

Setbacks

With hindsight, I saw that we in the support group were probably all too paternalistic. We had had no real preparation for the task of helping someone describe their own scenario, and I realize that, for example, in providing Silvia with sums of money that she knew she would want to repay, and in choosing something as personal as clothing for her (some of it second-hand), members of the support group caused her embarrassment and even humiliation. As a colleague and I would write later on the subject of identity in a handbook on working with refugees and asylum seekers, "The refugee is an individual who has been suddenly torn away from everything which is familiar and plunged into an unfamiliar world. All coherence and continuity that had once given the refugee his/her identity have disappeared, causing a lack of stability and continuity. Part of your old identity disappears, and you feel diminished as a human being. You may at times be aggressive, protesting about everything, while at other times you may become depressed, isolated, passive."

On the whole, Silvia was too gracious to complain. But as time went on, I was anything but God's good gift to her as a home builder and confidante: involved in the refugee crisis in South Asia, and obliged for months to slog on in the office until almost midnight, pacing the flat at 3 a.m. when unable to sleep, I was often tense and preoccupied. We were in 1978 and 1979, the period of the mass exodus from Vietnam, Laos and Cambodia. For months, I was the lone and heavily overburdened resettlement officer at UNHCR headquarters, a job that later (much too late, really!) was distributed to six professionals, all with their support staff.

Daily, Silvia was taking the train to Geneva for a morning of French lessons, then she would return to the village to eat in the flat and spend time with Valentine or other residents, take my dog for good long walks, and await my return from work. Though unfortunately this was at an increasingly late hour, by which time Silvia was usually asleep in bed, I nevertheless spent all the time I could with her, and noted the frequent seizures or epileptiform fits she had, which in one month totalled twenty-two. She would lose consciousness and fall down, then, appearing to come round after some time, she would seem to be conscious but was in reality only half-conscious. This whole process usually took between half to three quarters of an hour. On one weekend occasion, we were just drinking coffee in the nearby café when she had a seizure and then tried to climb on the table and start to undress.

Trying to create the conditions in which Silvia would feel she had support and friendship, we got together two young basketball teams in the village, Silvia having spoken of having a passion for this sport. With regular Sunday afternoon games and the subsequent refreshments for everyone in the flat, her spirits seemed to rise and for a record time – several months, in fact – there were no more fits. It seemed almost too good to be true! During this period, Silvia was invited to make a short speech of welcome in Geneva to the family of Viviane, the leftist militant who with her husband and two grown children had been accepted by the Swiss. But unfortunately, there were more troubles ahead. On the occasion that Silvia "blacked out" in the street in Geneva and passers-by called an ambulance, I received a call from the Cantonal Hospital asking me to go and explain what I knew about Silvia's illness, for the medical staff was simply baffled. I could only tell those doctors the little I knew!

Our young Chilean quite reasonably wished to find a studio flat in Geneva, and succeeded in due course in finding one and moving into it. It was in an old building in Geneva's St Jean area, near the River Rhone and quite close to the city centre. Now she was much nearer for the French lessons and for the series of appointments with the social worker of the aid agency with which she was registered. The young social worker, seeing an alert young woman in front of her, was totally uncomprehending with regard to Silvia's illness. Moreover, the girl's naivety in dealing almost patronisingly with someone ten years her senior with considerably more life experience was a minor source of vexation, as she was frequently being kept waiting. But determined to get her into work, she came to find her a first job – loading shelves in a shop. On the first day, Silvia unfortunately blacked out and was virtually kicked out, a blow for her already-low self-esteem. Another job subsequently found for her in Geneva also ended in disaster, as soon as she suffered a seizure – doubtless as a direct result of new stresses. Silvia then completed satisfactorily a three-month course intended to lead to a sedentary job – but technology was moving ahead so fast over that period that the elements she had learned to use were suddenly classified as redundant: this was in 1980–81 and we were on the brink of the computer age!

Those failed attempts to regain a place in society and financial independence were obviously counterproductive.

Matrimony And Motherhood

Meanwhile, however, two men in the French language class were, Silvia told me, attracted to her and wanted to marry her, one a good-looking young Egyptian who was in Geneva on a student visa, the other a Romanian, a slightly older man, perhaps a refugee.

Before long, Silvia decided to marry the Egyptian, who we can call Ahmed. We tried delicately to warn him about Silvia's psychological problems, not of course to try to break up the relationship but to be sure that the young man knew that he would have to be especially understanding and tolerant towards his future wife. Ahmed really seemed to have fallen in love. We then realized that not only could we not feel sanguine about Silvia contracting a marriage with a Muslim because of the cultural constraints, but that she was prevented by a disastrous prior marriage in Mendoza to an alcoholic fellow refugee from marrying legally in Switzerland until she could obtain a divorce. CEAS came to the rescue, but it took time, and although the couple went through a Muslim ceremony in Geneva, this was of course not sufficient for the Swiss authorities, and at the end of his study period (during which he had earned his living as a waiter) the young husband was obliged to go back to Egypt.

A son was born a few months later, Mohammed Luis (Mohammed to the father, Luis to the mother!). He was slightly premature, but made good progress and was much admired by us all. In time, Silvia felt sufficient pity for the baby's father, parted from his little son, for her actually to decide to go to Egypt and contract a legal marriage so that he could return to Geneva. Luis was an adorable thirteen-month-old toddler by this time. My husband and I, with a Romanian asylum seeker who was living with us, took care of the little fellow over that ten-day period while Silvia, though apparently rather perturbed with what she saw of the society she was marrying into, went through with the ceremony before getting back to us and the baby as fast as she could.

There were still too many setbacks to Silvia finding peace of mind, but she proved to be an excellent mother, despite her ongoing seizures. Soon after her husband returned to Geneva, the harmony the parents had found in the short term had vanished and the young man finally found a room elsewhere. A legal separation, with the father having regular access to his son, went well enough, until one day when Silvia received a call from him from Cairo, to tell her that he and "Mohammed" were there – a tremendous shock! But he said that he would be bringing the boy back in due course.

Silvia waited in a state of extreme anxiety for two long months, hoping that the little boy's father had financial reasons to return to Geneva and bring him back, which turned out to be the case. The infant was somewhat traumatized by his surroundings in Egypt and, above all, by a circumcision operation, but he was again safe with his mother.

A legal battle began, with the father (who did not hide from the child his intention of taking him to Egypt for good one day) seeking to have the terms of the custody of his son overturned in his favour. He claimed that the mother was mentally ill and unfit to look after him. In reality, Silvia excelled as a mother, as several people were able to testify, and the court concluded that she could not be faulted. Ahmed's reaction to his failure was not reassuring. Gradually, Silvia was driven to the conclusion that he was a harmful influence on the growing child, who since the kidnapping and his operation had been uneasy with his father, and that it might eventually be in her son's best interest to envisage a future in Chile. She could take no steps, however, before the Geneva courts, some years later, decided to give her unconditional custody of the boy. By this time, there had been moves within Chile to work towards a return to democracy.

While Silvia did not establish contacts with other Chileans, she became friends with the Swiss mother of two boys who were near in age to Luis and lived a couple of hundred yards away. The two mothers in fact soon helped each other, taking turns in looking after the three little boys for short periods. It was cheering that, in this regard, Silvia was close to leading a normal life. She brought Luis to stay with us in Céligny at regular intervals, and he became our little Claudia's very first friend. With his seniority of two years, he led their activities, watering the garden with minute red watering cans, building a Fisher-Price garage together and making sandcastles at Divonne lake. Winter after winter, swathed in woollen caps, scarves and mittens, they sledged together in our nearby mountains, and fed the ducks, swans and other lakeside birds at Nyon. They were excellent friends.

Although Silvia's integration might have appeared satisfactory to onlookers, there were nevertheless some unpleasant racist attitudes and behaviour on the part of one or perhaps two residents of the same block of flats that naturally upset her. She actually found excrement put down in front of the door of the apartment – a really shocking act of totally unjustifiable animosity. Like many people in her kind of situation, Silvia in any case mostly had rather negative feelings, finding it hard to feel happy, and becoming irritable and angry with relatively little provocation. For one reason and another, Switzerland never really endeared itself to her, and in fact she longed to be able to return to Chile one day. With this in mind, she managed to obtain a divorce from Ahmed, being given sole custody of their little boy.

Return Home After Sixteen Years Away

In April 1990, the glad day came in Chile that a democratic government was voted in, and Luis, who had been doing very well at school, stayed with us one last time while his mother travelled to Berne to get a Chilean passport. She knew that it was not going to be easy to start life back in her own country with a young son to educate. Her old support group in Céligny guessed that her needs would be considerable for a time, while the Swiss government, after some delay, came through with a small grant towards a project Silvia had outlined: she would rent a house large enough to accommodate guests, perhaps in a university town such as Valparaiso, and run it as a means of support for herself and young Luis.

165

At the airport, both our children (Luis, seven; Claudia, five) were bewildered, Silvia very nervous. We had already promised that one day, be it many years ahead, we would visit them in Chile. In ensuing years, we received good news of them, and Farmer Widmer's son Christian went twice to visit them. He found a different Silvia to the one he had known in Céligny, full of gaiety and fun. Her health had improved, while Luis turned out to be a brilliant schoolboy.

Claudia and I went, as promised, to see them. It was in early 2004: Luis was twenty, Claudia eighteen. Silvia's hostel was working out well, and Luis was now at university. When he was fifteen, he had gone to see his father, who had sent him an air ticket, but the boy found that he could not get on with him at all. Five years later, a similarly negative reunion took place and Luis spent several weeks with us – recovering, it seemed, from the shock of finding it very difficult to be with his father. Subsequently, he won a scholarship to go to Stockholm University to work on a master's degree in physics. This was in 2007/08. Some of us sent Silvia an air ticket to come over to Geneva during her son's year in Sweden, and she and I travelled to Stockholm together, staying with Swedish friends of mine. Day by day, Luis, living in a studio where he did not have the right to accommodate a guest, would come for her early each morning and they probably covered the whole of Stockholm on foot before that ten-day reunion came to an end.

Subsequently, Luis began on doctoral work in Valparaiso, and we gradually lost touch with the two of them. But, after all those years, Céligny residents as well as our family continued to think about the brave girl who had counteracted many an obstacle, and who finally, despite the unresolved burden of PTSD, got her wish to live her life back in her own country.

CHAPTER 9

Solidarity And Hope

In 1973, Dr Jorge Barudy, a Chilean psychiatrist and psychotherapist, was arrested and tortured by the Pinochet regime. But then, he soon managed to leave Chile for Peru, before setting up invaluable work in Belgium among refugees of several origins.[1] Here Dr Barudy, invited to the Vitznau workshop, gives us a masterly account of what disruption and exile can do to a family, and in particular to children, whose lives had hitherto been calm and uneventful.

The Therapeutic Value Of Solidarity And Hope

The most appropriate and creative form that help for the child can take is to enable him to regain his confidence in adults.

In all regions of the world, political repression and civil wars are the cause of a diaspora, the extent and complexity of which surpass all individual and even institutional efforts to find ways of predicting and treating the suffering of thousands of human beings. Children are also among them, victims of forces that have traumatized their existence and that compel them to witness the break-up of their familiar environment.

The purpose of this chapter is twofold: to propose an analytic model for the understanding of the psychological suffering of refugee children, and to present certain possibilities for prevention and treatment of this suffering, employing the resources of the refugee community in the refugee

---

[1] This chapter is a summary of experience gained in refugee camps in Central America and that obtained in Belgium by Colectivo Latinoamericano de Trabajo Psicosocial (COLAT) in the children's workshops, the purpose of which has been the prevention and treatment of psychosocial problems of refugee children.

camps or in the receiving country. Within this framework, we shall try first of all to demonstrate the use of a systemic and integrated approach to the understanding of the children's psychological disturbances; and subsequently to show the value of community action in mental health programmes for refugee children.

The Systemic Approach To The Understanding Of Suffering In Children

According to the systemic model, the child and the symptoms he/she presents are not viewed in isolation but in the context of a wider system of family and social networks. This means that we consider the problems manifested by child victims of political repression and war as the result of a multiplicity of factors and take into account the influence of various persons and human systems which have acted either to exacerbate or to mitigate the harm done. Within this context, it is necessary to describe the overall problem of the refugee child, taking into account all the events that marked his history prior to his arrival in a refugee camp or country of resettlement. Throughout the analysis the child is seen as interacting with other family members, who, in their turn, are in a process of interaction with other social systems (school, neighbourhood, refugee camp, social and medical aid systems etc.).

The Life Pattern Of The Refugee Child And His Family

The child within the context of a stable family environment

Prior to the events that created the situation of forced exile, the family lived in a state of equilibrium, interrelating with a variety of social systems that were important for the maintenance and development of normal family life. This state of equilibrium was subject to fluctuations only insofar as a family is never a static entity but rather a structure responding to the requirements of change from within (birth of a baby, growth of children etc.) and without (changes in socio-economic conditions etc.)

The family was also part of a wider social network, including, for example, the extended family, neighbours, colleagues and political organizations. This relationship with the outside world provided the family members with support and enabled them to experience the mutual "strengthening" of their individual identities, family identity and group images – a set of factors that make up social identity. This system of exchange of information and activities – which constitutes a real network of

168

interpersonal relations – was influenced in its turn by the context, culture and sociopolitical and sociocultural setting of the family of the future refugee child.[2] The family unit is, in effect, the basic reference point for each member of the family, determining their perceptions of appropriate role behaviour and social relationships.

During this initial stage, it can be said that the child and his family were living in a state of internal equilibrium, within the framework of a relatively stable environmental and sociocultural context. By way of illustration, let us take the case of a Chilean family followed by our centre. Before the military *coup d'état* of 1973, they lived an average working-class life. The husband, socially the head of the family, worked in a factory, maintained external social contacts, and was an active militant in his trade union. The mother, a housewife, carried out household tasks, was responsible for the children, and maintained an active and rewarding relationship with other mothers, organized in a mothers' group. She also received the assistance of her own mother, as well as regular visits from the rest of the family. The children (six, eight and ten years old when the coup occurred), attended school regularly, had friends in the neighbourhood, participated in a children's workshop organized by the father's trade union, and received the affection and support of the extended family, which consisted of a group of fourteen adults, including aunts, uncles, cousins, grandparents and godparents.

It was a family that functioned and evolved normally. It experienced moments of conflict and crisis, as do all families, but nevertheless had a sense of its own worth and identity in a well-defined environmental, sociocultural context. It is important to note that this family had learned, on a trial-and-error basis, ways of coping with problems and conflicts, so as to ensure the well-being of its members. Until the time of the coup, the family had always been autonomous and, despite its modest origins, had never needed to seek any form of social assistance. Analogous situations have been observed in families from other cultural backgrounds followed in our centre, although the environmental and sociocultural picture can be altogether different in the case, for example, of a Ghanaian, Iranian, Afghan or Salvadorean family.

The case under discussion clearly involves a family whose organization is considered functional. In other words, in the situation of relative equilibrium described above, none of the family members presented any symptom of mental illness. In the course of our work we have also encountered families that, even in periods of equilibrium, presented symptoms of varying degrees

---

[2] H. Aponte, Thérapie familiale et communauté, *Cahiers Gamma 2*, Paris (April 1980) 17–29.

of malfunctioning. In such cases, the events leading to the disruption of normal family life only aggravate these symptoms.

Repression: The Break-Up Of The Child's World Following Disruption Of Normal Community Life

Situations of organized violence[3] cause a serious disruption of the child's world insofar as the family and sociocultural group to which he belongs finds itself in a state of environmental disequilibrium. Political repression, arrests, torture, war, and religious persecution are events which affect the whole society, causing widespread social crisis. This crisis disrupts normal social networks and results in a situation of disequilibrium inside the family. In this situation, the family strives to find a means to counterbalance the negative effects that these external pressures are creating within the family in order to safeguard the well-being of its members.[4]

Also at this point, in terms of his physical, psychosocial and sociocultural needs, the child is in danger of being denied the essential components that ensure a healthy, happy development. Thus, the child is affected in both a positive and negative manner, not only by his personal history but also by that of the family, the community, the culture and the society to which he belongs. In this process of growth and development, the child assimilates and transforms the world around him so that it becomes part of his personality. For this reason, the child's experiences in the early years of his life play a fundamental role in the development of internal resources to which he can have recourse throughout this existence in order to be able to find creative solutions in situations of conflict. If his physical and emotional needs are unmet and he is confronted with a threatening life situation, then his process can be disrupted and his progress towards normal development may be adversely affected.

The Consequences Of The Disaster For The Child: Effects On Growth And Development

Situations of organized violence constitute a threat to the growth and development of the child. They cause disturbances not only at the level of material needs but also at the level of psychosocial and spiritual needs.

---

[3]   We use the term "organized violence" to mean situations involving massive political repression and civil wars, a definition accepted by the World Health Organization.

[4]   G. Ausloos, Systèmes-Homéostase-Equilibration, *Thérapie familiale*, Vol. 2 No. 3, Geneva (1981) 187–203.

With regard to material needs, many children experience hunger and a lack of physical care and protection prior to their arrival in a refugee camp and/or country of resettlement. There is very little data concerning the effects of inadequate physical care experienced by young children who have been victims of organized violence. There is, however, a relevant body of knowledge relating to the impact of negligence on young children. Research in this field has established a series of risks and harmful consequences for the child which are relevant to the situation we are considering, e.g. the risk of retarded growth due to malnutrition. Aside from its obvious physical effects, it can result in psychological symptoms such as depression, withdrawal, and lack of interest.

There are also effects of inadequate provision of psychosocial needs. As the child learns to interact with the significant adults in his world, he experiences a sense of satisfaction and fulfilment in terms of his need for love and affection. The development of this exchange between child and adult is essential for him to learn that not only is he a unique individual but also a member of a wider society. The consequences of a situation of organized violence on the development of this self-perception can be extremely harmful for the growing child.

There are a number of experiences that can cause disruption at the level of psychosocial needs. One is the experience of numerous and violent losses. The events linked to political violence signify, for a certain number of children, the tragic disappearance of parents or close relatives – tragedies to which unfortunately the child has often been an eyewitness. Thus, the child has observed the brutality and violence inflicted on his parents, which has very often resulted in death.

In these situations, the child is faced with the phenomenon of loss, of bereavement. In "normal" conditions, the mourning period goes through three stages: first, fear and anguish associated with the abrupt disappearance of the parent; second, anger towards the deceased parent and the persons seen as responsible; third, a period of despair and extreme distress combined with an acceptance of the reality of the situation. A favourable context can help the child to distance himself from the tragedy and start little by little to invest in relationships with other adults. If this context does not exist, there is a risk that the child will remain in a state of pathological mourning manifested by behavioural disturbance (aggression, violence, hyperactivity etc.), anguish (expressing itself by enuresis, encopresis, nightmares, etc.) and depressive symptoms.

Disorganization and breakdown of the family structure is another experience that can cause disruption at the psychosocial level. External aggression involves enforced and violent changes in family organization, with intra-family tensions caused by the redistribution of roles and tasks. In this situation, the child must often assume responsibilities beyond his years. In the case of the Chilean family described above, the father was arrested, brutally tortured, and sent to a concentration camp for four years. [We have called the circumstances experienced by political prisoners in the course of their imprisonment (i.e. the situation as a whole – the repressive events which have traumatized their sense of identity, the destruction of their self-esteem, and the devaluation of their personality) "the moral career of the political prisoner"][5]

Following the father's imprisonment, the wife had to assume all the family tasks, begin working to provide for the family, and assume an active role in efforts to defend and secure the release of her husband. With other prisoners' wives, she contacted human rights organizations associated with the Catholic Church. As a result of these experiences, the wife went through a process that increased her self-esteem, the opposite of what her husband was suffering in the concentration camp.

As for the children, the eldest, a boy of ten, assumed parental tasks to the extent that he started to exercise a certain level of authority, as well as being a support and acting as a spokesman for his mother. We can say that the children had to "grow up" through force of circumstances. This does not indicate, however, that the children were spared any of the effects of suffering, anguish, fear or feelings of marginalization. All such experiences will leave traces that will manifest themselves in ways peculiar to each child.

In the case of families who have been obliged to flee, exile brings a new crisis that once again disrupts any possibility of establishing a new equilibrium. Exile is never the fulfilment of a wish; it is a "forced choice", necessary to escape danger and survive. Exile is never an individual process, even if the fugitive arrives alone in the host country: it always involves a break or a repetition of the break in the individual's personal and social history that began with the repression.

In the host country, the refugee family is usually faced with an alien social and cultural environment. This challenge makes the refugee and his family aware, sometimes for the first time, of the discontinuity of their situation. The sensation experienced by each member of the family is one of uprooting.

---

[5]   J. Barudy and C. Vieytes, *El dolor invisible de la tortura: nuestras experiencias terapeuticas con ex-prisioneros políticos y sus familias* (COLAT Franja Ediciones, 1984) (French version available).

With exile, each family member is also undergoing a process of mourning, not only for friends, parents, or comrades who have died but also for the loss of a social and institutional sense of belonging. Each adult and child is once again in a state of disequilibrium,[6] i.e. each is searching for a new stability and a new orientation. This quest may be hampered by varying degrees of persecution, social discrimination, or racism directed against the refugees in the host community.

The Effects Of The Crisis Within The Family

For many families, exile corresponds to the moment when the whole family is reunited after a prolonged separation. But these reunions take place on alien soil and are characterized by the difficulties described above. In the absence of supportive social networks, each family member seeks points of reference and the satisfaction of his needs within the family. The more the environment is perceived as threatening, complex or unfamiliar, the more the family members will be dependent on each other for the satisfaction of their need for intimacy, security and recognition.[7] The family was subjected to many changes over the preceding years, and in exile it must once again face a new situation.

In the case of the Chilean family in which the father had been imprisoned, he was unaware of the reality of the new family situation. When he joined his family, he had to catch up with the other members; it was necessary for him to re-establish relationships and contacts and to make a place for himself in this family which had functioned without him for so long. During the period of imprisonment, for the first time in his life perhaps, he found himself in a position of dependence on his wife, who was taking steps to have him freed, visiting him in prison, arranging to send him parcels, and so forth.

When the couples meet again in exile, or in a refugee camp, they will usually try to resume the pattern of their relationship as it was before their forced separation. In an effort to integrate, the husband will probably want to resume his role as head of the family, facing the difficulties of exile, taking responsibility for legal and social steps, and so on.[8]

---

[6] J. Barudy, Integración critica: meta de une terapía liberadora en el exilio latino-americano, in *Asi Buscamos Rehacernos* (Colat-Celadec, 1980), pp.225–240.

[7] J. Barudy, J. Serrano et al., El mundo de exiliado politico latino-americano, in *Psycho-patología de la tortura y el exilio* (Fundamentos, 1982).

[8] J. Martens, De leefwereld van politieke vluchtelingen, *Kultuurleven*, No. 4 (1979) 327–334.

However, things will never be the same as before; the wife may refuse to resume her traditional role and relations between the couple may become strained. The children are also conscious of change within the family circle. The family is seeking a new equilibrium. The children may never actually have realized that their father was in prison, but they had become accustomed to the situation. As we saw with the Chilean family, the older children became responsible for looking after the youngest and for managing the household. Thus, often children are compelled by circumstances to assume a parental role.

The child will never have forgotten that one day his father went away, and in most cases young children feel guilty about what happens to their parents. They often think "If father left, it's because I was naughty", and sometimes the children continue to harbour this idea deep down. When the father joins the family again, the child experiences a complete change; he tries to re-establish a relationship and present his father with a positive image of himself. But, for a number of children, it is sometimes difficult; they reject their father and behave in a very aggressive manner when they are reunited with him. This is very distressing for the father, and makes his reunion with the child even more difficult. The children also suffer from their parents' resumption of their former roles; they feel rather lost. They are no longer obliged to be adults but have forgotten how to be children. We have seen children who refused to revert to being children and who were in open conflict with their parents. Others regress and play at being babies.

The child is confused by the changes brought about by exile; he has difficulty in adapting and finding a role for himself in the new state of affairs. Often he does not understand the changes, the meaning of so many frustrations, the reason why his grandparents, his friends, his dog are so far away. He does not understand why, in this new country, people look at his family askance and do not accept them, or why the authorities still pester them. The child feels all of these tensions and also the frustrations of his parents, but he does not know how to explain or express this. He does it in his own language, with his body, and it is thus that behavioural problems, aggressiveness, bed-wetting etc. may appear.

Taken as a whole, the situations of repression, persecution and exile, described above, result in a long period of insecurity, both for the child and for the family unit. The effects of their experiences are felt for a considerable period of time, with the result that the family unit is not in a position to recover the essential equilibrium that would enable it to reorganize and to utilize its innate resources in coping with the effects of the adverse situation in which it finds itself. For the child it is not just a question of inadequate basic needs but also of a situation which he/she perceives as a continuous threat.

Traumatization Of The Child's Sense Of Identity

Experiences of organized violence are destructive for any human being, but more so for children. One of the main objectives of the use of terror as a method of social control is the intimidation of the civilian population. Children frequently witness unspeakable cruelties, and these events can so traumatize the child that his very sense of identity is threatened. The situation is even more disastrous when the child has been a witness to brutalities inflicted on those he loves.

All these events – assassination, rape, torture, destruction of his home etc. – invade the child's sense of self in an insidious and silent way. If the child represses his memories of the events he has witnessed, they can appear in a disguised form as nightmares, delusions of persecution, a generalized sense of anxiety and/or somatic symptoms (enuresis, encopresis, abdominal pains etc.).

It is clear that children are the most liable to be affected by traumatizing experiences because their personalities and, by extension, their sense of identity are still in the stage of formation. As we have already indicated, refugee children have been profoundly affected by very serious losses, by having lived for long periods in threatening situations, and by having witnessed unimaginable barbarities. Children living in refugee camps or in exile in a far country also suffer from the uprooting. The child and his family find themselves in a different environment which, in most cases, is totally unfamiliar to them. Uprooting causes yet another loss: that of their own culture.

Why are the experiences associated with organized violence so profoundly traumatizing? They present problems difficult to grasp because the experiences related to organized violence transcend all human comprehension. Faced with such experiences, the child's psychological development may be arrested and he may lose confidence in himself. He can no longer differentiate between excessive aggression and aggression that is normal and constructive for his age. This may result in arrested development with regressive or stereotyped behaviour and the appearance of other symptoms as defence mechanisms against the horror he has witnessed.

Community Psychotherapeutic Models Of Assistance

Our model is the synthesis of a series of experiences carried out in refugee camps in Central America and with the Latin American exile community in Belgium. These experiences are based on an intervention model that uses the community's innate capacities, professional resources and the systemic approach to the understanding of children's suffering.

Methodology

Each project's basic core team consists of the professional resources existing on the spot: psychologist, psychiatrist, social assistant, nurse, teacher etc. The professionals must first of all examine the actual facts (number of children, sex, family situation etc.), prepare the therapeutic tools and create the practical conditions to start the work.

The professional coordinator then selects, from among those in the refugee camps or in the community of exile, persons who, by their sensitivity and interests, are disposed to contribute to the welfare of the child. A training period in which professionals and future "animators" work together is indispensable to ensure cohesion within the team.

The programme of therapeutic intervention comprises three levels of action which are related to each other in a circular way:

1. Psychotherapeutic help for children,
2. Assistance in family reorganization,
3. Reconstruction of the social network and preparation of collective projects.

Psychotherapy For Children

We opted for the creation of children's groups, structured and supported by adults. These structures enable the child to express his traumatic experiences, his fits of anger, and his sadness in a context of security, affection, respect and acceptance. Through the use of therapeutic tools such as games, drawing, modelling clay, dramatization, the employment of key words etc., the child can express himself in order to come to terms with what he experienced, what he lost, and what he feels.

It is vital that the child understands what he has experienced. Why did I have to flee? Who killed my father and why? Why did my father let it happen? Why didn't my mother protect us? Who were those men with blackened faces who destroyed our house?

It is important to emphasize that the child cannot attain acceptance of traumatic experiences if he tries to repress or deny them, or to provoke situations leading to forgetfulness. Mental health involves an understanding of the past experience. If the child does not understand what happened to him, or what he witnessed, he will never be able to rid himself of the horror. Moreover, his imagination will aggravate his suffering, making him feel guilty and abandoned, and may cause him to create fantasies, etc. As Dr Albert J. Solnit has remarked:

> Each human being, child or adult, wishes to see himself as a whole person, responsible for his life. One of the essential aspects of this feeling of free will is the knowledge of his own history, but a knowledge which is neither dominant nor destructive.

The child therapy groups are formed according to the age of the children. Usually we work with three categories of children: the youngest (aged three to six), the intermediate group (aged six to ten) and the oldest (aged ten to fourteen). For children under three years of age, we aim at affective and social care. We encourage parental involvement and the organization of a crèche in order to make up for the deficiencies in physical care and affection to which the children have been subjected as a result of the family's experiences.

We use a variety of therapeutic techniques in the workshops. The use of significant topics through key words is an adaptation of the methodology of Paulo Freire.[9] This aspect of the programme consists of introducing significant words in order to animate the group, to facilitate verbal expression, and to attribute new meanings to traumatic experiences, e.g. "war", "soldiers", "flight". With the help of comic strips and magazines, for example, the adult introduces a discussion involving the key words and encourages a group dynamic which enables the children to describe and accept the traumatic experiences they had previously repressed.

In the self-expression workshops, the children are divided into groups of ten, according to age or the problem involved, and are accompanied by one or two animators. The main methods of expression are usually drawing and the use of modelling clay, though one can also have recourse to games, puppet theatre or techniques similar to socio-drama. The animator plays a crucial role in these workshops. He is required to concentrate his attention on the particular experiences of one child, while at the same time ensuring an atmosphere of respect, acceptance, and empathy towards that child. With the help of background information on the child, and using the

---

[9]   Paulo Freire, *Pedagogia del Oprimido* (Signo XXI, 1976).

above techniques, the animator is able to help the child express and accept the traumatizing experiences.

The witness group method is used principally with children aged eight to fourteen. This consists of meetings involving verbal expression focused on the family history of each participant. How did they live before the emergency? How do they live now? What has changed? This type of therapy allows each child to reconstitute his personal history. At the same time it is possible to create a sense of support and solidarity among the children, which provides catharsis for the emotions and feelings associated with their traumatic experiences.

We also use a programme of workshops and holiday camps for children. This type of experience as carried out in Belgium, the Netherlands, Denmark and the Federal Republic of Germany is aimed at the refugee child. Initially, it was intended exclusively for Latin American children, but subsequently it was extended to refugee children of other ethnic origins.

The experience involves a framework of games and of expression within which the children of political refugees may encounter adults from their home community in a context in which the bonds of affection are strengthened and sociocultural ties acquire added value. The children have the opportunity to express themselves in their mother tongue, to become aware of the history of their people and of their parents, and to experience solidarity. The animators (professionals and non-professionals) and the children work closely together to promote a group dynamic that aims to ensure the well-being of all members of the group.

All of the experiences described above are the result of the creative talent of professionals and members of the refugee communities. They put to use the innate resources of their communities by creating a context in which the child succeeds in grasping the true nature of his history by reducing the harmful effects of his experiences. Additionally, he can come to trust in the therapeutic value of love.

Assistance With Family Reorganization

As indicated earlier, the effects of repression subject the family to numerous constraints and upheavals which may last for a considerable time. The problems involved in refugee camp life and/or in exile trigger a series of mechanisms aimed at establishing a new equilibrium.

The child also suffers from constraints and upheavals and is looking for a new equilibrium. He has not had time to understand why his father disappeared and has had to accept a new situation without having had the opportunity to find answers to the questions in his mind. Adolescents must often take over a paternal role and look after brothers and sisters as well as helping their mother. As we have seen, many children feel guilty about the arrest or flight of their father, thinking that if their father went away it was because they had behaved badly. If later on the father returns to the family in the refugee camp or in exile, this creates conflict situations for certain children in the sense that they are once again obliged to adapt to another role. Insofar as the father resumes his paternal role, the child is no longer compelled to play an adult role but, very often, he is no longer able to assume his previous role.

It is therefore essential to assist the family unit and to help it acquire a new equilibrium so that it may be able to provide its members with the indispensable support they need. Whether this aid is given to one or a number of families, we consider that family sessions are the best method to use in this type of situation. They are indispensable when a new family arrives in a camp or resettlement country.

Such sessions may be animated by a professional or a member of the community itself. The purpose of family sessions is to provide its members with a framework in which it is possible to come to terms with their experiences and the problems they present, but – above all – to stress the positive aspects of family relations and their own inner resources. Negative states of mind such as anxiety, despair, passivity and violence can be treated within the same context, enabling people to seek alternative solutions to cope with situations of conflict.

During these meetings the forces external to the family that have contributed and are still contributing to its destabilization – persecution and its consequences, flight, the change in living conditions etc. – are also analysed. This enables the family unit to understand and to redefine the behaviour of its members as the expression of their suffering.

Elements in the new social network itself, which can have a positive influence on the process of adaptation, are also outlined and analysed: organization of the refugee camp, assistance, institutions, self-help groups etc. Relevant and comprehensive information on the structure of the new social network also enables the family to determine effective coping strategies.

The family sessions also offer an opportunity to detect the personal difficulties of individual family members who may require more specialized assistance, e.g. a psychotherapeutic intervention for the child. In this type of activity, it is important to work with the families in seeking constructive solutions for the reintegration of unaccompanied children or orphans, so as to enable them to satisfy their need for security, education, and development. Finally, meeting as a family strengthens identity and increases cohesion, which will facilitate relationships within the family and improve communication with other families.

Reconstruction Of The Social Network And Preparation Of Collective Projects

As has already been said, life in a refugee camp and/or in exile is the consequence of breakdown. Paradoxically, it offers the child and his family an opportunity for security because it is precisely then that the first attempts to organize daily and cultural life are made; it is precisely then that solidarity with the community should be sought.

The most appropriate and creative form that help for the child can take is to enable him to regain his confidence in adults by mobilizing his own family and the whole community. The existence of a system of community self-help awakens a feeling of unity in the child. It involves the carrying out of community projects which make it possible to work with others to discover the realistic opportunities that are available in the new environment.

There are various ways of going about this:

- By giving community members training so that they may undertake certain tasks in the field of psychotherapeutic assistance and the reorganization of the family.
- By mobilizing mothers to create self-help centres.
- By mobilizing adults to establish cooperatives.
- By mobilizing youths to take charge of workshops for children.
- By simply appealing to existing institutions, such as the school or the church, instead of creating new structures foreign to community functioning.

Through working together, a sense of hope is established that has a therapeutic effect within the community. This community feeling enables the child to develop a sense of self-confidence and of coherence again, to the extent that his internal and external environments are predictable and that things will work out as well as can reasonably be expected for such vulnerable beings as children.

Although the past has been painful and the present is difficult, affective ties must be strengthened and hope for the future cultivated.

CHAPTER 10

Cambodia

The 1978–90 period started as one in which everyone on the international humanitarian scene was taken by surprise at the magnitude of the crisis suddenly afflicting the former Indochina in terms of its outflow of refugees. Both the massive exodus from Vietnam by boat and the 1979 massing on the Cambodia–Thailand border of over half a million Cambodians who had lived through years of trauma were of course unprecedented phenomena in that part of the world. As for Laos, an exodus had begun earlier, with tens of thousands crossing the Mekong to Thailand from May 1975 onwards.

Part I – Tragic Background

The country that was doomed to undergo radical change, literally overnight, as a result of the Khmer Rouge takeover of 17 April 1975, traces its history as a Khmer kingdom or empire back over more than a thousand years. The founder of the dynasty in the ninth century oversaw the development of an advanced system of agricultural hydraulics that served the rice fields upon which the prosperity of the kingdom depended. The Khmer Empire, once extending from the Annamite chain in the north to the Malay peninsula in the south was, over a period of time, territorially diminished until Cambodia found itself wedged between competing neighbours – Siam (Thailand) and the kingdoms that have been superseded by present-day Vietnam. In fact, there continued to be a latent fear of further domination by Vietnam.

Cambodia was to become the tragic victim of multiple forms of interference from the time in the nineteenth century that France established control over what came to be known as Indochina.[1] During the Second World War, Japan occupied Indochina, then following its defeat the French established the Federation of Indochina, to which Laos and Cambodia submitted, while nationalists in Annam, Tonkin and Cochinchina did not, demanding complete independence for a new state of Vietnam. In 1946, fighting broke out between Vietnamese nationalists and the French, which continued until the French were beaten at Dien Bien Phu in May 1954 and Vietnam was divided into North and South.

After Independence in 1953, the young Prince Norodom Sihanouk became Head of State, but he was soon frustrated in the exercise of sovereignty. Though it could have been little imagined that within a decade Cambodia would get pulled into the conflict initiated by President John Kennedy to try to save South Vietnam from communism, the North Vietnamese communists put the country's eastern flank into use as a supply route, and imported military supplies through the Cambodian port of Kompong Som. In 1969, US President Richard Nixon authorized devastating secret bombing raids that were to last until August 1973.

The Agony Of Cambodia And Its Inhabitants

Over four terrible years, carpet bombing by B-52 aircraft dropped a recorded total of 2,756,941 tons of bombs on Cambodia, substantially more than the volume of bombs (about two million tons) dropped on Europe throughout the Second World War. Experts have estimated that a hundred thousand Cambodians lost their lives and some two million became homeless. Meanwhile, the Head of State, Prince Sihanouk, while travelling to Moscow and Peking in 1970 in an effort to save his country from being drawn even further into the Vietnam War, was deposed by Marshal Lon Nol, a rightist general who had twice been prime minister. In a polarization of political attitudes, certain leftist deputies went underground, and the presence of Americans and large numbers of Vietnamese on their territory alienated many Cambodians from their government. In five years of violent civil war, more and more young men and boys joined the communist Khmer Rouge, while large numbers of the inhabitants of rural areas fled to the capital.

---

1 France retained the royal families of Laos and Cambodia. With regard to Laos, the king was still the head of state until communists took over the government in 1975. In Cambodia, Prince Sihanouk was revered by every Cambodian, but became the victim of the overthrow of his government in 1970 and, subsequently, a tragic figure trying to do his best for his country while a prisoner of forces far stronger than himself.

On 17 April 1975, the capital, Phnom Penh, was captured by the Khmer Rouge, who that same day began to implement their radical programme of transforming Cambodia into a rural society in which everyone would be harnessed to serve the State.

A few years later, Dr Haing Ngor,[2] a survivor despite subsequent periods of imprisonment and torture, wrote about that afternoon. He had been operating on a wounded soldier when two young Khmer Rouge jumped over the fence of the hospital compound, one holding a US-made M-16 rifle, the other a Chinese-made AK-47. Both of them, looking for the doctor, were violent, but neither, Dr Ngor thought, could have been older than about twelve. Other guerrillas in ragged black uniforms swarmed over the hospital grounds, and he saw that most of them held AK-47s, the communist assault rifle with its ammunition clip unmistakably curving out from the underside of the stock in the shape of a banana. They had the same fierce, angry expressions as the two in the operating room. There was something excessive about their anger, he thought. Something had happened to these people in their years in the forests. They had been transformed. They were not like the Cambodians I had known, shy and a bit lazy and polite. Dr Ngor bluffed the two youngsters, alleging that the doctor they were looking for had just left. "Get out," they then shouted at everyone in the ward. "Get out! Everybody has to move. *Now.*"

On the pretext that there might be more American bombs falling, the Khmer Rouge herded the city's two to three million residents at gunpoint onto roads leading out into the countryside, houses and schools being searched and emptied. The boy soldiers who had invaded the hospital forced everyone, even critically ill patients, out of their hospital beds onto the roads. They too had to leave the city – or die on the way, which of course many did. What searing sights must have met the eyes of every stressed and bewildered urban dweller! As no one was allowed to give other poor victims succour, many who were elderly and weak at the outset soon died along the roads leading out of the capital. Thousands of fitter people

---

[2]   Dr Ngor became famous both for his book, *Surviving the Killing Fields* (Chatto & Windus, 1988) and for his role in the film *The Killing Fields*. Despite his family's fear for his life, he campaigned throughout the USA for peace in his war-torn country, speaking in UN meetings and creating the Dr Haing S. Ngor Foundation with a view to improving the life of Cambodia's inhabitants. He was murdered in Los Angeles in 1996, a witness claiming that this had been on the orders of Pol Pot, still very much alive. The current goals of the Foundation include preserving the legacy of Dr Ngor's accomplishments and human rights endeavours as well as the promotion of Cambodia's history and culture through education, activism and the arts.

are believed also to have died too, in the utter chaos along the jammed roads that everyone was being driven along at gunpoint.

Once the Khmer Rouge soldiery had expelled every member of the diplomatic corps and all the Vietnamese and Chinese, who formerly had constituted the commercial backbone of society, Cambodia was completely sealed off from the rest of the world.[3] The usurpers of this hitherto most beautiful, ancient, highly cultured land then proceeded to wreak havoc. Intellectuals with names like Pol Pot, Khieu Sampan, Ieng Sary and Ta Mok, armed with university degrees from Paris but infected with Maoist ideas, attempted to reshape the country's economy on cooperative lines by driving everyone out of the towns to work in the fields while eliminating the upper strata of society. Prime targets for early elimination included all the previous government's armed forces and civilian employees, teachers, doctors and people in other professions – and their families. The Khmer Rouge regime was responsible for the death or disappearance of over 90% of Cambodian artists, including most of the dancers of the Royal Court Ballet. People in commerce and industry were liquidated. To be killed, without any form of trial, it was sufficient to wear glasses or to know a foreign language.

Horrific Measures

Dr Haing Ngor's book *Surviving the Killing Fields* goes a long way to explaining why educated men who had set themselves up as leaders of the nation murdered on that hallucinating scale. Gradually, a third of the population was eliminated. The new masters had the liberty, by force of arms, to do what they wished. AK-47s and other firearms, threats, deaths and torture were their only real tools, for they lacked a philosophy and they even lacked a real structure. Dr Ngor, who had realized instinctively that he could never reveal that he was a doctor, was among the masses who had to work as "war slaves". Continually moved from one place to another, living with no personal possessions, forced day after day to work and to attend propaganda meetings from four in the morning until midnight, people dropped from exhaustion after surviving for months on nothing but thin gruel dished out twice daily by the organization "Angka". Dr Ngor was forced to be yoked together with an ox to plough fields not yet softened by

---

[3]   A British diplomat friend of ours, after two weeks imprisoned in the French embassy compound with 2,000 other foreigners, was crammed with countless others onto the back of one of twenty lorries brought in to evacuate them. In the course of the next twenty-four hours before they reached the Thai border, they saw the same pagoda that they had passed the previous day.

the rains, and was whipped when the Khmer Rouge overseer thought he was not pulling hard enough.

He wrote years later that the victims of Khmer Rouge cruelty were told in propaganda sessions that the key concept for the new society was "independence-sovereignty", which for "Democratic Kampuchea" meant being absolutely free of other countries – free of their aid and even of their cultural influence. The deluded Khmer Rouge leaders seemed to imagine that, by reorganizing and harnessing the energy of the people and by eliminating everything that distracted from their work, Cambodia would become an advanced, developed nation almost overnight. That rapid development, or "great leap forward", as it was called, required, he wrote, our "correct revolutionary understanding" of many other concepts and terms. "For us it was almost like learning a new language. For example, there was the concept of 'struggle' – military talk, like 'front lines'. It reflected the idea that the nation was still at war."

They had already abolished religion, disrobing the monks (few of whom remained alive for long) and destroying the Buddha statues. The former surgeon wrote in his account that on the front lines they abolished the family too. They wanted people to renounce personal attachments of any kind, because those relationships interfered with their devotion to Angka. Children had to leave their parents, the elderly had to leave their sons and daughters, and if work assignments required it, husbands and wives had to split up too. "This was 'liberation', because it freed us from the time of caring for others and gave us more time to work."

Dr Ngor was in a group whose front lines leader was Chev. On a word from him, people were tied and taken to the forest, from whence they never returned. It was some time before the Khmer Rouge had succeeded in killing, or allowing to die from starvation and beatings, a third of the population. Then they turned upon one another. And so, reportedly taking their cue from China's Cultural Revolution and using arms and other equipment supplied by Peking (Beijing), the inhabitants of a peaceful Buddhist land enrolled as Khmer Rouge soldiers turned to mass violence. *Two million victims!*

The Khmer Rouge, like the Nazis before them, exercised unbelievable cruelty on millions of innocents. The term "holocaust" was to be used when the full horror came to light of Cambodia's suffering from the day of the Khmer Rouge takeover of 17 April 1975.

Collectivization was Angka's stated priority – second only to national security. In the interests of the former, Pol Pot's regime converted Phnom

Penh's secondary school, Lycée Tuol Svay Prey, into a prison, S.21 – and not just an ordinary prison. Grisly evidence of mass torture was found there after the Vietnamese overran Cambodia in December 1978 and found this place of horror, which they called Tuol Sleng.

What William Shawcross, in his book *The Quality of Mercy*, called "an organized assault" upon Buddhism was the desecration of the wats (Buddhist monasteries) and the violent treatment of the bonzes (monks). Buddhism "had been the glue which, together with the monarchy, held Cambodian society together", but that assault had the result of eliminating all but 3,000 of the 50,000 monks. The Catholic cathedral and the various churches in the capital were destroyed, while the regime cynically promulgated a constitution guaranteeing the right of every Cambodian "to worship according to any religion".

The Khmer Rouge surpassed all other communist regimes in their levelling of society by abolishing private households, forcing people to eat Angka's watery gruel in communal kitchens, and removing children from their parents to work in mobile agricultural teams. Schools had in any case been closed, most teachers liquidated. People were watched all the time by village presidents responsible for gathering security information about people under their surveillance, and by local informers, many of whom were children. Khmer Rouge troops were never far away. In the general atmosphere of fear that prevailed, as time went on partly accounted for by dissentions and purges within the ranks of the Khmer Rouge, implications that people were easily expendable discouraged resistance.

The population was forced not only to try to rehabilitate devastated stretches of the countryside, using only hoes and their bare hands, but also to work upon a new system of hydraulics introduced by the Khmer Rouge in defiance of the well-tested traditional methods. The wholesale destruction of centuries-old dykes was to make the country much more vulnerable in times of heavy rains. Floods, followed by drought, were to diminish the yields of two successive crops during those nightmare years. Severe economic hardship thus went hand in hand with the suppression of religion, education and indeed all that represented the former society, including traditional songs, festivals and modes of dress.

This was the country of which it was written:[4]

> The culture of Cambodia has always been central to the life
> of the people. A rich heritage in music, theatre and shadow
> puppetry has been surpassed only by the tradition of dance,

[4] *The Tenth Dancer*, BBC Education, IBT and Christian Aid, 1993.

which has inspired populations for centuries and to this day remains a strong symbol for the beauty of the spirit of the Cambodian people.

Originally influenced by Indian religion and art, the Cambodian people adapted the stories and movements by incorporating a wide range of mythologies to suit their own history and tastes.

Litany Of Even More Disaster

When on 25 December 1978 the Vietnamese invaded the country called "Democratic Kampuchea", the generalized violence intensified, and the Khmer Rouge took hundreds of thousands of people with them in their retreat towards the Thai border. Fighting between the Khmer Rouge and the Vietnamese would continue for ten further agonizing years.

As the Vietnamese consolidated their grip on the country, installing a regime headed by Heng Samrin, who was a former Khmer Rouge officer, there was a chronic shortage of food, and it was believed that the Vietnamese were looting a good amount of the relief goods sent in, including rice, sending some of the rice to Vietnam and using the rest for their own troops. Dr Ngor writes of people who for the most part were of rural origin, until the 1970s never previously uprooted: "The people were hungry, and they were tired of communism. They wanted freedom. They wanted rice. And all of Cambodia was on the move, fleeing, marching, stumbling, spilling over the border into Thailand."

It is estimated that between 600,000 and 750,000 "Kampucheans" staggered across the border in extremis, emaciated and no doubt in most cases deeply affected by their traumas. Among them were several thousand children of all ages, who had no idea where their parents were, or if they were alive at all. The existence on the border of large numbers of Cambodians not recognized as refugees posed very serious problems, particularly as they were under the control of Khmer Rouge cadres. They left behind a scattered population thought to number no more than four and a half million, who had at first pathetically welcomed the arrival of the Vietnamese as liberators and now suffered in extreme need. Their own "leaders" had forced them to experience a living nightmare, their bequest a country ravaged, famished and lost.

Fortunately, those monsters were in full control of Cambodia only from 17 April 1975 to the end of 1978, not quite four years. But ironically, through the most unfortunate contortions of international politics, far from being brought to account for their atrocities, they actually retained a seat in the United Nations for a number of years. What is more, by the force of arms, and trading on Thailand's disinclination to accept further refugees, they held a large displaced population captive on the Thailand–Cambodia border for fourteen terrible years, from 1979 to 1992–93. These were not the only tragedies besetting the Cambodian people. From April to June 1979, Thailand – unwilling, as it had said publicly, to afford a haven to more refugees unless they could immediately be moved to third countries[5] – forced well over 40,000 people back across the border to almost certain death for the majority, over precipices, through the minefields and at the hands of Khmer Rouge soldiery involved with fighting the Vietnamese.

Aid agencies – principally, to start with, the ICRC and UNICEF – found themselves in serious dilemmas. If they brought urgently needed food and medicines to the border populations where people were starving, they were seen by Phnom Penh to be helping the Khmer Rouge. Naturally, they wished at the same time to carry out urgent relief aid to the decimated population of the country itself, though their two senior representatives were allowed by the Vietnamese only a forty-eight-hour visit to Phnom Penh. William Shawcross wrote that that the two men's first impression of Cambodia was of overwhelming emptiness. On the short flight from Ho Chi Minh City they saw through the aircraft windows that almost all the fields below seemed to be untilled, though they should by then have been well planted if there was to be a 1979 main-season crop. The villages looked deserted, and no boats were to be seen on the rivers. Phnom Penh airport appeared abandoned, and in the town itself shops and houses were ransacked, the streets littered with rubbish and wrecked cars. The international representatives were shown an orphanage, where hundreds of children were in a pitiful condition, without food, without drugs, near death.

Shawcross writes that, on this first trip, Messrs Beaumont and Bugnion were lodged in the government guesthouse. Everything was ramshackle. Water and electricity were intermittent; food was very scarce. Their interpreters from the Foreign Ministry seemed so weak from lack of food that they occasionally fainted. The two international agency visitors shared with them whatever food they had brought and handed over suitcases filled with 200 kilos of medicines to officials from the Ministry of Health, who had tears in their eyes as they carried them away. One reportedly said, "For almost five years we have seen thousands and thousands of our people dying, while we were unable to give them any assistance. Now we are becoming doctors again."

---

[5]   From May 1975 onwards, Thailand had already received large numbers of lowland and highland Lao as well as thousands of Vietnamese "boat people".

Evidently, every Cambodian to whom the two men talked had a horror story to tell about life under "Pol Pot"; everyone, it seemed, had lost at least one member of his family, by murder, starvation or disease. At the end of their brief visit, Beaumont and Bugnion met President Heng Samrin, who did not impress them. He too had been an officer in the Khmer Rouge, until he defected to Vietnam in 1978. He spoke only in general terms, but he told them, with no trace of self-consciousness, that "two million people are starving as a consequence of the Pol Pot time".

A group of Scandinavian ambassadors from Peking (Beijing) made a brief visit to Phnom Penh, finding it "a ghost city". In the subsequent months, all the Western aid representatives were up against situations in which the ministries set up by the Vietnamese were staffed by people without experience (or much education), who it seemed lacked even pencils and paper to work with, let alone other equipment. There were no telephone lines. And there was maddening bureaucracy, all proposed measures having to be approved by Vietnam and agonizing delays occurring in the face of what was said to be a very high risk of mass starvation. "Two million dead by Christmas?" was a headline in not a few newspapers on both sides of the Atlantic. There were unverifiable claims by people in Ho Chi Minh City and Phnom Penh that considerable aid had already been provided by the "socialist countries". One had to hope that the claims were well founded.

At all events, the Phnom Penh government said that, in the previous four years, two to three million of the population, or up to 45% of a population of 7.5 million in 1975, were either deliberately exterminated or perished from physical exhaustion. "The remaining population of Kampuchea faces utter deprivation... with famine an ever-present threat. Most of the people are in rags, with no shoes, and even the government's civil servants have at most one shirt and one pair of pants."[6]

To make matters even worse, three opposition groups were now in existence: Pol Pot and his adherents headed the Kampuchea Democratic Party, still enjoying the support of China and managing for years to have the status of diplomats as representatives of the government of Kampuchea, which was still holding a seat in the United Nations; Prince Sihanouk and his partisans had created the National United Front for an Independent, Neutral, Peaceful and Cooperative Cambodia, FUNCINPEC; and Son Sann, a former minister of the royalist government, in 1979 founded the National Liberation Front of the Khmer People, FLNPK. For another ten

---

[6] From a widely circulated report by a UN official, Victor Umbrecht, quoted by Shawcross (*op. cit.*, pp.115–116).

years, there would be ongoing conflict across the north-western reaches of the stricken country, so there was no question of repatriation for the huge numbers of refugees at Khao I Dang and the "displaced persons" trapped on the Thailand–Cambodia border. It would be more than ten years before any of the criminals of the Khmer Rouge regime could be brought before an international tribunal.

Part II – Reaching Hundreds Of Thousands Of Cambodian Refugees In The Camps

Although UNHCR was not set up to be operational, on Monday 22 October 1979, a new field officer posted to Bangkok, Mark Malloch-Brown,[7] was taken by Thai officers to an empty field near a small town called Sa Kaeo, about forty miles from the Cambodian border. Mark, a twenty-six-year-old British journalist, had been among the dozen or so highly motivated young people recruited by UNHCR and coming through my door one by one in the late summer of 1979 to be briefed, ostensibly on the resettlement of Indochinese refugees. No one at headquarters had briefed him on how to set up a camp for 90,000 people from a stretch of bog and to do it in the space of forty-eight hours, and in fact no one had the slightest idea of how this could be done anyway. UNHCR was never supposed to become operational!

That Monday, he was told that he had to build a camp, for 60,000 "illegal immigrants" would be arriving en masse between Wednesday and Saturday. He did a fine job, aided by his Thai assistant, Kasidid Rochanakorn, and another UNHCR officer, Ted Schweitzer, obtaining a bulldozer and starting to carve roads in the mud. He contracted for a warehouse to be built, rented a backhoe to dig latrines, arranged for water to be trucked in from six kilometres away and hired a company to purify water. Then he hired 200 local Thais at $2 a day for construction work. Soon other international agencies joined in the effort: buying water tanks, bringing in huge quantities of bamboo and thatch to build a clinic and some huts, and so on. Many other people, Thais and foreigners, were coming from Bangkok volunteering their services.

The arrival of the first 15,000 people from the border area on 24 and 25 October led to a medical crisis, with no adequate medical relief measures

---

[7] Mark achieved a "tour de force" in creating the Sa Kaeo camp in the nick of time to receive the first 15,000 Cambodians. Over the intervening years, this resourceful and highly capable man, Baron Malloch-Brown, KCMG, PC, has run the United Nations Development Programme, served the UN as deputy Secretary-General and been a UK government minister.

as yet in the camp. Those brought in were people who had fled with the Khmer Rouge earlier in the year, and had lived in the forests for months with little or no food, prey to a fatal form of malaria. Some unfortunate people had been in such a very weakened state that they died in the trucks. At the beginning, thirty people were dying daily at Sa Kaeo, and for several weeks the situation was so serious that it discredited UNHCR and even the ICRC. Mark received critically needed help from the US embassy in the persons of three capable engineers, and in time, problems were overcome. At Khao I Dang, another camp established at virtually the same time under Mark Malloch-Brown's authority to receive further large groups of weakened Cambodian refugees arriving *in extremis*, parallel problems had to be faced and resolved, somehow or other.

In Khao I Dang, situated within six kilometres of the Thailand–Cambodia border and soon to become the largest refugee camp of all, there would be almost forty agencies working among the 130,000 refugees. The relief personnel coming to both these camps were part of an intense international effort mounted by the ICRC, UNICEF, UNHCR, the World Food Programme and a miscellany of NGOs. They provided immense quantities of medicines, foodstuffs, water, shelter and other support, and saved thousands of lives. A Swedish "Save the Children" agency (Rädda Barnen) provided a team of social workers to conduct interviews with thousands of unaccompanied children, with a view to providing information likely to be helpful in the tracing of any family members still living, and to make recommendations regarding the best long-term solution for each child. It was headed by Kate Tiborn, who had already documented thousands of children in the "boat people" camps in Malaysia. The young Swedes found that some of the children were listless, dispirited and despondent – which was of course to be expected, given what they had been through over the previous chaotic years. In two chapters of this book, Chapters 9 and 15, we can see the effect on children of war, abandonment and migration.

In the medium to long term, most of the refugees housed in Khao I Dang, Sa Kaeo and a third camp, Kamput, that was also run by the UNHCR with the Thai authorities, were eligible for resettlement in other countries. Over the years following their arrival in Khao I Dang (to which camp the populations of the two other camps, Sa Kaeo and Kamput, would be transferred at the end of 1982), appreciable numbers came to leave for resettlement in the West and large numbers of them went to the USA. But it would not be until 1991 that there would be any hope of repatriation to Cambodia of all those people who were not eligible (like those in the border camps), or not keen, to be resettled. On 23 October 1991, exactly twelve years after Sa Kaeo and Khao I Dang camps had been created on open Thai land, all parties except the Khmer Rouge signed a peace agreement in Paris, and in 1992–93 over 230,000 Cambodians left for home – the majority of whom had been stranded for about ten years in those insalubrious camps on the border ("Site 2" *et alia*) under the control of Khmer Rouge soldiery or representatives of the other two opposition parties.

Dr Jean-Pierre Hiegel

The International Committee of the Red Cross (ICRC) took the initial responsibility of providing medical services in the camps. Then early on, a French psychiatrist, Jean-Pierre Hiegel, became the ICRC's Medical Coordinator in all the Khmer camps, taking over the initial role of a senior ICRC man, Dr Rémi Russbach. The medical teams rapidly saw the need for a psychiatric ward, and to deal successfully with the problem of post-traumatic stress and other psychiatric disorders, Dr Hiegel opted for a solution involving the Cambodian traditional healers, people who he correctly assumed could be found among the tens of thousands of refugees. When his predecessor, Dr Rémi Russbach, head of ICRC's medical division in Geneva, gave his approval to this proposal, any doubts, fears and open opposition on the part of Western NGO medical practitioners had to be laid to rest.

Dr Hiegel had up to this point been first a member of a team of medical practitioners in France directed by a psychologist, Colette Landrac, then on leaving to explore Asia he had joined the team of Dr Bernard Kouchner, one of the founders of Médecins sans Frontières, on a rescue ship in the South China Sea. In the preface to the book published in the early 1990s by Dr Hiegel and his wife Colette,[8] Dr Bernard Kouchner heaps praise on his erstwhile colleague, particularly his ability to listen to survivors and to persevere in solving problems. He rated as a stroke of genius Dr Hiegel's idea of organizing for people who had lost everything – their families, their roots, their past, their hopes – a special physical environment in the form of a large airy bamboo edifice in which Cambodian traditional healers (the *kru* or *kru khmer*) and traditional midwives would provide suffering refugees with their various forms of traditional medicine. At the same time, Dr Hiegel and other Western medical practitioners would be taking care of aspects of people's health, such as tuberculosis, cancer or a broken limb,

---

[8]   Jean-Pierre Hiegel and Colette Hiegel-Landrac, *Vivre et revire au camp de Khao I Dang – une psychiatrie humanitaire* (Fayard).

found to require other forms of treatment. So a unique combination of traditional and Western medicine came into being.

Dr Russbach, in his introduction to the book, wrote of Jean-Pierre's early mind-searching combined with his basic certainty of the therapeutic value of people finding resources in their own deeply buried basic values. Given that the brainwashing of the Khmer Rouge had not achieved the destructive purposes intended (except, as it was to prove, insofar as young committed Khmer Rouge fighters were concerned), freedom of thought had been preserved to a marked extent, and the safeguarding of the considerable Khmer cultural wisdom and practice in the teeth of barbarity and violence had after all been assured.

When, after an introductory period of setting up essential medical services in Khao I Dang, the ICRC needed to hand over to another entity the financial responsibility for the planned activity, the Order of Malta[9] agreed to take it on for six months, provided Jean-Pierre Hiegel remained in charge. It was to extend its support, to which other organizations contributed, for over twelve years, until the repatriation operation ended in April 1993.

Jean-Pierre Hiegel worked in Khao I Dang from its conception to its closure fourteen years later. As time went on, his former boss Colette Landrac decided to travel to Thailand to visit him. She spent two weeks observing him at work, then she went back to Paris to give up her job and pack for Khao I Dang! The two of them worked closely together, got married, and went on with the work together year after year. Thanks to the meticulous records they kept (despite not having the use of a computer before late 1990) they brought out the book *Vivre et revivre au camp de Khao I Dang – Humanitarian Psychiatry* (500 pp, Fayard).[10] It is a unique record of pioneer work carried out along with traditional healers among traumatized people on the other side of the world. Describing numbers of those individuals who came in particular need to the Khao I Dang traditional medicine centre (TMC), it depicts the means found alongside the traditional healers, traditional midwives and other medical staff to relieve distress and psychiatric harm, enabling people to cope with their

---

[9] The Order of Malta is permanently present with medical, social and humanitarian projects in most countries of the world. Its 13,500 members, 80,000 volunteers and qualified staff of 42,000 professionals, mostly medical personnel and paramedics, form a network including everything from emergency relief for refugees and displaced persons who have lived through war and conflict to intervention in areas hit by natural disasters.

[10] It is a book that really deserved to be published in English. I offered to translate it, and did so, but unfortunately, Colette did not manage to find a publisher.

lives in the camp until such time as either resettlement or repatriation would take them forward.

Western Medical Personnel And Traditional Cambodian Healers

The Traditional Medicine Centres (TMC)

When it was realized that the state of mental and physical health of the Cambodian refugees called for the initiation of particular forms of support, the first purpose-built centre was designed for Sa Kaeo by a young ICRC architect, Jean de Spiegeler. It became the model for similar centres created in Kamput and Khao I Dang, in which programmes of traditional medicine and mental health were to be run by Jean-Pierre Hiegel. Dr Hiegel also worked in the camps of Phanat Nikhom, Ban Napho and Ban Thad, which housed for varying periods refugees of other ethnic groups, including lowland Lao, highland Hmong and Yao, and Vietnamese.

The Khao I Dang TMC, situated some way from the camp hospitals and dispensaries, was a huge hall in which, in the fullness of time, up to a thousand people could come per day for consultations and treatment. Its overall usefulness and its peaceful, harmonious nature evolved little by little as Dr Hiegel and others became increasingly aware of what it could become – a place of healing and, after a period of several years, even one of overnight accommodation for some of the most mentally ill.

The overall design, being devoid of partitions, meant that people could be observed conferring with the traditional healers or midwives, seated with them on raised platforms. They would be receiving counselling and appropriate treatment that consisted, for example, of massages, steam baths or the supply of different medicines based on plants. There were other raised areas for the preparation of ointments, powders or pills from fruit, flowers, seeds, roots and bark, mixed in accordance with age-old recipes. In a nearby kitchen, huge pots would be boiling a miscellany of ingredients as part of the preparation of ointments, which, before being applied to body parts, might be mixed with honey. The *krus* made the pills from various herbs, rolling them between their fingers and then leaving the resulting substance to dry before cutting it up into small pills.

The refugees were familiar from before the 1970s both with the *krus* and with the traditional midwives and their methods, and then everyone had after all been through the same terrible experiences in Cambodia, so they felt fully at ease with them, whether their ailments were physical or psychological (or both). This way, refugees suffering from post-traumatic stress and other psychiatric ailments were largely taken in hand by members of their own community, and helped in line with their own deeply held cultural beliefs, while benefiting as need arose from the support of modern psychiatry.

Dr Hiegel, before joining hands with traditional healers, had taken care to ensure that these were responsible, experienced men who fully deserved the trust and esteem of their fellow countrymen and women. In order to get to work closely with these men, who had probably never met a qualified Western doctor before, he demonstrated respect and humility, qualities that were in any case part of his approach to his mission. Gradually, the *krus* came to understand that they could not resolve all the health problems in the camp without recourse to modern medicine, so a unique partnership was established that lasted for the fourteen years of the life of Khao I Dang. The often vehement opposition voiced initially by Western medical practitioners and certain religious groups had to be tempered with reasoning and with the help of concrete examples of what the *krus* were capable of doing for the sick. Even so, Dr Hiegel, aware that the *krus* exercised a high standard of medical ethics,[11] sometimes found that he had to defend them from quarters that found unjustifiable ways of attacking them. But, fortunately, in time there was sufficient mutual respect for the traditional healers to refer cases to the qualified doctors – and even vice versa. And, on occasion, both parties would examine a patient together!

Working with the traditional healers involved a combination of the substantial knowledge and proven techniques of both parties – that is to say, the traditional healers on the one hand and the scientifically trained practitioners on the other. Maintaining the identity and the specificity of each would be a guarantee of safety. Furthermore, it was important to preserve the right of each individual to consult whom he or she wished; or, in the event of the person making the wrong choice, to be able to switch the type of treatment initially given to the only effective one (for example an operation for appendicitis) in order to save a the person's life.

We are again talking in this chapter about a period in which PTSD was only just being defined in the USA (1980) and its symptoms listed by the American Psychiatric Association (1987). Dr Hiegel, half a world away, noted the prevalence of somatic ailments, and if he did not necessarily attribute them to psychological (psychosomatic) causes, as a psychiatrist he probably understood, better than most other doctors could have done in the same circumstances, the depth of suffering, past and indeed present,

---

[11] There were some exceptions: Dr Hiegel had to watch the situation, and get rid of a few charlatans.

of practically every Cambodian admitted to the camps. In due time, with Colette, his wife, he recorded all the cases of overt mental illness. As for all the deep emotional scars that many people had, the treatments of the traditional healers seemed to go a long way to healing them, as would the longed-for chance to return to Cambodia. After all, the whole community was therapeutic, the TMCs being set up not only to heal physical wounds, sores or other ailments but to pour balm on bodies and minds that had been tested and tried beyond any reasonable limits.

Caring For The Mentally Ill

It was inevitable that there should be people, including children, who were psychotic and would probably need very careful treatment over a prolonged period. After the four agonizing years under the Khmer Rouge, people needed to get back to their traditions and their culture, even though their homes had remained far out of reach (if not destroyed). Many attributed both physical and psychological problems to the spirits, who had been forcibly neglected throughout those years of violent repression, and were now thought most likely to be wishing to remind people of their presence by causing health problems. For many, the magical treatment of the *krus* worked wonders, though for psychotic patients it was far from adequate.

Dr Hiegel was made aware of the extremely violent behaviour of a very sick woman, Mom, alone in the camp. He learned from others that she had been a French teacher in Cambodia, before losing both husband and baby through unimaginable atrocities at the hands of Khmer Rouge soldiers. In the camp, she had been so mentally ill that her mother and other family members had left without her to be resettled in the West. She had been taken in by a traditional midwife, who, over several years, cared for her in her own home, washing and feeding her, and repairing the clothes she had torn and the bamboo walls she had tried to tear down. Dr Hiegel began to treat her psychosis, but realized that, as soon as she seemed a little better, the intolerable scenes that had caused her madness came back and she took refuge in renewed lunatic behaviour. Realizing that this was her escape from the acute suffering of her unbearable recollections, Dr Hiegel delayed the treatment for quite some time, until the understanding and support poor Mom was receiving from other Khmers, and in particular from that kind midwife, seemed to warrant another attempt to deal with her psychosis. She then, under treatment, appeared to attain a state of serenity, spending days reading aloud in a strange, chanting voice to a group of children from a French book that she no longer understood. Finally, she asked about her mother, contact was re-established and she was able to join her abroad.

It appeared that for some mentally ill refugees, outbursts of schizophrenic behaviour could be a survival strategy, to stave off recollections of atrocities simply too painful to bear. Other cases were reported by Dr Hiegel of mentally sick patients who had no living relatives, either in the camps or back in Cambodia, being "adopted" by other Khmer, who eventually saw them through to a return home, even settling down with them in the same village.

Ways of accommodating mentally ill patients overnight came up as a real challenge after violent bouts of fighting just inside the Cambodian border between the Vietnamese army and opposition fighters brought to Khao I Dang a significant number of mental patients from among the many tens of thousands of new border-crossers. They were without any family members. At this point, the TMC was functioning well as a day centre, where hundreds of people came for traditional treatment of various kinds and, at the same time, a day hospital for mental patients. It was decided to let the mentally ill patients sleep there too. There were no rooms or beds, and each patient simply slept on a mat on the bamboo floor under a mosquito net, that was taken up in the morning. The traditional practitioners provided a kind of surveillance. So the TMC became a place where the mentally ill could actually live, at least for periods.

In a report to cover the year 1986, Jean-Pierre and Colette Hiegel described the TMC in these terms:

> The psychiatric patients are invited to stay in the TMC. Depending on their illness and their wishes, they stay part-time or full-time and may even spend the night there. In fact, the TMC has a role as day hospital or psychiatric hospital. It is a calm yet busy place where a large number of people of every kind live, work or simply come in and out: the traditional practitioners, midwives, masseurs, and traditional doctors who are usually mature people who command confidence and respect; the work people and assistants, engaged in the various tasks needing to be done in the preparation of the traditional remedies, in all about 80 refugees. Then the clients: every day hundreds of people – men, women, children, babies, old people – come in to consult the *krus* and receive traditional treatment. The whole of the TMC – the consultation area, entrance hall, garden, is a pleasant place where refugees come not only for treatment, but also for the pleasure of spending

a little time with people. In such an environment, the mental cases feel protected but also they get stimulation. All the patients who are ready and willing to work are invited to do so. About 30 of the work people on various tasks are actually patients who in the past, and sometimes the present, have psychiatric problems. But even if they are not ready (or not yet ready) to take on any work, they benefit from the psychological support of the community in which they can establish new relationships.

Khao I Dang's TMC in 1990 treated 538 mental cases, most of them from the border camps. There were sometimes 200 of them there are the same time, so with people accompanying them there were about 700 living and sleeping in the centre. In the same period, the twenty traditional practitioners received and treated daily an average of 130 patients coming to see them about physical complaints. It quite often happened that visitors, after looking round the TMC, asked "But where are the mentally sick?", some of them turning rather pale when they were told that they had been among them from the moment they arrived!

Many of the patients, from 1985 onwards and more particularly after 1989, were teenagers who had been suddenly thrown into the war and came to the TMC in a state of serious post-traumatic confusion or psychosis. Some of them had had experiences that had left them terrified, their facial expressions denoting horror. Everyone set about helping them, helping them to eat, to wash or to dress. They talked to them, and went out to bring them back to the TMC when they had got lost wandering about in the camp. If anyone had told these helpers that what they were doing was like a form of psychotherapy close to mothering, and actually just what good, ordinary people will do spontaneously in response to need, they might have started wondering whether to go on doing it!

One of those troubled youngsters was very agitated when he was brought in after undergoing surgery. He was violent and threatening, terrorizing everybody. One of his legs had been hit and had been put in plaster with an external attachment that he threatened to break, like everything else within his reach. He shouted that he didn't want to stay there, he was a resistance fighter, a Khmer Rouge warrior; he had to go and fight, free his country, kill the Vietnamese! … He pulled himself along on his bottom, shouting and threatening everyone. An elderly *kru* and an old midwife went over to him, talking to him in the simple language of country people, the *kru* putting an arm round his shoulders to get him to drink. The old midwife massaged him, talking gently to him. The little warrior broke down and cried. He was hurting, he was afraid, he was alone, he wanted his mother. The *kru* and the midwife stayed with him for a long time, until he quietly went off to sleep. He stayed in the centre for several days, calm and reassured. He kept on his plaster and the attachment.

There were children of all ages in the centre, belonging both to patients and to workers, as well as whole families living there. There were psychotics lulling babies that were not theirs. In a corner, forty or so severely mentally ill cases were continually involved with the production of the traditional medicaments, cutting up and crushing the different plants that were the basis of many powders or pills used by the *krus*.

Some of the help to traumatized Cambodians who had escaped to Thailand came from Dr Richard Mollica, who in 1981, with a small team, had set up the Indochinese Psychiatric Clinic in Boston. In 1988 he went to the border camps having been begged by some of the Cambodians being treated in the IPC to help their surviving relatives. Arriving in Site 2, which he first described in the terms used by its residents: "a place of rape, murder, and human cruelty", he became conscious that the camp authorities denied the pain and suffering of the 150,000 people virtually imprisoned there. But the young psychiatrist goes on to describe how, against all the odds – since any form of work was strictly forbidden by the Thai authorities – people were managing to get some healing for their indisputably severe emotional wounds by carrying out illegal activities: "Residents were out doing anything and everything to survive, from buying and selling chickens to engaging in prostitution, babysitting, taxiing aid workers on bicycles, and sneaking outside the camp to forage for firewood." In his book *Healing Invisible Wounds*, Dr Mollica writes very tellingly of the abject situation that these many tens of thousands of Cambodians were in, year after year, but also of the self-healing that he observed was a process of which he had been observing the reality back in the USA.[12] In Chapters 19 and 20, I shall try to describe ways in which from 1978 onwards, trauma came to be understood and ways found of assuaging or alleviating post-traumatic stress.

---

[12] Richard A. Mollica: *Healing Invisible Wounds – Paths to Hope and Recovery in a Violent World*, Chapter 4, pp.88–109.

Back In Cambodia

Many welfare agencies have done their best since the early 1990s to support both those who returned to their stricken country from the Thai camps and those who had never left Cambodia. One person whose story should be told is that of the late Dr Beat Richner, a Swiss who opened hospital after hospital where Cambodians could be treated free of charge. These hospitals were funded by private donations and by the sale of tickets to concerts that he, a very talented cellist, gave whenever he was back in Europe.

As a young man, Dr Richner, after obtaining his degree and specializing in paediatrics, had been sent to Cambodia by the Swiss Red Cross to work in the hospital of Phnom Penh, but he was forced to leave when the Khmer Rouge took over the country. Sixteen years later, the government in Phnom Penh asked Dr Richner to return to Cambodia and rebuild and manage the Kantha Bopha Hospital. He moved to Phnom Penh, where under his direction the hospital was rebuilt and soon cared for 1,000 outpatients, performing over 350 operations a day. In 1996, on being invited by Prince Norodom Sihanouk to build in the grounds of his palace, Dr Richner built a second hospital. He then gave the rest of his life to opening other hospitals in different parts of the country. He died in September 2018 at the age of seventy-one.

A Danish clinical psychologist, Dr Inger Agger, concluded a seven-month research project in Cambodia a few years ago in which she explored local Buddhist approaches to the healing of violence-related trauma. Her paper, published in 2015, is entitled "Calming the Mind: Healing after Mass Atrocity in Cambodia". As Dr Agger wrote in her abstract, a high prevalence of PTSD, depression and anxiety was found in surveys carried out in Cambodia that were based on the diagnostic categories we have seen earlier. Her study explored Cambodian approaches to healing trauma, "examining the ways in which Cambodians appeal to elements of Buddhism in their efforts to calm their minds, situating this mode of coping in the context of broader Khmer Buddhist practice and understandings."

People involved in treating Cambodians, Lao and Vietnamese – like Dr Hiegel – soon became aware that Western psychology had much to learn from local "contextualized" methods of dealing with the aftermath of trauma, including the Khmer understanding of distress and approaches to relief. In other words, as Inger Agger says, "methods of assessment and treatment of distress cannot be transposed wholesale from one cultural setting to another but require considerable cultural adaptation". Other researchers reached the same conclusion, for example Maurice Eisenbruch, who suggested that by suspending some of the Western preconceptions about suffering and mental health "and learning what we can of reality as it is experienced by our informants, insights that can help us critically evaluate and enrich our own models." This is of course what Dr Hiegel realized, and what Dr Mollica realized too early on, through the close contact he and the members of his small team at the Indochinese Psychiatric Clinic enjoyed from 1981 onwards. Eisenbruch went on to say that he had "noted the limitations of simply transposing Western diagnostic categories to characterize the distress experienced by Cambodian refugees."

Although several decades have passed since the Khmer Rouge terror, Cambodians continue to wonder how it could all have happened, and how to cope now.[13] Theravada Buddhism, formerly adhered to by a vast majority of the Cambodian population, has re-emerged, as Dr Agger found. There are indigenous practices that Cambodians can call upon to help calm their distressed minds.[14]

> The concept of mindfulness is central to the Theravada Buddhist tradition. Khmer Buddhism, an amalgam of pre-existing animist and Hindu traditions onto which Buddhism was later grafted, also offers numerous other approaches to healing, such as through medicinal herbs, spirit possession, and various "magical" practices.

We saw some of these approaches at work at the TMC in Khao I Dang camp. Dr Hiegel learned a great deal from the traditional Cambodian ways of tackling shock and distress, as demonstrated by the traditional healers and midwives. He doubtless could have written what the American psychiatrist Maurice Eisenbruch asserted in 1991 (over twelve years from the time Dr

[13] One researcher has written a six-part series that looks at the effects of PTSD on members of the Cambodian community in the USA, one part being entitled "At 92, she's still haunted by Khmer Rouge atrocities in Cambodia".

[14] practices that could have helped a deeply distressed young Cambodian (about whose life a film came to be made): given a scholarship in 1965 to study at Leipzig University, GDR, he went on to get a PhD in 1977 and did high-level research. Never having dreamt that he would be cut off from his roots for the rest of his life, he was numb on hearing that most of his family had been killed early in the Khmer Rouge years. Like many survivors, after that he was "thinking too much" – a key indicator of distress that neither his German wife (who finally wanted a divorce) nor the three daughters born to them could understand until after taking their father's ashes to Cambodia and participating in ceremonies, their father's funeral and a wedding, carried out entirely on the overwhelmingly beautiful traditional lines that the late Dr Ottara Kem must have been dreaming about.

Hiegel took over responsibility for the medical care of Cambodians in Khao I Dang and other camps), namely that approaches to calming the mind – through meditation, knowledge, and understanding – are particularly well-developed within the Buddhist canon and traditions.[15]

Dr Mollica and his team at the IPC realized early on how important it was to consider the ways in which Cambodians, as well as Lao and Vietnamese, *experienced, understood* and *coped* with their distress. The same is true of Swiss medical specialists who were involved over several years with the Indochinese taken in by Switzerland (Chapter 12 of this book).

Dr Agger came to realize that one mental health problem, "thinking too much", was a key indicator of distress – thinking about upsetting topics, past traumatic events and separation by death from loved ones. The Khmer expression *kut caraeun* could lead to headaches, dizziness, depletion of bodily energy and what Cambodians sometimes referred to as a heating of the brain or excessive heat in the head – symptoms indicating that the person, in distress, might experience anger that could be expressed in violent, antisocial behaviour.

Introducing the subject of nightmares, Dr Agger wrote,

> A second significant mental health problem among Cambodian survivors of the Khmer Rouge period is that of recurrent, disturbing dreams about loved ones who died untimely or violent deaths during the regime. In Cambodia, it is widely believed that the spirits of those who die a violent death may be unable to find peace. … The problem of restless and hungry ghosts is exacerbated when funeral rites were not performed according to proper Buddhist custom—something that was impossible under the Khmer Rouge, who banned Buddhism.

The IPC team in Boston had patients who were grieving for this very reason, their anxiety leading to the ambition to perform the funeral rites, be it decades after the deaths of their family members.

Dr Agger in the course of her detailed research work in Cambodia, learned of the following methods that Cambodians use for calming the mind:

---

[15] M. Eisenbruch, From Post-traumatic Stress Disorder to Cultural Bereavement. Diagnosis of South East Asian Refugees, *Social Science and Medicine*, Vol. 33, No. 6 (1991) 673–680.

Meditation:

Various forms of meditation are practiced [*sic*] in Cambodia, but two of the most commonly mentioned during the fieldwork were *samadhi* (stilling the mind through mental concentration) and *vipassana* (insight) meditation, which involves the acquisition of self-knowledge and insight into the true nature of reality. In interviews, people who had experienced Khmer Rouge atrocities sometimes described how they used meditation as a coping strategy. For instance, a middle-aged male survivor in Pursat Province described how he practiced *samadhi*:

> [To] calm my feelings and to cool my body. I noticed that if I was thinking too much I felt so hot in my head. Now it is released, even though there are still some family problems which make me feel a little bit of headache, but I can solve this.

A male teacher at a meditation centre in Siem Reap Province explained how meditation can help survivors:

> They do meditation or relaxation with breathing exercises until their breath becomes normal again. They come here to calm their feeling, so it can lead them to gain more energy inside and to push their nervous system to run more smoothly.

It became apparent that as in the USA, most survivors turned to monks for advice about how to deal with mental suffering, so as not to be overwhelmed by feelings about the past. Buddhism recognizes that suffering is an intrinsic feature of the human condition, and the objective of meditation is not to abolish suffering but to transcend it. "Meditation and mindfulness not only alleviate the suffering caused by 'thinking too much' but also lead to moral behaviour in line with the Buddha's teachings."

Making Merit For The Deceased

Dr Agger explains that in Cambodia, "it is recognized that healthy grieving involves maintaining a good relationship with the dead and perhaps assisting the dead towards rebirth. The spirits of those who died a violent death or whose bodies were not ritually handled by monks may continue to experience distress and unfulfilled needs even after death and they may continue to disturb their surviving relatives." Therefore, efforts to "calm the mind" may need to be directed not simply to the living individual but also to their relationship with the dead, and she gives the following examples:

> A middle-aged female survivor of the Khmer Rouge regime from a village in Takeo Province explained,
>
> They died and there were many victims killed during the Khmer Rouge regime. So we are here at the pagoda to let them know that the survivors care for them, to help their souls calm down and to assist them to find a place and be reborn. So we pray for them and make offerings to them.

Similarly, a middle-aged man from the same village said,

> Because we are Khmer Rouge victims and thinking too much about the past, about family members who were killed, they have rituals to make us feel calm and relief from pain and relief from grief. This is also to calm the spirit of the dead.

Another male survivor from the village elaborated,

> I think the dead are still here, because I often dream of them and maybe we have not offered enough for them to be reborn. They were killed, they are still out there, but if they had died naturally they could have been reborn. They are still calling for us, because we think of them and dream of them. Sometimes we sleep well, and sometimes we dream that they come to see us. Those who were killed, their souls are still out there and cannot find a place to be reborn.

Something else that is found to calm the mind, as Dr Agger reports, is the ritual chanting by the monks in Pali, a language that Cambodian lay people do not understand, but the rhythm and melody of the chanting gives them a feeling of inner peace.[16] Dr Agger included in her paper a

---

[16] I had the privilege of experiencing similar chanting in Laos, being invited to festivals such as a wedding and a funeral, and also in relation to a friendly little ceremony known as a *baci*, held fairly frequently within the UNHCR Regional Office, Vientiane, in relation to the arrival or the departure of people connected with our work in Laos.

description of the annual two-week Festival of the dead, that she writes is "the most spectacular instance of social healing that involves the dead."

Cambodian Parents and Cambodian Minors in the USA

The United States, heavily involved in Indochina in the 1960s and 1970s, opened generous resettlement quotas that enabled very large numbers of refugees from Laos, Vietnam and Cambodia to go the USA. In UNHCR's Geneva Headquarters, as the only resettlement officer concerned with the outpourings of Indochinese refugees across almost all of South East Asia and the obligation of "the West" to take them in, I was in daily contact with officers of the US Mission to the UN and their counterparts from other countries' missions, at the same time conscious that there were bound to be multiple problems of integration for these hundreds of thousands to be moved to new countries.

Given what we can believe about the Cambodians' state of mind on leaving Thailand, coupled (without a doubt) with the culture shock that most if not all of them who landed on the other side of the world must have felt, we can only too readily imagine that many of them came sooner or later to attend psychiatric clinics, and this has been confirmed by Dr Richard Mollica in his book referred to earlier.[17] The question then was, of course, in those early years, what treatment would be appropriate for these people from the other side of the world...

Quite a high proportion were diagnosed with PTSD. A report published in May 1986 of a study of forty young Cambodian high school children found that half of them developed PTSD four years after leaving Cambodia, where under Pol Pot they had endured separation from their families, forced labour and starvation. They had all witnessed many deaths. Their psychiatric problems were found to be more common and more severe when they were not with a family member.[18]

Most refugees are strong individuals, who may arrive in a country of resettlement with high hopes and yet be prepared for some setbacks. The chance to make a new start is sure to bring its challenges: how do you find your way around in a new society, forge links with strangers and find work when you hardly know the language? It's a long, slow climb back to

---

[17] Richard A. Molica, *op. cit.* (*Healing Invisible Wounds – Paths to Hope and Recovery in a Violent World*).

[18] David Kinziem, William H. Sack MD, Richard Hangell MD, Spero Manson PhD, The Psychiatric Effects of Massive Trauma on Cambodian Children, *Journal of the American Academy of Child Psychiatry*, Vol. 25, Issue of 3 May 1986, 370–376.

a decent way of life. Meanwhile, your damaged self-respect remains fragile, and the space needed to process grief for all that has gone before is still lacking. Most people don't recognize that you are a disaster victim, perhaps scarred for life by what you have been through.

As the late Dr Haing Ngor said: "They wanted us all to rebuild our lives. But we didn't have some of the pieces."

An article dated 22 April 2012 by Greg Mellen in the *Long Beach Press* spoke of the high incidence of PTSD among Cambodian refugees, featuring depression and anxiety in particular. He wrote that PTSD from Cambodia's killing fields affected kids who had never been there. Many had to deal with the fallout from a damaged generation of survivors who were now raising families, still struggling to fit into a new culture and inadvertently passing along much of the pain for their children to sift through. As Cambodian-Americans and children of refugees, he gave two examples in particular, Sin and Em, as carrying a difficult legacy. They "have borne trauma passed on from parents. They experience symptoms that can range from extreme anxiety to emotional numbness, from violence to withdrawal, from hyper-arousal and activity to clinical depression."

Sam Keo, a genocide survivor and licensed clinical psychologist, says kids who grow up around PTSD can't help but be affected. "It's not genetic, but if you hang around someone with PTSD, you're going to get something," he says. That something is called "intergenerational transmission of trauma". Em says she has had to miss school and other functions to take her parents to appointments to provide translation and fill out forms. "It gets passed down, all the symptoms," she said of PTSD. Sin has inherited characteristics of PTSD from her experiences. "I don't get over stuff," she says. "I find it hard to stay focused on the things I need to do."

Sin and Em are part of Khmer Girls in Action, a teenage advocacy group in Long Beach. Recently KGA, under the supervision of UCLA (University College of Los Angeles) conducted a wellness survey of about 500 Khmer youth in Long Beach. The study highlighted some troubling trends. It showed that nearly half the youth displayed symptoms of depression, including feelings of loneliness, fear and insomnia. Also, 56% of the Cambodian youth felt discriminated against in jobs, education and language access. "Many people have been racist toward me," said Lyiah Kai, a Poly High Student. "I felt scared and alone."

Many experts agree that knowledge is power in the fight against PTSD. And young people are often desperate to learn about and better understand their parents and their experiences. "I try to get them to talk about the genocide but it's so taboo to talk about," Em said. "But we have to deal with it."

Sam Keo says it is vital for parents to share their stories with their children, although he cautions that parents need to wait until their children are old enough to understand. But many Cambodian parents seem to be forever silently stuck in 1975. "They're not letting go of the past. They still feel they're victims."

It took Keo nearly twenty years to write his book. He said that at times it was so painful that he would break down after each paragraph. He says that understanding is the most important thing one can offer. "When you see the children of these refugees, perhaps already born in this country, please think that they too have some of these invisible scars," he says. "They witness their parents' reactions and internalize these as if they were their own. The horrors of war do not end with the refugees, but they continue to be lived by their children and their children's children."

Theanvy Kuoch, a refugee who lost nineteen relatives to starvation and abuse in Cambodia, works with Cambodian survivors after training in cross-cultural family therapy in the USA. She is the executive director of Khmer Health Advocates in West Hartford, CT. She says that survivors often keep silent about life under the Khmer Rouge. They fear upsetting their children and grandchildren with talk of the past. Or they may have been terrorized into silence. "The people who lived under the Khmer Rouge understood one hundred percent that you must not talk at all. If you talk, you die. In order for you to survive, you must not talk at all. When survivors don't talk, though, the trauma can overwhelm them and potentially deprive their children of nurturing."

Theanvy Kuoch practises "contextual family therapy", an approach that considers the individual, but aims to benefit all family members. "Cambodian families have very close ties," she says. "When you see Cambodians, you're not only seeing one member of the family, you're seeing the whole family. It's really 'a whole family' problem." It is tragic that so many youngsters from Cambodia lost their parents during the Pol Pot years, cheated of the family structures they had known up to 1975.

The problems of integration are certainly multi-faceted. A Swiss doctor told me years ago of a young Cambodian he was trying to give support to. The young man had been granted Swiss nationality, but now, like all Swiss men under forty, he had to report for compulsory military service, and he was apparently very nervous and even anguished about that, particularly in relation to firearms. The poor young man must have been a child in the

Khmer Rouge years, when scenes of shootings and death must have got permanently imprinted on his mind.

Healing Invisible Wounds

In Chapters 19 and 20, we will look at the wonderful discoveries made since the early 1980s both in understanding the hitherto unknown phenomena of the sequelae of trauma and in finding invaluable ways in which sufferers can hope to be dispensed of their PTSD symptoms.

CHAPTER 11

Laos And Vietnam

The tragic history of Indochina in the decades that preceded the year 1975, particularly in relation to the US role in support of the government of South Vietnam, may still remain in many memories. In any case, the heavy bombing of all three countries – Vietnam, Laos and Cambodia – and the strafing with napalm and other chemicals of much of Vietnam that caused massive displacement of populations, along with almost irreparable damage to the land – and to individuals – were the subjects of sensational reports in even the most serious newspapers and television newsreels.

Laos, a small landlocked and largely mountainous country through which the great Mekong flows, is bordered by China, Vietnam, Burma/Myanmar, Thailand and Cambodia. Its traditional economy was essentially rural, and, apart from the capital, Vientiane, none of the towns – Savannakhet, Paksé, Luang Prabang (the old royal capital) and Sayabouri – had more than 50,000 inhabitants. The country, a monarchy for 700 years and once known as "the land of a million elephants", was a protectorate throughout the French colonial period, with large numbers of Vietnamese and Chinese given the responsibility for much of the administration. In 1954 Laos obtained its independence, with King Sisavang Vatthana its ruling monarch. Within years, however, there were discussions under the aegis of the United Nations to try to resolve the country's future, given the growing strength of the independence movement under North Vietnamese influence.

The two main population groupings of this small country have been the lowland Lao, living along river valleys and in towns, and the Hmong (or Meo) and other hill tribes, whose traditional habitat was always the high mountain regions (often over 3,000 metres above sea level), with very different apparel and way of life from the people of the plains. There are still members of small tribal groupings living in those highland areas of Laos that are virtually above the clouds, their social customs markedly different from those of other Laotians.

Following the signing of the Vientiane Peace Agreement of 1973 between the former Vientiane government and the revolutionary forces of the north, the Lao Patriotic Front[1] (Neo Lao Hak Sat), a provisional government of national unity was set up, led by Prince Souvanna Phouma as prime minister, with his half-brother Prince Souphanouvong as head of the National Consultative Political Council. Hitherto, the two princes had been opposed to each other, Souvanna Phouma, appointed the country's prime minister several times previously, representing the Vientiane government, and Souphanouvong representing the Lao Patriotic Front (of which the Pathet Lao was the fighting force).

The United Nations High Commissioner for Refugees, Prince Sadruddin Aga Khan, was asked by the 1973 UN General Assembly to give assistance to people of the three countries of Indochina who wanted to return to their home villages after being uprooted for several years by the Vietnam War. This, a totally new departure for the Office, meant establishing "special operations" in all three countries, provided, of course, that the respective authorities would give the green light. There were still two Vietnams (North and South), and the High Commissioner was soon authorized to set up offices in both Saigon and Hanoi, under the overall supervision of a regional representative in a new office in Vientiane, the colourful capital of Laos. Negotiations with Phnom Penh to work with the displaced in Cambodia were at an initial stage and, in view of subsequent events, were of course not destined come to anything.

The UNHCR team in Laos that was to work with the coalition government's "Mixed Commission", consisted, in line with those in Prince Sadruddin's other field offices, of a minimum of individuals, of whom from 20 March 1975 I was one. Entranced from the first day by the country, its peoples and its culture, I was often in an exalted mood, until (very soon) the major process of change within both Laos and Vietnam meant that while some people were being settled after years away from their homes, many others were becoming uprooted.

Vientiane was an enchanting town in which you would see many races mingling in the streets and in the huge daily market. While the majority races were the lowland Lao and the upland Hmong, there were ethnic

[1]   Originally they were nationalists and anti-French, becoming close to the anticolonial struggle in Vietnam… and adopting the communist vision of how to build a society.

Chinese, Thai, Vietnamese and minority races such as the Thai Dam. The lowland Lao in particular, several of whom were on our staff, were relaxed and friendly, generally ready to return a smile, to laugh over an incident or to enter into a conversation. Many (or most) spoke a little English or French. Women's dress was very decorous.[2] There was almost continuous music in the town, for wherever you went lyrical Lao ballads would emanate from people's radios, or you would hear people making music spontaneously along the roadside. At that time, it was very romantic music that you heard – before the changes that brought to everyone's ears rather martial music broadcast from loudspeakers installed across the length and breadth of the town.

In those early months of 1975, the Mixed Commission's mobile units were busy determining which of the displaced wished to return to their villages in the north, and those who did were transported by air and given initial assistance to settle. By April 1975, several hundred people were being taken daily to the Plain of Jars,[3] from whence they were moved to their ancestral homes. Aircraft of the Royal Lao Air Force and the Australian Air Force, as well as aircraft from the USSR and Royal Air Lao, participated in the airlift and took on board not only people but a good deal of personal property, including bicycles, sewing machines and even poultry.

This was satisfactory. However, as related in Chapter 10, April 1975 turned out to be a really terrifying month in Cambodia, with the entry into the capital, Phnom Penh, of the Khmer Rouge after five years of fighting, and the immediate initiation of depraved measures to bring the whole population of the country under very strict control.[4]

But not only that: *no later than the following week*, Thai papers reported that communist forces in Laos had broken the ceasefire, seizing territory that included a strategic road junction ninety miles north of the capital – a manoeuvre by the Pathet Lao that all too clearly indicated that they were not satisfied with the terms of the peace agreement that they had signed (no doubt reluctantly) twenty-seven months earlier.

---

[2]   The Lao girls and women mostly wore a sleeveless blouse and straight skirt to mid-calf, the latter having a band five or six inches deep around the hem that they had embroidered themselves in petit point.

[3]   A megalithic archaeological landscape in Laos. It consists of thousands of stone jars scattered around the upland valleys and the lower foothills of the central plain of the Xieng Khouang plateau.

[4]   On the staff of UNHCR's small regional office was a vivacious Cambodian girl, who became very anxious about her mother in Phnom Penh. There was of course a total news blackout in Cambodia for four years, and none of us was in Vientiane long enough to learn whether the girl's poor mother had managed to survive.

And then *just days after that, on 30 April,* South Vietnam's capital, Saigon, fell to the Viet Cong soldiery, causing widespread panic. Virtually before the eyes of the world there was a stampede of men and women desperate to get out of the country by any means. On 1 May, newspapers the world over announced the surrender of South Vietnam. *The Bangkok Post* wrote – under a huge headline: "THE WAR IS OVER: Communists in full control!"[5] – that the longest war in modern times had ended the previous day when South Vietnam surrendered unconditionally. It reported that, despite pockets of resistance fr om diehard troops of the Saigon regime, the capital fell virtually without a struggle. It depicted the scenes, with barefoot teenage guerrillas and heavily armed regulars in jungle fatigues riding in triumph through the streets bedecked with white surrender flats and thronged by cheering residents relieved that the end had come without a bloodbath. The collapse of South Vietnam came only hours after the Americans completed their disorderly pull-out, which President Ford described as closing a chapter in the American experience. Alistair Cooke in a *Letter from America* on BBC radio recalled how, ten years earlier in 1965, President Lyndon Johnson simply ridiculed his suggestion that eventually the United States might consign three or four hundred thousand troops to Vietnam. The idea was preposterous! He held out his arms reprovingly to Cooke. "Not 400,000", he smiled. "Not 300,000, not 200,000 – not even anything like 100,000 – I give you my word." But, in the end, the American presidents sent no fewer than 543,000 troops to Vietnam, and a new word, "escalation", was born.

Not everyone understood how it had all started. As Louis Heren indicated in *The Bangkok Post* on 1 May 1975, the American war in Indochina began on President Kennedy's New Frontier, as a liberal reaction to Khrushchev's support for wars of national liberation. The Special Forces were formed, and thousands of military advisers were sent to South Vietnam against the advice of the generals. Americans, brought up in suburbs and on the Great Plains, were to teach Asian troops, whose language they did not speak, to fight General Vo Nyuyen Giap, one of the greatest guerrilla generals in modern history, in paddy fields and jungles half a world away…

President John Kennedy was assassinated in November 1963, and when Johnson succeeded to the presidency he did not seize the opportunity to withdraw.

But 1964 was an election year. Johnson was not prepared to quit, if only because with countless other Americans he could not bring himself

---

[5] A few passages based on some in an earlier book of mine, *Faith, Hope and Courage, the Great Strengths of Refugees* (1995) follow here.

to believe that the United States could be defeated by a bunch of Asian guerrillas in black pyjamas. France, yes, but not the United States.

The first heavy air assault was mounted against North Vietnam in 1963. The first American combat troops were landed in the South. Two jumps had been taken up the escalator in a matter of hours. There was no going back. McNamara said that it was a test of will and of the political purpose of the United States. With those fatuous words began the greatest tragedy in American history since the Civil War.

The Bangkok Post, under another headline, "Human Cost of Bloodbath", reported that both sides committed war crimes, but the brutality of war was greater because of the guerrilla tactics used by the North Vietnamese and the American counter-measures.

According to the Indochina Resource Centre in Washington, the total casualties, dead and wounded, from January 1961 to January 1975 were 5,773,190. Excluding American casualties, this was rather more than 10% of the population of South and North Vietnam, Cambodia and Laos. The dead totalled 2,122,244, including 56,231 Americans. Before the final collapse, the South Vietnamese authorities estimated that 55% of the population, about 10 million, were refugees. The number of orphans was thought to be in the region of 900,000.

There were other terrible statistics: the United States Air Force flew 1,899,668 sorties and dropped 6,727,084 tons of bombs on Indochina. In comparison, the Second World War was a minor operation. The combined British and American air forces dropped only (*sic*) 2,700,000 tons of bombs on Germany.

For the moment, it seemed that foreigners in Saigon, soon renamed "Ho Chi Minh City", were not under threat. However, it would not be long before most of those who had not yet left would be obliged to do so. The UNHCR secretary in the Saigon branch office, Norma Fraser, who loved the country so much that she had ignored the High Commissioner's instruction to evacuate, finally found herself being taken out with only her handbag. She never saw the rest of her lifetime's belongings again.[6]

Within a week or two, an exodus would begin from Laos too.

* * * * * *

---

[6] Norma had no family back in her native Scotland, so everything she possessed was with her in Saigon! Incidentally, we in Vientiane were advised to be ready to evacuate in case the sudden need should arise.

To start with, the rumblings consisted of vigorous student demonstrations in Paksé and in Vientiane. Before the weekend of 8/9 May 1975, which was expected to be momentous, with students pressing for the Americans and others to leave, hundreds if not thousands of foreigners, including missionaries who had lived and worked in Laos for years, opted to cross the Mekong to Thailand. Most of them had not intended to leave for good, but they were not allowed back unless it were on seventy-two-hour visas, of which few decided to make use.[7] I was left as the only resident of a block of eight flats that, hitherto, had all been occupied.

Despite all the disruption, the United Nations High Commissioner for Refugees, Prince Sadruddin Aga Khan, came for meetings in Vientiane and on the Plain of Jars before going on to Hanoi. UNHCR's presence in Vietnam, albeit only with a small office in the Hotel Thong Nyat, was the only United Nations body represented so far in North Vietnam, and so had some importance at that fraught time. Sadruddin was taken down the celebrated Route No.1 to view damage done by the bombings. His visit led to his being instrumental shortly afterwards in facilitating delicate contacts between the United States and the Vietnamese authorities to resolve the problem of repatriating the remains of US servicemen killed in Vietnam.

On 23 May, the very balanced *Far Eastern Economic Review* published a two-page article headed "Laos: The Silent Surrender", which suggested that the once-powerful rightist faction in Laos could "look to the failure of their own political machinations when searching for reasons why they were driven from the ruling coalition" and why the country went under the effective control of the Pathet Lao.[8]

---

7 A young British photographer connected to the Christian and Missionary Alliance (CAMA) came back to see me in the office, handing me the keys of no fewer than seven households, inviting me on behalf of their erstwhile residents to help myself to anything that could be of use, supposing that as UN staff, I would be staying. In the event, I was able to sell off the contents of those houses and flats as well as mission cars and motorbikes, after carrying some of the more personal items across the Mekong to their respective owners, along with the church's hymnbooks that it seemed the refugees wished to use in the camps.

8 A journalist who in 1972 wrote an article entitled "Laos 1972: The War, Politics and Peace Negotiations" had already shown how the United States and North Vietnam were major participants with troops, supplies and support in the war that had continued despite the Geneva Accords of 1962. Laos, just like Cambodia, was most important to North Vietnam as a land access to the South through the Ho Chi Minh Trail. Hence the very heavy bombings that left an untold number of bomb craters across the land, thousands of displaced people and animosity towards the USA. The Vientiane Peace Agreement of 1973 was unlikely to hold.

The article then related how the rightists made two mistakes, one moving General Van Pao's troops (former members of the CIA-trained "secret army") to a new location, the other devaluing the kip. "Both schemes backfired, and the rightists were on their way to being tumbled out of office", with the Americans receiving shocks when rioters captured three US AID officials in Savannakhet, and ransacked the US AID offices in the royal capital, Luang Prabang.

As the panic developed, wealthy Laotians fled abroad, as did Vietnamese and Chinese businessmen. This caused another drop in the value of the kip. Many rightist army officers fled abroad under their own steam, while another group of military men and politicians, including General Vang Pao, were reportedly lifted out of the country into Thailand aboard US helicopters. A royal prince even swam across the surging waters of the Mekong to the other side!

As it became clear that the communists had virtually taken over government, the Lao population began to be increasingly nervous. Many Lao who had worked for the Americans saw that their future in their home country might be far from bright, and started leaving, crossing to Nong Khai in Thailand on the Mekong ferry, while, after General Vang Pao's sudden departure, tens of thousands of his followers, the Hmong hill people, also left, on other boats from a different crossing point. Apparently the latter imagined, even after it was rumoured that the general had left for the USA, that he would be able to look after them. By mid-July, having paid large sums[9] to cross the Mekong, the 40,000 Hmong in northern Thailand were virtually destitute – and hungry.[10] They were informed that they could not remain there, yet they had practically no prospect of being accepted by the US or any other country – not yet, anyway. But, of course, they were afraid to go back. The gifted ladies who only a short time earlier had sat on Vientiane pavements embroidering exquisite cushion covers were now obliged to produce saleable work in order to survive, though the quality of their work could never be the same.

---

[9]   Fifty thousand kip (about US$83) per person.

[10]   As reported by the *Far Eastern Economic Review*, three months after the Hmong had fled Laos, the Thais provided one kilogram (2.2 lb) of rice for two Hmong families per day, but, considering the size of families, this was not enough. Refugees complained of hunger and many were sick. Sixteen people had already died of sickness, the hot, humid climate having aggravated the food problem. These were people who had always lived at very high altitudes. Before long, the phenomenon of sudden death occurred in those camps.

As for King Sisavang Vatthana and Queen Khamboui, they and Crown Prince Say Vongsavang were first put under house arrest in Luang Prabang, where they lived quietly until they were reportedly sent some two years later to a remote area for political indoctrination, and there they died.

On 5 September 1975 we heard over Vientiane radio (broadcast in French as well as in Lao) that six former rightist Laotian leaders had been sentenced to death and five others given life prison terms (all in their absence). Under the circumstances, it could not be wondered at that our subsequent reporting had some unusual elements. The first few lines of one of our project reports for Geneva Headquarters on the "Agreement with Department of National Defence for Participation of Two C-123s of the Royal Lao Air Force in the Airlift Operation" explained that no report was available from the Ministry of Defence as required by the agreement signed between the regional representative and General Oudone Sananikone, the then director general, Ministry of National Defence, for the use of military aircraft in the repatriation of displaced persons between Vientiane and the Plain of Jars. We explained that it was most unlikely that any such report could now be obtained, since General Oudone had left the country and had been condemned to death in his absence. The minister, Sisouk Na Champassak, had also left Laos (and been condemned in his absence to hard labour for life).

It was apparent that more and more Lao were finding it difficult to live in their own country. We heard that it was enough to have the same name as those being condemned to death or to life imprisonment to be watched. Our Lao colleagues, with most of whom we had ties of friendship, told us that from now on they must avoid having contact with us outside work hours. Certainly the invective against the "American imperialists" went on and on, over loudspeakers, on posters. "Lackeys of the CIA" were warned that they would be hanged if discovered. Gone were those wonderful Lao lyrics we used to hear over the soundwaves, and no doubt to the approval of Lenin, Marx and Engels, who made their appearance on several mammoth posters, revolutionary songs made their entrée, and stayed. The Pathet Lao stressed that everyone must be concerned with politics, and the Buddhist priests were not exonerated but were made to attend seminars to help them change their religious methods to suit the new realities. People in full-time jobs were expected to attend political seminars which were run from 7 p.m. to midnight.

One by one, members of our local staff – in fact, all of them except for one, a communist – were gradually to leave. I would hear footsteps on the staircase leading up to the door of my flat, and guess that this would again be someone wishing to tell me that they were leaving at dawn. Belongings of quite a few people got left with me, to be taken, if possible, to them in the Nong Khai camp across the Mekong at some future date. Orapanh, our secretary-interpreter, in earlier years a student at Moscow State University, told me about a woman she knew who was so traumatized by the departure of her husband, who she knew had been successful in getting to France, that she had bought poison to commit suicide after poisoning her three children. Obviously, we could not let that happen, and, months later, the woman and the children were reunited with the husband near Paris.

This is only a brief sketch of what happened in Laos, leading to the exodus of countless thousands of people who would be accepted by the Thai only on condition that they would be resettled elsewhere. Unfortunate Laos, unfortunate Vietnam.

* * * * * *

For one or two days and nights from that dramatic 30 April 1975, many thousands of Vietnamese reached US vessels that willingly took them on board, while others somehow managed to get onto the roof of the US embassy and to clamber onto helicopters as they lifted into the air. Headlines worldwide spoke of the drama. The island of Guam was the first destination of many of these people who, if they changed their minds about having left Vietnam, would find that there was no way back. There followed, slowly at first, then in an unending torrent from mid-1978 onwards, an exodus by small boat of an almost unbelievable number of Vietnamese who were willing to risk their lives at sea, in the belief that they could start much better lives in the USA or other countries of the West. "Boat people" camps sprang up all along the Malaysia's eastern coastline, as well as on Indonesian islands, in southern Thailand and in Hong Kong. Some of the "boat people" who had set out in fishing boats, drifting without fuel and water before reaching land, ended up in the depths or on remote islands or – when they were lucky – got rescued *in extremis* by merchant shipping.

Whether or not because of my earlier headquarters experience in refugee resettlement, I was appointed on return from an assignment in Africa to replace a resettlement officer, Anne-Marie Demmer, who in August 1978 was going on maternity leave. She could not have "timed" her maternity leave better, for a crisis was erupting and the work actually quadrupled within less than a month. I soon needed to work fifteen-hour days in the hope of keeping up with the incoming telexes that arrived in sheaves, while the telephone rang as soon as I put the handset down from previous calls coming from all over the world. From the handful of countries that previously accepted Indochinese refugees (essentially USA, France and the UK), there were suddenly thirty of them starting to get involved in the "boat people crisis" that had just erupted. New "general services" staff had to be recruited and trained, senior staff had to be kept informed, and news and guidelines needed to be sent out to all the new branch and sub offices...

No sketch of the "boat people" crisis in South East Asia would be complete without reference to the big freighters. On 8 November 1978, the first of these appeared at Port Klang, on the west coast of Malaysia. Bearing the name of *Hai Hong*, it had 2,387 persons on board, whom the captain alleged he had rescued at sea – but, as Bernard Kouchner remarked later, he and his masters in Vietnam probably made more money from that one voyage than they had throughout the old hulk's lifetime, for people reported that they had paid 1,200 American dollars per person to get onto the ship – so, while being pressured to leave, they were also held to ransom! The Malaysian authorities refused to allow these people to disembark. But the passengers, mostly ethnic Chinese, were crammed together in insanitary conditions, in intense heat, without sufficient food or water. No medical personnel were allowed on board. While it is probably a miracle that no epidemic broke out, there were many cases of malaria, diarrhoea (especially among the children, some of whom were in a critical condition) and serious skin conditions resulting from severe sunburn. Urgent measures had to be taken to get these poor people off through concrete offers of immediate resettlement. By the end of the month, more than half had left for Canada, France and Germany. The US agreed to take 553 of them, but they had to wait (on board) for four months in those dreadful conditions. The Swiss acceptance of the fifty-three people no other country would accept was a real boon.

But no sooner had the excitement over the *Hai Hong* begun to die down than two other large freighters appeared: the *Huey Fong* carried 3,318 people and was first sighted 145 miles from Hong Kong on 22 December 1978. Five days later, the ship was at anchor in Hong Kong harbour, having somehow evaded port controls under cover of night. The Hong Kong authorities allowed everyone onto land. The very same day, the *Tung An*, with 2,318 people crammed together on board, appeared outside Manila harbour. The Government of the Philippines did not authorize disembarkation, and the *Tung An* remained in Manila harbour for a period of months, the last passengers finally being allowed on land in

June. A fourth big freighter, carrying the name of *Sky Luck*, then surfaced in Hong Kong harbour on 7 February 1979 with 2,637 people on board. Not surprisingly, perhaps, the Hong Kong authorities did not this time allow disembarkation, and it was not until 30 June – almost five months later – that the Vietnamese, by now quite desperate, set foot on land, and then only because they contrived to cast the moorings adrift and the vessel drifted onto rocks, with the help of engines that the Hong Kong authorities believed they had immobilized.[11] Most of the passengers in every case were ethnic Chinese, and few had any connections whatsoever in other countries, so their resettlement proved far from easy. It may be largely thanks to the stern measures of the Hong Kong authorities, imprisoning captain and crew of the *Sky Luck* and exacting heavy fines that no other large freighters crammed with Vietnamese ever appeared. But *how* crammed some of those small fishing boats were: while some of them, built only to hold a team of fishermen and their catch, had no more than a couple of dozen people on board, others had several hundred (in one case 630).

* * * * * *

In 1987, Ms. Dao Tu Khuong,[12] a psychologist who had been working in "boat people" camps in Malaysia and other parts of South East Asia, gave the following testimony at our Vitznau workshop (her text albeit somewhat reduced in volume for the purposes of this book):

Flight From Vietnam And Victims Of Violence In The South China Sea:

Running like a thread through the saga of the boat people, as depicted in the accounts of men, women, children, and whole families, is evidence of deep schisms at the level of the personality, the family, and the population as a whole.

Before taking to their boats, most Southern Vietnamese lived in daily uncertainty and fear under a totalitarian system devoid of clear laws.

---

[11] We thought that the *Sky Luck* must be the same ship that, carrying the name *Ky Lu*, clandestinely landed 604 Vietnamese at Palawan Bay, the Philippines, on 2 February, that is to say, five days before it reached Hong Kong with an "S" painted on in front of "KY" and "CK" added to the "LU".

[12] Dao Tu Khuong, who is Vietnamese, worked as a UNHCR consultant in 1982–86, spending periods in camps in Malaysia and Thailand, revisiting them regularly to follow up on people previously seen or to assist new arrivals. She worked specifically with refugee women and girls subjected to violence at sea.

Anyone, it seemed, could suddenly be found at fault. Living in constant fear... they spent months or even years in a permanent state of alert. To a great extent, the people of South Vietnam had had to live with permanent hunger. ... For years afterwards, many Vietnamese would suffer deeply from this lack. Everyone had endured losses, decades of war had decimated human and plant life. Frequently the fields were sown not with life-giving seeds, but with mines, still capable of taking their toll. People had lost loved ones, their home, which was far from being just a roof over their heads – it was the place of their ancestors, from which they drew their strength.

In the harsh light of day-to-day life, questions of life and death, of humanity and inhumanity, had an unreal quality, and the unreal became the norm which eroded their existence. Having the will to survive, they needed an antidote to despair; so the people of South Vietnam turned to an illusion – that of a western paradise. The more the object of one's dreams is remote and inaccessible, the more it is longed for and the more one is prepared to go to any lengths to get it. The illusion was reinforced by the fact that hundreds of thousands of people in South Viet Nam lived a decent life – even a good life by local standards – thanks to the gifts of money, medicaments, and other items which arrived from abroad.

Thus the Vietnamese boat people leave having suffered heavy losses which there has been no opportunity to lament because it is all they can do to survive. They have lived through years of uncertainty, fear, humiliation, and frustration, losing trust in those around them and often in themselves. They have nothing to pack on leaving but their illusions and a spirit of sacrifice. They will sacrifice the present for the future, sacrifice themselves and their needs and personal wishes to guarantee continuity of the family and a place to substitute for the land of their ancestors. The spirit of sacrifice has been inculcated over centuries, drilled into them almost like a religion.

The other side of this deeply-rooted conviction about personal sacrifice is a kind of disregard for one's own needs and one's very survival, a denial even. A sudden confrontation with one's inner self in a time of crisis may shock people and deepen their sense of humiliation and loss of personal integrity.

In my mind's eye is the haunting expression in the eyes of a very young girl who had been raped at sea by pirates in front of her father, he having been rendered powerless to do anything to help her. Some months later, the father and the daughter felt the need to speak of this painful experience in my presence. The girl said that in the hands of the pirates, death seemed so imminent and so desirable that she felt no fear for herself, but only for her father. Her father, still affected by what he had just heard, confessed to having hoped, at the moment when all his inner resources failed him, that she could save the rest of the family – be sacrificed for them. But looking back, had he not left Vietnam to assure his children of a future? How could father and daughter ever face each other after this? For several months the girl enclosed herself in an almost total silence. But her expression spoke for her; I could see that something had been shattered forever – a loss much more serious than that of her personal integrity.

In a first asylum camp I worked with two young women who had attempted to take their own lives. Both had been raped at sea. In my capacity as counsellor to these distraught young women, I tried to discern what factors would have reactivated their emotions to the extent that they would seek to do away with themselves. The first girl was in the camp with her elder brother and his wife and children, the second with her elder sister. In both cases, the relatives were giving none of the usual support the girls needed more than ever before –rather the contrary, in fact.

The evaporation of this support had occurred at sea and continued in the camp. … In the situation in which a person has been the subject of an attack and is at the same time the victim of a family split, it seems that just one more setback will tip the balance and precipitate a person already reduced to a state of vulnerability into a suicidal act.

The psychological deterioration of families and of a people can be illustrated only too poignantly by the experiences of the unaccompanied children and by the profile they present to us of their parents in relation to their parental role and responsibility for the migration of their offspring. The psychological circumstances prevailing at the time of flight from Vietnam create a high probability that these children will suffer psychological problems later on. Their lack of preparation for what is to happen to them is a dangerous negative element: frequently parents have withheld from their young children (even children under thirteen) the fact that they are going to have them flee by boat. The children realise only once they are out at sea amongst many strangers, that they have unknowingly been sent on a nameless, endless journey. One child told me "My mother lied to me." She had told him that they were going to see his grandmother.

Perhaps the silence of the girl brought face to face with her father's tenacious will to survive is symptomatic of the state the boat children are in: they stifle their pain, but it will emerge in physical form. And when their bodies cannot cope with such a burden of human distress, they create a world of their own into which they can retreat and dream their dreams, safe from the torments of the real world.

On the all-too-common rape (often multiple rape) of women and young girls fleeing Vietnam by boat, we heard that while for any woman, rape is a deep wound, the cultural tradition in Vietnam reinforce the meaning of its being an irremediable stain. The Cult of Ancestors remains fundamental for all Vietnamese, including those who recently turned to Christianity.

People in Vietnam have heard of piracy and rape of women and young girls. Some believe in their luck or in the ability of the boat leader to avoid pirates on. … They have often come to the point of accepting rape as an unavoidable accident. They know that not only may they encounter robbery and rape of their women, but also that the pirates can wound them, throw them into the sea or even kill them. It is also common that the boat people, obsessed with their desire to flee, manage to convince themselves that piracy will not happen to them but only to other people.

The Victim Becomes The Scapegoat And An Outcast

When boat people meet pirates, the women are often told to obey them and not to provoke their anger. "Use women to assuage the pirates" may then become an unspoken thought. B.T, a 20-year-old girl who left Vietnam alone, experienced what it is to be the scapegoat. After five days on the high seas, her boat met with pirates who offered the passengers three options: if they showed any resistance, they would all be killed; or the young Vietnamese who spoke Thai and was serving as interpreter would be killed; or they should offer the pirates a young virgin girl, in which case they would all be set free.

It seems that the pirates, being Asian, know how to play on the humiliation of the boat people. They make the boat people participate in or consent to the sacrifice of their own virgin girls. They force them to become accomplices in their own humiliation. This leads to a loss of self-esteem of the whole group, not just the rape victims; all the boat people will suffer a loss of integrity.

For Vietnamese girls, becoming the ones to be sacrificed is quite coherent; this way of seeing things cuts down much of the potential anger or revolt they might feel. Such a sacrifice makes more sense to the victim, however, if there are members of her own family in the boat whom she will be instrumental in saving. If the women are single or unaccompanied, to become the scapegoat in a sense appears to be purposeless. It seems all the more absurd since she will have the impression that she is the scapegoat for a whole group or all of society, only to have it reject her and her whole family. Indeed, according to certain opinions, "by this tragedy, a woman pays for the misdeeds of her own family".

Once they are released by the pirates, the young women have tremendous difficulty in readjusting to the crowded conditions on their boat. The sanitary conditions on the boats after four or five days at sea are terrible, but it is a commonly-shared filth of all those on board. A young rape victim said, "I had the impression that my very presence soiled the boat in a different way, especially when the others let me have more space than before... out of pity, or because I was dirtier than they; I was glad that some men avoided looking at me, thus sparing me the shame of looking them in the eyes." The idea of suicide, or the wish that a storm would swallow all of the passengers and the pirates, have come to more than one woman who has been raped.

Dao Tu Khung went on to report the experiences of children who were raped by pirates. Some of them lost their reason. ... The mother of a ten-year-old who was raped said, with despair and revolt, "I was afraid for my sisters and myself, and we thought of protecting ourselves. But how could I have expected that they would touch a child?"

Conclusions: The Psycho-Social Effects Of Rape On The Women And The Community Of Boat People

It is thus easily understandable that the rape of Vietnamese and Chinese boat people is a humiliation, a form of mental and physical torture imposed upon women directly and upon their families indirectly, including the children. One can consider it also as a form of torture of a whole people, because the circumstances and context of the rape of boat people make everyone participate in their own debasement, destroying something that is an integral part of their cultural and moral foundations and making them accomplices to that destruction. One may say that the boat people are, at the outset, travellers without any physical luggage, without any cultural luggage, or at the very least they are deeply shaken to the very roots of their beliefs and their cultural models. It will thus be all the more difficult for them to assimilate and to integrate new models in a totally different environment.

Yet women rape victims, as well as the other boat people on Pulau Bidong,[13] appear to be surviving quite well. ... It is important not to forget, however, that these people are still in a situation of shock and trauma,

---

[13] Pulau Bidong is a waterless island of about one kilometre square situated nineteen miles from the Malaysian coast, on which the Vietnamese boat people, including many taken from other camps on the coast, had to manage until such time as visas

after years of uncertainty and humiliation in Vietnam and after awakening from the nightmare of their sea voyage. On top of that is the insecurity and uncertainty of the present and the future. These people are merely surviving on the island.

This means that the psychological repercussions of their past will only appear later. One might very wonder why they have not lost their reason, or sink into depression. ... There is a risk that the violence that the rape victim has experienced and her desire for revenge will rub off onto those who surround her. Instead of expressing open-mindedness, confidence and love, her approach could be inspired by suspicion and rapports of strength.

* * * * * *

At the same workshop, the plenary session, "Disruption, Uprooting and Flight" was also addressed by Dr A.G. Rangaraj.[14]

The Health Status Of Refugees In South East Asia

Health is a state of complete physical, mental and social well-being and not merely the absence of disease or infirmity. World Health Organization

Accepting the definition of health given by the World Health Organization, that Health is a state of complete physical, mental and social well-being and not merely the absence of disease or infirmity, we can examine the health status of South East Asian refugees in the first asylum countries, under two categories: *medical* problems and *psycho-social* problems.

If you go to any camp in South East Asia and ask the doctors, "What is the principal public health problem?" they will say "Tuberculosis, tuberculosis and tuberculosis." This is because one per cent of the refugees have active tuberculosis (TB). ... We treat all TB cases before they leave the country of first asylum, which usually takes six to twelve months. ... The second disease which might be of interest is hepatitis B. ... Then some thirty per cent of the refugees suffer from anaemia, ... The fourth common problem is intestinal parasitic infection. Other problems, such as malaria and venereal diseases, are

---

to a third country had been issued in their name. At one point, there were 46,000 of them on that island.

[14] Dr Rangaraj, an Indian national, had an extensive background in medicine, public health and epidemiology. He served as a special consultant to WHO, UNICEF, UNHCR and IOM in Africa, Thailand, Afghanistan, Bangladesh and South East Asia.

hardly worth mentioning because they are local problems which are detected, treated, and tested before people leave for other countries.

Psycho-Social Problems

What are the mental problems of these refugees? The predominant symptoms we find in the camps are mainly somatic complaints; next we have suicide attempts. Then we have abnormal forms of behaviour, instances of antisocial behaviour, and of course blatant cases of anxiety and depression.

Now I am neither a psychiatrist nor a psychologist, but if you categorise them diagnostically, sixty percent of the symptoms can go under depression and anxiety – predominantly the former. Functional psychoses which need psychiatric intervention and drug treatment range between a quarter and a half of the cases. Thirdly we have cases of adjustment reactions. We know about the refugees' suffering causing grief, mourning, and loss; added to that, the uncertainty about the future places a burden of anxiety upon them. Here I would like to highlight three or four aspects of the mental health problem with a few case illustrations.

1. Long stayers

Refugees who have been in the camp for a long time – five, six or seven years sometimes – seem to die internally. Outwardly, they have lost everything – family, country, culture… and suddenly they find they are nobody. Everything is done for them – they are not left to do anything for themselves, and there is no future for them – nobody wants them, and years have gone by. Some of them who came as youths are now young men who should be marrying, having children, working, building up a life – but there is nothing. They have lost everything and gained nothing. Decay seems to set in and they seem to disintegrate, day by day.

2. Victims of violence

Because of what happened in their country, I know that the Khmers all consider themselves victims of violence. With regard to pirate attacks on Vietnamese boats in the South China Sea, the woman may be raped and others may also be assaulted physically. But because all the people in the boat are forced to witness what goes on without being able to do anything to help, I would say that they are all psychologically affected – they are all in a sense victims of violence.

We found a family of three who had three pirate attacks on their way from Vietnam, and three times the poor woman was raped. The husband, the navigator of the boat, could do nothing to prevent it. Ultimately they arrived, completely exhausted, in the camp. They were so traumatised and shocked that they could not do anything to help each other. The husband felt that he had led them into all this trouble; he suffered from severe guilt feelings and wanted forgiveness from his wife. The wife was so shamed and damaged and dispirited that she could not make a move towards him, but wanted his understanding. Because they could not do anything for each other, each became completely isolated in his or her own misery and felt only resentment of the other. Meanwhile, the boy – who was only six years old – began to show signs of disturbed behaviour. He would cling to his mother, but she was so preoccupied with her problem that she almost neglected him. He was sent to the camp school, but because of disruptive behaviour he was sent back.

Complete disintegration of the family was imminent. We took them into the family centre and found that the mother was still interested in the child – she wanted him educated. So there was a spark still left. Our psychiatrist asked a Vietnamese teacher if he would teach the mother, who would then be the one to teach the child. This was done and the mother developed her interest in the boy, feeling responsible and caring for him once again. As a result, her status improved. Her husband thought that perhaps she was beginning to forgive and to forget, so he also improved. Actually the whole family benefited from the astute intervention of the psychiatrist.

* * * * * *

UNHCR reported in 2000 that in nearly a quarter of a century of displacement within and from Indochina, more than *three million* people fled their countries, of whom some 2,500,000 found new homes elsewhere and 500,000 returned. Resettlement countries made extraordinary commitments, while fortunately, Cambodia, Laos and Vietnam all eventually accepted repatriation and reintegration programmes. On the negative side, however, UNHCR wrote of "the countless people who drowned at sea, or who lost their lives or suffered in other ways from pirate attacks, rape, shelling, pushbacks and long-term detention in inhumane conditions."

Another "negative side" appears now, in late 2019, in the form of the apparently somewhat widespread longings that many people in Vietnam harbour for a better life, which has resulted in many young people attempting the long and dangerous journey to the United Kingdom. According to investigations made in Britain, some Vietnamese families have been ready to stint themselves, perhaps in the extreme, to hand over to members of the young generation and/or to "people smugglers" all the money that they can put together to finance the journey of a single member to what appears to be looked upon as a promised land. I write this only days after thirty-nine bodies were discovered in a sealed refrigeration truck parked half way between the Channel and London: those who died so tragically, ostensibly young Vietnamese, had, it was said by other Vietnamese, typical longings to get established in Britain so as to send money back to their families.

Integration

One does not need to have lived for a time in the former Indochina to imagine the myriad of problems liable to perplex and unnerve people arriving in Western countries from the other side of the world. For many who got to be "resettled" before the end of the twentieth century, there are problems for two (if not three) generations, that is to say, for those who crossed the Mekong or left Vietnam by boat (or ship!), and for their children – and possibly even for their grandchildren.

Some of their children have evidently built up successful working lives. A top British tennis umpire whom we see on televised tournaments such as the Australian Open, the US Open or Wimbledon has such unmistakable Lao features, not to mention a typical Lao name, that we can be happy that he has "made it", functioning at such a high level in international sport. A radiologist attending to my health here in Fribourg Canton, Switzerland, is the son of a boat refugee (a man still active in his profession), while a colleague of his, a young anaesthetist, has cousins who left Vietnam by boat.

However, PTSD is still reportedly widespread among the Vietnamese American population, and has been found difficult to treat as far as the older generation, reluctant to talk about their traumatic experiences, is concerned. They can commonly complain to their doctors about headaches, dizziness, fainting and body pains, and when no physical problems are detected, they may simply be given painkillers, which of course does nothing to cure post-traumatic stress. Alternatively, they may be sent to psychiatric hospitals.

The parents' secrecy, and their nightmares and depression, have visibly affected many of the second generation, as we have seen (Chapter 10) has been the case among the Cambodians. The concept of intergenerational transfer of trauma first documented among some of the children of

Holocaust survivors (Chapter 3), has been found to affect Vietnamese survivors too.[15]

Obviously, there has been quite some research carried out in the USA on these questions, duly recorded at the US National Library of Medicine and National Institutes of Health. Progressively, means are explored to relieve many of these refugees of their recurring somatic complaints along with, as far as is found possible, the post-traumatic stress that for some, diminishes with time and care – while for others, unfortunately, it does not. In any case, those who have had access to the Indochinese Psychiatric Clinic in Boston, created by Dr Richard Mollica and his team that from the start was largely composed of Indochinese, have certainly been greatly helped, along with many thousands of others. More will be said shortly about the wonderful Boston IPC.

The next chapter gives us a thorough explanation of, on the one hand, the characteristics of the "boat people" who were admitted to Switzerland, and on the other, the work carried out to accompany them through their difficulties in the first few years: Switzerland at the end of the 1970s and beginning of the 1980s was exemplary in accepting people who because of a physical, mental or social handicap had been rejected by every other selection team, and by setting up new, well-thought-out measures to assist with integration.

As stated in some of the other chapters, Chapters 19 and 20 of this book feature discoveries made over the last thirty to forty years in relation to trauma and its effects, and to a number of methods that can lead to healing.

---

[15] Julianne Pham, *Secrecy Behind PTSD Among Vietnamese Elders Affecting Second Generation* (Chopsticks Alley, 2018).

CHAPTER 12

South East Asian Refugees And Mental Health

Following the two chapters on Cambodia, Laos and Vietnam, although it makes for a rather long chapter, I decided to quote *in extenso* the observations and findings of two Swiss specialists, Dr Hans-Rudolf Wicker and Dr Hans-Karl Schoch, who were involved in the 1980s with the reception and treatment of Indochinese refugees. They worked with a newly created agency called "An Lac",[1] a psychosocial counselling service seeking to improve the psychosocial assistance for Indochinese refugees in Switzerland, and through community work to prevent individual social and psychological crises among the roughly 9,000 refugees from Vietnam, Cambodia and Laos admitted to Switzerland by the early 1980s. Theirs was not an easy task, given that they were dealing not only with ethnic Vietnamese, Cambodians and Lao but also with ethnic Chinese from those three countries, speaking various Chinese dialects. The 7,000 Vietnamese and ethnic Chinese made up the largest category. Here is the two specialists' scholarly paper:

The goal at An Lac, both in theory and in practice, was to gain an inside understanding, however incomplete, of the socio-cultural and ethno-psychological structures of the refugees they were working with on a daily basis. The ethnic factor was considered of overriding importance in working with refugees, and more specifically, with South East Asian refugees. The rest of this chapter is the paper delivered at Vitznau. Research

---

[1] The name, meaning "living in peace and working in tranquillity", was suggested by a Buddhist monk. Dr Hans-Rudolf Wicker is a social anthropologist who was in charge of the An Lac project of the Swiss Red Cross (to which other agencies subscribed). Previously, he worked with Eskimos in Alaska and for a period of six years with Indians of the Guarani tribe in Paraguay in the framework of a project to preserve their land rights and provide medical, agricultural and literacy assistance. Dr H.T. Schoch is a psychiatrist who was accredited to the An Lac project.

and experience with previously little understood trauma needing to remain on record to serve as reference in other contexts, readers will doubtless keep in mind the fact that these experiences were first presented in 1987.

Psychological Vulnerability Of Refugees

The experience of World War Two refugees has taught us that a refugee's problems are far from over once he/she is provided with food, clothing, shelter, and work in the country of refuge. Consciously or not, the loss of familiar socio-cultural surroundings remains a problem for decades, if not for life. First-generation refugees hardly ever attempt what seems practically impossible anyway: complete assimilation into the host population. Instead, in an effort to preserve their identity, they usually try to reconstruct some semblance of their native socio-cultural infrastructure. Cholon, the twin-city of Saigon almost exclusively populated by Chinese refugees and immigrants, is a prime example of such a process. So, by the way, is Orange County in Southern California.

Whatever the form of integration in the country of refuge – whether tending towards assimilation or towards the creation of socio-cultural enclaves – being a refugee means being engaged in a kind of lifelong psychological balancing act. Torn from their native surroundings and traumatized by the events, before, during and after their displacement, refugees become highly susceptible to psychological disorders. The "displacement syndrome" is a standard term in psychiatric diagnostics, and psychiatric statistics show a marked increase of psychological vulnerability in refugees. In a series of Norwegian studies from the 1950s, L. Eitinger proves that the rate of psychiatric breakdowns among refugees from the East is five times higher than among the native population (Eitinger 1958, 1959, 1960, 1960a).[2] At the time it was suggested that the high incidence of reactive psychoses among refugees would tend to disappear as integration and the re-establishment of a personal identity progressed. Years later, however, the ratio was still four-to-one (Eitinger and Grunfeld 1966).[3] ...

---

[2] L. Eitinger, *Psychiatric Investigations Among Refugees in Norway* (Oslo University Press, 1958); L. Eitinger, The Incidence of Mental Disease Among Refugees in Norway, *Journal of Mental Science*, Vol. 105 (1959) 326–328; L. Eitinger, The Symptomatology of Mental Illness among Refugees in Norway, *Journal of Mental Science*, Vol. 106 (1960) 947–966; L. Eitinger, Psychiatric Investigations Among Refugee Patients in Norway, *Mental Hygiene*, Vol. 44 (1960) 91–106.

[3] L. Eitinger and B. Grunfeld, Psychosis Among refugees in Norway, *Acta Psychiatrica Scand.*, Vol. 42 (1966) 315–328.

Based on the available data, we can safely conclude that in general, groups of refugees are more susceptible to psychological disorders than native populations. Caution is indicated, however, when interpreting these findings. The prevalence of a paranoid symptomatology among such refugees (Hitch, 1983)[4] tends to suggest that previous political persecution would noticeably influence the course of the subsequent disease. In some individual cases this may undoubtedly be true. Generally speaking, however, there is no evidence that refugees without direct political persecution are more stable in the integration process. None of the psychotic refugees supported by An Lac were politically active in the past. In many cases, however, their parents had come under intense political pressure before they fled and had suffered substantial material losses in the course of the government's nationalization programmes. Moreover, findings indicate that an increased susceptibility to psychological disorders coupled with a paranoid symptomatology is not confined to refugees alone. Forced urbanization and migration for economic reasons have had similar effects on the populations concerned.

Therefore, the increase in reactive psychoses among migrating populations can be said to be primarily socio-cultural rather than political in origin. The destabilization and destruction of functional systems that existed in the home country – such as family, village, neighbourhood, or even pedagogical concepts – is an inevitable by-product of refugee movements, as well as country-city migrations, or economic migrations leading to a socio-cultural crisis. As an individual the refugee has to make an enormous effort to integrate into his new surroundings – defining "integration" here primarily as reducing structural insecurity in a new environment. As a group, the refugees have to re-establish some kind of sociocultural orientation (Devereux, 1982),[5] in order to find new models for identification. Whether or not they actually succeed remains questionable. However, it is between these two types of friction – individual insecurity in the new surroundings and collective socio-cultural insecurity that the problem of increased psychological vulnerability must be located.

Before we go on, let us have a closer look at the problem of trying to establish a new socio-cultural identity. Since models of identity are not created and perpetuated by the individual but only by the group as a whole,

---

[4]   P. Hitch, The Mental Health of Refugees: a Review of Research, in Baker, R. (ed.), *The Psychological Problems of Refugees* (The British Refugee Council and the European Consultation on Refugees & Exiles, 1983).

[5]   G. Devereux, Normal und anormal, *Aufsätze zur allgemeinen Ethnopsychiatrie*, Frankfurt (1982) 173–217.

the cultural aspect is of utmost importance. In other words, depending on the ethnic origin of the group, different forces are mobilized in establishing a new identity. Sometimes the religious aspect is dominant, sometimes the political or the economic. Among refugees trying to establish a new identity, secondary migration always plays a very important part. There are many examples of this. The Vietnamese refugees in Switzerland, for instance, demonstrate a marked tendency towards secondary migration to the United States, Canada, and Australia, since Swiss conditions make it extremely difficult for them to manifest themselves as an ethnic group, thereby reconstructing their own identity.

The approximately 60,000 Laotian Hmong refugees living in the US have become famous for their strong sense of regrouping.[6] Between October 1981 and October 1983, 20,000 of them regrouped by means of secondary migration (Fink 1986).[7] Within a few years the cities of Fresno, Stockton, and Merced in the Central Valley of California witnessed the growth of large Hmong communities, comprising today far more than half of all Hmong refugees in the US.

The social structure of the Hmong is characterized by large kinship groups, so-called lineages. Reconstruction of these lineages and sub-lineages as a reconstruction of social relations must be seen as an important attempt on the part of the Hmong to re-orient themselves and to mobilize current energies for the preservation of their psychological welfare. Embedded in these lineages are all the elements the Hmong rely on in times of social or psychological crises, such as the old, respected men and women for counselling in social matters, the shamans who have their own way of being therapeutically active, or the simply neighbourly assistance, based on kinship, which ca be relied upon in certain situations.

As we have seen, the mobilization of energies needed to re-establish a group identity follows specific cultural patterns. The same can be said

---

[6] Hereby hangs a tale: at the height of the crisis in South East Asia, Argentina offered to take 1,000 refugees from the camps in South East Asia (on condition that UNHCR covered all the expenses of a selection mission). We suspected Argentina of having not the purest motives for making this offer, and strongly advised the deputy high commissioner, Dale de Haan, an American, to decline it when the Argentine ambassador called on him. Unfortunately, the advice was not followed. The programme went ahead, and the refugees selected soon found themselves scattered all over that huge country, sometimes with a thousand kilometres between one family and the next. They too were Hmong. They too could not stand such a degree of isolation.

[7] J. Fink, Secondary Migration to California's Central Valley, in G.L. Hendricks, B.T. Downing and A.S. Deinard (eds.), *The Hmong in Transition* (Centre for Migration Studies of New York, 1986), 184–187.

for models of failure. This may sound confusing at first, since from our point of view failure in the process of integration is inevitably associated with unhappiness and frustration, irrespective of whether the people concerned are refugees from Poland, Chile, or Vietnam. However, looking at different groups of refugees who have failed in the integration process, we can see that their reactions can differ considerably depending on their origin. Models of failure are developed long before a person becomes a refugee. They are embedded in the personality structure of the refugee and are brought along from the native country. Among Tamil asylum seekers in Switzerland, for instance, personality disorders are most often connected with sudden, excessive alcohol consumption. Among Vietnamese and ethnic Chinese refugees from South East Asia, alcohol plays no part in coping with the stress of integration, whereas paranoid schizophrenia and other forms of schizophrenic reactions are frequent. Cambodians do not take to alcohol, nor do they develop psychoses. Their inability to cope in the country of refuge is often connected to unresolved traumas of loss and fleeing. Psychiatrists call this a post-traumatic stress syndrome.

One particular reaction to displacement and integration stress among the above-mentioned Hmong refugees in the US became known as "sudden death syndrome", a term coined by R.G. Munger (1986):[8] a person, irrespective of age or state of health, will die a sudden death without apparent reason, usually at night. Between July 1977 and April 1983, 79 such cases came to light among Hmong refugees in the US. Although autopsies were carried out, the phenomenon has not yet been explained in medical terms. A 1982 study among the Hmong at the Ban Vinai refugee camp in Thailand also revealed an alarming increase in the rate of sudden death cases. Interpreted by the Hmong themselves as a specific loss of soul within the framework of their animistic beliefs, the increase of sudden death cases among them seems to be a reaction to their displacement. Small numbers of sudden death cases do occur among other South East Asian groups as well; we know of some cases in Switzerland.

Psychodynamic Aspects Among Vietnamese And Sino-Vietnamese

The preceding section showed that an increased rate of psychological disorder among groups of refuges must be expected. Yet as counsellors

---

[8]   R.G. Munger, Sleep Disturbances and Sudden Death of Hmong Refugees. A Report on Fieldwork Conducted in the Ban Vinai Refugee Camp, in G.L. Hendricks, B.T. Downing and A.S. Deinard (eds.), *The Hmong in Transition* (Centre for Migration Studies of New York, 1986), 379–398.

and social workers, but also as physicians and psychiatrists, we are not necessarily equipped to cope with this situation.

If we are going to deal with this problem seriously, we have to make every effort to familiarize ourselves with the personality structure of the different ethnic groups of refugees in order to assess and understand their reactions to the problems of displacement and understand their reactions to the problems of displacement and re-integration. Otherwise, any aid programme we might come up with – informed by European modes of thinking as they inevitably will be – will be doomed to failure.

Since we approach the topic of refugee integration from an ethno-specific viewpoint, in this section we shall discuss some specific aspects of the personality structure of the refugee groups we are working with at An Lac. For the sake of simplicity we will concentrate on the two main groups: the ethnic Vietnamese and Chinese refugees from Vietnam, Cambodia and Laos. In our opinion, three topics are central to the understanding of the psychological structure of these groups: orality, authority and role adaptation.

Orality

Scientific authors have repeatedly pointed out that the orality in the basic psychological structure of Vietnamese and Chinese is more pronounced than, say, in Europeans or North Americans (Wulff, 1987, Muensterberger, 1984[9]). This is seen primarily as a result of a distinctly permissive education during infancy, described very vividly by the Vietnamese author Phan thi Dac in her book *Situation de la personne au Viet-nam* (1966).

Until the age of four or five. Vietnamese children are practically exempt from disciplinary measures of any kind. Long nursing periods and immediate gratification, intensive physical contact, 24-hour care at the hands of the biological mother, as well as a number of substitute mothers within the extended family (grandmothers, aunts, older sisters) characterize their education at this age. The mother in such a family constellation is the symbol of care and nurture. Adults often reactivate this role situation aimed at care and nurture during periods of illness. Vietnamese psychiatric patients in Swiss clinics are known to complain about hunger in an almost stereotyped manner, even though they are being served three sufficient meals a day like all other patients. Mothers of such patients will not be

---

[9]   E. Wulff, *Psychiatrie und Klassengesellschaft* (Fischer Verlag, 1977). W. Muensterberger, Transcultural Pschoanalysis: The Case of a Chinese Army Officer, *The Journal of Psychoanalytic Anthropology*, Vol. 7, No. 1 (1984) 3–21.

discouraged from bringing their adult children full meals to the hospital – usually much to the dismay of the whole staff.

To South East Asians, preparation and intake of food do indeed have a significance which goes far beyond anything we are accustomed to in European countries. This is as true in everyday life as it is in the realm of the symbolic. Therapeutic work among Vietnamese and Sino-Vietnamese refugees is bound to fail if this aspect is not sufficiently taken into account. Heavy emphasis on anything connected with food is part of the oral development of the personality structure of these refugees. Existential anxieties and paranoid perceptions are often expressed in the context of eating. An individual may complain about being hungry even though there is sufficient food; he may express fears that his food is poisoned; or he may be compulsively stockpiling foods that must not be touched by anyone else.

In the cultural realm, elements expressing the significance of the oral aspect abound; an adequate discussion of the subject would call for a separate study. May it suffice at this point to recall the food sacrifices common at Buddhist funerals, or the fruit sacrifices on the Buddhist altar. One Vietnamese expression for soul is even a derivative of the word for the steam produced in cooking rice (Cadière 1915).[10]

The Vietnamese language is particularly expressive of all things oral. A number of Vietnamese expressions for actions only remotely related to intake and incorporation begin with the root for "eating" (*ăn*), that comes into the expressions "to get dressed, to live, to learn, to steal, to take advantage, to make love, to be bribed or gamble etc." Even the expression "to feel safe" (ăn *chăc*), includes the root for "eating", originating no doubt in the security needs of early infancy.

The oral fixation in Vietnamese social structure provides the foundation for the individual's lifelong identification with the extended family, the clan, and the whole line of ancestors. The Vietnamese or Chinese psyche does not demand independence and autonomy like its western counterpart but seeks close group and family ties. To some degree this explains the tendency towards secondary migration among south East Asian refugees. ...

Authority

As a social and moral philosophy, Confucianism still plays a vital part in establishing important everyday hierarchies in Vietnamese and Chinese society: the unquestionable loyalty of subject to ruler, son to father, younger

---

[10] L. Cadière, Anthropologie Populaire Annamite, *Bulletin de l'Ecole Française de l'Extrême Orient*, Vol. XV, No. 1 (1915) 67.

brother to older brother, and wife to husband. To this day, subordination and adaptation to a strict hierarchy are important elements in the contexts of family and school, even though the old rulers have been replaced by party cadres. Of course, authority in these countries never meant the mere exercise of individual power but was seen as vital for the preservation of the larger social units, such as the extended family, the village, or the state. A person may exercise authority and power in the name of these entities, but such exercise must, above all, be aimed at the perpetuation and preservation of the larger social unit. In the present context we are less concerned with the sociological forms of authority than with its influence on the psychology of the individual, its effects on the integration process and, particularly, on the resulting psychological problems.

A child first gets acquainted with the different forms of authority within his own family. Parents in Vietnamese and Chinese families are revered in a way that is closely related to the ancestor worship still being practised today. This reverence manifests itself not only in a lifelong positive attitude towards one's own parents, but also in the fact that negative feelings towards them are strictly taboo. ... Lack of respect and admission of hostile feelings towards one's parents have always been two of the gravest offences within Vietnamese and Chinese family structure. As late as 1896 a new Vietnamese law stipulated that children should be hanged if they disgrace their parents and beheaded if they exhibited violence towards them (Forrest 1982).[11] Social change has relaxed some of these attitudes over the past decades and among Vietnamese refugees in the West ancestor worship has been reduced to the level of the purely symbolic, due to the simple fact that the graves of the ancestors were left behind in the old country. Nevertheless, the loyalty of children towards their parents among first-generation refugees remains a central problem with far-reaching consequences in any kind of psychosocial work with these groups. Below are some of the more important points:

- Refugee families from South East Asia are generally very tolerant of family members with psychological problems. This tolerance abruptly ends if the latter show verbal or physical aggression towards older family members. Our experience tells us that this only happens in acutely psychotic phases.
- Family therapy is practically useless with South East Asian families, in spite of their family-centred way of life, because during such

---

[11] D.V. Forrest, The Eye in the Heart. Psychoanalytic Keys to Vietnam, *The Journal of Psychoanalytic Anthropology*, Vol. 5, No. 3 (1982) 269.

therapy sessions participants will invariably try to protect the family reputation. Individual problems are verbalized only inasmuch as they do not touch on the family. Children in particular would never say anything negative about their parents in such sessions (Tran Minh Tung 1986).[12]

- Our experience with the mentally ill also indicates that therapy should never be directed at loosening family ties, even if, based on western understanding, deep-seated, hidden family problems may be influencing the course of the illness or may even be the cause of it. In the long run, powerful guilt feelings – inevitable in children of such families – will dominate all other psychological problems and will send the temporarily estranged patient back into the bosom of the family.

- The taboo on negative feelings towards parents and other persons of authority within the same ethnic group leads to the construction of imaginary enemies outside of one's own group. Such stereotyped projections are common among Vietnamese and Sino-Vietnamese refugees, both on an individual and on a collective level. Any further discussion of this point would go beyond the scope of this report. Let us just add that the western counsellor, helper, or physician – as an individual or as a member of the institution he represents – frequently finds himself part of these projections, which does not facilitate his work.

Role Adaptation

As we have seen, the Vietnamese infant is rarely disciplined. Instant gratification is the guiding principle of the first years. This changes at around age five, when the child must learn to speak properly; among other things, this means learning the standardized expressing of respect for one's parents, one's older brothers and sisters, and one's surroundings in general. In Vietnamese and Chinese families early education is concerned less with notions like hygiene, independence, and achievement. What counts instead are respectful speech and behaviour, as well as finding one's place in a clearly-structured community. Educational sanctions are provoked by failures in these areas.

A brief look at the structure of the Vietnamese language will give us an idea of what is hidden behind such a system, and of the consequences

---

12 Tran Minh Tung, *Südostasienflüchtlinge in Psychiatrie und Psychotherapie – wie anders ist anders?* (Dôc-Lâp-Zentrum, 1986).

of this educational concept for the individual. In Vietnamese, abstract personal pronouns such as "I", "you", "he" are practically non-existent. Instead, terms expression relationships are used and these, in accordance with Confucian thought, are hierarchically structured. If a Vietnamese speaks to a brother older than himself, or to a non-related person of equal status as his older brother, then he addresses this person with the term for "older brother" (*anh*), while referring to himself as "younger brother" (*em*). Female persons do the same with the corresponding terms for sister. Talking to their parents, children refer to themselves as "children" (*con*); in conversation with their grandparents, children refer to themselves as "grandchildren" (*cháu*) Other words used instead of "I" include *ông* (grandfather), *bác* (uncle), *cô* (aunt), etc.

In Vietnamese society a person is never just "I", but – depending on the conversation partner – a father, a daughter, an aunt, a younger brother, a master, or an apprentice. This type of socialization and communication operates with constantly changing roles and obviously involves a long learning process. Placing oneself and others correctly within the social hierarchy amounts to recognizing and confirming pre-existing and community-oriented social norms. Intentional or unintentional failure to do so, however, will provoke the community and inevitably draw sanctions of some kind. This is the true domain of children's education. After a certain age children will be disciplined for failing to observe these rules.

The individualized "I" of European culture has a definitely negative value in Vietnamese and Chinese society. The few words denoting "I" in modern Vietnamese make this plain: *Tôi* and *Tô*, for instance, originally meaning servant or slave, denote a definite social standing. Thus in Vietnamese, the direct term of "I" is used only by someone trying to express distance from the person he is addressing. …

As we can see, role adaptation based on given social entities is very important in Vietnamese society. The individual exists not for himself but, first and foremost, for and through the community. Individuality, creativity, and a strong ego are not in demand and therefore receive little encouragement in Vietnamese education. Integrating and adapting to social norms, as well as taking on responsibilities within the community, are paramount. It should be obvious, then, that for Vietnamese refugees the change from a community-oriented society to an extremely ego- and achievement-oriented society is bound to be very difficult. The implications of such a change will probably never be fully recognized. Nevertheless, we would like to add some points that should be borne in mind in future psycho-social work with these refugees.

After many years of psychiatric experience in Vietnam, the German Eric Wulff (1977)[13] concluded that, from a European point of view, it was very difficult to reconstruct a case history with a Vietnamese patient. His experience seems to match ours. Vietnamese and Sino-Vietnamese are not in the habit of definitely organizing past events within a fixed framework of space and time. Rather, depending on the audience and his own situation, the speaker's view of past events will change. He will give two totally different accounts of the same event at different times or under different circumstances. A European doctor might be inclined to qualify such behaviour as devious, or else as a symptom of a specific illness. In reality, the patient is simply changing his role depending on the situation and the listener, as he has been taught since childhood. To him it is not the past event that is of prime importance but the situation in which it is recalled.

- In the European psychological context, the therapist by definition meets the client on an equal social level while keeping personal distance. In a Vietnamese context this constellation is unthinkable; psychotherapy as we understand it cannot ever really be carried out with South East Asian refugees. Instead, psycho-social work with these ethnic groups implies establishing a basic rapport of confidence with the client so that the therapist or counsellor can act as an authority in the positive sense.
- Ego strength and ego weakness are concepts frequently used in European diagnostics. With South East Asian patients they seem pointless, since the education of these patients is aimed at subordinating the individual ego to the collective ego. Asian therapies are frequently based on the premise that overwhelming ego strength is dangerous to the community and must be reduced in order to make the individual more functional. Such contradictions originating in a cultural context should be taken into account when working with mentally ill refugees.

Obviously, the insights gained from our discussion of oral development, authority, and role adaptation are insufficient for a comprehensive definition of the Vietnamese and Sino-Vietnamese personality. They do, however, indicate the complexities of psycho-social work with ethnically

---

[13] E. Wulff, *Psychiatrie und Klassengesellschaft* (Fischer Verlag, 1977).

and culturally different groups. In order to conceptualize this kind of work, we will have to gain a certain measure of independence from our own traditional techniques of social work and psychotherapy and at least partly revise the. It is our only chance of being of any help at all to these people.

An Lac As A Model Of An Ethno-Centred Psycho-Social Service

Let us now turn to the actual An Lac project. Since the late 1970s staff members of Swiss aid organizations had been reporting difficulties in their work with South East Asian refugees. In particular, they pointed out the increase in psychological disorders among the refugee population. Thus in 1981, the Swiss Red Cross commissioned a psychiatrist to conduct a study to gain a clearer understanding of the nature and extent of the problem.

The study showed that 83 South East Asian refugees had already been hospitalized or were receiving outpatient psychiatric treatment, and that in all likelihood the number of cases would continue to grow. At that time the group of psychiatric patients included the so-called "mental cases" – refugees who were already mentally ill when they arrived in Switzerland – and refugees who had developed psychological disorders in the course of primary integration in Switzerland. Therapy and counselling facilities were totally inadequate then, and the central question was whether and how the psycho-social treatment of these refugees could be improved at all. Two main proposals were discussed.

The first suggested that all hospitalized south East Asian psychiatric patients then scattered in clinics all over Switzerland – be grouped together in a separate ward in one psychiatric hospital and put under the care of South East Asian hospital staff. ... The second proposal involved the creation of mobile, interdisciplinary, and ethnically mixed teams to provide direct counselling to refugees and staff to create consulting and coordination services in psychiatric hospitals, and to undertake crisis intervention. This proposal was eventually developed further (Wicker and Haug, 1983)[14] and put into practice at An Lac.

Although An Lac's approach is definitely psycho-social, care had to be taken to avoid a psychiatric image as this might discourage the South East Asian refugees from approaching the service. An Lac was therefore conceived as a mixture of community centre and psycho-social service with a kind of Buddhist interpretation. Criteria for the selection of staff members

---

[14] H.R. Wicker and W. Haug, *PSIND – Projekt zur Verbesserung der sozialpsychiatrischen Betreuung von südostasiatischen Flüchtlingen in der Schweiz* (Swiss Red Cross, 1983).

includes ethnic origin and language on the one hand, and interdisciplinary cooperation on the other. Presently working at An Lac are one ethnologist in charge of coordination; one Vietnamese psychologist; two Vietnamese and one Swiss social workers; two ethnic Chinese acupuncturists who, besides speaking Mandarin, are fluent in the Chinese dialects Kuangtung and Trieu Chau; one Vietnamese secretary; and one Swiss psychiatrist for case discussions who, in cooperation with the other members of the team, treats refugee outpatients in his private office. Altogether An Lac has 6.2 full-time jobs. It is based in Berne but as a mobile team it works throughout Switzerland. In terms of methods, An Lac favours forms of conversation and therapy familiar to the refugees from their own tradition. Although in no way dismissing European knowledge of psychological problems and psychiatric treatment, we do start from the assumption that South East Asian refugees with psychological problems are often involved in a process of recalling their cultural origins, and that they should be supported in this before any attempt is made to improve their integration.

This phenomenon of trying to recall one's own socio-cultural origins does appear as regression in the course of psychological disorders. For instance, in the course of his personal destabilization a patient may lose his grip on languages learned in Switzerland and proceed to communicate in his other tongue only. Sometimes this process goes to extremes, as in the case of a young Sino-Vietnamese refugee who, in the course of his illness, first lost his knowledge of German, then forgot his Vietnamese, and now only speaks Chinese. This example shows the importance of a differentiated ethno-specific procedure if one is to be in a position to give psycho-social help.

Activities at An Lac can be roughly divided under the headings "prevention" and "therapeutic case work". Below we take a brief look at these two types of activity.

Prevention

Preventive work at An Lac is roughly equivalent to what social workers call community work, the only obvious difference being that for An Lac the community is not a neighbourhood or a village district but the South East Asian refugee population of Switzerland. Community work allows us to gain access to the refugee population, to take up general problems, to support self-help initiatives, and to have contacts with well-integrated as well as poorly-integrated refugees. For many refugees, An Lac comes to life not primarily because of the psycho-social case help offered but through community work involving their active participation.

Activities in the field of prevention at An Lac include the following:

- Language courses for different levels, as well as courses designed specifically for women and illiterate refugees;
- Holiday weeks for single and elderly refugees and those of moderate means;
- Youth recreational activities;
- Regular Buddhist meetings, usually for meditation;
- Organization of festivities according to the Vietnamese and Chinese calendars.

The An Lac building contains a library, a sewing machine, a Chinese chess set, a ping-pong table, and other games. Of course there is also a much-frequented kitchen.

Community work should provide the refugees with the opportunity to learn and be active within their own cultural context. At the same time it serves an important function in the prevention of psychological problems. Our experience tells us, however, that this aspect is limited. We must realize that even a well-developed community network will hardly ever reach a majority of refugees living in Switzerland. Moreover, the very refugees who are having social and psychological difficulties often avoid contact with other refugees out of a sense of shame and therefore are not in a position to use the facilities offered by An Lac.

Thus whether the community work at An Lac is effective in preventing psychological disorders remains an open question. Still, for refugees with psychological problems these opportunities for encounters are very important, not so much in terms of prevention as in terms of resocialization. For those refugees who specifically come to us for counselling (whose number is already quite sizeable), the various in-house and outside activities at An Lac provide a welcome opportunity to build up contacts with healthy individuals of the same ethnic group, which is essential for the process of rehabilitation. Even though An Lac primarily works with refugees who suffer from psychological disorders, they are not noticeable as a separate group.

Therapeutic Case Work

Community work at An Lac addresses specific groups among the South East Asian refugee population. Therapeutic case work, on the other hand, is designed to assist refugees or refugee families with social and psychological problems. Past experience indicates that these are usually serious problems. Considering the disastrous consequences a divorce in a Swiss family often has for all persons involved, it is easy to imagine how much more difficult relationship problems can be in a refugee family. Or consider how difficult it is to deal with Swiss mental patients, and how therapeutic success is in no way guaranteed – and then think about dealing with refugee mental patients who, due to their communication difficulties, are already isolated within their Swiss surroundings.

Moreover, it is natural for South East Asians to consider an individual's psychological problems or family problems as very intimate matters that must at all costs be hidden from the outside world. Often help is sought much too late or not at all. In such cases only crisis intervention can prevent the worst. Additional difficulties are caused by the fact that autochthonous self-regulators that may have existed among the refugee population in their native country are no longer operative due to the lack of an adequate social infrastructure. In Vietnam a battered woman, for instance, will seek refuge in her parents' house or with other relatives of the older generation. Marriage problems will then be discussed between her relatives and those of the husband, and jointly a solution will be sought. Where is this woman to go in Switzerland if her parents are in Vietnam, one aunt is in the United States, and her one brother in Australia?

Furthermore, first generation refugees are hardly in a position to make use of the large selection of counselling services and therapies in Switzerland because they lack both knowledge and confidence, not to mention their communication problems.

In many respects, therefore, An Lac is the only place in Switzerland where South East Asian refugees can turn in a time of crisis (not counting the two centres in Lausanne and Zurich, run by Buddhist nuns and monks, which in their own way serve an important religious-educational and therapeutic function). It is no coincidence that An Lac has become the focus for all the most serious problems among South East Asians in this country.

The clients An Lac cares for and counsels over varying periods of time can be roughly divided into three groups: (a) people with social and relationship problems, (b) people with psychosomatic problems, and (c) psychiatry patients. Obviously, there can be no clear division between these groups, as problem areas often overlap. Common to all clients are problems of displacement and integration.

Marriage problems and generation conflicts are predominant in the first group. Many refugee families cannot cope with the pressures of displacement and integration – an inability resulting in strong family conflicts. Typically, such conflicts are characterized by autochthonous cultural elements as well as integration stress. On a cultural level, parents and husbands often desperately try to hold on to their traditional authority over children and wives respectively. Status symbols play an important role here. Family conflicts will be denied by the people involved for long periods of time, to themselves as to the outside world.

Speaking in terms of integration, one marriage partner frequently succeeds much better in adapting to Swiss conditions than the other, thus gaining an extremely dominant position within the relationship. Over extended periods of time, such an imbalance becomes humiliating for the other partner. Fathers often cannot cope with their reduced social status, just as they cannot accept the growing independence of their children, who often integrate more easily and more quickly than their parents. So far An Lac has had to deal with 25 such family and marriage conflicts, eight of which ended in divorce.

Social problems are also frequent among refugee youths who come to Switzerland alone. Included in this group are refugees who were under twenty years of age when they arrived in Switzerland and whose families stayed behind in South East Asia. Unlike other European countries, we have no official data concerning the number of unaccompanied South East Asian youths in Switzerland. We estimate their number at 300 to 400. In one way or another, An Lac has come into contact with more than 40 of these youths, who in the meantime have become young men. Usually they had problems with the law or with psychiatric institutions, or integration problems at work. These unaccompanied youths must be considered particularly vulnerable in the integration process. This is particularly true in Switzerland, where no special effort was made to support them. Too old for regular schooling, they rarely have access to vocational training and develop into a marginal group with its own dynamics. In working with them we have come to the conclusion that misdirected integration is practically irreversible, even with subsequent counselling or therapy.

Refugees with psychosomatic problems make up our second largest group of clients. Psychosomatic problems are practically ubiquitous among South East Asian refugees of all ages. Most common are sleep disturbances, concentration difficulties, headaches, migraines, back pain, braced shoulders, tinnitus (ringing in the ears), articular pains, and depression. Quite frequently psychosomatic reactions in men around fifty lead to job loss and a general inability to cope.

It is a known and scientifically proven fact that Vietnamese and Chinese tend to somatise conflicts (Kleinmann, 1980).[15] Traditional Chinese and Sino-Vietnamese medicine takes this into account and emphasizes the close connection between psychic and somatic factors. In the treatment of refugees with psychosomatic problems, An Lac has recourse to Chinese medical methods by suggesting acupuncture treatment in addition to improving the actual resettlement situation. At present, An Lac offers regular acupuncture treatment in Lausanne, Berne and Zurich. The popularity of our Chinese acupuncturists may serve as an indication of the interest among South East Asian refugees for their own traditional forms of medical treatment. Between January 1986 and June 1987, more than 150 refugees underwent acupuncture treatment, requiring on the average ten sessions per patient.

For An Lac both the largest and the most difficult category of clients are the mentally ill. We use the term "psychiatric cases" for those refugees who – based on the diagnosis of past years, whether in Switzerland, or in their native country, or at a camp in a country of transit – have been hospitalized for psychiatric reasons or received psychiatric outpatient treatment. Also included are refugees whose mental health, as diagnosed by specialists, would require treatment but who for various reasons have not yet received such treatment. At the moment, An lac is in contact with 53 people in this category, 43 of whom have received one or more treatment sessions. These 53 live in 15 different Swiss cantons.

A majority of psychiatric cases are people with psychoses. Without guaranteeing an assured diagnosis in each case, we assume that 37 people were or are psychotic, and of these 36 are schizophrenic and only one is depressive. Four more people have been diagnosed as suffering from organic brain disturbances and seven people manifest neurotic disturbances.

The predominance of schizophrenic psychoses over affective psychoses is striking. People who know the South east Asian refugee might be surprised to hear this, since depressive moods are very frequent among these refugees. However, it is important to make a clear distinction between processes of mourning caused by the loss of native surroundings and family on the one hand, and depression as an illness on the other. Based on the clinical picture, schizophrenic disturbances clearly outnumber affective disturbances, as Tran minh Tung (1986),[16] a Vietnamese psychiatrist living in the United States, has also shown. A count of psychiatric cases according to ethnic origin gives

---

[15] A. Kleinmann, *Patients and Healers in the Context of Culture* (University of California Press, 1980), pp.146–178.

[16] Tran Minh Tung, *Südostasienflüchtlinge in Psychiatrie und Psychotherapie – wie anders ist anders?* (Dôc-Lâp-Zentrum, 1986).

the following picture; 28 Kinh or ethnic Vietnamese, 20 ethnic Chinese from Vietnam, three ethnic Chinese from Cambodia, and two ethnic Chinese from Laos. Even though (for reasons too involved to be presented here) these numbers are not necessarily representative, they do show that Vietnamese and ethnic Chinese refugees are more susceptible to mental illness than ethnic Cambodians or Laotians – despite the fact that the problems of integration in Switzerland are much the same for all of these groups.

In working with schizophrenic South East Asian refugees, it has been our experience that the combination of serious mental illness and a difficult integration process is particularly harmful. Refugees almost invariably express fears and delusions originating in ideas of being persecuted and feeling threatened by their Swiss surroundings. At the same time, based on their delusions, they construct unreal relationships to their native country. The bi-cultural elements in the clinical picture make it extremely difficult to work towards improving the mental and social condition of such persons.

Even in the planning stages of An Lac, we observed that mental illness among South East Asian refugees follows a definite pattern. The acute psychotic phase is marked by strong conflicts between the patient and his family, who will try their best to master the situation alone. The patient will be shielded from the outside world for as long as possible. Only when the situation becomes intolerable for everyone concerned will he be committed to a hospital.

In the hospital the patient will receive treatment by medication – most refugees react favourably to medication, whereas other therapies are usually not possible. Conversation between psychiatrist and patient is difficult, since in most cases the refugee will not be fluent in any European language. Invariably, South East Asian patients find it difficult to understand rehabilitation measures such as ergotherapy, protected workshops, etc., because their wildly unrealistic income expectations prevent a slow and constant personality build-up aimed at increasing self-confidence. In the minds of refugee patients, work is always tantamount to making money. As a result, occupational therapies during hospitalization go unused.

As the psychosis slowly subsides under the influence of medication, the patient will be released into his former surroundings. However, more often than not family members will not have had the benefit of extensive discussions to prepare them for the situation. Psychiatric treatment usually ends here since the family assumes that the patient has recovered. The game is ready to begin again, as conflicting family relations and integration problems persist. Outside assistance is rarely sought, and it will only be a matter of some months before the patient has a relapse and is hospitalized again. The result is a kind of revolving-door effect which contributes significantly to making the illness chronic. We have met patients who have been hospitalized up to five times since their arrival in Switzerland.

At An Lac, work pertaining to mentally ill refugees can be summed up in two points:

1. It is our task to detect mental illness in the early stages. We try to accomplish this through contacts with refugee families and by using the existing network of relations and communication among refugees. Reactive psychoses, in particular, can be curbed by early intervention and subsequent psychiatric outpatient treatment. By avoiding hospitalization we can prevent the patient from dropping out of his social and professional context.

2. In the case of hospitalized refugees, An Lac will contact the patient as well as the psychiatrists in charge to prepare the patient's release and such rehabilitation measures as are indicated. In such situations An Lac often mediates between patient and family. Post-clinical assistance designed to give support to the patient and his family is one of the crucial points in working with the mentally ill. This usually includes continued psychiatric outpatient treatment. If conditions are right and the patient succeeds in his transition from clinic to private life, long-term chances for his stabilization are much improved.

Working with mentally ill refugees is not easy. It requires much patience and sympathetic understanding on the part of An Lac staff members, as well as a knowledge of the culturally-determined, characteristic clinical pictures. Needless to say, patients must be given the opportunity to discuss their problems and aspirations with people from their own culture. An Lac assists them in going back to their own cultural background. The high rate of suicides among such refugees – resulting from the hopelessness with which mentally ill refugees tend to view their situation – only underlines the importance of An Lac's efforts in this area. Between April 1985 and august 1987, we recorded three suicides and two attempted suicides among psychotic patients.

Even though assisting mentally damaged refugees is primarily the responsibility of our ethnically-mixed team, which is oriented towards social work, the presence of a psychiatrist is important With his assistance, aims and limits of therapeutic work are adapted to the limits given by the client's illness, a line is drawn between overtaxing and spoiling the client, and signs of approaching crises are detected in time to intervene – by medical means as well, if necessary.

Therapeutic Work

In our dealings with mentally damaged refugees in our therapeutic work at an Lac, we soon realized the importance of an explicitly socio-psychiatric approach. On his own, no refugee will seek psychiatric advice or therapy, certainly not in any western sense of the word. Most clients with psychological disorders who voluntarily come to An Lac or are referred to us do not come because they feel mentally ill, but because they feel tired, excited, sad, angry, or even possessed, or because they have problems with their family or with Swiss people – their social worker maybe, or their employer.

The An Lac psychiatrist's work is of an unusually specific nature. For most South East Asian visitors he will be a somewhat alien element, a representative of Swiss authority who intervenes at times, for example sending an acquaintance who is unwell to hospital, or giving someone an injection, or having long discussions with An Lac staff. But for most refugees the psychiatrist is not a person with a clearly-defined role, except perhaps when the problem at hand is of a physical nature.

Actual psychiatric work takes place very much behind the scenes. For visitors, An Lac is primarily a social space where Buddhists meet and language courses take place, and where elderly or lonely people go for company. All this makes the position of the psychiatrist a peculiar one. He appears mostly as counselling and instructor and, sometimes, as supervisor of the ethnically-mixed team. His diagnoses or therapy recommendations are based on second-hand information from the team, and he delegates the actual therapeutic work back to the team, i.e., primarily to its Vietnamese members. In the eyes of the patients they are the real authorities who can be approached for advice or assistance. The psychiatrist does not become very involved personally, yet it is his duty to be fully informed about the patients at all times.

A similar situation holds true for long-term treatments. These are usually administered through the team, or through volunteer counsellors, or through social workers employed by aid organizations. On the one hand, there is the importance of regularly administering any medication that may be necessary in certain cases. This usually presents no problems, as South East Asian patients do not differ significantly from Swiss patients in their readiness to cooperate. On the other hand, we have the more psychotherapeutic parts of the treatment, which fall into basically two different categories: work involving the patient's family, which can be very demanding and means being confronted with rigid structures, and work involving individual patients.

The latter is based on a behaviour-therapeutic approach involving training in social competences and is aimed at improving the patient's grasp of reality. This kind of therapy seems particularly important in the case of mentally-handicapped refugees who have just arrived in Switzerland. They are confronted with the double stress of having to cope and integrate into new surroundings while at the same time being handicapped by the disturbance of vital psychological functions. Not infrequently, this situation results in psychological breakdowns.

It is easy to see that working with mentally-ill refugees at An Lac requires a common learning process for all concerned as well as a constant exchange of information. In particular, non-medical staff members have to familiarize themselves with the basics of psychopathology. For this purpose we have an ongoing educational programme conducted by the An Lac psychiatrist on the basis of case-related background information.

Psychiatric work with South East Asian refugees is not easy. Having to do with interpersonal conflicts, individual problems, inner needs and external norms, it requires a clear understanding of culturally-shaped social rules, principles, codes, and structures of thought. Language and related semantic problems are only one part of the difficulties arising in a therapeutic context, we are also up against a variety of meta-psychological problems. Think of the therapeutic goals usually applied to Swiss patients: autonomy, ego significance, terms like individual development and self-realization, delimitation and self-responsibility – and then put these against the traditional values of our South East Asian clients, where individuality counts for little and the family means so much, and where hierarchy, tradition, and the ancestors play such vital roles.

We are confronted with the problem of formulating for our clients (and not just the mentally ill) goals that do justice to Swiss realities – which now are theirs too – without suggesting that they completely abandon their traditional values. Although by now a still rather slim body of literature dealing with ethno-psychiatric work exists, we cannot at present follow one particular school of psychotherapy. It is necessary to break ground, and to collect and valuate the results. At this point, any other approach would strike us as being unrealistic.

Conclusion

An Lac certainly does not resolve all the psychological problems of South East Asian refugees living in Switzerland. However, with our ethno-centres approach we do try to meet the specific needs of the refugee population and particularly of those refugees who are failing in the process of integration. In doing so, we also try to go beyond the methods commonly used in refugee work. It is our experience that psycho-social work must increasingly be based on the ethnic factor. The same is true for planning implementing general integration measures for refugee groups.

The term refugee as such is clearly a political term and conveys no information about the cultural, social, or ethnic background of a refugee. However, these very factors are of the greatest significance in the process of integration and in dealing with the social and psychological problems arriving from it – much more so than the mere fact of being considered a refugee. For us "helpers", paying more attention to ethnic and cultural factors entails a learning process that will give us more assurance in dealing with foreigners – which is precisely what refugees are in the first stage of their integration.

CHAPTER 13

Faith, Hope And Courage –
The Great Strengths Of Refugees

Over recent years, millions of people have crossed "to the other side" (i.e. the other side of a border) without necessarily knowing what to expect once they have managed it. When all one's thoughts are concentrated on escape from circumstances that for whatever reasons have become intolerable, I dare say that a refugee is almost oblivious as to what may be met with after the escape. His or her thoughts are probably focused on the dangers of flight and on everything being left behind, or may be focused even on a hypothetical return. I once asked a Chilean refugee at what point he had decided he would return to Chile. His answer was "The day I left!"

It has taken this man, this woman, that family, a lot of courage to leave, and they will have to muster both courage and faith to move ahead with their lives. No one who does not go through the experience of fleeing conflict and persecution can really imagine either the probable trauma of flight or the bitterness of life in a camp. The inevitable closeness to hundreds or thousands of others, uncertainty about the future, homesickness, despair about what has been lost and even possible doubt as to whether the decision to take one's family into the unknown (or, in a few cases, to leave the family behind) was the right one are elements that will all weigh on one's mind. Emotional torture may be very real and a kind of camp psychosis may ensue.

While in many refugee camps there is much that speaks of courage and hope and of people's belief that despite the hardships they now encounter, they have taken the right step, the psychological consequences should not be underestimated. We can return to this theme shortly.

Mass Exodus From Syria, Allied With That From Countries Like Afghanistan, Iran And Iraq, And The Migrant Crisis Involving Libya And The Mediterranean

The unprecedented exodus of the last few years from Syria and other countries in conflict has brought about unquantifiable levels of homelessness. After fleeing their ruined cities, their homes, schools and hospitals wrecked by bombs, huge numbers of people of all ages have mostly found nowhere to live other than tented camps in a surrounding country.

At first, the world did not altogether turn its back on these desperate Syrians, and at the same time there was an outpouring of sympathy for all the people who were risking their lives by trying to cross the Mediterranean to safety.

In 2015 I had occasion to write the following about the events of a single week:

Week of 22–29 August 2015

Frantic people fleeing, fleeing war and loss, repression, terrorism, hunger, seeing in Europe their only hope of survival

For many weeks now, the media had brought us film sequences of Italian crews bravely struggling to wrest thousands of stricken people from the sea. These desperate migrants have left Libya in unsafe boats, having often found themselves in the clutches of traffickers who promised to take them to safety – at a price. Now – this very week – Greece is suddenly faced with the same kind of emergency: large numbers of people are rescued and disembarked on the Island of Kos, or on the Greek mainland, who then set off on foot to Macedonia, to Serbia and on towards the north-west, trekking for weeks without belongings but with their children, hoping to survive with only their determination to drive them forward. They are desperate to reach Europe at the rate of 1,500 per day on this route. Some, trusting in salvation from terror and loss, drown in the sea off the Greek coast; some are met by barbed wire after weeks travelling on foot over hundreds of kilometres, some are even sprayed with tear gas, so unwelcome are they, but oh how desperate. … Today (22nd August 2015) we have seen the police of Macedonia spraying crowds with tear gas

252

to try to repel them. What a shocking reception for desperate people who have managed to survive the war in Syria and the terrible conditions of the very long, harrowing journey from their stricken country.[1]

Most of us can probably remember these scenes, these tragic facts, and realize that large numbers of Syrians have not got to Europe at all, being housed "temporarily" in tented camps nearer their shattered country. The exodus has continued, and the countries surrounding Syria, sheltering people from at least a dozen countries (including Iraq, Iran, Afghanistan, Bangladesh, the DRC and other African countries) are commendable for their willingness to allow countless thousands to eke out a pitiful existence on their territories. But for how long? these governments must perpetually wonder. Presumably it has to be until such time as a miracle may enable there to be large-scale reconstruction in those countries devastated by conflict, above all (we must hope) in beleaguered Syria, and consequent repatriation of masses of refugees.

In any case, the 2015 upsurge in the numbers of people wishing to give their seriously disrupted lives the chance of a new start in Europe caused European governments "alarm and despondency" (to use a time-honoured phrase). Only Germany and Sweden were exemplary and made it easy for a million or so Syrians to move to potential new homes. However, various social and work pressures, combined with a few very unsavoury incidents, then caused public opinion, particularly in Germany, to swing right away from the kind of generosity and openness that Chancellor Merkel expressed at the height of the migrant crisis and that, for a time, seemed to be that of the German public. As practically everyone is now aware, governments have since been giving more serious thought to questions of immigration, in general finding it impossible to equate migrant need with migrant intake, even though the European Union worked out a scheme – later aborted – in which each government would accept a proportion of the needy people at Europe's gates.

The merciless war in Syria has gone on and on, joined by Russia and recently by Turkey, that is anxious to protect its borders. The level of bombing simply defies description, as do the awful numbers of stricken uprooted populations of the Turkey–Syria border areas. Yet again we are faced with unbearable scenes of suffering families leaving their bombed-out homes, not knowing where they can go to be safe.

---

[1]   An extract from *Prince Sadruddin Aga Khan, Visionary and Humanitarian* (2017).

As for the migrant crisis affecting Africa in particular, fifty years ago the then United Nations High Commissioner for Refugees, Prince Sadruddin, gave clear warnings that there would be mass south–north migration unless the developed countries did far more to help struggling African countries develop their economies and their infrastructures. Sadruddin, a man of great compassion who gave seventeen years of his life to serving refugees through the United Nations and many more to other delicate UN missions, was throughout his adult life concerned in the extreme about the disparities between rich and poor. He spoke of the problems on many occasions, one of the first of which was in a radio interview in 1972 in the Palais des Nations, when he said:

> The rich countries should understand that if you don't promote development, either through UNCTAD or the other UN channels, or bilaterally, we are going to go towards a head-on clash, a head-on collision with a major disaster. Because the struggle today is against illiteracy, against disease, against over-population, against a low standard of living, and if that gap between the rich and poor is not narrowed somehow, *the rich countries will perhaps suffer even more than the poor countries in due course.*[2] (my emphasis)

Again, in 1981, Sadruddin made it perfectly clear in his report to the United Nations Commission on Human Rights that, inevitably, mass exodus would be the pattern of the future unless development activities on a hitherto unimagined scale were rapidly planned and executed, naturally in close cooperation with the countries concerned. For the rest of his life, the theme cropped up again and again in his reports and speeches.

Of course, Sadruddin was a visionary, and of course it is a pity for the world, as one journalist put it,[3] that he did not come to be in a position – as he had hoped he might one day[4] – to take initiatives of a kind that would transform the international community's attitude towards the poorer countries and their populations, and ensure that billions (or trillions) of dollars, francs or euros got channelled into programmes of a kind that

---

[2] Interview with a Dutch journalist, Palais des Nations, Geneva.

[3] "A pity for the world, whose hunger and homelessness and vandalism, Sadruddin's issues..." Neal Ascherson, Why the UN Should Choose a Prince, *Observer*, 28 September 1986.

[4] He would have made a great UN secretary-general, and had received a majority vote in the Security Council – only to have the USSR, for unknown reasons, use its power of veto.

would transform the economies of those needy countries. If this sounds over-ambitious, we have only to think of the trillions devoted to developing and multiplying nuclear weapons, and of other trillions devoted to space research – to what end, we may well ask.

Greece had already reached saturation point in relation to accommodating refugees. And now, with the February 2020 action of Turkey in opening its border to Greece to refugees from the tented camps, and despite the efforts of Greek coastguards (abhorrent to witness on our TV screens) to prevent distressed people in pitiable dinghies from landing, thousands more of these uprooted people have managed to cross the short stretch of sea to reach Greek shores. Lesbos, featured in innumerable reports, is said at the time of writing to have thirteen times more people in its camps than it was ever intended, but in the eyes of refugees it is a gateway to Europe.

What hopes can these people realistically entertain of a future in Europe? The period of several decades (broadly speaking from 1975 to the 1990s), in which very large numbers of refugees were accepted by thirty or so countries, came to an end after hundreds of thousands of people born in Vietnam, Laos and Cambodia, as well as many Latin Americans, had been taken in. The huge numbers of Syrian and Afghan refugees are likely to be in limbo for a very long time, along with refugees from some African countries, from Iran, from Iraq... The list of uprooted people of different nationalities unfortunately seems endless, the apparent hopelessness of their situation heart-rending. For over very many years, the hardening of European countries' attitudes to refugees has continued despite each one's international treaty obligations, in particular the 1951 Convention Relating to the Status of Refugees. Asylum laws and procedures have been made more stringent, with asylum seekers often being sent back to countries through which they had transited and even, on occasion, to their countries of origin. New restrictive policies have been implemented not only at the national level but bilaterally and regionally as well.

A close observer put it this way quite some time ago:

We can have the most impressive and distinguished national legislation incorporating the internationally-accepted human rights standards, including the principles of the 1951 Geneva Convention Relating to the Status of Refugees, yet we can still deny asylum to the obvious victims of repression and persecution, and violate the dignity and integrity of the individual who seeks security. This is the connection between law and procedure and the concerns that one has specifically with people suffering exceptional human distress. ... An obvious conclusion that one can draw is that despite many positive examples of solidarity and care, the growing failures in the system must be contributing to the distress of individuals already under psychological pressure through their experience of violence, loss, insecurity, and disorientation.

Thirty years ago the United Nations High Commissioner for Refugees, in a Note on International Protection, referred to a growing tendency by some States to assimilate the problem of refugees and asylum seekers with that of *terrorism, narcotics trading or violence* (my italics). "There is no evidence of any link between one set of problems and the other, and it is to be regretted that a sense of insecurity among States is contributing to an erosion of minimum standards for the treatment of refugees and asylum seekers," he said. By now, Europe has practically closed its doors to people longing to find asylum from violence, and a way to start a new life. The situation is heart-rending. And, at the same time, the flow of migrants into Libya, where they have been mercilessly robbed and exploited, has continued. The dangerous sea voyage to Europe from Libyan shores has been as unsafe as ever, in the absence of rescue vessels that hitherto lifted survivors from the angry waves and took them to safe shores – measures that were stopped when European ports, one after another, decided not to let any more migrants disembark.

Nowadays, presumably because of the sudden blight on practically every country of the world of the Coronavirus, the media rarely have us see more of the uprooted masses of unhappy, stateless people. But these people are just as much a target of that frightening virus as the rest of us are. One trembles on trying to imagine what their fate in those terribly basic camps is likely to be, how much greater than ever before their inevitable distress…

A Very Bleak Future; Psychological Consequences Of Life In Refugee Camps

It would be difficult to over-emphasize how debilitating years in a camp situation, en route to nowhere, can prove. When there are the daily food distributions, people at the end of the queue sometimes have to go back to their tents empty-handed. Those at the front of the queues have perhaps waited for hours, having arrived long before the expected time of the distribution to be sure of getting their rations; then, somehow, the food

256

can run out before everyone has been served. There is probably a disturbing lack of hygiene and of everyday commodities, however valid the efforts of various NGOs to meet the human needs of huge numbers of refugees. There is nothing much to do in a refugee camp, even if some of refugees have managed to organize at least a little language training. An experienced observer of mankind, Stefan di Mistura, noticed as a young man that the most important element in the life of a refugee was to retain his dignity, and he never failed to use this perception throughout more than forty years as a senior UN representative (for eight of those years endeavouring to find solutions to the problems of Syria). To retain your dignity, month after month, year after year, in a refugee camp must undoubtedly be the most difficult achievement of all.

Present in any case are anxiety and frustration, and there's probably mourning too for what has been left behind – "cultural bereavement", as someone pertinently put it: grief that one may never see one's relatives, friends and pets again, grief that the children have no schooling. The situation today is such that, on Lesbos, it is reported that even some of the *children*, who represent 30% of the refugee population, actually contemplate ending their lives, so conditions are clearly unbearable. And there are very many such camps in Turkey and the Middle East – in Jordan, Lebanon, Gaza – each with its load of uncertainty, of noise, of poor hygiene: a nightmare existence for everyone.

Perhaps it is the fate of refugees to be plagued by psychological problems rooted in the guilt feelings often experienced by those who have managed to escape from persecution. They know their present state is not particularly enviable, but realize that those they had to leave behind are probably even worse off. They are among the privileged few who have escaped prison and torture. The grief they go through thereafter is perceived by them to be a sign of weakness.

Nevertheless, a visitor to a camp in Malawi for Mozambicans who had fled terrible violence said that the more time one spent in the camps, the more one became aware of the amazing spirit of human endurance, and this was particularly noticeable among the women, symbols of continuity. Thousands of women had retained their dignity in spite of degradation, and toiled all day long to hold the community together, sometimes spontaneously breaking out in traditional singing and dancing to keep their spirits up in songs and gestures of love for Mozambique and their desire to return to their homeland.[5] Dr Bernard Kouchner, instrumental back in the

---

[5]   Janet Hawley, Women Do the Work, *Refugees* (September 1990).

1980s in the rescue at sea of many Vietnamese "boat people", contrasted the creative spirit of those he subsequently visited (marooned on a waterless island far from the Malaysian coast) with that of French people who he found complaining about traffic jams and the increased cost of petrol.

Living In A Vacuum

Even if admitted by a "country of resettlement", in certain circumstances a refugee may be far from (re)settled, as the following account demonstrates.[6]

In a men's hostel located in a depressingly unattractive area of the outskirts of Frankfurt, a suicide letter was found, written by a thirty-year-old Eritrean. He was a recognized refugee. In his country of origin he had been a bank employee. He had sent out dozens of job applications to German banks. "Dear brother," he wrote in his suicide note, "I haven't been murdered. I've killed myself." He ended the note with the following sentence: "I'm not angry at anyone, only myself."

Was this an isolated incident? And why did it happen?

The young man in question had left behind him a life in Eritrea. Behind him lay his escape to the free world, motivated by political and religious persecution, compulsory service in the Ethiopian militia, the re-education camps for captured freedom fighters, the official ban on the use of the Eritrean language, the use of poison gas, the drought and general hopelessness.

We cannot reconstruct the details of the way he had lived and the dangerous conditions under which he had escaped. All we know is that he was a bank employee and, as such, a member of the middle class of his country – a country with a rich historical tradition and one of the first to be Christianized, but also one of the world's poorest. Then our young Eritrean went to the Federal Republic of Germany. There, in 1981, after he had been given recognized refugee status, his luck (if we can call it that) ran out altogether.

What he wanted was to be able to live and work under conditions in keeping with his dignity as a human being. He had already sent out countless job applications in vain. In the last one he sent before he died, he had written the following to the prospective employer: "I would like a job, but if that is not possible, then I would be willing to work for nothing, just to be able to gain some experience, to keep up my morale and to keep going physically."

---

[6]   An account that speaks of an Eritrean who arrived in a still-divided Germany. Cf. *Refugees, the Trauma of Exile* (IFRC Geneva).

An occupant of one of the adjoining rooms at the hostel in which he had lived said of him: "He did a lot of thinking." He thought about his parents and sisters and the extended family at home, about compatriots who had lost their lives, and those who had managed to survive but felt guilty as a result. He thought about what it would be like to go back to Eritrea some day...

He was described by his fellow countrymen as having been reserved and sensitive – as a loner. He reached a point at which he was no longer able to bear the uncertainty of his situation. Alas, his faith, his hope and his courage finally forsook the dear man. His choice to escape from death in Eritrea led to his choice to escape from life in Germany.

The Psychosocial Consequences

Most refugees have been exposed to violence in one way or another. They or their families may have been victims of violence, or they may have witnessed or heard about horrific events. Many of us who have worked with refugees have heard over and over again about terror, rape, physical abuse and other forms of humiliation.

Violence has, of course, its immediate consequences: death, mutilation, pain, despair, terror. But there are also the consequences that come later – the psychological consequences – for those who are lucky enough to survive. Characteristic symptoms are the re-experiencing of traumatic events and a numbed responsiveness to the external world, as well as a variety of other symptoms such as pains, dizziness, insomnia or moodiness.

Emotional numbness manifests itself in feelings of detachment, or in a loss of ability to develop an interest in enjoyable activities. The patient has trouble feeling emotions, especially those of intimacy, tenderness and sexuality. Often at the root of this are painful guilt feelings about surviving when others did not.

Emotional instability and irritability can result in unpredictable explosions of aggressive behaviour with little or no provocation. Subsequent guilt feelings may in some cases lead to suicidal actions.

Hostility, although a frequent trait in refugees, is sometimes difficult to discern because the cultural background of some refugees may require a display of politeness and motivate them to try to hide their suspicions and their hostile feelings. These feelings of hostility are rooted in a fear of betrayal. Refugees often show a profound distrust of representatives of authority – policemen, civil servants, or even uniformed postmen, and social workers. Doctors, too, may be viewed with the same kind of suspicion, which is understandable when one remembers that, where these people came from, doctors and nurses may have monitored torture sessions, or even played an active part in them.

Confronting Adaptation

The causes of psychic disturbances are often rooted not only in traumatic experiences that occurred in connection with escaping the country or origin (civil strife, war, loss of family members) but also in the process of dealing with problems that occur during the period of integration in, and adaptation to, the country of asylum. The major factors are differences encountered in the social system of the host country, in the mentality of the people, in the lifestyle of the people, and – more than anything else – in the language. We have seen something of this in the experiences of Silvia (Chapter 8).

In the initial adaptation phase, the new rhythm of life, different climatic conditions and coping with everyday problems in general are a considerable burden. But, gradually, these sources of stress diminish.

A much more serious problem is the lack (or often almost total absence) of communication with the population of the host country as a result of the language barrier. Even patterns of non-verbal communication – such as gestures, intonation, ways of showing gratitude, affection, approval or disapproval – are very different and can easily lead to misunderstandings. The powerlessness felt at not being able to understand or be understood results in pent-up frustration, which may lead to explosions of anger or to depression. The strong pressures to adapt and to "achieve" that exist in our society stand in contrast to the much more flexible system the refugees were used to, namely that of organizing themselves and reaching their goals by different routes. All this has a detrimental effect on contacts with other people. Feelings of isolation and loneliness are reinforced. Nevertheless, adverse circumstances can bring out hidden resources and strengths we never knew we had. They teach us to adapt to a whole new set of variables. A former minister of justice, now a refugee, told someone (a senior government representative for whom, years earlier, he had given an official dinner in his home) that yes, thanks – he had a good job: he was washing dishes in a restaurant.

Many refugees have made an outstanding contribution to their societies of adoption, even if at first it is a long slow climb to a decent way of life, for it takes years to reconstitute a real home and attain an acceptable quality of life. This will of course be all the more difficult if the climate should be one of rejection and even xenophobia. A refugee begins to realize there is a stigma attached to being labelled "refugee" or "asylum seeker" – he has a minority status no one admires.

The fact that asylum seekers are mostly not allowed to work during the eligibility process, which may mean several years, is a particularly grave problem. This only adds to the already enormous burden of adjustment. Once they are entitled to work and find jobs, refugees may have quite considerable difficulties in adjusting to the different kind of work environment they encounter in Western societies. They have problems coping with large amounts of work-related stress, inflexible work standards, and a lack of friendship and supportiveness among their workmates. They develop feelings of inferiority as a result of humiliation, loss of dignity and loss of social prestige.

The confrontation with new values, behavioural norms and adjustment pressures has a destabilizing effect on family structures. Traditional roles and family hierarchies are questioned. There may be a gradual breakdown in the traditional sense of family identity. Feelings of insecurity and anxiety motivate conflicts within the family.

Young people demand greater freedom in making their own decisions, but their parents may not be equipped to deal with such changes. The young people in question are under mental and emotional stress. The parents, in turn, have a hard time identifying with Western educational patterns, thus there is a gradual loss of family cohesion and of the unconditional loyalty of family members to one another. This is a heavy emotional burden for everyone involved. Traditional male and female roles are almost bound to change in the new social environment. In the case of women, there is a gradual development towards emancipation; in the case of men, on the other hand, the traditional authority of the husband and family head is eroded. Marital conflicts are the consequence.

A progressive loss of identity, the lack of opportunity to speak their language and the inability to engage in traditional cultural activities and lifestyles reinforce the refugee's feeling of being uprooted and lead to severe identity crises. In cases where symptoms of behavioural problems existed before he or she arrived in the new environment, psychological pressures are increased and symptoms are aggravated, so that there are hardly any reserves left for developing a positive attitude towards integration.

How Can We Help?

The question arises as to how these people can be helped and what preventive measures can be taken with a view to avoiding a further increase in the incidence of behavioural disturbances among refugees, thus eliminating the need for them to be treated in psychiatric clinics. What can our society at large do for the refugees?

At the very least, we need a policy on asylum seekers that is based on realistic and humane objectives and that takes integrative factors into account more strongly than has been the case in the past. It must be aimed at helping refugees to cope mentally and emotionally with their situation as refugees. At the same time, it should provide constructive approaches for dealing with life. Ideally, above and beyond the safeguarding of material needs, the policy should assure provision of the kind of cultural and educational assistance that will enable refugees to live a life relatively free of tensions and conflicts. This statement presupposes a change in public attitudes so that more attention can be given to solving refugee problems than has been the case in the past. Contributing towards this necessary change in public thinking is a constant challenge for all the organizations and institutions working with refugees.

The prospect of refugees returning to their countries of origin would be improved if, in addition to providing them with more humane living conditions, the countries of asylum were to assist them in acquiring job qualifications and experience (for example, in starting their own businesses). This would be fully consistent with the much-promulgated principle of helping people to help themselves; moreover, it would also be much more likely that integration in the host society would lead to reintegration in the society of origin.

Across the Atlantic, it is obvious to the world at large that President Trump has been taking extreme measures to prevent stricken Central Americans from getting a foothold in the USA – further proof, if proof were needed, that, in our Western societies, sympathy for uprooted people has very much been on the wane. This is a rather sad note on which to bring this chapter to an end.

CHAPTER 14

Rwanda - Ethnic Violence And Genocide

Part I – November 1959 To 6 April 1994

The story of uprooting and genocide in Rwanda is a long and complex one. It is also distressing, so it is only appropriate to warn readers that they may wish to skip parts of this chapter that deal with most of the violence (especially part II).

What happened from the late 1950s to the end of the 1990s had repercussions that continue to be dramatically felt to this day, as we shall see.

Background Up To The Late 1950s

Rwanda, known for decades as "the land of a thousand hills" and a home of the increasingly rare mountain gorillas, is a small but beautiful highland country in the Great Lakes region of Africa. If we compare its size with that of one of its neighbours, the Democratic Republic of Congo (DRC, for a time called Zaïre), we see that the 26,338 square kilometres of the former, against the 2,344,900 sq km of the latter, make the DRC eighty-nine times bigger – quite an astonishing fact![1] But its small size has not prevented Rwanda from being in world news at fairly frequent intervals since 1959.

People who knew the country in the days when it was half of a League of Nations (and subsequently a United Nations) Trust Territory of Ruanda-Urundi[2] headed by a *mwami* (king) found that they were in a charming country, one that was at peace with the world, where herders of long-horned

---

[1]   The respective areas in square miles are 10,173 and 905,366.
[2]   First awarded to Germany at the Berlin Conference of 1884–85, at which Africa was parcelled out to European powers, then taken from Germany in 1916 and entrusted to Belgium as a League of Nations Trust Territory.

cattle and agriculturalists led a satisfying life of hard work interspersed with festivals. An American woman, Rosamond Halsey Carr, who made her life in Rwanda after falling very much in love with the area of Africa's Great Lakes early in her marriage, wrote about how life had been in the late 1940s on the shores of Lake Kivu.[3] If I reflect this person's appreciation of the Rwanda of yesteryear, it is to show that before the country was subjected several decades later to massive violence, it was a truly lovely place to live in, whether one was born Rwandan or came to live there from far away. Mrs Halsey Carr was still writing about Rwanda fifty years later (cf. our Chapter 14 part II and Chapter 15).

On the eastern side of the immense Lake Kivu, at over 1,500 metres above sea level, there were small coffee plantations. The steep hills were terraced with crops, and the valleys were pastures for the long-horned cattle of the Tutsi herders. With bougainvillea and climbing roses growing in abundance, there was colour everywhere. The attractive little towns at the northern tip of Lake Kivu, lying side by side on the Rwanda-Congo border, Kisenyi (in Rwanda) and Goma (in the Congo), were then Belgian government posts. Kisenyi, since renamed successively Gisenyi and Rubavu, was principally a residential town, with large villas and several hotels fronting on white sandy beaches. Europeans who were resident in other parts of the Belgian Congo would come to this highland area to enjoy the cool air, swim in the lake, dine on French cuisine and enjoy a rich social life.

Eight conical peaks towering more than ten thousand feet above sea level – the Virunga volcanoes – form the backdrop for the two towns. Goma, the commercial centre for North Kivu, stands in the shadow of the Nyiragongo (3,469 m), an active volcano called "the burning mountain", because its rim has continually glowed red at night, as I well remember from the times spent in the area in 1964/65 and 1976/77.[4] Some of the people of Ruanda-Urundi were Tutsi or Watutsi cattle-herders, who represented roughly

---

[3] Rosamond Halsey Carr with Ann Howard Halsey, *Land of a Thousand Hills* (Plume, 2000).

[4] The Nyiragongo was to erupt violently in January 1977, spilling twenty-two million cubic metres of lava across a wide area and threatening to engulf Goma airport, over ten kilometres to the south. Six hundred people as well as countless cattle were killed; thousands of others were displaced and were later found by the Red Cross to be trying to survive by eating grass and the leaves of trees. The eruption left a crater 900 metres deep, at its base a lava lake, and the surrounding desolation was impressive to see: a moon landscape with blackened trees sticking out of the mass. Back in 1965, the French consul had taken me by boat around the northern edge of Lake Kivu, to see the result of earlier lava flows.

15% of the population, while the Hutus (85%) and the Twa or Batwa (1%), agriculturalists and hunter-gatherers, respectively, made up the rest.

The inhabitants of these two small countries had never attached importance to their tribal identities, whereas first the Germans, then the Belgians, the latter administering the joint trust territories largely along the lines that they had adopted in Congo, unfortunately did. Initially looking on the Tutsi as racially superior to the Hutu and imagining them as likely to be people of some northern race, the colonial powers at first ruled through the existing structures, that is to say, the monarchy and the structures basically created by the Tutsi. What would eventually lead hundreds of thousands of Tutsi to their deaths was a racially conceived system of issuing every Rwandan with an identity card denoting their origins, keeping lists of every inhabitant in the government offices – and propagating their notion that the Tutsi had actually come from elsewhere. Little by little, the colonial methods based on race led to an upsurge of animosity on the part of Hutus towards the Tutsi, which spelled danger when Belgium started – rather suddenly – to put its weight behind the Hutu.

May I say here that for most of my adult life, I have had links with Rwanda that have included lifelong friendships with Rwandans, and that – more to the point – before writing this chapter I read or re-read a wide range of books about the country and its sufferings. There is a tremendous wealth of material on Rwanda, and on the 1994 genocide, published in both French and English, books and learned articles continuing to appear year after year. All in all, I found that the story of Rwanda, expertly told by a young American author, Stephen Kinzer, gives such comprehensive coverage of the whole story of the country from colonial times to the present that it is tempting to draw frequently on his well-documented factual account: *A Thousand Hills: Rwanda's Rebirth and the Man Who Dreamed It* (John Wiley & Sons, Inc., 2008). It is tantamount to a serious biography of Mr Paul Kagame, based on the ready access the author had to the president, a rich assortment of other interviews and a host of relevant publications.

At the time of writing, Paul Kagame, who in the 1960s and 1970s was a refugee child in Uganda, is in his third term as president of Rwanda. He explained to Stephen Kinzer how, as a two-year-old taken outside by his mother with her other children to face the death she expected from an advancing mob intent on killing them, he vividly remembers how the family was saved *in extremis* by the *mwami's* terrified chauffeur. The queen, a cousin of Kagame's mother, had learned of the day's spreading violence, and had sent the royal chauffeur to rescue them. It seems that, when the

265

violent crowd saw the car coming, they charged ahead even faster, "hoping to reach and kill their victims before he could arrive. They were closing in as the chauffeur screeched to a halt, pulled the intended victims into his car, and sped away." He took them to safety at the royal palace. This was on 9 November 1959. The husband had been absent that day. A few months later, the reunited family took refuge in Uganda.

What some survivors have referred to as the start of the genocide was carried out by death squads that rampaged through the country for several months, and resulted in the flight of tens of thousands of people to Congo, Uganda, Tanganyika (as it then was)[5] and Burundi. Unfortunately, violence of that kind was to erupt periodically over the next forty years. A United Nations Commission of Inquiry was sent to Ruanda-Urundi in April 1960 and meetings were organized between the political parties – both the Hutus and the Tutsis having set them up in the meantime – to arrange for elections. The UN Trusteeship Council put out that year a report rather full of foreboding:[6]

> The developments of these last eighteen months have brought about the racial dictatorship of one party. An oppressive system has been replaced by another one. ... It is quite possible that someday we will witness violent reactions against the Tutsi.

Events moved on fast: in October 1960, a provisional National Assembly was constituted, naming a Hutu prime minister, Grégoire Kayibanda, and three months later Rwanda was declared a republic. On 1 July 1962, in a period in which very many (in fact most) African countries were claiming independent status from the colonial powers, Rwanda and Burundi were separately granted full independence by the Belgian government. Hutu power was now becoming a reality in Rwanda.

The December–January 1963/64 Crisis

In September 1963, the UNHCR established a regional office in Africa, the capital chosen being that of Bujumbura, largely because of its geographical proximity to the refugee concentrations in the four countries of asylum. "Regional Office for Africa" was actually a very grand name for a couple of expatriates operating from a small villa in a quiet sandy road of a relatively

---

[5] Zanzibar and Tanganyika would unite on 29 October 1964, when the name of the country was changed to "The United Republic of Tanzania".
[6] https://research.un.org/en/docs/tc/ruanda-urundi: 1960: T/1583/28th and 29th sessions.

insignificant capital. UNHCR's regional representative was a Swiss, Jacques Cuénod. Two community officers, Arthur Rose from the USA and Rachel Yeld from Britain, were recruited to advise on the creation of the rural settlements that UNHCR, trying to tackle an entirely new sphere of activity, planned to set up in the four asylum countries in cooperation with the governments. A further officer, François Preziosi, was in post in Bukavu, in the adjoining Kivu Province of Congo. It was a UNHCR presence in the very heart of Africa, at least – a modest start.[7]

Three months later, in December 1963, poorly coordinated groups of refugees attacked Rwanda from Uganda, Congo and Burundi, and it was believed that the government in Kigali actually fled. However, the attack was abortive and resulted in a new upsurge of Hutu violence, triggered by increasingly intense tribal hatred and sheer panic. Inevitably it led to new refugee flows and this seemed to be a whole new chapter in the Tutsi–Hutu saga.

Jacques Cuénod cabled for staff reinforcements, as it happened giving my name. I was soon en route for Africa for the first time. Arriving in Bujumbura airport in 30°C heat – a great contrast to Geneva's sub-zero January temperatures! – to be met by a UN volunteer and taken into the small town, I was struck by the beauty of the surroundings of Bujumbura. This small capital stands at the head of Lake Tanganyika, by far the longest lake in Africa, a magnificent expanse of water 770 metres (2,500 feet) above sea level in the Great Rift Valley, bonded by those imposing volcanic mountains to the west and north, and by the highlands of Burundi to the south. Impressive also were the panoply of colours and the vociferousness of young street vendors who jostled for our attention to the marvels of carving in ivory, malachite and ebony, the brightly coloured, tightly woven baskets and the tropical fruits of every description of which they hopefully offered their entire stock. "Cent francs, Madame, d'accord – alors soixante francs, d'accord! Cinquante, cinquante, d'accord, Madame!"

In contrast, the little UNHCR regional office was besieged by people newly arrived from terror. Refugees massed around the little building, queueing at the front and back doors, standing on the lawns and flower beds, spilling over into the road. Thin old men stood leaning both hands on the top of their five-foot staffs. Young women sat feeding their infants. Toddlers solemnly held onto their mothers, and school-age children grouped together to try to play, somewhat half-heartedly. Young men jostled a little for a better place in the queues.

---

[7] Years later, there would be UNHCR branch offices in a number of African countries, with a combined staff of several hundreds.

News Of Killings

The evening of the next day, a Sunday, Arthur Rose took me to Vugizo Mission, which stands among local people's homes on the crest of one of the hills above Bujumbura, and heard chilling accounts of what was beginning to be known of the recent massacres of Tutsis. The mission radio links carried reports of houses burning, people fleeing, and dozens of bodies floating down rivers. A particularly poignant report from Ibuye, the Ruanda Mission headquarters in Burundi, had it that a Pastor Yona had been murdered. "But surely not," people whispered. "Yona was helping displaced Tutsis living in Nyamata, in the south of Rwanda. He could never have had anything to do with any invasion…" But the rumoured report was only too true. The Ibuye Mission in the north of Burundi, seen as a safe haven by hundreds of desperate people fleeing for their lives, was reached by a distressed young schoolmaster from Nyamata, who had seen it all happen three days earlier, and had then managed to escape. Soldiers had taken the pastor, who would die praying for his captors, to a bridge over the river and there they had shot him and thrown his body into the water.

Among the thousand Tutsis I subsequently saw at the Ibuye Mission was the young mother of seven children who was expecting an eighth. Her husband had been killed, possibly in the presence of his wife and children, who then joined the stampede of crowds trying frantically to reach the border to safety. Subsequently, the poor mother, falling desperately ill in the refugee camp, had to agree that her newborn baby should be given for adoption. But how distraught she must have been before she died at the thought that her seven bereft children, once so happy and confident in their hilly homeland, would have to be looked after by relatives, themselves homeless refugees.

Not for the first time – and unfortunately, not for the last – Ugandans living round Lake Victoria saw bodies floating in the lake, brought in by its major affluent, the Kagera River, a tributary of the Nile. Tens of thousands more Tutsis were now in all four countries surrounding Rwanda.

UN's Efforts To See The Rwandan Tutsis Settled

In the asylum countries, land settlements were gradually being created for the destitute refugees by the respective young governments in cooperation with international agencies. First of all, emergency relief programmes had been set up by NGOs on behalf of the UNHCR in Burundi, Congo, Tanganyika and Uganda as precursors to those rural settlement programmes. Some of the refugees, however, were already making it clear that they were not all sure that they wanted to settle in these four countries. They were not agriculturalists anyway, and they believed that the Hutu government would suppress the traditional culture and institutions of Rwandan life. Many of them vowed to return, and they would continue to make sporadic attempts to take the country back. As Prince Sadruddin Aga Khan, UN High Commissioner for Refugees,[8] had once remarked, "There's a linkage between the presence of refugees and the problems of peace and security", and this was certainly true where agitators were already going to the settlement area to harangue their fellow countrymen, advising them not to even think of planting crops: *they were all going to be returning to Rwanda* – somehow!

Nevertheless, the land settlement areas put at the disposal of the refugees by the governments of the four asylum countries were beginning to take shape. For the three being established in Burundi – Kigamba, Kayongozi and Muramba – a Dutch programme officer arrived and was put in charge of liaising with the local authorities and overseeing the development of the refugees' plots. We would be receiving nine "VSOs"[9] (volunteers) from Britain, three of them to live in each centre and oversee the distribution of food, tools and seeds until the government was ready to take over the settlements. In the area called Kalonge, in the heights many miles north of Lake Kivu (Congo), refugees had been obliged to clear forested areas before they could have land to cultivate.

We were notified that three new Land Rovers that UNHCR Geneva had put on order, one for each of the centres, were now available in Kampala to be picked up. Peter Boswell, one of the English VSOs, Jean Durand, a newly arrived French driver from UNHCR Paris, and I flew to Kampala to fetch them and to be given the opportunity to see something of Rwanda. On the three-day drive to Bujumbura, Peter and I (having lost Jean, the truant) visited one of the refugee settlement areas at Oruchinga, in southern Uganda, extremely impressed to see what a young VSO, Tony Winterbotham, was managing to do in looking after the basic needs of a suddenly inflated number of refugees (15,000, in fact). We were

---

[8] From 1962 to December 1966, Sadruddin Aga Khan was Deputy UN High Commissioner for Refugees before becoming High Commissioner in January 1966, serving for twelve further years. He oversaw the refugee situations in Africa, starting with that of the Algerians, and soon that of the Rwandans and others.

[9] VSO stands for Voluntary Service Overseas. UNHCR had applied for mature men, to come for one year. We received eighteen-year-olds who had six months to offer before going to university. At least they all held driving licences! And knew a little French.

accommodated that first memorable night by a Russian lady, Toni Nuti, whose house was on a minute island in the middle of the Kagera River at a point at which the river, forming the boundary between Uganda and Rwanda, swirls by in a series of rapids. Mrs Nuti received overnight guests, in this case ourselves and two veterinary officers, by our being winched in a steel cage across the surging waters by a night-watchman. Darkness had fallen some time earlier, so it was only the next morning that we found what a little paradise this was, full of colour and small animal life. The next night, we got rooms in the Kagera National Park Lodge, hearing hyenas barking through the night but having to drive on without seeing any of the animals. Kigali was then just a modest settlement chosen at independence barely two years earlier to be Rwanda's capital, and we saw no one except the UN representative, a young volunteer, Robert Teare. If it was stimulating to drive right across Rwanda from the north-east to the Burundi border in the south to see much of the beautiful country from which thousands had fled in terror, our exhilaration was naturally tinged with deep sadness that there had been such violence and uprooting. I picked up a young hitchhiker who had not seen her parents for several years, for they had fled Rwanda in 1959. She was just going back to her boarding school, having no thought of crossing the border. The whole experience was unforgettable.

Turbulence In Congo

Our subsequent experiences came as a series of shocks, for the Congo was going through some of its darkest hours. In the fifty-six years since European states had parcelled out Africa at that Berlin Conference, handing over this vast territory to Belgium's King Leopold, it had never really had a chance of fulfilment, much less tranquillity. As a state pushed suddenly into independence in 1960, it was in its infancy but already in the throes of violent convulsions. Pierre Mulele, the young former education minister in the rapidly formed Congolese central government, was leading a rebellion said to be receiving support from Peking. Rebels controlled a large area of Kwilu Province and neighbouring Kasai, as well as parts of the Kivu, including Bukavu, the provincial capital with its 80,000 or so inhabitants. We had already actually seen some of the Mulelist rebels, armed to the teeth and far too dangerous for border officials to stop, charging through to Bujumbura in their Jeeps to stock up on provisions.

And now the majority of the Europeans still living in the Congo (said to number 100,000 before independence, though large numbers had already fled) were escaping from potentially murderous bands. Bujumbura began to be flooded with these poor distressed people, who had had to leave everything they had built up over many years. The new arrivals included Ann Preziosi, the wife of our colleague François Preziosi, and the wife and children of another UN staff member, Jean Plique. The two hotels were soon overcrowded, and people were glad of any accommodation, even floor space, in the homes that people like ourselves were only too glad to offer them.

Then came the rumour that François Preziosi and his ILO colleague Jean Plique had been killed in or near one of the Kalonge refugee settlements.[10] Their driver had left the Land Rover where it stood and had fled on foot to Bukavu. The rumour came to be confirmed two agonizing weeks later. Sadruddin Aga Khan came to us immediately from Geneva, to convey the condolences of the UN family to the two widows and the two Plique children, and probably to see how we were holding up. He stayed three or four days; then and later, he was wonderfully supportive of his staff. There were tensions in Bujumbura too, between the Chinese and the Americans, and between Tutsi and Hutu. Just as in Rwanda, Burundi has had to contend since independence with the aspirations of both groups.[11]

Within a few weeks of these events, UNHCR needed to evacuate from Bukavu, now back in government hands, white-collar Rwandan refugees and their families who had been served with an expulsion order. A scheme was rapidly worked out to take them by boat along Lake Kivu to Goma, by air to Tabora and from thence, on the backs of lorries to an area in the Mwesi Highlands of Tanzania. The UN and certain NGOs (the Lutheran World Federation in Tanzania and the Red Cross in Congo) were doing what they could for the Rwandan refugees, hoping against hope that these uprooted and possibly traumatized people would settle down in the countries neighbouring their own to which they had fled.[12] That, of course, was what the Kigali regime was hoping. But would they?

---

[10] Jacques Cuénod and I had visited these settlements a few weeks earlier, and but for a warning from a coffee planter would have run into rebels that day.

[11] On the evening of 7 January 1965, Pierre Ngendandumwe, the young Hutu recently commissioned by the king, Mwami Mwambutsa, to serve as prime minister, was shot on the steps of the hospital where he had visited his wife and their newborn baby. We heard the shot from the office. Subsequently it was found that a Rwandan Tutsi had fired the shot. Someone came by the office when I was there alone, to say that we were on a hit list because we were helping Rwandan Tutsis.

[12] That first mission of mine to Africa took me (several times) to both Bukavu and Goma, towns that have often been in the news – never more than in recent years, as we shall see. And purely by accident (for UNHCR kept few records at that time) Geneva headquarters appointed me eleven years later as UNHCR representative in the Kivu, stationed in Bukavu. Destitute Hutu refugees from Burundi needed help to settle.

As Stephen Kinzer wrote, Rwandan exiles and their children never managed to adjust to their status as refugees and never forgot the country they had been forced to leave. The Tutsi who fled their homeland after 1959 were not only eager to return but were angry at the way their brethren were repressed at home. Exile intensified their attachment to Rwanda, rather than weakening it, and in places as far apart as Uganda, Belgium, Quebec and California they formed cultural groups, published newspapers and magazines, and passed their traditions on to their children. Always they returned to the question of how they might finally return home.

Paul Kagame's Boyhood In The Camps

The years passed. Stephen Kinzer writes of Paul Kagame's boyhood and adolescence. He declares that the raid he survived as a small boy with his mother and siblings "set the rest of Rwandan history in motion. From it grew decades of impoverished exile, a far-reaching conspiracy that ranks among the most audacious plots in the annals of covert action, an insurgent army that deposed a dictatorship, and a new order determined to rebuild a shattered nation." With his bosom friend, Fred Rwigyema, the adolescent Paul would sit at the feet of men who had taken part in *inyenzi*[13] raids, and spoke of their dreams of reclaiming Rwanda. He would explain to his biographer, "You're a child when these things happen, but you grow up in an environment that affects you in such a fundamental way. There is a lot of thinking, and raising questions in your mind. As you grow, you discuss the whole history with your parents and friends and others… You are actually somebody with very little, if anything…"

While Paul Kagame's mother set aside her memories of privilege and worked in the fields alongside other refugees to feed her children, her husband, who had been a hereditary noble and the owner of many cattle, never got over their loss, and he died when Paul was only fifteen. Paul's best friend Fred Rwigyema then suddenly disappeared, and he became rebellious, sometimes picking fights with Ugandan counterparts who taunted and insulted him and his fellows as refugees. He said "You were always reminded, in one way or another, that you didn't belong there, that you were not supposed to be there. You have no place that you can call yours… (it was) nothing anyone could get used to."

---

[13]   The invaders called themselves "cockroaches", possibly because of their stealth, acting under cover of darkness. The label stuck to the Tutsis, used in the most derogatory way, of course, by the hostile Hutus.

Kagame was sixteen when Juvénal Habyarimana, Rwanda's defence minister, who in the early 1960s had been one of the very first recruits into the new country's army, overthrew the first president of Rwanda, Grégoire Kayibanda, in what was given out as a bloodless *coup d'état*.[14] Henceforth, Habyarimana, heavily backed by France and Belgium, claimed 99% of votes in every election, and there was no way that any Rwandan Tutsi could return.[15]

Paul Kagame, after several years in which he did not distinguish himself at school (rather the reverse because his mind was so troubled), worked assiduously in his last secondary year, and subsequently passed an East African Airlines examination to become a pilot – but was contemptuously dismissed by the selectors because he was not Ugandan. That and other rebuffs set him thinking about going into Rwanda more or less clandestinely. Ineligible for a passport from either Rwanda or Uganda, he obtained a travel pass that did not mention his background, and got to Kigali by taxi. Once there, he spent several weeks, more or less out of sight but having long conversations with an uncle who earlier had been imprisoned for a year for entering Rwanda, and listening in a remote corner of a hotel bar to the conversations of politicians, civil servants and police officers who gathered there after work.

On a second visit to the land of his birth, Kagame got further insights into Rwandan life and found a thrill in this kind of intelligence gathering, at a time that exile was proving intolerable but return home was out of the question. Then suddenly his close teenage friend Fred Rwigyema resurfaced! He came with heart-stopping news: he had been recruited by followers of Yoweri Museveni, a Ugandan rebel determined to overthrow the violent, illiterate dictator Idi Amin. Fred had been training over the last year at a base in Tanzania, and now an invasion of Uganda was planned. *Amazing!* This military training and experience of Fred's seemed to open a way forward for Kagame and for other young exiles. In effect, it was in this period, without anyone noticing, that Rwandan exiles began learning how to fight.

---

[14] Various sources report that officials, lawyers and businessmen close to Kayibanda as well as a selection of army officers were executed, and that he and his wife were imprisoned at a secret location, said to be a house near Kabgayi, where some sources claim that they were starved to death. Habyarimana was apparently a product of cults that were powerful in his native north-western region and he relied heavily on the advice of soothsayers and shamans. He was afraid of spilling the deposed president's blood in case spirits would plague him. Cf. InformationCradle and Dhimbaia.

[15] We learn that an uncle of Kagame's did go back, but was imprisoned for a year. When the UNHCR posted me to Bukavu in 1976, my friend Matthieu Gasana, a bank employee in Bujumbura, wished he could come to see me there. But the only way to Bukavu to Bujumbura passed through a strip of Rwanda. "I don't think Mr Habyarimana is keen to see me," Matthieu joked.

Rwanda's government remained stable during these years, counting as always on more or less unconditional support from its colonial patrons in Belgium and France – who, however, while urging President Habyarimana from time to time to introduce some measures of democracy, had planted the seeds of the regime's destruction. "They imagined Rwanda as a colonial success story. In fact, they had set in motion forces that would propel it beyond the edges of imaginable horror."[16]

Covert Military Training Of Rwandans

Fred Rwigyema and Paul Kagame were at first the only two Rwandans training and fighting for Yoweri Museveni, along with Ugandans and Tanzanians similarly anxious to see Idi Amin removed from power. Their efforts were rewarded. But then the question arose of how to depose the restored Milton Obote, who though receiving general acceptance in the world was also a despot. Museveni, a man of a different type, started to build up a sufficient revolutionary force to overthrow Obote as well. He knew how to do it, he knew that the methods he proposed to use had been successful elsewhere, and he was conscious that it would take several years.

For five years, during which time Paul Kagame became a senior intelligence officer and close protégé of Museveni's, he learned all about going without food and travelling great distances on foot without being seen. Other Rwandans joined the "National Resistance Army" after Obote began serious repression of the refugees in the settlements. All of them were initiated into their leader's code of conduct and his thinking. They all became hardy guerrillas and, finally, Museveni took Kampala in January 1986 with his force of 14,000 fighters, 500 of whom were Rwandan. He remains president of Uganda to this day.

Meanwhile, in refugee settlements and further afield, a Rwandan network was gradually being created of people who believed in an eventual return, and raised funds under the umbrella of a so-called "Rwandan Refugee Welfare Foundation". Later, the name changed to the "Rwandan Alliance for National Unity" (RANU), the forerunner of the Rwandan Patriotic Front (RPF), which before it was ever ready to take on the dictator in their homeland developed support groups across Africa, Europe and North America.[17]

---

[16] Kinzer, *op. cit.*, p.20.

[17] The elder son of Matthieu Gasana and family, my Rwandan friends in Bujumbura, was two years old in 1964, an affectionate little fellow who, as a student of banking in Germany, was a member of one of these groupings. Eugène Richard Gasana and I

Both Paul Kagame and Fred Rwigyema entered the new Ugandan army as senior officers, in company with about 1,500 Rwandans secretly preparing, like themselves, for a different role. The former was put in charge of sixty-seven intelligence officers whom the Museveni government sent to Cuba for training. By mid-1987, the two friends began to conceive a daring, large-scale covert operation, to get more and more Rwandans trained within the Ugandan army over a period of years. Following criticisms from Kigali about the senior level of the two men in the Ugandan army, they were both demoted but continued in active duty, Fred Rwigyema secretly taking over the title of RPF chairman. These events coincided with a weakening, from several causes, of the government in Kigali. A dangerous foray into Rwanda on the part of a few dozen RPF men who did not realize that there was a grand plan for taking over Rwanda naturally had grave repercussions. Both that abortive attack and criticism levelled at Museveni about the number of Rwandans in his army were factors precipitating the decision that Rwigyema and Kagame took to invade Rwanda soon: they would be defecting from the Ugandan army along with valuable military supplies!

Museveni continued to suspect the two top officers of hatching plans to invade Rwanda – as did the government in Kigali – and decided to assign them elsewhere. Fred Rwigyema was told to go to the USA and Kagame believed he was being sent to Nigeria, in both cases for extended periods of military training. At this critical time, Kagame persuaded his friend to plead family reasons for not going to the USA: he had to head the invasion! The Ugandan president reluctantly accepted Fred's arguments, and the training in the USA now fell to Kagame, just after he had met and married a lovely Tutsi girl, Jeannette Nyiramongi, whose life so far had been lived in Kenya. She had seen her prospective husband only briefly, but had heard enough about him to be seriously interested. Their first married home was rather surprisingly – especially for the bride – at Fort Leavenworth, the US Army Command and Staff College.[18] Kinzer writes that Paul Kagame's assignment in the United States did not in any way weaken his obsession with returning to Rwanda. In fact, although it took

---

met again in Brussels in 1985, but then did not manage to link up before 2015, when he was the Rwandan ambassador to the United Nations, New York. Our reunion in Kigali when one of my return visits coincided with one of his meetings with President Kagame was short but meaningful! I had been with Matthieu, his father, in a Turin hospital on his fiftieth birthday in 1986, a few days before he died after receiving ineffectual treatment for cancer.

[18] Kinzer, *op. cit.*

him away at an important moment, it was also a chance for him to learn skills that he knew would prove valuable in the war to come.

On arriving in Kansas, he found an apartment, began his coursework, and arranged for his wife to join him. He spoke with Fred by telephone almost daily, the two senior army officers orchestrating the final phase of their plan. They planned to launch the invasion on 1 October 1990, when the presidents of Uganda and Rwanda would both be in New York, attending a UN World Summit for Children. General Fred Rwigyema, in charge of all forces in northern Uganda, moved 2,000 soldiers, all of them of Rwandan origin, to the south of the country along with vehicles and ammunition, with no one objecting! Then the assault took place across a road bridge into Rwanda, past a lightly guarded customs post. With news of the invasion spreading, volunteers were joining them from all parts of Rwanda, so the hoped-for momentum was building up.

The Invading Force

Unfortunately, the well-trained, highly motivated men met with two monumental setbacks. The first was that Maj. Gen. Fred Rwigyema, the overall commander highly respected by every man under his command, was killed on the second day by a sniper's bullet, just six miles inside Rwanda – devastating of course for the RPF troops who saw it happen, and for Paul Kagame when he got the news. Rwigyema's death was kept a secret from most of the men for a month, for fear that they would lose morale and desert the war.

The second setback was met with after the two planners had reckoned on the inadequacy of the Rwandan army to mount much of a counter-offensive. But they had been far from imagining that the RPF on its very first incursion would face attacks from Gazelle helicopter gunships, supplied by France.

Paul Kagame, within several weeks at the US staff college, had already explained to his shocked military hosts that he would soon be obliged to leave, and why. And now, knowing that East African governments as well as that of Belgium would have been warned that he might try to travel and take over the rebel forces, he used subtle and daring means to join the men, narrowly escaping arrest. However, he found the revolutionary army in serious disarray, many valuable fighters (*inkotanyi* – "those who fight bravely") dead. In fact, it was a situation of devastation that greeted him.

Kinzer relates that President Habyarimana had immediately appealed to France for urgent help, untruthfully alleging that there had been heavy fighting in the capital, Kigali. It seems that in fact he had even ordered his own army to stage a night attack on Kigali that he could blame on the RPF, and President Mitterrand was more than ready to bale his friend out. We learn from various sources that, in the early 1990s, France sold the Rwandan regime more than $20 million worth of weaponry and helped it buy five times that amount from arms dealers in Egypt and South Africa, a French bank standing as guarantor. On 6 October the French prime minister, Michel Rocard, announced Opération Noiret – Operation North Wind – under which 600 elite paratroopers would be rushed to Rwanda. They deployed close behind government battle lines, taking over management of the campaign, directing artillery attacks, advising Rwandan commanders on field tactics and supplying essentials. To bolster the French force and to symbolize a continuing interest in a former "colony", Belgium sent 400 soldiers of its own.

Determined to keep Rwanda within its "Francophonie", the collection of some eighty French-speaking States, the French president, François Mitterrand, was ready to go to great lengths to keep hold on it (and prevent it, with its English-speaking invaders, from falling into the hands of the dreaded "Anglo-Saxons").

The Odds Stacked Against Kagame And The Depleted Revolutionary Army

Kagame, known to every senior RPF officer from the previous few years in Uganda as an excellent strategic thinker, experienced fighter and strict disciplinarian, had to think how to rebuild the decimated force, whose future hung on his decisions. No one could have anticipated that he would move the force, apart from a few units left behind as decoys, to several months' cover in the Virunga volcano range that rises to well over three thousand metres above sea level (Karisimbi is the tallest at 4,507 m). It is an intensely cold area deserted by human beings, except for the few researchers at the Dian Fossey mountain gorilla research centre, and, inevitably, some notorious poachers.

The experiment proved successful, though accompanied by a severe lack of food and warm clothing, so the terrible cold was responsible for a number of deaths. The rest of the hardened young men survived the months of Kagame's intensive training, getting to understand their daunting mission more fully. Operations began by taking the government soldiery by surprise in Ruhengeri, in the north-western corner of Rwanda, a vitally important strategic area that saw them achieve success to an almost unimagined degree. No one in the ruling group had realized that the rebel fighters had not simply disbanded.

Then, after a series of other successes, the RPF found an ideal headquarters in an abandoned tea plantation in the north of the country, Mulindi. Kagame could now direct his side of the war from there, and receive visitors. He again had unofficial support from Museveni, who, after recovering from his initial shock over the defections, could see advantages in there being, quite possibly, a RPF government in Kigali. Meanwhile, despite the initial drawbacks of shocking living conditions in the heights, many Tutsis from Rwanda and further afield, and even some Hutus, had joined the ranks while supporters around the world now stepped up their collections of funds, clothing and footwear.

However, the government in Kigali, and in particular a nucleus called the *akazu*[19] that was concentrated around the dictator's extremist wife, now stepped up the gradual brainwashing of the whole Hutu population. A document entitled the "Hutu Ten Commandments" was propagated through an extremist newspaper and was broadcast repeatedly on radio programmes, inciting hate and fear – the start of a process that would end in genocide. Tutsi civilians were attacked, again and again, in waves of massacres, at first in response to the October 1990 invasion, then following the January 1991 raid on Ruhengeri. Kinzer quotes this later conclusion of Human Rights Watch: "Habyarimana's supporters perfected some of the tactics they would use during the genocide: how to choose the best sites to launch attacks, how to develop the violence – both in intensity and extent – from small beginnings, how to mobilize people through fear … and how to build cooperation between civilian, military and militia leaders to produce the most effective attacks."[20] Youth gangs developed into militia squads, being told that killing Tutsis was merely a form of communal work, called "clearing the bush". But, as the regime became more radical and violent,

---

[19] *Akazu*, literally the little house, was the core of the concentric webs of political, economic, and military muscle and patronage that came to be known as Hutu Power, otherwise "Le clan de Madame" (Habyarimana's wife). In his book *Stepp'd in Blood: Akazu and the Architects of the Rwanda Genocide against the Tutsi*, published in April 2019, Andrew Wallis publishes plenty of evidence of the workings of that group of extremists. Another British writer, Barrie Collins, had published a book in 2014 contradicting the nevertheless well-documented facts of the responsibility of the Rwandan *akazu* for the extremist theories and activities.

[20] Kinzer, *op. cit.*, pp.99–100.

some of the Hutu elite distanced themselves from it, a number fleeing the country, some deciding to join the RPF.

While all this was going on, from June 1992 to August 1993 talks were being held in Arusha (Tanzania) between the Rwandan government and the RPF, with a view to ending the civil war and creating a representative government. Members of the international community, in particular France, hoped that an Arusha Accord, if signed, could bring about peace between Tutsis and Hutus. However, tension was building up day by day, and French army officers, some of whom had earlier trained the Presidential Guard in advanced killing tactics, were helping their Rwandan counterparts with the training of new militias, called *interahamwe* ("they who work together"). The Rwandan government tripled the number of men serving in the army, but these youngsters were poorly trained and far from being as motivated as their adversaries, who, two years from the date of the 1990 invasion by 4,000 men, numbered 12,000 *inkotanyi*.

The time came when the invading force was within relatively easy reach of Kigali, having covered a very great distance on foot over six days. The commanders believed that they could even have captured the capital, but Kagame would not authorize a final push, and pulled his puzzled troops back. He had to take the larger picture into account: international pressures had been exerted for some time both on the government and on the RPF to envisage a peaceful settlement, though it appeared that neither side really believed in the Arusha talks. Nevertheless, on 4 August 1993, both sides signed peace accords that catered for a future government in which both sides would play an active part. Earlier, President Habyarimana, under pressure from France, had agreed to legalize opposition parties, and several had emerged, some aiming for democracy. But a violently racist CDR, run by the president's extremist wife, denounced the Arusha Accords, which would give the party no say in the future government, and poured blame on the RPF, the Tutsi, Hutu "traitors" – and also *on their president*.

This seems to have been a parting of the ways – President Habyarimana was beginning to lose control, and the *akazu* was now set on the path to genocide. It used a radio station, Radio-Télévision Libre de Mille Collines (RTLM), to broadcast its venom, giving tips on efficient ways to kill with homemade weapons. All the most ordinary inhabitants of one of the poorest countries in Africa got to hear what that radio station wanted them to hear. The brainwashing would soon be only too effective.

DIANA MISEREZ

The Downhill Slide To Chaos Reported By The Un Special Rapporteur

Warnings of trouble brewing were given inter alia by two United Nations Special Rapporteurs (1991 and 1993), and by the British NGO Oxfam, the latter reporting that Rwanda "stands at the brink of an uncharted abyss of anarchy and violence, and there are all too many historical, ethnic, economic and political pressures that are likely to push it over the edge."[21]

The 1993 Special Rapporteur, Mr B.W. Ndiaye, had carried out a mission to Rwanda in April 1993, reporting back to the Commission on Human Rights which took his report at its fiftieth session in August 1993.[22] In Mr Ndiaye's succinct prose, we read that, during 1992, he had "received reports and allegations relating to extrajudicial, summary or arbitrary executions of unarmed civilians by the Rwandese security forces in connection with the armed conflict between government security forces and the Rwandese Patriotic Front (FPR) since October 1990". He had also received information concerning "killings of members of the Tutsi minority... allegedly perpetrated with direct or indirect involvement of the security forces" (para. 2). He wrote that his work had been greatly facilitated by the considerable amount of information brought to his attention by various human rights organizations, both Rwandan and international, which he said was on the whole sufficiently convincing and precise to be taken into account. Making special mention of the report of the International Commission of Inquiry, which he was able to use as his main working document because of its methodical and specific nature and the diversity and consistency of the testimony it contained, he had concluded after cross-checking that the substance of the allegations of human rights violations and in particular of extrajudicial, summary or arbitrary executions could be regarded as established.

The Special Rapporteur related how, after Habyarimana's 1973 *coup d'état*, regional rivalries were added to the existing ethnic antagonism, with the north-west, the home region of the president, enjoying privileges in relation to the rest of the country. While the majority of the population reportedly considered "that it is possible for the two main ethnic groups to live together peacefully, there is a certain élite which, in order to cling to power, is continuing to fuel ethnic hatred, for instance by spreading rumours prejudicial to the Tutsi" (para. 20). He reported that the situation had become particularly explosive with the distribution of weapons

[21] Quoted by Kinzer, *op. cit.*, p.115.
[22] Economic and Social Council: Document E/CN.4/1994/7/Add.1 of 11 August 1993: Commission on Human Rights, fiftieth session, item 12 of the provisional agenda.

to civilians by the authorities (paras 21–22). The report referred to the number of displaced persons, between 900,000 and one million, adding "an indeterminate number of persons who, as a result of local acts of violence whose presumed perpetrators are still at large, live in a permanent state of terror and dare not move back into their homes, cultivating their fields in the daytime and spending the night in the open or with members of their families" (para. 23).

In the section of the report labelled "A. Types of violations", the Special Rapporteur wrote that killings had been taking place not only in the combat zones during or after clashes but also in areas situated some distance from the hostilities. "In the latter case, it has been shown time and time again that government officials were involved, either directly by encouraging, planning, directing or participating in the violence, or indirectly through incompetence, negligence or deliberate inaction." The number of victims had sometimes reached tragic proportions, as for example in Kibilira, where at least 348 persons were said to have been killed in forty-eight hours shortly after the outbreak of war in October 1990 (para. 28). In the following paragraph, Mr Ndiaye reported that death threats and "political" assassinations had been used to intimidate or eliminate the regime's opponents, witnesses of human rights violations, or human rights activists. Such violations of the right to life had sometimes been committed by government officials.

In the section of his report labelled "B. Persons responsible for violations", he reported inter alia in relation to the hurried recruitment campaign after the start of the armed conflict, increasing numbers from 5,000 to 40,000 men within a few months. The undue haste with which recruits had been selected and instructed had, he said, had negative repercussions on the discipline of the combatants and on their training in the rules of war. These inadequacies, combined with the low wages received by the soldiers, facilitated the crimes committed, such as the endemic practice of raping Tutsi women (cases of twelve-year-old rape victims have been reported), looting, armed attacks, revenge killings and murders of civilians (para. 33). "Soldiers of Bigogwe camp (Mutura Commune) are said to have organized fake attacks by rebels during the night of 4 February 1991, so that they could then unleash indiscriminate and bloody reprisals against those alleged to be responsible. The Forces Armées Ruandaises are also accused of incitement to murder and of giving logistic support to the killers... setting up roadblocks" (para. 35).

The report went on along similar lines for another twenty paragraphs, each tending to be quite as alarming as the others (under headings "Violations attributable to local government officials", "Violations attributable to political party militias", "Violations attributable to clandestine organizations", "Violations attributable to private individuals, to the Rwandese Patriotic Front", "Absence of the rule of law", "Tradition of impunity", "Judicial system (lamentable)", "Absence of any system for the protection of ethnic minorities" and "Injurious propaganda"). Then came the Special Rapporteur's conclusions and recommendations.

The word "genocide" was brought into use by the Special Rapporteur before the much larger-scale violence began, and unfortunately, there was no time to implement the recommendations before April the following year, when all hell would be let loose – even had the UN had the will to try; for they would have required years rather than months, and, furthermore, they would of course also have required the goodwill of the authorities, which patently was not available. The Special Rapporteur must have realized that there was little hope of action being taken on his recommendations before things got out of hand, although his paragraph 60 and the first line of his paragraph 61 remain significant in the circumstances:

> These recommendations take as their starting-point the principle that although their country is poor and overpopulated and they are exposed to all the evils of underdevelopment, Rwandese citizens, whatever their ethnic group, political affiliation or social origin, have the same fundamental rights as all other citizens throughout the world. There is no reason why their lives should not be as precious and well protected as the lives of citizens of the Netherlands, for example.
>
> The international community cannot remain indifferent to their situation and must therefore provide its assistance wherever that of the Rwandese State is inadequate or non-existent.

The Un's Failure To Keep The Peace

A UN Peace-keeping mission *(too small)* was sent to Rwanda in October 1993 *(too late),* with at its head Major General Roméo Dallaire, an experienced and highly conscientious Canadian officer *(poorly briefed,* however, in New York). Very soon after he arrived, and almost daily from then on, he provided UN New York with graphic accounts of the dangerous way in which events were moving towards some sort of climax.

Over months prior to its getting off the ground, the United Nations Assistance Mission for Rwanda, UNAMIR, set up by the UN Department of Peacekeeping Operations headed by Kofi Annan, had had its strength cut back successively by the Security Council to one *that was almost meaningless in the circumstances*. General Dallaire, far from getting a thorough briefing for his mission, was nowhere near grasping "the intensity of the maelstrom into which he was stepping", as Kinzer put it. Like his boss Kofi Annan, he was forced to accept the drastic cuts in manpower that both France and the United States had worked resolutely to bring about. It so happened that Rwanda had a seat on the Security Council at that time, occupied by a representative of the country's extremist faction, in a position to deliver misleading information about the government's intentions to the assembled diplomats.

The reluctance of Western political elites to provide political and material support for the UN Assistance Mission for Rwanda meant that it lacked the backing to undertake population protection and weapons raids. Members of the Secretariat adopted a defeatist approach to the UNAMIR commander's calls for a liberal interpretation of his mandate.[23] As a result, under the authority of Kofi Annan and his team at UN Headquarters, who unfortunately were handling several crisis situations at the same time so cannot have focused sufficiently on the mounting dangers in Rwanda, Dallaire had to proceed with a mission to do nothing more than "monitor observance of the ceasefire agreement" recently signed at Arusha, "monitor the security situation" and "report on incidents". "UNAMIR was deployed naively and undernourished, a deadly combination", an American diplomat wrote afterwards. It simply had no teeth. The day after a formal ceremony to inaugurate the UNAMIR headquarters – and this was many weeks before the fateful day of 7 April 1994 when things got out of hand – death squads attacked in five places and killed more than twenty Tutsi. "The swiftness, the callous efficiency and the ruthless number of men, women and children murdered principally by machetes and bayonets characterized this well-orchestrated operation," General Dallaire reported to New York.

Two weeks later the Force Commander reported another massacre in which eighteen bodies were found with "hands cut off, eyes pulled out, skulls crushed in and pregnant women cut open." Over the next few months, he sent many anguished cables like these. Kinzer surmised that their only

---

[23]   Michael Pugh, Peace Enforcements, Key Developments, in *The Oxford Handbook on the United Nations*, p.379.

effect in New York was to contribute to a spreading sense that Dallaire was an excitable type, overly energetic, and not experienced enough to place African violence "in its tribal context". They must have overlooked the very explicit contents of the report of Mr Ndiaye, UN Special Rapporteur in 1993. One even wonders whether they shared his high-minded principles.

General Dallaire, in his own account of events,[24] relates how in January 1994, an informer whose name was simply given as "Jean-Pierre", a man hitherto seriously involved with the extremists, came to him with an astonishing offer: to reveal the plans by which death squads in Kigali could slaughter 1,000 people in twenty minutes and the places where the army was hiding four large caches of rifles and grenades that were soon to be distributed to *interahamwe* [25](extremist) gangs. The Force Commander prepared a two-page cable outlining his plan to raid the arms depots whose existence violated a provision in the Arusha peace accords, which banned the storage of weapons in Kigali. A few hours later, he was stunned by a return cable from New York that ordered him to suspend his planned raid on the grounds that it "clearly goes beyond the mandate entrusted to UNAMIR".

Other informants came forward in the weeks that followed, all of them warning that powerful Rwandans were methodically preparing to exterminate both the country's Tutsi population and the moderate Hutus. Maj. Gen. Dallaire in a series of cables to New York pleaded for permission to conduct "weapons search and seizure operations". Kofi Annan reportedly turned down these requests, insisting that the UN force "cannot take an active role" and must limit itself to "a monitoring function". Dallaire was warning that a catastrophe was imminent, but his superiors did not want to listen. We now know that Kofi Annan made sure that no ambassadors ever saw the "genocide fax", as Dallaire's cable about Jean-Pierre came to be known. That cable was, as one American diplomat later wrote, "a starkly written warning sign, a scarlet message of danger to civilians, to the peace process, and to peacekeepers… [a] graphic cataloguing of detailed plans for violence and sedition". It is mind-numbing that, to the few UN officials who saw it, it was inconvenient and it proposed an operation that would make the Rwanda mission more complex and therefore more controversial. So to the eternal shame of the United Nations, it was buried.

"We were cautious in interpreting our mandate," Mr Annan's deputy at the UN peacekeeping office, Iqbal Riza, explained afterwards (weakly, it seems, under the circumstances), "because we did not want a repetition

---

[24] Maj.-Gen. Roméo Dallaire, *Shake Hands with the Devil. The Failure of Humanity in Rwanda* (2004).

[25] The word means "those who attack together".

of Somalia." The Clinton administration had been deeply scarred by the Somalia debacle, so, following President Clinton's lead, the Washington officials, despite the clear warnings of the 1993 special rapporteur, kept themselves in wilful ignorance of the looming crisis. Meanwhile, the desperate Dallaire received conflicting instructions.[26] As emerged from a French TV documentary about the genocide screened in early 2019,[27] the Czech President of the Security Council at that time said that had the Security Council been given sight of the "genocide fax", without any question it could have decided to take decisive action. It seems an eternal tragedy that a UN official could take responsibility for suppressing it.

Various testimonies show that the Security Council was seriously concerned with the coming genocide, meeting daily for hours, once it had started to try to decide what to do. It nevertheless reduced the "peacekeeping force" to 400, so no wonder General Dallaire was frantic! Throughout the most critical period, the American delegation steadfastly expected everyone to avoid the word "genocide", given that were it to be accepted that a genocide was being perpetrated, it would automatically bring about some energetic action.[28]

Kinzer raises the question we may all have in our minds: what drove so many Rwandans to become murderers during the terrible spring of 1994? He points out that the various theories include the culture of obedience to authority that has long shaped Rwandan life, overpopulation, the decline of world coffee prices, and the country's long isolation, which "made it easy for uneducated people to believe the monstrous propaganda they heard on the radio". One root cause of the slaughter was "a colonization process that introduced myths of a superior race".

Of course, in essence, this crisis was political. Until the refugees were back and reaching for power, the ruling elite steadfastly refused for three decades to confront the refugee crisis. Powerful Rwandans were determined to stop them at any cost. "Violence intensified as the Arusha process reached its climax. So did the virulence of anti-Tutsi propaganda."[29] To add to the tragic potential of the situation, very many Hutus were keeping aside

---

[26] Just a year later, a UN peacekeeping force, mandated under the same UN Secretary-eneral, Boutros Boutros-Ghali of Egypt, was reduced to equivalent powerlessness in Bosnia and Herzegovina (Chapter 16).

[27] Jean-Christophe Klotz *Retour à Kigali, une affaire française (Back to Kigali, a French Crisis).*

[28] Michael Pugh, *op. cit.*

[29] Kinzer, *op. cit.*, p.132.

from the extremist propaganda. They would meet their deaths along with hundreds of thousands of Tutsis.

Too Late To Prevent The Genocide

On 5 April – two days before the start of the genocide (the term that for a very long time the UN managed to avoid using), the Security Council met to authorize an extension of the UNAMIR mandate. But it seemed impossible at that late stage to do much about it. It was week in which the UN peacekeeping mission in Somalia was collapsing, and in Bosnia, Serbian troops were storming across UN lines to attack the "safe haven" of Gorazde. No one wanted more bad news, and in his report on Rwanda, it appears that the Secretary-General, Mr Boutros-Ghali, did not give any. Reportedly, despite the Force Commander's explicit reports, he attributed much of the violence in Rwanda to banditry, claiming that the country's leaders were committed to the peace process. Belgium, France and the United States skilfully evacuated their soldiers and nationals, reinforcing General Dallaire's conviction that the rapid deployment of just 5,000 well-trained and well-armed professional troops in the first days of the genocide would have stopped or substantially reduced the tragedy. Later, Mr Boutros-Ghali reportedly claimed that if he misled the Security Council, it was only because he had been away from New York for weeks and was not well briefed on what was happening in Rwanda.

French interference was soon to have tragic consequences not only for Rwanda but also for the Congo. When on 6 April 1994, the aircraft bringing the presidents of both Rwanda and Burundi back from the peace talks in Arusha was shot down over Kigali Airport, the French joined the Hutu government in blaming the RPF. No investigation was authorized, but it has seemed more than likely ever since that the Hutu extremists eliminated the Rwanda president as a signal to the masses to begin the killings.

An eminent French journalist, Jean-Christophe Klotz, one of the few to go to Rwanda during the 1994 genocide, brought out in spring 2019 a ninety-minute television documentary entitled *Retour à Kigali, une affaire française* (*Back to Kigali, a French Crisis*) that reproduces many convincing elements on France's role in Rwanda. It shows how deeply implicated the French government seems to have been in Rwandan affairs. We learn that, throughout the genocide, the Rwandan president had daily access by telephone to the Elysée – to President Mitterrand and his top advisers. We see him warmly welcomed at the Elysée Palace, and he probably believed that no matter what his regime did, French support would always be forthcoming. We see top politicians, such as François Léotard, France's Minister of State and Minister of Defence, Hubert Védrine, Secretary General of the Elysée, and many of the top army men of that period speaking about the tragedy.

Rwanda has accused France of complicity in the mass killings – a charge repeatedly denied by Paris.[30] We know that influential NGOs such as Médecins sans Frontières appealed in vain for measures to be taken to stop the killings. The truth should emerge when the serious investigation ordered by President Emmanuel Macron reports, a panel of experts having been appointed to investigate France's role in Rwanda's genocide.

Part II – 7 April 1994 To The End Of The 1990s

7 April 1994

This date will forever be remembered in Rwanda, and by all others who love the country. When on 6 April the aircraft bringing back from Arusha the presidents of both Rwanda and Burundi was shot down, this is thought to have been the signal[31] for the ready-prepared genocide plans to be launched without delay. Perhaps it was, for although the RPF was immediately accused of causing the death of Mr Habyarimana and his counterpart from Bujumbura, others have believed that it was the *akazu* that so wanted the country's president out of the way that they decided to kill him – and so have a free hand to carry out their plans.[32]

---

[30] The experts will now consult archives to analyse France's role. They will have access to presidential, diplomatic, military and intelligence archives, Mr Macron's office said in a statement. Julien Allaire of Survie, a Paris-based NGO that focuses on relations between France and Africa, told the BBC that there was already ample evidence of "France's diplomatic, military and economic support for the Rwandan government before, during and after the genocide". A French author, Patrick de Saint-Exupéry, wrote in *Le Figaro* of 12 January 1998 that François Mitterrand had remarked to his aides, "Dans ces pays-là, un génocide c'est pas trop important" (In those countries, a genocide isn't anything very much). One can scarcely believe it.

[31] Hugh McCullum, a Canadian author working in 1994 for the All Africa Council of Churches, wrote later, "What happened in Rwanda was premeditated murder, a genocide with clear motives, means and opportunity to carry it out. The plane crash was merely the signal."

[32] Kinzer tells us that a Belgian scholar, Filip Reyntjens, had asserted at a press conference in Brussels in 1993 that powerful Rwandans, members of the *akazu*, among them Madame Habyarimana, her three brothers and a powerful military

The "hate radio", "Mille Collines", announced the death of the president, naturally attributing it to Tutsi rebels and inciting the population to rise up to avenge it. As per the prearranged plans, the Presidential Guard and gangs of young *interahamwe* militia set up roadblocks across Kigali, getting some of them in place within an hour of the plane crash. Now the death lists prepared ahead of time came into rapid use as part of the meticulously planned brutal campaign to eliminate the Tutsis by any foul means – some of which would turn out to have been previously unimaginable. Maj. Gen. Dallaire relates in his book[33] how Colonel Bagasora, head of the army, called a meeting on the evening of that 6 April at which he claimed to have events under control. Dallaire protested that the Prime Minister, Madame Agathe, should be in control, at which Bagasora curtly replied that Mme Agathe "didn't enjoy the confidence of the Rwandan people and was incapable of governing the nation". Hours later, thugs arrived to capture, rape and kill the poor woman, whose five children managed to hide and were later picked up by a brave UN peacekeeper. A contingent of ten Belgian UNAMIR peacekeepers who had arrived just too late to try to save her were ordered by a Rwandan officer to surrender their arms and were taken to Camp Kigali, the military base in the centre of town. There they were held for several hours, before being tortured, murdered and mutilated.[34] Maj. Gen. Dallaire had probably the worst of his many shocks on coming upon their remains, having gone to look for his men.

The American woman mentioned earlier, Rosamond Halsey Carr, who spent her life farming in Rwanda, wrote that as of 7 April, gangs of militant Hutu extremists spread across the countryside, rounding up tens of thousands of young men and inciting them into a frenzy of hatred toward the Tutsi. And that the following morning she awoke to find the house surrounded by twenty of more teenage fanatics wielding clubs and shouting wildly. "I had known some of those boys since they were babies. They stormed through my house and searched the grounds, looking into cupboards and under beds for people who had been their neighbours and friends all their lives. I could do nothing but watch in silent fury…" and as she learned weeks later, after she had been forced to leave the country,

---

commander, Colonel Théoneste Bagosora, had secretly established a "Zero Network" of militias and death squads being trained to commit mass murder. Bagosora, a graduate of the French military academy, had been involved with the first waves of Tutsi massacres from 1959 to 1963.

[33] Dallaire, *op. cit.*

[34] As a result of this atrocity, Belgium recalled the rest of its peacekeepers – another shock for Dallaire.

"Kigali dissolved into a state of anarchy and terror, as soldiers and guards loyal to Habyarimana went on a rampage, rounding up opposition leaders and their families. Cabinet ministers were abducted and the acting prime minister was executed. Amid the violence, ten UN Belgian peacekeepers and seventeen Jesuit priests were tortured and killed."[35]

Rosamond, the last remaining expatriate farmer, was evacuated on Sunday, 10 April. "I was awakened at six o'clock on Sunday morning to the sound of Belgian soldiers banging on my front door, ordering me to leave immediately. 'You have exactly five minutes to pack!' they shouted. This time I did not hesitate. Dazed and still in my nightgown, I hastily stuffed precious papers and photographs, my jewel case, and a few articles of clothing into a small suitcase. ... Numb with grief and sorrow, I left my beloved Rwanda. ... During April and May, the genocide escalated to horrific proportions. I spent hours glued to the television watching images that will haunt me for the rest of my life. ... People were dragged from houses, offices, and churches and were executed by gangs of drunken young men using guns, grenades, machetes, and axes to carry out their deadly mission. Patients were slaughtered in hospital beds. Mutilated bodies littered the streets of Kigali and piled up in every building."[36] She went on to describe the situation in Kigali, the food shortages, the scarcity of drinking water, the fact that power lines were cut and phone lines down. "Chaos reigned, and the air was thick with smoke from burned-out villages and the stench of thousands of rotting corpses. Amid the carnage, there were also moments of extraordinary bravery and sacrifice, as many Hutu risked their lives to protect Tutsi friends and neighbors. Two wars raged simultaneously in Rwanda, one was the battle between the two armies – the Rwandan military and the RPF for control of the country, and the other was the systematic slaughter of all ethnic Tutsi by the *interahamwe*. The streets were ruled by hostile young thugs urged on by government radio and fuelled by cane liquor or banana beer, greed, and tribal hatred."

In the first twenty-four hours after the plane crash, the Presidential Guard, the army and *interahamwe* units killed 6,000 Rwandans, among them almost every opposition figure in the country. Three days later, the death toll had reached 20,000. In the ensuing days, weeks and months hundreds of thousands of Tutsi and moderate Hutu – half of them children, no doubt – came to be killed. People were killed in their homes, at roadblocks

---

[35] Rosamond Halsey Carr with Ann Howard Halsey, *My Life in Rwanda* (2000).

[36] This brave woman, absolutely devoted to Rwanda and its people, had been advised earlier to leave, but had adamantly refused. Rosamond Halsey Carr, *op. cit.*, pp.207–209.

and in churches where they had believed they might be safe. Some hid in the bush, but were found and slaughtered. With the abominable violence was the equally abominable deception. People naturally believed that if they could only reach the inside of a church, they would be safe. But many of the priests – naturally not all – were actually with the killers.

In New York there was talk of withdrawing UNAMIR, and Dallaire referred to "the Security Council and all its dithering".[37] Before long, as he wrote, "The Council had finally voted for the skeleton force option. The resolution's phrases were pure UN-ese: 'having considered... express regret... shocked... appalled... deeply condemns... demands... decides... reiterates... reaffirms... calls upon... invites... decides to remain actively seized of the matter.'" All peacekeepers were to be pulled out of Rwanda, except for 270 whose main job would be to observe the slaughter. With Resolution 912[38] now in writing, Dallaire had to explain to his troops – many of whom were very tired and sickly because of the lack of proper food and medicine, while others were in a zombie state after living horrific and traumatic experiences in this cesspool of guts, severed limbs, flesh-eating dogs and vermin – that although acts of heroism had been performed by many of them, "the world had decided not to support us in our efforts but instead to pull most of us out to safety".[39] And he also said, "Ultimately, led by the United States, France and the United Kingdom, this world body aided and abetted genocide in Rwanda. No amount of its cash and aid will ever wash its hands clean of Rwandan blood." Despite the exceptional dedication of those making up the peacekeeping force – many in the end severely traumatized and unfit for further service – the UN failed Rwanda ignominiously.

With almost all the foreigners evacuated from Rwanda and the UN force reduced to almost nothing, the killers resumed their activities with awful efficiency. An ICRC statement quoted by Kinzer declared, in uncommonly straightforward terms, "Whole families are exterminated. Babies, children, old people and women are massacred in the most atrocious conditions, often cut with a machete or a knife or blown apart

---

[37] Dallaire, *op. cit*, p.308.
[38] Dallaire, *op. cit.*, p.322. What Kinzer termed "an ignoble document... agreeing to emasculate the peacekeeping force". The result would undoubtedly have been different if Kofi Annan or Boutros Boutros-Ghali had shown Security Council members copies of Dallaire's cables, for they made it unmistakably clear what was happening. "The message Boutros-Ghali sent to the Security Council before its vote, however, said something very different: that the violence in Rwanda was 'indiscriminate' and the product of 'chaos'." Kinzer, *op. cit.*, p.156.
[39] Dallaire, *op. cit.*, p.323.

by grenades or burned or buried alive. The cruelty knows no limits." Tens of thousands fled to churches, but many clergymen did not protect them, several of the Catholic bishops being close to the regime. A few days after the genocide began, Archbishop Vincent Nsengiyumva of Kigali, chairman of the president's political party for over a decade, issued with other bishops a statement supporting the government and urging Rwandans to respond favourably to its programme.[40]

While some Rwandan priests, nuns and lay workers saved lives, often at the cost of their own, as Kinzer relates, many cooperated with the killers, some turning away Tutsi families seeking refuge. "Others gave refuge but then summoned militia gangs to kill those they were sheltering. In the western town of Nyange, Revd. Athanse Seromba's church was packed with two thousand refugees when a gang of *interahamwe* killers appeared on April 12; he showed them how to break in and after they had finished throwing grenades into the huddled crowd encouraged them to finish off survivors. At a church complex in the south-central town of Nyamata, ten thousand people were slaughtered..."[41]

Philip Gourevitch gives us in his book[42] the terrifying story of what happened to seven Adventist pastors from the area near Kibuye, a town on Lake Kivu, who had addressed a respectful letter to the head of the church, telling him that they had information that they were to be killed the following day with their families, and begging him to intervene with the mayor. "We believe," they wrote, "that with the help of God who entrusted you the leadership of this flock, which is going to be destroyed, your intervention will be highly appreciated, the same way as the Jews were saved by Esther."

---

[40] The *New York Times* published a report by Paul Lewis on 10 June 1994 stating that the Roman Catholic Archbishop of Kigali, two other bishops and ten priests had been killed by soldiers of the RPF. "Lieut.Col. Frank Mugambata, the rebel commander in the western town of Gitarama, said that the bishops and priests were killed by 'undisciplined soldiers' who had been sent to guard them. The soldiers thought these clergymen had been implicated in the earlier massacre of their own families. He said the soldiers would be severely punished."

[41] Kinzer, *op. cit.*, p.160, and Gabriella Venturini, *The Hague Justice Portal* (http://www.haguehisticeportal.net) "Rwanda's Unanswered Screams: Still Seeking Justice after the Seromba Trial", 28 February 2007. Athanse Seromba had escaped and lived quietly near Florence, Italy for several years working as a parish priest, before in 2002 appearing for trial by the International Criminal Tribunal, Arusha. He was first sentenced to fifteen years' imprisonment, then following the prosecutor's appeal, to life imprisonment.

[42] Philip Gourevitch, *We Wish to Inform You that Tomorrow We Will Be Killed with Our Families* (Farrar, Straus and Giroux, 1998).

The seven signatures followed, perfectly visible on the photocopy that Philip Gourevitch was given a couple of years later when he located the former pastor Ntakirutimana at his home in the USA.[43] The author had heard in Rwanda in 1995 the whole story about the seven pastors and the 2,000 members of their flocks who were all killed in the hospital where they had taken refuge. Fifty thousand people were killed in Kibuye before the killers eventually left for Zaïre.

As most of the world turned away from the crisis, the RPF advanced, its force swelling to over 20,000. By the beginning of June, more than half of them were fighting around the capital, and reportedly, French leaders were horrified. A confidential memorandum Stephen Kinzer quotes, after remarking that not since France's humiliations in Indochina and Algeria had it faced such a complete defeat, said:

> Considerable political and geo-strategic interests are hidden behind the Rwandan heap of corpses. The region cannot be left in the hands of an English-speaking strongman completely aligned to American views and interests.[44]

And Kinzer continued to relate that, determined to prevent this outcome, President Mitterrand sent a steady stream of supplies to the Rwandan army, in mid-June dispatching two planeloads of weaponry, "including thousands of the fragmentation grenades that *interahamwe* killers liked to throw into huddled crowds of refugees. In the end, though, no amount of armaments could stop an attacking enemy with the advantages the RPF enjoyed."

Of these advantages, the deputy UNAMIR commander, General Anyidoho, wrote that the force "was very cohesive and disciplined. They received no salaries, but had a vision and purpose for going into guerrilla warfare. ... The RPF soldier was alert, day and night. He lived a life of

---

[43] This man after all the killings, in which clearly he had participated, had fled Rwanda and had managed through a son who was a cardiologist in the USA to get US residence permits ("green cards") for himself and his wife. The following year, he was accused by Tutsi survivors who had managed to track him down of having been involved in the criminal killings of the 2,000 people who had taken refuge in the hospital of Mugonero, where another son of his was a doctor. To Gourevitch, he did not deny having received the letter, but he made up a story about what he had done after going to see the mayor (if indeed he ever went) and about sending a message to the seven pastors that the mayor had said that he could do nothing. He was very indignant that some Rwandan Tutsis had found him and accused him of responsibility for thousands of Tutsi deaths (he actually spoke to Gourevitch of it being 8,000). Later, he was arrested by the FBI, released and, after another period, arrested again.

[44] Kinzer, *op. cit.*, p.172.

deprivation but remained steadfast to his cause. He received no pay, wore any type of clothes and footwear, but his determination to have a home and a country spurred him on to success."[45]

Day in, day out throughout those terrible weeks of April and May, then throughout June and into July, the regime's "Mille Collines" radio broadcasts continued to whip up hate, convincing the population that the invading Tutsi army would rape and murder them all. It was not long before the radio called for the murder of General Dallaire too. Kagame and his fellow commanders, who had observed the ceasefire provided for by the Arusha Accords, had no choice now but to push forward with all speed to try to stop all the killings –going on all over the country except in those areas already captured by the RPF. Afterwards, it was estimated that between a quarter and a half million women were raped and mutilated before they were killed.

Unfortunately, there were other churchmen heavily involved in the genocide. For example, while Father Pierre Ngoga, a local priest, had sought to defend threatened people and paid for it with his life, another local priest, Father Thadée Rusingizandekwe was described by survivors as one of the leaders of several *interahamwe* attacks. The Bishop of Gikongoro, Monsignor Augustin Misago, was often described as a Hutu Power sympathizer, and had been publicly accused of barring Tutsis from places of refuge, criticizing fellow members of the clergy who helped them. On 4 May, accompanied by policemen, he told a group of ninety Tutsi schoolchildren not to worry, because the police would protect them. But, three days later, the police helped to massacre eighty-two of the children.[46]

The horror that had begun in earnest – a 100-day paroxysm of state-sponsored killing – would cost the lives of a million people,[47] killed in the most horrifying circumstances. Rape was one form of murder widely used, the HIV virus being transmitted to many women, not all of whom died despite their awful wounds.

All that remains as disturbing as ever in the minds of many Rwandans and all those who love the country and its people. Today one cannot travel far in the country without coming across one genocide memorial after another. My Tutsi friends, Damien and Thaciana Ngabonziza, now living in Kigali after years in exile,[48] accompanied a friend and me on a journey in the direction

---

[45] Kinzer, *op. cit.*, p.172.

[46] Related by Philip Gourevitch, *op. cit.*

[47] The Rwandan government put this figure at over one million, even if the UN and others often use the figure of 800,000.

[48] They had fled in 1973 through forest at the foot of the volcanoes after receiving a compelling warning. Damien later became secretary-general of the International

of Lake Kivu in March 2015. They pointed out a place where they said that 50,000 people had been massacred in the space of two weeks, and it was not only Tutsis who were massacred; all the moderate Hutus were killed too, along with Hutus married to Tutsis – as has been confirmed by many sources.

Further French Interference

By mid-June, the RPF seemed to be so much on the verge of taking over the whole country that the interim government fled to Gisenyi at the tip of Lake Kivu, mentioned at the beginning of this chapter as Kisenyi. Enormous masses of Hutu, estimated at two million, were fleeing along the roads in advance of the RPF, believing them to want to kill them – since that is what they had been told repeatedly. President Mitterrand, still determined to prevent an RPF victory, decided to order the French army to Rwanda, as a last-ditch effort to save its besieged client regime. General Dallaire was told by Bernard Kouchner, well known from other humanitarian theatres, that it was sending a force into Rwanda to stop the genocide and deliver humanitarian aid, setting up a safe haven in the west of the country where Tutsis fleeing could find refuge. Dallaire was shocked in the extreme:

> I began to swear at the great humanitarian using every French Canadian oath in my vocabulary. He tried to calm me with reasons that probably sounded high-minded to him but, considering the track record of the French in Rwanda, struck me as deeply hypocritical. Surely the French knew that it was their allies who were the architects of the slaughter… I could not believe the effrontery of the French. … The *génocidaires* believed the French were coming to save them, and they now had carte blanche to finish their gruesome work.[49]

The embarrassment of diplomats and world leaders that had amplified as news of the slaughter in Rwanda spread led to a unanimous Security Council vote to approve a sixty-day French mission, and the next day French troops began arriving at airstrips in eastern Zaïre (today's DRC), to bring a fleet of helicopters, fighter-bombers, armoured vehicles (100) and a battery of 120 mm machine guns to their self-proclaimed "Turquoise Zone" in Rwanda. One and a half million people flooded into the "Turquoise Zone".

Social Service, Geneva. He told me how he felt when he had to go to Rwanda on mission, soon after the genocide, visiting one or two remote areas.

[49] Dallaire, *op. cit.*, p.422.

Most were of course Hutus who had actively or passively participated in the genocide, Kinzer writes. "Announcers from the Mille Collines hate-radio station even turned up with their transmitter, so the station was able to continue broadcasting as if nothing had happened. Dallaire was outraged. ... France's claim that the Turquoise Zone was created to save innocent lives, though, was only for public consumption. It was above all a safe haven for the defeated regime and its army." The killing of Tutsis in that zone went on unchecked until the end of August, despite the presence of French soldiery.[50]

Dallaire realized the nature of the catastrophe that seemed to loom ahead. He was quite right: these disastrous measures initiated by President François Mitterrand were the beginning of a process that would end with huge numbers of terror-stricken Hutus being ushered by the French into Zaïre ahead of the *génocidaires* or *interahamwe*, where they would be trapped for some two years, closely controlled by the latter. The heavily armed extremists would be free to enjoy the indefinite use of the weaponry they had taken with them, even managing to import ammunition, and as General Dallaire explained to a senior US State Department official whom he went to Nairobi to meet, would regroup and prepare to fight again.

As usual, Dallaire was right. Thus began the chaos and the never-ending violence in Kivu to be reflected on further in Chapters 15 and 17, "Children" and "Rape as a weapon of war".

Could It Not Have Been Different?

Well, of course it could. Michael N. Barnett published in 2010 a series of essays on the UN and humanitarianism,[51] in which the question of ethics came up, not least in relation to what he called "one of the twentieth century's darkest chapters: the genocide in Rwanda". He writes that working at the US Mission to the United Nations and assigned to cover Rwanda, he like many others had grave doubts as to whether a humanitarian intervention might stop the genocide, and he and others spent considerable energy debating how to justify non-intervention. But, in due course, he learned that Secretary-General Boutros-Ghali and Under-Secretary for Peacekeeping Operations Kofi Annan had been receiving detailed recommendations from General Roméo Dallaire, including a fairly well-conceived plan for intervention,

---

50 Colette Braeckman, *L'Homme qui répare les Femmes* (2015).
51 *The International Humanitarian Order Security and Governance* (Routledge), Introduction, p.13. See also Michael Barnett's Chapter 6, The UN Security Council, Indifference, and Genocide in Rwanda, pp.111–139 in the same publication.

while consistently and repeatedly telling the Security Council that it had not received any concrete suggestions from General Dallaire, intimating that he was too overwhelmed by events to develop any contingency plan. Barnett writes that reasons for the Secretary-General's office withholding information that would provide fuel for an intervention became something of an obsession for him for several years.[52]

There is another angle to which I will hold for the rest of my life, namely that given the reputation of Prince Sadruddin Aga Khan, an outstanding UN High Commissioner for Refugees, UN Special Rapporteur and top UN trouble-shooter, it is grievous that he was passed over for the "top job" because of a Soviet veto (never explained). He was ready, if elected as Secretary-General of the United Nations, to take initiatives and to use diplomacy in tricky situations. He had had considerable experience in the 1960s and 1970s of Rwanda, its colonial and neo-colonial background and its refugee flows. Had he *only* been appointed Secretary-General in 1981 when a majority of nations voted for him, I know that he would have seen to it that he was consistently briefed[53] and would have devised measures on the one hand to give greater support to the *moderate* Hutus and, on the other, to restrain France from giving unlimited support to the presidential family. We know that the escalating Hutu extremism stemmed from that presidential family and gradually stifled all attempts to build a fairer society.

Even if this extraordinarily able man had been elected Secretary-General of the UN only ten years later, in 1991 (when Mr Boutros Boutros-Ghali was appointed), his influence would surely have saved those 800,000 to a million lives and intolerable, incalculable suffering on the part of survivors. The trauma of people who saw their families hacked to death, who themselves were amputated and scarred by machetes and who lost their homes, would never have occurred. Had Sadruddin been at the helm in the UN when the situation in Rwanda deteriorated to the extent that it did under Mr Boutros-Ghali, surely the Security Council would have felt bound to agree to realistic measures being put in place – instead of there

---

[52] In 2002, Michael Barnett published *Eyewitness to a Genocide: The United Nations and Rwanda* (Cornell University Press, 2002).

[53] In pages 200–202 of the biography, *Prince Sadruddin Aga Khan Humanitarian and Visionary* (2017) we read of measures he envisaged in 1981 to analyse such a situation well in advance and plan a contingency action. "What is the ethnic composition (of a country)? What are the cultural and social realities? Where might a clash arise? Where would a spark be that could ignite a major crisis?" all combined with "the strengthening of the UN's peacekeeping and peace-building role." He was a great believer in taking initiatives in preventive diplomacy, as his record shows.

being "too little, too late". However, this was not to be, as several members of the Security Council, not to mention the UN Secretariat, were unwilling to attribute weight to the terrible warnings of the UN Special Rapporteur, Mr Ndiaye, and as we see, they were not given all the facts anyway.

As it was, the Force Commander in the conclusion to his long account of the very traumatic time that he was in Rwanda wrote, "Could we have prevented the resumption of the civil war and the genocide? The short answer is yes. If UNAMIR had received the modest increase of troops and capabilities we requested in the first week, could we have stopped the killings? Yes, absolutely. ...If UNAMIR 2 had been deployed on time and as requested, would we have reduced the prolonged period of killing? Yes, we would have stopped it much sooner."[54]

How tragic that the world remained blind, week after week, to what was happening in that little overpopulated country. It is surely no wonder that the new Rwanda government, facing utter chaos and hardly knowing where to begin to rebuild the country, had no confidence whatsoever in the international community. It had to take over the abject ruins of a severely traumatized, dysfunctional country that was now short of not only the million or so killed in the previous hundred days, but also of about two million who had fled in terror into neighbouring countries, a majority into Congo (then called Zaïre) along with the defeated army, the Presidential Guard and the *"génocidaires"*, who had been allowed by the French military on the border to take their arms and equipment with them. These armed men threatened their unfortunate charges with death if they did not flee into Zaire, while keeping up the fiction so long propagated by the hate radio "Mille Collines" that the Tutsi army was bent on massacres.[55]

These dangerous men and their charges overran the border town of Goma, filling the limited lakeside area of barren volcanic rock at the base of the Nyiragongo volcano. The hitherto pure water of Lake Kivu was soon

---

[54] Dallaire, *op. cit.*, p.514.

[55] Kinzer gives the following disturbing account: "On the 17th of July, twenty thousand soldiers arrived in Goma as intact fighting units. Their leaders said they had run out of ammunition to fight the RPF, but they had in any case retained much of their hardware. Their equipment included sixty-two armored cars with either cannon or machine guns mounted, over 250 mortars, twelve howitzers, thirty-five air defense weapons, fifty anti-tank guns and six helicopters, some of which were armed as gunships. Once regrouped with the militias, in September 1994 it was estimated that the total forces available around Goma from the losing side in the Rwandan civil war numbered between 34,000 and 37,000 fighting men. ... For the hard core of defeated Hutu leaders and their murderous militia cohorts, the determination to finish off a bloody mission which had begun in April 1994 remained undiminished."

polluted by dead bodies and human waste. Desperate from hunger and thirst, many died of starvation and of cholera, and a Canadian relief worker wrote, "Overnight the pleasant resort town of about 150,000 on the shores of a lovely lake became an indescribably filthy, sick city of eight hundred thousand or more desperately poor people stretched out to the edges of the lake as far as one could see through the stench and smoke." By the end of July, 3,000 people were dying every day in those insalubrious camps around Goma. President Bill Clinton was finally pushed into action by what people now saw on television (having seen nothing of the genocide…)In a three-day airlift, waves of American planes landed at Goma, bringing 4,000 fully equipped soldiers to build shelters, dig latrines and distribute relief supplies worth nearly half a billion dollars.[56]

UNHCR would try to ensure, with the World Food Programme and a host of NGOs, that these people would not starve, although the situation was unique and judged to be far from being in conformity with UNHCR's original mandate, the first Statute of which lays down that it "under the authority of the General Assembly, shall assume the function of providing international protection… to refugees who fall within the scope of the present Statute". For this mass of Hutus was not the kind of refugee exodus that seemed to justify UNHCR setting up refugee camps in terms of its mandate to protect and assist refugees: it was a huge mass of fearful people whose fears had been initiated and intensified by the military factions that had driven them across the borders, and who very soon turned out to be the people running the camps – before long carrying out cross-border raids to kill some of the remaining Tutsis.

There were NGOs whose staff very quickly realized that far from being standard refugee camps, these settlements were army camps holding civilians, and some of them left. It has been pointed out that, once it became clear in mid-to-late 1994 that the settlements along the Zaïre–Rwanda border were and would remain either militarized bases for armed operations or sources of supplies, including recruits, for such activities, UNHCR had no lawful basis upon which to continue its presence. It is beyond doubt that the servicing of combatants and non-combatants contributed to, even if it was not directly responsible for, the decision to neutralize those settlements as threats to the security of Rwanda.[57]

---

[56] It is a bitter truth that a military deployment on that scale could have stopped the genocide. Leaders of the new regime in Kigali were naturally outraged by this injustice.

[57] From an offprint from *Refugee Rights & Realities: Evolving International Concepts and Regimes*, edited by Frances Nicholson and Patrick Twomey (Cambridge University Press, 1999).

At all events, the UN High Commissioner for Refugees, Mrs Sadako Ogata, having involved UNHCR in the care and maintenance of this tremendous number of Hutus, resisted the idea of repatriation. There is after all the sacrosanct principle that all refugee repatriation must be voluntary. As the criminals in charge of the camps would not allow people to exercise their will in the matter, and in fact threatened people with death if they attempted to go back – just as they had threatened them with death if they did not flee – everything stayed the same for two years.[58] It was then as a result of Paul Kagame's determination to bring them back, connected with the intended campaign of Laurent Kabila to overthrow the Zairian dictator Mobutu, that the camps were suddenly dismantled militarily, and from the north of Lake Kivu huge numbers streamed back into Rwanda, where they were received very peaceably. Unfortunately however, from the southern end of the lake, huge Hutu crowds accompanied by the armed contingents fled *westwards*, into forested areas of a region that the most dangerous of them would now infest. Inevitably, there would be cross-border raids from Zaïre/Congo, and the new Rwandan government would not be given the chance to tackle in peace the immense challenges it was facing. At the same time, Kivu became an area far more dangerous than it had been in the 1960s.

Similarly impressive numbers of Rwandan Hutu were made to repatriate from Burundi and Tanzania at around the same time.

How To Breathe Life Into A Devastated Rwanda...

Paul Kagame and his fighters took over a country totally drained of life, shattered morally, politically, socially and economically. The UNAMIR peacekeepers were shattered too, some of them palpably damaged mentally, perhaps traumatized for the rest of their lives. The whole scenario could not have been more appalling. And to think that had some of the people in New York taken their responsibilities seriously, the whole abhorrent tragedy need not have happened. Some of them, when they began to take stock of their inaction and of what had led up to it, understandably felt sincere contrition – but naturally far too late, of course, for it to do any good.

Kinzer writes that everyone who made it to Kigali in July 1994, including every RPF soldier, was shocked by the piles of decomposing corpses. "In the city, on the outskirts, and in most of the surrounding

---

[58] Hutu leaders had issued radio broadcasts inciting their countrymen to flee. "If you stay in Rwanda", they threatened, "the RPF will kill you in revenge – or we will kill you as traitors." Rosamond Halsey Carr, *op. cit.*, p.210.

countryside, bodies lay in ravines, in half-dug graves, and heaped atop each other inside churches. Many were mutilated."[59] He went on to say that the murder of so many people in such a short time (100 days) was too overwhelming a reality for most Rwandans to grasp – far beyond the scope of human imagination, in fact.

> Beyond the impenetrable tragedy of mass murder, beyond the looting that had left Rwanda with no foundation on which to build a new state, lay another, more ghostly challenge. It was buried within the broken hearts and spirits of survivors. They moved, walked, and spoke, but few were truly alive. To call them traumatized would be to trivialize their anguish.

Kinzer compared what he called "the teeming chaos of sprawling refugee camps" with its surreal counterpart in an empty Rwanda, where half of those who had been alive three months earlier were either dead or in flight. Whole regions were left without a single inhabitant. ... "Amid this spectral emptiness, the new regime in Kigali struggled for its bearings."

In the USA, Rosamond Halsey Carr, a few weeks from her eighty-second birthday, wrote that she was sick with worry for the people she loved and wracked with guilt for abandoning them in such haste – although she had certainly had no choice! Consumed by unbearable heartache and an irrepressible desire to go back, she decided in the teeth of opposition from her family to return, although she realized that the Rwanda she had known was gone forever. "Somewhere in the back of my mind," she wrote, "I had the crazy idea of converting the old pyrethrum drying house into a shelter for lost and orphaned children. I didn't know how I was going to do it. I didn't even know if any of my workers were still alive or if my house was still standing. I only knew that I had to go home."[60]

In the next chapter, we shall see the results of this extraordinary determination to do everything she could for the young survivors of the horror.

After The Savagery, The Duplicity, The Looting... Trauma And Instituting A Justice System

To attempt to show how Paul Kagame succeeded against heavy odds in rehabilitating Rwanda and gradually making it admired by people across the world would take several chapters. But let's turn to the judicial efforts

[59] Kinzer, *op. cit.*, pp.181–182.
[60] Rosamond Halsey Carr, *op. cit.*, p.212.

that came to be made to pin down and to sentence perpetrators of the overwhelmingly tragic events.

The Gacaca Court System (Pronounced GA-CHA-CHA)

The new regime arrested tens of thousands of people identified by neighbours as killers, having to wait a long time however for those who had fled abroad. Government investigators soon named more than 800,000 suspects, but the true number of killers turned out to be considerably higher than that. As there was far from enough space in prisons for all those arrested, many had to be left to return to their communities to await trial, and gradually, though the process took years, they were all tried.

As Rwanda's legal system – like everything else – was left in ruins after the genocide, most of its lawyers having been killed, the UN set up the International Criminal Tribunal for Rwanda in neighbouring Tanzania, described briefly below. But this left so many hundreds of thousands of people accused of involvement in the killings and other forms of violence with whom it was imperative to deal that it was decided, after years of study and debate, to revive the ancient *Gacaca* or community courts, which used in the past to take care of family disputes or other grievances of a local nature. Several judges would sit in the presence of a crowd from the community.

In the *Gacaca* system, communities at the local level elected judges to hear the trials of genocide suspects accused of all crimes except the planning of genocide. The courts gave lower sentences if the person was repentant and sought reconciliation with the community. Often, confessing prisoners returned home without further penalty or received community service orders. More than 12,000 community-based courts tried more than 1.2 million cases throughout the country.

Paul Kagame said, "The trauma, the results of these horrible events – we are trying to find some silver lining and build on it. ... The process of healing is proceeding probably better than I expected at the time of the liberation, but it will take a long time." Writing in 2008, Kinzer quoted these remarks of Kagame's, while going on to say that in his view, "Rwanda has barely begun to confront the mental illness that envelops the country like an oppressive black cloud, unseen but unavoidable." Nevertheless, while he thought that most victims had no access to counsellors, therapists or antidepressant drugs in a country with "a nationwide mental health crisis" (as the Harvard programme in Refugee Trauma had put it), the Gacaca courts (2001–12) had become, as he said himself after attending one, "group therapy sessions as much as judicial proceedings. They are cathartic and often excruciating. Nowhere else do Rwandans have a chance to mourn together while confronting those who terrorized them."[61]

The Gacaca trials also served to promote reconciliation by providing a means for victims to learn the truth about the death of their family members and relatives. At the same time, they gave perpetrators the opportunity to confess their crimes, show remorse and ask for forgiveness.

A BBC staff member in Kigali, Prudent Nsengiyumva, spoke about the weekly Gacaca courts held in villages across the country, usually outdoors in a marketplace or under a tree. One of the main aims of the *gacaca* was, she said, to achieve truth, justice and reconciliation among Rwandans. The courts gave lower sentences if the person was repentant and sought reconciliation with the community. Often, prisoners who confessed returned home without a further penalty, or received community service orders. The Gacaca trials served to promote reconciliation by providing a means for victims to learn the truth about the death of their family members and relatives, while giving perpetrators the opportunity to confess their crimes, show remorse and ask for forgiveness in front of the whole community. The hearings gave communities a chance to face the accused and give evidence about what really happened and how it happened. Many people in Rwanda say that this process helped to mend the wounds of the past. The judges, mostly lacking legal qualifications, were elected from within communities, and were given a few weeks' training before the dates of hearings.

These courts functioned for just over ten years, being closed officially in June 2012. Kinzer again quotes Paul Kagame as having said that the backdrop in relation to dealing with crime and coping with trauma was that the whole population should be involved and be seen to be buying into the process of justice and reconciliation. Historically, he said, Gacaca meant people sitting on the grass to discuss and resolve problems, as part of Rwandan culture. "Conventional systems have not provided a solution for us. They do not come close to giving us a solution. *Gacaca*, with all its weaknesses – and there are not so many, fewer than in a conventional system if you're dealing with our problems – opens up opportunities for us."[62] In those ten years of existence, almost two million cases (involving a little over one million *génocidaires*) were prosecuted in more than 11,000 Gacaca courts for crimes such as killings, rapes, torture and property crimes (in fact all except the planning of the genocide, tried in a higher court). The

---

[61] Kinzer, *op. cit.*, pp.255–256.
[62] Kinzer, *op. cit.*, p.257.

conviction rate was high, at one stage mentioned as being in the region of 65%. Between 250,000 and 500,000 girls and women, mostly Tutsi, as well as boys and men, were raped by Hutu extremists. Many were also tortured and mutilated. Hundreds of thousands of children were orphaned. These figures show the magnitude of the genocide in which a majority of the population participated.

Everyone from a particular community during the genocide was eligible (or even expected) to be present at the Gacaca, and to participate during the proceedings. In all, 254,000 judges were elected by the population and given a few weeks of training, but, according to one report, some 40% were found to have been involved in the genocide and had to be replaced. "Confessions, guilty pleas, repentance and apology played an important role, and influenced decisions about the length of a sentence or community service. The *Gacaca* courts were set up to allow the population of the same community to work together, to judge those who had participated in the genocide, to identify the victims and rehabilitate the innocent. The Gacaca court system was therefore a basis for collaboration, reconciliation and unity among Rwandans."[63]

Depending on the measure of the sentences, those with light convictions were allowed to return to their communities; the others went to prison and were made to work in agriculture. Travelling along a valley from Kigali towards the west of Rwanda in March 2015, I saw large numbers of these men, dressed in pink and well guarded, toiling in the fields. Of those who were released and sent back to help rebuild communities, some brought problems: "Survivors are worried about their security because they are living side by side with those who had wanted to previously exterminate them," Albert Gasake, the legal Advocacy Project Coordinator at the Survivors' Fund Organisation told the BBC's *Network Africa* programme. "Suspicion is very high," Mr Gasake said, and added that failure to compensate survivors for the loss of their properties posed another threat to genuine reconciliation.

There would appear to be a huge amount of grieving still needed in Rwanda, grieving for the people who were massacred – partners, children, parents, siblings... grieving for lost limbs and disfigured faces, grieving for the homes and belongings set on fire, grieving for the understanding that used to exist between people of different ethnic backgrounds. How could any community come to terms completely with all the hate-induced violence of 1994, and of the subsequent years that the *interahamwe*

---

[63] A.M. de Brouwer and E. Ruvebara, *International Criminal Law Review*, Vol. 13 (2013) 937–976.

continued to attack some of the peaceful communities of north-western Rwanda. Indications still abound of very painful memories of the genocide, for example the birth twenty-five years ago of children born of rape, a major feature of the genocide. Today neither they nor their mothers are accepted by society, for they are ostracized largely because of what happened, not so much, probably, because of who they are now.

The International Criminal Tribunal for Rwanda (ICTR) was established by the United Nations Security Council on 8 November 1994 (Resolution 955):

> International Tribunal for the Prosecution of Persons Responsible for Genocide and Other Serious Violations of International Humanitarian Law Committed in the Territory of Rwanda and Rwandan Citizens Responsible for Genocide and Other Such Violations Committed in the Territory of Neighbouring States, between 1 January 1994 and 31 December 1994

The first trial started in January 1997, and by December 2012 the Tribunal had completed the trial phase of its mandate. During its two decades of work in Arusha, Tanzania, the ICTR sentenced sixty-one people to terms of up to life imprisonment for their roles in the massacres. Fourteen accused were acquitted and ten others referred to national courts. The ICTR held 5,800 days of proceedings, indicted ninety-three people, issued fifty-five first-instance and forty-five appeal judgements, and heard the "powerful accounts of more than 3,000 witnesses who bravely recounted some of the most traumatic events imaginable during ICTR trials," ICTR President Judge Vagn Joensen told the UN Security Council in December 2015. The ICTR was formally closed on 31 December 2015.

The Mechanism for International Criminal Tribunals (MICT), set up by the Security Council in December 2010, took over the remaining tasks of the ICTR, as well as of the International Criminal Tribunal for the Former Yugoslavia (ICTY). The Mechanism plays an essential role in ensuring that the ICTR's closure does not leave the door open to impunity for the remaining fugitives. The ICTR branch of the Mechanism began to function on 1 July 2012.

The Tribunal issued several landmark judgments, including:

- In the first judgment by an international court on genocide, a former mayor, Jean-Paul Akayesu, was convicted in 1998 of nine counts of genocide and crimes against humanity. The judgment was also the first to conclude that rape and sexual assault constituted acts of genocide insofar as they were committed with the intent to destroy, in whole or in part, a targeted group.[64]

- The conviction of the prime minister during the genocide, Jean Kambanda, to life in prison in 1998 was the first time a head of government was convicted for the crime of genocide.
- The Tribunal's *Media Case* in 2003 was the first judgment since the conviction of Julius Streicher at Nuremberg after the Second World War to examine the role of the media in the context of international criminal justice.[65]

The National Court System

A national court system was also at work, prosecuting those accused of planning the genocide or of committing serious atrocities, including rape.

---

[64] The Case of Jean-Paul Akayesu: after an intense and precisely targeted campaign of a number of international non-governmental organizations, which aimed at raising awareness of gendered violence at the ICTR, the trial of *Jean-Paul Akayesu* established the legal *precedent* that *genocidal rape* falls within the act of genocide. "the [Trial] Chamber finds that in most cases, the rapes of Tutsi women in Taba, were accompanied with the intent to kill those women. ... In this respect, it appears clearly to the chamber that the acts of rape and sexual violence, as other acts of serious bodily and mental harm committed against the Tutsi, reflected the determination to make Tutsi women suffer and to mutilate them even before killing them, the intent being to destroy the Tutsi group while inflicting acute suffering on its members in the process."[Presiding judge *Navanethem Pillay* said in a statement after the verdict: "From time immemorial, rape has been regarded as spoils of war. Now it will be considered a war crime. We want to send out a strong message that rape is no longer a trophy of war." (Found on Wikipedia). Nick Louvel and Michele Mitchell made a film about the former mayor, Jean-Paul Akayesu. In the *New York Times* of 20 October 2016, Ken Yaworowski relates how the film, entitled *The Uncondemned* and running for one hour twenty-one minutes, was made about this man who encouraged and ordered rape. He writes that witnesses had been intimidated and killed, while others held back. But eventually Akayesu was given a life sentence.

[65] The Case of Ferdinand Nahimana and Jean Bosco Barayagwiza The trial against "*hate media*" began on 23 October 2000. It was charged with the prosecution of the media which encouraged the genocide of 1994. On 19 August 2003, at the tribunal in Arusha, life sentences were requested for *Ferdinand Nahimana*, and *Jean Bosco Barayagwiza*, persons in charge for the *Radio Télévision Libre des Mille Collines*, as well as *Hassan Ngeze*, director and editor of the *Kangura* newspaper. They were charged with genocide, incitement to genocide, and crimes against humanity, before and during the period of the genocides of 1994. On 3 December 2003, the court found all three defendants guilty and sentenced Nahimana and Ngeze to

By mid-2006, the national courts had tried approximately 10,000 genocide suspects. In 2007, the Rwandan government abolished the death penalty, which had last been carried out in 1998, when twenty-two people convicted of genocide-related crimes were executed. This development removed a major obstacle to the transfer of genocide cases from the ICTR to the national courts at the end of its mandate.

Unity And Reconciliation In Rwanda

The reconciliation process in Rwanda focuses on reconstructing the Rwandan identity, as well as balancing justice, truth, peace and security. The Constitution now states that all Rwandans share equal rights. Laws have been passed to fight discrimination and divisive genocide ideology.

Primary responsibility for reconciliation efforts in Rwanda has rested with the **National Unity and Reconciliation Commission**, established in 1999. It makes use of the following approaches:

- **Ingando**: A programme of peace education. From 1999 to 2009, more than 90,000 Rwandans participated in these programmes, which aim to clarify Rwandan history and the origins of division among the population, promote patriotism and fight genocide ideology.
- **Itorero**: Established in 2007, the Itorero programme was a leadership academy to promote Rwandan values and cultivate leaders who strive for the development of the community. From 2007 to 2009, 115,228 participants took part in the Itorero program.
- **Seminars**: Training of grass-roots leaders, political party leaders, youth and women in trauma counselling, conflict mitigation and resolution, and early warning systems.
- **National summits**: Since 2000, several national summits have been organized on topics related to justice, good governance, human rights, national security and national history.
- **Research**: The National Unity and Reconciliation Commission has published a number of studies investigating the causes of conflicts in Rwanda and how to mitigate and resolve them.

---

life imprisonment and Barayagwiza to imprisonment for thirty-five years. On 28 November 2007, the Appeals Chamber partially allowed appeals against conviction from all three men, reducing their sentences to thirty years' imprisonment for Nahimana, thirty-two years' imprisonment for Barayagwiza and thirty-five years' imprisonment for Ngeze (Wikipedia).

When I was about to fly to Kigali with a friend (March 2015), my Rwandan friend Damien wrote, "You're not going to recognize Kigali!" Of course, he was right. Though I had been there in 1986 to run an eight-day International Red Cross training course, a magnificent modern city of one million inhabitants had now replaced the quiet dusty place I had first seen when driving the new Land Rover through in 1965 and the modest capital of the 1980s. The Rwandan ambassador to the United Nations (mentioned in a footnote) instructed his driver to show us all of Kigali. We were impressed beyond words.

Stephen Kinzer wrote in the introduction to his remarkable 2008 book about the country, "It has recovered from civil war and genocide more fully than anyone imagined possible and is united, stable, and at peace. Its leaders are boundlessly ambitious. Rwandans are bubbling over with a sense of unlimited possibility. Outsiders, drawn by the chance to help transform a resurgent nation, are streaming in", and Bill Clinton, Bill Gates and Howard Schultz (the chairman of Starbucks) were among those mentioned.

President Paul Kagame said at the twentieth anniversary of the genocide, "Rwandans were made to think of their weakness instead of their strength. Raising the level of dignity so that know they are capable – this is what our concept is about." Kagame the visionary, the former guerrilla fighter in Uganda, the inspiring leader of the forces that overthrew the dictatorship and the long-term president, has been keen on having his country move ahead, asserting that democracy and development go hand in hand – as he says, "complex, but there it is!" Rwanda has been hailed as a model of transformation, "a development miracle, a success story." In a round-table television discussion on Rwanda just last week, the majority opinion, voiced inter alia by Jonatan Rosenthal, chief Africa editor of *The Economist*, was that Rwandans are generally happy with the progress in their country.

But the cost of the years of violence, in particular of course 1994, comes in terms of post-traumatic stress, suffered by an unknown proportion of the population, some of whom must still be suffering from physical wounds too, having suffered amputations or other forms of maiming during the atrocities of April–June 1994 – not to mention the women who became pregnant as a result of rape, and now live with the twenty-five-year-olds they bore, ostracized by the general population.

What Can Be The Extent Of Post-Traumatic Stress?

In March 2013, an article was published online entitled: Rwanda – Lasting Imprints of a Genocide: Trauma, Mental Health and Psychosocial Conditions in Survivors, Former Prisoners and Their Children by *Heide Rieder* and *Thomas Elbert, University of Constance*. It is a long, scholarly paper for which there would be insufficient room in this book, but the authors are happy to have a few extracts included here. The focus of the study, carried out six years after the genocide, included former prisoners, i.e. people who may well have been perpetrators of the genocide and who subsequently spent two stressful years in camps before returning to Rwanda, often to prison.

Abstract

Background

The 1994 genocide of the Tutsi in Rwanda left about one million people dead in a period of only three months. The present study aimed to examine the level of trauma exposure, psychopathology, and risk factors for posttraumatic stress disorder (PTSD) in survivors and former prisoners accused of participation in the genocide as well as in their respective descendants.

Methods

A community-based survey was conducted in four sectors of the Muhanga district in the Southern Province of Rwanda from May to July 2010. Genocide survivors ($n = 90$), former prisoners ($n = 83$) and their respective descendants were interviewed by trained local psychologists. The PTSD Symptom Scale Interview (PSS-I) was used to assess PTSD, the Hopkins Symptom Checklist (HSCL-25) to assess symptoms of depression and anxiety and the relevant section of the M.I.N.I. to assess the risk for suicidality.

Results

Survivors reported that they had experienced on average twelve different traumatic event types in comparison to ten different types of traumatic stressors in the group of former prisoners. According to the PSS-I, the worst events reported by survivors were mainly linked to witnessing violence throughout the period of the genocide, whereas former prisoners emphasized being physically attacked, referring to their time spent in refugee camps or to their imprisonment. In the parent generation, when compared to former prisoners, survivors indicated being more affected by depressive symptoms ($M = 20.7$ (SD = 7.8) versus $M = 19.0$ (SD = 6.4),

$U = 2993$, $p < .05$) and anxiety symptoms ($M = 17.2$ (SD $= 7.6$) versus $M = 15.4$ (SD $= 7.8$), $U = 2951$, $p < .05$) but not with regard to the PTSD diagnosis (25% versus 22%, $\chi^2(1,171) = .182$, $p = .669$).

A regression analysis of the data of the parent generation revealed that the exposure to traumatic stressors, the level of physical illness and the level of social integration were predictors for the symptom severity of PTSD, whereas economic status, age and gender were not. Descendants of genocide survivors presented with more symptoms than descendants of former prisoners with regard to all assessed mental disorders.

Conclusions

Our study demonstrated particular long-term consequences of massive organized violence, such as war and genocide, on mental health and psychosocial conditions. Differences between families of survivors and families of former prisoners accused for participation in the Rwandan genocide are reflected in the mental health of the next generation.

Introduction

In April 1994, Rwanda was immersed in a brutal wave of organized violence that left an estimated one million people dead in a period of only three months. Civil war, genocide against the Tutsi minority group and violent reprisal attacks until 1998 horrified its inhabitants. The thoroughly planned and state-monitored genocidal violence was specifically marked by the extensive participation of the local population: neighbors went after neighbors by means of guns, machetes or sticks during house to house searches, at roadblocks or at central congregation points. Looting, destroying property and genocidal acts including murder and sexual violence were common [1]. Overall, more than 10% of the country's 7.8 million population and approximately 75% of the Tutsi ethnic minority were killed and a huge number of people ended up widowed or orphaned. In the direct aftermath of genocide, two million people took refuge in the neighboring countries. Many of them did not reenter Rwanda prior to 1996, when the refugee camps began breaking down and people felt encouraged and/or coerced to return. In many cases, a return to Rwanda was followed by immediate incarceration. The release of these prisoners did not begin before 2002 when *Gacaca*, a judicial initiative based on a traditional Rwandan mechanism of local conflict resolution, was implemented to confront the estimated 1.2

million cases [2]. Until the present day, genocide survivors and those who participated in the genocide continue to live next door to each other.

In the aftermath of 1994, genocide survivors showed high rates of mental health and psychosocial problems due to the inconceivable, dehumanized brutality that the majority of them had been exposed or witness to. Entire family systems as well as the general social fabric that formerly provided support were destroyed due to losses of family members and growing mistrust and fear following the genocide. A great majority of the survivors were female and woman-headed households proved to be especially vulnerable, suffering from the effects of economic deprivation, which included a lack of food, housing and money for the education of their children [3].

1. Straus S. How many perpetrators were there in the Rwandan genocide? An estimate. Journal of Genocide Research. 2004;6(1):85–98. doi: 10.1080/1462352042000194728.
2. Human Rights Watch. Justice Compromised. The Legacy of Rwanda's Community-Based Gacaca Courts. New York: HRW; 2011.
3. Kumar K. In: Women and Civil War. Impact, Organizations, and Action. Kumar K, editor. London: Lynne Rienner; 2001. Civil Wars, Women, and Gender Relations: An Overview; pp. 27–38.

Apart from general population samples, studies analyzing the mental health situation in Rwanda following the genocide have mainly focused on groups of widows and orphans or children living in child-headed households. An elevated level of depressive and anxious symptoms as well as PTSD was found in each of these groups [4-7]. On the other hand, little to nothing is known about the mental health situation of former prisoners in Rwanda, many of which spent several years in refugee camps after 1994. It is assumed that former prisoners – that is, accused perpetrators and their respective families – also present with mental health problems, whether due to their participation in [8,9] or exposure to violence, genocide and their refugee status. Concrete data on this is, however, currently lacking.

4. Straus S. How many perpetrators were there in the Rwandan genocide? An estimate. Journal of Genocide Research. 2004;6(1):85–98. doi: 10.1080/1462352042000194728. [CrossRef]

5. Human Rights Watch. Justice Compromised. The Legacy of Rwanda's Community-Based Gacaca Courts. New York: HRW; 2011.

6. Kumar K. In: Women and Civil War. Impact, Organizations, and Action. Kumar K, editor. London: Lynne Rienner; 2001. Civil Wars, Women, and Gender Relations: An Overview; pp. 27–38.

7. Dyregrov A, Gupta L, Gjestad R, Mukanoheli E. Trauma exposure and psychological reactions to genocide among Rwandan children. Journal of Traumatic Stress. 2000;13(1):3–21. doi: 10.1023/A:1007759112499. [PubMed] [CrossRef]

8. Schaal S, Elbert T. Ten years after the genocide: trauma confrontation and posttraumatic stress in Rwandan adolescents. Journal of Traumatic Stress. 2006;19(1):95–105. doi: 10.1002/jts.20104. [PubMed] [CrossRef]

9. Brounéus K. The trauma of truth telling: effects of witnessing in the Rwandan gacaca courts on psychological health. Journal of Conflict Resolution. 2010;54(3):408–437.

The above is nothing more than a somewhat tantalizing glimpse of the effects of massive trauma on the Rwandan population as detected by researchers a few years ago. To know more about how people are progressively recovering from their extremely damaging experiences, we would need to extend our search to other sources of data. However, despite it being impossible ever to account fully for that inconceivable violence, it did seem essential before reaching this point to devote space to relating the events that led up to the genocide, which is why Chapter 14 is the longest in this book.

Going on to feature children, we turn to Chapter 15, "Children".

CHAPTER 15

Children

**Trauma amongst children and the psychological
consequences for children of war trauma and migration**

In one case out of two, "refugee" also means "child". UNHCR

Refugee children are children without a country or a home. Sometimes they no longer even have a family. They are children without a childhood, as Sybella Wilkes wrote after spending some time among refugee children in Kenya, who had fled terror in Sudan, Ethiopia and Somalia. It was evident that it was very difficult for those children, robbed of their childhood innocence, to deal with the emotional horrors they had experienced. So they were reluctant to talk about their experiences, but after a time, supplied with paper and paints, many of them expressed what they had been through in pictures.[1] Then a few of them did manage to talk about what they had been through.

As we all know, childhood is the time when we form our view of the world and how to act within it; whether to trust others or to fear them; whether to seek love or avoid pain; whether to use force or kindness to achieve our goals. What happens in childhood generally shapes the people we become. In Chapter 9, Dr Barudy gave us plenty of insights into the situation of children in situations of uprooting. Refugee children are in double jeopardy, because they are children and because they are refugees. What can be more bewildering to a child than to know that there are people seeking to take their parents away, or to be caught up in war, or to be taken over mountain passes at night – or to be put on frail boats,

---

[1] Sybella Wilkes, *One Day We Had to Run!* (Evan Brothers Ltd., in association with UNHCR and Save the Children).

sometimes without a parent. Drawings refugee children make, sometimes years after these events, illustrate all too plainly that these experiences leave an indelible mark. It is unacceptable that children, the most innocent of victims, should be so scarred by violence and uprooting.

A young Sudanese boy eventually came to speak of what had happened.

It was something like an accident when I ran away from my village. We were playing at about 5 o'clock when these people, the soldiers, came. We just ran. We didn't know where we were going to, we just ran. My brother helped me to run. We didn't know where our mother or father were, we didn't say goodbye. I didn't see the soldiers, I just heard the shooting, the screaming and the bombing that went DUM, DUM, DUM like this and killed many people. We ran without anything – no food, no clothes, nothing.

In the day the sun is hot and your feet burn. So we walked at night when it is cold, because then you don't say all the time, "I want water, I want water." Wild animals, lions, killed many people. We ate soil and the leaves of trees. The big boys knew the way. I think God showed us the way.

People died of hunger. I saw many dying. Even my friend died. There was no water, no food. When I saw my friend dying, I carried on walking. You see sometimes you can help, and then sometimes you can't.

After two months, we came to the Anyak tribe who knew the way to Ethiopia. They helped us get fish, we would catch the fish standing in the river. To go to Ethiopia, to the Panyido refugee camp, there was a big river we had to swim across. Many people drowned on the way. ... In Panyido, we did not have food for two months, but at least there was peace. Then the United Nations, he came, he saw the people, he went to Geneva to find food and he came back.

This boy related how, after three years in Ethiopia, where the refugee children could eventually go to school, they and the UN were expelled by the new Ethiopian authorities and they had to face a long series of other calamities. But he wrote, "One day I will be an engineer to build Sudan. I don't know whether my mother and father are dead or alive. I was nine when I left Sudan. I am 14 now."

An appalling fact is that some of the people of South Sudan have been forced to leave their homes up to four times, as victims of the civil war that has now raged for several years. Since South Sudan became independent, the rest of the world naturally hoped that the suffering southern Sudanese would at last be able to live in peace.

Such Losses…

It is difficult to express all the losses that a refugee child can suffer. Many lose their parents and others who had been close to them. There is the void that is left when refugee children lose their culture, language, school, friends, toys and pets. The community that offered a place for the child outside of the family had gone, along with personal possessions, familiar foods, even the usual skills and games learned in childhood. However resilient children are often found to be, even childish spirits can reach breaking point.

In an international seminar the president of the Erikson Institute for Advanced Study in Child Development in Chicago said that young children can cope well with the stress of social disasters like war if they retain strong positive attachments to their families, and if parents can continue to project a sense of stability, permanence, and competence to their children. The homelessness that comes to the children when the family becomes refugees creates vulnerability that often gets translated into developmental harm. Chronic danger imposes a requirement for developmental adjustment – particularly when that danger comes from a violent overthrow of day-to-day social reality, as is the case in war and communal violence. A severely traumatized child is likely to draw conclusions about self-worth, about the reliability of adults and their institutions, and about the safe approaches to adopt towards the world.[2]

Several other speakers stressed that in a war or refugee situation, it is the mother's attitude, her own ability to cope, that will determine the coping mechanisms of the child. Margaret McCallin, the moving spirit for the seminar, remarking on the strength and fortitude of refugees and displaced people, urged that one should not equate resilience with *invulnerability*. She pointed out that in the initial stages of an emergency, or upon arrival at a camp or settlement, some people may seem to be coping well. But one should not assume that their capacity to cope will continue unaltered.

And that includes children. The research carried out among Mozambican and Salvadoran refugees – both groups with multiple traumatic events

---

[2] *The Psychological Well-Being of Refugee Children – Research, Practice and Policy Issues* (International Catholic Child Bureau, 1992).

behind them – indicated that the children were significantly affected by the mothers' emotional well-being. Refugee women who have been victims of traumatic events are subject to a range of stressful daily life events, and both conditions cause the women considerable emotional distress: they worry constantly about their present situation, and added to this they are troubled by the frequent intrusion of memories of the traumatic events they have experienced. Such flashbacks, rather like reliving those events all over again, bring with them all the feelings of fear, horror and personal vulnerability that were present at the time. So women exposed to extreme situations of generalized violence might be exhausted through trying to cope with the consequences of these experiences, and find that their capacity to cope with everyday life has been severely curtailed. This is what happened with numerous women in territories of the former Yugoslavia in the 1990s, and doubtless is the situation of millions of Syrian and Yemeni women today.

Children's Rights

Children of course have rights – the right to love, understanding and affection, the right to appropriate food and medical care, the right to education, the right to have access to games and recreation, the right to a name and a nationality, the right to be assisted in case of disaster, to learn to be a full member of society and develop one's full potential, to be brought up in a spirit of peace and universal brotherhood, and the right to exercise those rights without distinction as to one's race, colour, sex, religion, nationality or social group. These rights are enshrined in the United Nations Convention on the Rights of the Child of 1989 (of which 196 countries are "States Parties", while the USA has simply signed it). Article 22.1 of the Convention confirms the right of the refugee child to "receive appropriate protection and humanitarian assistance in the enjoyment of applicable rights" and Article 39 proclaims that "States Parties shall take all appropriate measures to promote physical and psychological recovery and social reintegration of a child victim of any form of neglect, exploitation, or abuse; torture or any other form of cruel, inhuman or degrading treatment or punishment, or armed conflicts. Such recovery and reintegration shall take place in an environment which fosters the health, self-respect and dignity of the child."

UNICEF wrote on the appropriate website:

> In 1989 something incredible happened. Against the backdrop of a changing world order world leaders came together and

made a historic commitment to the world's children. They made a promise to every child to protect and fulfil their rights, by adopting an international legal framework – the United Nations Convention on the Rights of the Child.

Contained in this treaty is a profound idea: that children are not just objects who belong to their parents and for whom decisions are made, or adults in training. Rather, they are human beings and individuals with their own rights. The Convention says childhood is separate from adulthood, and lasts until 18; it is a special, protected time, in which children must be allowed to grow, learn, play, develop and flourish with dignity. The Convention went on to become the most widely ratified human rights treaty in history and has helped transform children's lives.

The Convention is the most widely ratified human rights treaty in history. It has inspired governments to change laws and policies and make investments so that more children finally get the health care and nutrition they need to survive and develop, and there are stronger safeguards in place to protect children from violence and exploitation. It has also enabled more children to have their voices heard and participate in their societies.

South East Asian Child Refugees

I would like us to contemplate the situation of the children who had belonged to their Vietnamese families before being sent out to sea, who got involved with the Khmer Rouge, or who belonged (or belong) to victims of rape. We have seen in Chapter 9 what measures are beneficial for children once they are in a more settled situation after knowing fear and flight from countries like Chile. Over and above these categories are other children caught up in severe repression, overt violence and even (and especially) genocide (Chapter 14).

In Chapter 11, we saw that large numbers of Vietnamese chose to take the risk of leaving their country in fishing boats. Some parents thought that their children would have a better future if they got to the West, and, as a result, many of the boats carried youngsters whose parents had sent them out from Vietnam, just with an older sibling or with a neighbour. Some of those children did not even know that they were being sent out to sea. This was a particularly sorrowful aspect of the whole exodus.

It seems incomprehensible that parents could do that. Some of the children had experiences that they would never be able to forget. One eleven-year-old girl who had left Vietnam alone had fallen victim to the pirates' violence. She said "I feel as if I were stripped of being as child. My classmates back in Vietnam are still like I was before. I wonder how they will learn about growing up." This poor girl was one of the few children who would talk about the violence at sea. Their childhood and innocence had been torn away at a stroke.

Some Western practitioners, because they are generally rather overworked or because their training has not alerted them to the particular situation of refugees and refugee children, may tend to react to them as if their life began only when they reached our shores. Many have tried to help refugees start a new life in the expectation that the traumatic past would be put behind them and forgotten. But a psychiatric consultant, clinical psychologist and paediatrician for the Paris Hospitals, Dr Kim Nguyen Ba Thien, spoke at Vitznau[3] of how she and her staff aimed to focus practitioners' attention on the supportive role they can play, both through practical measures and through psychological support, thus helping prevent the development of psychiatric problems. But she pointed out that this can be achieved only through familiarity with each child's personal history, supposing that they have been given proper information as to how best they can help.

Caught up in a historical process, these children have been plunged abruptly into the twofold drama of war and exile. Both bring about the destruction of established patterns, and hence the need for psychological adjustment, so both should be recognized as potentially traumatizing and may lead to the onset of mental disorders of varying severity, depending upon personality, earlier experiences, age, family and social fabric. As these events are risk factors for psychological breakdown; the child needs to establish a personal space that is sufficiently safe and in which he can maintain his identity and come to terms with the shattering of his past, restructuring himself if need be, so that his development can proceed smoothly. But if the child fails to make the necessary psychological adjustments, what help can be given, and above all, what can be done to forestall such failure. This is a crucial question and, in response to it, a British social worker, Rosalind Finlay, said:

[3] The five-day Red Cross workshop on psychological problems of refugees and asylum seekers mentioned earlier in this book. I quote here and again later in the chapter several paragraphs from a comprehensive account, Dr Nguyen Ba Thien and Dr Brigitte Malapert, The Psychological Consequences for Children of War Trauma and Migration, in *Refugees, the Trauma of Exile*, ed. Miserez (1988).

Of course, the children's new school is of considerable influence and importance in their development. It is in school that they may be pressured to deny their heritage as well as the violent disturbances which have brought them there. It is the school that must share the responsibility for validating their life, their personal and national identity, their language, customs and ways of life, in order to help them adjust – however temporarily – to their new circumstances.

To encourage the acquisition of a new culture and identity through school by denying their past is to encourage untold problems for them later in life, precisely to do with their confused sense of identity.

It is important to see the child in the whole context of his past and his present and to help him or her adjust to the present by going through the mourning process so essential to psychological well-being, by understanding what are the bases for his or her life now, and by learning what he or she can expect life to bring in the future.

Dr Ba Thien underlined the importance of that mourning process:

> Mourning over the trauma experienced, mourning for the actual death of parents, siblings, extended family, compatriots, mourning for the loss of a homeland and for family and friends left behind, mourning for the part of oneself which has gone, for a past that is lost. The child victim of war must bear all these sorrows and share in those of the people around him...
>
> Every refugee child needs to work out his mourning, not in order to forget what happened, but to come to terms with it so as to achieve release from anxiety and be able to invest in a new life. This need for psychological adjustment is compounded by the need for adjustment imposed by *exile*. Migration launches the child and his family into a whole new space/time dimension and into a different socio-cultural environment. ... New behaviour and thought patterns have to be worked out, and even further efforts of psychological adjustment are needed to bring about a new equilibrium. Behind the refugee child lies the land he or she has had to leave and a traumatic past, and before him lies an unknown destiny in a new land, a present situation to cope with, and a future to be traced out.

Children – like adults – can have delayed psychological reactions to earlier traumatic experiences. Some Cambodian children developed psychological problems years after leaving their country. Perhaps the young Cambodian refugee in Switzerland who had been glad to be granted Swiss nationality had an unpleasant shock when he was called to undertake the military service that is compulsory for men at the age of eighteen. I was told that he was palpably traumatized by the sight of firearms.

There are unfortunately situations in which children find they are on their own. It's a bewildering time, a distressing time for orphaned and exiled children – far more so, of course, than for those sharing exile with their parents. It cannot be other than a damaging time, even though in adversity the child may develop qualities of resourcefulness and courage that will serve him or her well later on. But, even when the family nucleus remains intact, the adults may find that their parental role, to care for the child, to guide and direct, to protect and shield, to be seen by the child to be in control of the circumstances of their lives, is to some degree (and sometimes to a very marked degree) stripped away. Before flight some children see their parents growing increasingly powerless to control events, humiliated, and perhaps arrested. Their confidence in the adult world is shaken. Intuitively, they become aware of strange and mounting tension in the family context, and their own anxiety mounts. There are children who are forced to witness events no child should ever have to see.

And now these children have neither home nor country. They have to rely on outsiders for food, shelter and clothing. They are vulnerable to nutritional deficiencies and to the diseases which poor nutrition, combined with water shortages and cramped, overcrowded camp conditions, can foster. The children often have to assume tasks normally carried out by adults, while contending with the dilemmas created by their propulsion into a different culture. They have few opportunities for play – a fact which represents another hindrance to each child's rehabilitation and development. Yet this is the lot of half of the world's refugees.

Some have been born into the refugee camps, and have known no other life – as has happened with young Afghans, spending their formative years in tented camps along Pakistan's border, seeing their mothers constrained by the mullahs to remain hidden in the tents. The presence along the border of millions of mines has sometimes turned nightmare into stark tragedy. A similar fate was that of Cambodians trapped for so long on the Thailand–Cambodia border. Years ago, a visitor to one such camp for Cambodian refugees spoke in an international meeting of the nine-year-old boy whose foot was blown off by a land mine when he was looking for fresh vegetables on the outer perimeter of the camps, going on to talk of other maimed children, for example the twelve-year-old refugee girl who had been gang-raped by armed camp guards, and the six-year-old boy whose leg was severed by a hand grenade in the early hours of Christmas Day...[4]

What will be the social development of children growing up in an environment which is tantamount to that of a prison camp – particularly those children without a close bond with a parent?

Dr Ba Thien spoke of the clinical study that she and her staff made of thirty cases of children referred to their psychology and psychiatry consultancy service at the Trousseau Hospital in Paris. They were aged between five and eighteen, with adolescents in the majority. In most cases, they had started to have problems between one and three years after arriving in France. The most common pathology found was a *temporary state of depression* (nine cases), shown in the form of difficulties at school (intellectual blockage, lack of interest, and behavioural disorders leading to failure). Seven of the nine had had to face the loss of parents, and were living in institutions. They responded to therapy, which consisted essentially of helping them to work through their uncompleted process of mourning. Then there were *temporary behavioural disorders* (three cases), taking the form of aggressive attitudes towards others and/or withdrawal, mutism, and deteriorating school performance. They were rapidly amenable to simple treatment through short periods of supportive psychotherapy. *Psychoses* (five cases): the doctors retained the classical term of *acute paranoid disorder* to describe the abrupt onset in two adolescents of initial episodes of behavioural disorders, accompanied by pervasive delusions and failure at school. In both cases, this indicated a transition to a psychotic state, and the boys were hospitalized, one with a follow-up for three years as an outpatient with medical treatment as indicated. His recovery was satisfactory. The second case was an unaccompanied minor, taken into a psychiatric hospital and the outcome was not known. Of the other cases, one was of an adolescent girl who had attempted suicide on her arrival in France, and a little girl of seven who had presented dissociative pre-psychosis detected at nursery school, but, again, follow-up did not prove to be possible.

Somatic illness (five cases): sudden outbreaks of profuse sweating, fits of vomiting, difficulty in breathing, repeated fainting fits, secondary

---

[4] Dieter B. Scholz, An Eye-Witness Account: The Wounds of Refugee Children, *Children Worldwide*, Vol. 14, No.2 (International Catholic Child Bureau, Geneva, 1987)

incontinence: the spectacular nature of the symptoms and their interference with daily life was noted. The children had had to be hospitalized before they were referred to the consultancy. In all cases, the onset of the symptoms was directly connected with an event (life in a prison camp, start of the exodus etc.) The evolution of the five cases was satisfactory, with supportive psychotherapy for periods ranging from a few months to a year.

Anxiety neurosis (one case): this unaccompanied minor was referred by a psychiatric service following violence towards himself and others, and epileptiform fits. The evolution of the rather spectacular disorders was satisfactory: psychotherapy for eighteen months, a new approach to schooling, being looked after by siblings.

Four of the others had *learning problems*, the difficulties arising from bilingualism and late schooling (for, of course, many refugee children miss out on education for several years).

Difficulties at school: twenty-two of the thirty children in the study presented difficulties at school (the reason for consultation or an underlying cause). The geographical displacement resulting from migration means a change of country and hence of language and sociocultural values. Every refugee child immediately has to face the language problem. Mastering a new language means acquiring the power of communicating with others, and forging a possible link between the world of the child's country of origin, with its sociocultural reference from the past, and the world of the host country in which the future will lie, for he has to move from one to the other.

Gaining access to this new value system through the acquisition of the new linguistic code in which it is encrypted means being able to interpret the new environment, and this understanding in turn facilitates new learning and hence better integration. But this confrontation may pose problems, for the child is caught between two cultural systems and is forced to define his own position. It is obviously impossible for him to abandon his original frame of reference completely. A little Vietnamese girl was asked by her Swedish teacher why she did not walk home with some of her schoolmates, who lived in the same part of town, perhaps even in the same street. She explained that she needed this lone walk to change from "being a Swede" (which she had been all day) to "being Vietnamese" (as she was of course at home), and vice versa each morning. She was probably one of countless refugee children who have had to rely on such astute solutions in their daily lives.

Rwandan Displaced Children

Several years ago, Paul Kagame, naturally very concerned with the mental health of Rwandans, said, "It's a seriously wounded society that we're managing." As in Cambodia, the violence deeply affected everyone, including (and perhaps especially) the children. To understand, as Westerners, the measure of the horror, we probably don't need to see either the film *The Killing Fields* (1984) about the death and destruction in Cambodia, or the film *Hotel Rwanda* (2005) about the experience of people saved, against the heaviest odds, from the genocide brutality by being sheltered for several weeks in the "Hotel des Mille Collines" (to give it its proper name). In any case, the stark statistics compiled by the United Nations may confirm what we could have supposed in relation to child survivors of the Rwandan genocide: 99.9% of Rwandan children witnessed violence during the period, 90% believed they would die, 87% saw dead bodies, 80% lost at least one relative, 58% saw people being hacked with pangas, and 31% witnessed rapes or other sexual assaults.[5]

So, as we could have expected, practically all the children who survived the 1990–94 war and above all, the genocide were lost and traumatized. Of course, after all the horror help did start coming, above all from the International Committee of the Red Cross, CARE and the Save the Children agency, and from the remarkable Rosamond Halsey Carr, who at the age of eighty-two managed to get back to Rwanda against the stiffest of odds (and apparently against the strongest advice of her friends and family). She left New York on 10 August 1994 and found Rwanda a war zone. "Kigali's beautiful airport – once the pride of Rwanda – had been ravaged by mortar shells and riddled with bullet holes. The windows had been blown out, and broken glass littered the floors. … Kigali was unrecognizable. The city was in shambles, with rubble everywhere. Every house, hotel, and business had been damaged and looted. Every building bore the scars of shelling, and some were simply heaps of stones. Street lamps had been wrenched from the ground and were lying helter-skelter on the sidewalks. There was no running water and no electricity. Nothing remained of the beautiful city I remembered. Apart from the soldiers, the streets were deserted."

On reaching her lifelong home, Mugongo, a few days later, stunned and shaken by what she and a companion had seen at a former university campus not far from her house, she found complete devastation, with everything she had possessed gone or irrevocably damaged. "A lifetime of

---

[5] Quoted by Kinzer, *op. cit.*, p.253.

hard work and memories was all gone. ... I wept with shame for the people who had done this, and I wept with anger at the utter violation of my life and the senseless destruction of the country I loved." But suddenly, her two half-starved dogs found her! Though they had not been fed for weeks, they had survived, as had her cat. "That was perhaps the defining moment, when my thoughts turned from leaving in defeat to believing that I had a reason to stay. Amid the throes of our joyful reunion, I looked up and saw the dear face of Biriko, my old cook. He was thin and dressed in ragged clothes, and his face bore the haunted look of a man who had returned from the bowels of hell. With what little strength I had left, I threw my arms around him and wept with sorrow and untold anguish."[6]

Many of the other members of the former staff also returned after weeks in the camps in Congo (Zaïre), especially her principal assistant, Sembagare – weak and haggard, and with eight orphaned children to look after. Rosamond's dream of opening an orphanage with him began to take shape. Through thick and thin, for she had returned to a country where nothing worked and where almost everyone had lost everything, she and Sembagare, with her niece Ann from the USA and with enormous help from UN military personnel, the Nigerian Medical Corps and a number of relief organizations, managed after four and a half months from the date of her return to Rwanda to get the old drying house renovated and ready to take in children. She said, "I can only surmise that God didn't feel I was ready to have children until I was eighty-two years old. Then he sent me forty all at once." The name chosen for the orphanage (after a competition among the numerous staff, and a vote) was *Imbabazi z'i* Mugongo: "Mugongo is a place where you will receive all the love and care a mother would give."

The first group of children was brought by Save the Children and ICRC. Many were unaccompanied children who had left Zaïre on their own, hoping to find relatives still alive in Rwanda, but most of the younger ones had no memory of who their parents were. We read:

> Our very first child (brought to me before the orphanage opened) was a little boy named Gahungu, later called Sammy, who was four years old. His mother had dropped dead on a path near the house of a man who had ten children of his own and didn't want the little boy. We happily took him in, and he is very proud of his distinction as being our "first child".
>
> Among our original group was twelve-year-old Nizeyimana, called Commander, who is particularly loved and admired by

---

6 Rosamond Halsey Carr, *op. cit.*, pp.216–217.

the other children. His father was killed when his family fled to Gisenyi, and he was separated from his mother and sister when RPF soldiers began firing at crowds of refugees trying to flee to safety in Goma. Although several of his family members have been located, Commander steadfastly refused to leave the loving environment of the *Imbabazi* and has told me that he wants to stay here "until he is all grown up". We have made a special exception in his case and allowed him to stay.

Soldiers found four-year-old Kadendeza in April of 1994, lying across the body of his dead mother. They brought him to their camp and kept him for several weeks. When their unit was relocated, they handed him over to a foster family in Ruhengeri. The head of the family was a drunkard who beat the little boy. He was so badly mistreated that neighbors reported this to Save the Children, who rescued him and brought him to us. For some time Kadendeza had spells of crying and clung desperately to anyone who picked him up to comfort him. After several months, he was laughing and playing happily with the other children. His traumatism had faded, but he still needs more caresses and affection than many of the others.

The book goes on with descriptions of two or three more individual cases. A girl of eleven, Ishimwe Pacifique, saw both her parents killed in Kigali during the genocide. She took her baby sister Clemence and began walking towards Gisenyi, where she believed she had a grandmother named Agnes. With the one-year-old baby tied to her back, the girl walked nearly seventy miles over a period of weeks, slept in fields and begged for food just to survive. They were brought to *Imbabazi* by Save the Children, after a period in hospital when both were ill. "Ishimwe is an exceptionally lovely girl and is doing well at school. Clemence is now a chubby four-year-old who has many 'sisters and brothers' and is adored by everyone. We have never been able to locate their grandmother."

These are perhaps typical cases of the hundreds who came to be cared for at *Imbabazi*. Some left after family members had been traced, which happened in about half the cases. As for their health situation, "Many of the children we receive come to us with worms and scabies, and some are terribly malnourished. We are fortunate in that none of our children have series physical disabilities, but they all bear deep emotional scars and demonstrate, at one time or another, symptoms of posttraumatic stress. There are cases of chronic bed-wetting, occasional outbursts of violence or uncontrollable crying, and some simply refuse to speak at all for long periods of time. It takes an enormous amount of patience, tenderness and loving care before they begin to feel safe and secure and learn to laugh and play and be children again." It was, she wrote, under Sembagare's careful supervision that the children received enormous amounts of love and comfort, spiritual guidance, emotional support, and discipline when necessary. "He was father to all the children."

The children came from all three ethnic groups – Hutu, Tutsi and Batwa (pygmy). Many of the Tutsi children had seen their parents, brothers and sisters killed during the genocide, and many of the Hutu children lost their families to the cholera epidemic that had swept through the camps in Zaïre. "They are all very brave and have enormous faith in God. Their love for one another is extraordinary, and it is our fervent prayer that this love will last all their lives and that the Banyarwanda will one day live together in peace." After all that these small human beings had been through, the attachment that they could have to the *Imbabazi* carers was critical to their emotional health and physical development. As an American child psychiatrist has written, "The more healthy relationships a child has, the more likely he will be to recover from trauma and thrive. Relationships are the agent of change and the most powerful therapy is human love."[7]

What *resilience* was demonstrated both by these little orphans, and by the dedicated American lady who at over eighty dedicated the rest of her life to them! Towards the end of her book she wrote, "Our children are happy and healthy, and they are dearly loved. One of the few regrets in my life is that I never had children of my own. Today, at the age of eighty-five, I am blessed with seventy-two. Mugongo has been my home for forty-three years now, and it is here that I intend to spend the rest of my days. The little orphanage that began as a dream has become a haven of love and laughter and a symbol of hope to all who have been part of it."

As though these children – and Rosamond and her staff – had not suffered enough, *interahamwe*, who had returned from Zaïre among the huge crowd of Hutus repatriating, resumed their murderous activities. Countless massacres occurred in October and November 1997, and new orphans arrived at *Imbabazi* nearly every day. Everyone lived under threat, and in January 1998 the whole Mugongo/Imbabazi population had to be evacuated by UNICEF. Violence continued in that north-western area of Rwanda for several years. But, despite it, and despite a second move, the

---

[7]   Dr Bruce D. Perry and Maia Szalavitz, *The Boy Who Was Raised as a Dog* (2017). The same authors write, "The most traumatic aspects of all disasters involve the shattering of human connections. And this is especially true for children."

work with the orphans went on. Rosamond Halsey Carr lived on until 2006, and was buried in her beloved Mugongo.

Studies On Trauma

There appear to have been all too few studies of the psychological effects on children of the Rwanda events of the 1990s. But one, published by the US National Library of Medicine, National Institutes of Health, entitled *Post-traumatic Stress Reactions among Rwandan Children and Adolescents in the Early Aftermath of Genocide* (1995),[8] turned up some disturbing figures. It was found that over 90% of the children in the study witnessed killings and had their lives threatened, 35% lost close family members, 30% witnessed rape or sexual mutilation, and 15% had hidden under corpses. A very high rate of post-traumatic stress disorders prevailed. The researchers concluded that, at the limits of catastrophic man-made violence, psychological resilience among youth is all but extinguished.

A UNICEF Assessment (Also Going Back Years)

6 April 2004 – "Ten years after the genocide in Rwanda that took the lives of 800,000 people, the country's children continue to struggle with the lingering impact of the atrocities", UNICEF said today. UNICEF's Executive Director Carol Bellamy said

Ten years later, the children of Rwanda are still suffering the consequences of a conflict caused entirely by adults. For them, the genocide is not just a historical event, but an inescapable part of daily life today and tomorrow.

By the end of the genocide in 1994, 95,000 children had been orphaned.

The children of Rwanda witnessed unspeakable violence. Tens of thousands lost their mothers and fathers. Thousands were victims of horrific brutality and rape. Many were forced to commit atrocities. The impact of the tragedy simply cannot be overstated.

Today, Rwanda's children face extreme challenges:

---

[8]   R. Neugebauer, P.W. Fisher, J.B. Turner, S. Yamabe, J.A. Sarsfield and T. Stehling-Ariza.

- Rwanda is home to one of the world's largest proportions of child-headed households, with an estimated 101,000 children living in some 42,000 households. These children are on their own either because their parents were killed in the genocide, died from AIDS or have been imprisoned for genocide-related crimes.
- 2000 women – many of whom were survivors of rape, were tested for HIV during the five years following the 1994 genocide. Of them 80 per cent were found to be HIV positive. Many were not sexually active before the genocide.
- By 2001, an estimated 264,000 children had lost one or both parents to AIDS, representing 43 percent of all orphans. This figure is expected to grow to over 350,000 by 2010.
- More than 400,000 children are out of school.
- Rwanda has one of the world's worst child mortality rates – 1 in 5 Rwandan children die before their fifth birthday.

UNICEF's Executive Director added that the anniversary must be marked with renewed concern for those continuing to suffer from the genocide. "We are all still accountable for supporting reconciliation and healing, and for ensuring that such atrocities never happen again," she said. "Never again" means holding perpetrators accountable and restoring the dignity of victims by commemorating or alleviating their suffering.

* * * * * *

The 2013 paper of which I quoted extracts in Chapter 14 (Rwanda – Lasting Imprints of a Genocide: Trauma, Mental Health and Psychosocial Conditions in Survivors, Former Prisoners and Their Children by Heide Rieder and Thomas Elbert, published in *Conflict and Health*) tells us this about the children:

With regard to the group of descendants, our study revealed that 16% of the descendants of survivors compared to only 1% of the descendants of former prisoners (and none of those born after 1994) fulfilled the DSM-IV criteria for the diagnosis of PTSD. In a study on a general sample of Rwandan youth interviewed during the direct aftermath of the genocide, Neugebauer et al. [39] reported a PTSD rate of 62%. Recent research on vulnerable groups such as orphans showed lower PTSD rates, between 24% and 34% [5, 7, 40]. With regard to those born before 1994, our sample of descendants of survivors manifested a similar level of PTSD to those reported by these last studies. Among these descendants, a particularly high trauma load was found and 50% showed to be half-orphaned. Their specifically vulnerable and life-threatening situation in 1994 and afterwards was strongly shaped by their families' experiences. Due to persecution and death, parental protection throughout the period of violence was often missing. In the aftermath of the genocide, their families had to cope with severe circumstances and descendants often took over great responsibilities, which often continue today and might explain the ongoing sequelae of distress as depressive and anxiety symptoms [7].

5. Human Rights Watch. Justice Compromised. The Legacy of Rwanda's Community-Based Gacaca Courts. New York: HRW; 2011.

7. Dyregrov A, Gupta L, Gjestad R, Mukanoheli E. Trauma exposure and psychological reactions to genocide among Rwandan children. Journal of Traumatic Stress. 2000;13(1):3–21. doi: 10.1023/A:1007759112499.

39. Neugebauer R, Fisher PW, Turner JB, Yamabe S, Sarsfield JA, Stehling-Ariza T: Post-traumatic stress reactions among Rwandan children and adolescents in the early aftermath of genocide. International Journal of Epidemiology. 2009, 38 (4): 1033-1045. 10.1093/ije/dyn375.

40. Sydor G, Phillipot P: Conséquences psychologiques des massacres de 1994 au Rwanda. Santé mentale au Québec. 1996, 21 (1): 229-246.

Children, Adolescents And Torture

Although one finds it hard to accept the notion, the atrocious fact is that children and adolescents can be subjected to torture. The United Nations Voluntary Fund for Victims of Torture has reported on the work of its Expert Workshop on redress and rehabilitation of children and adolescents victims of torture and the intergenerational transmission of trauma, held in Geneva on 6 and 7 April 2016. We are allowed access to the summary of the proceedings:

International Human Rights Frameworks For Protection, Rehabilitation And Redress For Children Affected By Torture[9]

Participants recalled that the international community has recognized the absolute prohibition of torture as a fundamental principle and an unequivocal obligation under customary and international law. In addition, the Convention against Torture and other Cruel, Inhuman or Degrading Treatment or Punishment (CAT) and the Convention on the Rights of the Child (CRC) provide that torture is a crime and is prohibited under all circumstances, without exception. There is no justification for torturing a human being, including for reasons of national security, the fight against terrorism, the threat of armed conflict or a public emergency. Participants stressed that because children and adolescents are already in a situation of vulnerability, the consequences of torture can have a cumulative impact on that vulnerability. The short- and long-term effects of torture for children and adolescents are often further exacerbated due to their experience with multiple and intersecting grounds of discrimination, such as disability, gender, ethnic origin, nationality and sexual orientation. These factors need to be taken into account in the process of seeking justice, redress and rehabilitation for children and adolescents. Participants indicated that the specific threshold for pain and suffering is lower in children than in adults due to the vulnerability of the child. Further, these levels will vary according to the age and maturity of the child. Participants also noted that there is an important gender dimension that needs to be taken into account as girls and boys do not necessarily experience torture in the same way.

States should demonstrate their commitment to ending torture and ensure that the rights of victims to redress and rehabilitation are enforced. (A. Pinto, Trustee of the Fund)

---

[9] Quoted with the permission of the UN High Commissioner for Human Rights.

Finally, participants recalled the legal obligation of States under international law to provide assistance to victims of torture. Specifically, article 14 of CAT stipulates that States must ensure that a victim of torture in its jurisdiction obtains redress and has an enforceable right to fair and adequate compensation, including the means for as full rehabilitation as possible. Likewise, article 39 of the CRC provides that States shall take all appropriate measures to promote the physical and psychological recovery and social reintegration of child victims of torture.

I would submit that, for a child, witnessing violence and even the murder of a parent or sibling is a form of torture. Being abused by an adult is surely another. This is a question raised by S. Jabbour, Subcommittee on Prevention of Torture: "Who will be responsible for a generation of millions of children undergoing trauma and suffering of extreme forms of human rights violations in different regions? The world is silent."

We can, I suppose, only hope that those children whose trauma is very present with them, will – sooner rather than later, through all possible means being taken for them – be in the hands of people qualified to ease their pain and set them back onto the road to recovery.

CHAPTER 16

"Ethnic Cleansing", Uprooting And Genocide In Europe

Those of us who have memories of terrible violence being perpetrated in the Balkans in the 1990s while the rest of Europe wondered what it could do about it – but on the whole held back – may still wonder how and why it can all have happened. I believe that some of the survivors are still wondering too.

Brief Background History Of The Area

To gain insights into at least part of the very sad reality, perhaps we should go fairly far back in history, to when Bosnia and Herzegovina, once part of the Roman province of Illyricum and later for several centuries an independent state, was conquered by the Ottoman Turks. At the height of its power in the sixteenth and seventeenth centuries, the Ottoman Empire was a multinational, multilingual empire controlling territories of south-east, central and eastern Europe, western Asia, the Caucasus, north Africa and the Horn of Africa.[1] Not until the late eighteenth and early nineteenth centuries did it face strong military defeats from its European rivals, the Habsburg and Russian empires,[2] after being at the centre of interactions between the Eastern and Western worlds for six centuries. In the course of the nineteenth century, the Ottoman State suffered further territorial losses, especially in the Balkans.[3] But Turkish influence and religion remained in

---

[1] Ottoman Empire. Oxford Islamic Studies Online, 6 May 2008.

[2] Virginia Aksan, *Ottoman Wars, 1700–1860: An Empire Besieged* (Pearson Education Ltd, 2007), pp.130–135. Romanian friends when I first visited them talked quite a lot about the victorious battles of their brave forces waged against the Turks.

[3] Donald Quataert, The Age of Reforms, 1812–1914, in Halil İnalcık and Donald Quataert, *An Economic and Social History of the Ottoman Empire, 1300–1914, Vol. 2* (Cambridge University Press, 1994), p.762.

parts of the Balkans, including significant parts of Bosnia and Herzegovina and Kosovo.

The country which from its establishment in 1929 was called Yugoslavia was rarely without tensions arising from the different aspirations of Serbs, Croats and Muslims. During the Second World War it was occupied by Nazi Germany when, with resistance activities spearheaded by Serbian-based "Chetniks"[4] on the one hand and communist Partisans led by Marshall Tito on the other, an estimated 900,000 people were killed. In 1945, Tito was at the head of a Yugoslavia Federal People's Republic, and became president in 1947, holding the country together until his death in 1980. Tito was a strong man who resisted Soviet influence, and it was under his leadership that the non-aligned movement was formed.[5] But without Tito, Yugoslavia was destined to break into several parts, six republics and two autonomous regions.

Paul Garde in his book *Fin de Siècle dans les Balkans* points in his preface to elements that were the basis for the mounting tensions and conflicts in the 1990s: the takeover of power in Belgrade by Slobodan Milosević, a communist (1986), Serbian nationalist meetings (1988), the abolition of Kosovo's autonomy (1989), elections in the various republics all won by the nationalists, and the first outbreaks of violence (1990). In 1991 in Croatia, the series of horrors began that would persist for years in other parts of the former Yugoslavia: the siege and destruction by Serbian forces of Vukovar, the attack on the historic port of Dubrovnik, and the "ethnic cleansing" of innumerable villages. "The die was cast, the time bomb had already exploded, and as for our governments, they were again behindhand by two or three wars."[6]

---

[4] The Oxford English Reference Dictionary gives: "Chetnik, from Serbo-Croat četnik, četa, band, troop, a member of a guerrilla force in the Balkans. During the Second World War, the term referred to the group of royalist Serbs... fighting the Germans, while it has recently been used of Serbs fighting in the former Yugoslavia."

[5] The Non-Aligned Movement (NAM) is the group of countries that do not want to be officially aligned with or against any major power bloc. In 2018, the movement had 125 members and twenty-four observer countries. The group was started in Belgrade in 1961.

[6] Paul Garde, *Fin de Siècle dans les Balkans* (2001). Professor Garde, professor of Slav languages and literature in the universities of Provence, Yale, Columbia and Geneva, has published several books including *Vie et mort de la Yougoslavie* (*Life and Death of Yugoslavia*).

The Tragic Events In Bosnia And Herzegovina:
Siege Of The Capital City And "Ethnic Cleansing"

It has been said of Bosnia and Herzegovina that standing at one of the world's great crossroads it was "a great melting pot" of cultures with its three ethnic groups, the Muslims, Croats and Serbs, and citizens from other parts of the world. Sarajevo, its capital, was known as a city of beauty and of culture. In 1984, it hosted the Winter Olympic Games.

However, in the first few years of the 1990s political upheavals, basically brought about by Serbia's unrealistic, frustrated dream of a "Greater Serbia", caused widespread trauma, loss of life and the displacement of over two million people, of whom some 700,000 sought asylum outside the borders of Yugoslavia. After the clashes between Croats and Serbs, ethnic violence between Serbs and Muslims also erupted in 1991, and the dreadful term "ethnic cleansing" eventually came to be familiar to the ears of almost every European. The Serbian forces elevated rape and sexual violation of Bosnian Muslim women as an instrument of terror to levels not seen in Europe since the Nazi concentration camps. The term "ethnic cleansing" came to be defined by a Commission of Experts established pursuant to the United Nations Security Council Resolution 780 of 6 October 1992 as "a purposeful policy designed by one ethnic or religious group to remove by violent and terror-inspiring means the civilian population of another ethnic or religious group from certain geographic areas." The methods used during the Bosnian ethnic cleansing campaigns included "murder, torture, arbitrary arrest and detention, extra-judicial executions, rape and sexual assaults, confinement of civilian population in ghetto areas, forcible removal, displacement and deportation of civilian population, deliberate military attacks or threats of attacks on civilians and civilian areas, and wanton destruction of property".[7]

Subsequent reports established that widespread ethnic cleansing occurred between other groups.

In a 1992 referendum that the Serbs boycotted, Bosnian Muslims and Croats voted overwhelmingly for independence, and the result was recognized by the USA and the European Community. It may have seemed that here was a last chance of peace, with the country being admitted to the United Nations. But violent civil war broke out, as the Bosnian Serbian political leader Radovan Karadjić proclaimed, with Serbian backing, an

---

[7] Report of the Commission of Experts Established Pursuant to *United Nations Security Council Resolution 780* (1992), 27 May 1994 (*S/1994/674*), English, p.33, para. 129.

independent Serbian Republic of Bosnia and Herzegovina, and set up a siege of the capital, Sarajevo. The army of the so-called Republika Srpska had the backing of the Yugoslav army, and committed mayhem from its various vantage points: stationed mainly in the surrounding hills, it held vastly superior strategic positions and military supplies. For three and a half years from 5 April 1992 to October 1995,[8] when a ceasefire was proclaimed, while Serb snipers inside the city attacked individuals daily, 13,000 soldiers from their vantage points on the surrounding hills assaulted the city with artillery, tanks and small arms. Shelling innumerable buildings and on one occasion the busy morning market, they caused terrible carnage and terror.

Civilians knew they were never safe, and the atmosphere was terrifying throughout all those years. A psychiatrist, Liljana Orue, quoted in UNHCR's *Refugees* magazine, said "The Sarajevans have a problem. They are clinically insane. If they were normal, they would sit terrified in the basement rather than risk being blown to bits on the streets." But it was also surmised that the crazy defiance helped Sarajevans retain a certain dignity in a city that had once hosted the Winter Olympics. One defiant old man said, "The worst that can happen to you is getting killed."

UNHCR, assuming tasks to assist a civilian population (as opposed to refugees) was involved with humanitarian needs in the situation described as "the most savage carnage in Europe since World War Two when millions of people were ruthlessly denied even their most basic human rights. In 1995 the Serbs tried to strangle Sarajevo totally, blocking the daily humanitarian airlift and attacking overland convoys. The only lifeline to the outside world was a winding dirt road over Mount Igman. The Serbs targeted it with their heavy machine guns and artillery and the road was quickly strewn with the carcasses of trucks and cars. … A group of Danish drivers vividly recalled being seized by Bosnian Serbs in the summer of 1994, robbed, blindfolded and lined up against a wall in a mock execution."[9] Of the estimated pre-war Sarajevo population of 435,000, the siege cost the life of 5,434 citizens and 6,137 defending soldiers (against a loss of 2,241 Serb soldiers).

---

[8]   The siege of Sarajevo lasted three times longer than the *Battle of Stalingrad* and more than a year longer than the *Siege of Leningrad*. As in the other two sieges, many people died of hunger. The Serb forces had for a time even occupied the upper floors of the city hospital, using them as a base to shoot citizens in the streets. After the war, the hospital buildings were "pockmarked with bullet holes as a reminder of a time when an enemy tried to destroy a healing institution, its staff, and its patients." Dr Richard F. Mollica, *Healing Invisible Wounds – Paths to Hope and Recovery in a Violent World.*

[9]   *Refugees*, No. 111, spring 1998.

Sarajevo was left with all its fine buildings extensively pockmarked by bullets, if they had not been reduced to rubble or left practically uninhabitable by mortar fire, or by grenades hurled inside by Serb "chetniks". The handsome Executive Council building had been set on fire. Other signs of the war were the many high-rise buildings across the river, emptied of their erstwhile residents.

After the war, the *International Criminal Tribunal for the former Yugoslavia* (ICTY) convicted four Serb officials for numerous counts of *crimes against humanity* committed during the siege, including *terror*.

There can be no possible doubt that the level of post-traumatic stress in the Sarajevo population must have been high, both throughout the siege and afterwards. As in Syria in recent years, people never knew when their homes would be bombed, or when they would be caught in crossfire in the streets. Most of the houses had their windows smashed in the violence, most households were without water and heating. These poor people clung to life as best they could, as a resident explained to me when I was lodged in his home in the course of 1996.

A 1993 UN–EC Peace Plan had failed, as had a Croat–Serb partition plan. The years of inter-ethnic conflict had caused untold damage across the whole country to both civilians and the country's infrastructure, quite apart from the soldiery of all three ethnic groups. Many fine buildings and vital bridges had been shelled. The lovely city of Mostar, probably the most-damaged city of the late twentieth century, had been rendered practically unrecognizable, its ancient arched bridge over the River Neretva that connected the two halves of the city destroyed on 9 November 1993 after relentless shelling by the Croats.[10]

The criminal "ethnic cleansing" by the Serbs had started in 1991, leading to massive displacement not only of Muslims but also of Serbs. While whole areas of Sarajevo formerly inhabited by Serbs were emptied of their residents, Radovan Karadjić and his Bosnian Serb army commander

---

[10] *The Independent* reported on 10 November 1993 that the "Stari Most", Mostar's spectacular sixteenth-century stone bridge and one of Bosnia and Herzegovina's greatest architectural treasures, had collapsed the previous day in a barrage of Croatian shells. Bosnians, particularly those under siege in east Mostar, had prayed that this would never happen. "For at least 25,000 Bosnians trapped on the city's east side the collapse is a disaster – a tremendous blow to morale and a strategic victory for the Croats. The bridge was the only access to a source of drinking water which people retrieved by scurrying across at night under threat of sniper fire. It was also the main route to the places where the front line crossed into west 'Croatian' Mostar." The bridge was listed by UNESCO.

Ratko Mladić worked in tandem, backed (as came to be widely understood) by the president of Serbia, Slobodan Milosević, to "flush out" by violent means the Muslim populations in the areas they had decided to incorporate into their Republika Srpska. In the atmosphere of violence and death, six "safe areas" were designated by the UN for Muslim civilians, one of which was Srebrenica, a small mountain town not far from the eastern border with Serbia. The UN Security Council voted to send heavily armed peacekeepers to protect all six designated "safe areas" – Sarajevo, Tuzla, Bihac, Srebrenica, Gorazde and Zepa – and a Dutch contingent of 600 UN peacekeepers arrived in the Srebrenica area.

But with or without safe areas, 1995 was to be a fatal year for Bosnia and Herzegovina. For Srebrenica, under siege for three years, it was from July onwards an unimaginable nightmare that seemed to have no end. In the atmosphere of dread, tens of thousands of Muslims had been leaving the captured villages of the surrounding areas, flocking to hoped-for safety in the UN safe haven. But with his dreams of a "Greater Serbia", the Bosnian Serb leader Radovan Karadzić, who would be tried for genocide years later by the International Criminal Tribunal for the Former Yugoslavia and sentenced to forty years in prison,[11] proceeded with the Bosnian Serb army commander, Ratko Mladić, to remove all the Muslim inhabitants of Srebrenica and its surroundings, and to arrest and kill men aged between seventeen and seventy. How did they perpetrate such an enormous atrocity? How could the psychiatrist that Radovan Karadzić was bring himself to order mass murder?

To deal with the UN Dutch peacekeeping force, Mladić's soldiers threatened the 600 Dutch soldiers with dire consequences if they did not relinquish all their weapons and keep away from the town. So the UN force sent to make Srebrenica a "safe haven" came to be rendered absolutely ineffectual by the Serb army.[12]

---

[11] On 20 March 2019, the ICTY changed this sentence, following appeal, to life imprisonment. Judge Vagn Joensen said that, earlier, Karadzic's systematic cruelty in committing his crimes of genocide, persecution, murders, rapes, inhuman treatment, forced transfers, the siege of Sarajevo and the murders of the men of Sarajevo had previously been underestimated. Karadjić's sentencing came years after he had been sought, but he managed to live heavily disguised from 1996 to 2008 before being arrested at last in Belgrade.

[12] As had happened with the Belgian peacekeeping corps in Rwanda the year before (Chapter 14). The Dutch force was subsequently heavily criticized both in the Netherlands and further afield. See for example Joyce *van de Bildt, Srebrenica: A Dutch National Trauma* (PDF), *Journal of Peace, Conflict & Development, Vol. 21 (March 2015)* and Kristen Boon, *Supreme Court Decision Rendered in Dutchbat*

Ratko Mladić, referring to the Muslims as "Turks", then instructed his forces to converge on Srebrenica and to take the town, congratulating them when they succeeded. All the inhabitants were turned out of their houses at gunpoint, and once they were all outside, Mladić,[13] using the kind of duplicity earlier practised on a huge scale by the Nazis, spoke through a megaphone attempting to reassure all the inhabitants that they would come to no harm as long as they cooperated. Then all the thousands of men and boys of between twelve and seventy were separated from the women and children in a situation of virtual panic. The men were told to disarm and to be "ready for questioning".

Aware that they were probably in great danger, approximately 15,000 men and boys from Srebrenica and area set off on foot in an attempt to reach safe territory seventy miles away. Despite the care they took to penetrate woodland, over the next few days the Serbs intercepted and captured over 8,000 of them, taking them by truck to locations where they killed them with point blank machine-gun fire or with firing squads. While all this was happening, the 23,000 women and children were loaded onto buses and taken to Tuzla, but not before many of the girls and women were taken and raped, sometimes in full view, reportedly, of members of the Dutch contingent or of other women.

The total number of deaths was subsequently put at 8,373. We have the testimony of two of the young men who, against tremendous odds, managed to escape.

The overall death toll resulting from the conflict in Bosnia was 200,000 dead, while another 200,000 were injured and as mentioned earlier, two million people were displaced.

After The Terror

In December 1995, a US-sponsored peace accord was signed at Dayton, Ohio, providing for two sovereign states – one Muslim-Croat, one Serb. A 60,000-strong NATO peacekeeping force was deployed for the country.[14]

Case: the Netherlands Responsible, Opinio Juris (6 September 2013), quoted on Wikipedia's page on Srebrenica 2015.

[13] The ICTY found Ratko Mladić guilty in December 2017 of eleven of the twelve prosecution counts and sentenced him to life imprisonment. Like Karadjić, he had managed to evade arrest for years – sixteen in his case!

[14] The NATO-led Implementation Force (IFOR) was deployed in December 1995 to implement the military aspects of the Dayton Peace Agreement and was replaced a year later by the NATO-led Stabilization Force (SFOR). SFOR helped to maintain

In 2004, the Appeals Chamber of the ICTY, located in *The Hague*, ruled that the massacre of the enclave's male inhabitants constituted genocide, a crime under international law. The ruling was upheld by the *International Court of Justice* (ICJ) in 2007. The forcible transfer and abuse of between 25,000 and 30,000 Bosnian women, children and elderly that accompanied the massacre was found to constitute genocide, when accompanied with the killings and separation of the men. The *Preliminary List of People Missing or Killed in Srebrenica* compiled by the Bosnian Federal Commission of Missing Persons contains 8,373 names. As of July 2012, 6,838 genocide victims have been identified through DNA analysis of body parts recovered from mass graves; as of July 2013, 6,066 victims have been buried at the *Memorial Centre of Potočari.*[15]

Twenty years on, we have testimonies from some of the people who were very radically affected by the Serb repression. In videos, we see prisoners who are almost walking skeletons, like the Belsen camp survivors of Nazi atrocities in 1945. We see women still grieving for the people so abruptly taken from them.

There are reports of mass rape, and someone says, "The rape of Bosnian Muslim women cannot be compared with rape used as a weapon of war. It was a project designed many years earlier, to be used as a weapon of ethnic cleansing. By destabilising women, they were destabilising society." It was combined with the genocide, which was planned at top level.

One man admitted that there had been atrocities committed not only on the Serb side. But what suffering, what horrors! Let us try to take in what some of them have said.

---

a secure environment and facilitate the country's reconstruction in the wake of the 1992–95 war. A BBC country profile of 2018 on Bosnia and Herzegovina reads: It is now an independent state, but remains partially under international oversight under the terms of the 1995 Dayton Peace Accords. Its three main communities are Bosniak Muslims, Croats and Serbs. More than 100,000 people were killed and around two million displaced in the war, which also left the infrastructure and economy in tatters. The peace agreement set up two separate entities – the Bosniak-Croat Federation and Bosnian Serb Republic – overarched by a federal government and rotating presidency. Peace has not brought the two entities closer together, and Bosnian Serb leaders often raise the possibility of seceding from what they call a failed state.

[15] Extracts from Wikipedia's very substantial coverage of all the above events, supplemented with photographs, no fewer than 355 references, and incorporating some harrowing testimonies.

Testimonies Of Survivors

In a video entitled *Remembering Srebrenica 20 Years On*, we hear of how the powerful military Serb contingents flushed all the Muslims out of the area of eastern Bosnia and Herzegovina, tens of thousands of them fleeing to the "safe area" of Srebrenica, where they lived in cramped conditions and some starved to death. The Serb military was not allowing any transportation of food on the roads to Srebrenica, and air drops did not meet the need, so people were desperate – as had been happening elsewhere in the stricken country.

Hatidja Mehmedović, a widow, speaks of her happiness when she was first married, and the birth of two sons. "Srebrenica used to be a nice little town, each house had a balcony that was full of flowers. My first son, Azmir, was born in 1974, the second, Almir, in 1977. I thought that my happiness would last for ever. But in the 1990s in Bosnia and Srebrenica it all changed. Mladić on 11th July forced us out of our homes." She was one of the 23,000 women the Serbs deported from the Srebrenica area. We see photographs of the three she lost in 1995, her husband and the two sons. Then she went on:

> In 2010 I buried both my sons and my husband. Only two leg bones of the older son were buried, the same of my husband. My younger son has a complete body, only his left arm is missing and half of his little finger. Sorry for my tears, but when I speak of my children it is very difficult for me...
>
> My younger son begged me to go to Potočari, "You won't manage the trek through the woods. Please go Mum, go quickly. I don't want to see you go," and he gently pushed me away from him, and put his hands over his eyes. We thought we would see each other after a couple of days...

Mrs Mehmedović never saw any of the three again.

> They weren't guilty of anything except their Islamic religion. They somehow got separated. They had all left together, so I don't how they got split up. What happened was that my husband Abdulla and my elder son were together. They stood in front of a firing squad and waited. It's impossible to imagine how it must be to look into the eyes of death. My youngest son got to the Pilica Cultural Centre. I heard this from a witness. He and others hid under the stage. They were about 500, all of them got killed.

I returned to the house, our family home. ... We can't change the past but we can learn from it.

Hassan Hasonović is one of the guides at the memorial just a few miles north of Srebrenica. "My twin brother, my father, my younger brother and my mother went to Poticari. We didn't have time to say goodbye, it was all chaos." He explains how it was that as the men and boys of the Srebrenica area had been afraid of what the Serbs could do to them, they had formed into a column of 15,000 aiming to get to the next safe area, seventy miles away. He had managed to work his way to the head of the column, and escaped. He could hear the shooting seven kilometres behind him. But he found out later about his family members, and saw the school where his twin brother and 500 other boys had been killed.

> There was chaos everywhere, we didn't even have time to say goodbye to one another when they separated us. The UN handed over their weapons and it was a most horrific week of slaughter.

Nezad Abrić, who eventually returned to Srebrenica to live, spoke to a British representative of a support agency, also called "Remembering Srebrenica", and showed her where he and thousands of others got intercepted:

> I have never talked about all this before. But more and more people are denying that it happened. Srebrenica was given to those who committed genocide. My children will attend school here, the situation is not very simple.
> I was 17 at the time. We were ambushed, there were one or two thousand men and boys behind me. Where the column was broken, the Serbs called us out of the woods with a megaphone. We didn't have any choice. We went down this hill, through forest and across that meadow. We were loaded onto a truck that took us some miles and stopped in front of a school building. We could hear soldiers ordering the people to come out from the upper classrooms, two by two, and after some time, the time it took them to go down the stairs, we heard bursts of gunfire. It lasted until midnight, then it was our turn. We came out and went down the stairs. To the left and right from the front door we could see heaps of bodies. I was barefoot and felt something sticky on my feet, it was probably human blood. We got into a truck, for ten minutes it followed a road, suddenly it stopped. We could hear machinegun fire.

I saw five people getting out. After they left, it took about a minute before the machinegun fire started. It was my turn, I got out and they told us to find our place. I didn't know what place they meant. Behind the truck as we were walking, we saw lines of dead bodies. These were just moments, everything was happening so fast while we were heading to those lines. At that moment, my only thought was that I am not going to suffer, it will be a quick death. As we got down, shooting started, I cannot remember the moment I was shot, I felt pain in the right side, I was down and trembling, I felt pain in my right side, stomach and head. Bullets around me hit the stones. I didn't dare to cry out, I suppressed the urge to scream, I was trembling. While they were killing the people around me, a bullet hit my leg. I asked God to send the soldier back to kill me, I didn't dare to ask the soldier myself.

Then one soldier said to the other, "Jovo, we'd better check that they're all dead, if any of the bodies are warm they need another bullet in the head", and the other swore and said "They're all dead, come on, let's go."

Somehow, in spite of being in terrible pain, the boy managed to walk miles to safety. Just seventeen years old, and involved in such violence and death, a witness to genocide, as the young Muslim Englishwoman he had been talking to said.

There are naturally other witnesses from whom one might be able to hear accounts, and countless reports and research papers exist on what happened to Bosnia and Herzegovina. The above can be only a summary. But it should reflect the circumstances in which many of the millions deeply affected, including all those who went as refugees to countries as far away as Australia, remain troubled, longing for a fuller understanding of how and why it happened, perhaps returning to try to find any living relatives. And some of these people may well be afflicted with lasting post-traumatic stress.

The task of unearthing bodies and the identification has been going on for years, and is rendered incredibly difficult by the fact that very few bodies or skeletons are intact. There have been cases in which no fewer than *seven* DNA matches on some bones have been necessary (normally there needs to be only one) before they have been identifiable and reconstruction of the remains can be effected, the families notified.

Srebrenica has been called "the black hole of mankind".

Rape As A Weapon Of War

In the above, there are already indications that during the Bosnian War, Bosnian Serb forces and Serb paramilitary units used genocidal rape as an instrument of terror as part of their programme of ethnic cleansing. Estimates of the number of women raped during the war range between 12,000 and 50,000.

On 6 October 1992 – three years before the "rape" of Srebrenica, the *United Nations Security Council* established a Commission of Experts chaired by *M. Cherif Bassiouni*. The Commission found that rape was being used by Serb forces systematically, and had the support of commanders and local authorities. Among the perpetrators apprehended, some claimed they were ordered to rape. Others said that the use of rape was a tactic to make sure the targeted population would not return to the area.

The ICTY declared that "systematic rape" and "sexual enslavement" in time of war was a *crime against humanity*, second only to the *war crime* of *genocide*. Although the ICTY did not treat the mass rapes as genocide, many have concluded from the organized and systematic nature of the mass rapes of the female *Bosniak* (Bosnian Muslim) population, that these rapes were a part of a larger campaign of genocide. … The *trial of VRS member Dragoljub Kunarac* was the first time in any national or international jurisprudence that a person was convicted of using *rape as a weapon of war*.

In the horror of that war the Serbs set up a series of infamous, unhygienic "rape camps" in different parts of the country under their control, where women were subjected to being raped repeatedly. Their suffering defies imagination. Amnesty International has declared that the use of rape in times of war is a pre-planned and deliberate military strategy, the first aim of which is to instil terror in the civilian population, with the intent to forcibly remove them from their property and their roots. In the war crime trials subsequent to the Dayton Accords, the ICTY handed down seven long sentences against Serb rapists, and the court of Bosnia and Herzegovina six. One can estimate that long prison sentences were as nothing compared to the lifelong trauma likely to affect those thousands of women (to the extent that they survived).

My Unexpected Involvement In Post-War Measures To Help Women Survivors

UNHCR was involved in the former Yugoslavia because the United Nations Secretary-General asked the High Commissioner to assist displaced persons. This was in the autumn of 1991, four months to the day after Croatia and Slovenia had proclaimed their independence and fighting had broken out. Over the ensuing months, television crews covering events in the former Yugoslavia frequently filmed UNHCR convoys travelling to various parts of Bosnia and Herzegovina (in particular), or standing at road blocks when armed elements would not let them through with their tons of humanitarian aid. It was a dramatic, difficult and extremely delicate involvement, with the Office of the High Commissioner, which had always been apolitical, having to play a more assertive role in Bosnia than perhaps anywhere previously. It had to detail several hundred staff members and spend huge sums of money – not least to help Sarajevans stay alive, if possible, during the Serbs' long siege. It was costly in other ways too: lives were lost by the UN, the Red Cross and other relief agencies as they went about their missions of humanitarian assistance.

Long after I had left UNHCR in 1981 to work with the International Red Cross, and even after I had left the International Red Cross for health reasons, UNHCR invited me in the summer of 1996 to plan and set up an aid programme in Bosnia and Herzegovina intended to help the worst-affected women of the tragic conflict to get on their feet. The women displaced from Srebrenica a few months earlier were particularly in the mind of the initiator, US President Bill Clinton. To be asked to do this was a great privilege.

Leaving the family and arriving in Geneva on the prescribed date, I had to be given, all within a few hours, a rushed "briefing",[16] a series of injections and a contract, prior to the flight to Zagreb next day. The only flights between the outside world and Sarajevo at that time were those of UNHCR, ferrying people from and to Zagreb. In the Zagreb hotel at breakfast, it was fortunate that a fellow guest warned me about the rather high danger, even in Sarajevo, of stepping on a mine.[17]

The Dayton Peace Accord had been signed eight months earlier in Ohio. The massacre of men and boys of Srebrenica had occurred thirteen months earlier. The origin of what was called the Bosnian Women's Initiative was the creation by US President Bill Clinton of a fund of five million dollars. Via

---

[16] This was with the UNHCR desk officer (an Italian recently returned from representing UNHCR in Sarajevo, and years earlier my assistant in Congo), the person in charge of women refugee affairs (who was Indian, I believe), the tall Austrian Deputy High Commissioner (who gave me a very warm hug!) and a delegation from the United States Mission to the UN Geneva.

[17] Just a few weeks later, three children playing on grass in Sarajevo were killed by the explosion of a mine.

his ambassador in Vienna (a friend of his), Bill Clinton had sent a signed letter to the stricken women promising this help, and I remember very well that it said in rather unmistakable terms that he was sending these women these millions of dollars. The lady ambassador, proud to announce at a meeting with hundreds of the uprooted, distressed women that help was en route, waved the famous letter in the air but did not explain to them how the funds were likely to reach them. On my arrival, travelling to Tuzla, where hundreds of women awaited me with tremendous expectancy, I had the delicate and in fact rather difficult task[18] of having to convince them that I had no banknotes to hand out, and that they would have to create project plans for activities that would then receive this funding via UNHCR.[19] As a matter of fact, at the end of my mission these funds had not yet reached UNHCR Geneva! The intricacies of bureaucracy were not what these damaged women could be expected to understand. No wonder they were more or less in revolt when I first opened my mouth to give them bad news!

Nevertheless, before that momentous meeting, I had met with the US Embassy mission officer who was to be my counterpart for the Bosnian Women's Initiative (BWI). His name was Andrew Erickson, son or grandson of a Swedish immigrant to the USA. We saw eye to eye, and as the weeks went by, Andrew sent periodic reports to his bosses in Washington. Busy in and out of the office space allocated to me on the seventh floor of a modern fine-looking but damaged building with non-functioning lifts, I had met the leading spirits of the women's organization Zena 21 (Women 21), discussing with them the urgency of planning and holding a major meeting at the (undamaged) Holiday Inn in Sarajevo, to consult the women themselves over their priorities in relation to the US/UNHCR funds. We lost no time in issuing invitations through UNHCR's offices (numerous in the country at that time) for three representatives to come from each town or major village in both parts of the stricken land, i.e. the Federation of Bosnia and Herzegovina (FBiH, with mostly Bosnian and Croat residents), and the Republika Srpska (RS, with mostly Serbs) to come to Sarajevo for consultations. The future exchanges would include guidelines as to how to apply for funding.

When the time came, I had the extraordinary good luck to receive the offer of an experienced expatriate social worker to set up and run the whole-day meeting, with the help of her half dozen young staff. The preceding

---

[18] I saw Bill Clinton's letter that day for the first time!

[19] After the first period, further funds came to be donated to the BWI, fortunately – for five million dollars could only go so far among so many. Some of the subsequent funds were donated by the government of Japan.

afternoon they prepared the huge hall with areas marked "Health", "Training", "Livestock" and "Accommodation", while I was documenting what I had learned through a series of visits to women in FBiH towns,[20] to hand out at the meeting.

Some Very Resilient Women

Over that initial period, I had been up at 5 a.m. daily to travel to meet as many people as possible in Tuzla, Gorazde, Mostar and Zenica. In Mostar, I met with women who said they needed bed linen, hoping to establish modest little guesthouses as a means of income, for Mostar is a tourist destination. In Gorazde, there were women wishing to get financing for a poultry project, maybe a donkey or two, or a few sheep. There were women who wished to get onto an IT course and receive funding for home computers. Then, in Tuzla, there was a teacher who, like all the others, had lost husband and sons in the July 1995 massacres of the Serbian forces. She spoke to me of the events of the previous year, recalling how she had been obliged at gunpoint to leave her home without any belongings, not even a pair of shoes. With her forced evacuation to Tuzla with thousands of other women, she was in fact in a refugee-type situation without having fled her country.

Courageous and resilient, this former teacher with a command of English had talked with a representative of the aid agency Oxfam, to try to create some form of help for the other distraught women. At that point, there were no actual proofs of the massacres, so the anguished women could only suspect that their husbands, sons, fathers and brothers might have been killed. Thanks to this initiative, large quantities of brightly coloured wool were sent in to establish a handicrafts activity, principally knitting, until such time as some kind of future could evolve from the tragedy of the Balkans conflict. Given weight restrictions on international flights, I could buy only a few of the beautiful pullovers from these ladies!

Subsequently several other women I was to consult in the course of that first week of the mission had been paramount in creating other measures to help one another after they had not only lost their loved ones, their homes and their belongings, they had in very many cases suffered violence at the hands of the Serb soldiery. In Zenica, a two-woman team of doctors told me at some length about their mobile service to victims of rape, that

---

[20] Unfortunately, for reasons I was not given, I was not invited to visit any place in the Republika Srpska, either that week or subsequently, however earnestly I offered to cross the borderline.

included operations conducted in the relatively basic conditions provided in their mobile clinic.

The day-long meeting at the Holiday Inn went well. It had been up to me to open the proceedings and explain to everyone how in general international funds were donated and how distributed: in this case it would be on the basis of valid project submissions that they should work up, along with a version in English to send through to us in the Sarajevo office of UNHCR for consideration. We would be a very small group examining these future submissions, and we promised to take decisions rapidly, and make the funds available just as rapidly.

I liaised with the UNHCR Sarajevo office's finance officer, a Japanese, seeing about streamlining the BWI procedures as far as possible, and with (Dr) Ulrike von Buchwald, until recent months my successor at the International Red Cross but now back in UNHCR, where earlier, she had acquired valuable experience in fundraising work. Ulrike and Andrew would form the nucleus of the project committee, along with a Thai staff member of UNHCR who had been in Bosnia and Herzegovina for some time, in theory now working alongside me.[21] In the event, soon after my mission ended it became evident that Ulrike and Andrew, more than sufficiently competent, would have to manage the job between them, after the Thai officer had notified certain applicants that their project would be funded, when actually it had been turned down. A fiasco... In vain had I recommended, very strongly, the involvement in the BWI of a young Bosnian woman, with relevant know-how, some of it from the Refugee Studies Programme of Oxford University. Her NGO employer was ready to second her to UNHCR at the very time that she would have made all the difference to the BWI programme.

Towards the end of my seventy-five-day mission, we had the visit of Ms Phyllis E. Oakley, Under-Secretary of State for Population, Refugees, and Migration in Washington. She travelled with me and met many of the women. Every trip in Bosnia involved seeing graveyards round practically every second bend. One imagined the hundreds or thousands of young lives brought so needlessly – as it seemed – to a sudden end.[22] We were

---

[21] Under a woman UN High Commissioner, Mrs Sadako Ogata (1991–2000) it happened that many women, particularly it seemed Asian women, received rapid promotions that it could be said took them to levels that perhaps exceeded their real ability. In a few cases, though, women's promotions were seriously overdue at that time.

[22] I walked round one or two of these. All the names on the concrete pillars, without exception, proved that they were the tombs of young males.

driven down steep inclines to cross rivers at the lowest point because the modern road bridge had been blown to bits. Of course, we passed a lot of empty houses, some of them gutted.

We knew by this time that the women were responding energetically to the guidelines and that the project submissions received so far were likely to be approved.

I was fortunate to be accommodated in Sarajevo by a Muslim couple in their sixties. The husband, despite permanent injuries from a stroke suffered just before the conflict, told me how they had lived through those war years. All their window glass had been blown out by the blasts of mortar fire from the nearby hills, but UNHCR had supplied plastic sheeting to keep out the worst of the cold. However, there was no heating fuel, so he and his wife had gradually burned most their furniture, as well as their books, clothes and even shoes, to keep alive throughout the cold months, living just in the one room they were trying to keep warm. There was no water supply, and even when I was renting one of their rooms, the brave husband limped daily down to a pump ten minutes away, to fill a bucket, or perhaps two, with water that had to suffice for twenty-four hours. I loved this dear couple: he with his winsome English, acquired at school, no doubt, and used throughout the years that he had been a high-level businessman; she with her very warm smile. On the days that I was not picked up by a UNHCR driver for a long trip, when setting off on the twenty-five-minute walk to the office I would pass the remnants of a neighbour's house that my host told me had been blown open by a grenade, or maybe a bomb, thrown in by a *chetnik*.

Thirteen years later, I was to return briefly to countries of the former Yugoslavia, with my daughter Claudia, who had been only eleven when I left home for Sarajevo in 1996. From Switzerland and northern Italy, we crossed a section of Slovenia and reached Croatia, where we drove past many ruined houses – Claudia's first experience of seeing war damage. Then, crossing into Bosnia and Herzegovina, we came to Mostar and walked round the town so shockingly stricken during the war, crossing the bridge that is a perfect replica of the world-famous one. Reaching Sarajevo as darkness fell, we found a hotel and then I rang the doorbell of my former hosts, but a neighbour advised us that the husband had died and the wife had moved away. This gentleman urged the two of us to spend the evening at his house, with his wife and mother. Though we at first demurred, we did go, and they gave us wonderful Muslim hospitality. It happened to be the end of Ramadan, and at a well-laden table we ate and talked for hours.

Then next day we drove on, crossing part of Serbia with its signposts in Cyrillic script, reaching Kosovo, where we had a special friend to see.

The second part of this chapter is about what happened to Kosovo in the 1990s.

Kosovo

Kosovo, a small, landlocked Balkan country with its capital in Pristina, has a beleaguered past that is far too long to go into in any depth in this book. Basically, its Albanian population, numbering about 1.8 million, compared to about 210,000 Serbs, suffered enormously in the 1990s from Serbian ambitions and Serbian military might.

The country was declared in the Yugoslav constitution of 1974 an "autonomous region of S. Serbia", one of the eight constituents of the Yugoslav Socialist Republic. It seems that all went comparatively well for fourteen years. Then, in the late 1980s, Serbians started objecting to Kosovo's virtual independence, agitating for it to be merged with the rest of Serbia. The Albanian-speaking population in their heart of hearts were longing for a Kosovo Republic, comparing their status with that of Macedonia and Montenegro, both full "republics".

In 1989, the Serbs suddenly brought in measures of segregation, using "emergency legislation" to rid industry and public services of Albanian-speaking employees at all levels, to prevent their children from having schooling and outlawing their language from the media. The new Serb Constitution confirmed these measures, dissolving the Kosovo parliament and government in July 1980 and formally annexing the country.

In 1991 the Kosovo assembly, though still technically dissolved, organized a referendum on sovereignty that received 99% support. The Kosovar majority then held unsanctioned elections, choosing Ibrahim Rugova as president and selecting a 130-member parliament. Serbia regarded the elections as illegal but allowed them to proceed. Rugova exercised a policy of peaceful resistance, while a degree of impatience over the situation led to the creation by 1995 of a Kosovo Liberation Army, UÇK, soon branded by the Serbs as a terrorist organization. Repression of civilians that had probably been prepared long in advance was set in motion, and the threat of ethnic cleansing – perpetrated in nearby Bosnia and Herzegovina – seemed real.

This time, the Europeans and Americans did not wait before reacting. Negotiations over Kosovo took place in February 1999 at Rambouillet near Paris. The two sides – Rugova/the UÇK and Serbia – accepted the fundamental principles, including the fact that Kosovo had to be granted greater autonomy, but the Serbs refused to sign the Rambouillet Accord, which, if implemented, would have provided for NATO control of Kosovo by the stationing of 30,000 NATO forces – a totally unacceptable provision for the Serbs. Meanwhile, in those early months of 1999 an estimated 300,000 Kosovars (15% of the population) were violently evicted from their homes to be sent into exile, their houses burned behind them.

It appears that Slobodan Milosević had lost face with his public over signing the Dayton Accords that ended the Bosnian conflict. His intransigence now, which the Serb public applauded, led to NATO starting to launch the threatened air strikes in an attempt to force Serbia to halt its repression of ethnic Albanians in Kosovo. These strikes, far from impressing Milosević, were used by him as an excuse for a strong upsurge in the expulsion and killing by Serb military forces of many thousands of Kosovo Albanians. The widespread killings emptied villages and even towns (Pristina, Mitrovica, Pec, Djakovica, Prizren): according to innumerable testimonies, the Serbs systematically emptied one village after another, road by road, house by house, using local Serbs too, former neighbours of the expellees, to harass and kill. People had their identity papers taken and were given only a few minutes to leave their homes before their houses were set on fire. Young men were often held and taken away, or were even killed on the spot.

Our son-in-law Isa and his siblings and parents were in among all this mayhem. Isa had already been pulled from a bus, questioned and beaten up by Serbs when he was about fifteen. By 1999, he had joined the UÇK, the only alternative being to surrender to the Serb military. Ferida, Isa's elder sister, alone with two babies to carry on the exodus and deprived of food or drink, survived against what seemed like heavy odds, and remains traumatized by the experience. Expellees were herded onto buses or farm trailers drawn by tractors, then forced to go the rest of the way to the border on foot on rough roads, in some cases in snow. On the way, many were again robbed, raped or murdered. They were forced into Macedonia, Albania, Montenegro and even Bosnia. The numbers of uprooted reached almost one million.[23]

Milosević, like an expert chess player (remarks the author Paul Garde), knew that he could withstand the bombing of Yugoslavia and as it gave him the opportunity he sought to clear Kosovo of Albanian speakers. The

[23] Garde, *op. cit.*: 986,979 (of whom 444,200 were in Albania, 247,400 in Macedonia, 69,700 in Montenegro and 21,700 in Bosnia, according to a UNHCR estimate quoted by *Le Figaro* on 10 June 1999.

Western politicians had not foreseen such a move, nor did they imagine that he would play such a strong hand. Of course, he had allies, such as Russia and even China...

Kosovo remains damaged by all those events, by the flight of very large numbers to countries of Europe as well as by the lack of meaningful investment. Switzerland admitted some 200,000 people, most of whom – hard-working people – have succeeded in leading active lives here, while some have returned to Kosovo, taking with them expertise acquired over the years as farmers, carpenters or restaurant employees. Many, including our son-in-law, have now acquired Swiss nationality, consoled to a degree over the dramatic circumstances that changed their lives by the stability they have found, and by frequent interactions both with their fellow countrymen living in this country, and with family back in Kosovo.

CHAPTER 17

Rape As A Weapon Of War In Kivu (Congo)

This chapter is likely to be one of the most disturbing in this book, and one of the most difficult to write, so because parts of its content are simply horrifying, some readers may prefer to skip it. The reality of Kivu today for hitherto peaceful communities, above all for the women and girls, is appalling.

Before writing about one of the twenty-first century's greatest heroes, Dr Denis Mukwege, I recall something of the nature of this "Switzerland of Africa", as the colonials used to call it. A green mountainous region around Lake Kivu, one of Africa's "Great Lakes" that divides the Kivu Province of Congo from Rwanda, was peopled by agriculturalists and herders, the latter related to the Tutsi of Rwanda. Having at its northern tip (as described in the first part of Chapter 14), the once attractive twin towns of Kisenyi (Gisenyi) and Goma, each overshadowed by the great volcanoes, one of which arises to over 4,500 metres (almost 15,000 feet) above sea level. At Lake Kivu's southern tip, on either side of the Ruzizi River that flows on down to Lake Tanganyika, lie Bukavu, the provincial capital, and Cyangugu. Bukavu, where Denis Mukwege was born in 1955, stands at 1,460 metres (almost 5,000 feet) above sea level, and enjoys an equatorial climate. Much of the town was built on seven fingers of land that thrust out into a lake that is so full of islands that one cannot really see where its actual bounds lie. Kivu, apart from the dramatic events of the early 1960s, was basically peaceful.

I was there several times in 1964, both before and after the tragic death that August of our UNHCR colleague François Preziosi. Goma, the town built at the foot of the Nyiragongo volcano, subsequently became familiar territory, the Hotel des Grands Lacs the obvious (or only) place to stay, when we were evacuating threatened Rwandans to Tanzania by boat from Bukavu and plane to Tabora. Eleven years later, UNHCR asked me to go

351

on an extended mission as head of the Bukavu office, their representative having had to be evacuated through utter exhaustion, brought on while trying to find ways of helping Hutu refugees from Burundi to settle on the land (but, unfortunately, no land was allocated before she was evacuated). Both North and South Kivu became increasingly familiar to me on trips to the former, a highland area adjacent to the volcanoes with representatives of the local authorities to issue Rwandan Tutsi refugees with identity cards, years after they had taken refuge there. Sometimes, travelling north from Bukavu, our Congolese driver would take the Cyangugu–Kisenyi road, in no worse state than the road on the Congo side of the lake.[1] The Nyiragongo erupted during that period, having for many years sent fiery sparks into the air, as we could see from Bukavu, many miles to the south. The new lava flows reportedly killed countless animals, but people somehow managed to escape, although many were displaced and were left destitute, miles from Goma, before being found by an International Red Cross delegate, Sven Lampell, to be eating grass and leaves to stay alive.

As for South Kivu, an area of unoccupied land had at last been granted on which, four years after their flight from widespread massacres in Burundi, the Hutu refugees could settle. The frequent eight-hour Land Rover journey I had to make along the shore of Lake Tanganyika leading to and from the settlement area, though far from comfortable, gradually had the effect that Kivu, like Rwanda, got under my skin! So now, when I see names like Masisi, Mwesi, Uvira and Fizi in relation to some of the thousands of women and girls whose lives, and bodies, have been torn apart, I can visualize the peaceful populations once familiar to me, and the contrast is overwhelming.

* * * * * *

Whether we like it or not, we are forced back to the unfortunate initiatives that the government of France took during the genocide in Rwanda, both to provide the losing Hutu army with more arms and to create that "Turquoise Zone" – ostensibly to protect Tutsis from further massacres but in reality to save its "client", the former extremist Hutu government, from capture by the RPF (Chapter 14, part II). This is how the *génocidaires* (*interahamwe*), armed to the teeth and absolutely determined to wreak more havoc on the unfortunate Tutsis, came to be ushered into Kivu, in and among the hundreds of thousands of their countrymen, who, with their

[1]   To think that, in Kisenyi, I was within six miles of the wonderful Rosamond Halsey Carr, who ran a pyrethrum and flower farm, and who many years later saved hundreds of Rwandan orphans! But I did not know of her existence then.

relentless propaganda, they had rendered first murderous, then absolutely terrified that the pursuing Tutsi army would kill them and rape their women; terrified also, we can assume, by their participation in the massacres of Tutsis, for which they surely realized that they would have to answer one day.

It is the reprehensible failure of the "international community" to prevent firstly the genocide, secondly the escape into the Kivu province of the Congo of some of the most dangerous men of our planet, herding with them between a million and a half and two million terrified Hutus, and, thirdly, the logical early repatriation to Rwanda of all those Hutus that led to the present situation. The Hutu killers were let loose in the Kivu Province of Congo,[2] forcing UNHCR and NGOs to acquiesce with their control of the camps, although these organizations were providing billions of dollars' worth of humanitarian aid for over two years to the perpetrators of the genocide and their captives. So those camps, which after the first shambolic weeks came to be amply supplied by UNHCR and other agencies with necessities (and apparently receiving also supplies of ammunition, though through other mysterious channels), provided the base for violent attacks on Rwanda. After two years, the new Rwandan government, determined to create circumstances in which the cross-border attacks would no longer be so frequent and masses of Hutus would have to return to Rwanda, found allies to take vigorous action. Among them were people of Banyarwanda origin living in Kivu, whose cattle had been decimated by the Hutus, and the Congolese politician Laurent-Désiré Kabila, who had been dreaming of overthrowing the dictator Mobutu. The strong force that took action on the Kivu side of the border, ostensibly setting off to dislodge Mobutu, had as its first priority the dissolution of the camps.

This was the beginning of the chaos that has subsequently reigned uninterruptedly in Kivu, with repercussions deeper into the country. Mobutu was ousted and Kabila took over in Kinshasa. But what came to be called the "First Congo War" had the largely unforeseen though catastrophic result that fragmented bands of militants roamed the country, and there began to be in Kivu the hitherto unknown mass rape of women and girls by bands of armed men. The atrocious violence has continued to this day.

Such are the circumstances in which the beautiful, mostly peaceful (albeit poor) province of Kivu was transformed into a living hell. All the violence and viciousness that Kivu has known since the end of the 1990s are attributable to the circumstances briefly described above. All the sufferings

---

2   Still called Zaïre then. At the time of the genocide, the convenor of a New York Round Table discussion quoted missionaries who had said to an international magazine journalist, "There are no devils in hell now – they are all in Rwanda."

of fragmented Kivu communities, because of the abominable attacks on their women and female children, all the annihilation of hospitals and the murder of their staff, as well as all the murders of Congolese, can be laid at those doors. For chapter and verse, one has only to read the very recent book by Colette Braeckman, *L'Homme qui répare les femmes – le Combat du Docteur Mukwege, Prix Nobel de la Paix 2018*. But there are plenty of other sources that bear out the above.

Other destructive factors were yet to come into the picture, as we shall hear from Dr Mukwege himself, who will first testify to the events of 1994–96.

Dr Denis Mukwege, Healer Of Thousands Of Women And Girls

Before 1994

Denis Mukwege's father was a Pentecostal minister, and Denis at a young age decided to study medicine, after learning through visits to parishioners with his father that many women, in the absence of specialist health care, endured complications in childbirth. He graduated with a medical degree from the University of Burundi, Bujumbura. From 1983, he worked as a paediatrician in Lemera Hospital that stood in the hills some miles above. However, after seeing women patients who in the absence of proper care often suffered pain, genital lesions and obstetric after giving birth, he went to France, to study, completing his medical residency in 1989. He and his family (now with three children) were encouraged to stay on in Angers, but, after much thought, always aware of the needs of his fellow countrymen and women, the doctor opted to return. Like his father, he too was a Pentecostal minister. A fervent believer, he would say that his faith enabled him to do the work he did.

Back in Lemera Hospital as head doctor, he treated people of many different backgrounds, including Banyamulenge pastoralists, who were long-term settlers akin to the Tutsis of Rwanda, Babembe people who live along the shores of Lake Tanganyika, the Bafuliru farmers from the Ruzizi Plain, and the Barundi Hutu refugees with whom UNHCR had been concerned in the 1970s. And now there were recently arrived Tutsi refugees too, accommodated at a camp in his community. "*As the person in charge of health questions,*" he said, "*I naturally looked after the refugee camp at Nyangezi, 22 km. from Bukavu. We welcomed these people with open arms after they had managed to get across the border."*[3]

After 1994

The people of the Congo had always respected newcomers, but suddenly, in 1994, they were about to be overwhelmed by them. First, in July, over a million Hutus crowded into Goma, with the dreadful consequences we have seen – the outbreak of cholera that cost thousands of lives, and the camps set up in great haste getting to be controlled by the extremists. Then, the following month, when the French military contingent was about to leave Rwanda, it saw to the safe departure of the remaining Hutus, who crossed over the Ruzizi River to Bukavu. Dr Mukwege noted, *"The Hutu were coming in from Kamanyola, the border posts of Ruzizi I and Ruzizi II. Soldiers, military vehicles, top officials, cattle, villagers, intellectuals and farming people, a whole country was migrating, landing on us with arms and belongings. What amazed me was that the soldiery made no attempt to hide and did not seem to be fleeing. On the contrary, they came over in good order, commanded by their officers, and they had kept their arms and their uniforms..."*

UNHCR, headed throughout the 1990s by Mrs Sadako Ogata, appeared to have no hesitation in treating these masses of Hutus as refugees. Yet, the camps defied international refugee law, in that they were not at the required distance from the border, they accommodated murderers, and the armed men were not disarmed and separated from the rest of the camp population. In no time, the UN agency was overwhelmed and appealed for help. Protestant entities called on Dr Mukwege to go Goma to evaluate the medical needs. He went accompanied by a Swedish doctor, and would report, "It was absolute horror. I've never seen anything like it. We saw people walking on the road who stumbled, then collapsed – and died. Everyone was agitated, running hither and thither, like ants. No one was paying any attention to people who had collapsed on the road. We had to be careful not to drive over bodies..." After a few days, the two doctors realized they could do nothing about the immense public health needs, especially the need for clean water. The experience they had traumatized them, so much so that the Swedish doctor soon went back to Sweden with a nervous breakdown, and cut off all his contacts with the Congo, while Dr Mukwege destroyed all the photographs he had taken. "I had to get those scenes out of my head," he explained.

---

[3]   Colette Braeckman, *L'Homme qui répare les Femmes* (2015). Much of the content of these paragraphs is based on this book.

In the Bukavu area, it looked as if the needs could be more manageable, and he sent to Norway for a mobile hospital which as he reported, arrived with 100 beds, radio, an operation theatre, a maternity area and a laboratory. "We set this hospital up in the town centre, to relieve the Congolese hospitals that were snowed under." So before long, he and his staff made a major contribution to the health needs of the escapees (otherwise known as refugees) in South Kivu.

Gradually, the Hutus put down roots in the area. Dr Mukwege, increasingly aware of the danger they represented, began to be seriously concerned. "Those soldiers of the former regime didn't even try to hide their arms or change out of their uniforms. There was no control over them at all – the situation was really abnormal."[4] It was obvious that in parallel to UNHCR's supposed authority, the Hutu officers were really in charge of the camps, to the point that they had to be consulted if one wanted to go in there. Other commentators have stated that UNHCR did not appear to be exercising any pressure on these men, such as threatening to withdraw aid if they did not give up their military activities in the camp. There was apparently the very same degree of authority in the camps – exercised over the camp populations by members of the former Kigali government, officers and soldiers of the Forces Armées du Rwanda (FAR), *interahamwe* and militiamen – as they had exerted on the Hutu population throughout the genocide. Two major NGOs, Médecins sans Frontières and International Rescue Committee, withdrew, seeing that the camps were in the hands of the extremists.

Over the next two years, from that angle the situation got worse. Mukwege could see here *"one of the causes of the Congolese people's misfortune. At first, the Congolese received all these people without any hostility. They gave them work. I never heard of any killing,"* and, furthermore, there was a high birth rate. *"I was treating the refugee women. Births were normal, and after all, the refugees were well fed and they had nothing special to do, so there was any number of new births. … Neither amongst Congolese women nor in the refugee population did I find any genital lesions resulting from rape."*[5]

Braeckman suggests that the "baby boom" was official Hutu policy, aiming to build up Hutu strength for the future. As for the idea of going back to Rwanda, it was out of the question, for anyone wishing to leave the camps was considered to be a traitor to the (Hutu) cause. Well-trained youngsters were involved in military cross-border operations just inside Rwanda, where

4   Colette Braeckman, *op. cit.*, pp.44–46.
5   Idem.

the surviving Tutsis lived in terror. Meanwhile, the Congolese Tutsi pastors in North Kivu, the Banyamulenge, were being robbed of all their cattle – and facing ruin. The North Kivu Breeders' Confederation applied in vain to the international organizations for compensation for 30,000 head of cattle stolen from their area.

War And Loss

A very dangerous period lay ahead when 1994 and 1995 gave way to 1996. In the meantime, Dr Mukwege had moved his family to Bukavu for safety, and for a long time he would walk to Lemera every second Monday, after spending alternate weekends with his family. Without public transport and also without any protection, he undertook the long, lonely two-hour walk back to the hospital.

In mid-1996, heavily armed men began to be seen crossing the Ruzizi Plain and disappearing into the mountains. Paul Kagame, Rwanda's defence minister,[6] had frequently warned the international community over those two years that if the Hutu camps were not relocated away from the border areas he would impose a solution himself. Dr Mukwege was advised by the authorities to barricade the hospital, but being far from imagining that violent conflict might be imminent he refused, wishing the hospital facilities to still be available to all. It seems that this open-mindedness led to his now being suspected of being in league with the armed men in the mountains. These included some of the Banyamulenge, who, robbed by the Rwandan Hutus of their herds of cattle and means of subsistence, and furthermore ostracized, as had never happened before, by Congolese who had started to absorb Hutu propaganda, had joined the Rwandan Tutsi army that was preparing to dismantle the Hutu camps.

Lemera Hospital, writes Colette Braeckman, unfortunately became a strategic area where Mobutu's government troops clashed with the new force. In the process, the hospital itself was violently attacked at the very time that a wholesale evacuation was about to take place. As it happened, Dr Mukwege had just got onto the road to take a chronically sick Swedish colleague down to Bukavu for safety. To his everlasting regret, just after he left unlimited force was used against the hospital and everyone in it. However, he could of course have done nothing to save his colleagues or his patients, and undoubtedly he would have been killed too, for everyone was killed and the hospital was completely demolished, its contents looted.

---

[6] Though Paul Kagame had directed affairs from 1990 onwards, he became president of Rwanda only in 2000.

While one could now see that there were more than enough highly dangerous actors in this scenario, the reality is that more fighting groups had got grafted onto Paul Kagame's army, some from Uganda – certainly sufficient fighters to defeat General Mobutu's fainthearted troops and remove him for good from his long-held power base.[7] Meanwhile, Dr Mukwege had received warnings that he was in danger, and just in time before it fell to the rebels he, his wife and children, his sister and a large group of colleagues got out of Bukavu, evacuated by air to Bunia, thanks to the Missionary Aviation Fellowship that sent three aircraft to take them to safety.

Such is the background to all the future horror that confronted everyone from that time on.

Hutu Escapees Depart In 1996 – But Not All Go Back To Rwanda

The multinational force put together by Paul Kagame surrounded the Hutu camps, attacking with explosives and causing mayhem on a terrifying scale. But, from the burning camps at the northern end of Lake Kivu, an orderly departure of hundreds of thousands of Hutu civilians could be seen, walking through the intended gap in the circle of Rwandan soldiery. Leaving Goma behind and crossing into Gisenyi, they had to keep moving but members of the government had come from Kigali to welcome them back. Fresh drinking water was available at this and at subsequent points along the routes that the estimated one million people took, on into the hills they had left over two years earlier.

The situation in and around Bukavu was very different with regard to the Hutu escapees. Half a million people stampeded in the direction of the forest, racing through the national park, aiming to get to Kisangani (the former Stanleyville), as far as possible from the avenging force that had set the camps on fire. Not only were Rwandan Hutus fleeing but large numbers of terrified residents of Bukavu also took to the roads. Dr Mukwege remembers all this only too well, and how a new humanitarian emergency came about – in which he had no choice but to play an important part, called upon by Scandinavians based in Kenya to make an assessment of the situation.

Over the ensuing months and years, political realities were rapidly coming into play. First of all, as Mobutu had to be removed, the strong force that Paul Kagame had put together moved in the same direction as

---

7   Mobutu was the tyrannical dictator of Congo/Zaïre for thirty-one years, from his *coup d'état* of 1965 throughout all the years in which the country could have been developing (receiving international funds to do so!).

the runaways before going on to Kinshasa. Laurent-Désiré Kabila then took over the reins of government, changing the country's name to that of the Democratic Republic of Congo, intending simply to thank Kagame and the other men for their support – and see them leave! Unfortunately, the Rwanda government had the aim of keeping its big neighbour under its wing. Political tensions became rife over the ensuing years, until what came to be known as the Second Congo War, an attempt made by President Kabila to push the unwanted military groups out of the country.

This was far easier said than done. Armed men had discovered great riches waiting to be mined, so they could now oversee the extraction – often by young children – of valuable minerals such as coltan. Ever since those dangerous years of the 1990s, they have looted without compunction and preyed upon local people, causing the most extreme distress in the villages. Furthermore, as they had intended all along, extremists carried out military cross-border operations against Tutsis in western Rwanda, for a time still benefiting from humanitarian aid organized to keep civilians among them alive. Nothing stopped them from operating in murderous bands from their hideouts in the dense forest.

Throughout the intervening years, Dr Mukwege has frequently faced exhaustion, both working fifteen-hour days in the operating theatre and denouncing the criminal attacks on the Kivu's people and its natural resources in major world fora. For a long time, he had the grinding impression that his was a voice in the wilderness – for while people were listening, there was no action.

Pioneering Work To Rectify Diabolical Injuries

With Lemera Hospital gone, Dr Mukwege managed to find a plot of land in Panzi, one of the poorer parts of Bukavu, to build a modest hospital. He founded the new hospital in 1999, with the financial help of Swedish Christian aid organizations and the Swedish International Development Cooperation Agency, giving it the name of the district. The Panzi Hospital has since become world famous because of the unique work carried on there, and because of Mukwege's tireless testimonies to the world about the intense physical and psychological suffering of the victims of savagery. Not all those who have been attacked in their homes have chosen to talk about these rapes: it is often too hard to admit what happened, especially when husbands and children have been forced to watch.

Over the twenty years that he has performed operations on women at the Panzi Hospital, in countless interviews and speeches – for instance in the United Nations General Assembly in 2012 and at the Nobel Peace Prize ceremony in Oslo in October 2018 – Denis Mukwege has consistently testified to the appalling violence, and I will give his testimony (like previous quotations of some of his words) in italics:

> *When I built the hospital, it was to help mothers with the delivery of their babies, but the first person to come for treatment was a woman who had been raped with firearms. And very soon I found that this was not an isolated case, and three months later I had helped forty-five women with the same story, collective rapes, the torture of genitals.*

He was devastated at what he found, and after several months of listening with empathy to his patients he had to arrange for them to talk to someone else, because what he heard was drastically affecting both his sleep and his surgical work. One question put to him in a BBC interview on the day before the award on December 2018 of the Nobel Peace Prize to him and to Nadia Murad was about the age of the victims. He replied that the youngest was six months old. But there were also women of eighty and over; all ages were taken, he said.

It seems inconceivable that men in any part of the world, however cruel their background, can use their male organs, rifles, razor blades and other instruments of torture and destruction in violent attacks on hapless women and children. Both the victims of these attacks and their whole communities are traumatized. Many of the husbands who have been forced to watch what was been done to their wives and daughters have lifelong repercussions in the form of total impotence. "I've lost my self-respect, and can no longer feel I'm a man. As for my children, who have seen their mother raped, have witnessed my humiliation, can I still say that I'm a father?"[8] Others reject their wives, or disappear.

Testifying To The World

> *It's a strategy of destruction, a strategy of war, rape as a form of terrorism, attacking where life comes from. You traumatize the whole population, and of course this leads to people losing self-confidence. There are infections, there is the destruction of the ability of women to give birth. You can destroy the economy this way, and they do it in total impunity. I would say that the*

---

[8]   Braeckman, *op. cit.*

military chiefs decide what's to be done with the women, so they do it because it was planned that way. We see that different groups have been doing the same things. They act as if they have the right to do what they want with women's bodies. We feel that the victims are left to their fate.

Readers will find the following extracts from the preface to the book *Rape – A Tool of Terror*,[9] recently published in Brussels, both moving and revealing, in line with the content of Dr Mukwege's many addresses to audiences in cities like New York, Brussels and Olso.

We are unfortunately living through a time of increasing tensions in the world coupled with the negation of values. Violence has become commonplace, assuming ever more loathsome forms.

I come from an area, the East of the Democratic Republic of Congo, that is one of the richest in the world. Yet the vast majority of its inhabitants live in extreme poverty. If sometimes people show interest in us, it is because of the violence inflicted on Congolese women and the disgrace of our daughters, sisters and mothers, whose bodies have been turned into battlegrounds.

When news of rapes in Kivu first came to be spoken of, at first people shrugged their shoulders, it was only what might have been expected… And it's probably because of that indifference that it was so difficult to mobilize the international community to tackle the war and the violence being visited on women. Politicians and international organizations lack courage and their silence is sometimes deafening. And what is more disturbing is that the outside world seems not to recognize its share of responsibility for what is happening in Congo.

I will mention again here that President Emmanuel Macron has ordered a government enquiry into the activities of France under François Mitterrand vis-à-vis Rwanda in the 1990s.

Coltan[10] *– such a tempting product*

---

[9] *Le VIOL Une Arme de Terreur*, In Koli Jean Bofane, Colette Braeckman Guy-Bernard Cadière, Jean-Paul Marthoz, Damien Vandermeersch, 2019 (my translation).

[10] Coltan (short for columbite–tantalites and known industrially as tantalite) is a dull black metallic ore, from which the elements niobium and tantalum are extracted. The niobium-dominant mineral in coltan is columbite (after niobium's original American name columbium), and the tantalum-dominant mineral is tantalite (Wikipedia).

Few countries possess as many natural resources as does the Congo. With an area equivalent to that of Western Europe, its resources in water, forestry, land, and minerals ought to make for a prosperous nation. But this has never been the case. The riches of the Congo have on the contrary been a curse. It was thanks to the huge deposits of minerals, especially copper, that Mobutu could become one of the richest men in the world. The East of the Congo is without any doubt one of the richest area in terms of minerals. One can find gold, diamonds, tin, and coltan. I am pretty sure that in your computer, as in mine, and in our mobile phones, there are a few grams of tantalum. Eighty percent of coltan world deposits are here in the Congo.

Mukwege goes on to explain how since the beginning of the twenty-first century there has been such a demand for coltan that a market sprang up that was based on violence, with armed groups taking over control of the mining areas and using the profits for arms purchases. It was at this same time that, apart from the cynical abuse of Congolese children forced to work in the unsafe coltan mines, women and even children began to come under more frequent attack.

Our first patients at Panzi were women and girls who were victims of sexual violence perpetrated with unheard-of violence. We had to deal with the consequences of this barbarity, and treated thousands of women for both the physical and the psychological damage done to them.

After that, when some of these patients came back to Panzi having been attacked again, when babies we had delivered who were the result of rapes were also raped, I realized I had to stop performing operations and inform international opinion and policy-makers of these terrible truths. In this I was helped by people in civil society, in academia, in international NGOs and in the media, and this book is in line with these efforts to inform opinion.

Schools must be the places where we get the new generations to react against situations in which –

- *violence becomes the norm;*
- *multinational bodies enrich themselves, in league with unscrupulous national and local authorities;*

- *a peaceful community is forced into exile, to leave its territory open to armed predators who ransack the mineral resources;*
- *electronic devices stained with blood are openly sold on the European and world markets without anyone worrying about it.*

I have been able to speak in such fora as the UN General Assembly. I have been glad to be able to talk, and with much humility to accept many distinctions such as the prestigious Sakharov Prize, awarded by the European Parliament. But every time, two or three days after these lovely, heart-warming ceremonies, I am back in the operating theatre, facing the cruel reality of women, girls and babies who have been the victims of sexual violence...

Time to act...

It's time we dealt with the causes. Thanks to a report by UN experts, the "Mapping Report" of the High Commissioner for Human Rights as well as many other documents that denounce the perpetrators, no one can hide behind the argument that all this is too complex. The motivation and the responsibilities of those concerned are now very well known, but what is lacking is political will.

Dr Mukwege has often spoken of the need to restore the authority of the State and to reform the army, the police and the justice system. Impunity has been a basis for lawlessness and has to be tackled as a priority. *"We in Congo for the time being have neither peace, nor justice,"* he has said, *"and we continue to see what the eyes of a surgeon should never have to see. How can I keep quiet when we know that these crimes against humanity are carried out on the basis of financial gain? Our country is sick, but with our Congolese women and our friends around the world, we can and must make it well."*

The courageous doctor has used all the funds coming from his many awards to improve the Panzi Hospital's services. Since its foundation, the hospital has treated more than 85,000 patients with complex gynaecological damage and trauma.

Danger To His Person Once Again

In September 2012, in the impassioned speech the doctor made at the United Nations he condemned the mass rape occurring in the *Democratic*

Republic of the Congo and criticized the Congolese government and other countries "*for not doing enough to stop what he called an unjust war that has used violence against women and rape as a strategy of war*". He called for an end to impunity, demanding that rapists face justice for their crimes. Possibly as a direct result of this outspoken address, four armed men entered his house on 25 October and held his daughters hostage. When he returned home, his bodyguard ran out to warn him, and was shot dead. Mukwege threw himself to the ground and escaped injury. The gunmen, possibly believing they had killed him, fled and were not found subsequently.

It was not the first time that the brave doctor had narrowly escaped death. The shock was such that, in an ongoing atmosphere of death threats, Dr Mukwege took his family and went to live in Europe. But he was so acutely missed by the Congolese women that they actually managed to raise sufficient funds for his airfare, begging him to return and promising round-the-clock protection if he would return. This caring man was moved to return, and found to his amazement that all along the twenty-mile route from Kavumu Airport to the city there were women lining the road to welcome him back. This was on 14 January 2013.

He said in a speech soon afterwards, on accepting that year's Human Rights Award, "*I studied medicine to bring life into the world, but much of what I see today is about the destruction of women, of families, of communities. Our hospital was established for pregnant women, but we were confronted by an urgent need, because of the pyramid of brutality, using rape as a weapon. Women had devastating internal injuries, some had been shot in the genitals, raped repeatedly by gangs, forced into sexual slavery and made pregnant by violent men and boys. Often they were infected by HIV Aids, as well as their babies. Sometimes we've been reduced to tears,*" and he went on: "*What's worse – we have children born after a rape, who are also raped. It's a vicious circle that has no end. I don't know what else to say to make people more aware, it's a war taking place on women's bodies. ... You traumatise the whole population, and this leads to people losing self-confidence, and so you destroy the economy, with consequences for future generations – a vertical effect. I would say that the military chiefs decide what's to be done with the women, they do it because they planned to do it. And we see that different military groups have been doing the same things. They do it in total impunity, they act as if they have the right to do what they want with women's bodies. The women have to keep quiet about what they have been through, but some, courageously, have pointed to the military chief, 'He's the one who killed our husbands, our children.' We feel that the victims are left to their fate."*[11]

Five years and very many other honours after that Human Rights Award, the joint winners of the 2018 Nobel Peace Prize, Dr Mukwege and Nadia Murad, were interviewed by the BBC on *HARDtalk*. Each was asked about their reaction when they learned about the award. Dr Mukwege said, *"I was working in the hospital when my anaesthetist came in and hugged me, then all the women hugged me too, I didn't understand. There was tremendous excitement – it was a complete surprise!"*

Massive Trauma

In an interview with Al Jazeera, Dr Mukwege said, *The medical treatment is only a small part in the handling of victims of sexual violence. When we started, their trauma was so strong that they could not continue a normal life, so we included psychological handling. But when they are excluded by the family, by the community, by the husband, if you leave them in the street they will be raped again. So we must support them to be re-integrated into society.*

He and his staff from that time on have devoted a great deal of care and attention to the psychological needs of the women victims of rape, encouraging them not to lose hope. Many were suicidal on arrival at Panzi Hospital, with their bodies indescribably damaged, knowing that they had been repudiated by their community, so there would be no way back. But, however long it was going to take, they have gradually been nursed back to health of both mind and body.

With some of the funds donated to Panzi Hospital, and subsequently to his Foundation, the doctor has had houses built where up to a thousand women, chosen from among the most vulnerable, can live with their children, and receive therapeutic help: three "Dorcas" houses. In the course of three months that each woman can stay there, they are helped to see how they can manage to face the future. In some cases, they are given micro credits to start up small businesses, and, little by little, the women acquire confidence in themselves and in one another. Dr Mukwege says how impressed he is with the women he has been treating, with their determination to take their lives into their own hands. *"They amaze me, just a small loan of 50 dollars is enough for them to get going. When I see that, I realize that people are courageous, all is not lost, there is still hope for the Congo.*

---

[11]   These and subsequent quotations come from Colette Braeckman's book, *L'Homme qui répare les femmes.*

I feel sure, despite what everyone has been through, that people can go on with their lives in rebuilding it together."[12]

"I think sexual violence has always been denied in our society. It must not be the victim that bears the suffering of having been raped. We must be able to change this suffering of the victim and turn it towards the aggressors and the torturers." His Foundation bears the expense of employing lawyers to take testimonies from women – those who are ready to talk and perhaps identify their rapists.

There has been limited success in eliminating a degree of the violence, but it has been estimated that there remain about one hundred dangerous bands that have found satisfactory hiding places in the dense forest of the Kivu, from which of course they can emerge to wreak more damage on communities. It has been stated that year by year, 400,000 women are raped – again, a very shocking fact.

*   *   *   *   *   *

Speech At The Nobel Peace Prize Ceremony

This exceptionally qualified, extraordinarily compassionate doctor, while continuing his strenuous work at Panzi and speaking out about these atrocious human rights abuses, has received honour after honour from virtually every part of the world. On 11 December 2018, five years after his rousing speech at the 2013 Human Rights Award ceremony, six after his appeal to the United Nations General Assembly in 2012, he made an impassioned speech at Oslo to the distinguished Nobel Peace Prize audience, who listened raptly to every word. The Nobel Peace Center has given authorization to quote from that speech here.

He began by recalling the attack, on 6 October 1996, on Lemera Hospital, when at least thirty patients were murdered in their beds, and the staff, unable to stop the gunmen, were also killed. *"It was the start of all the violence,"* he said. *"We opened the Panzi Hospital and were ready to start delivering babies. But the first patient we received had received a bullet in her genital organs. Then one day came an urgent plea for an ambulance. We sent the ambulance, and it returned just over two hours later and the patient it brought in was a little girl only 18 months old, bleeding profusely after being raped by an adult. Everyone was crying, praying inwardly 'Oh please, please let*

---

12   Braeckman, *op. cit.*, p.135.

this be a nightmare, not reality', but this was now the reality, the new reality in the Democratic Republic of Congo."

He said that when another baby was brought in just as tragically damaged, he realized that we could not solve the problem in the operating theatre; it was essential to get at the root causes. So he went to the village the babies had been brought from, asking the men, *"Why haven't you protected your babies, your girls, your women, from these atrocities? and the response we got was 'We know who did it, everyone's afraid of him, he even killed a human rights worker who had been denouncing the violence, he's a member of the provincial parliament and has immunity.' We were desperate. Dozens of other children were raped. But in the end, we went to a military tribunal, these crimes were judged and it was given out that they were crimes against humanity."*

But, as Dr Mukwege then said, the cruel violence not only damages people sexually; it also damages them psychologically and genetically. In the absence of law and order in the country, the spiral of violence goes on, crime becomes organized and as a result, he said, four million people have been uprooted and six million have died. He accepted the Nobel Peace Prize in the name of the victims of violence, thanking all those who had helped Panzi Hospital. But he went on to say that while the Democratic Republic of the Congo is the richest country in the world, its population is the poorest. He spoke of the abundance of mineral riches, such as gold, cobalt and coltan, which are mined by children who are forced into this work. He pleaded that consumers of products such as smartphones and new cars should insist that those mineral ingredients be mined in conditions of human dignity. But he said that for so long, people had looked the other way while the country was being plundered in full view of everyone, huge profits ending up in the bank accounts of oligarchs.[13]

"Over exactly 20 years that we have been working in Panzi hospital, we have seen all the proof of poor government. The people of the Congo have been humiliated in full view of the international community," he said. He claimed that the citizens are capable of transforming the country, and he gave the example of a remarkable woman who, despite having been gravely damaged,

---

[13] As I write this (20 July 2019) the Swiss daily news features the fact that millions of children in the DRC are deprived of schooling because, while attendance at school is free for every child, the costs of compulsory school materials are beyond the pitiful budget of millions of parents. At the same time, the international mining conglomerates are failing to pay taxes on the billions of dollars' worth of minerals they are extracting from the country. If they were to be made to pay what they owe, there would no longer be any need for any of those millions of children to miss school – which shows us the scale of the scandal.

had recovered her full physical and psychological health and had started helping others. But the international community should come to grips at last with the fact that the violence has gone on unchecked for so long, and should pull together with the DRC government to create democracy and establish law and order. The criminals had immunity now, but they certainly should get arrested and be charged with their crimes.

"It is obvious that the current situation must not be allowed to go on. The rapes, murders and torture disgrace our world, while very large numbers of small children are exploited in the process of multinational companies, bent on making huge profits at the expense of the health and well-being of little Congolese children, getting their hands on cobalt." A recent British report gave the age of one small child involved in the perilous mining work as four years, while other tiny children were crying because of pain, because of the awful strain of having to do this work under duress while earning only a few cents a day to help their families – putting their health at risk and naturally, missing out on schooling.

We can look out for moves to help the DRC to overcome these traumatic situations that have certainly gone on for far too long.

In September 2019, news media including the BBC reported the launch by Dr Mukwege of an international fund to help victims of rape. We read that the doctor, who attributes the prevalence of mass rapes to the existence of conflict, hopes to be able to extend the sexual violence victim treatment programme developed at Panzi Hospital to other countries hit by conflict such as the Central African Republic, Burundi and Iraq.

Some Good News At Last!

1. On 7 November 2019, the International Criminal Court sentenced to thirty years' imprisonment one of the most notorious warlords of the last two decades, Bosco Ntaganda, forty-six, found guilty on eighteen counts of war crimes in DRC: murder, rape, the recruitment of child soldiers and illegal exploitation of minerals in Eastern Congo.

The ICC had in fact issued a warrant for this man's arrest in 2006 (thirteen years ago!), when he was alleged to have been recruiting children of under fifteen as soldiers in the Forces Patriotiques pour la Libération du Congo (FPLC) in 2002–03. In July 2012, it issued a second warrant for his arrest based on allegations of murder, rape and sexual slavery in those same years. Despite these arrest warrants, Bosco Ntaganda was never picked up by the Congolese authorities or by the UN, but on the contrary he was made a general in the Congolese army from January 2009 within the framework of a peace agreement between the authorities and armed groups – while the Congolese populations continued to bear the brunt of his criminal activities.

A Global Witness report written when Bosco first stood trial[14] states that this former Rwandan soldier got rich from Congo's minerals, owning mines and illegally taxing mineral trading routes. "The fluctuating nature of Congo's war alliances – where enemies can quickly become partners and vice versa – allowed Bosco to become extremely powerful and wealthy. Crossing over from rebel to army general in a 2009 backdoor peace deal cemented his control over lucrative mining zones, allowing him to effectively run his own state-within-a-state. This despite the fact Congolese law deems the involvement of the army in the minerals trade illegal." The report goes on to say that armed control over Congo's minerals continues, Bosco's story being powerfully emblematic of the impunity warlords and members of Congo's national army enjoy. Bosco's arrest two years ago and his condemnation on 7 November 2019 should help damage some of the determination of other armed criminals.

2.   Here is another item of good news: French triple world karate champion Laurence Fischer has devoted a good deal of time to giving women in Dr Mukwege's Foundation months of expert instruction on self-defence. In a film shown on Swiss television on 7 March 2020, we see Laurence Fischer starting to turn the tide for hundreds of the women, converting their earlier fear to a fierce determination not to let anyone overpower them ever again. Three of the women have even decided to become karate instructors. The movement is gaining strength and could well result in the saving of many lives.

Psychosocial Help With The Women's Trauma

There is little doubt that Dr Mukwege and his staff have inculcated a spirit of resilience, and that the women are managing to help and encourage one another to cope with the psychological sequelae of what they have been through. Gradually, with more awareness of the burdens the Kivu has had to carry alone, outside aid has come in that contribute to the recovery of very many women, along the lines of the following.

---

[14]   Patrick Alley, co-authored with Norbert Mbu Mputu, *Global Witness* (2 September 2015).

Minova, Sud-Kivu, Democratic Republic Of The Congo.

Volunteers from the DRC Red Cross who work in a sexual violence counselling centre brief displaced persons on the issue of rape and other forms of sexual violence. The centres provide support for many women in the two Kivus. Psychosocial assistants look after the victims of sexual violence and other types of trauma, referring them to medical facilities where necessary.

The International Committee of the Red Cross (ICRC) carries out a variety of activities, including involvement in forty "listening centres", where victims of violence can come and talk about what they have been through.

Described by the UN Office for the Coordination of Humanitarian Affairs (OCHA) on its website, but without giving a date:

> More than 1 million women and girls have been raped in the Democratic Republic of the Congo (DRC) during the past 20 years of violent conflict, according to estimates by UN Women. Beyond physical pain, they suffer emotional trauma and the fear of rejection. But with support from the OCHA-managed DRC Humanitarian Fund (DHF), the non-governmental organization Hope in Action is helping survivors of sexual violence in eastern DRC to recover and thrive.
>
> In 2015 Hope in Action received US$600,000 to build/ rehabilitate four community-counselling centres in DRC's North Kivu Province (in Masisi and Walikale territories). Survivors of sexual violence meet compassionate listeners at the centres and find help in their uphill battle to recover. Women are also offered free medical assistance through local health centres where they can receive post-exposure prophylaxis (PEP) kits, which, if taken within 72 hours of an assault, reduce the risk of HIV transmission.
>
> [Two Kivu women,] Anne and Colette, who were trained as counsellors for a Hope in Action *Maison d'Ecoute* (Listening House [a safe place to tell their stories, which is a simple but crucial part of recovery]) ... feel they needed "to be involved in the fight to stop sexual violence within [their] community", but they are worried that some survivors do not seek assistance out of fear of stigmatization and rejection by their husbands.
>
> "In some cases, we hear of a sexual assault and visit the survivor if the security situation allows it. Then we do the

utmost to convince her to come with us to seek medical assistance at the health centre," explained Colette.

A Helping Hand

In April 2016, Hope in Action also began supporting income-generating activities to help survivors get back on their feet. By providing access to farmland and agricultural inputs or financial assistance to start small businesses, 120 women were again able to provide for themselves and their families.

One of those women is 63-year-old Nana.* "I received financial assistance from Hope in Action to help me start selling charcoal at the local market," she said. "Now, thanks to the profit I make, I eat three meals per day and can meet my basic needs, as well as those of my family."

Renée,* 39, said: "Thanks to this activity, I own and cultivate my own field and sell vegetables at the local market. Now, I can feed myself and my children and send them to school."

The Hope in Action project also supports community outreach and training activities to help break stereotypes, inform people about gender and sexual violence, and help communities heal. The active involvement of men has been central to these activities.

Le Grand and Jackson, both 30 years old, explained that the DHF-funded training changed their perception of their roles as husbands and fathers. "The training really contributed to opening our minds and understanding the importance and benefits of considering ourselves as part of a family that functions best as a team rather than as a dictatorship," explained Le Grand.

"I noticed a positive change in my husband's behavior towards me. Before the training, he never used to ask for my [sexual] consent," added 25-year-old Adeline.

Medical Attention And More

Espérance, the Head Nurse at the health centre in Loashi village, Masisi Territory, North Kivu Province explained that with DHF funding, Hope in Action was able to provide the centre with critical antiretroviral medicine, PEP kits, maternity and baby kits, $50 per month for operational costs and a mill for survivors to process their crops. Profits from the mill are distributed equally among the survivors, and they each receive 50,000 Congolese Francs ($30) per month.

The Hope in Action project will soon end, but Anthony Musafiri, Coordinator for Hope in Action in North Kivu, noted that its positive effects would be long-lasting.

"These DHF-funded activities have strengthened the resilience of beneficiaries," he said. "Women who were long marginalized and survivors of sexual violence are smiling again because of their extraordinary courage and a response that was adapted for sound social cohesion."

He added: "We are also delighted to note a real change in men's attitudes. An increasing number of men no longer consider the role of women as limited to work in the house and in the fields. They now see women as true partners who can play the same role as men within their community."

Since 2011, the DHF has allocated just over $1 million to Hope in Action to support more than 90,000 people.

The DHF allows donors to pool their contributions into a single, unearmarked fund to support the highest-priority humanitarian projects in DRC. So far this year, the fund has received a total of $15 million from Belgium, Germany, Ireland, Luxembourg and Sweden.

A Final Word

Dr Denis Mukwege has done such remarkable work that it is no wonder he has been given so many prestigious awards. The list, found easily on a search engine like Google, seems unending! He must be very glad that the ICC has just condemned one of the most notorious criminals to thirty years in prison. We know that he would prize, above any award, concrete action to capture and then send for trial all those other violent men who come out of hiding to molest and ill-treat women who want nothing more than a peaceful life of hard work in the fields and the care of their families. We must hope that world authorities will at long last find effective methods to restore the DRC's easternmost province and its inhabitants to the original calm that some of us once observed, but that most of them have never even known.

CHAPTER 18

Victims Of Terrorists In Northern Iraq

I began to write this book in the week that two remarkable people who were joint Nobel Peace Prize winners made very moving speeches in Oslo about the atrocities of which both had had searing experience in their respective countries: Dr Denis Mukwege, the famous Congolese gynaecologist and surgeon who is the subject of the previous chapter, and Nadia Murad, a young Yazidi woman who has now acquired well-deserved fame too. These two exceptional people are alerting the world to situations that should never have arisen, to suffering that it is beyond the capacity of most of us to be able to imagine. Courageous, selfless people like the 2018 Nobel Peace Prize winners help the rest of us to retain at least some faith in human nature in a world that is so very far from perfect.

On 3 August 2014, fanatical, heavily armed Islamists began to bear down on the town and region of Sinjar, the part of northern Iraq that has always been the home of large numbers of peaceful Yazidi agriculturalists, a place of memory, full of vital monuments, mausoleums and shrines. ISIS proceeded to destroy the whole area: both its inhabitants and its infrastructure.

After a few agonizing days of terrible uncertainty during which huge numbers of Yazidis fled to the commanding heights of Mount Sinjar, a nineteen-year-old farm girl, Nadia Murad, and thousands of other Yazidi girls and young women were taken prisoner and forced to become "wives" and sexual slaves of ISIS fighters. They were driven from their homes on the very same day that all their men, including six of Nadia's brothers, and older women – her beloved mother among them – were taken and summarily executed. From that day on, and for months, Nadia was to experience daily brutality in a variety of forms so excruciating that she wished her torturers would kill her. But one day – against enormous odds – she managed to escape, receiving a tremendous measure of help and support from a family that, had it lacked humanity, would have handed her straight back to her torturers. These people took a terrible risk in taking her in, but they were determined to see her to safety.

Nadia remained acutely conscious of the sufferings of thousands of her fellow victims, who experienced the same tortures day after day throughout the intervening years, unless they managed to escape – but only very few did, other than by taking their lives rather than submit to the extreme cruelty of their captors.

This is another chapter making for perturbing reading, though I imagine that most readers will have become acquainted over the last few years with the incredible violence and cruelty of ISIS fighters, the media having provided innumerable accounts of their atrocities – including some that the terrorists, filming their own murderous deeds, seemed only too keen to show the world. In the event, the media deemed most of those scenes to be too terrible to convey to the public, and certainly, no reasonable person can ever get accustomed to hearing about such barbarity.

The Yezidis (or Yazidis) are a people recognized in writings from at least the twelfth century, living across a wide swathe of Middle Eastern countries: Turkey, Syria, Iraq, Azerbaijan, Georgia and Armenia. Yezidism, as a serious researcher writes, "is very much reliant on an oral tradition, which is somewhat vague as to the genesis, history and evolution of its current form."[1] Birgül Açikyildiz writes that she began her research in the province of Sinjar – the province of Nadia Murad, which when she was there in 2002 still "had a very heterogeneous population: Yezidi Kurds and Muslims as well as Sunni Arabs and Shi'ite Turkomans and finally, a minority of Assyro-Chaldeans. ... During the actual (then current) conflict in Iraq, the population mix in the province of Sinjar played into the hands of all the extremist groups, who stirred up inter-ethnic and interreligious rivalries and feuds and played upon nationalist and religious aspirations." This was before the August 2014 attack by ISIS that left huge numbers of dead and thousands of women taken into sexual slavery.

In her autobiography *The Last Girl*,[2] Nadia describes in some detail how she and her community lived before that fateful date. She wrote of her family's harmonious and meaningful life in the village of Kocho,[3] which "had grown to about two hundred families, all of them Yazidi and as close

---

[1]   Birgül Açikyildiz, *The Yezidis, The History of a Community, Culture and Religion* (I.B Tauris, 2010).

[2]   Nadia Murad, *The Last Girl. My Story of Captivity, and my Fight against the Islamic State* (Tim Duggan Books, 2017).

[3]   Often written as "Kojo".

as if we were one big family, which we nearly were. The land that made us special also made us vulnerable. Yazidis have been persecuted for centuries because of our religious beliefs and, compared to most Yazidi towns and villages, Kocho is far from Mount Sinjar, the high, narrow mountain that has sheltered us for generations. For a long time we had been pulled between the competing forces of Iraq's Sunni Arabs and Sunni Kurds, asked to deny our Yazidi heritage and conform to Kurdish or Arab identities."

Nadia goes on to explain how their daily life was before the genocide:

> Muslim doctors travelled to Kocho or to Sinjar City to treat us when we were sick, and Muslim merchants drove through town selling dresses and candies, things you couldn't find in Kocho's few shops, which carried mostly necessities. Growing up, my brothers often travelled to non-Yazidi villages to make a little money doing odd jobs. The relationships were burdened by centuries of distrust – it was hard not to feel bad when a Muslim wedding guest refused to eat our food, no matter how politely – but still, there was genuine friendship. These connections went back generations, lasting through Ottoman control, British colonization, Saddam Hussein, and the American occupation. In Kocho, we were particularly known for our close relationships with Sunni villages.

Nadia explains that despite those good relations, when there was fighting in Iraq – and she said there always seemed to be fighting in Iraq – those villages dominated their smaller Yazidi neighbour, and old prejudice began to harden into hatred. She had seen that from that hatred came violence. "For at least the past ten years, since Iraqis had been thrust into a war with the Americans that began in 2003, then spiraled into more vicious local fights and eventually into full-fledged terrorism, the distance between our homes had grown enormous. Neighboring villages began to shelter extremists who denounced Christians and non-Sunni Muslims and, even worse, who considered Yazidis to be *kuffar*, unbelievers worthy of killing…"

Before going into some detail on the events leading up to the capture and death of thousands of Yazidis, Nadia wrote about her people's religion.

> Yazidism is an ancient monotheistic religion, spread orally by holy men entrusted with our stories. Although it has elements in common with the many religions of the Middle East, from Mithraism and Zoroastrianism to Islam and Judaism,

it is truly unique and can be difficult even for the holy men who memorize our stories to explain. I think of my religion as being an ancient tree with thousands of rings, each telling a story in the long history of Yazidis. Many of those stories, sadly, are tragedies.

Birgül Açikyildiz over the course of three years (2002–04) travelled to innumerable places where Yazidis were the dominant populations. For example, "During my week-long stay in Sinjar I visited ten villages located in the mountains where the mausoleums of Yezidi saints were situated. These mausoleums had all been destroyed during the campaign of the 1970s[4] and only recently restored by the Yezidis themselves." In her book she writes, "After many similar meetings and conversations, it was abundantly clear to me that Yezidism is very much reliant on an oral tradition which is somewhat vague as to the genesis, history and evolution of its current form." The author was to refer in some detail to the Yazidi religion (for example on pages 35–37, and 71–113), but she gives a summary in the first two pages of her book:

> This book explores what makes Yezidism a separate and unique religion. It principally focuses on the Peacock Angel (Tawûsi Melek), the main character in Yezidism, and explores his relation with the Creator and the Yezidi people. Yezidis believe in one eternal God *(Xwedê)* who is the creator of the universe. He is Good and the owner of every motion and sensation on earth. He is all-forgiving and merciful. According to the Yezidi belief system, God manifests himself as a Holy Trinity in three different forms: the Peacock Angel, Sultan Êzi and Sheikh ʿAdī (d.1162). Furthermore, God has delegated his earthly powers to seven angels led by the Peacock Angel, who have responsibility for human and worldly affairs.

In a later reference, Birgül Açikyildiz writes that some Yezidis she met called themselves Dāsinī or Dāsin, a name derived from a Kurdish dynasty of the Hakkari region; today they are entirely Yezidi. According to one eastern Christian tradition, she explains, Dāseni or Dāsaniyat is the name of one of the churches of the East (Nestorian) dioceses, a church that disappeared when the Yezidis first appeared. Another Christian tradition suggests that the Yezidis were originally Christian but were reduced to their

---

[4] Meaning Saddam Hussein's campaigns. Birgül Açikyildiz, *op.cit.*, p.22.

present condition at the beginning of the twelfth century by ignorance. It may be that the eastern Christians came to this conclusion because, like them, Yezidis practise baptism and consume wine and other alcoholic drinks. "In order to support their claims, local people of the Church of the East assert that Sheikh 'Adī was Addaï, the legendary Christian Apostle of Mesopotamia. This idea may correspond to the tradition that the sanctuary of Sheikh 'Adī at Lalish was originally a monastery."

In her autobiography, Agatha Christie lists as the first of all the delights she remembers from her early years "walking up through a carpet of flowers to the Yezidis shrine at Sheikh 'Adī."[5] She then went on to write of the beauty of the great tiled mosques of Isfahan – a fairy-story city... a red sunset outside the house at Nimrud, and other unforgettable experiences.

"The epicentre of the Yezidi faith is in Lallish," writes another author,[6] "not far from the city of Dohuk in Iraqi Kurdistan. Lallish is made up of the collection of temples set in a forested valley around the tomb of the Sufi mystic Sheikh Adi ibn Musafir, who died in the twelfth century and is revered by Yezidis. Every Yezidi must make a pilgrimage to Lallish at least once in his or her lifetime."

* * * * * *

Nadia wrote, "Today there are only about one million Yazidis in the world. For as long as I have been alive – and, I know, for a long time before I was born – our religion has been what defined us and held us together as a community. But it also made us targets of persecution by larger groups, from the Ottomans to Saddam's Baathists, who attacked us or tried to coerce us into pledging our loyalty to them. They degraded our religion. ... Before 2014, outside powers had tried to destroy us seventy-three times. We used to call the attacks against Yazidis *firman*, an Ottoman word, before we learned the word *genocide*."

The author Cathy Otten wrote her recent book[7] after spending a considerable time among survivors of the ISIS attack of August 2014 on Sinjar, and reported, quoting authoritative sources, "An estimated 6,383 Yezidis – mostly women and children – were enslaved and transported to ISIS prisons, military training camps, and the homes of fighters across eastern Syria and western Iraq, where they were raped, beaten, sold, and

---

[5]   There is a detailed description of that visit on pages 87–88 of her autobiography.

[6]   Cathy Otten, *With Ash on Their Faces – Yezidi Women and the Islamic State* (OR Books, 2017), essentially about the Yezidis of the Sinjar region, in particular from Kocho.

[7]   Otten, *op. cit.*, p.15.

locked away. By mid-2016, 2,590 women and children had escaped or been smuggled out of the caliphate and 3,793 remained in captivity. Around three thousand Yezidis were killed, half executed in the days following the ISIS attack, with the rest left dying on Sinjar Mountain from injuries, starvation, or dehydration." The individuals whose stories she tells were, like Nadia, from Kocho.

Before the ISIS onslaught of early August 2014, Nadia relates that the villagers heard of the kidnap of two farmers, along with a hen and some chicks. "Soon afterward Dishan, a man employed by my family, the Tahas, was abducted from a field near Mount Sinjar where he watched our sheep. It had taken my mother and brothers years to buy and breed our sheep, and each one was a victory. We were proud of our animals, keeping them in our courtyard when they weren't roaming outside the village, treating them almost like pets." Nadia affirms that one of her brothers raced to see whether their sheep had been stolen, and returned saying "Only two were taken, an old, slow-moving ram and a young female lamb. The rest were grazing contentedly."

We can picture the peaceful life of the Yazidis before ISIS came to kidnap and murder. But "The day after Dishan was taken, Kocho was in chaos. Villagers huddled in front of their doors, and along with men who took turns manning a new checkpoint just beyond our village walls, they watched for any unfamiliar cars coming through Kocho. Hezni, one of my brothers, came home from his job as a policeman in Sinjar City and joined the other village men who loudly argued about what to do." Nadia writes that life went on; people scaled down their dreams, aware that they were again going to have to adjust to new threats. They saw news of attacks on television, but sometimes they shut out politics completely. … With Dishan still captive, I returned with my siblings to the onion fields."

Then comes a painfully telling paragraph at the end of the first chapter of Nadia's autobiography:

> We wouldn't find out why the kidnappers stole the animals – the hen, the chicks, and our two sheep – until almost two weeks later, after ISIS had taken over Kocho and most of Sinjar. A militant, who had helped round up all of Kocho's residents into the village's secondary school, later explained the kidnappings to a few of the village's women. "You say we came out of nowhere, but we sent you messages," he said, his rifle swinging at his side. "When we took the hen and the chicks, it was to tell you we were going to take your women and

children. When we took the ram, it was like taking your tribal leaders, and when we killed the ram, it means we planned on killing those leaders. And the young lamb, she was your girls."

* * * * * *

For days the Yezidis dared hope that help would come from some quarter. "Near Sinjar, an uneasy stillness hung in the air like a tension headache that comes before a storm. Frantic rumors circulated. ISIS declared the birth of their caliphate across Syria and Iraq."[8] But, suddenly, Kocho was surrounded, and people were herded to the school. Eighty pages after the shock of the above chilling paragraph in Nadia's autobiography, we read, "I didn't know how much ISIS hated us and what they were capable of doing. As scared as we all were, I don't think any of us on that walk could have predicted how viciously they would treat us. But while we were walking, they had already started to carry out their genocide", and she describes how ISIS set fire to a woman who had lost her husband and sons in the Iran–Iraq war and become a recluse, when she refused to leave her little house.

Nadia could not know then that among the thousands of people who on 3 August had tried to flee to Mount Sinjar, many had been intercepted by Daesh (ISIS) and had been either captured or killed, while some of the others, for lack of food and water in the heights, had not survived – despite some food drops by coalition aircraft. Cathy Otten, in her book *With Ash on Their Faces*,[9] writes that when the road to Kurdistan (along which people had hoped to walk to safety) became inaccessible because of fighting, approximately 130,000 people were left stranded on Sinjar Mountain, where, as we have just seen, many did not survive. However after a time, despite the proximity of ISIS fighters, most of the surviving Yezidis on the mountain managed to escape across the desert to Syria, under the guard of the YPG and frequently aboard vehicles that had to weather both sandstorms and violent attacks.[10]

Nadia wrote of how in the school that fateful day, the men were separated from the women and children. Once ISIS knew that no Yazidis

---

[8] Cathy Otten, *op. cit.*, p.31.

[9] Cathy Otten, *op. cit.* We hear how Yazidi and other fighters managed, after severe initial setbacks, to establish a corridor along which over a fifteen-day period the escapees could walk to safety, although hardships such as the scorching August sun, hunger and thirst proved to overwhelm some of them even then.

[10] The YPG is the armed force, an affiliate of the PKK, that benefits from security cooperation with the US in the war against ISIS.

were willing to convert to Islam, the men were forced to walk a short distance before being shot. The women and children heard the gunshots from where they were being held captive, but how could they imagine that all their menfolk were now dead?[11] Now ISIS told their captives to hand over their mobile phones, jewellery, watches, money, ID papers and ration cards. Even small children were searched for valuables. Then the girls were driven not to Mount Sinjar, where they had believed they were to be taken, but to Mosul, the second city of Iraq, which had been in ISIS hands since June.[12] They were taken in groups to different addresses, to be presented in the slave market, where they would be sold and forced into a mockery of a marriage with one or other ISIS fighter.

A report by the UN Commission for the Inquiry on Syria that designated the ISIS crimes against the Yezidis to be genocide said, "In jails across Iraq and Syria, where the women were being held, they felt a sense of abject terror on hearing footsteps in the corridor outside and keys opening the locks. The first twelve hours of capture were filled with sharply mounting terror. Many of the women and children had seen or heard their male relatives being killed by the armed ISIS fighters who now surrounded them. The selection of any girl was accompanied by screaming as she was forcibly pulled from the room, with her mother and any other women who tried to keep hold of her being brutally beaten by fighters. Women and girls began to scratch and bloody themselves in an attempt to make themselves unattractive to potential buyers. ... To avoid being raped, some of the girls killed themselves by slitting their wrists or throats, or hanging themselves, or throwing themselves from buildings in Tal Afar, Mosul and Raqqa."[13]

Nadia testified in her book:

> Over the past three years, I have heard a lot of stories about other Yazidi women who were captured and enslaved by ISIS. For the most part, we were all victims of the same violence. We would be bought at the market, or given as a gift to a new recruit or a high-ranking commander, and then taken back to his home, where we would be raped and humiliated, most of us beaten as well. Then we would be sold or given as a gift again, and again raped and beaten, then sold or given to

---

[11] Just a few individuals, taken for dead, somehow managed, though riddled with bullets, to survive after easing their way from under the mass of dead bodies and walking a great distance under cover of night.

[12] Eight hundred thousand people fled Mosul when ISIS took it over.

[13] Quoted by Otten, *op. cit.*, pp.103–104.

another militant, and raped and beaten by him, and sold or given, and raped and beaten, and it went this way for as long as we were desirable enough and not yet dead. If we tried to escape, we would be punished severely. As Hajji Salman had warned me (her first "owner", a vicious man who commanded the fighters in Mosul), ISIS hung our photos at checkpoints, and residents in Mosul were instructed to return slaves to the nearest Islamic State center. They were told there was a five-thousand dollar reward if they did.

The rape was the worst part. It stripped us of our humanity and made thinking about the future – returning to Yazidi society, marrying, having children, being happy – impossible. We wished they would kill us instead. ISIS knew how devastating it was for an unmarried Yazidi girl to convert to Islam and lose her virginity, and they used our worst fears – that our community and religious leaders wouldn't welcome us back – against us. "Try to escape, it doesn't matter," Hajji Salman would tell me. "Even if you make it home, your father or your uncle will kill you. You're no longer a virgin, and you are Muslim!"

Nadia referred to ways the captives tried to defend themselves, even while they were being raped, feeling just a little proud if they managed to draw blood by scratching their attacker. "Of course, it was the voices of the women who were not there, who had killed themselves rather than be raped, that spoke the loudest." And she described how she tried to escape at the first opportunity, climbing through a second-floor window. But she was caught, whipped, then raped by her captor, before being given to the guards in his house to gang-rape her. There were six of them.

She had already said, "Without my family, captive in Mosul, I felt so alone that I barely felt human. Something inside me died. ... Back then, I didn't understand how cruel one man could be. Hajji Salman was the worst man I had ever met, and after he allowed his guards to rape me, I prayed to be sold. I didn't care to whom and I didn't care where they took me. ... When I fantasize about putting ISIS on trial for genocide, I want to see Hajji Salman captured alive. I want to visit him in jail, where he will be surrounded by Iraqi military officers and guards with guns. I want to see how he looks and hear how he talks without the power of ISIS behind him. And I want him to look at me and remember what he did to me and understand that this is why he will never be free again."

It was agony for Nadia to imagine what the other women prisoners were going through. Cathy Otten gives us some real-life examples in the DP camps spoken of by some of the survivors. The young ISIS fighter, who had tried so hard to be first in his class at school but was picked up by mistake when it was his elder brother who was being sought, and who gradually allied himself with ISIS: after a time he became notoriously vicious towards his victims, as well as incredibly possessive. The other one, who when his *sabaya* did not obey a command immediately slammed one of her legs so violently with a heavy piece of wood that he broke it. The one who took the three youngest children of his captive and poisoned them: they were brought back to their mother vomiting, and died before her stricken eyes. She was denied any part in their burial (if indeed they were buried. She feared that their little bodies may simply have been thrown away somewhere). Stories of the slave markets, of women who were sold and resold ten or fifteen times… of rape, rape, rape…

* * * * * *

9 And 10 December 2018

The day before Nadia Murad came to make her speech of acceptance of the Nobel Peace Prize, she told a BBC interviewer of her astonishment on hearing about it. This was several months before the Kurdish Peshmerga, backed by the Western coalition led by the USA, managed to free from the terrorists the last of the areas that they had held since an Islamic State "caliphate" was proclaimed in June 2014 and became known as "Islamic State".

She said, "I didn't know about the Peace Prize. The journey I chose to take was very difficult, for three years I have tried to tell the world what is happening, but now I have no energy left. The prize has come after major suffering. I talked to governments, to law courts, to the press, and each time was difficult, I felt the suffering and pain over and over. I am talking now and thousands of women are suffering. They haven't the freedom to talk. ISIS did this, they took everything, my sisters, my mother. It didn't matter to ISIS if you were only a young girl. They only aim to dishonour us. It's happening to 3,000 of us."

She said at the Nobel Peace Prize ceremony in Oslo:[14]

---

[14] Nobel lecture given in Oslo on 10 December 2018, Nobel Media: https://www.nobelprize.org/prizes/peace/2018/murad/lecture.

I want to talk to you from the bottom of my heart and to share with you how the course of my life and the life of the entire Yazidi community has changed because of this genocide, and how ISIS tried to eradicate one of the components of Iraq by taking women into captivity, killing men and destroying our pilgrimage sites and houses of worship.

I lived my childhood as a village girl in Kocho, in the south of Sinjar region. I knew nothing about the conflicts and killings that took place in our world every day. I did not know that human beings cold perpetrate such hideous crimes against each other. As a young girl, I dreamed of finishing high school. It was my dream to have a beauty parlour in our village and to live near my family in Sinjar. But this dream became a nightmare. Unexpected things happened. Genocide took place. As a consequence, I lost my mother, six of my brothers and my brothers' children. Every Yazidi family has a similar story, one more horrible than the next because of this genocide. The social fabric of a peaceful community has been torn apart, a whole society that was carrying high the banner of peace and the culture of tolerance has become fuel for a useless war.

In our history, we have been subjected to many campaigns of genocide because of our beliefs and religion. As a result of these genocides, there are only a few Yazidis left in Turkey. In Syria, there were about 80,000 Yazidis, today there are only 5,000. In Iraq, the Yazidis face the same fate, their number is decreasing significantly. The goal of ISIS to eradicate this religion will be achieved unless the Yazidis are provided the appropriate protection. This is also the case for other minorities in Iraq and Syria.

After the failure of the Government of Iraq and the Government of Kurdistan to protect us, the international community also failed to save us from ISIS and to prevent the occurrence of the genocide against us, and stood idly by watching the annihilation of a complete community. Our homes, our families, our traditions, our people, our dreams were all destroyed.[15]

---

[15] Air strikes against ISIS in Iraq actually began in August 2014, but it was only four years and seven months later, in March 2019, that the badly damaged territories in which ISIS had established itself in were fully taken back – even if then, large numbers of terrorists were still on the loose.

One could see that many women in the audience were wiping their eyes as she spoke.

> After the genocide, we received international and local sympathy, and many countries recognized this genocide, but the genocide did not stop. The threat of annihilation still exists. The predicament of the Yazidis in the prisons of ISIS has not changed. They have not been able to leave the camps, nothing of what ISIS destroyed has been rebuilt. So far, the perpetrators of the crimes which led to this genocide have not been brought to justice. I do not seek more sympathy; I want to translate those feelings into actions on the ground.

In her speech, Nadia Murad pleaded for international protection, asylum and immigration opportunities, while recognizing that, at last, Iraqi territory was gradually being liberated from ISIS. She said how important it was for the crimes of ISIS to be investigated and for those who welcomed, helped and joined the terrorists in controlling vast areas of Iraq to be prosecuted.

> There should be no place for terrorism and extremist ideas in post-ISIS Iraq; we must join forces in building our country; we must contribute together to achieve security, stability and prosperity for the benefit of all Iraqis. In the 21st century, in the age of globalization and human rights, more than 6,500 Yazidi children and women became captive and were sold, bought, and sexually and psychologically abused. Despite our daily appeals since 2014, the fate of more than 3000 children and women in the grip of ISIS is still unknown. Young girls at the prime of life are sold, bought, held captive and raped every day.
> Every day I hear tragic stories. Hundreds of thousands and even millions of children and women around the world are suffering from persecution and violence. Every day I hear the screams of children in Syria, Iraq and Yemen. Every day we see hundreds of women and children in Africa and other countries becoming fuel for wars, without anyone moving in to help them or hold to account those who commit these crimes.
> For almost four years, I have been travelling around the world to tell my story and that of my community and other vulnerable communities, without having achieved any justice. … Thank you very much for this honour, but the fact

remains that the only prize in the world that can restore our dignity is justice and the prosecution of criminals.

A London newspaper reported Nadia Murad as saying that change can happen when one least expects it. "I know this to be true because my life changed in an instant. One moment I was a farm girl, going to school in my village in northern Iraq and the next I was an ISIS sex slave, 'owned' by militants. My peaceful existence was shattered simply because my religious beliefs were deemed sub-human by a group of men who believed they were superior." She told the reporter how ISIS murdered her family and took her captive, exposing her to horrors which would be impossible to imagine had she not endured every moment and felt each brutal blow. "My story is not unique", she said. "I am only one Yazidi woman. ISIS's terror rained down on all of us. It was not a slow drizzle but a thunderous storm that moved through my community, destroying everything. Make no mistake: ISIS planned to exterminate the Yazidis, ISIS planned a genocide." She said that people were herded out of our homes like animals going to slaughter, and she went on to say that survival came with a purpose and an obligation. "I have travelled the world to seek justice, pleading with global leaders to help the Yazidis who remain in dire need. My pleas have been met with expressions of sympathy but little action. More than 3,000 Yazidi women are still in captivity. More than 300,000 Yazidis live in squalor in refugee camps in the Kurdistan region of Iraq, without basic human necessities."

Nadia Murad has been quoted by an impressively wide range of newspapers and magazines, often in relation to how much Yazidis want to return to Sinjar and to have bright prospects for their children. However, as ISIS destroyed everything, they cannot have this unless Sinjar – the Yazidi homeland – is rebuilt. "Let hope unite us. Let humanity unite us," she said.

* * * * * *

Nadia's Very Special Lawyer, Amal Clooney, Barrister

In the Foreword to Nadia's autobiography, Amal Clooney, a specialist in public international law, human rights, international criminal law and extradition, wrote that Nadia Murad was not just her client; she was her friend. Nadia, on asking Mrs Clooney if she would act as her lawyer, had explained that she would not have funds at her disposal, and that furthermore the case would probably be long and perhaps unsuccessful. But she urged her to listen to her story.

Amal Clooney wrote, "She was forced to watch her mother and brothers marched off to their deaths. And Nadia herself was traded from one ISIS fighter to another. She was forced to pray, forced to dress up and put makeup on in preparation for rape, and one night was brutally abused by a group of men until she was unconscious. She showed me her scars from cigarette burns and beatings."

Ms Clooney went on to say that the atrocious beliefs instilled into many immature minds since Abu Bakr al-Baghdadi announced his Islamic State had it that the Yazidis, as a Kurdish-speaking group that did not have a holy book, were non-believers whose enslavement was a "firmly established aspect of the Shariah." This was why, in line with the warped morality of ISIS fighters, Yazidis could be systematically raped – a way of destroying them.

She explained how, when the two women met, it had been almost two years since ISIS's genocide against the Yazidis had begun. Thousands of Yazidi women and children were still held captive by ISIS, but no member of ISIS had been prosecuted for these crimes in a court anywhere in the world. Evidence was being lost or destroyed. And prospects for justice looked bleak.

Amal Clooney took the case. She and Nadia began to campaign together for justice, and in April 2019 at the UN Security Council, in company with Dr Mukwege, they participated in the launch of a draft resolution that would have ensured that the perpetrators of sexual crimes as tools of warfare would be charged with their crimes. The resolution included a proposal for an investigative team to be established to collect evidence of the crimes committed by ISIS in Iraq since 2014.

Unfortunately, the resolution was passed only after it had been considerably watered down, the USA, China and Russia having objected to parts of it, including a provision for survivors of rape to be given adequate help and support. A *Guardian* article of 22 April had the headline "US Threatens to Veto UN Resolution on Rape as Weapon of War", and went on to say "The US is threatening to veto a United Nations resolution on combatting the use of rape as a weapon of war because of its language on reproductive and sexual health, according to a senior UN official and European diplomats."[16] It went on to say that the German mission and others hoped the resolution would be adopted at a special UN Security Council session on sexual violence in conflict, but the draft resolution had already been stripped of one of its most important elements, the establishment of a formal mechanism to monitor and report atrocities, because of opposition from the US, Russia and China.

---

[16] Julian Borger, *The Guardian* (22 April 2019).

"Even after the formal monitoring mechanism was stripped from the resolution, the US was still threatening to veto the watered-down version, because it includes language on victims' support from family planning clinics" and so on. The Resolution was finally passed in its watered-down version. Manon Schick, head of Amnesty International Switzerland, commented on the television news that evening that the survivors of the systematic ISIS rapes, which were tantamount to acts of torture, deserved better than that. She added that human rights have little chance of being upheld in the world if the US is starting to ally itself with Russia and China.

Amal Clooney wrote movingly that Nadia "has defied all the labels that life has given her: Orphan. Rape victim. Slave. Refugee. She has instead created new ones: Survivor, Yazidi leader, Women's advocate, Nobel Peace Prize nominee, United Nations Goodwill Ambassador. And now author," and that she is the voice of every Yazidi who has been a victim of genocide, every woman who has been abused, every refugee: "Her spirit is not broken, and her voice will not be muted. Instead, through this book, her voice is louder than ever." Nadia's special lawyer has succeeded, with two German lawyers, in bringing to trial a German woman citizen who joined ISIS in 2014 and has been accused of crimes including that of murdering a five-year-old Yazidi child. This is the first trial of an ISIS member, and could well lead to a sentence of life imprisonment. Meanwhile, Iraq has offered to put on trial large numbers of ISIS fighters who are in the custody of the Kurdish army, and who their countries of origin are unwilling to allow back.

* * * * * *

Nadia's Initiative

Nadia lost no time in creating "Nadia's Initiative", a foundation that she presides over and from which she continues her advocacy work. It is dedicated to rebuilding communities in crisis and advocating for victims of sexual violence. Her director and one of her co-founders is Abid Shamdeen, a global development specialist, like her born and brought up in Sinjar. He co-founded Yazada, a leading Yazidi non-profit organization formed to assist survivors of the Yazidi genocide, and as a key member of the management team he is establishing strategic priorities and determining emergency response initiatives. Shamdeen previously worked for the US Army in Iraq as a cultural adviser and translator.

Then there's Elizabeth Schaeffer Brown, co-founder, special adviser and board member of Nadia's Initiative, an entrepreneur with expertise in advocacy, communications and strategic partnerships. She was part of the original team that initiated the campaign to bring ISIS before the International Criminal Court on charges of genocide and crimes against humanity and launched Yazda's Genocide Documentation Project, which has been collecting evidence of human rights violations committed against the Yazidis.

Two other board members and co-founders, Elizabeth Bohart and Kerry Propper, also bring considerable skills and experience to Nadia's Initiative. The former is a social impact strategist, working internationally with start-up organizations to build community-driven initiatives that focus on addressing the critical needs of highly vulnerable communities. Kerry was part of the original team that initiated the campaign to bring ISIS before the International Criminal Court on charges of genocide and crimes against humanity, initiating Yazda's Genocide Documentation Project that should supply evidence to support the international legal case against perpetrators, both individual ISIS fighters and ISIS as a whole.

* * * * * *

The Beekeeper Of Sinjar[17]

In a book of this name, an author and poet, Dunya Mikhail, who had had to flee Iraq some years earlier after working as a journalist for the *Baghdad Observer*, tells the story of a Yazidi man, Abdullah Shrem, who until 2014 had made his living as a beekeeper – and who devoted himself from that fatal August to rescuing as many Yazidi women as he possibly could. Dunya Mikhail kept in touch over a prolonged period with this remarkable man, who had told her,

> I used to be obsessed with beekeeping, but ever since we've had our Daesh problem I've been distracted from the bees. Freeing people from those savages has become my daily concern. I used to have a huge garden in Sinjar where I would tend to the beehives for hours on end, discovering the secrets of the bees, their meticulous organization, their harmony with nature. The movements of the queen bee up above, her superior flying abilities compared to the males amazed me, made me

---

[17]   Dunya Mikhail, *The Beekeeper of Sinjar* (Serpent's Tail London, 2018).

profoundly appreciate all the women in my life. ... In our society women work and sacrifice for others without getting what they deserve, without enjoying the same privileges as men. Women are oppressed even outside the world of Daesh, which has nothing whatsoever to do with rational human life, of course.

This remarkable Abdullah told Dunya Mikhail that he relied upon the same skills in his new work. "I cultivated a hive of transporters and smugglers from both sexes to save our queens, the ones Daeshis call *sabaya*, sex slaves. We worked like in a beehive, with extreme care and well-planned initiatives. Our hive includes women, too, and they have a big part to play in the rescue operation. At the moment I need to be careful not to talk about the specifics of our work, for their own protection. Beekeeping's just a hobby. What I'm doing now can't be described. I can't explain the feeling I get when I welcome back runaway girls, when they are reunited with their families. We all cry together, overcome with a mixture of joy and outrage. For the sake of that moment, that moment of reunion, I spend most of the day answering calls for help from voices that tell me where their prisons are located. ... The smugglers who help us are working for a wage, and that's their right."

The beekeeper said that the people in the region were helping one another, but that sometimes he paid the drivers out of his own pocket. "Anyway money's not going to stop us from doing whatever we can, even if we have to make special arrangements. Our work isn't without danger, of course. Daesh gruesomely executed one of our drivers when he was caught. ... In fact up to now, we've lost twelve smugglers."

The additional measure of tragedy is of course that – as was the case with Nadia Murad – the rest of the family, or most of it, has been eliminated. Abdullah put Dunya in touch by telephone with a man whose little daughter of nine, intended to be kept as a *sabaya*, had escaped from an ISIS house just after seeing her mother beaten almost to death and taken away with her younger children. Her father was among hundreds of men from Kocho and other villages who had been ordered by ISIS men to line up in pits in such a way that their execution with bullets would be swift. He was one of the only survivors: at the cost of careful hiding by day and an agonizingly painful journey over two or three successive nights, he reached a man who gave him the generous help he desperately needed, including clothing to replace his blood-soaked clothes, and undreamt-of hospital treatment for his gaping wounds that were such that he could no longer stand. The poor man, who

Abdullah said also lost his mother and his siblings and their families, was now in a DP camp without any news of his wife and younger children. At least he could be reunited with his little Nazik.

A recording made by a journalist and communicated to Dunya Mikhail was of a three-year-old, Hoshyar, kidnapped from Raqqa and since rescued from an ISIS house in Syria where he had been taught Islamist ideology by a Russian Islamist, and made to build rockets. Asked what he had been given to eat, the child replied "Bones. Abu Jihad would eat meat and then give me the bones. I couldn't eat the bones but he used to make me stand on one leg for an hour. He told me he could cut my head off if he wanted to." Now his sister Rula, seven, testified to the journalist over the telephone:

Can you tell me what you did when you were with Daesh?
They beat me while we made rockets for them.
What kind? And how did you make them?
TNT. From chemicals.
Did you also study Quran and prayer?
Yes.
Who was your teacher?
Daesh.
What was the name of the person who taught you?
Abu Jihad.
Did you learn how to pray?
Yes, but now I want to forget.

The journalist then had the testimony over the telephone of the children's mother. She related how they had fled Kocho but were surrounded by Daesh and a lot of their people were killed. "First they took the men and killed them. They held us in a building until one in the morning. Then they brought a bus and took all of the girls away, and separated the elderly." Sixty or seventy were left. "They took us to Sinjar, where they'd also taken the rest. Then to Talafar. They kept us there for three months. We were thirsty and hungry the whole time. They would only give us one chunk of bread per day. Then they took us to Syria. In Syria, they sold us from one person to another, until Abu Jihad held onto us so that we could make rockets. We boiled them on the stove – chemicals, refined sugar powder and chemicals that they told us they got near the Turkish border. I made ten or twelve rockets a day for five months. ... They forced Rula and Hoshyar to make four rockets per day. If there was any defect in the rocket he'd beat them with electrical cables. That was the hardest thing for me. I wanted to kill myself. I pleaded with him not to beat them but he told me he didn't care about anything but the rockets."

The man had spoken Russian with his friends and Arabic with her. She and her two children were able to escape thanks to a link that a woman fellow prisoner had with Abdulla, so that both women and their children all got away.

We see from what women affirm after their rescue how they and their children were exploited, abused and traumatized when in the hands of ISIS terrorists. One can easily imagine the levels of post-traumatic stress that these women and children must have been prone to after months of hideous treatment by merciless men.

* * * * * *

An indissoluble problem that remains, over and above PTSD, is that of children born of rape – particularly the children of Yazidi mothers. The *Sunday Times* published on 17 March 2019 the current predicament of an eighteen-year-old girl, Jehan, captured at the age of thirteen from Sinjar and forced into sexual slavery and motherhood. Living under the self-proclaimed caliphate with her "owner", a Tunisian jihadist, she and the three tiny children she had borne in the four years since her capture had the experience of sheltering from bombings, but then managed to escape when Kurdish forces advanced on Baghuz, one of ISIS's very last strongholds.

The newspaper report affirms that Jehan said she had no choice but to abandon her three children, all aged under three. Her relief at being freed was short-lived, for, as she prepared in a refugee camp for the journey back to her homeland in Sinjar, northern Iraq, she was presented with an ultimatum: she could not take her children. If she wanted to keep them, she would have to stay in Syria, living in penury as an ostracized single mother. Although her daughters, Hafsa, four months, and Juairia, fourteen months, and two-and-half-year-old son, Qahqa, had been conceived by force, she had raised and loved them. But, faced with this wrenching dilemma, she handed them over to a charity. "I wanted to see my family, that's why I left them," Jehan explained last week, back home in northern Iraq. "I was thinking to bring them, but they told me it's not good to take them, that they'll have a better life here. My family would not have accepted them." How agonized that young teenaged mother must be.

"Jehan, who looks and seems young for her age, struggled to speak about the children she had left behind." The two eldest, she said, would remember her. They did not know that she was a slave or was Yazidi – only that she was their mother. The fate of hundreds of ISIS children is one of the tragic legacies of the caliphate. The children of sex slaves face a particularly distressing plight as they are not wanted by the Yazidi community. After ISIS swept into Sinjar in 2014, capturing more than 6,000 Yazidi women, Baba Sheikh, the Yazidi spiritual leader, ruled that they would be welcome back. But nothing has been said about their children with ISIS fathers. "These kids aren't allowed in Yazidi culture," said Tahseen Murad Haider, a Yazidi activist. "Many people tried with Baba Sheikh. You allowed the women to come back. Why not the children? It's not the kids' fault, it's ISIS." Any children who appeared to be under four and a half – born after ISIS took Sinjar – were routinely removed from their mothers before they returned home, he said. "They (the women) get upset when they lose their kids," said Haier. His account was confirmed by others in the Yazidi community. "The children are spread across Iraq and Syria, according to Yazidi charities and activists. Some get taken to Yazidi House, a charity in Syria. …"

There is yet another terrible problem, that of the hundreds of thousands (if not millions) of mines scattered by ISIS across the length and breadth of the territories they had occupied. Brave Kurdish women, trained and salaried by a Swiss demining foundation, are hard at work day after dangerous day on demining operations that look very much like being needed for an incalculable number of years. A Swiss weekly news magazine of 14 August 2019 published a rather terrifying eight-page article that features both the brave women involved in demining work and the many forms of life-destroying explosives indiscriminately left half-buried across the broad sweep of those territories. An army colonel is quoted as saying that the mines gave ISIS protection for a long time. But there is no protection for civilians wanting to return to their home areas. In 2018, no fewer than 2,510 people were killed and wounded in Iraq by explosive devices. The work goes on…

Meanwhile, in a report to the UN Security Council released in February 2019, the UN Secretary General, António Guterres, said that, in Iraq, the jihadist groups have already "substantially evolved into a covert network". Europeans can still fear that these bloodthirsty men will still create havoc in our own countries unless they can be stopped through uncannily effective police work. And not only Europeans, for on 17 August 2019 a devastating attack was made on a huge wedding party in Kabul, Afghanistan, soon claimed by Islamic State, that killed over sixty people and wounded countless others. As though it was not sufficient that the Afghans have somehow to cope with the Taliban...

* * * * * *

The Appeal Of Hrh The Grand Duchess Of Luxembourg

On 26 and 27 March 2019, HRH the Grand Duchess launched a vigorous appeal on behalf of the countless victims of rape as a weapon of mass destruction, in the company of many people gravely concerned about sexual violence – including fifty survivors. Among the participants were the United Nations High Commissioner for Human Rights Dr Bachelet, Nadia Murad, Dr Mukwege, and dozens of people who, we hope, will find means both of counteracting the hitherto uncontrollable phenomenon of widespread rape and capture, and of arresting and bringing before international tribunals many of the perpetrators of these crimes. It is distressing to learn how many countries across the world have become infected with this atrocious scourge.

Describing what has been happening as "spreading like an epidemic through fragile environments around the world... more than ever used as a weapon of mass destruction against whole populations, condemning victims and their families to a life of suffering and desolation, as well as devastating the body and mind", the appeal set out what was needed from now on. It urged everyone to "Stand Up with survivors, Speak Up for justice and Rise Up to end rape as a weapon of war".[18]

The appeal of Grand Duchess Maria Teresa stated that, despite the best efforts of the international community, the world has failed to protect the most vulnerable among us – women and girls in particular – from the savagery of men who target their bodies and seek to dehumanize them. It said that we cannot remain silent in the face of such violations, against hundreds of thousands of civilians in fragile environments. We must draw attention to this major humanitarian crisis, of which the international community does not fully comprehend the extent. It called upon all the citizens of goodwill to join the movement Stand Speak Rise Up! and to express solidarity and support for the survivors.

Let's raise our voices for the prevention of sexual violence to
become a priority in the eyes of the international community

---

[18] Details of the Women's Forum can be seen on Stand up Speak up Rise up (Google and other search engines).

and leaders throughout the world. Let us ensure that substantial means are given to the fight against rape as a weapon of war, as well as to the support of victims, wherever they may be. We refuse to believe that rape is an inevitable consequence of war, a mere case of collateral damage. Inaction and passivity are not an option. The first thing we can do is wage a war on indifference. Silence, negligence and normalization of sexual violence must be replaced by the strong and united voices of survivors. Their voices must be heard.

We can no longer accept the fact that rape is one of the crimes that is least frequently reported and punished; that its victims are silenced by their fear to speak up, making them invisible. Society must offer them spaces that protect and amplify their voices and give them the means to assert their human rights.

In order to break the vicious cycle of sexual violence we must tackle the culture of impunity that protects it and transform it into a culture of dissuasion Collectively and globally, we must denounce this code of silence.

And so on. Let us hope that initiatives like this one will make all the difference.

Yazidi Women And PTSD

As Cathy Otten has written, "the battle for survival of the women and girls who were taken by ISIS continues long after their return". At the end of her introduction, she wrote, "I've tried to work in a way that doesn't cause further harm, by listening, particularly to ISIS survivors, most of whom are dealing with PTSD."[19] The result of various studies illustrates the devastating psychological consequences of genocide and enslavement.

For example in one study by Hawkar Ibrahim *et alia*,[20] published in 2018, entitled "Trauma and Perceived Social Rejection among Yazidi Women and Girls Who Survived Enslavement and Genocide", 416 Yazidi women and girls living in a displaced persons camp in the Kurdistan region of Iraq were assessed for PTSD and depression symptoms. More than 80% of girls and women, and *almost all participants who had been enslaved*, met

---

[19] Otten, *op. cit.*, pp.10 and 11.
[20] *BMC Medicine*, Vol. 16, Article 154 (2018), https://doi.org/10.1186/s12916-018-1140-5.

criteria for a probable DSM-5 PTSD diagnosis. The researchers concluded that, in a context like that one of maximum adversity, enslavement and war-related events often led to high levels of PTSD and depression. Furthermore, as one could expect, perceived social rejection featured in the relationship between trauma exposure and mental health among abducted genocide survivors. The provision of psychosocial support and treatment for Yazidi people was seen as essential and as urgently required.

The researchers applied the same conclusions to the survivors of equivalent traumatic events in Congo, Rwanda and Uganda.

A survey was made in February and March 2016 on the effect on Yazidis living in Germany of the ISIS attacks of August 2014 on Yazidi settlements in northern Iraq, when 3,100 Yazidis were killed and 6,800 kidnapped. In a brief report published in 2017,[21] we read that 512 people took part in the survey. Their average age was twenty-six and they had lived in Germany for an average of not quite twenty-five years. Almost all of them learned about the genocide from the media. Twenty-nine per cent had relatives who were victims. There were 132 participants (25.8%) fulfilling criteria for PTSD, more common among the women. According to the Hospital Anxiety and Depression Scale, 201 (39.3%) had clinically relevant scores for anxiety and 95 (18.9%) clinically relevant scores for depression.

The BBC recently reported that a former ISIS victim who had gone to live in Germany (where an estimated 25,000 Yezidis now live) had the shock of finding herself face to face with her torturer. The man called her by name as she came out of a supermarket and terrified her by telling her that he knew everything about her life in Germany. Unfortunately, such encounters are reportedly not rare. The trauma can continue and, as in this case, cause further uprooting: the girl and her parents, because of her shock encounter, are now, as I write, trying to emigrate to Australia.

It is good to be able to end this chapter with the recent news of the death on 26 October 2019 of the founder of the so-called Islamic State and leader of ISIS, Abu Bakr al-Baghdadi, after an operation coordinated between several States and led by crack US military units with their dogs. We have to hope that ISIS will soon no longer be a threat to so many across whole swathes of our world. However, the damage they wrought on the defenceless Yazidi community is to a degree beyond repair, especially of course the psychological damage.

---

[21] The 2014 Yazidi genocide and its effect on Yazidi diaspora, *The Lancet* (28 October 2017), https://www.thelancet.com/journals</lancet/article7PHS0140-6736(17)32701-0.

With regard to the material damage, Amnesty International (Switzerland), in its March 2020 magazine, quotes a report by Adiba Qasim, a woman of Yazidi birth, that gives scant news of any improvement whatsoever in the state of the wrecked town of Sinjar – just the reverse. In her resume of the perpetually troubled lives of Yazidi people, one whose history goes back 6,000 years, Adiba Qasim states that the genocidal attack of IS was the seventy-fourth attempt to "ethnically cleanse" northern Iraq of these people who were (who are) far from being true Muslims. IS destroyed the wells and the agricultural infrastructure, the crops and the cattle. She states that there are still 2,800 women and children missing from the community, while the insecurity and the lack of infrastructure in their ancient lands precludes a return of all those living in miserable camps whose needs are far from being met. The ruined state of their towns and villages means that any return is out of the question, and increasingly, some – even children – are taking their lives. Meanwhile, Turkish bombs falling on these areas add to the terror and absolute uncertainty of the Yazidi survivors, whose testimonies on the atrocities IS committed have not been taken into account in legal processes concerned with captured IS fighters.

Despite the tragic nature of the ongoing situation, Haidar Alias, director of an agency in the United States that has been documenting the genocide and helping survivors, thinks that a third of surviving Yazidis may well try to return to the Sinjar area once Turkey is no longer dropping bombs on it. But they would need support from the international community that has so far not been available. We must hope that sooner or later, this help will be forthcoming and will enable the community to return to Sinjar and resume their traditional way of life once again.

CHAPTER 19

Discoveries: Research And Practice, 1978 Onwards

From the beginning of this book, we have recognized that trauma, once an unknown quantity as long as the conclusions of those trying to draw attention to it were not really taken seriously, has come about in a wide variety of situations often involving the break-up of communities and the loss of homes as a result of one form or another of organized violence. The statistics of refugee numbers issued by the UN Refugee Agency, UNHCR, are more horrifying year by year.

At the same time, we have to brace ourselves to accept that, quite aside from conflict situations and terrorist actions that overwhelm whole communities, all is not well in our Western societies. The Council of Europe has stated that one child in five in Europe suffers abuse or neglect,[1] while research by the US Centers for Disease Control and Prevention has shown that one in five Americans was sexually molested as a child; one in four was beaten by a parent to the point of a mark being left on their body; and one in three couples engages in physical violence.[2]

As we have to take on board these unpalatable facts, we can at least be consoled by the fact that tremendous discoveries have been made in the last thirty to forty years in relation to trauma. Thanks to a number of dedicated, hard-working and inspirational people in the medical fields, particularly in the USA, there is the realization that while trauma and its consequences are an important factor in our societies, we now know enough to be able to start dealing with it. Although this may not mean that there is always a cure for everyone affected by the sequelae of traumatic experiences, more and more indications have come to the fore that different methods can be adopted to lessen – or even eradicate – the manifestations of PTSD.

---

[1] International television news, 13 November 2018.
[2] Quoted by Dr van der Kolk in *The Body Keeps the Score*, p.1.

At the very least, many of those with terrifying experiences behind them, who find they are suffering overwhelming perplexity, fear, shame and other emotions, can reach out to a person or persons who know about post-traumatic reactions and can provide some adequate form of support. Above all, family members or friends whose understanding and love are essential to healing, need to be there to help.

Dr Bessel Van Der Kolk, The Body Keeps The Score (Penguin Books, 2014)

On receiving this book I was really bowled over on reading the most complete account of how the author, often seconded by other researchers and above all helped by his own patients, got to the bottom of the mysteries surrounding trauma and post-traumatic stress. I make no apology for quoting extensively from his book, which has been acclaimed far and wide. For example the *New Scientist* noted that, drawing on thirty years of experience, Dr van der Kolk, in a book packed with science and human stories that gives moving evidence of the struggle and resilience of the patients, argues powerfully that trauma is one of the West's most urgent public health issues.

The European Journal of Psychotraumatology marvelled at the astonishing amount of information on almost every aspect of trauma experience, research, interventions and theories, concluding that the book was a veritable goldmine of information.

Nature quoted Dr van der Kolk's assertion that severe trauma is "encoded in the viscera" and requires tailored approaches that enable people to experience deep relief from rage and helplessness. The magazine liked Dr van der Kolk's tracing of the evolution of treatments from the "chemical coshes" of the 1970s to neurofeedback, mindfulness, and other nuanced techniques.

There are six further pages of similarly appreciative evaluations. Dr Judith Herman, clinical professor of psychiatry, Harvard Medical School and author of *Trauma and Recovery*, wrote that "Dr van der Kolk's masterpiece combines the boundless curiosity of the scientist, the erudition of the scholar, and the passion of the truth teller." Dr Rachel Yehuda, professor of psychiatry and neuroscience, director of the traumatic stress studies division at the Mount Sinai School of Medicine, New York, called *The Body Keeps the Score* an "inspirational work which seamlessly weaves keen clinical observation, neuroscience, historical analysis, the arts, and personal narrative". She said that Dr van der Kolk had created an authoritative guide to the effects of trauma and pathways to recovery. It was a "must read" for mental health and other health care professionals, trauma survivors, their loved ones, and those who seek clinical, social or political solutions to the cycle of trauma and violence in society.

Before writing about other prominent figures in this whole expanding picture, I'd like to outline something of the life and work of Dr Bessel van der Kolk.

Early Background And Initial Confrontation With Trauma

Dr van der Kolk grew up, as I did, in war-torn Europe, he in Nazi-occupied Holland, I in badly bombed Britain. His father, like mine, was tormented by what decades later would be termed PTSD. Other coincidences in our backgrounds include our both having had an uncle forced into slave labour by the Japanese to build the infamous bridge over the River Kwai, and extend even to the fact that in our very different spheres, we both met with badly traumatized individuals in the year 1978. The similarities end there, though I lived in Holland throughout 1966 for UNHCR on the coordination of a twenty-country campaign to raise funds for Tibetan refugees, while the future Dr Bessel van der Kolk, then about twenty-three, must just have been starting out on life in America.[3] I shirked scientific studies, while Dr van der Kolk excelled in them, and thanks to his subsequent research and practice over more than thirty years he has given us in his book, published in 2014, quite incomparable insights into the multiple effects of traumatic experiences. I have been given the great privilege of quoting extensively from his book.

Bessel van der Kolk studied surgery, cardiology, paediatrics and psychiatry in the USA. He found that "the key to healing was understanding how the human organism works", but on coming to observe the complexity of the mind he realized that psychiatrists knew very little about the origins of the problems that they were trying to treat. We can probably imagine how daunting it was for him, as he relates at the very beginning of his first chapter,[4] to be confronted one day by a young man who was causing a commotion in the hall of the Boston Veterans Administration Clinic before bursting through his door. Dr van der Kolk describes him as "a large, dishevelled man in a stained three-piece suit, carrying a copy of *Soldier of*

---

[3]   He writes that, in the late sixties, he took a year off between his first and second years of medical school, and worked as an attendant on a research ward at the Massachusetts Mental Health Center, in charge of organizing recreational activities for the patients, a period that, as he wrote, "exposed me to things the doctors never saw during their brief visits." *The Body Keeps the Score*, pp.22–23.

[4]   Ibid., *Lessons from Vietnam Veterans*, pp.7–12.

Fortune magazine under his arm… so agitated and so clearly hungover that I wondered how I could possibly help this hulking man. I asked him to take a seat, and tell me what I could do for him."

It is a fascinating story, one that goes to one's heart, of how this man, Tom, like so many others, had had intensely traumatic experiences in Vietnam in which, on a single day, he had lost every man under his command in grisly circumstances. Despite returning to a life as a newly married well-qualified lawyer and father of two small boys, he felt deadened inside – but was suddenly capable of such violence that he had moved out of his own home for fear of attacking his own family. On his second consultation, he admitted that he had taken none of the tablets Dr van der Kolk had prescribed two weeks earlier to deal with nightmares, claiming that if he took the pills and the nightmares went away, "'I will have abandoned my friends, and their deaths will have been in vain. I need to be a living memorial to my friends who died in Vietnam…' Tom's need to live out his life as a memorial to his comrades taught me [writes the young psychiatrist] that he was suffering from a condition much more complex than simply having bad memories or damaged brain chemistry – or altered fear circuits in the brain. Before the ambush in the rice paddy, Tom had been a devoted and loyal friend, someone who enjoyed life, with many interests and pleasures. In one terrifying moment, trauma had transformed everything."

Dr van der Kolk must have been at his wits' end to know what to do about this man and other veterans who, faced with even minor frustrations and beset by powerful flashbacks, "often flew instantly into extreme rages". Nothing in his psychiatric training had prepared him to deal with any of these challenges, and "five years after the last American soldier left Vietnam, the issue of wartime trauma was still not on anybody's agenda". He searched in Harvard's Medical School library for any books on war neurosis, shell shock, battle fatigue or any other term of diagnosis he could think of that might shed light on his patients – at first in vain. But then he did find one author, Abram Kardiner, who reported the same phenomena after the First World War, and his observation on what he called "traumatic neuroses" caught our doctor's eye, namely "The nucleus of the neurosis is a physioneurosis."[5] "What Kardiner called 'traumatic neuroses' today we call posttraumatic

---

5   Quoted from A. Kardiner, *The Traumatic Neuroses of War* (P. Hoeber, 1941), with the comment: "Later I discovered that numerous textbooks on war trauma were published around both the First and Second World Wars, but as Abram Kardiner wrote in 1947: 'The subject of neurotic disturbances consequent upon war has, in the past 25 years, been submitted to a good deal of capriciousness in public interest and psychiatric whims. The public does not sustain its interest, which was very

stress disorder – PTSD", Dr van der Kolk affirmed, and he went on to say that Tom and his fellow veterans became his first teachers in his quest to understand how lives are shattered by overwhelming experiences, and "in figuring out how to enable them to feel fully alive again."

He reported that Tom had experienced the death of his friend in the paddy fields "as if part of himself had been forever destroyed, the part that was good and honourable and trustworthy." He had gone into a frenzy afterwards and was desperately ashamed of the violence he had perpetrated there. The sobering truth is that, as Dr van der Kolk explains, trauma, whether it is the result of something done to you or something you yourself have done, almost always results in its being difficult to engage in intimate relationships. "After you have experienced something so unspeakable, how do you learn to trust yourself or anyone else again? Or, conversely, how can you surrender to an intimate relationship after you have been brutally violated?"[6] He came to realize, through his patients, that it takes enormous trust and courage to allow oneself to remember, to confront the shame about the way one behaved during a traumatic episode.

These were very important discoveries, and Dr van der Kolk speaks of a colleague, Sarah Haley, who wrote an article entitled "When the Patient Reports Atrocities", which he says became a major impetus for the ultimate creation of the PTSD diagnosis. In it she discussed "the almost intolerable difficulty of both talking about and listening to horrendous acts that are often committed by soldiers in the course of their war experiences. It's hard enough to face the suffering that has been inflicted by others, but deep down many traumatized people are even more haunted by the shame they feel about what they themselves did or did not do under the circumstances."[7] The consequent loss of self-esteem may be considerable – and lasting.

Dr van der Kolk went on to relate that he subsequently encountered a similar phenomenon in victims of child abuse. Most of them were found to suffer from agonizing shame about what they did to survive and maintain a connection with the person who abused them. He said that this was particularly true if the abuser was someone close to the child, someone the child depended on, as is so often the case. The result in the mind of the child would most likely be confusion about whether one was a victim or a willing participant, "which in turn leads to bewilderment about the difference between love and terror; pain and pleasure."

---

great after World War I, and neither does psychiatry. Hence these conditions are not subject to continuous study.'" *Op. cit.*, p.373n.

6   *Op. cit.*, p.13.

7   Ibid., also on p.13.

The Complexity Of The Human Being

In the Prologue to his book, Dr van der Kolk wrote that in the course of years of medical studies:

> I was struck by the contrast between the incredible complexity of the mind and the ways that we human beings are connected and attached to one another, and how little psychiatrists knew about the origins of the problems they were treating. Would it be possible one day to know as much about brains, minds, and love as we do about the other systems that make up our organism?
>
> We are obviously still years from attaining that sort of detailed understanding, but the birth of three new branches of science has led to an explosion of knowledge about the effects of psychological trauma, abuse, and neglect. Those new disciplines are neuroscience, the study of how the brain supports mental processes; developmental psychopathology, the study of the impact of adverse experiences on the development of mind and brain: and interpersonal neurobiology, the study of how our behaviour influences the emotions, biology, and mind-sets of those around us.
>
> Research from these new disciplines has revealed that trauma produces actual physiological changes, including a recalibration of the brain's alarm system, an increase in stress hormone activity, and alterations in the system that filters relevant information from irrelevant. We now know that trauma compromises the brain area that communicates the physical, embodied feeling of being alive. These changes explain why traumatized individuals become hypervigilant to threat at the expense of spontaneously engaging in their day-to-day lives. They also help us understand why traumatized people so often keep repeating the same problems and have such trouble learning from experience. We now know that their behaviours are not the result of moral failings or signs of lack of willpower or bad character – they are caused by actual changes in the brain.[8]

My cousin Peter Handford and his colleagues in the Law School, Perth, came to some of the same conclusions in their consultations with eminent Australian psychiatrists (see Chapter 5).

---

[8]   *Op. cit.*, pp.2–3.

* * * * * *

Early on in the research that Dr van der Kolk was keen to do, a team experimented with Rorschach tests, and he wrote, "The Rorschach provides us with a unique way to observe how people construct a mental image from what is basically a meaningless stimulus: a blot of ink. Because humans are meaning-making creatures, we have a tendency to create some sort of image or story out of those inkblots, just as we do when we lie in a meadow on a beautiful summer day and see images in the clouds floating high above. What people make out of these blots can tell us a lot about how their minds work."[9]

One of the men, Bill, on seeing the second card of the Rorschach test, exclaimed in horror, "This is that child that I saw being blown up in Vietnam" (he described the dreadful scene in detail). Dr van der Kolk said that experiencing Bill's flashback first-hand in his office helped him realize the agony that regularly visited the veterans he was trying to treat, and helped him appreciate again how critical it was to find a solution. The traumatic event itself, however, horrendous, had a beginning, a middle and an end, but he saw that flashbacks could be even worse. "You never know when you will be assaulted by them again and you have no way of telling when they will stop. It took me years to learn how to effectively treat flashbacks, and in this process Bill turned out to be one of my most important mentors." Other veterans reacted dramatically to the Rorschach test given subsequently, the majority of them upset by what they saw. "We learned from these Rorschach tests that traumatized people have a tendency to superimpose their trauma on everything around them and have trouble deciphering whatever is going on around them. There appeared to be little in between. We also learned that trauma affects the imagination: … In viewing scenes from the past in those blots they were not displaying the mental flexibility that is the hallmark of imagination. They simply kept replaying an old reel."

He wrote that the Rorschach tests also showed that traumatized people look at the world in a fundamentally different way from other people. "For most of us, a man coming down the street is just someone taking a walk. A rape victim, however, may see a person who is about to molest her and go into a panic. A stern schoolteacher may be an intimidating presence to an average kid, but for a child whose stepfather beats him up, she may represent a torturer and precipitate a rage attack or a terrified cowering in the corner."

---

[9]   Ibid., pp.15–17.

We read that meanwhile, "Our clinic was inundated with veterans seeking psychiatric help. However, because of an acute shortage of qualified doctors, all we could do was put most of them on a waiting list, even as they continued brutalizing themselves and their families. We began seeing a sharp increase in arrests of veterans for violent offenses and drunken brawls – as well as an alarming number of suicides. I received permission to start a group for young Vietnam veterans to serve as a sort of holding tank until 'real' therapy could start."[10]

Obviously, it was frustrating for the doctors to have no sound basis to go on. Dr van der Kolk writes that in this period in those early days at the VA the veterans received all sorts of diagnoses – "alcoholism, substance abuse, depression, mood disorder, even schizophrenia, and we tried every treatment in our text books. But for all our efforts it became clear that we were actually accomplishing very little. The powerful drugs we prescribed often left the men in such a fog that they could barely function. When we encouraged them to talk about the precise details of a traumatic event, we often inadvertently triggered a full-blown flashback rather than helping them resolve the issue. Many of them dropped out of treatment because we were not only failing to help but also sometimes making things worse."[11]

We then read that a turning point was reached in 1980, when a group of Vietnam veterans, aided by two New York psychoanalysts, lobbied the American Psychiatric Association to create a new diagnosis: PTSD. Describing a group of symptoms more or less common to all the veterans, it led to a name being given to the suffering of people overwhelmed by horror and helplessness. I still find it strange that in Argentina *two years earlier*, a young psychologist had been able to explain to me in simple terms the reality of post-traumatic stress. This was the principal element in my determining to try to make known in Europe, as best I could, the reality of trauma by the setting up in Vitznau in 1987 of an International Red Cross workshop on refugee trauma and by the consequent publication.[12] I found out only many years later that efforts were then being initiated by a concerned person within UNHCR, a clinical psychologist, Mary Petevi, soon to be transferred to the World Health Organization (WHO), to tackle the so far largely unrecognized fact of refugee trauma. Thanks to Mary's convictions and determination, along with those of a young American psychiatrist, Dr Richard A. Mollica with whom she came to work closely,

[10] *Op. cit.*, p.17.
[11] *Op. cit.*, p.19.
[12] As mentioned earlier, *Refugees The Trauma of Exile* (Nijhoff, 1988) and *Réfugiés Les Traumatismes de l'Exil* (Emil Bruylant, 1988).

great strides were made in having refugee trauma become a concern of governments worldwide (see Chapter 20).

Early Research And Practice

In the USA, we read that the conceptual framework of PTSD led to an explosion of research and to attempts to find effective forms of treatment. Dr van der Kolk put in a research proposal to the VA, which disappointingly was turned down with the unimaginative assertion that "It has never been shown that PTSD is relevant to the mission of the Veterans Administration." Before long, the VA was to do a dramatic "about face", but too late for Dr van der Kolk, who in 1982 took a job at the Massachusetts Mental Health Center, the Harvard teaching hospital where he had trained as a psychiatrist.

Dr Judit Herman, whose book *Trauma and Recovery* was first published in 1992 (before being reprinted numerous times), makes invaluable assertions in relation to some of the root causes of PTSD. Stating that belief in a meaningful world, initiated in the earliest stages of our lives, is formed in relation to others, she observes that the violation of human connections is highest of all when survivors have been not just passive witnesses of violence but active participants – possibly guilty of atrocities. In the Vietnam War, it seems without question that soldiers' serious demoralization sometimes became the seedbed of meaningless acts of serious harm to innocent civilians – rendering the men vulnerable to lasting psychological damage. Nine per cent of the veterans in one study acknowledged having committed atrocities, while another study found that every one of the men who acknowledged participating in atrocities had PTSD, more than a decade after the end of their service periods.

At the MMHC, Dr van der Kolk now found himself facing issues that he had thought had been left behind at the VA, for he received depressed and anxious patients coming to him with stories of molestation and family violence, many female patients speaking of having been sexually abused as children.[13] He found that contrary to bland statements in the textbook, incest had devastating effects on women's well-being. "In many ways these patients were not so different from the veterans I had just left behind at the

---

[13] He writes of how he was struck by how many women spoke of being sexually abused as children, in the light of assertions in the standard textbook of psychiatry that incest was extremely rare in the USA, occurring about once in every million women. He writes "Given that there were then only about one hundred million women living in the United States, I wondered how forty seven, almost half of them, had found their way to my office in the basement of the hospital."

VA. They also had nightmares and flashbacks. They also alternated between occasional bouts of explosive rage and long periods of being emotionally shut down. Most of them had great difficulty getting along with other people and had trouble maintaining meaningful relationships. As we now know, war is not the only calamity that leaves human lives in ruins."[14]

Dr van der Kolk continues (pages 20–21 of his book) with very disconcerting information that leads us to realize how common domestic violence has become in our westernized societies. He gave some statistics, and continued, "In other words, for every soldier who serves in a war zone abroad, there are ten children who are endangered in their own homes. This is particularly tragic, since it is very difficult for growing children to recover when the source of terror and pain is not enemy combatants but their own caretakers."

* * * * * *

The days, weeks and months passed, and three decades after Dr van der Kolk met Tom, he could write under the heading "A new understanding":

> We have learned an enormous amount not only about the impact and manifestations of trauma but also about ways to help traumatized people find their way back. Since the early 1990s brain-imaging tools have started to show us what actually happens inside the brains of traumatized people. This has proven essential to understanding the damage inflicted by trauma and has guided us to formulate entirely new avenues of repair.
>
> We have also begun to understand how overwhelming experiences affect our innermost sensations and our relationship to our physical reality – the core of who we are. We have learned that trauma is not just an event that took place sometime in the past; it is also the imprint left by that experience on mind, brain, and body. This imprint has ongoing consequences for how the human organism manages to survive in the present.[15]

On page 314 of *The Body Keeps the Score*, Dr van der Kolk quotes something said in 1889 by Pierre Janet, the French doctor once famous when he associated closely with doctors Charcot and Freud on the phenomenon

---

[14] *Op. cit.*, p.20.
[15] *Op. cit.*, p.21.

of hysteria: "Traumatic stress is an illness of not being able to be fully alive in the present." With hindsight, I realize that Silvia, the Chilean woman refugee who had befriended the UNHCR envoy to Mendoza in 1978 and whose story appears in an earlier chapter, had ongoing problems as a result of her PTSD over and above the very troubling epileptiform fits that never really spared her.

After thirty years of research and practice, our Dutch-American psychiatrist could write that trauma results in a fundamental reorganization of the way our minds and brains manage perceptions. It changes not only how we think and what we think about, but also our very capacity to think. His book makes absolutely fascinating reading. He and other writers became aware of the fact that the natural animal response to crisis, *flee, fight or freeze*, is also ours. But, unlike animals, for real change to take place our human bodies need to learn that the danger has passed and to live in the reality of the present. Dr van der Kolk explained that the search to understand trauma has led us to think differently not only about the structure of the mind but also about the processes by which it heals.

* * * * * *

Gradually Finding That New Understanding

All the above (and more) comes within the first twenty-one pages of this exceptional book. Chapter 2 moves onto "Revolutions in understanding mind and brain".

Over the years, Dr van der Kolk's readiness to listen to patients was an essential element in his understanding of mental illness – allied to his approach to the work inspired by a great teacher, Elvin Semrad, who "actively discouraged us from reading psychiatry textbooks during our first year. ... [He] taught us that most human suffering is related to love and loss and that the job of therapists is to help people 'acknowledge, experience, and bear' the reality of life – with all its pleasures and heartbreak. ... I remember being surprised to hear this distinguished old Harvard professor confess how comforted he was to feel his wife's bum against him as he fell asleep at night. By disclosing such simple human needs in himself, he helped us recognize how basic they were to our lives. Failure to attend to them results in a stunted existence."

But obviously, not everyone had the ethos of Prof. Semrad. "Our profession, however, was moving in a different direction. ... The way medicine approaches human suffering has always been determined by the technology available at any given time."[16] Dr van der Kolk writes, quoting sources, "A major textbook of psychiatry went so far as to state 'The cause of mental illness is now considered an aberration of the brain, a chemical imbalance'." But he suspected that what was often recorded on patients' files as "hallucinations" could well have been the true stories – namely of real experiences of terrible violence in the home setting. "There was no question that many patients on the ward[17] engaged in violent, bizarre, and self-destructive behaviours, particularly when they felt frustrated, thwarted, or misunderstood. They threw temper tantrums, hurled plates, smashed windows, and cut themselves with shards of glass. ... I was surprised and alarmed by the satisfaction I sometimes felt after I'd wrestled a patient to the floor so a nurse could give an injection, and I gradually realized how much of our professional training was geared to helping us stay in control in the face of terrifying and confusing realities."

In 1984, the young psychiatrist came to be forcibly struck by the testimony of Steven Maier of the University of Colorado on "learned helplessness", seen in experiments with electric shocks on dogs in which Maier had participated with Martin Seligman of the University of Pennsylvania. "The mere opportunity to escape does not necessarily make traumatized animals, or people, take the road to freedom. Like Maier and Seligman's dogs, many traumatized people simply give up. Rather than risk experimenting with new options, they stay stuck in the fear they know. I was riveted by Maier's account. What they had done to these poor dogs was exactly what had happened to my traumatized human patients. They too had been exposed to somebody (or something) who had inflicted terrible harm on them, harm they had no way of escaping. ... Their fight/flight response had been thwarted, and the result was either extreme agitation or collapse."

This fact may have been one of the most important discoveries, and certainly is frequently mentioned in other literature on trauma, for example Peter Levine's book *Waking the Tiger*, which has been translated into twelve languages.

Dr van der Kolk narrates how he and others gradually plumbed the depths of psychological suffering, for from the late 1980s onwards, newly found trust in pharmacology resulted in a real upsurge in research. "Psychiatry departments, which had always been located in the basements of hospitals, started to move up, both in terms of location and prestige."

---

[16] *Op. cit.*, p.27.
[17] i.e. at the MMHC, the Massachusetts Mental Health Center.

That was very promising. Nevertheless, as he wrote, "the drug revolution that started out with so much promise may in the end have done as much harm as good. The theory that mental illness is caused primarily by chemical imbalances in the brain that can be corrected by specific drugs has become broadly accepted, by the media and the public as well as by the medical profession. In many places drugs have displaced therapy and enabled patients to suppress their problems without addressing the underlying issues."[18] We read shocking facts about the proliferation of drugs at enormous financial cost – and human cost too, evidently. "Half a million children in the United States currently take antipsychotic drugs. Children from low-income families are four times as likely as privately insured children to receive antipsychotic medicines. These medications often are used to make abused and neglected children more tractable"[19] (and so on).

Dr van der Kolk reasons that "the brain-disease model overlooks four fundamental truths: (1) our capacity to destroy one another is matched by our capacity to heal one another. Restoring relationships and community is central to restoring wellbeing; (2) language gives us the power to change ourselves and others by communicating our experiences, helping us to define what we know, and finding a common sense of meaning; (3) we have the ability to regulate our own physiology, including some of the so-called involuntary functions of the body and brain through such basic activities as breathing, moving and touching; and (4) we can change social conditions to create environments in which children and adults can feel safe and where they can thrive."[20]

The doctor was starting to wonder if "we could find more natural ways to help people deal with their post-traumatic responses". He then moved on (in Chapter 3) to "Looking into the Brain: The Neuroscience Revolution", speaking of the novel brain-imaging techniques of the early 1990s, that "opened up undreamed-of capacities to gain a sophisticated understanding about the way the brain processes information". Among the many astounding findings resulting from his brain scans was "visual proof that the effects of trauma are not necessarily different from – and can overlap with – the effects of physical lesions like strokes" (page 43). So many very rich discoveries were being made! but in relation to the dread that traumatized people may have, that of recurring flashbacks, or of recurring violence, "our scans had revealed how their dread persisted and could be triggered by multiple aspects of daily experience. They had not integrated

---

[18] *Op. cit.*, p.36.
[19] Ibid., p.37.
[20] Ibid., p.38.

their experience into the ongoing stream of their life. They continued to be 'there' and did not know how to be 'here – fully alive in the present."

* * * * * *

Moving On...

All the above serves, I hope, as an introduction to the remarkable discoveries made by Dr van der Kolk and others over the initial years from the landmark year 1978. There is naturally no way of incorporating here the very many other newly understood certainties that can be found in the subsequent 320 pages of *The Body Keeps the Score*, though there are further elements from the book in our Chapter 20. But, at the end of it all, the brilliant doctor could supply us with these edifying statements in his Prologue:

> This vast increase in our knowledge about the basic processes that underlie trauma has also opened up new possibilities to palliate or even reverse the damage. We can now develop methods and experiences that utilize the brain's own natural neuroplasticity to help survivors feel fully alive in the present and move on with their lives. There are fundamentally three avenues: 1) top down, by talking, (re-) connecting with others, and allowing ourselves to know and understand what is going on with us while processing the memories of the trauma; 2) by taking medicines that shut down inappropriate alarm reactions, or by utilizing other technologies that change the way the brain organizes information, and 3) bottom up: by allowing the body to have experiences that deeply and viscerally contradict the helplessness rage or collapse that result from trauma. Which one of these is best for any particular survivor is an empirical question. Most people I have worked with require a combination.[21]

Dr van der Kolk went on to say that this had been his life's work. In this effort he was supported by his colleagues and students at the Trauma Center that he had founded thirty years earlier. Together they had treated thousands of traumatized children and adults: victims of child abuse, natural disasters, wars, accidents, and human trafficking; people who have suffered assaults by intimates and strangers. "We have a long tradition," he wrote, "of discussing all our patients in great depth at weekly treatment

---

[21] *Op. cit.*, p.3.

team meetings and carefully tracking how well different forms of treatment work for particular individuals."

Their principal mission, he wrote, was to take care of the children and adults coming to them for treatment, but he and his staff have always been dedicated to conducting research to explore the effects of traumatic stress on different populations, and to determine what treatments work for whom. "We have been supported by research grants... and a number of private foundations to study the efficacy of many different forms of treatment, from medications to talking, yoga, EMDR, theatre, and neurofeedback."[22]

The Dutch-American psychiatrist affirmed that the challenge was for people to gain control over the residues of past trauma and return to being masters of bodies and minds. He explained that "Talking, understanding, and human connections help, and drugs can dampen hyperactive alarm systems... but the imprints from the past can be transformed by having physical experiences that directly contradict the helplessness, rage, and collapse that are part of trauma, and thereby regaining self-mastery."[23] He said that he preferred no particular form of treatment, but in his work all the forms of treatment described in the book come into use, each which can produce profound changes, according to the nature of the particular problem and the make-up of the individual person.

At the end of his Prologue, Dr van der Kolk wrote, "I wrote this book to serve as both a guide and an invitation – an invitation to dedicate ourselves to facing the reality of trauma, to explore how best to treat it, and to commit ourselves, as a society, to using every means we have to prevent it. We are on the verge of becoming a trauma-conscious society. Almost every day one of my colleagues publishes another report on how trauma disrupts the workings of mind, brain and body,"[24] and "Trauma is now our most urgent public health issue, and we have the knowledge necessary to respond effectively."[25]

His book, evidently, repays reading (and re-reading). Furthermore, there is a very great number of apposite references contained in the three pages marked "Resources" and the four marked "Further Reading", besides all those in his fifty pages of notes.

In addition, on the one hand YouTube makes available a number of videos, one lasting one hour and forty minutes, in which Dr van der Kolk describes his work; and on the other, one can find through Google no fewer

---

[22] *Op. cit.*, pp.3–4.
[23] Ibid., p.4.
[24] Ibid., p.349.
[25] Ibid., p.358.

than twenty-nine illuminating quotations from his book, three of which are reproduced here:

- The single most important issue for traumatized people is to find a sense of safety in their own bodies.
- Trauma really does confront you with the best and the worst. You see the horrendous things that people do to each other, but you also see resiliency, the power of love, the power of caring, the power of commitment, the power of commitment to oneself, the knowledge that there are things that are larger than our individual survival. And in some ways, I don't think you can appreciate the glory of life unless you also know the dark side of life.
- People have a range of capacities to deal with overwhelming experience. Some people, some kids particularly, are able to disappear into a fantasy world, to dissociate, to pretend like it isn't happening, and are able to go on with their lives. And sometimes it comes back to haunt them.

* * * * * *

Four Other Pre-Eminent Us Researchers/Practitioners In The Field Of Traumatic Studies

I believe that the following are among the most pre-eminent US researchers and practitioners in the field of traumatic studies. Their interest and involvement are recorded in truly fascinating publications such as these – real *treasure troves* of vital and still-recent knowledge:

Judith Lewis Herman, MD, *Trauma and Recovery From Domestic Abuse to Political Terror* (Pandora, 1992).

Richard F. Mollica, MD, *Healing Invisible Wounds – Paths to Hope and Recovery in a Violent World* (Harcourt, Inc., 2006, and Vanderbilt University Press, 2009).

Peter A. Levine, PhD, *Waking the Tiger, Healing Trauma* (North Atlantic Books, 1997) and *Healing Trauma A Pioneering Program for Restoring the Wisdom of Your Body* (Sounds True, 2008).

Bruce D. Perry, MD, PhD, and Maia Szalaitz: *The Boy Who Was Raised as a Dog and Other Stories from a Child Psychiatrist's Notebook* (Basic Books, 2006 and 2017).

Dr Judit Herman

Dr Herman has been mentioned earlier in this chapter. Her very considerable contribution to the whole area of traumatic studies is certainly no less remarkable in its way than that of Dr van der Kolk, with whom she worked closely over a seven-year period. Her book, first published as early as 1992 and reprinted frequently thereafter, has been called "one of the most important psychiatric works since Freud".[26] Dr Herman, working for twenty years as a psychiatrist at a feminist mental health clinic, and for ten years a teacher and supervisor in a university teaching hospital, has as the principal focus of her book the survivors of incest, along with the role of childhood trauma in the condition known as borderline personality disorder. However, she deals also with suffering brought about by torture, in its dreadfully varied forms, including that of long-term incarceration, and she frequently quotes the work of other researchers and practitioners.

In her introduction, Dr Herman refers to the psychological harm that predictably affects people who have experienced a single overwhelming event, and the more complicated harm caused by prolonged and repeated abuse. In both cases, the fundamental stages of the recovery process are, she writes, establishing safety, reconstructing the trauma story and restoring the connection between survivors and their community. On page 121 of her book, she sets out the diagnosis of complex post-traumatic stress disorder. In the second part of her book, she develops an overview of the healing process, and offers a new conceptual framework for psychotherapy with traumatized people. The testimony of survivors of traumatic experiences is at the heart of her book.

Dr Herman, in her first chapter, "A Forgotten History", sets out the "episodic amnesia" relating to the study of psychological trauma, when periods of active investigation in the 1880s by doctors and psychiatrists like Jean-Martin Charcot, Sigmund Freud, Pierre Janet and some of their contemporaries alternated with periods of oblivion that she attributes to the fact that the subject provoked "such intense controversy that it periodically becomes anathema". She writes that the study of psychological trauma has repeatedly led into realms of the unthinkable – bringing researchers face to face both with human vulnerability and with the capacity for evil in human nature. When the traumatic events are of human design, she remarks, those who bear witness are caught in the conflict between victim and perpetrator, and it is morally impossible to remain neutral. It was undoubtedly the

---

[26] From the *New York Times Book Review*.

case over very many years, and it can still be the case today, that opinion frequently weighs in favour of the perpetrator.

We read the fascinating story of how Freud's investigations into women's lives led into the unrecognized reality of childhood sexual exploitation, a discovery that "crossed the outer limits of social credibility and brought him to a position of total ostracism within his profession". Freud retreated into a rigid denial, as did another researcher, Dr Joseph Breuer, whose principal patient, however, Bertha Pappenheim, had the extraordinary courage some time later to travel throughout Europe and the Middle East to campaign against the sexual exploitation of women and children.

In writing on "the Traumatic Neuroses of War", Dr Herman comments that the reality of psychological trauma was forced upon public consciousness by the appalling losses of over eight million men in the four years of the First World War. She remarks that one of the casualties of the war's devastation was the illusion of manly honour and glory in battle. Men were breaking down as a result of the horrors of trench warfare, and she writes that they began to act like hysterical women, screaming and weeping uncontrollably, becoming mute and unresponsive, losing their memory and their capacity to feel. According to one estimate, mental breakdowns, initially attributed to shell shock, represented 40% of British battle casualties, but unfortunately these men were generally treated with scorn, suspected of cowardice and often treated with electric shocks, and it was only gradually that a more liberal point of view was entertained. But as Dr Herman writes, within a few years of the end of the war, medical interest in the subject of psychological trauma faded once again, and she goes on to explain how it was that as a result of the experiences of combat during the Vietnam War, discoveries were made that led gradually to the present-day awareness of trauma – vindicating the much earlier discoveries of people like Pierre Janet.

Speaking of the effects on former combatants of traumatic experiences, Dr Herman records the fact that in a study of 100 combat veterans with severe post-traumatic stress disorder, 85% developed serious drug and alcohol problems after their return to civilian life, whereas only 7% had used alcohol heavily before they went to war. Tragically, their drug abuse simply compounded their difficulties and alienated them from others. Studies carried out in parallel came to similar conclusions.

The expert researcher, practitioner and writer describes in the next hundred pages of her book under chapter headings "Terror", "Disconnection", "Captivity", "Child Abuse" and "A New Diagnosis" the other aspects of traumatic disorders that afflict people of all ages. Then she turns to writing on "Stages of Recovery", on which in our Chapter 20 we shall hint at her innumerable pearls of wisdom.

Dr Richard F. Mollica

It is thanks to a conversation with Dr Herman that I first became aware of the remarkable work of Dr Richard Mollica, professor of psychiatry at Harvard Medical School, directing the Harvard Program in Refugee Trauma that he had founded in the early 1980s. Richard Mollica's preparation for the unique work he has carried out for well over thirty years is also remarkable.

He writes that he discovered early on that science does not address the moral and humanistic issues of society, and he majored in chemistry and religion, believing that in medicine he could apply his interests in science, religion, philosophy and the arts to better the human condition. As a medical student in New Mexico, he worked in remote Hispanic villages and in Indian reservations, "serving poor patients within a rich cultural and natural environment". Subsequently, he managed to combine residency training in psychiatry with an advanced degree in religion and philosophy. It is hard to imagine anyone more highly motivated to serve the poorest people in communities, and he soon found as a young Harvard doctor in the early 1980s that newly arrived refugees from South East Asia were both extremely poor and at the same time, almost totally excluded from the existing medical systems. Without altogether realizing the lasting significance of what they were doing, Dr Mollica with other dedicated individuals set up what was initially the Indochinese Psychiatry Clinic. On the staff were a dedicated young social worker, Jim Lavelle; a Hmong chief from Laos, Ter Yang; a Vietnamese former soldier, Binh Tu; and a young Cambodian woman, Rosa Lek. Their motivation, clearly stated on their website, was:

To bring the advances of modern medical science to those members of our society who in spite of their great suffering have little access to care.[27]

The mental health clinic was initially open one half-day a week, the staff (none of them paid) offering free services to people referred at the rate of perhaps twenty refugee patients in a single afternoon by medical colleagues in the public or private medical system. Dr Mollica worked very closely with the Indochinese members of the group, who, as he writes, were able to contextualize for him the past history and suffering of these patients. They

---

[27] http:/hprt-cambridge.org.

provided also insights into the cultural manifestations of suffering in different South East Asian communities.

As we have seen, in the early 1980s Western health workers did not have the capacity to identify and treat psychological problems in even the former combat soldiers who were clearly seriously destabilized by their trauma. Even less could American psychiatrists and psychologists expect to be able to relate to the sufferings of people from the other side of the world, such as the huge numbers of Cambodians, Vietnamese and Lao who were admitted to the USA from the late 1970s onwards.[28] Moreover, as Richard Mollica asserts, there was a deep belief in medicine and psychiatry that people who had experienced horrific atrocities could not be rehabilitated. However, he adopted the basic principle of the "phenomenological method", developed and widely applied in Europe: that a fresh approach to human behaviour and relationships can be obtained by the psychologist or doctor by abandoning all currently held theories opinions, prejudices, and biases. He wanted to make his own discoveries about how best to help people without being misled by the observations of standard medical providers. In this, he acted very much like Dr Jean-Pierre Hiegel in the Thai refugee camps that held huge numbers of severely damaged Cambodians.

Over the next two decades the Indochinese Psychiatric Clinic, later renamed the Harvard Program in Refugee Trauma, successfully treated more than 10,000 survivors of mass violence and torture. Over thirty years of clinical work with survivors of genocide, torture and abuse in different parts of the world, including Cambodia, Bosnia and Herzegovina and the USA, Dr Mollica came to realize the surprising capacity of traumatized people to heal themselves. As he wrote, "The capacity of persons to recover from violent events and to engage in self-healing is, in fact, the major discovery celebrated in this book."[29]

---

[28] At the time, I was the lone UNHCR Geneva resettlement officer involved with the quotas that, finally, no fewer than thirty Western countries were opening to try to meet the needs of the huge numbers of "boat people" arriving on the shores of South East Asian countries and of the Lao and Cambodians crossing into Thailand. In 2000, UNHCR announced that since 1975, over three million had fled their countries, of whom 2.5 million were taken for resettlement and the remainder were allowed to repatriate. The USA accepted the largest number.

[29] Richard Mollica, *Healing Invisible Wounds Paths to Hope and Recovery in a Violent World* (Harcourt, Inc., 2006), p.15.

Dr Peter A. Levine

Once again, we are in the presence of a most remarkable researcher and practitioner, whose book *Waking the Tiger* has been affirmed by senior medical practitioners to be extraordinarily valuable in relation to trauma, bringing new thinking and new concepts to the fore.

Dr Levine, like Dr van der Kolk,[30] is a dog-lover and perhaps this was in some way fundamental to some of his thinking about the animal world. "We are more akin to our four-footed friends than we might wish to think," he writes, telling us that his study of the origins of trauma led him into studies in a very wide range of fields. He states that he came to view PTSD not as pathology to be "managed, suppressed or adjusted to" but as a natural process gone awry.[31] Increasingly, he became convinced that "the instinctual repertoire of the human organism includes a deep biological knowing which, given the opportunity to do so, can and will guide the process of healing trauma" and as he worked to heal clients, he came to acquire new understanding, and reports that people were very "relieved to finally understand how symptoms were created and to learn how to recognize and experience their own instincts in action" – instincts that in reality have parallels to those of other animals.[32]

In a video we can view on the internet, Dr Levine, who received doctorates in medical and biological physics from the University of California at Berkeley and in psychology from International University, says that he began his investigations into mental illness a long time before there was any definition of PTSD. Over years, he watched innumerable animal videos and talked with wildlife workers to see, and to get to understand, how it is that animals subjected to intense fear and helplessness manage to move from their heightened state of arousal to one of normality – literally by "shaking off" the trauma.

Dr Levine's first chapter is entitled "Shadows From a Forgotten Past". In it, he reminds us that primitive men and women were hunters and gatherers, living as predators but at the same time, as prey to fierce animals. He states that the key to healing traumatic symptoms in humans is in our physiology. "When faced with what is perceived as [an] inescapable or overwhelming threat, humans and animals both use the immobility response," he writes, and he takes the example of an impala chased by a cheetah that at the

---

[30] Bessel van der Kolk in *The Body Keeps the Score* says that he loves dogs and could never have participated in experiments using dogs.

[31] Peter A. Levine, *Waking the Tiger Healing Trauma* (1997), p.6.

[32] Ibid., p.7.

crucial moment, "falls to the ground, surrendering to its impending death. Yet it may be uninjured. The stone-still animal is not pretending to be dead but it has instinctively entered an altered state of consciousness shared by all mammals when death appears imminent. … Physiologists call this altered state the "immobility" or "freezing" response."[33] Dr Levine tells us that the other two responses of the three that the practitioners all talk about (*fight* and *flight*, the third being *freeze*), are much more familiar to most of us, but he believes that the third really is of paramount importance in relation to the onset of post-traumatic stress.

Explaining this, Dr Levine suggests that, in the event that an unguarded moment comes about on the part of the hunter, "the impala could awaken from its frozen state and make a hasty escape", and, "when it is out of danger, the animal will literally shake off the residual effects of its immobility response and regain the full control of its body, resuming its normal life as if nothing had happened".[34]

But alas, human beings cannot benefit from this advantage. "We avoid it because it is a state very similar to death. This avoidance is understandable, but we pay dearly for it. The physiological evidence clearly shows that the ability to go into and come out of this natural response is the key to avoiding the debilitating effects of trauma."[35]

Whoever the survivors of organized violence or of terrible accidents may be, traumatic symptoms "stem from the frozen residue of energy that has not been resolved and discharged; this residue remains trapped in the nervous system where it can wreak havoc on our bodies and spirits. The long-term, alarming, debilitating, and often bizarre symptoms of PTSD develop when we cannot complete the process of moving in, through and out of the 'immobility' or 'freezing' state."[36]

Dr Levine writes of the shamanic approaches to healing in communities where people are traumatized. "In contrast to Western medicine, which has taken its time in recognizing the debilitating impacts of trauma, shamanistic cultures have acknowledged such wounds for a very long time",[37] viewing illness and trauma as a problem for the whole community. We have seen in our chapter in Cambodia that when people, fervent Buddhists, are completely overwhelmed, they may consider that their souls have become separated from their bodies, so they want there to be attempts, in the

[33] *Waking the Tiger*, pp.15–16.
[34] Idem.
[35] Idem., pp.16–17.
[36] Ibid., p.19.
[37] Ibid., p.57.

presence of those close to them, to capture them and get them to return. The traditional healers in that huge Khao I Dang refugee camp duly attended to the mental health needs of tens of thousands of distraught, traumatized Cambodians. "Shamanism recognizes that deep interconnection, support, and social cohesion are necessary requirements in the healing of trauma. ... In acknowledging our need for connection with one another, we must enlist the support of our communities in this recovery process."[38] He refers to the behaviour of people from the Third World in relation to the 1994 Los Angeles earthquake, less troubled than the average Americans, and that of large goldfish that ahead of the actual quake, formed into tight groups and remained like that for hours after it.

Peter Levine points out how cultures that use ritual and shamans to heal trauma are sometimes looked upon as primitive and superstitious, but they address the problem directly, openly acknowledging the need for healing when someone in their community has been overwhelmed, whereas most modern cultures take the line that it is heroic to carry on as if nothing much has happened, as in the example I gave earlier of my uncle returning from Japanese slave camps being "shielded" by the family from questions that he told me decades later he would have been glad to respond to. As Dr Levine observes, "these social mores do great injustice to the individual and the society. If we attempt to move ahead with our lives, without first yielding to the gentler urges that will guide us back through these harrowing experiences, then our show of strength becomes little more than illusion. In the meantime, the traumatic effects will grow steadily more severe, firmly entrenched, and chronic. The incomplete responses now frozen in our nervous systems are like indestructible time bombs, primed to go off then aroused by force."[39]

Dr Bruce D. Perry And Maia Szalavitz

Fulsome praise of the book *The Boy Who Was Raised as a Dog and Other Stories from a Child Psychiatrist's Notebook*, compiled by child psychiatrist Dr Perry with the help of an experienced science writer and reporter, confirms its great value in helping us understand trauma. Dr Perry is senior fellow of the ChildTrauma Academy, a non-for-profit organization based in Houston, Texas, and an adjunct professor in the Department of Psychiatry and Behavioral Sciences at the Feinberg School of Medicine at

---

[38] *Waking the Tiger*, pp.59–60.
[39] Ibid., p.62.

Northwestern University in Chicago. Maia Szalavitz is an award-winning New York journalist and author who specializes in neuroscience.

In his introduction, Dr Perry affirms, in company with other experts, that in the early 1980s little attention was paid to the lasting damage that psychological trauma can produce. "Even less consideration was given to how trauma might harm children. It wasn't considered relevant. Children were believed to be naturally 'resilient', with an innate ability to 'bounce back'." While not setting out to refute this misguided theory, Dr Perry observed in the lab that stressful experience in early life could change the brains of young animals. Numerous animal studies, he wrote, showed that seemingly minor stress during infancy could have a permanent impact on the architecture and the chemistry of the brain and therefore, on behaviour. He wondered whether the same could not be true of human beings. Then he found when he began his clinical work with children that the vast majority of his patients "had lives filled with chaos, neglect and/or violence. Clearly, these children weren't 'bouncing back'" and had they been adults, they could have been diagnosed with PTSD – something still seen as rare, affecting only a minority of former soldiers. Only gradually did it begin to be realized that catastrophic events can leave indelible marks on the mind – and that the impact is actually far greater on children than it is on adults.

Dr Perry quotes disquieting statistics about official reports of child abuse or neglect, of children spending time in foster care and of victims of natural disasters and devastating road accidents. He concludes that as moderate estimates suggest, at any given time more than eight million American children suffer from serious, diagnosable, trauma-related psychiatric problems. In his descriptions of lives touched by desperation, loneliness, fear and other damaging elements, Dr Perry reports on hope, survival and triumph, remarking that sometimes, he has chanced upon the best of humanity in the midst of some of the worst. Some of his experience has been truly unique. He states that many of his contacts have been with tortured, terrified children, including some who witnessed their parents' murders, and others who had spent years chained in cages or locked in closets.

In the author's note, preface and introduction to the 2017 edition, we read that the stories in this book are all true, but in order to ensure anonymity and protect privacy they have naturally altered identifying details. The sad reality, the authors tell us, is that these stories represent only a tiny percentage of the many they could have told. Within the last ten years, the clinical group at the ChildTrauma Academy has treated over a hundred children who have been through extreme experiences. The authors had had no idea of the magnitude of interest in the many aspects of trauma that could lead to their book becoming "used as a textbook in undergraduate and graduate classes in sociology, neuroscience, psychology, criminology, and many other disciplines". Little had they expected to hear from so many people apparently affected by trauma and neglect ("parents, teachers, social workers, police officers, military personnel, child welfare workers, juvenile justice officials, judges, coaches, psychiatrists, nurses, psychologists, paediatricians…").

This recent second edition notes that, over the previous ten or so years, awareness of adverse childhood experiences (widely referred to as "ACEs") and developmental trauma has grown "almost explosively" to affect public systems and the lay public, their book having played a part in that. Having sought a balance between detailed stories and the teaching of scientific material, they say that they decided to use a series of clinical narratives about patients whose experiences illustrated key concepts about the brain, development, or trauma. Though the book contains extremely disturbing material, the authors sought a combination of emotionally intensive and novelty material, for optimal learning.

I feel sure that we can interpolate that child survivors of genocides have had very similar problems (that in very many cases have probably not been detected).

* * * * * *

This story of trauma and uprootedness cannot be concluded without reference to the all-important area of *recovery* from traumatic experiences. A final chapter, based on the above publications, is therefore an attempt to encourage the reader to read on to the very end.

CHAPTER 20

Part I – Towards healing

The young Argentine psychologist in our conversations in 1978 about those of the Chilean refugees in Mendoza who were damaged by their traumatic experiences offered the opinion that, in most cases, they would probably recover their health once they were in a secure environment, able to find fulfilment in work and in relation to the communities that would take them in. We have seen in previous chapters of this book how much usually depends on environment, fulfilment and in particular, warm relationships. The Rwandan orphans in Chapter 15 who had survived the most devastating conditions imaginable seemed to come back to life in the loving environment created by Rosamond Halsey Carr and Sembagare at the Mugongo *Imabazi*. Cambodians cared for in camps like Khao I Dang, Thailand after being exposed for four Khmer Rouge years to diabolical cruelty were gradually nurtured back to health by teams of wise traditional healers. Conversely however, what was without any doubt the most devastating element in the lives of Holocaust survivors after their liberation was the absence of the family members whom they had somehow imagined they would manage to find – but who they were then forced to realize had almost all been murdered by the Nazis. And furthermore, the war had changed practically everything else that they had once known.

Back To Chile

Writing in Chapter 8 about the state terrorism of the Pinochet regime in Chile, I wanted to let readers of this book know of the valiant efforts made, from 1974 onwards, i.e. within months of the *coup d'état*, to help people very seriously affected by the violence. "An important element related to the mental health area was a strong Chilean tradition for social and preventive health care," Inger Agger and Søren Buus Jensen reported in their 1996 book referred to earlier, *Trauma and Healing under State Terrorism*. They painted a picture (of which the following can of course be only a part) of what happened in the unprecedented circumstances of that period to try to meet the needs of people radically affected by the violence.

Immediately after the *coup*, doctors, psychologists and psychiatrists found that they had been dismissed from their jobs. While the Catholic Church was ambivalent about the coup (some of its dignitaries supporting the military while many priests were trying to help the persecuted), the Catholic Archbishop of Santiago in conjunction with Protestant and Jewish leaders established two committees: the National Committee for Refugees (Comité Nacional de Refugiados) and the Committee for Peace (Comité pour la Paz). Though the members of these bodies, all volunteers, were in danger of arrest (and ten of the latter were arrested within the first few weeks), they did their best, looking for relatives (husbands who had been arrested during the night, sons or daughters who had disappeared), or getting people into the safety of European embassies or across the border to safety.

On 1 April 1975, based on the activities of the Comité Nacional de Refugiados, the Fundación de Ayuda Social de las Iglesias Christianas, FASIC (Social Aid Foundation of Christian Churches) was founded. UNHCR was active in Chile and FASIC was its implementing partner, thanks to which fact its activities were tolerated by the military. A few months later, the Catholic Church established the Vicaria de la Solidaridad, forming a medical team that referred patients to the private practice of psychiatrists and psychologists who, while usually working secretly, were part of a network of solidarity. Little by little, a nationwide network grew up of people whose human rights had been violated and who dared to look for help and to demonstrate peacefully in the streets: they were able to give one another a degree of comfort by sharing their grief and anxiety. Then in 1976/77, a psychiatrist newly returned from exile in Argentina developed a FASIC medical-psychiatric programme with professionals who "did an outstanding job in formulating the first theories about psychotherapeutic assistance to victims of the repression". They observed that giving testimony in a meaningful context seemed to have a beneficial effect on survivors, and from this the testimony method as a psychotherapeutic tool was developed, and described in a key paper from those early days of the repression.

All these people, without always realizing it, were permanently in danger, while at the Vicaria several members of the staff went on trial, some were imprisoned and a social worker was murdered. With the authorities further perfecting their methods, it became more and more difficult to bring help and solace to people suffering anguish and loss. Nevertheless, the work went on, often in secret, and from 1978 to 1980 new survivors' groups were organized, among them one of "witness-survivors", survivors of torture who could now use communication in the group as rehabilitating and reparative – no doubt people with a lot of spirit, like the Chilean refugees in Geneva who I remember chanting in unison at rallies "*Un pueblo unido jamás sera vencido!*" (A united people will never be beaten), and the energetic Dr Jorge Barudi of our Chapter 9.

Turning Again Now To The Five North American Specialists

The five experts who have worked out how to help seriously traumatized individuals and whose books I began to feature in the previous chapter deserve our fullest esteem and admiration (as no doubt do yet others). The extremely stimulating material that their books present is of course far too comprehensive to reflect in this closing chapter other than in the most cursory manner. They are real treasure troves! but here are a few notes that I wanted to put together in relation to the critical question of healing or recovery, thereby offering readers a glimpse into material that calls for the highest possible attention.

Dr van der Kolk in *The Body Keeps the Score* entitles Chapter 13 "Healing from Trauma: Owning Your Self". He begins by observing that, while nothing can be done about the traumatic experiences – they have happened and they have no doubt radically changed people – "what *can* be dealt with are the imprints of the trauma on body, mind and soul", and recapitulates with a list of what can be expected: "the crushing sensations in your chest that you may label as anxiety or depression; the fear of losing control; always being on alert for danger or rejection; the self-loathing; the nightmares and flashbacks; the fog that keeps you from staying on task and from engaging fully in what you are doing; being unable to fully open your heart to another human being."[1] He goes on to assert that the challenge of a person's recovery is to re-establish ownership of his or her body, mind and self, and in this, after an acute trauma, it is critical to communicate with loved ones, for nothing, he says, calms us down when we are terrified like the reassuring voice or the firm embrace of someone we trust. So we need to reunite as soon as possible with family and friends in a place that feels safe. Our attachment bonds, he writes, are our greatest protection against

---

[1]   Van der Kolk, *The Body Keeps the Score*, p.205.

threat, and recovery from trauma involves (re)connecting with our fellow human beings.[2]

In his inimitable style that reflects the wisdom acquired over more than thirty years, the Dutch-American doctor describes in this and subsequent chapters the many measures that can be undertaken to lessen and perhaps finally eradicate the principal effects of trauma. Sub-headings such as "Integrating traumatic memories", "Cognitive behavioural therapy (CBT)", "The unspeakable truth", "Breaking the silence", "The miracle of self-discovery" and "Art, music and dance" are indicative of some of these measures. Chapter 15, entitled "Letting Go of the Past", introduces us to a procedure called "eye movement desensitization and reprocessing (EMDR)",[3] now used quite widely by psychologists and psychotherapists to help patients bring forth painful memories that their brains have not integrated, and start to deal with them. Chapter 16, "Learning to Inhabit Your Body: YOGA" goes in depth into the need for the kind of exercises that yoga leads us to make. Chapter sub-headings such as "The legacy of inescapable shock", "The numbing within", "Exploring yoga", "Learning self-regulation", "Yoga and the neuroscience of self awareness" and "Learning to communicate" are indicative of the broad sweep of that chapter. And there are still four other chapters to be explored and perhaps acted upon!

Dr Judith Herman's far-ranging book *Trauma and Recovery From Domestic Abuse to Political Terror* (1992) sets out in her part II the stages of recovery, under the chapter headings "A healing relationship", "Safety", "Remembrance and mourning", "Reconnection" and "Commonality". She observes that "the core experiences of psychological trauma are disempowerment and disconnection from others", so that recovery has to rely on the empowerment of the survivor and the creation – and I'm tempted to suggest possibly the repair – of relationships. The faculties originally formed in relationships with others, including trust, autonomy, initiative, competence, identity and intimacy, have often been damaged by the traumatic experience and need to be reformed or retrieved. The survivor needs to be the author and arbiter of her own recovery, and this is something that all those who offer support need to take on board, even if they are well-trained, experienced therapists.

Dr Herman writes in some detail about the role of therapists in relation to the different needs of survivors of traumatic experiences. Then at the beginning of her chapter on safety, she suggests that in the course

---

2   Ibid., p.212.
3   EMDR was invented in 1989 by Francine Shapiro, a psychologist and member of the Mental Research Institute in Palo Alto, USA.

of a successful recovery "it should be possible to recognize a gradual shift from unpredictable danger to reliable safety, from dissociated trauma to acknowledged memory, and from stigmatized isolation to restored social connection".[4] It is terribly important to establish a safe environment, but as the author says, with survivors of chronic childhood abuse, establishing safety can become a very complex and time-consuming task – and even restoring self-care can be problematic for some survivors, who, like the late Diana, Princess of Wales, may indulge in self-harming behaviour. Creating a safe environment may call on the person to make radical changes in her life.

In the second stage of recovery, remembrance and mourning, Dr Herman writes that the survivor has to tell the story of the trauma, completely, in depth and in detail. The bystander, perhaps a therapist, plays the role of a witness and ally in whose presence the survivor can speak of the unspeakable. A hundred years earlier, a gifted, intelligent and severely disturbed young woman found an apt designation for her intimate dialogue with Dr Joseph Breuer in Vienna in the mid-1890s: a "talking cure". We read that the reconstruction of the trauma story should begin with a review of the survivor's whole life before the trauma, her relationships, ideals, dreams, problems and conflicts, creating the context within which the significance of the trauma can be understood. Mourning can be the most dreaded task of this stage of recovery, but it is certainly necessary, even though it can often call forth strong desires (or fantasies) for revenge, retaliation or compensation.

In the subsequent stage, "reconnection", many survivors may choose different means of ensuring their self-defence. Some seek to give further meaning to their personal tragedy by making it the basis for social action – transcending it and putting her in contact with the best in other people. Some will decide to pursue justice. Though recovery is never complete and some symptoms may return, Dr Herman writes that the survivor who has accomplished her recovery faces life with gratitude. In restoring social bonds, some survivors find that they are not alone. Belonging to a group, sharing experience of past trauma, can be beneficial and possibly even rewarding, contributing to the power of the healing relationship.

Dr Richard F. Mollica, *Healing Invisible Wounds – Paths to Hope and Recovery in a Violent World* (2006). From the time he was a medical student, Richard Mollica acquired very valuable experience in working among different cultures. He speaks of the fact that there are hundreds of examples of insights gained by managing to interpret the meaning of certain words,

---

[4]   Judith L. Herman, *Trauma and Recovery*, p.155.

and he speaks of "brainwashing" as an example of a term that has different connotations from one culture to another. He affirmed that "when you abandon old ideas, you permit intuition and imagination to lead you to something entirely new" – which turns out also to have been the experience of the other adventurous researchers we are concerned with here. Dr Mollica said that during his time caring for people affected by extreme violence, he had moments of revelation that completely transformed his manner of thinking and working as a doctor. "It is important [he wrote] to listen to the patient and also to the prejudices and the boundaries of knowledge in your mind. We have… to be ready to receive new knowledge."

One of the salient examples of this was the team's firmly held notion that it would be unethical to ask traumatized refugees to describe their experiences to a filmmaker. They were loath to let a film director, involved in producing a serious documentary on torture and torture treatment, interview any of their patients, but in the end two patients *were* invited to be interviewed on camera. They had both been tortured, and both were eager to tell the world what they had been through. This event led to a multi-year programme, the Cambodian-American Women's Oral History Project, of in-depth listening to the stories of ten Cambodian women, and to unsuspected healing as they recalled in detail all the beautiful features of their years in Cambodia before the traumatic events that overturned their lives.

We read that those two patients' trauma stories became and remained a centrepiece of their healing process.[5] If the trauma story remains hidden until the patient finds the opportunity to reveal just a fragment of it, this, he affirms, is part of the most surprising and revolutionary discovery of all those that he and his team made in the clinic – the fact that patients have the ability to heal themselves. He provides the moving story of a Cambodian woman who "showed me the power that all patients hold for self-healing. … We must look carefully for efforts at self-healing and strongly support and nourish all who have survived extreme violence." He writes that "the healer has to place himself as close as possible to the pain and suffering of the traumatized person in order to take in the revealed truth. This process becomes the foundation of all healing actions."[6]

Dr Mollica goes on to record that in Bosnia, efforts at self-healing flourished among the citizens of Sarajevo as a whole. "Sarajevo, a beautiful city of Orthodox Christian, Muslim, and Roman Catholic religions,

---

5   Richard Mollica, *Healing Invisible Wounds*, pp.19–21.
6   I am reminded of the work of Helen Bamber (my Chapter 4), whose gift for listening was no doubt the tool that virtually brought many survivors back to life, as several of them testified. Neil Belton's biography of Helen is entitled *The Good Listener*.

experienced one thousand days of barbarism unlike anything seen in Europe since the atrocities of World War II. Even after this terrible attempted murder of an entire city, Sarajevo's citizens never gave up their fight for survival," and Dr Mollica quotes a statement written by an artist, C. Boltanski, that clarified for him the collective power of self-healing, in which he read "What I've seen here, and what they have taught me is that life, the desire to live, is always stronger than barbarism, and that people can go on despite shelling and life without anything, hoping, creating, living."

The doctor found a similar collective emphasis on self-healing during his work in New York City immediately after the attacks on the World Trade Center, "when the solidarity among New York City residents from different races, ethnic backgrounds, and social classes was extraordinary. As in Sarajevo, everyone was in alignment, each contributing to the safety and security of others."

In his exciting book, Dr Mollica continues to show how the force, called self-healing, is one of the human organism's natural responses to psychological illness and injury. We can notice the body's elaborate process of self-repair when physical wounds heal, but "the healing of the emotional wounds inflicted on mind and spirit by severe violence is also a natural process" and he elaborates on this on page 94 of his fascinating book. Everyone concerned about trauma should read this book (and the others I so highly recommend!) But there is much more, and I will revert to the Harvard Program in Refugee Trauma later in this chapter.

Dr Peter A. Levine, *Waking the Tiger, Healing Trauma* (1997) and *Healing Trauma A Pioneering Program for Restoring the Wisdom of Your Body* (2008). Both in *Waking the Tiger* and in the videos we can access on the internet, Dr Levine explains how it is that when we human beings are subjected to traumatic events, we reach what psychiatrists refer to as a heightened state of arousal, and get stuck in fear and helplessness – though we have an innate capacity to heal. A short synthesis of Dr Levine's work was given in the previous chapter.

He tells us in terms that we can understand without possessing a degree in physiology how the brain is impacted, and what we would need to do to "shake off" the trauma as animals are capable of doing, and usually do. Incidentally, Dr Levine was told by someone caring for rescued wild animals that the "shaking off" is essential to their well-being for without it they will probably die. He believes that the key to healing traumatic symptoms in humans lies in our being able to mirror that behaviour of wild animals to become fully mobile and functional again.

In *Healing Trauma A Pioneering Program for Restoring the Wisdom of Your Body*, Dr Levine has created a programme in twelve phases to be followed with the help of audio exercises, the object being that of "getting unstuck", as he puts it, and "restoring feelings of wholeness".

Dr Bruce D. Perry, *The Boy Who Was Raised as a Dog and Other Stories from a Child Psychiatrist's Notebook. What Traumatized Children Can Teach Us About Loss, Love, and Healing* (2006), written with Maia Szalavitz. Dr Perry who founded the ChildTrauma Academy, an interdisciplinary group of professionals dedicated to improving the lives of high-risk children and their families, said, "Our work brings us into people's lives when they are most desperate, alone, sad, afraid, and wounded, but for the most part the stories you'll read here are success stories – stories of hope, survival, triumph." He and his co-writer added, "Surprisingly, it is often when wandering through the emotional carnage left by the worse of humankind that we find the best of humanity as well."

One of the important conclusions Dr Perry has drawn is that what determines how children survive trauma is whether the people around them – particularly the adults they should be able to trust and rely upon – "stand by them with love, support, and encouragement". The good doctor whose work, he writes, has taken him to the intersection of mind and brain, has found that despite their pain and fear, the children in his book, and many others like them, have shown great courage and humanity. "And they give me hope. From them I have learned much about loss, love, and healing."

It is evident from Dr Perry's stories that the lack of parental (and particularly maternal) love and care is catastrophic for any infant. One little girl was treated in hospital for a miscellany of ailments because her weight was unacceptably low, despite her regular food intake. It was found after investigations by Dr Perry that what she had lacked all along was straightforward maternal love and care, for her young mother, deprived herself of the kind of physical contact mothers usually give their newborn babies, cradling them when they are distressed and seeing that they have sufficient food, fun and care, did not know how to act as mothers normally do! As soon as she took her little daughter in her arms, sharing meals with her tenderly and starting to play with her, the child started to put on weight and began to thrive. This was, however, after it had been arranged that she and her little girl should live with a woman who had extraordinary success with ailing children, pouring abundant love over them, if necessary day and night.

Love was what was missing totally from the world of the little boy Dr Perry was asked to meet most of whose first six years had been catastrophic.

We read how this unfortunate small boy had been born to a fifteen-year-old girl who left the baby with her mother, but when his grandmother died unexpectedly only a few months later, he was simply left with an elderly man, the mother's boyfriend, who knew only about dogs.

All Dr Perry's stories are fascinating, some tear-jerking, some heart-rending, and this one is no exception. It certainly deserves to be read, along with the ten other stories in the book. In 277 pages, we read the stories with the headings "Tina's World", "Skin Hunger", "The Coldest Heart", "The Boy Who Was Raised as a Dog", "'Mom is Lying. Mom is Hurting Me. Please Call the Police'" and The Kindness of Children. After the twelve stories, the last with its focus on NMT, we come to "Chapter Commentaries for the 2017 Edition" (pages 305 to 347), "Study Guide and Comments for Group Leaders" (pages 349 to 360) and "Group Leader Comments for Discussion Questions" (pages 361 to 384).

* * * * * *

Further References To Good News

There are by now other books as well as videos that are liable to be helpful to people seeking to be cured of trauma. Here are some examples.

Pete Walker, *Complex PTSD: From Surviving to Thriving: A Guide and Map for Recovering from Childhood Trauma* (2013). Judging by the five pages of fulsome appreciation and thanks expressed in testimonials about Pete Walker's first book, *The Tao of Fully Feeling*, and his website, the contents of this book must be meeting the mark for many people who, like the author, have had to contend with desperately damaging childhoods.

The book, one of the first to talk of "Complex PTSD", which Pete Walker in his thesis refers to as Cptsd, covers a lot of ground. Much of its content is to be found in the books that feature earlier in Chapters 19 and 20, but there are other observations worth noting, such as this (in the chapter on "Levels of Recovering", page 32): "Perhaps never before has humankind been so alienated from its normal feeling states, as it is in the twenty-first century. Never before have so many human beings been so emotionally deadened and impoverished." He designed the book (335 pages) in such a way that by using the very detailed table of contents, people can find quite easily what they are looking for and turn to the appropriate pages.

Pete Walker has practised as a senior psychotherapist for thirty-five years.

* * * * * *

Dr Arielle Schwartz, *The Complex PTSD Workbook – A Mind–Body Approach to Regaining Emotional Control and Becoming Whole* (2016). Dr Arielle Schwartz is a clinical psychologist whose book focuses on unresolved childhood trauma, and aims to empower readers with a thorough understanding of the psychology and physiology of trauma so that they can make informed choices about the path to healing that may be right for them. The author in *The Complex PTSD Workbook* "helps you navigate the complicated, and often overwhelming, terrain of complex PTSD (C-PTSD)." She writes that, as people learn to understand the symptoms of C-PTSD, they will also gain valuable knowledge about common misdiagnoses and co-occurring disorders such as bipolar disorder, learning disabilities, anxiety disorders, major depressive disorder and substance abuse. The exercises and examples are intended to safely guide readers to explore the emotions and manifestations of their PTSD.

* * * * * *

Dr Richard P. Brown and Dr Patricia L. Gerbarg, *The Healing Power of the Breath, Simple Techniques to Reduce Stress and Anxiety, Enhance Concentration, and Balance Your Emotions* (2012). Doctors Brown and Gerbarg, by offering a range of simple breathing techniques drawn from yoga, Buddhist meditation, the Chinese practice of qigong, Orthodox Christian monks and other sources, provide an alternative to taking medication for stress-related issues including anxiety, depression, insomnia and trauma-induced emotions and behaviours.

* * * * * *

Jonathan Hoban, *Walk with Your Wolf: Unlock your Intuition, Confidence and Power* (2019). Jonathan Hoban is a psychotherapist who specializes in walking therapy: delivering psychotherapy in the great outdoors. This is something that some people wishing to overcome trauma find stimulating and far preferable to sitting in a therapy room, where everything remains the same from one session to the next – and where, reportedly, many feel trapped or intimidated. In nature, there is variety that lifts the spirit and encourages conversations. It seems that recall is easier when we are walking, and most of us agree that nature is a great healer!

* * * * * *

Phakyab Rinpoché with Sofia Stril-Rever, *Meditation Saved Me: A Tibetan Lama and the Healing Power of the Mind* (translated from *La meditation m'a sauvé*) (2014). The testimony of a Tibetan monk, a refugee torture survivor, who when suffering from severe gangrene of a foot was advised by the Dalai Lama to cure himself through meditation. Doctors at the New York Centre for Torture Survivors were anxious to perform an urgent amputation of the foot, but the Dalai Lama sent the monk this message: "Why are you looking for healing from outside sources? You have in yourself the wisdom that heals, and once you are healed, you will tell the world how to get healing." For many people, the spiritual dimension should not be discounted.

* * * * * *

Part II - The Remarkable Expansion In The Consciousness Of Trauma Worldwide

1. The Harvard Programme In Refugee Trauma:
Department Of Psychiatry, Massachusetts General Hospital,
Cambridge, Massachusetts, USA

I n this and the previous chapter, we have learned something of Dr Richard A. Mollica's work in a team of highly motivated individuals whose vision, from their creation in late 1981 of the Indochinese Psychiatry Clinic (IPC), was, and has remained, *to bring the advances of modern medical science to those members of our society who in spite of their great suffering have little access to care.*

The Harvard Program in Refugee Trauma (HPRT/IPC) uses multidisciplinary methods of inquiry and unconventional treatment strategies. It has actually defined a new approach to the identification and treatment of torture and mass violence, while demonstrating for the first time, along with other scientists, the enormous psychiatric distress and disability associated with mass violence and war. As Dr Mollica has asserted:[1]

> The discovery and evaluation of culturally effective treatment now called evidence based medicine was always an essential aspect of IPC/HPRT's working methods. The clinic, especially in its early days, no matter how small its size and budget, always used its clinical experience and knowledge as a springboard to a greater scientific understanding of refugee mental health. This science oriented methodology led to many

---

[1]   http:/hprt-cambridge.org, viewed in July 2019.

major discoveries that have transformed the care of refugees and traumatized populations worldwide.

It is now thirty-eight years since those Indochinese paraprofessional staff and American health care professionals began their work at the newly created IPC. The evolution in terms of the huge geographical area covered over the intervening years that have seen so much devastation resulting from violence is truly remarkable: we learn how HPRT has expanded its clinical role by introducing public health science to the emergency phase of refugee and humanitarian relief and to the international reconstruction activities in the *more than sixty nations* devastated by violence. Therefore, governments and international agencies should no longer deny or ignore the long-term morbidity associated with the social and psychological consequences of war.

We read that "HPRT came out of a powerful tradition of public psychiatry rooted in the scientific and clinical traditions of some of the world's greatest psychiatrists and mental health scholars". Many of these experts were unconventional, and achieved great things with their (seemingly) far-fetched ideas. One of them was the British psychiatrist Professor Douglas Bennett, who coined the term "upside down" psychiatry, and thanks to whose inspiration large numbers of mentally ill patients were freed from mental hospitals (popularly known to the public as "lunatic asylums") and introduced (or reintroduced) into communities, where they held jobs and were given support by nurses and non-professionals, rather than by psychiatrists. I well remember all this happening in Britain.

Then there was Professor Fritz Redlich, one of the leading psychiatrists in America, a refugee from Nazi Germany, who in a 1950 study called *Social Class and Mental Illness* that he carried out with sociologist August B. Hollingshead revealed that patients from the lower social classes received very different treatment from that given patients from higher social classes – a disparity shown to include African-Americans, Hispanics and refugees and torture survivors. The HPRT realized fully that refugees were "low-status" patients and that it would have to overcome enormous barriers in order to provide high quality care to these patients. The initiators of that study helped HPRT/IPC produce successful treatment outcomes in caring for America's new low-status patients – the refugees!

Among other leading psychiatrists whose influence on HPRT proved meaningful was Professor Franco Basaglia, who lectured in Rome on "Psychiatria Democratica" – and thanks to whom HPRT adapted its knowledge of "democratic psychiatry" to provide culturally effective community-based mental health care in the United States and abroad, including Cambodia.

Two women leaders in the development of the women's oral history tradition in America, and five other major scholars and intellectuals, all made major contributions over two decades to the pioneering work of HPRT. HPRT's creative vision and activities grew out of these people's brilliant and generous support, that soon did away with the earlier criticism and limited support that had characterized the early life of the IPC.

I will try to indicate the key measures of the last three decades that have resulted in there being much more international understanding of mental health needs, marking in bold type the years in which relevant progress has been made.

Training Work

Among the early HPRT projects were those on Cambodian mental health and Reconstruction in Bosnia.

Cambodian Mental Health

In 1991, after a visit by Dr Mollica to the Thailand–Cambodia border, HPRT first trained a group of refugee survivors to provide their fellow refugees with mental health assistance. After the repatriation and elections in 1992, HPRT was invited by the Ministry of Health (MOH) of the Royal Cambodian Government to initiate a pilot community mental health project in Siem Reap Province, the site of the historic Angkor Wat temples. Then HPRT developed the first community mental health clinic in Cambodia using Siem Reap's primary health care system. Over the past eight years, this clinic, staffed entirely by local Cambodian mental health professionals, has treated over 2,000 mentally ill patients.

Subsequently, the Cambodian MOH asked HPRT to train 100 primary care physicians throughout Cambodia's twenty-one provinces. This effort transferred necessary mental health skills, knowledge and behaviours to more than 10% of Cambodia's primary health care system. Highly vulnerable groups traumatized by war and poverty could now receive culturally effective treatment within their local communities.

Bosnia Reconstruction

In 1995, HPRT's training approach was adapted to help the medical and psychiatric practitioners caring for traumatized persons during the Balkans conflict. With the collaboration of local experts from Croatia and Bosnia, HPRT designed a curriculum and trained almost one hundred primary care practitioners from both countries. An extensive one-year training of Croatian and Bosnian mental health practitioners followed.

In recent years, HPRT and its Bosnian colleagues established a training model that is being replicated throughout Bosnia and has been accepted by the region's Stability Pact. This model includes a methodology, curriculum, and training approach that was successfully administered by HPRT to almost all primary care practitioners in Middle Bosnia Canton, a canton notorious for the intensity of local ethnic violence and devastation.

Concurrently with its activities in Middle Bosnia Canton, HPRT produced a curriculum on the care of traumatized persons that is now being integrated into Bosnia's three medical schools (Sarajevo, Tuzla, Mostar), as well as its faculties of social work (Sarajevo), philosophy and psychology (Sarajevo), and the Franciscan Theological Seminary.

Guidelines And Reference Materials

Invaluable guidelines in many forms have been elaborated by experts – revolutionizing the whole overall area of response to human need at times that serious traumatic events have dislocated communities and caused untold suffering. One set is called the **Utrecht Guidelines (1993)**.

It was not far into the war years in the former Yugoslavia – June 1993 – that some twenty-five European mental health experts and staff of the UNHCR and HPRT met in Utrecht, along with representatives of the Harvard School of Public Health, the World Federation of Mental Health USA, the International Organization for Migration (IOM) and the World Health Organization (WHO) to see about streamlining care and rehabilitation measures needed by victims of rape, torture and other severe traumas of that conflict. UNHCR and the government of the Netherlands co-funded the consultation, which was organized by the Pharos Foundation and entitled "Care and Rehabilitation of Survivors of Extreme Violence of Rape, Torture and Other Severe Traumas of War in the Republics of Ex-Yugoslavia".

In the introduction to the Utrecht Guidelines we read:

The need for practical, widely relevant guidelines for the mental health evaluation and care of refugees and displaced persons has never been greater. The current more than 100 violent conflicts around the world have produced some 44 million displaced individuals, roughly 2 million of whom remain within the confines of their own states. The twentieth century has seen over 140 million forcibly uprooted persons for whom the detrimental effects of the experience have long been recognized, some have estimated mortality in such populations to be 60 times the normal during the acute phases of displacement.

While the strong initial impetus for this work derived from the highly visible plight of refugees in former Yugoslavia, its authors recognized a deeper need to disseminate more consistently the information and measures necessary in the mental health evaluation and care of those exposed to the hardships and trauma of forced displacement worldwide."

And this was before the genocide in Rwanda!

One of the conclusions reads "In the majority of instances, individuals possess the resilience and adaptiveness to avoid the long-term effects of forcible displacement and trauma." But the next paragraph reads "Within a population of such individuals it is possible to recognize the full spectrum of psychosocial and behavioural responses to trauma, including 'normal', short-lived and widely occurring responses, as well as those causing significant impairment and long-term suffering."

The Utrecht Guidelines, with the conclusions and recommendations of the consultation, can be found easily on the internet.

Another set of guidelines was the **Tokyo Guidelines (1997)**.

The 1995 Great Hanshin-Awaji (Kobe) earthquake, known as the Kobe earthquake, was a natural disaster of extraordinary proportions for Japan. It was responsible for 6,437 deaths and 43,792 casualties. The Harvard Program in Refugee Trauma and Waseda University's Institute for Asia-Pacific Studies received funding to organize a symposium addressing the following issues, described in the introduction to the subsequent "Tokyo Guidelines":

Assistance in these "complex humanitarian emergencies" has remained largely unchanged or unchallenged since the end of World War II. One dilemma for international policy makers is that they do not have a scientific methodology for assessing the cultural, political, and social meanings of trauma in the lives of civilian populations and how these traumatic experiences alter the everyday lives of the affected individuals. Little empirical research assessing outcomes is conducted and humanitarian goals are often subordinated to political agendas. Although the magnitude of the problem is becoming clearer, methods for prevention and reconstruction of damaged societies have remained elusive. As a consequence, the enormous burden of human suffering and loss of social and economic productivity remains hidden behind a veil of neglect, ignorance, and denial.

Meeting in May 1997 in Tokyo, innovative thinkers gave equal time to Bosnia and Herzegovina, Croatia, Cambodia, and Kobe. Under the following titles, the participants drew up conclusions and recommendations:

1. Definitional Issues
2. Ethical Decision Making
3. Evaluation and Assessment Issues
4. Emergency Phase to Reconstruction Continuum
5. The importance of Altruism and Self-Help
6. The Importance of Work
7. The Importance of Home
8. Vulnerable Groups
9. The Role of the Mental Health System in Reconstruction

The Tokyo Guidelines were no doubt critically useful in relation to the tsunamis of this century and the Fukushima tragedy.

2. The World Health Organization Comes Alongside, As Does The European Parliament!

Over and above the foregoing, the last thirty or so years have seen other notable efforts made to explore, understand and disseminate the reality of trauma in many different contexts.

In relation to man-made trauma, Dr Mollica observed, "In the early 1980s, the mental health impact of war, torture and mass violence, was completely unknown and consequently neglected by those policy pioneers who had influence over the lives of refugee communities. An essential element of achieving this mission was a science based methodology that could for the first time describe the trauma experienced by refugees and civilian populations as well as the medical and psychiatric sequelae associated with these events."[2]

Someone who became intensely aware of these realities and who saw that worldwide consultations on the subject were called for was a Cypriot clinical psychologist who had acquired field experience as a UNHCR consultant. Her name is Mary Petevi. For a short period in the early 1980s, she and I shared certain concerns in the UNHCR Resettlement Section that I was soon to leave, but neither of us then spoke of the concern each had: refugee trauma, – *yet this was the very topic on which each of us would soon get involved*, I within the Red Cross/Red Crescent Movement, she within UNHCR and WHO. What Mary came to achieve, often in close cooperation with Dr Richard Mollica, is really remarkable.

1988 Onwards

After the World Health Organization established an Advisory Group on Mental Health of Refugees within its Department of Emergency and Humanitarian Action, Mary was appointed WHO technical officer for mental health in conflict and disasters. She was involved, with interested parties, in convening a series of seven important international consultations on the impact on survivors of massive violence and uprooting, covering subjects such as *Health Hazards of Organized Violence in Children* (London and Bergen), *Ethical Standards in Mental Health Care for Asylum Seekers, Refugees and Displaced Persons* (Zeist, The Netherlands) and *Health Situation of Refugees and Survivors of Extreme Violence* (Gothenburg, Sweden). While the consultations were held in Europe, participants came from all over the world and from a very wide range of backgrounds – from disciplines such as psychiatry, psychology, social work, anthropology, sociology, education, public health, nursing, law, management and human rights. They represented UN agencies, NGOs, academic and research institutions, donors, ministries of health or foreign affairs, and other bodies concerned with the subject matter of each consultation.

From these high-level consultations, 700 conclusions and recommendations emerged. Mary Petevi, who in due course would edit the all-important *WHO Declaration of Cooperation in Mental Health of Refugees, Displaced and Other Populations Affected by Conflict and Post-Conflict Situations*, first succeeded in condensing these to seventy. The seventy were then sent worldwide to relevant agencies, mental health associations,

---

[2]   From the Harvard Programme in Refugee Trauma website, http:/hprt-cambridge.org.

academic or other institutions and professionals, with the request to review and condense them further – the aim being to find and to publish twenty over-ridingly important principles. Hundreds of eminent people were involved in reviewing this material that was to lead to the final document.

An analysis of the responses enabled a draft Declaration to be prepared, and then circulated within and outside WHO for review. At a "Second Meeting on Community-Based Rehabilitation in Post-Conflict Countries", held in Harare, Zimbabwe, from 21 to 23 February 2000, the new draft was reviewed and adopted. Finally, WHO held from 23 to 25 October 2000 an International Consultation on Mental Health of Refugees and Displaced Populations in Conflict and Post-Conflict Situations, and adopted the *WHO Declaration of Cooperation: Mental Health of Refugees, Displaced and Other Populations Affected by Conflict and Post-Conflict Situations,*[3] with its twenty salient principles. It is a technical consensus-building document in mental health policy, strategies and programmes.

Furthermore, a technical document, entitled *Rapid Assessment of Mental Health Needs of Refugees, Displaced and Other Populations Affected by Conflict and Post-Conflict Situations and Available Resources* (*RAMH*), was endorsed at that same WHO consultation. It had been jointly developed by the WHO technical officer with the IFRC and the Disaster Mental Health Institute, University of South Dakota, USA. Then it had been further elaborated with contributions from ministries of health, ministries of cooperation, United Nations agencies, humanitarian agencies, NGOs, WHO collaborating centres, international mental health associations, international human rights societies, academic and research institutions, and experts from countries in several WHO regions, including countries in conflict and post-conflict situations.

Dr Gro Harlem Brundtland, director-general of WHO at the turn of the century, said in introducing the "Declaration of Cooperation" at the International Consultation, "We are proposing this document as a contribution towards obtaining international consensus in policy, strategy, and programmes, and as the guiding principle for our efforts in this field. ... It is our moral and professional obligation to provide the resources, to preserve mental health, restore dignity, and create hope and self-confidence for fellow human beings." In the introduction to the Declaration, the World Health Organization called upon "all governments, organizations and institutions to adopt and implement the following concrete steps, in

---

[3] WHO Declaration of Cooperation: Mental Health of Refugees, Displaced and Other Populations Affected by Conflict and Post-conflict Situations, Department of Mental Health and Substance Dependence, World Health Organization, January 2001.

taking up the challenge to prevent and reduce mental disorders and mental health problems, to restore hope, dignity, mental and social well-being, and normality to the lives of refugees, displaced and other populations affected by conflict."

So we see that at the beginning of this twenty-first century, the mental health of people affected by massive violence acquired – for a time at least – a high profile worldwide.

In its *World Health Report 2001, New Understanding, New Hope,* Dr Gro Harlem Brundtland stated that mental health, a long-neglected subject, was crucial to the overall well-being of individuals, societies and countries and needed to be regarded in a new light. She referred to 2001 being the tenth anniversary of the United Nations General Assembly's determination that the mentally ill have the right to protection and care. In 2013, the WHO Regional Office for Europe, asserting that "Mental disorders are one of the top public health challenges in the WHO European Region, affecting about 25% of the population every year", issued its European Mental Health Action Plan 2013–2020.

In Europe, the European Parliament on 19 February 2009 adopted an important resolution on mental health. The document begins with eleven statements that begin with "having regard" and twenty-four statements beginning with "whereas", before it launches into its fifty articles, of which these are the first two:

1. Welcomes the European Pact on Mental Health and Well-Being and the recognition of mental health and well-being as a basic priority for action;
2. Firmly supports the invitation to cooperate and foster action between the EU institutions, the Member States, the regional and local authorities and the social partners on five priority areas for the promotion of the mental health and well-being of the population, including all age groups, and different genders, ethnic origins and socio-economic groups, combating stigma and social exclusion, strengthening preventive action and self-help and providing support and adequate treatment to people with mental health problems and to their families and carers; stresses that any such cooperation must fully comply with the principle of subsidiarity;

We learn from the Harvard Program in Refugee Trauma (HPRT) how in 2002 seven ministers of health from Afghanistan, Bosnia and Herzegovina, Cambodia, Indonesia, Peru, Rwanda and Uganda and WHO mental health representatives met in Sarajevo, Bosnia and Herzegovina, and drafted a Global Mental Health Action Plan, outlining the vision and mission statement that would lead to an unprecedented textbook edited by Dr Richard Mollica that should meet the needs for both training and practice in the wide field of displacement: *The WHO and HPRT's Global Mental Health Action Plan; Textbook of Global Mental Health: Trauma and Recovery, A Companion Guide for Field and Clinical Care of Traumatized People Worldwide* (Paperback, 12 July 2012).

Then the Sarajevo consultation was followed two years later, on 3–4 December 2004, by an international congress of ministers of health for mental health and post-conflict recovery, again with WHO mental health representatives. Both these meetings had a direct impact on the 2013 WHO Mental Health Action Plan that the Harvard Program in Refugee Trauma sees as a framework for all those interventions related to man-made and natural disasters that call for a multidisciplinary response, starting with the complex emergency phase and going on to the recovery stages of healing.

Such (as far as I can see) have been the principal developments since the 1980s, along with the contributions to the current wealth of material made by the Red Cross and Red Crescent Movement and other NGOs. So it really seems that mental health has come to be recognized in the international arena. World Mental Health Day is celebrated each year on 10 October, with the overall objective of raising awareness. In 2018, the theme of the WMH Day was "Young people and mental health in a changing world", and for 2019 it had a focus on suicide. The efforts of many indefatigable individuals, not least Mary Petevi, based in Geneva, and Dr Richard Mollica, based in Boston, have made all the difference in relation to people liable to be affected in future by organized violence.[4]

Nevertheless, two experts have written within recent years that over one billion people are estimated to face abyssal levels of suffering and dysfunction. They assert that there are increasing levels of poverty and dependency, that the absence of a social human-centred approach in humanitarian response keeps mental health a low priority. They go as far as to say that humanitarian policies and action are "subjected to double

---

[4] On 4 September, I was with Mary Petevi in one of Geneva's lakeside cafés for our first meeting since I left UNHCR all those years ago! Then, the same afternoon, Dr Mollica called me and said that, on the whole, refugee mental health "is doing pretty good", with a lot of ministries of health using the guidelines relating to emergency measures, though he said that there remains serious concern about the safety of women refugees in camps.

standards in moral values and to geopolitical, military, financial and other interests of powerful states, of local governments and regimes".[5]

The Harvard Program in Refugee Trauma is approaching its tenth year of training professionals in Orvieto, Italy, through the Department of Continuing Education at the Harvard Medical School. It states on its website that "it is honored that WHO has responded positively over the past decade, and has promoted a Mental Health Action Plan, which in partnership with HPRT's Global Mental Health Action Plan creates the excellent opportunity for policy change and culturally effective mental health projects worldwide."[6]

Further training and reference materials deserving of recognition and use are:

International Federation of Red Cross and Red Crescent Societies (IFRC), *Community Based Psychological Support, A Training Manual* (1st edition, January 2003)

International Federation of Red Cross and Red Crescent Societies (IFRC), *IFRC Framework for Community Resilience* (2018)

Both the above, mentioned earlier in this book, are briefly described in Annex 1C.

Gerard A. Jacobs and Gilbert Reyes (eds), *Handbook of International Disaster Psychology (Contemporary Psychology)* (Praeger, 2005). Editorial reviews that describe this four-volume publication tell us that "This multivolume set emphasizes programme design and evaluation, coordination of humanitarian organizations, rapid response, assessment of needs, and cultural sensitivity to groups." Volume 3 focuses on refugee mental health.

The two authors, Gilbert Reyes, associate dean for clinical training at Fielding Graduate University in Santa Barbara, and Gerard A. Jacobs, director of the Disaster Mental Health Institute and a professor of psychology at the University of South Dakota, have had considerable experience at various disaster sites, including the 11 September 2001 attack on the World Trade Center. In the course of the last fifteen to twenty years both have worked closely with the International Red Cross, Prof. Reyes in the drafting of the 2003 IFRC Training Manual.

More books on trauma are coming onto the market year by year. And now, one should be able to buy (or rent!): *The Encyclopedia of Psychological Trauma* (1st Edition) by Gilbert Reyes, Jon D. Elhai and Julian D. Ford.

---

[5]   Mary Petevi and Heidi Kerko, J.D., *Human Rights and Mental Health in (Post) Conflict Situations.*

[6]   http:/hprt-cambridge.org.

ANNEX 1A

Conclusions And Recommendations 1–20 Of The Red Cross Workshop On Psychological Problems Of Refugees And Asylum Seekers, Vitznau, Switzerland, 6–11 October 1987

Overview

1. Psychological problems are by far the most important health concern of refugees and asylum seekers. Even those who fled their countries as much as forty years ago may still suffer from trauma, while refuges and asylum seekers from Latin America, South East Asia, Africa, the Near or Middle East, and Europe may have considerable psychological problems on arrival in receiving countries. Children are not exempt from such trauma; in view of their vulnerability, particular attention should be paid to the danger that the stress of adjustment to the new society may affect their progress towards a balanced development.

2. A disturbingly high proportion of refugees and asylum seekers have undergone torture or other forms of inhuman or degrading treatment in their countries of origin and/or during flight.

3. Psychological trauma are frequently compounded by the circumstances which confront refugees and asylum seekers in the receiving countries. For asylum seekers, the agonizing uncertainty attending the process of eligibility determination, conditions in reception centres, family separation, and in many cases severe restrictions on any reasonable form of activity of self-expression exacerbate trauma caused by previous events. For those admitted as

refugees under government quotas or family reunion arrangements, stress factors accompanying the process of acculturation or integration (for example, lack of meaningful work or any work at all, communication difficulties, secondary migration and other factors) add to those trauma arising from experiences in the country of origin, in flight, or in a transit situation prior to arrival. Those whose applications are rejected and who face deportation are subject to very severe stress, while those who are not given refugee status but who are allowed to remain in a receiving country temporarily, often in very uncertain conditions, may be found to manifest anxiety, fear, and paranoid reactions.

4. In Europe, against a climate of increasing restrictiveness on the part of governments, both in their interpretation of the 1951 Convention and in terms of national asylum law, public opinion has changed markedly in the last few years, sometimes causing refugees and asylum seekers to feel unwelcome and the butt of extremist feeling.

5. It is obvious that National Red Cross Societies and all those concerned with the welfare of refugees and asylum seekers must consider the social and psychological needs of these people as the highest priority. Planning for the material and non-material needs of those who seek help must take full account of this from the very beginning. Assistance to those who have suffered massive trauma will require a multi-disciplinary approach, possibly on the part of several agencies working in close coordination. The needs of vulnerable groups, in particular children, elderly persons, and the handicapped, should be of prime consideration.

Situation Of Refugees/Asylum Seekers Prior To Their Arrival In Europe

6. Medical screening carried out by ICM in countries of South East Asia immediately prior to departure, and by Red Cross personnel in countries receiving refugees/asylum seekers, demonstrates beyond any doubt that refugees/asylum seekers are generally in good physical health on reaching Europe. This contrasts with views frequently held in receiving countries, both within the medical profession and amongst the general public.

7. All the evidence shows however that a significant percentage of asylum seekers have undergone torture and other forms of organized violence in their countries of origin. According to Amnesty International, torture is practised in more than ninety countries, most of which deny that they use torture – a fact which will have implications for the victims' credibility when they come to register an asylum request.

8. Most refugees/asylum seekers have a history of suffering and deprivation which may include the sudden dissolution of their traditional way of life, the leaving behind of family members and the tombs of ancestors, incidents on the high seas or elsewhere in which they are victims of physical and psychological violence, and long periods of uncertainty in first asylum camps. They have few moral or material resources left. Many of them – including children – are found to suffer from psychological trauma and depression.

Psycho-Social Situation Of Asylum Seekers And Of Recognized Refugees Following Their Arrival In Europe; Provision Of Services

9. Asylum seekers reaching countries of Western Europe from nearly one hundred other countries have totalled some 200,000 over the last three years, according to figures quoted by UNHCR. While this number represents only a small proportion of the foreigners granted admission annually (600,000 to 900,000), it has represented a three-fold increase and receiving mechanisms have not been able to keep pace. Red Cross representatives are concerned that asylum seekers have been accommodated frequently in makeshift shelters such as ships or ferry boats, overcrowded hostels affording little privacy, or in old people's homes or other institutions. They have continuously observed that administrative procedures for dealing with asylum requests have caused long delays in pronouncing a decision, while appeals procedures may extend the period of uncertainty to several years, during which time the asylum seeker has few of the rights normally associated with residence.

10. Participants at the workshop have seen how delays and uncertainties, coupled in all too many cases with uncomprehending treatment by representatives of receiving countries, exacerbate existing trauma. What the exile is going through, if he has been a victim of persecution, is a de-structuring of mind and body, of personal

relationships, and of the total social situation. These factors demand of those caring for the refugee/asylum seeker an understanding of the various somatic, cultural, social and psychological elements which come into play and which contribute to a de-structuring or a restructuring of the personality.

11. Studies carried out and experience gained show unequivocally that it is essential for torture victims or others suffering from trauma – and for their families – to be supported through the provision of adequate care and understanding. If trauma exists, the effects of it will persist throughout life unless it is addressed. This may have serious consequences for family unity; many cases have been observed of violence displayed by the sufferer, particularly towards his wife and/or children.

12. Studies reveal also that most of those who have undergone torture find it difficult to speak of it until a climate of confidence has been established. Moreover, torture victims do not all bear the same psychological consequences. They must certainly not be considered mentally ill; however, research has demonstrated the need to discern the intensity of the trauma, the person's personality, and the psychological forces with which he/she has to cope. It has also shown the need for the children's psychological health to be addressed. Many children have been found to have suffered more from the silence of their parents on what the latter have been subjected to (torture, etc.) than had they been allowed to face the facts at the time – however unpalatable.

13. It should be noted that even if refugee children are not manifesting adverse behavioural symptoms, the assumption must not be made that they have necessarily adjusted to their new environment. The demands made upon them by the changes involved in, for example, family structure and role behaviours as a result of their experiences will have been considerable. They may appear to be coping but this does not necessarily imply satisfactory adjustment. Programmes directed at the special needs of the children should be developed and should include an evaluation component, so that the effectiveness of different methods and approaches may be assessed and add to the level of preparedness for the reception of future refugee groups. In addition to the above, special consideration should be given to the situation of unaccompanied minors.

14. In the light of this knowledge, it is clear that attitudes of the past which expected those who had been through traumatic experiences to forget about them must be discarded. The Red Cross has a role to point to the needs of such persons, at the same time demonstrating concrete, pragmatic ways of catering for them and of combating human rights abuses.

15. It is recommended that National Societies act upon Recommendation XI of the Twenty-fifth International Red Cross Conference which urged them "to take the initiative to give, either independently or in cooperation with their governments, humanitarian, legal, medical, psychological and social assistance to victims of torture in exile and, whenever possible, in their own countries".

16. Assistance to refugees/asylum seekers having psychological problems is best rendered by multi-disciplinary teams which may also be multicultural. It is often an advantage to include personnel who are compatriots of the sufferer and who may themselves earlier have been victims of similar persecution, including torture. Where specialized personnel are required who are not part of the multi-disciplinary team, sensitization is essential to prevent further psychological damage being unintentionally inflicted. (Dentists and gynaecologists are amongst those who should receive special briefing.)

17. It is recommended that the multi-disciplinary teams should work in centres (or networks) which should address the physical, mental, and social situation of the whole family, which would be characterized by a lack of sentimentality, full respect for the situation of the sufferer, and complete honesty and openness on the part of both refugee and the personnel. Furthermore, where possible, anything which could remind the torture victim of his earlier experiences should be avoided (for example being kept in ignorance of events concerning him, being kept waiting, being sent to an uninitiated specialist for treatment).

18. A range of therapies is found useful by practitioners – usually starting with individual therapy, then including the spouse, and the children. Group therapy may prove beneficial. Teaching positive elements – such as how to take physical exercise, how to find expression in art forms or in music, how to "have fun" – is important, while the active participation of the refugee in his/her own therapy is essential.

19. With regard to those needing to obtain refugee status after arrival in Europe, the Red Cross may render important services. In order

to qualify for political asylum, the individual asylum seeker must provide evidence that he/she has been the subject of persecution, or has a "well-founded fear of persecution". Whereas many asylum seekers have suffered torture, they may have difficulty in disclosing sensitive details of this to busy immigration officials. (Some may fear reprisals on family and friends at home.) This may lead to poor decisions based on misunderstandings and insufficient documentation. It is recommended that all asylum seekers should have the right to legal representation and medical examination by independent and impartial bodies, and should be referred to a competent body, for example the Red Cross, UNHCR, or another independent humanitarian organization, for advice and assistance.

20. It is recognized that if the first interview of an asylum seeker is with the police, there will be an inevitable association with the forces of repression in the country of origin which could call up recent persecution trauma. Police and immigration officials should be sensitized to the real plight of the asylum seeker, as should those put in charge of reception facilities. The presence of a neutral observer at a first interview would put the asylum seeker more at ease.

ANNEX 1B

A Red Cross And Red Crescent Guide: Working With Victims Of Organised Violence From Different Cultures (1995 - Second Part)

NB the first part, omitted from this annex, is a resume of situations that refugees and asylum seekers often meet with.

8. Psychosocial Approaches That Can Be Used In Different Cultures

All cultures have developed ways to provide support for emotional healing. They include gaining control over violent memories; seeking meaning; maintaining a "connection" with memories of the departed; and using traditional social support, traditional healing, activity and support groups, behavioural/educational models, self-expression, psychotherapy, storytelling, systems models, folk traditions, ceremonies and religious rituals.

Culturally meaningful strategies and approaches are needed because survivors may not be responsive to ideas **foreign to them and their cultures**. For example, in many cultures people are not used to speaking about themselves or their feelings, but often feel comforted in the presence of others who they believe understand them, even if little verbal communication occurs. Non-verbal activities, in general, may be more culturally acceptable.

Most survivors of organised violence will not have the opportunity to receive comprehensive individual care. Strategies which are **group and community oriented** are required because individual approaches are often impractical or impossible, given the large number of victims and the limited resources available.

Small positive changes will have positive effects and can help people to escape unhealthy patterns. Any small positive change can affect a person's life and may promote healthy functioning. When individuals are successful at solving small problems or having brief positive experiences, they begin to believe their life can change. In addition, they begin to think differently by seeing alternatives to their situations and possibilities for change. They see that their actions can affect their lives and that they can have control again.

8.1 Gaining Control Over Violent Memories
(Reduces Anxiety, Fear, Intrusion)

Flashbacks, anxiety and avoidance are common among victims of violence. Usually, people desperately **try to forget** violent memories and control them. These memories, however, are normally vivid and strong and break through into consciousness both while awake and during dreams.

When people are able to "face" their memories and fears in safe, supportive and relaxed surroundings, they may be able to **gain control** over them because they are no longer **threatened** by them. Also, people can be taught to reduce their reaction to these memories and fears through behavioural methods. Studies indicate that the majority of victims who are able to talk about their traumatic experiences in a safe and supportive environment eventually reduce their fears and anxiety regarding such experiences.

Not all victims want to talk about their experiences or verbalise their pain. It is very important that people who are working with them do not see this reluctance as "resistance" but rather as **a coping strategy which is necessary for that person at that time**. People should be given the opportunity to talk about their experiences but **never forced** to do so.

Some cultural traditions encourage sharing traumatic experiences in supportive surroundings. Among Guatemalan refugees traumatic "stories are often retold in the evenings as the group sits together in the candlelight before retiring. It is impossible to tell how much these children remember on their own and how much the story, elaborated by the group as a whole, has become part of their general recollection" (Melville and Lykes, 1992). See below for Gaining Control over Memories One and Two.

Panic

There is some debate as to whether support workers should encourage victims to talk about their painful experiences. When people go over terrible memories they naturally become extremely upset. In rare cases, some people react by becoming violent or attempting to withdraw from the outside world. An individual having a violent reaction may scream continuously, run around, destroy property, or try to injure himself or others. A person undergoing extreme withdrawal may be unable to speak, seek safety (hide under large objects or in a corner), curl up in a foetal position or cry quietly in terror. It is important that support workers learn how to handle these reactions should they occur.

Such reactions often indicate that the individual is "out of control". When this happens, it is important that just a few people, preferably friends, use **gentle but firm** physical strength to remove the person to a quiet and calm place where they can remain with him until he relaxes. They must also make sure that the person can't injure himself in this environment. It is often helpful to aid the person's recovery by reminding him what has happened, what day it is and where he is. People who have these reactions may need to be referred to resource personnel if they have difficulty in resuming normal functioning.

8.2 **Traditional Social Support** (Provides Support, Fights Isolation)

Social support from family, friends and community members is one of the most important resources for an individual struggling with the consequences of organised violence. Caring people help victims in their adjustment process by:

- Providing individual and group support (which substitutes for their emotional losses and fights isolation and loneliness);
- Helping them understand what has happened;
- Aiding in solving problems;
- Maintaining hope (which encourages the desire to survive).

Traditional social support includes:

1. Listening to the victims describing their experiences and expressing their feelings;
2. Staying with the person and providing comfort;
3. Participating in ceremonies or rituals;
4. Giving cultural meaning to the events and the person's responses;
5. Supporting values and social ties from the culture and religion;
6. Eventually encouraging the person to join his community and go on with his life by participating in common life activities.

Examples of common life activities are: going to school or work; maintaining a daily schedule; carrying out household responsibilities; caring for others; observance of religious traditions; maintaining an interest in the world through listening to radio or reading; passing on or receiving cultural or religious beliefs and participating in social activities.

Copying Traditional Support

When these social supports are unavailable, it may be possible to develop resources for victims of violence by copying some of the above activities. Trained personnel, field workers and volunteers (e.g. Red Cross/Red Crescent staff and volunteers) may initially perform some of these activities. Their goals should include finding people from the victim's community or culture who are good listeners and caring people, and training them to provide social support and teach self-help skills and techniques.

8.3 Traditional Healing

In traditional cultures, people's opinions about their problems are very strongly influenced by traditional beliefs and religious views. People may believe in and trust folk healing, and consult indigenous healers because they are a part of the people's culture. Folk healing can provide comfort and support to some survivors of violence, including people who do not regard most of the traditional beliefs as true.

In traditional belief systems throughout the world, the community may consist of the individuals, the dead and the spirits. The goal of individuals is to live in equilibrium with this spiritual dimension.

Traditional healers offer four kinds of treatment for people who are emotionally distressed – physical treatment, magic healing methods, counselling and medication. Physical treatment may consist of painful experiences which are supposed to shock the patient. These can frighten the patient and may be dangerous. Magical treatment usually involves communication or ceremonies involving spirits or the dead. "In one type of treatment the spirit is asked to speak through the person and explain his problems. This encourages the person to say things he may have been ashamed to say and can have a healing effect. Healers may pour magic water on a person's head or blow on the person while saying special prayers or words. People often find this relaxing and calming." (Refugee Mental Health, 1992).

453

Traditional healers from different regions of the world may use similar counselling techniques because they are responding to important and **basic human needs**. They may provide a caring, trusting relationship in which the sufferer can talk about his traumatic experiences and his pain. Healers may also take on the role of teachers and give helpful suggestions or use the power of a group to provide support. They may help the survivor to give meaning to his experiences by offering cultural explanations about why the victim has suffered, which may reduce shame and guilt. The often give specific directions about ways to reduce suffering (e.g. performing rituals and ceremonies) and encourage the person to return to his social and cultural group.

Healing treatments include "steaming" (steam baths), massage, directing people to participate in religious ceremonies or ritual activities, and teaching self-help activities such as meditation or yoga. Traditional healers usually offer remedies for many kinds of physical complaints.

Folk Medicine Can Be Dangerous

Some traditional/folk healers, who may have not been trained in traditional medicine, can be dangerous and may take advantage of people who are desperate because of their suffering. Also, certain folk practices may cause severe physical pain, injury or even death. It may be difficult to determine whether certain practices are dangerous. The following questions may be helpful:

1. Is the healer or particular practice putting a person's health in danger? (e.g. burning skin)
2. Is the healer attempting unusual and spectacular cures? (perhaps to gain fame)
3. Is the healer requesting larger fees than normal?

When practices or certain healers are thought to be dangerous, support workers should communicate this concern to the community of healers. Efforts should be made to protect people through information about dangerous practices. Genuine healers can be organised to discuss these practices and encouraged to take action against fake healers and dangerous practices. Healers will understand that dangerous practices can threaten or damage their reputations also, support workers can contact local authorities or organisations which are responsible for protecting victims.

The community of traditional healers may itself have suffered violent trauma. They may be unable to learn methods correctly or find materials such as plants for their remedies and ceremonies. It is important to support the remaining genuine traditional healers. When this community cannot function, traditional healers from similar cultures may be helpful in training community members or providing care.

8.4 Seeking Meaning

Victims of organised violence have usually had their family, work and community lives significantly disrupted. They often need to rediscover how to live their lives and how they fit into a changed world. It is important to help them recreate daily routines, participate in meaningful work, and resume personal responsibilities, religious and folk traditions. Survivors will find comfort, sense and meaning through these activities.

Some victims of organised violence find meaning through bearing witness to the horror of their experiences and establishing a historical record of what happened to them, their communities and their country. Others may find meaning by participating in social action to help other victims and prevent further violence.

8.5 Changing Attitudes Through Relationships And Daily Experiences

People working with victims of violence need to be sensitive to the attitudes victims have learned from their experiences, and understand ways they can help victims to relearn positive and hopeful feelings towards the world around them.

Survivors will develop positive attitudes only through their relationships with others and by their daily experiences. Their feeling states will slowly change in response to a different reality: where they are **no longer** in danger; where they have a **future**; where they can become socially and emotionally connected to others; where they can **participate** in constructive work or activities; and where they can **grieve** with cultural support.

Several different approaches may reduce the feeling of helplessness. One is providing ways in which people and their communities can improve their situation through education, vocational skills, commerce or production of goods. Another is involving people in constructive activities which improve their environment and give a sense of being productive, needed and effective. Some examples include organising schools and activities for children, developing family or community gardens, producing important materials for the community, arranging better health care, and teaching culturally important skills such as farming and traditional crafts.

Genuine and caring interactions are necessary to encourage the development of trust. In addition, stable relationships with caring people over long periods of time provide the victims with a structure they can trust. Children and adolescents especially need to re-establish a regular daily routine and build relationships with peers and adults. Support workers must be willing to help them with whatever problems they have and should be available to them.

People who have suffered similar experiences and have become active and hopeful about their future can provide encouragement and hope to those suffering from hopelessness. Stories, traditions, and cultural beliefs may give them a sense of purpose, explain why they survived, and reduce feelings of guilt or shame. Victims are usually comforted when significant others genuinely forgive them or reassure them that they should not feel guilt or shame.

In addition to self-expression, physical activities (e.g. sports and construction-type activities) may reduce anger and aggressiveness by redirecting explosive energy through socially acceptable activities.

8.6 Psychotherapy

Psychotherapy is one way in which Western cultures provide help for emotional healing. The relationship with a trained therapist is central. During the process of therapy, the client and therapist review the client's past, his family relationships, feelings, thoughts and experiences. The client's goals are insight and understanding. In cultures where people are comfortable talking about their inner feelings and analysing them, psychotherapies can help them in their healing process and are used in most comprehensive care centres. In many non-western cultures, however, the individual exists not for himself but for the community: his role is to adjust to social norms and perform his responsibilities and duties in his family and community.

8.7 Medication

Medication may provide relief to some victims of violence. Some forms of psychological problems respond very well to medication because they are caused by biochemical problems regardless of the person's culture. Examples are people who exhibit severe symptoms which interfere with their thinking and feeling. Victims who are reacting with severe depression or severe anxiety may also benefit from medication.

Doctors and some medical workers can prescribe medication and should supervise its use. People may abuse medication by taking too many pills, taking them when they don't need them or even using medication in suicide attempts.

8.8 Educational Approach To Reduce Anxiety And Fears

People benefit from learning about **normal or expected reactions and responses** to their violent experiences. Many victims worry that they are "going crazy" because of their reactions. They may be terrified by the intrusion of their memories into their conscious life, troubled by their physical symptoms and disturbed by feelings they have difficulty controlling.

Basic ideas that should be included in training material are:

1. Survivors have struggled to survive terrible events.
2. Their reactions to these experiences may appear strange and abnormal.
3. Their painful feelings and behaviour are usually understandable reactions to brutal events. Most survivors are not going "crazy".
4. They may experience shock, denial, anger, depression, anxiety and fear. They may even deny that violent events have happened and try to avoid people or things that remind them of their brutal experiences.
5. They may be unable to control their horrible memories that may wake them up at night and burst into their mind during the day (flashbacks).
6. They may feel unhealthy and complain of different physical problems.
7. They may feel ashamed even though they know they were victims. What happened to them was not their fault.
8. They may experience serious problems which are reactions to their violent experiences but which they may not connect with their experiences (e.g. domestic violence and alcohol or drug abuse). Normal life changes or life crises may also trigger painful reactions.
9. Some of the following activities may help them to heal: talking to others about their experiences, participating in cultural or religious rituals, establishing a safe environment and protecting themselves,

using self-help skills, expressing their feelings in culturally acceptable activities, understanding what has happened to them and why they have the feelings they do, and allowing themselves to mourn for their losses.

10. Most of these feelings and behaviours will eventually disappear and they will begin to feel differently. But this healing will take time.

11. They should try to be with other people, participate in normal activities and talk to caring listeners.

This information will help them to understand the **range of reactions** that most people experience, support the notion that their **reactions are understandable**, and **prepare them** for confusing or difficult feelings in the future. People will benefit from such information throughout their lives because they will go through different stages of reacting to their trauma and will find some information more important at different times of their lives.

8.9 Groups – Activity And Support
(Reduces Isolation, Provides Support And Feeling Of Belonging)

Studies indicate that groups are one of the most successful approaches for survivors of violence.

Activity and support groups provide members with an immediate **community**. Activity groups focus on specific activities, and support groups on providing support to their members. Both kinds of groups reduce isolation and provide a feeling of **belonging and support**. An activity or support group may fulfil an individual's immediate emotional need for a sense of caring and belonging. For example, a women's activity group which focuses on traditional crafts may also be a place where people talk about their feelings and experiences and provide support to others. Similarly, many support groups focus on activities which the members can do together.

Since it is unacceptable in many cultures to talk about one's feelings, activity groups are excellent ways to reduce isolation and encourage a sense of belonging. Also, in many cultures membership in a support group might cause social problems for the individual (i.e. stigmatise them) while activity groups are generally more accepted.

Support groups should focus on **clear goals**. For example, if members are in the initial stages of recovery, group goals may include learning about symptoms, controlling intrusive symptoms, establishing physical safety, learning about self-defence and solving problems. When these goals have been achieved, a new group may form for those wishing to tell their stories in culturally acceptable ways or to grieve with support. At the stage of reconnection, group members may work on learning to trust others, establishing relationships and learning skills. Group leaders are responsible for establishing clear goals for the group, organising each meeting and for creating an atmosphere of safety and trust. Leaders must not force ideas and beliefs on others, nor force members to share experiences.

Being with other people who have had similar painful experiences allows group members to feel **accepted and less isolated, secretive and ashamed**. Participating in activities together builds a sense of group belonging. Listening to others as they describe their traumatic experiences, responses and efforts at coping encourages members to feel that their reactions, feelings and thoughts are understandable and acceptable. Sometimes a sense of belonging in the group encourages group members to continue the group and participate in a wide variety of activities, including productive projects which benefit other members of the community.

8.10 **Self-Help Skills Or Behavioural Techniques**
(Reduce Anxiety, Intrusion Symptoms, Feelings Of Isolation)

The teaching of self-help skills enables individuals to learn techniques which **reduce symptoms of stress** with which they and their families are living. Behavioural techniques are usually simple exercises that most individuals can learn. Examples of techniques include breathing control, relaxation techniques, meditation, physical exercises, active listening and storytelling.

In cultures throughout the world, women usually assume the central role in providing health and education to their children and in helping vulnerable members of the community. In addition, they often help to support their families. As a result, the teaching of self-help skills to women will have an important impact on any community.

8.11 **Communication And Emotional Expression**
(Reduces Isolation And Encourages Connection With Others)

Much distress is due to the inability to understand and express one's thoughts and feelings and to listen to and understand others. In many families, people are unable to share the pain of what they have seen or suffered. They may want to protect their family and at the same time need comfort and understanding from them. Often family members have also suffered and fear to talk about their experiences. They may be afraid that communicating their painful feelings may cause others to feel responsible for their pain. This unspoken agreement not to share their feelings and be silent prevents the very comfort and closeness that they may desire. In some cultures they can benefit from learning communication skills and expressing their feelings in culturally acceptable ways.

8.12 **Storytelling** (Encourages Hope For The Future, Reduces Fear And Anxiety, Encourages Connectedness With Culture And Ancestors)

Throughout history, individuals and communities have told stories about their history and gods, common life problems and experiences. Sometimes these stories are shared through traditional art forms such as theatre, dance, puppetry, song and religious ceremonies. Stories can create a sense of **pride and self-confidence** in one's people, pass on certain **values and traditions** and suggest a **hope for the future** of the community or society. In addition, they try to explain common human experiences that every person faces, teach people how to live their lives, and bring the community together through their common bonds of ancestry, belief and values. Usually there are good storytellers and traditional artists in the community.

Storytelling can be a very constructive and useful method to use with people who have been victimised by organised violence to encourage positive coping attitudes and pass on healthy community values and beliefs. Such attitudes include believing you can trust others, that people are trying to help you and that people care for you and each other. Other positive attitudes are feeling hopeful about the future, that you are not alone, and that you are capable of doing useful things. Positive behaviours include trying to understand and solve your problems, performing useful tasks and participating in everyday activities.

8.13 **Self-expression**

People need opportunities to show and express their feelings about the violence that they have suffered, whatever those feelings may be. Family and community members, however, may have difficulty accepting these feelings because they may remind the community of terrible memories and frighten others. People who have suffered need to have the opportunity to express their feelings in **acceptable ways** or otherwise they may choose socially unacceptable ones.

Acceptable methods of self-expression are defined in most cultures. People are usually permitted to express intense feelings in structured ways, such as through theatre, dance, puppetry, music, drawing and painting, sculpture, wood carving, poetry, singing songs and religious or traditional ceremonies. These methods allow individuals to express a wide range of feelings without being afraid or ashamed of their feelings. Support workers should also encourage stories and descriptions about the courage people showed in their struggle to survive. In many cultures people are not used to sharing or expressing their feelings with others. Structured methods may encourage people to communicate their feelings in non-threatening ways. Physical activity and exercise is another structured medium in which people can relieve tension and act out their intense feelings in a socially acceptable manner.

8.14 **Systems Models** (Reduce Feelings Of
Hopelessness, Helplessness And Isolation)

Systems models focus on the individual's social systems that **shape and influence** his behaviour rather than on the internal thoughts and feelings of the individual. Social systems include families, school classes, work or peer groups and institutions such as schools, hospitals and refugee camps. Support workers have many opportunities for intervention using systems models, because any change in the social system will influence the behaviours and the attitudes of its members.

Suggested interventions are usually small positive changes in the system. Examples include: changing an institutional regulation; encouraging individuals to try new behaviours or institutions to be more flexible; and redefining behaviours or regulations in a positive way.

Changes may be introduced in a social system or institution to promote positive attitudes, caring interactions, self-respect and control over one's environment. For example, support workers and survivors may examine the physical organisation of a school, hospital or refugee camp to improve safety or train personnel to promote positive interactions. They may organise participation in meal planning and food preparation to promote positive attitudes towards eating, continuation of cultural traditions, control over one's environment, personal competence and job skill development.

When working with children and adolescents, support workers may promote activities that help children to develop self-confidence and competence. They may look at projects and daily activities as a way of reducing feelings of isolation and encouraging a sense of belonging. For example, sports activities, small competitions, cultural celebrations and group activities are activities found in most cultures. From a systems perspective, they also promote positive attitudes.

Systems ideas encourage support workers to look carefully at the reality of people's daily lives in addition to the emotional pain they may be suffering.

> For example, support workers may have the tendency to discount complaints (quality of food, availability of resources, problems like theft) because they assume that these complaints reflect general negative attitudes rather than real and important concerns. In fact, solving these real problems can have a significant impact on people and their daily lives.

8.15 Maintain A Connection With Memories Of The Dead
(Reduces Grief)

Intense emotions help to maintain most significant relationships; the death of one member doesn't eliminate the feelings and attachment that the other has felt and can continue feelings beyond his or her death (Shucer and Zisook, 1988). In situations of organised violence, where most deaths are unexpected and usually unnaturally caused, the grieving may benefit from maintaining ties with memories of the dead. This process may offer the grieving a period of emotional protection from the finality of death.

Continuing contact with memories of the dead is common across cultures both in waking, conscious states and in dream states. Examples include speaking to or hearing from the dead, "seeing" lost loved ones and having a "sense" of their presence. In some traditional cultures, the spirits of the dead are thought to be present for days or weeks after the death, and certain prescribed behaviours are required to ease their transition to death.

In certain East European folklore, the dead are always watching over the living and "participating" in their lives. Some cultures associate the dead with the protective relationship they expect from a god; praying to or speaking with the dead is considered necessary when faced with important decisions or crises. People can also maintain a connection with memories of the dead through continuing activities, interests and beliefs of the deceased.

Ceremonies and rituals associated with death exist in all cultures, including taking care of the body, the use of death in religious observances and the required mourning activities. Death anniversaries which are recognised in many cultures stimulate memories of the dead, provide an opportunity to express sadness and grief through cultural traditions, and connect the living with their memories of the past and the departed.

Many survivors have lost so many relatives, friends and neighbours that they feel overwhelmed by their inability to mourn for them all. One suggested approach is the drawing of a family map or family tree, a map of friends or a map of neighbours who have died. Individuals and families can fill in all the names of those who have died and create a record at the same time. For some survivors, this record, picture, drawing or song can become an important memory and may even help them to fulfil cultural traditions for mourning.

> For example, certain cultural traditions require that the dead person's name be included in a prayer or ritual activity in order to satisfy their god or the dead person's spirit.

This list or map may enable survivors to mourn in culturally acceptable ways. It is also equally helpful to create a drawing or map of the survivors.

8.16 Traditions And Rituals
(Reduce Isolation, Encourage Cultural Identity)

Traditions and rituals can provide comfort to people during difficult times in their lives. They provide a structure and order for people's family lives through: explaining common human experiences, teaching people how to live correctly in their societies, and defining the relationships and responsibilities that family members have to each other and to their communities. They may also direct people to participate in specific activities during important life experiences, including birth, puberty, marriage and death. These activities may help people to anticipate and prepare for these experiences, give meaning to their experiences and receive family and community support. In very traditional cultures, people's opinions about their problems are strongly influenced by traditional beliefs and religious views. Traditions and rituals should be encouraged and supported when they provide comfort to victims.

9. Red Cross and Red Crescent Guide Annexes

A. Communication exercises

i) Active Listening One
Active listening is different from normal listening, because in active listening, listeners don't ask questions, make judgements

or tell people what to do. Active listening is a proven technique which encourages people to sort out their feelings, find new ways of interacting and begin to solve their own problems.

In most cultures, people understand that listening to others who are upset, nervous, anxious or depressed is comforting. Listening allows the person to express his pain, suffering, sadness and shock and tell his story to someone who cares. Often the person feels immediate relief and comfort. You can use active listening with individuals and in groups.

The person may not want to talk about his experiences or may want to establish a relationship with you first. You may need to talk about things which do not threaten him first. He usually will talk to you when he is ready and if he learns to trust you. It may take weeks or longer.

You may need to help the person or group relax if they are breathing quickly, talking fast or in an excited state. (See Basic Breathing Technique below.) Secondly you need to establish a caring and genuine physical connection to the person by looking at them, keeping your attention on them and maintaining a culturally acceptable distance between you and the person.

Active listening involves listening very carefully to the person and responding by summarising what they have said. This shows the person that you are really with him and caring about his feelings and thoughts. When talking with the person you should always allow for periods of silence, and for the person to talk about what he wants to without questions from you. Let him lead the conversation. Respond after the person expresses an idea, thought or feeling and then pauses.

Do not interrupt him, try to interpret what he has said or give advice. Do not reassure him that everything will be okay or that he shouldn't be upset, because he may feel that you don't really respect his pain. You should talk in short and simple phrases and with genuine feeling. The person must be certain that what he says to you remains private or he will not be able to trust you. When the person feels you have really understood him, he will often say yes or continue with his story. If you have not, he may say "No" and explain.

You must practise to learn this skill. Sit down with others and practise sharing stories and feelings. Honestly respond when the person has understood and when they have not.

ii) Active Listening Two

Read Active Listening One and practise until you are really good at listening and understanding others. If may be difficult for some people to talk about their violent experiences, think about their problems and make decisions. They may feel overwhelmed and confused.

Through the process of active listening, you help the person to sort out his feelings and begin to solve his problems. Listen to his words and feelings. Watch his body movements, because they add information to your understanding. A person may move his arms violently, sit and stare with no emotion, clench his fists, etc.

People will feel you are really listening if you use some of their words when you respond. It is better to respond with genuine emotion and repeat than to add your own feelings or thoughts to their expressions. When people are expressing their feelings, you must be committed to stay with them and let them finish. If they can count on you for support, they will learn to trust you.

You need to learn about their culture and beliefs or you may not understand their feelings and conflicts. Support positive beliefs and attitudes like: feeling that people can take actions to solve problems; hoping that time will help solve some of the problems; recognising individual and community strengths and resources; being hopeful about the future; and that people are capable of doing useful things.

It is important to try to find something positive in their stories. Use anything, even if it is a small event, thought or feeling to support the positive beliefs and attitudes mentioned above. Emphasise the positive to help them look at their story with some hope for the future. These small positive experiences can become the building blocks of their recovery. For example, you may find a moment of courage, compassion, caring or support in their stories.

Panic – in rare cases, a few people may "panic" or behave in inappropriate ways because their feelings are so upsetting. They may react by becoming violent or trying to withdraw from the outside world. If they have a violent reaction they may scream continuously, run around, destroy property or attempt to injure themselves or others. If they undergo withdrawal they may seek safety (hide under large objects or in a corner), curl in a foetal position or cry quietly in terror. If this occurs, it is important that a few people, preferably friends, use gentle but firm physical strength to remove the person to a quiet and calm place where they can remain with him until he relaxes. They must also make certain that the person can't injure himself in this environment. If the person has difficulty resuming normal functioning, they need to be referred to resource personnel.

iii) Gaining Control Over Memories One

Learn by following techniques from the annexes: Active Listening One and Two, Basic Breathing Technique, Simple Relaxation Technique and Understanding Reactions to Violence. This method takes a lot of time because many meetings are required. Make sure that you can finish what you have started.

Steps for helping survivors to gain control over their violent memories:

1. Develop a safe environment in which victims can talk about their experiences.
2. Develop a relationship so people are comfortable. Allow enough time so that discussions are not rushed. Listen carefully. Treat people with respect and try to understand what they are saying.
3. Encourage them to talk about what they are feeling and thinking now.
4. Tell them about normal reactions to violent experiences.
5. Tell them that they will feel less frightened if they can tell their stories to other people. Suggest close family members or friends. If they do not know anyone with whom they are comfortable sharing their experiences, suggest that you can help them to overcome their fears. If you are in a group situation, using a radio, a theatre or other group approach, you can use stories you have heard to reduce the fears of your audience or other group members. If you use a story you have heard, make it general so that the person who told you cannot identify it as his or her story.
6. Teach basic breathing and simple relaxation technique, and practice until they can relax. Encourage them to

use these techniques when they are having difficulty controlling their memories.

7. Ask them to use a breathing technique to relax. If they are still anxious, ask them to use simple relaxation technique. Ask them to talk about what happened to them, their friends and families. They may prefer to present their story in dance, song, art or theatre.

8. Encourage them to give more details and point out any positive actions or behaviour of individuals (e.g. courage, compassion, sharing, protecting). Ask questions about what they felt and thought during their experiences. Suggest that they are recovering and healing when they can tell their stories.

9. Repeat the exercise several times.

10. If they are still suffering from fears and nervousness, see Gaining Control Two.

iv) Gaining Control Over Memories Two

If survivors are still suffering fears and nervousness after using Gaining Control One, you can use relaxation techniques to help them control their memories.

Steps to follow:

1. Make a list with them of their painful experiences. Look at the list together and help them decide which experiences were painful, very painful or the most painful.

2. Start the process with one of the least painful experiences. Ask them to use the basic breathing technique until they feel calm and relaxed. If they are still anxious, ask them to use simple relaxation exercise. Ask them to talk about the experience you have chosen, and tell them that they can stop any time by indicating that they are getting upset (touching their face, lifting their hand, closing their eyes). Use details from their story to help them to recreate the experience and their feelings and thoughts at the time.

3. When they stop talking, suggest that they can calm themselves. First tell them that they were just telling a story about a memory and that they can let the memory

go away. Ask them to continue using their breathing or relaxation technique until they are relaxed.

4. Stop as long as is necessary until they are calm and feel comfortable.

5. When they are ready, ask them to continue the story where they stopped and repeat stopping and relaxing. When they are finished with their first experience, ask them to repeat the story until they are able to tell the story without wanting to stop.

6. Repeat a few times. Tell them they have learned to control their memories and are beginning to recover.

7. Choose a more painful experience on their list and repeat the above process. After each session, emphasise how they have learned to control their memories. Tell them that each success will make them strong and more in control. Suggest that they are recovering and healing when they learn to control their memories.

8. Continue until they are more comfortable in their daily lives.

v) **Storytelling**

Read annexes on active listening and practise until you are good at listening to others.

Storytelling can be a useful method to use with victims to encourage positive attitudes and pass on healthy community values and beliefs. Good stories try to explain common human experiences which every person faces, teach people how to live their lives, and bring the community together through their common bonds of ancestry, belief and values.

Positive stories can be presented in theatre, puppet or dance presentations, in song, on the radio and in traditional or religious ceremonies. Find people from the community who are good storytellers or who have experience in any of these different forms. Encourage people of all ages to tell stories.

Storytelling can also be used interactively with individuals of all ages or groups. Encourage someone to tell a story about another person, animal or object. In that way, he will not feel personally threatened. Some people may prefer using stories from their community, religious stories or folk tales. When he is finished it is your turn. Use his stories and add to them or tell a similar story to support positive beliefs. Your story should be very general and end with the possibility of several things happening. Then the person is asked to tell another story or continue the story already told.

Whenever the person uses negative attitudes in a story, you should use characters and action to suggest positive attitudes and behaviours. Positive attitudes are: feeling that people can take actions to solve problems; hoping that time will help solve some of the problems; being hopeful about the future; feeling that you can trust others; and that you are capable of doing useful things. Examples of negative attitudes including feeling nothing can be done about pain, blaming one's self or others and feeling aggressive towards others.

You must practise to learn this skill. Sit down with others and practise sharing stories. Honestly respond when the person has encouraged positive attitudes. You will certainly have much experience with stories from your own childhood, family, religion and community.

vi) Self-expression

Self-expression gives people opportunities to show and express their feelings about the violence they have suffered, whatever those feelings may be.

Most cultures define acceptable methods of self-expression. People are usually permitted to express intense feelings in structured ways, such as through theatre, dance, puppetry, music, drawing and painting, poetry, singing songs and religious or traditional ceremonies. These methods allow individuals to express a wide range of feelings without being afraid or ashamed of their feelings. In many cultures people are not used to sharing or expressing their feelings verbally. Non-verbal methods may encourage them to communicate their feelings. Encourage individuals to share life stories with friends, family or group members.

Find those methods that the people know and believe in, and encourage them to express their pain, grief and hopes. Here are two simple exercises that can fit in most cultures. The can be done individually, in groups, in families and as a community event:

1. Ask children to draw, sketch, paint, draw in sand, carve on wood, etc. their home, their family, stories about themselves or dreams. Their art may show fear, sadness or anger, or may describe what happened. It may also include descriptions of good experiences. The purpose is to encourage children to express themselves. They don't have to understand what they have produced or explain it to others. Sometimes, though, they will be very excited and want to discuss their art. Children will enjoy seeing each other's pictures. Some children will be very controlled with their own art and will benefit from seeing other children's drawings. Children can take drawings home; sometimes they encourage families to share their stories. They may want to continue drawing or practise other methods of self-expression. Through self-expression they can review memories and express intense feelings, which helps them to heal and recover.

2. Ask people to draw (sing, dance, carve) the story of their lives. Remind them that their life experiences have included good times as well as bad. Ask them to relax or close their eyes as they remember their childhood, happiness, good times and bad times. Suggest they mark the time in their life story when their trauma occurred. Encourage them to see the joy as well as the sadness in their lives.

B. Group Work

i) Social Support

Read Active Listening One and Two and practise until you are good at listening to others. People who genuinely care about others and are good listeners can learn to provide social support. Caring people can help victims of violence to fight their feelings of loneliness, understand what has happened, solve problems and maintain hope which encourages the desire to survive.

Some common ways of providing support include: listening to people describing their experiences and expressing their feelings; staying with the person and providing comfort; participating in ceremonies or rituals; giving meaning to the events and the person's responses; supporting positive beliefs; assisting in solving problems by making lists of important concerns; helping the person to maintain relationships with the community and encouraging the person to participate in common life activities.

Examples of common life activities include; work; school; being useful to the family or others; participating in social activities like celebrations, entertainment, sports; following religious traditions; and maintaining an interest in the world through talking about events, listening to radio or reading. Solving daily life problems can prove overwhelming to some people suffering from trauma. Help people discuss their problems and realistic solutions. Encourage any positive effort at solving problems because it will promote feelings of confidence.

One method for solving problems or making small positive changes can be done in simple steps and with limited resources. Survivors may need assistance at first by learning to:

1. Make a list of serious and small problems or goals;
2. Number the problems in order of difficulty;
3. Choose one small practical problem at a time;
4. Think of several different ways to solve the problem;
5. Try one way until the problem is solved or improved;
6. Choose another problem and continue the process.

Some people will want you to tell them what to do or what is right. Although it is better to encourage them to solve their own problems, you should do what the people in the culture expect. Encourage positive attitudes and beliefs, but do not deny their pain by telling them that they shouldn't be upset.

Practise supporting others. Tell each other when you feel comforted and accepted. You yourself have experience supporting family members, friends, neighbours; try to remember how others have made you feel better.

ii) **Activity Groups**

Groups can provide support and a feeling of belonging by creating an immediate community. Activity groups generally offer interesting activities that the members enjoy and can do together. Participating in useful activities will show members that they can still do important and necessary things for themselves and their community. Since it is uncommon in many cultures to talk about personal feelings, activity groups are excellent ways in which people can feel supported and accepted.

When you encourage people to join your group you need to be clear to them about why they are being asked to be members, what they will do in the group and for what period of time. You should try to make membership a positive idea.

As the group leader, you are responsible for organising specific activities for each meeting, arranging a meeting place and providing materials. It is very important to be flexible and let the group members participate in deciding the activities of the group. For example, many activity groups may choose a different activity if one is too difficult or has been already achieved; may continue to meet because they like each other; or may choose to work on a specific community problem like recreation programmes.

It is important that you are genuinely interested in the members and can feel comfortable with many kinds of comments and behaviours. Just as good parents encourage acceptance of all family members, a good group leader needs to support acceptance of all kinds of members.

As the group leader, you must make sure that the group and its members do not force members to participate in activities, share their feelings or talk about their experiences. Members need to feel respected and in control of their activities in the group.

Practise being in a group of your own, learn about how groups work and the effect of groups on members. Meet as often as possible in a group of your own over a period of time until you are comfortable with starting your own group. You yourself already have group experience as a member of your family, in your class at school and at work.

iii) **Support Groups**

Read the pages on Activity Groups and Active Listening.

Groups can provide support and a feeling of acceptance and belonging by creating an immediate community. Support groups are created to provide support to people who have had similar experiences or problems, such as rape victims, torture victims, children 8–11 years old, adolescents and mothers.

Group leaders should have experience in the particular problem area. Some of the best group leaders are people who have gone through similar difficulties, can be genuine and open about their problems and struggles, and can serve as a "model" to the other members.

Members gain an immediate sense of acceptance by being with others who have similar problems. Sharing experiences, stories and feelings in a supportive environment comforts group members by helping them realise that they are not "crazy" and that others can actually understand the pain they may have experienced. Members can also discuss ways of solving problems and learn to give support to others.

Group members and leaders should not question other members, criticise or judge them; analyse or interpret what they say. Nor should they force their ideas, feelings or solutions on other group members.

At first, discussion should be general and members should talk about everyday activities. Group members need to feel comfortable with each other before talking about personal matters. This may take several meetings. It is important to have a specific subject each meeting and to make meetings interesting so that people will want to attend. If the members want to talk about something different, follow their needs and wishes. It is your responsibility to keep the discussions going and encourage support of each other.

It is essential that group members are never forced to talk about painful experiences. As the group leader, you must make sure that members feel respected and in control at all times. Many members may never be able to share stories but will still benefit from listening to others.

Some members will want you to tell them what to do or what is right. Usually, group leaders are careful not to tell members what to do, and encourage them to solve their own problems. Sometimes you may need to give advice because the people in the culture expect it. As members begin to give support to others and to resume normal activities, you know that they are healing. Members who are genuinely concerned and supportive of others may start groups of their own. Group leaders should meet regularly to discuss their groups, learn from one another and give support to one another.

NOTE: C. Educational approach: the seven pages under this heading in the Red Cross/Red Crescent Guide are omitted for lack of space, as are D(i) on Physical Exercises for Reducing Anxiety and D(iii), (iv) and (v) Simple Relaxation Techniques.

D. Relaxation exercises

ii) Basic Breathing Technique

Relaxation techniques help individuals reduce their nervousness and feel calm by themselves. They are good skills because they help people relax when they are upset, when they are afraid and when they are in a situation which reminds them of bad experiences in the past.

Relaxation techniques are simple to learn if you take the time to follow the direction carefully, practise the technique until it works for you and use it regularly. You should practise this technique until you can relax easily before trying to teach someone else. You will find that the more often you practise the technique, the shorter time it takes for you to feel calm and relaxed.

One simple way to relax someone who is nervous or excited is to ask him to breathe slowly and rhythmically for a few minutes. This usually calms him and teaches him a skill he can use anywhere. It is important that you breathe rhythmically with him and also concentrate on relaxing.

Basic Breathing: Make yourself comfortable. Close your eyes if this makes you more comfortable. Put your hands on your stomach and breathe slowly with your stomach, not your chest. Each time you breathe think about how your stomach is getting full with air and then letting the air out. Feel how relaxed you feel with each breath.

With each breath, think how you are bringing in energy and good feelings. When you breathe out, think how you are getting rid of your bad feelings and nervousness.

Concentrate on each breath. In – energy and good feelings. Out – emptying my body of bad feelings and nervousness. In, out; in – good feelings, out – bad feelings; in – energy, out – nervousness; in, out. Feel how relaxing it is to bring in energy and bring in good feelings. In, out. Follow each breath. Continue for a few minutes until you are relaxed and calm.

D(iii) is similar to the above, but it adds "Let the relaxation spread to your stomach, your waist and back. ... Relax the lower part of your body, your behind,... knees,... feet... and all the way down to the tips of your toes. Take a deep breath and hold your breath for a couple of seconds... and let the air out slowly... slowly... Notice how you relax more and more." **D(v)** suggests the following, once the basic breathing technique has started to have its effect:

"Think of a calm and relaxing place you have been in the past. Imagine you are there right now. Let your mind rest safely in this relaxing place. Remember what this place looks like – the sounds, smells, colours and feeling of this place. Rest there for five minutes at first and then longer each time you do this exercise. When thoughts rise up in your mind, let them go out. Leave our special place. Breathe slowly and evenly, and open your eyes."

10. References And Future Reading

- Agger I. and Jensen S.B. Testimony as Ritual and Evidence in Psychotherapy for Political Refugees. Journal of Traumatic Stress 3 (1990)
- Basoglu M., Prevention of Torture and Care of Survivors. JAMA, Vol.270, No. 5, August 1993
- Benedict Helen, Safe, Strong, & Streetwise. Little Brown and Company, Boston, 1987
- Caplan G., Loss, Stress, and Mental Health, Community Ment. Health J., 26/1, 1990
- Doerr-Zegers, et al., Torture: Psychiatric Sequelae and Phenomenology. Psychiatry, Vol.55, May 1992
- Eiseman Jr. F., Bali: Sekala & Niskala, Vol. 1: Essays on Religion, Ritual, and Art. Periplus Editions, Singapore, 1989
- Eisenbruch M., From Post-Traumatic Stress Disorder to Cultural Bereavement, Soc. Sci. Med., Vol.33 (6), 1991
- Health Hazards of Organised Violence. Working Group on Health Hazards of Organised Violence, WHO regional office, Europe, 1986

- Herman Judith Lewis, Trauma and Recovery. Basic Books, New York, 1991
- Hoffman, Lynn, Foundations of Family Therapy. Basic Books, New York, 1981
- Horowitz M., Post-traumatic Stress Disorders: Psychosocial Aspects of the Diagnosis. Int.J.Ment.Health, Vol.19, No.2, 1990
- Lister E., Forced Silence: A neglected dimension of trauma. Am. J. Psychia, 139:7, July 1982
- Macksoud M., Helping Children Cope with the Stresses of war: A Manual for Parents and Teachers. UNICEF, New York, 1993
- McCallin Margaret, Ed., Psychological Well-Being of Refugee Children: Research, Practice and Policy Issues. International Catholic Child Bureau, Geneva, Switzerland, 1992
- Melville M. and Lykes K., Guatemalan Indian Children and the Socio-cultural Effects of Government-Sponsored Terrorism. Soc.Sci. Med.Vol 34, No. 5, 1992
- Miserez D., Ed., Refugees – The Trauma of Exile, League of Red Cross and Red Crescent Societies. Martinus Nijhoff Publishers, The Netherlands, 1988
- Mollica R., et al., Repatriation and Disability: A Community Study of Health, Mental Health, and Social Functioning of the Khmer Residents of Site Two, Vols. 1 and 2. Harvard School of Public Health and World Fed.Mental Health, 1992.
- Mollica R., et al. Assessing Symptom Change in Southeast Asian Refugee Survivors of Mass Violence and Torture. Am.J. Pschiatry 147:1, January 1990
- Ost L., Applied Relaxation: Description of a Coping Technique and Review of Controlled Studies. Behav.Res.Ter. Vol 25, No.5, 1987
- Pascalis G., Transcultural Psychiatry in Afghanistan, Psychol.Med., Paris, 13:10, 1981
- Pelzer K., and Ebigbo P., Clinical Psychology in Africa. Chuka Printing Co Nigeria, 1988
- Protacio-Mercelino E., Children of Political Detainees in the Philippines: Sources of Stress and Coping Patterns. Int.J.Ment. Health, Vol.19, No.1. 1989
- Refugee Mental Health, Draft Manual for Field Testing. WHO and UNHCR, Geneva 1994

- Report on Meeting of Advisory Group on Health Situation of Refugees and Victims of Organised Violence. WHO Regional Office Europe. ICP/HSR 813/19, 1988
- Ressler E., Totorici M., Marcelino A., Children in War – A Guide to the Provision of Services: A Study for Unicef. UNICEF, New York, 1993
- Sande Hans, Palestinian Martyr Widowhood – Emotional Needs in Conflict with Role Expectations. Soc.Sci.Med., Vol.34, No.6, 1992
- Shanan J., Surviving the Survivors: Late Personality Development of Jewish Holocaust Survivors, Int.J.Ment.Health, Vol.17, No.4, 1989
- Shucter S. and Zisook S., Widowhood: The Continuing Relationship with the Dead Spouse. Bull Meninger Clinic. 52/3, 1988
- Solomon S, Gerrity E., Muff A., Efficacy of Treatments for Post-traumatic Stress Disorder. JAMA, Vol. 268, No.5, August 1992
- Toole M. and Waldman R., Refugees and Displaced Persons. JAMA, Vol.270, No.5, August 1993
- Weigel Marion, Unpublished papers. Final Report, Delegation Zagreb,Croatia. International Federation of Red Cross and Red Crescent Societies, 1993
- Wikan Unni, Bereavement and Loss in two Muslim Communities. Soc.Sci.Med, 27(5), 1988
- Zyi A and Ugalde A., Political Violence in the Third World: a Public Health Issue. Health Policy and Planning. 6(3): 203-217, 1991

ANNEX 1C

Community Based Psychological Support, A Training Manual, IFRC, 1st Edition, January 2003; IFRC Framework For Community Resilience, 2018

These two valuable publications, unlike Annexes 1A and 1B, have no overall focus on uprooted populations, but this does not of course mean that they cannot be vital in relation to the work of coping with refugee crises. Incidentally, each carries the following statement: "Any part of this publication may be cited, copied, translated into other languages or adapted to meet local needs without prior permission from the International Federation of Red Cross and Red Crescent Societies, provided that the source is clearly stated."

In a general introduction to *Community Based Psychological Support, A Training Manual*, the IFRC states that, in today's world, the need of communities for psychosocial support along with the traditional relief aid (shelter, food distribution and basic health care) has increasingly been recognized. Therefore psychosocial support has become an integral part of the IFRC's emergency response, helping individuals and communities to heal psychological wounds and rebuild social structures in the wake of one or other form of emergency. It can help change people into active survivors rather than passive victims.

The Reference Centre For Psychosocial Support (PS Centre)

Founded in 1993, the PS Centre works with National Red Cross and Red Crescent Societies all over the world to promote psychosocial well-being of beneficiaries, humanitarian staff and volunteers through operational assistance, capacity building, competence development of staff and volunteers, advocacy and knowledge.

The PS Centre is hosted by the Danish Red Cross, and supported by the Canadian Red Cross, Finnish Red Cross, French Red Cross, Hellenic Red Cross, Icelandic Red Cross, Norwegian Red Cross and Swedish Red Cross. It has worked with several research institutions.

The PS Centre and the Health in Emergencies Unit in the IFRC Health and Care Department have guided the work on the Psychosocial Support Programmes and supported National Societies with relevant tools and inter-agency work. The regional Red Cross Red Crescent Psychosocial Support Programme networks that exist in several zones are a key resource.

Examples of PS work around the world:

- support to PS delegates in Sichuan, Mongolia and Myanmar
- PS assessment in Georgia and Beslan
- Tsunami lessons learned project
- development of a PS component to Emergency Response Units (ERU)
- training and workshops in Israel, Russia, Uganda, Syria
- facilitation of Health ERU and Health in Emergencies training in China, France, Germany, Hong Kong and Norway
- psychosocial film *Rebuilding Hope*
- a psychosocial toolkit (CD-ROM),
- programme assistance in a number of National Societies, including the Palestine Red Crescent Society and the Danish Red Cross
- a community-based PS support training kit and a handbook on PS interventions

The IFRC Training Manual has six modules on training health volunteers to provide basic emotional and psychological support to children and adults in emergencies. The modules are on *psychosocial well-being, stress and coping, supportive communication, promoting community self-help, populations with special needs* and *helping the helper*. Professor Gilbert Reyes, mentioned earlier, took part in the preparation of this training manual.

* * * * * *

In the introductory paragraphs to the *IFRC Framework for Community Resilience* (24 pages, 2018), we read that the IFRC, "the world's largest

479

volunteer-based humanitarian network", reaches "97 million people annually through long-term services and development programmes as well as 85 million people through disaster response and early recovery programmes. ... Guided by Strategy 2020 – our collective plan of action to tackle the major humanitarian and development challenges of this decade – we are committed to 'saving lives and changing minds'. ... For the IFRC, the concept of community resilience represents a unique opportunity as this approach in many ways captures the totality of what the IFRC is working to achieve" and "this is in fact what many National Societies have been doing over the course of many decades by supporting their local communities." The IFRC defines resilience as "the ability of individuals, communities, organizations or countries exposed to disasters, crises and underlying vulnerabilities to anticipate, prepare for, reduce the impact of, cope with and recover from the effects of shocks and stresses without compromising their long-term prospects".

The IFRC's Framework for Community Safety and Resilience (FCR) published in 2008, evolving over subsequent years into the Framework for Community Safety and Resilience (with the same initials, FCR), holds that community safety and resilience approaches provide National Societies with an opportunity to build on, enhance and adapt activities that they had already been carrying out. The FCR has gone through an extensive consultation process, both within the IFRC and externally, for example National Societies participating in two-day workshops in the four zones, and seventy-seven National Societies participating in community resilience workshops at the 2013 General Assembly. Suggestions from a number of external organizations and private sector partners have informed the FCR, and *ipso facto* this *IFRC Framework for Community Resilience.*

ANNEX 2

United Nations Voluntary Fund For Victims Of Torture - What The Fund Does

The UN Voluntary Fund for Victims of Torture is a unique and universal humanitarian tool available to the UN and OHCHR providing direct assistance to victims of torture and their family members wherever torture occurs – as outlined in its Mission statement. The Fund aims at healing the physical and psychological consequences of torture on victims and their families, and thus restoring their dignity and role in society.

Since its establishment by the General Assembly in 1981 (resolution 36/151), the Fund has made awards to more than 620 organizations and rehabilitation centres around the world, reaching out to over 50,000 victims every year. It is managed by the Office of the United Nations High Commissioner for Human Rights, with the advice of a Board of Trustees composed of independent experts from the five world regions.

The overarching objective of the work supported by the UN Torture Fund is to assist victims of torture and their family members to rebuild their lives, providing immediate and accessible remedies. This is implemented through the award of grants to a variety of channels of assistance, including, civil society organisations, associations of victims and their family members, private and public hospitals, legal clinics, public interest law firms and individual lawyers.

Types of assistance

Direct humanitarian assistance is provided in the following fields:

Medical assistance, includes residential treatment, referrals to specialists and mobile health clinics. The medical assistance treats the physical after-effects of torture. Following diagnosis by a general practitioner, treatment is provided by medical specialists in the fields of orthopaedics, neurology, physiotherapy, paediatrics, sexual health, urology as well as traditional healing and complementary medicine.

The grants are therefore used for example for doctors' salaries, laboratory tests, diagnostics, ambulances and transportation of victims, medical expertise for tribunals, medicines, and surgery.

Psychological assistance for individuals, couples, groups and families to enable victims of torture to overcome the psychological trauma they have experienced: therapy counselling, art therapy (theatre, painting, sculpture), occupational therapy, meditation/acupuncture and other culturally sensitive and appropriate techniques, psychological support in preparation for attendance at trials. Individual therapy, whether based on clinical, psychoanalytical, behavioural or other therapy, seeks to assist victims with their gradual reintegration into society. Psychiatric therapy may be combined with medication to alleviate physical and psychological symptoms.

Grants are therefore used, for example, for salaries of psychiatrists, psychologists and other types of mental health professionals, medicines, referral to specialists, interpretation costs, preparation and submission of expert reports for tribunals.

Social assistance, includes vocational training, material assistance for basic needs, such as accommodation, food, clothes and utilities, on the basis of needs and vulnerability. Organisations are required to establish a transparent mechanism for the provision of social assistance and effective monitoring procedures.

The social assistance complements the above-mentioned forms of assistance by providing various services to reduce the sense of marginalization that many victims experience. Due to the disproportionate number of persons with physical and/or mental disabilities in the population of torture survivors, social assistance ensures that victims have access to a minimum of basic services, including housing, health care, education, language classes and employment training.

Legal assistance may be provided in a number of ways. For torture victims seeking asylum, legal assistance can be crucial in the preparation and follow-up of asylum applications in a host country. The Fund also contributes to combating impunity. Grants are used to seek reparation and compensation for victims through claims before competent national, regional and international bodies.

Legal aid supported by the Fund includes:

- Litigation of torture cases, filing complaints against alleged perpetrators in order to seek prosecution and/or obtain redress, including compensation for torture victims;
- Defence of torture victims in criminal cases brought against them (for example in cases where a confession extracted under torture lead to self-incrimination);
- Legal assistance and counselling on medical, social, economical of family issues. For example, issues such as family reunification applications, accessing housing, obtaining medical or social benefits, obtaining work and residence permits;
- Legal assistance to victims of torture who are asylum seekers or internally displaced, in asylum and/or non-refoulement procedures;
- Legal assistance to family members of enforced or involuntary disappearances (Habeas Corpus cases, obtaining remains or ordering autopsy, documentation of disappearance, litigation to obtain death certificates to solve inheritance issues.
- Indirect legal assistance such as referrals to pro-bono lawyers;
- Documentation of torture, for future prosecution of perpetrators.

Grants are therefore used for, **inter alia**, lawyers' fees, transportation of lawyers, victims and experts, expertise by forensic and ballistic experts, interpretation, printing of documents, additional investigation costs, court and legal fees and prison visits.

Financial assistance enables victims to meet their basic needs and to gain access to other types of assistance, such as health care. In some cases, nominal assistance is distributed to unemployed victims, particularly when they are unable to work as a result of the serious physical and psychological effects of torture. Financial assistance may also be used to offset the costs of educating their children.

The excellent web site invites us to view examples of projects funded (PDF), and to see and read stories from projects supported by the Fund.

The Fund Today

At its thirty-ninth session in March 2014, the Board of Trustees took stock of ten years of activities of the Fund and determined the objectives of the Fund for the next years, which are reflected in the Fund's Mission Statement and Guidelines:

- Introducing a competitive process in the review of project proposals, based on merit and documented needs, as well as years of continuous support by the Fund to the same project;
- Setting a maximum number of projects to be managed on a yearly basis and a time-bound support to selected projects;
- Ensuring a more balanced geographic distribution of resources among the five regions of the world;
- Increasing the average grant size;
- Generating closer alignment with GA resolution 36/151, which encourages prioritized assistance to countries whose human rights situation is under United Nations scrutiny.

At its 40th meeting, in October 2014, the Board examined and evaluated more than 257 project proposals aimed at providing direct assistance to victims of torture and their family members, amounting to a total request of $14,796,502.

As a result of the review, a total of 187 grants were awarded in 2015 for a total of $6,260,000.

Grants awarded by the Board for 2015 directly assist victims of torture in more than 81 countries in the five regions of the world.

Monitoring And Administration Of The Fund

The Secretariat of the UN Torture Fund has a sophisticated monitoring and evaluation methodology to ensure the accountability on the use of grant.

As a rule all new applicants are visited before any application is presented to the Board of Trustees for its consideration. Evaluation reports are prepared, with details on the type of assistance to be provided, notes on the meetings with staff and victims and a description of existing internal financial procedures and management.

Field visits are conducted by the staff of the Secretariat of the UN Slavery Fund, Board members and OHCHR Field Presences staff. A monitoring and evaluation manual, with details on how to conduct an evaluation, has been developed for this purpose. A total of 35 projects were visited amongst the 44 awarded projects for 2015.

Information on results of the visits can be shared, as appropriate, with other Institutional Donors to projects co-funded by the UNVTFCFS.